One in a Million

With my best wishes

Bill.

One in a Million

That *Bill Taylor*

Sir Bill Taylor

Matador
Unit E2 Airfield Business Park
Harrison Road, Market Harborough
Leicestershire LE16 7UL
Tel: 0116 279 2299
Email: books@troubador.co.uk
Web: www.troubador.co.uk/matador
Twitter: @matadorbooks

ISBN 9781803137018

British Library Cataloguing in Publication Data.
A catalogue record for this book is available from the British Library.

Printed by TJ Books Ltd, Padstow, UK
Typeset in 12pt Adobe Jenson Pro by Troubador Publishing Ltd, Leicester, UK

Matador is an imprint of Troubador Publishing Ltd

Acknowledgements and Appreciations

Throughout my life I recognise thousands of people who were challenging, awkward, enriching, and fun. Family, friends, neighbours, colleagues and beyond – met and yet to be met.

Our two very much grown up "kids": Matt & Kit, hard-working, thoughtful, funny, married to two great people and now each with two excellent kids of their own, all always reverently respectful. NB one of these qualities is a complete lie.

Lady Anne Taylor: Wife, mother, former secondary school Head of Science teacher. Loving and loved, she is extremely patient, respected and popular especially with former (of 9,000?) pupils she regularly "bumps into".

Dr Mike Davis, former secondary school teacher, HE & NHS consultant. Mike hung on in with me throughout!

Graeme Edwardson from Tecchies IT support and hero.

Rev Chris Chivers, formerly of Blackburn Cathedral. Thinker, writer and teacher of Christian theology. Sadly slipped under my radar.

Advisors & main damp shoulders
+ Pete Graham, photography guru.

- Cassandra Boderke (professionally Murray), former journalist and sub editor.
- Mike Murray, former successful entrepreneur and Chair of Community Business Partners.
- Nick Nunn, former Dep Editor *Lancashire Telegraph* and national journalist trainer.
- Young people and Youth Workers, who taught me so much.
- Councillors and public service staff – so hard working and resourceful.

Legions of private and voluntary sector folk all with their shoulders to various wheels.

Associate Advisors & occasional damp shoulders
Steve Almond, recently acquired friend.
Dr Kate MacFarlane (Blackburn HE, Sunderland and now Manchester).
Mick Seedall and Stuart Gregory, Tutors, Blackburn College, who initially set off with students Sarah and Sean to offer help when and where it was abundantly needed.
Jonathan Bond at the college from way back.
Linda Harling, Rossendale Council.
Neil Johnson, former Pictures Editor, *Lancashire Telegraph*.
Neil Matthewman, NHS and 3rd Sector.
Pauline Milligan, NHS Business Support.

And dozens, hundreds of others who told me stories, got me into scrapes, and out of them. I have mainly loved all the folk I've come across, with almost no exceptions.

Charities
There is a cover price for this *self published* book. Anything above that will find itself shared between our local hospice and Save the Children. For young and old, nearby and across our difficult world.

Contents

Chapter 1

Prologue – Setting the Scene

Our story's seldom told.

> *'It is not the critic who counts; not the man who points out how the strong man stumbles, or where the doer of deeds could have done them better. The credit belongs to the man who is actually in the arena, whose face is marred by dust and sweat and blood; who strives valiantly; who errs, who comes short again and again, because there is no effort without error and shortcoming; but who does actually strive to do the deeds; who knows great enthusiasms, the great devotions; who spends himself in a worthy cause; who at the best knows in the end the triumph of high achievement, and who at the worst, if he fails, at least fails while daring greatly, so that his place shall never be with those cold and timid souls who neither know victory nor defeat.'*
>
> THEODORE ROOSEVELT AT THE SORBONNE, 1910.

*   *   *

On a beautiful bright and sunny winter's day in December 2003 I was knighted with HM.

Most readers will think that's Her or His Majesty, and indeed it was Prince Charles, Prince of Wales, heir to the throne who came at me with a sword that morning. Was this really me? Not bad for a boy who didn't get his first shop-bought jumper till he was twelve, I thought to myself at the moment of dubbing.

But for me, my HM was Helen Mirren, the multi award winning actress. We spent two or three hours together that day. To my way of thinking her elevation to royalty was retrospectively endorsed three years later when the Academy (of Motion Picture Arts and Sciences) awarded her an Oscar for Best Actress for her eponymous film depiction of Queen Elizabeth II.

I was accompanied to Buckingham Palace by my wife, Anne, our twenty-two-year-old son, Matthew, and our eighteen-year-old daughter, Katherine.

I have begun with this little anecdote, which I'll return to later in more detail, because that might be all that people 'know' about me. Without really knowing very much.

But this story isn't about getting a knighthood.

It's about a little boy, born in Leeds not really very long after the end of World War II. Aged three, he moved with his mum and dad to Birmingham and went to primary and secondary school there. He went on to spend three years at university in Lancaster and then settled into a working life as a youth worker in Blackburn, Lancashire. Many, many other things happened too!

People who think they know me will almost certainly only know some tiny elements of that story.

Across the road from our first married home lived a little girl called Joanne, aged four, five perhaps. One day she said to me, 'Hello, **THAT** Bill Taylor'. I asked her why she called me so. 'It's what my mummy calls you.' 'I see!' I replied and I did.

Joanne with Mum Norma, Dad Martin and brothers Damian and Kieran Reeves emigrated to Australia in 1981. She's now Spicer, in her forties I'm told. She lives in Melbourne, married and a mother to two boys.

There's an intricate and complex story to be told here about THAT Bill Taylor. But I'm not sure which Bill Taylor is THAT one!

We are all different actors in all the life dramas in which we have roles. Sometimes doesn't it feel that we're on the stage, others, sat in the audience? It's not just our work, our family situation, community setting, faith or other life-shaping factors that define us. We are all complex cocktails of things that go to make up who and what we are. What we present or what others see is only on the surface.

Take me as only one example:

- Most won't know me as a spouse, a parent, a friend or acquaintance to many.
- I've also been a face-to-face youth worker and worked in classrooms across Lancashire, Europe, the world.
- I have managed, trained or spoken with and for youth workers – including community volunteers, part-time, trainees and university students, tutors and trainers.
- Most will have no experience of me as a public speaker addressing Cabinet Ministers, high-ranking Whitehall civil service *Mandarins* and/or several hundred fellow council leaders.
- I have also worked with school classroom and head teachers, chairs and members of governing bodies; those in further education (mainly sixteen-nineteen-year-olds) and higher education (mainly university based) principals, vice chancellors and other educationalists; but most especially *kids*, children, students, young people – particularly pleasing if it's presenting them, in the presence of their peers and parents, with prizes or awards for effort or achievement that motivate them to try harder or go further.
- Some will know me as the chap speaking on the radio, being quoted and photographed in local, national and *trade* papers.
- I've worked in a leadership role and alongside beat and high-ranking police officers, doctors, other clinicians and senior NHS officers, trade unions, staff and MDs (managing directors) in the private sector of companies both small and stock-market quoted. I've chaired a small, a few-thousand-pounds-a-year voluntary group at one end of the scale through to leading the 'umbrella' organisation for Lancashire's 4,500 voluntary organisations and groups.

- There's also me as a guy in the pub telling or listening (and laughing) to stories or jokes over a pint or two or more, a former keen amateur golfer and photographer and all those kinds of things that go to make up not just me, but every one of us.

This has all occurred over several decades and in different civic and academic venues locally, in London, around Britain, Europe, and beyond.

I did not do any of the above alone; I worked in some great, hugely successful teams, we gained reputation and recognition, and many were recognised with national awards and personal honours from the Queen. Talented, visionary, imaginative and creative; committed, principled but not dogmatic; determined, hard-working, articulate, leaders and team players.

As well as THAT Bill Taylor, there's Councillor Bill Taylor, but that's not one monolithic being either. All of us are different people at different times and different people to different people at different times.

Many things determine how we are. Being a councillor is one of the things that determined me, but I don't think it would be easy to pick that out from any of my other forming factors.

Just a word on my intended style. I read a story attributed to no longer Labour supporting actress Maureen Lipman. She quoted a stock saying of her dad, Maurice, '*Hak mir nisht keyn tshaynik!*' (literally 'Don't bang the teakettle at me!'). I'll try not to bang on about things, try not to spell things out for you. My intended style is for us: for me to write and you to read this together. As the chorus urges the audience to be imaginative in the opening prologue to Shakespeare's *Henry V*, 'Admit me, Chorus, to this history, Who prologue-like your humble patience pray.'

*   *   *

At any one time across the UK there are over 100,000 elected councillors. On average they serve for a little less than ten years. This means, in most of our lives, over 900,000 different folk will act as our local elected members! They will spend thousands of billions of pounds of our money on our behalf.

That's nearly one million people from all kinds of backgrounds, with all kinds of experiences and all kinds of aspirations. As in any human activity there is not one way of doing things, no right way or wrong way, no workshop manual. I was one of these elected members for twenty-five years, not just successful across most council activity, but also in education, schools and colleges, crime and disorder, community safety, the NHS. I strived to always do my best and it was completely enjoyable.

THEIR story is seldom told! I'm not sure it's ever actually been told before!

This is the story of one of them.

Just one in a million.

Chapter 2

Bill is Born. Leeds, 1952-55

Born at the right time.

10 April 1952 fell on a Thursday. Thursday's child has far to go?

Babies born on and around that date, and indeed between 1946 and 1964, went on to become known as Baby Boomers.

It was on that day that William George Taylor was born in St James's Hospital, Leeds, in Yorkshire. So, why William George?

*   *   *

Billy (William) Yule Selkirk 1890-1941 was my mum's dad, I never met him. He had been professional soldier in the Cameron Highlanders, a sergeant in the 2nd Battalion. Stationed during World War One in Poona, India, then Western Front (including the 2nd Battle of Ypres, then Salonika, Greece. He served for eight plus years, was hospitalised for 19 days, and then invalided out with colitis in 1916. He became a tram driver in Edinburgh. We believe he died of cancer.

George was my never met uncle, a Royal Marine (No. Ply/X 1550), who perished, blown to Kingdom Come on *HMS Spartan*, off Anzio in 1944, aged twenty-eight. Recently we had found out that George Hopper Hogg (not Selkirk) had been born illegitimate in 1917. George's mum, my grandmother, Isabella Hogg, had married Billy Selkirk in 1923. George had met and married (in late 1942) a corporal in the Women's Auxiliary Air Force (WAAF) from Ladywood, Birmingham. They had a fourteen month long wartime marriage. Miranda Maud Selkirk (née Waters) returned to Birmingham soon after being widowed. Little or nothing was ever heard of her again.

*　*　*

I was to return to St James's quite soon after being born to be treated for a condition my mum called pyloric stenosis.

St James's Hospital was a National Health Service provision, or NHS as it's come to be known. When I was born, the NHS was less than four years old!

The significance of the NHS is generally not lost on Baby Boomers, but subsequent generations may take this globally revered social institution as the norm and even take it for granted.

The NHS came into being in July 1948, its underlying ethos being that healthcare should be freely available to all at the point of service delivery.

It was created as part of a comprehensive 'cradle to the grave' welfare state to combat and eradicate five major problems as identified in Britain by the Beveridge Report published in 1942.

Its full title embraced Social Insurance and Allied Services and it had five key principles:

1. The approach must be comprehensive to cover all problems relating to poverty, from birth to death.
2. Provision must be universally available to all.
3. Provision must be contributory, with everybody who benefits from it contributing to it from their income.
4. Services at the point of delivery must be non means-tested and available to all.
5. Involvement in this comprehensive social provision was compulsory and all had to contribute.

This was never seen, set up or intended to be a feather bed. This was a safety net for all.

So, what did Beveridge and his committee concentrate upon?

Again, there were five problems to be addressed. The report referred to these as the five 'giants':

1. Many were in poverty and so suffered 'want'.
2. Many were ignorant and so needed better educating.
3. Many lived in squalor and so needed better housing.
4. Many were unemployed due to a lack of employment opportunities or their ability to gain employment.
5. Many were ill or infirm or exposed to diseases due to inadequate healthcare provision.

As a young baby, not realising it at the time, I was soon to benefit from the slaying of at least three of these five 'giants'. These human rights or privileges of living in a more fair and just society were gifted to and instilled within Baby Bill. In my later life, the need for me to both recompense for them and ensure they were just as available to future generations, became and remains crucial to me.

There's a very strong case, in my opinion, to revisit Beveridge eighty years on, reaffirming and re-examining the long-term needs of a civilised, caring society. More than a decade of Tory-driven austerity has meant fewer doctors and nurses and police, low morale across our depleted public sector and insufficient investment in health and social care, transport, environmental and educational matters.

*   *   *

What was the world like that spring morning?

Having been generally recognised as being pivotal to the victory in World War II, Winston Churchill was defeated in a landslide by Labour's Clement Attlee in the July 1945 General Election. Churchill bounced back at the General Election in October 1951. He remained in office until 1955, when he was succeeded by the short-lived and unsuccessful Sir Anthony Eden.

Queen Elizabeth II's father, George VI, died on 6 February 1952, and although her coronation wasn't held until 2 June 1953, she immediately succeeded as sovereign. She went on, of course, to become our longest-reigning monarch.

In 1951/2 Manchester United, yet to be rocked by the 1958 Munich air crash, won the English football league under manager Matt Busby. Of the two dozen or so footballers who played in his team that season, nearly all of them were English with two Scotsmen and one Irishman in their ranks.

The FA Cup Final in 1952 was staged at Wembley on 3 May between Newcastle United and Arsenal. A nearly-all-standing crowd of 100,000 people saw ten-man Arsenal (no substitutes allowed in those days) go down 1-0 to the Geordies, the winning goal coming from George Robledo, who surprisingly came from Chile, as did his brother Ted who was also in the team.

The first-class cricket county championship in 1952 was won by Surrey. The Surrey team included both Bedser twins, Jim Laker, Peter May and Stuart Surridge. Surrey dominated domestic cricket in the 1950s winning seven times on the trot. India toured England for a four-match test series in 1952. England won three of the games with one draw. Led by Len Hutton, the England team included Fred Trueman, Jim Laker, Tom Graveney, Dennis Compton and Godfrey Evans.

So, what sort of world was this bairn, born to three Scottish grandparents and one from Yorkshire, to be set upon?

Well, this William George was born in pounds and ounces. There were sixteen ounces in a pound and fourteen pounds in a stone. When I needed this information, it would bewilder me. I would never quite get why it was known as 'imperial'!

But it wasn't just the calibration of weight that was out there to beguile me. The decimalisation of our currency was nigh on twenty years into the future. At that time, the smallest coin was a ¼ penny known as a farthing. Double that for a ½ penny, known as a ha'penny and double it again for a penny. Then silver coinage took over from those 'coppers'. There were twelve pennies in a shilling known colloquially as a 'bob' and six pennies in a sixpence, with the nickname of a 'tanner'. Below the tanner there was a coin for three pennies, a very heavy multisided coin known as a 'thrupence'. Above the bob, came the florin, worth two bob or two shillings. There then came the half a crown, two shillings and sixpence, known colloquially, purely to confuse the people, as half a dollar!

The half a (dollar) crown was the largest coin in daily use. At the other end of the scale, the farthing was ¼ penny, meaning there were 960 farthings to a pound, usually referred to as a 'quid'. That's nearly 1/1000th of the basic denomination pound. These days we only have a coin, the one penny, that is 1/100th of a pound and even that is rarely used.

The lowest bank note back then was for ten shillings known as a ten-bob note! After that came the pound note, £5.00, £10.00 and so on!

Confused? So, you should be!

But this labyrinthine approach to things didn't rest with weights and monies. Take lengths, for example: someone had gone to even greater lengths to ensure that this was incomprehensible too.

A basic unit was the inch. Twelve inches to a foot. Three feet to a yard. Twenty-two yards in a chain (the length of a cricket pitch). Ten chains to a furlong (useful in horse racing). Eight furlongs to a mile. It couldn't be any easier! Could it?

We even got in hot water when it came to temperatures! Using the Fahrenheit scale, for some reason, or perhaps for no reason, freezing point was 32° and boiling point 212°! It was all very baffling!

How we measured volume spoke volumes itself! A pint was the standard measure, two pints to a quart, and eight pints to a gallon. I am not going to the mystical intricacies of gills, firkins and hogsheads here!

But what other factors shaped the world that I was born into?

How much did people earn? How much did people spend? How did they spend their time?

According to the *Daily Mirror*, a good wage in the 1950s was just less than £10.00 a week.

An average house was worth just over £2,000. Back in the 1950s less than 10 per cent of the population owned their own house. That figure is around 65 per cent these days!

Using today's decimal currency to make things easier, half a dozen eggs would cost 8p, a loaf of bread 4p, twenty cigarettes 18p and a pint of beer 6p.

Some food items were still luxuries. For example, when Elizabeth II became queen in 1952 sugar, butter, cheese, margarine, cooking fat, bacon, meat and tea were all still rationed and had been since World War II. Sugar was rationed until 1953 and finally meat was no longer rationed in 1954.

How widespread was owning and watching a television in the 1950s? TV broadcasting started in 1936, but it was suspended during the war and resumed in 1946. It's commonly thought that broadcasting the Queen's Coronation in 1953 acted as a catalyst for TV ownership. In 1952 14 per cent of homes had a television, rising to 31 per cent two years later. This proportion rose to 75 per cent by the end of the decade.

Few people owned cars, all British made, many around Birmingham. Popular models were the Morris Minor and the Austin A30. Depending upon the specification, one of these, brand new, could cost between £300 to £500 or £600!

Most people lived very near to where they worked. I'm talking here about the same street, the next street or in the immediate local vicinity. Few people, a very few people, commuted. Train users were by and large business people or holidaymakers. Except for the big cities, there were few black taxi cabs and private hire vehicles were non-existent. The bus was the king of public transport in both urban and rural settings. Buses took factory workers, office and shop workers, the school kids and housewives about their business and leisure.

What about people's leisure time? Before television ownership became more widespread, listening to the radio, ironically known to that generation as the wireless, was the main source of family home entertainment.

Teenagers had not yet been invented, so neither had 'pop' music! However, the *New Musical Express* did publish the very first record chart in 1952. It included songs by Mario Lanza, Bing Crosby, Nat King Cole and Vera Lynn! As you can see, the youth market did not exist, so young people were not yet targeted for exploitation. It really took the dawning of the so-called Swinging Sixties to see the development of a youth counterculture and then capitalism saw its exploitable consumerist potential.

Going to the cinema was the main silver screen activity. The popular films in 1952 included: *High Noon, Singin' in the Rain, The Importance of Being Earnest, Ivanhoe* and *The Story of Robin Hood and his Merrie Men.*

*   *   *

So, the scene is set. The recent world war had ravaged Britain, much of Europe and many other parts of the world. Soldiers, sailors and airmen returned to their hometowns unsure of what to expect. Two million homes had been destroyed in Britain alone. There was much to do.

The Beveridge Report 'mapped out' what needed to be done. Hundreds of thousands of new homes were needed. The National Health Service would be created. The 1944 Education Act, still known as the Butler Act, after the Conservative politician RA Butler, would create new types of schools in a new education system, but the act wasn't necessarily designed to directly promote greater social mobility. School dinners and free school milk too! Can't learn when you're hungry.

This was the world that we Baby Boomers were born and grew into. The balancing point of gender equality shifted, mainly due to the realities of world war. Women went out to work, 50 per cent more after the war than before. Ninety per cent of single women and 80 per cent of married earned a pay packet, many taking previously traditionally 'male' jobs.

There was a lot to be done and many challenges and opportunities to be faced.

*   *   *

My early years, just over three of them, were spent in Leeds.

My mum and dad married in Holyrood Abbey Church, Edinburgh, in 1949 and after a honeymoon on the Isle of Man, began their married life lodging with my dad's mum, Agatha Taylor, in the Roundhay area of Leeds. I never heard my nan called by her real name as she was always called 'Tiny' (because she was very tiny). To my knowledge I never met my paternal grandfather, Frank. I believe he was a travelling salesman.

My mum found father-in-law Frank polite, charming, a real gent, but she never spoke fondly of this period in her life, indeed, quite the opposite. I guess three generations under the same roof is never ideal.

Listening to my mum some decades later, I got the impression that her marriage was never a happy one, although lasting some eighteen or so years. I was told later that at one stage, probably pre-me, my mum went back home to Edinburgh telling her mum she'd had enough. She was sent packing back to Leeds, being told you've made your bed so go and lie on it. Perhaps that's how things were, rightly or wrongly, back then.

I think we left Roundhay when I came along and moved to rented accommodation, part of a big old house on the Brudenell Road in Leeds, in the Hyde Park area near to Headingley.

I assume Dad continued to work in the housing department of Leeds City Council. I don't know where or for how long, but my mum used to talk about working for Mrs Wagstaff in a wool shop somewhere in Leeds.

Again, I don't recall the actual experience, but we moved to a council flat on a large estate called Tinshill. This is situated in north-west Leeds not too far from Yeadon, now Leeds/Bradford Airport.

In later life my mum would speak fondly of our time in Tinshill. It was the first real home of her own, where she could start to make her family nest. This would have been like a Parker-Morris standard home, about which I will speak later.

My dad then must have got a new job, presumably a promotion, to work in Birmingham for their city council. This meant a move of some 120 miles south to the West Midlands.

The stories I have been told about my dad would depict him as the archetypal (that is, tight-fisted) Yorkshireman.

Little hope for me then, three-quarters Scottish, the other quarter Yorkshire? But here I would make a little plea. For people with these ethnicities and blends of them, it isn't that we don't like spending money, rather we are extremely loath to waste it!

During World War II a very small motorbike called a Corgi was built, intended to make paratroopers more mobile when they were dropped behind enemy lines. These were single seaters, with a 98cc two-stroke engine and were foldable. It was just the job for the job for which it was intended! But not just the job for which my dad acquired one. No helmet of course, flat cap reversed with me strapped behind my dad on his chosen conveyance by a large suitcase strap! Economical? Yes. Safe? Not in the slightest!

I'm told that as the furniture van rolled out of Leeds, my dad asked the removers if they could drop his wife and child at the railway station, their means of transport to the Midlands. 'Well, how are you getting there?' asked the guys in the van. 'I'd rather hoped to travel with you guys to save a few bob!' No gratuitous waste there, eh!

We must all have arrived safely in England's second city. It was the summer of 1955.

Chapter 3

Early Brum Days

This is the story about how we begin to remember.

563 Bordesley Green East, Birmingham, was a fairly unassuming two-bedroomed semi-detached council house, well built by the city council in 1952, presumably in anticipation of Parker-Morris standards. It was situated on the south-east side of the city not far from Elmdon Aerodrome now known as Birmingham International.

So, what were Parker-Morris standards? In 1961 Sir Parker-Morris and his committee, published minimum standards for new housing. These rigorous standards included how many square metres per person should be allocated in new homes, that every home should have a flushing toilet, with designated storage spaces and heating systems to maintain a reasonable temperature (13°C, I believe, was seen as ample!). Hundreds of thousands of homes were constructed pretty damn quickly and, in an era where fossil fuels, mainly coal, were deemed abundant, there was little or no home insulation. Many of these homes designed and destined for heroes were single-storey Emergency Factory-Made Homes, EFMH, more lovingly known as prefabs. Over 150,000 were built, with an intended life span of ten to fifteen years. Many lasted twice that! The mass-produced steel-framed Crittall windows transferred heat, well, cold actually, such that severely frosted up windows were quite normal, on the inside.

Birmingham is Britain's second city by population (certainly not by footballing prowess or performance). The city's population these days is about 1-1¼ million, over 3½ million including the whole of the West Midlands region.

'Ham' means the home, 'Ing' of the people and 'Birm' of the seventh-century Anglo-Saxon tribal leader or Prince Birm or Beorma.

Birmingham claims, from its leading involvement in the Industrial Revolution from the eighteenth century and beyond, to be 'the workshop of the world' or 'the city of a thousand trades'. The early construction and development of the canal network in the late 1700s gave Birmingham a transport 'edge'.

Looking back, there was a great sense that Birmingham's civic leaders or 'City Fathers', and I'm assuming here that they were all, or nearly all, male, were people of great vision and determination (and wealth?).

Famous Birmingham industrialists included James Watt (chemist and engineer – steam engine), Matthew Boulton (partner with Watt and creator of the Soho mass-production factory), Joseph Priestley (chemist) and William Murdoch (steam engine and gas lighting). Harness their success with the ambition of a dynasty of usually Liberal local city politicians such as Thomas Attwood, Joshua Scholefield, Joseph Chamberlain, followed by his son Austen, and Birmingham was set for an ambitious and successful future.

Many beautiful parks and public buildings such as the Council House, Saint Philip's Cathedral, the museum and art gallery, the 1834 Roman architecturally styled town hall (location for the performing arts and venue for the world premieres of Mendelssohn's *Elijah* – *1846* and Elgar's *The Dream of Gerontius* – *1900*) gave 'Brummies' a sense of civic pride and leadership – and an well-illuminated path to follow?

I never did figure out Birmingham's main market hall, in this still post-war period. It was a building, had been a building, but had no roof or glazed windows. I'd not been witness to Blitz and bomb-destroyed Britain so few years before. The damage done by the Luftwaffe and all other bombers wreaked such damage that took so long to rebuild.

We went there most Saturday mornings by the number 53 or 54 bus. Travelling by bus at the weekend was totally different to midweek journeys. Monday to Friday children and ladies travelled downstairs; upstairs seemed to be men only. If you had to venture to the upper deck, a perilous trip, children were usually confronted by row upon row of four large men occupying the two double seats, rendering the central passageway along the bus non-existent. Smoking was allowed upstairs and indulged in by all, it would appear. Even by the smoking standards of the day, this travelling ball of fog seemed impenetrable. I never understood the need for an official sign on the top deck stating 'Spitting is prohibited'! My wife tells me that the presumably posher citizens of her childhood Bolton were instructed that 'Expectoration is strictly prohibited'!

Back to the visit to the market, hoses with low-pressure jets of water stemming from them, were everywhere on the market walkways. It was such fun and the source of much maternal telling off to hop and skip over, across and through these jets.

One mission to the market, always undertaken by my dad, was on Christmas Eve to obtain our Christmas Day chicken, always attempting to be successful in a kind of bargain-basement 'chicken run'. His strategy was to secure the last-minute, last chicken in the whole of the city of Birmingham at a knockdown price. Sadly, one year his Yuletide brinkmanship fell 'fowl' of his penny-pinching ways. All his chickens had(n't) come home to roost or roast. He wasn't half going to cop for it when he got home. My mum would not see any funny side to his caper with(out) the capon!

We had a very quiet Christmas Eve, very quiet indeed. The seasonal argument exploded the next morning, Christmas Day. My mum had purchased and prepped all 'the trimmings'. There was only one thing irretrievably missing – the bird. My dad stormed out of the house. 'I'll get a bloody bird,' he said with little confidence.

Now, in those days there were no supermarkets, just specialised small shops like greengrocers, butchers and more general purveyors with corner shops. The disgraced 'head of household' was quite a while. He came back some considerable time later clutching a paper bag and emitting foolhardy and triumphalist bravado.

How had he achieved whatever he had achieved? He'd had to resort to last-gasp, backs-against-the-wall tactics. In a final roll of the dice, he had gone to a local, and closed for Christmas Day, corner shop. He knocked desperately on the door, somebody eventually came to remind this unwelcome caller presumably in most unseasonal language that it was December 25th. My dad daren't take no for an answer and appealed to the shopkeeper. He gained access to the shop, asking for the nearest thing they had to a full chicken. These small family businesses were run on an 'open all hours' shoestring basis with little refrigeration and rarely any freezer. Frozen foods were nearly all Birdseye brand and restricted to a narrow range. Fortuitously, mainly for him, my dad had stumbled upon a shop with a modest freezer. He made a purchase and scurried home.

That Christmas lunch was probably the most notable (and quiet) in Taylor family history. Alongside my mother's lovingly prepared 'trimmings' lay the nearest thing to roast chicken that could be found. A packet of ten fish fingers, three for Baby Bear, three for Mummy Bear and four for Daddy Bear adorned our plates.

Christmas food shopping was better preorganised in future years.

* * *

563 was my mum's dream home of which she was very proud. A decent-sized front garden positioned the house set well back from the main road. Inside, upstairs had a separate toilet and bathroom and two decent-sized bedrooms with storage areas. Downstairs 'boasted' a 'through' (talked up as being 'contemporary') lounge, kitchen with washing boiler, more storage and an outhouse with coal store. Our back garden was immense, the width of the house and running back some 100 to 120 feet. These really were intended to be homes for heroes.

All around us our neighbours were blue or white-collared workers. Engineers, office workers, librarians, architects and other professional, skilled and semi-skilled workers busying themselves at home-making. In those days finding yourselves in a modern council home was seen very much as a step or three up the ladder of social mobility.

One chap directly across the road wore an eye patch permanently. He was a Chindit my dad would affirm, without any further but much hoped for explanation. So, you know a little more, the Chindits, formally known as the Long Range Penetration Groups were special operations units of British and Indian troops that operated totally unconventionally way behind Japanese enemy lines in Burma in 1943/5 under the command of Major General Orde Wingate DSO and bars. Chindit comes from the Burmese word *chinthe*, the lion on their unit badge.

One must also report and record the presence of a great community matriarch, Mrs Paine. Mrs Paine seemed exceedingly old. She lived next door and always wore a pinafore apron, always. Now we children of this era always wore shorts and usually sported cuts, grazes, bruises and scabs, bumps to heads were frequent. The injured were routinely sent to see Mrs Paine, who, for some reason, would rub best butter on the wound or bump. Ask me not why.

*   *   *

And so, the Taylor family had arrived in Birmingham in 1955. Colin, the dad with his vestigial Yorkshire accent working for Birmingham City Council as a district housing officer (aka the council rent man) and mum, Isobel, with a much stronger Scottish accent, which in truth never really left her from my recollection, staying at home until I could start school.

My main playthings were my three-wheeled tricycle and cowboy outfit, complete with cowboy hat, waistcoat, chaps, spangly (Roy Rogers-like) cuffs and six-shooter in holster. Being an only child, with few other youngsters around, and having strictly imposed and closely monitored maternal restrictions on where I could play and who I could play with, my main plaything was my imagination.

That meant spending hours, usually in my own creative solitude, as a cowboy, in the US cavalry, aboard a World War II naval ship, in the trenches of World War I. Any of these scenarios and many more were the backdrop enabling my imagination to run its course.

Sometimes my mum would take me to the local cinema. One such time in 1956, we travelled by bus to the Swan, Yardley, two or three miles away. This was to see the film, *Reach for the Sky*, a biopic depicting the life of the RAF's Douglas Bader, starring Kenneth More. The story of the dashing, but headstrong RAF pilot who lost both his legs in a 1930 air display crash fascinated me. Bader, of course, went on to overcome disabilities, meet and marry the girl of his dreams, join the RAF as a fighter pilot and attain the rank of wing commander. As the war progresses Bader is shot down over France, bails and parachutes out, is captured, escapes and is captured again. Eventually, Bader is such a pest to the Germans (remember of course that Bader is reliant on his two, often confiscated, prosthetic legs) that he ends up incarcerated in the notorious Colditz Castle POW prison, from where he is liberated at the end of the war. This truly 'Boy's Own' real-life adventure fascinated me and most other young boys of my generation.

However, fast-forwarding to the later confession by my seemingly guilt-ridden mother.

The Taylor family had the habit, verging on a tradition, of not being punctual at cinemas. The practice of quitting the cinema when the main feature film got to the point where they had started watching it, was normal, with the accompanying statement 'this is where we came in'.

That afternoon, it was later admitted, this point in the film was reached and my mum announced 'this is where we came in', got up, left the cinema and caught the bus home.

That's all well and good, the bus journey was barely fifteen minutes long and Mrs Taylor got home to 563, made a cup of tea and sat down to enjoy it. It was only then in a moment of reflection that she realised she left something at the cinema – her pride and joy, her little boy William George.

The neglectfully forgetful parent got her coat back on and rushed for the bus in a panic. Retracing steps, explaining in the foyer and to the usherette, Mum found me illuminated in both senses of the word by the silver screen, still enthralled by the film, elbows on knees, head in hands. Some years later I was told by my mum that, as I was so lost in the film, she slipped in beside me and feigned similar immersion until its conclusion.

David Cameron did a similar thing with one of his children several decades later. One can only assume that if that practice is acceptable enough for a prime minister and his family, it's good enough for us!

Now the cinema incident was not the only time my mum invoked the ire of her family in 1956. Any self-respecting student of international relations would recall that April 1956 of that year witnessed the UK state visit of the Soviet officials Nikita Khrushchev and Nikolai Bulganin. The Ukrainian Khrushchev was First Secretary of the Communist Party of the Soviet Union, effectively the leader of the USSR. His travelling companion was a full member of the Politburo. These global political heavyweights spent eight days in Britain mainly in Whitehall but fitted in a trip to Birmingham aboard a Vickers Viscount turbo prop aircraft. Alighting at Elmdon, the entourage had an eight-mile car journey to the town hall in central Birmingham. This we can only assume was a high-security cavalcade.

Somehow, a local thirty-year-old housewife got wind of this international event occurring right on her doorstep of Bordesley Green East. One can imagine her tidying her hair, straightening her clothes, before venturing onto the pavement to wave a welcome to the passing entourage. We were told later that the welcoming committee numbered exactly one person!

Now, my mum was in the habit of a weekly, Alistair Cookesque missive back home to her mum in Edinburgh; a letter from Birmingham? Her mum would reply promptly. I would expect their exchanged news was mainly mundane and about trips to the shops, radio programmes listened to, and I guess what I had been up to. But not this time. My mum related this international drama played out on her very doorstep to what she assumed would be her receptive mother. She had waved at all the VIP crammed cars and had received waves back. Grandmother didn't contact her daughter for several weeks for consorting with communists.

*   *   *

The job of a council rent man appeared, through childlike eyes, to be twofold. On Monday, Tuesday and Wednesday he would walk around council estates (these days these would be called challenging social housing) often entering homes left unlocked by trusting tenants to collect their rents. By the end of any one day, a thousand pounds, more than most would earn in a year, would be being carried in a leather cash bag. Remembering that he, like most people, didn't have a car, this was done in a repetitive set order, almost like clockwork, day after day, unaccompanied and on foot, or at best travelling by bus.

On Mondays to Wednesdays, whilst 'on the streets' the rent man donned a (Attaboy brand) flat cap, presumably for protection. Thursday and Friday were 'office days', entailing a bus trip to Bush House, the housing department headquarters in the centre of the city. This more administrative role necessitated the switching of headgear to a rather more dashing trilby, for some unknown reason. Even through such young and untrained eyes, this switch of headgear seemed pompous.

* * *

My pre-school life carried on in this carefree manner until my first big rite of passage, going to primary school!

Chapter 4

My Early Primary Years

I'm on my way, I don't know where I'm going.

Of course, 1957 was a very important year in the history of education in the United Kingdom.

Why specifically, you might ask? The simple reason being that this is the year, in September, when I began my thirteen-year (primary, secondary and sixth-form tertiary) 'career' in state-school education.

My primary school from the age of five until eleven was Church Road Primary, later to be known as Yardley Primary. It was a typical Edwardian-designed school, built in beautiful red brick. Each of the three interlinked school halls had six classrooms opening onto them. So that's eighteen classrooms in all. From my recollection, each classroom accommodated in excess of forty to forty-five pupils. So that means that the school housed some 800 pupils! Quite a big school back then and even by today's standards.

The toilets were 'housed' a fifty-yard dash across the playground. There was no toilet paper in the toilets; it was too damp. Should a pupil have need to uneasily request such a deluxe facility, they would be issued with exactly six sheets of tracing paper-like material. Each sheet had imprinted on it 'Birmingham City Council Education Committee. Now wash your hands'. I'd like to thank the powers that be for this call to arms, well, hands, but the sink taps were usually either frozen or untwistable and there were never ever any soap or towels.

On the other hand, neither was the perpetual Olympian-style contest of who could wee the highest up the boys toilet wall facilitated. Like most things that little boys go on to engage in and enjoy, each generation thinks they've invented it. A calibrated wall, in feet and inches, of course, would have measured and recorded all optimum achievements for all to know and aspire to.

I was joined, admittedly with a gap of some quarter of a century, at Yardley Primary, by writer and actor Adil Ray, better known as the character and Sparkhill Community Leader, Mr Khan. Everybody knows him! I didn't know it but several decades later I would meet quite a few of his inspirations.

Now about my first day at school. This is one of my 'I don't know whether I remember this or the recollection is retrospectively implanted in my mind via parental anecdotal moments'.

My mum and I travelled to school by Birmingham City Transport bus, the iconic Outer Circle No. 11. The twenty-six-mile circular route, in service since 1926, was later regaled on stage at the Birmingham Repertory Theatre in 2014 in the celebrated young playwright Rachel De-lahay's semi-autobiographical drama *Circles*.

It was, of course, on a corporation bus that youngsters would encounter much-feared municipal officials for the first time, in the shape of the bus inspector. He was scary, hopping on the bus without warning and announcing 'Tickets, please'. One would feel guilty even when the evidence of purchase was plainly there gripped firmly in front of you or even more safely, inside your glove. Elsewhere was the other to be greatly feared municipal tyrant, the park keeper or parkie. His word was the law unless you fancied chancing it.

Anyway, four or five stops later, we alighted ('alighted' is one of those words that an eager to learn youngster would come across in officialdom and find them both baffling and mesmerising) and made our way, as instructed by official letter, to the headmistress's study.

This was a short journey of trepidation, not only for my mum but me too!

The infants' headmistress was called Miss Jones, from memory. She had a formidable persona or so that timorous first-day boy thought! My mum was very quiet too.

'Good morning, William,' Miss Jones said. Now to all of us Baby Boomer Bills, the use of the lengthened version of our names, aka our 'Sunday' names, was limited and reserved only for when we were being told off. Not a good start then to my school career.

'William, as your headmistress I am a very busy person and I won't be able to know and remember all pupils' names. When you see me you must say good morning or good afternoon, Miss Jones. In return, I will smile at you like this.' I was to find out decades later that Miss Jones, who retired in 1963, was actually Miss Elisabeth R U Jones. Teachers didn't have first names as far as pupils and parents were concerned then.

Now please remember I was the little five-year-old boy on his first day at school meeting his new headmistress. Without a trace of warmth and affection Miss Jones distorted her face into a forerunner emoticon; it was surreal and scary at the same time!

Miss Jones then wrote something on a scrap of post-war austerity, recycled, but neatly trimmed exercise-book paper. 'I've written your name, 'William Taylor', on here. Please hand it to your new class teacher.'

'But, Miss Jones, I know that already and also nobody calls me William. I'm called Bill.' I then realised that I'd expressed my thoughts out loud. Miss Jones replicated her earlier 'smile' and repressively instructed her new charge to 'take this slip of paper to your class teacher please, William'. I did as I was told!

Is this my first run in with authority? Authority 1, Bill, or should I say William, 0?

But what the unsuspecting Miss Jones didn't know, and neither did I until relatively recently, is that this wasn't William Taylor's first foray into the world of education!

* * *

Not so many years ago, perhaps fifteen or twenty, my mum told a story about her mum, my gran gran.

Seemingly once or twice every year gran gran would travel from Edinburgh to Leeds to see her now only child (my Uncle George died off

Anzio in 1944) and family. This entailed having her old age pension paid cash into a local post office for the duration of her two-week stay.

I'm told this was all a bonus to me for two very good reasons. The first one, a mint Yo-Yo (the chocolate-covered biscuit) and secondly a very small photograph of Prince Charles, heir to the throne. A very small photograph of Prince Charles, you may wonder. Exactly right!

Apparently, there was a ritual in our family that every week, my mum would take me to the local post office and acquire for me a 6d National Savings stamp. (The d was for old pence, confusingly.) This featured an image of Prince Charles's younger sister, Princess Anne. They were both to meet me some three or more decades later.

However, when my gran gran was in Leeds the trip to the post office reaped new and far greater rewards.

The co-conspirators would set off together on their mission. The much (cupboard?) loved grandparent would secure her then in cash payment pension and three-year-old William George his fivefold increased 2/6, half a crown National Savings Stamp, adorned with an image of Princess Anne's older brother and heir to the throne, Charles. The grateful recipient of this huge cash input had no concern for a possible gender imbalance at the time. And anyway, munching the delicious minty chocolate-covered biscuit on the way home was distraction enough.

However, the plot thickened one day and the older partner in crime became an unwilling and unsuspecting accomplice.

Seemingly the trip to the post office took a given amount of time, straight there and straight back. One day the notionally allocated time slot was exceeded by nearly two hours! Grandmother and grandchild where in deep doo-dah with the intervening generation family member.

Poor old gran gran returned exceedingly late with her grandson and was comprehensively dressed down by her daughter. What could have caused this great fallout?

I am told that the route to the post office passed the local junior school. Returning from the post office, laden with our spoils, gran gran made the mistake of taking a breather near the school railings.

The yet to be identified aspirant school pupil took his chance. 'gran gran, I've decided I'm ready for school, I'm off.' I was through the gate, across the playground and into the building before my grandmother could say Jack Robinson!

Now schools being the institutions that they are, welcoming signs such as 'No Trespassers' and 'Family members to remain outside school gates' dissuaded my grandmother from setting foot beyond these restrictions.

The hopeful new acquisition to the school's roll, aka her grandson, was nowhere to be seen. My grandmother panicked, assessed the situation, her predicament and possible solution. She would have to go in!

With trepidation she entered the totally unfamiliar building and looked lost, which was apt because she was lost! Eventually the school caretaker discovered and took pity on her. She was led to the school office and eventually the headmaster's study! What would become of her?

She was interrogated by the head teacher, an ordeal she had not experienced for fifty or more years. The two of them then searched the school on a classroom by classroom basis, looking for the errant child. Quite some time later I was found in a classroom, where the nonplussed class teacher hadn't a clue what to do with the situation that confronted her.

Seemingly I'd knocked on my chosen classroom door, entered and announced to the teacher (thereby bypassing the later life official interview with the head and note with my wrong name on it), 'Hello, I'm Bill Taylor and I'm ready for school!'

I'm confident these were the days before child protection, safeguarding and risk assessments were prevalent in all schools and other educational establishments, so did the unsuspecting class teacher have an off the shelf solution?

I'm told I was sat down and the head teacher was summoned. Talk about a drama! The three grown-ups concerned eventually took charge of the situation and determined a plan.

'Bill, you're little too young to be starting school yet, but we admire your eagerness. Please will you now go home with your grandma. She will explain what's happened to your mum. When it's time for you to start school you'll be very welcome, we'll send a letter inviting you to start to your mummy and daddy.'

Perhaps then, Miss Jones only scored an equaliser?

*   *   *

I enjoyed the six years at primary school learning new things and having a wider circle of friends. Sometimes lessons took place in one of the school halls. These included, after the school's only loudspeaker was mounted in its place on the wall, tape-recorded BBC radio programmes for schools such as *Music, Movement and Mime* and *Singing Together*.

On one occasion *Music, Movement and Mime* included *In the Hall of the Mountain King*, a piece from Peer Gynt, we were told. We were instructed to find space, and then make movements inspired by the music. I frenziedly dashed round the hall in my interpretation of the music and gained the teacher's approval.

Singing Together was entirely different. Songs that we learned to sing included 'What Shall We Do With the Drunken Sailor?', 'The British Grenadiers', and some lamenting tune 'Blow the Wind Southerly'. Teacher was at great pains to stress that the song was sung by the world's best singer Kathleen Ferrier, who we were (mistakenly) told came from a place called Blackburn.

On another occasion as many of the school's pupils as possible were paraded into the hall. With us all sat cross-legged, our head teacher, Mr Aspinall, announced we were about to witness a great historical event. I discovered much later that Mr Aspinall was actually L J Aspinall B.Sc. Teachers didn't have first names in those days! The loudspeaker was turned up to full volume. Cosmonaut Yuri Gagarin had been the first human being to travel in space in *Vostock 1* on the 12 April 1961. Gagarin's flight lasted more than an hour and a half. His Space Race rival, US astronaut, Alan Shepard, did similarly three weeks later, on 5 May. Shepard's *Freedom 7* venture into space lasted less than fifteen minutes. I'm afraid it's not clear to which of these two brave spacemen's courageous adventures we listened. Indeed, given the almost incomprehensible electronic noises being broadcast to us, it wasn't much of a momentous event at all.

But there was an event in the school's history of far greater moment, that captured the imagination and the awe of the pupils. Again, this was heralded by a suddenly sprung upon us whole school assembly in the main hall. Mr Aspinall demanded silence and the full attention of everyone there and waited till he got it. 'Children', his voice was appropriately stentorian for the auspicious announcement he was about to make, 'this is a great day in the history of the school and one which you will remember for a long time. At last this school will have inside toilets for all children.' The sea of beaming faces opened wide, agog with incredulous excitement. Mr Aspinall then used that well-known but divisive primary teacher's selection ploy. 'When you have all quite finished chattering, boys and girls will be chosen, six at a time, to go and examine our new indoor facility and use it if they wish. I will be selecting the order of this privilege by those children who are sat up the straightest.' All the assembled children then folded their arms as tightly as they could and sat as bolt upright as they could too.

The process took most of the afternoon. It felt like the zenith of our school lives. The new toilets were gleaming, the tiles sparkled, the whole room smelled of liberally applied and probably 'Birmingham City Council Education Committee' issued bleach. The paper towels in their wall-mounted holder looked resplendent and we graced the novelty of their presence by actually using them and the blocks of carbolic soap. Could things really get any better in our school?

*   *   *

It was whilst at junior school that I took up the mind-blowingly boring pastime of collecting corporation bus numbers. No need to re-read. I had and have no idea why. It entailed sitting on the kerbside waiting for the cream and blue vehicles to go by, noting the fleet number and later underlining it as bagged in an official paperback book listing all buses. For example, bus registered as JOJ 283 would be fleet number 283 and so on. My greatest proud pleasure was that every bus had a sign written on its side, Director of Transport, W G Copestake. I had no idea what Mr Copestake actually did, but us sharing a WG-ness was enough for me. One day, perhaps?

Every year 'the school trip' occurred. This generated much excitement and anticipation as well as preparatory lesson time. The trip to nearby

Blakesley Hall, a Tudor hall built in 1590 by Richard Smallbroke for his successful merchant family, was only a twenty-minute walk away. This would be conducted walking in twos with each pair of partners intent on trying to make each other tread on the gaps in the paving stones.

A visit to Jacobean Aston Hall, built for Sir Thomas Holte between 1618-35, architecturally incongruous to the nearby Villa Park football stadium, meant hiring a coach, which added to the adventure of the trip.

Other school trips were far more ambitious in their scope entailing very early coach trip starts, every pupil's duffel bag laden with packed lunches and sweets. These were often eaten before the coach had even set off from school and resulted in manifest nausea. I can recall trips to Warwick Castle, Kenilworth Castle and the Roman historical site of Verulamium near St Albans. But mainly I remember the anticipation, the grub, the singing and laughing and a long, exhausted sleep on the way home.

The greatest school trip ever must have taken place in 1962. England schoolboys versus West Germany to be held at Wembley Stadium. We could hardly believe this opportunity. It must have been an early start on the coach. The sandwiches wrapped in that waxy paper that sliced bread came in (we always had Co-op bread, others in Birmingham chose rivals Hawley's. 'Hawley's bread, Hawley's bread, eat one slice, and you'll drop down dead!' we would chant). We would examine and compare each other's sandwiches, the odd swap might be negotiated, but they wouldn't last long.

I don't recall if there were any motorways fully open in 1962, so the journey could have been a mixture of motorway, with the odd bit of dual carriageway and A roads. We did make a stop however at something resembling a motorway services at Newport Pagnell. We were allowed half an hour. Those thirty minutes were to expose us to a brand new, but to become a lifetime, pastime – the vinyl record. In the corner of the cafe was a huge, gleaming silver machine. I'd had my first sighting of a jukebox. I was mesmerisingly fascinated by its workings, all encased in glass. People who had one, slotted sixpence into the machine. Then there was quite a selection debate. Records, and for the record I'd never seen a seven-inch single before, had their titles displayed from which selection could be made. I just stood there and watched. The chosen buttons were pressed. A metal arm inside the jukebox curved along and then upwards to where the records were vertically stored. The selected disc was grabbed, it was twisted horizontally and placed on the already spinning record deck, and the arm removed itself automatically. Another arm came over, holding the needle which placed itself on the outer edge of the record, then, after a little initial scratching, the music began. We all crowded nearer. I heard my first seven-inch record and my love of pop music had begun. I can still hear 'Telstar' by the Tornados ringing in my ears.

Our half hour was up and our teachers dragged us away from our first fleeting immersion into the 'Swinging Sixties'. The day was yet to offer even more new experiences.

I've had to rely on black and white Pathé news footage from the time to tell me what happened. It reports that 95,000 screaming schoolboys packed Wembley that day and shows that the then twin-towered Empire stadium had virtually no seating or covered roofs. England scored first quite early on, with West Germany equalising just before half time. The visitors then scored early in the second half and England lost one goal to two!

I don't remember a thing about the match, before which I bought an England rosette. All that we did for the whole game was the nine-hand clap followed by the 'England!' high-pitched chant. By the end of the game we simply had no voices left. We climbed aboard our coach and slept most of the way back to Birmingham.

An introduction to the world of pop music and, albeit schoolboy level international football all in one day took its toll on the young boys.

*   *   *

What were teachers like in the late 1950s and early sixties? First of all, we being so young, they all seemed ancient, but most likely were all in their thirties and forties. Many of the post-war intake into this profession had served in the armed forces, possibly in the Army Education corps, the culture of which many brought to their professional duties. There was an element of emergency to the recruitment and training of teachers which ran until 1951. Teacher training lasted one year. Fifty-five new temporary colleges were opened offering 13,500 places. By 1951, there were over 120 state and voluntary, usually church-based, colleges training around 25,000 new teachers.

Teachers were held in deferent, respectful high regard, some in fearful trepidation. Inflicting corporal punishment was an option. I once got the cane for something I thought trivial both then and now.

On a different occasion, on church parade with my Wolf Cub pack in Yardley Church, we mucked about a little, as nine/ten-year-olds can do. The next day in school I was summoned to see the senior teacher and admonished for my behaviour in church, which he was attending as a parishioner. My defence, had I been legally sharper aged ten, would have been that I was there with the Cubs and not with school and therefore the case should be deemed inadmissible. I was warned that 'I was being watched'.

Sometime later in a queue at a schools sports event, I was singing and mucking about again. The same teacher required that I went to see him the next day. I duly reported to his classroom where he was teaching his class at least one year older than me. 'Why were you behaving like that yesterday?' he asked. Well, at the time, being nine or ten, I was no child psychologist. 'I don't know, sir, I think my friends made me do it. They told me to do it!' His interrogation continued, 'So, you do everything you're told to do?' He'd outmanoeuvred me, had me on the ropes. 'Yes, sir.'

His class had just had their art lesson and clearing up was taking place. This included taking all the unused liquid paints and jettisoning them into a two-gallon bucket. 'OK,' he said, 'plunge your head into that slops bucket!'

His class, some forty-five eleven-year-olds, like eighteenth-century witnesses to the French revolutionary 'Reign of Terror', watched on. I did as instructed and totally plunged my head into this messy quagmire. A total immersion into the art world? The displaced liquid spilled over the classroom floor. I was told to go to the toilets to clean myself up, my public ignominy complete. It took a long time to recover from this humiliating punishment. I'm not sure that the punishment fitted the crime. Was I bullied? Did he really expect me to act as instructed or exercise some judgement? A lose-lose situation.

We had a student one time and her role was to teach us a little bit of French as a modern language. She must've dobbed me in to our actual class teacher (Mr Bucketgate), as he suddenly appeared and weighed into me once again. 'Guillaume', that's me, 'tomorrow morning you will stand in front of the class and tell us all the names of the four seasons in French'.

I wasn't going to let him or his student get one over on me. The next morning I was stood in front of the class, things were said to me in a language I had little handle on, to which I replied: 'le pranton, letty, low tan and leaver'! Both teacher and student were dumbstruck! I was rarely asked again!

I think it was in my penultimate year at primary school when, aged ten, I got into another scrape with my class teacher. It could have been described, perhaps, as a conflict of artistic opinion. I think her name was Miss Cawley and one afternoon she announced that we would have a library lesson. Our set task was to visit the school library just down the corridor, choose a book and a drawing or photograph from within it and return to class to copy it into our exercise books. This I duly did.

I must have spent a good hour, if not more, replicating my chosen photograph into my exercise book. Miss Cawley circled her class observing her pupils' work. She arrived at my desk and went instantly, ballistically berserk at me and my plagiarised effort. 'You filthy, disgusting little boy. Go straight to the headmaster with your exercise book and text book and show him what you've done.' I hadn't a clue what I'd done wrong. In tears, anticipating the impending rollicking, I went to the headmaster's study. I was instructed to 'Enter'.

Seven years later, aged seventeen, on a school trip that included Florence, this earlier incident came flooding back. I was stood in the Galleria dell'Academia in Florence, looking up in awe at the extremely life size Renaissance sculpture by Michelangelo of the biblical figure David.

That was 1969. Going back outside Mr Aspinall's study in 1962, I entered at his behest. 'Yes, boy, what have you done?' I explained the task set and undertaken. He pondered for a while. He then removed the offending page from my exercise book. 'I'm taking you back to Miss

Cawley now to tell her you've been dealt with and that is all you will tell her too.' We returned to the classroom, Mr Aspinall told my class teacher I'd been dealt with and that appeared to be the end of that. I had the distinct feeling that Mr A was on my side but took the view that discretion was the better part of valour.

My introduction and immersion to the more classical world of art did not stop with my newly gained appreciation of Michelangelo or my unwittingly Warholesque pre-Pop Art full head paint plunge, sadly not appreciated or shared by my teachers. For some reason and by some other and more cultured teacher, the identity of whom escapes me, we were taken to see opera in the centre of the city, at the Hippodrome Theatre. Here we saw *Carmen* by Bizet and *The Mikado* by Gilbert and Sullivan. All I can remember is being astounded at the costumes, singing and general razzmatazz. Whoever had the chutzpah or the vision to get this group of council-house kids to witness opera at the age of ten? Thank you.

As fate would have it, my last year at primary school was spent in Mr Bucketgate's class. There were forty-four pupils in the class; Teresa Zemlak held the coveted number forty-four in the class register. It felt like our class teacher had his favourites and perhaps I wasn't among them. At the end of every school day he would say to my walk-to-school and playground pal, Keith Ginsberg, 'garrulous Gaston Ginsberg, please go and titivate the tintinnabulum'. Keith would dash from class grasping the handbell and ringing it through all three school halls. This gave the local GP's son a much-coveted headstart in the post-school dash for the nearest sweet shop.

Our school was very close to the communal playing fields for a number of local schools, only a three-minute walk away. Our cricket team's match night was Monday, the day we were allocated the use of the league's only proper cricket ball. The cherished 'cherry' had to be passed on the next day to Tuesday's custodians and so on. No ODIs or 2020 inspired slogging in those days, so shots were more circumspect. Anything that strayed beyond the relatively kempt playing area into the very long and untended rough meant the local rule 'lost ball stopped play' was invoked. This meant all players, teachers and spectators, sometimes on all fours, were immediately deployed to search exhaustively for the coveted ball until it was found. Was this over obsession with the welfare of balls to come back to haunt me in my later, youth work career?

*   *   *

Outside of school, what else happened? I loved reading; I loved reading anything, everything. There were some huge, almost too heavy to hold books that I must have inherited, called something like *The Golden Treasury of Knowledge*. These were hardbound in blue with golden edges to the pages, published in the 1930s perhaps, and inside revealed stories of invention and discovery. I loved them.

Then there were trips to the library at the Swan, Yardley. I think we were restricted to three books issued each visit. That meant two visits to the library every week. I don't really recall what books I read. There would definitely be *Just William* books by a lady called Richmal Crompton, a few Enid Blytons, and later, the boarding school-based novels featuring Jennings and Darbishire.

Comics were popular and I progressed from the *Topper* to the *Victor*. The latter crammed with true and fictional war stories and of course, the celebrated middle-distance runner and welder, Alf Tupper, 'The Tough of the Track'. I believe I then added a more encyclopaedic magazine entitled *Look and Learn* to my portfolio.

There was also a 'sick box' of comics including some American ones, that circulated the street to those youngsters who fell ill with childhood infections. Perhaps that very circulation was the source of them?

We did eventually get a TV too. A fourteen-inch, British-made PYE. Its cabinet was constructed in beautiful real wood, the screen occupying a very small part of the whole appliance. The TV, valves, a cathode ray tube and all other pre-transistorised components meant it would take some five minutes to warm up. Like many, we rented our TV from a company incongruously known as Radio Rentals. The two reasons for this were the cost of the initial outlay on one of these coveted contraptions and their persistent failure to work reliably. This meant regular visits by the brown-overalled and multi-screwdrivered Radio Rentals repair man. I loved his visits and as soon as the back cover was off I was squeezed between him and fascinating, strange smelling and very dusty illuminated glass things that made or didn't make our prized possession function. So much so that once my hero in brown had me parentally extricated from this pole position.

And then there were bikes, proper two-wheeler bikes known, for some reason, as 'push' bikes. Perhaps aged nine or ten, I was presented with one for Christmas or my birthday. This was a splendid model, a BSA (the initials of course, of Birmingham Small Arms, the manufacturer's three rifles insignia resplendent just under the handlebars). Initially, as always, I had to 'grow' into this bike. The solution to this juvenile lack of leg length back then was to put wooden blocks around the pedals, but that wasn't all, the aspirant and novice cyclist had to solve the question of balance. This in most cases was achieved by the poor old dad running behind their child with a steadying hand under the saddle. This took a matter of minutes or hours. Once achieved, offspring was ungratefully off as though the newly acquired skill was a God-given innate gift.

The ability to cycle meant an opportunity to cycle to school and back. But not before I'd spent a requisite Saturday morning being trained and then tested and then resplendently awarded, complete with embossed certificate, my National Cycling Proficiency badge, a red and green triangular badge, if I remember rightly.

So, the newly accomplished cyclist had: triumphed over challenge, acquired a new skill, and gained not only confidence but also new-found freedom. Some may think that not every child needs to experience and sense these challenges and build upon them, but every child, every single child, must have these opportunities not once, but time and time again.

*　　*　　*

At the age of eight I began my three year stint in the Wolf Cubs, later going on for five years or so in the Boy Scouts.

The 'Scout hut' was a ten-minute walk away on nearby Yardley Fields Road. I don't remember knowing many of the boys there, which was good; new friends to make. On arrival I was introduced to a lady in uniform who called herself 'Our Kala' which I later found out was actually Akela. Another lady called herself Blue (Baloo). All the other boys, having done their month's trial, were in the uniform: green jumper, neckerchief, green cap with gold braiding I think, and some odd-shaped green things protruding from below the turns in their full-length grey socks.

As a Tenderfoot, aka rookie, of course, I only had my school cap which I wore all the time. 'Excuse me, Miss,' (Oops!) I asked in my parentally honed politeness, 'where do we hang our caps?' My second scouting gaffe! 'We keep our caps on in the Cubs, outdoors or in!' I felt admonished. But not too much as I then kept on my green and red Church Road Primary cap all that first night.

The trial month negotiated and enjoyed, I was taken down to the Scout shop in central Birmingham and togged out as a fully-fledged Tenderfoot member of the 261st Birmingham, St Edburgha's Cub Pack. Their neckerchief was red with a grey trim. I was allocated to Yellow Six led by a Sixer and a Seconder.

Looking back, the Wolf Cub experience was a bit like Freemasonry for boys, although isn't it likely that Robert Baden Powell or his colonial acolytes were members of 'the Craft'? At the beginning of the evening, we would all circle up, Akela having introduced a *Lord of the Flies*-style totem topped with a wooden head of a wolf. Akela would indicate to the chosen duty Sixer in charge of proceedings to begin. He would bang the totem three times on the floor and chant 'DYB DYB DYB', the assembled and circled pack would drop into the crouching position and respond 'Akela, we'll DOB DOB DOB!'. To the uninitiated this was all quite bizarre. It was a while before I found that DYB is Do Your Best and DOB was Do Our Best! And a further while before I discovered that this ceremony which opened every pack meeting was entitled the 'Grand Howl'. I suppose if you're going to have a howl, you might as well have a grand one.

The rest of the pack meeting was fine. After the opening ceremony and the breaking of the flag, we indulged in some activities and also 'badge work'. A game of Battleships and Kim's (O'Hara) observation game were de rigueur for the evening. I really very much enjoyed it.

Akela, Baloo and others gave of their time freely as volunteers. As we got to know them as people it seemed they were all called Dadd. Akela, aka June Dadd, was married to Scoutmaster, aka Skip, Bob Dadd. His brother Bill Dadd was Assistant Scoutmaster. Baloo was really trainee teacher Kath Treadwell. The hours and hours, day in, day out, week in, week out that these people gave, were priceless. I and millions of others and their families owe them a great debt of gratitude.

Two big highlights in the Wolf Cub year were the Birmingham-wide rally which I think was held in Cannon Hill Park, and cub camp.

The rally in the park was immense; thousands, if not tens of thousands of Cubs and Scouts, all in uniform, gathered to use the group fund-generating attractions, sideshows and food stalls. The culmination of the day was the all-member march past of the guest of honour, who stood on the dais with other dignitaries acknowledging the cheering and saluting throng of Cubs and Scouts. From memory, one year it was the World Chief Scout, Sir Charles MacClean, another time Princess Margaret.

Our annual pack Cub camp was much looked forward to, enjoyed and talked about fondly for weeks after. It was always held at York's Wood, Birmingham's Scouts' camping ground. Cars and vans of Cub leaders, parents and other helpers were packed with the excited boys and their equipment. The journey didn't take long; fifteen to twenty minutes. We always twigged when we were close to our destination as the vehicles rattled over the World War II Bailey Bridge that straddled the nearby River Cole. We were allocated tents, laid out our groundsheets, rolled out our sleeping bags and surveyed the tuck we'd brought with us. Every meal seemed to be jam butties, from those large catering-sized tins of cheap and nasty jam, but I'm sure we had 'square' meals too – Spam fritters, stew and mash, apple pie and custard from recollection.

We didn't sleep very much all weekend, probably not at all on the first night. They kept us very busy with the activities planned all day on the Saturday culminating on the Saturday evening with a mass campfire sing-song in one of the campfire hollows constructed from tiered logs. We were wrapped in our campfire blankets and plied with piping hot and sickly cocoa. We then sang ourselves giddy and ging ganged our goolies in the dark night. This communal event didn't last much later than nine o'clock, but the lack of sleep and day's activities soon took their toll and off to our tents we went, not stirring until our freezing cold, character-forming, early morning wash, followed by porridge, and a fried breakfast with towers of toast dripping with lavishly trowelled-on cheap marg to be devoured.

Later that afternoon, the Sunday, beaming parents arrived to collect their much missed charges, who may well have dropped off to sleep on the short journey home or were soon wrapped up in their own beds. Don't worry, back again next year.

I really did enjoy my time in the Cubs. I got my first star, then the second. Finally, with the requisite number of proficiency badges in things like first aid, cook and similar, I qualified to become a 'Leaping Wolf' the highest attainment level of Wolf Cub. Staying in Yellow Six for all three years, I was promoted to Seconder and then the full leadership role of Sixer. So, aged eleven, I progressed via the Going-Up ceremony, into the then named Boy Scouts.

*　　*　　*

Saturday mornings became the ABC Minors mornings, held about a mile and a half down the road at the long-gone Ritz cinema. For 6d we went into the cinema from 10 a.m. till about midday. It was bedlam in there; hundreds of kids, in the dark, virtually unsupervised, having a whale of a time. Disney cartoons, Laurel and Hardy, Abbott and Costello, some cowboys and Indians and a cliff-hanging weekly rocket man-type serial were all on the programme. The half-time interval heralded tubs of ice cream, ice lollies or Kia-Ora orange drinks to be consumed. And to end this morning? The Queen. The final game of the morning was to get to and out of the hurriedly stewarded emergency exits during the opening bars of the National Anthem. Our haste to leave was less an unpatriotic act, more a final demonstration of supervision intolerance.

*　　*　　*

What else do I recall from my primary school years? The corporation bus in its blue and cream livery was the dominant mode of transport for us in the late fifties and early sixties, but then people around us started to get their own vehicles. My dad's pal from his Leeds days, Uncle Reg, seemed always to have had a car. (I need to explain here that during my formative years, all adult males and females close or familiar to the family, were usually universally known, out of respect, as Uncle This or Auntie That.) No one on our section of Bordesley Green East, a hundred or more houses, had a car. That was, of course, until our next door neighbour, Uncle Arnold, got one. The whole street came out to admire his Thames Trader van! Uncle Arnold was a private sector professional architect. Not so long later the family moved not too far away to their own 'private' home on Church Road.

Perhaps this spurred my dad to acquire his own vehicle. This he did in the late fifties, when he acquired a second-hand GPO van. The body had been painted grey and the four mudguards maroon. It's number plate was TOX 283.

Let me describe this van in more detail. Anyone under the age of fifty may find this hard to believe. This was way before seat belts had even been thought of. There were two proper seats in the front of the van. Any passengers in excess of two, and by that I mean me, had to clamber over to the relative danger of the flat rear space. This danger began were I to dare getting any dirt or mud on the front seats resulting in a maternal slap on my calves.

So, two proper seats, three gears, two flag-like indicators that popped up horizontally but didn't always return to the vertical down position until the driver stopped, got out of the vehicle and encouraged the indicator to return to the retracted position. The windscreen wiper, singular, was driven from a large black box just above the driver's head. If the driver accelerated, so would the speed of the windscreen wiper, going slower would mean the wiper going at a slower speed including stop.

I haven't mentioned the heating; there wasn't any. But there was air conditioning, if you count a little ratchet handle at the base of the windscreen in the middle. Twiddle it one way and the entire windscreen, hinged at the top, would travel a couple of inches forward – this caused a face-chilling gale to blow through the vehicle. Twiddling it the other way would more or less guarantee the windscreen was weather and watertight.

The in-car entertainment was me. I knew three songs: 'The Man From

Laramie', 'Robin Hood (riding through his glen)' and 'Davy Crockett (King of the Wild Frontier)'. It must have got quite monotonous for my fellow travellers!

Cars, and especially former GPO vans, broke down with great regularity, the only reliable feature of these vehicles. This meant that being in membership of one of the two rescue services at the time was prudent. We were members of the AA or Automobile Association, others joined the rival RAC, the very grandly named Royal Automobile Club. AA men would travel on the roads in Britain on a motorcycle with a bright yellow sidecar containing tools. All fully paid-up members of the AA sported a yellow badge on the front of their car broadcasting their membership. AA men were expected to salute every oncoming vehicle displaying this badge. If the AA man didn't fulfil this custom, the ignored member was expected to stop and ask why his 'knight of the road' had been derelict of his duty. The only acceptable reason for this discourtesy was because the dutiful patrol man was tipping his loyal member the wink that he was heading towards a police speed trap. There was method in this oddness, deviously cynical though it might have been!

Fairly soon the van was replaced by a Ford Prefect, a Ford Popular, then a Vauxhall Victor. All these cars shared a facility long gone these days, a little slot near the front bumper. When, after being left out overnight (i.e. most mornings) the vehicle wouldn't start, a handle had to be inserted and hand-cranked into action. This was a regular occurrence and was accompanied by fear of losing thumbs and quite a lot of cursing. Eventually, however, the car would splutter into life and the journey could commence.

*   *   *

All of a sudden these cars were followed by a caravan, the acquisition of which was shared with another 'Uncle', Uncle Malcolm, who was a school caretaker I think in Northfield, another part of Birmingham. This joint venture was stored at school.

Now, caravans these days have fridges, freezers, ovens, electric lighting, flat-screen satellite TV, hot and cold running water, flushing sanitation, even blown hot air central heating; all very mod cons.

This twelve-foot-long home from home boasted a sink for washing up and a two-ring gas cooker. It was lit by a single gas mantle.

The caravan never went very far; indeed it only ever went to a site at Symonds Yat near the River Wye, Herefordshire. I think towing the caravan made it a journey of about a couple of hours. Quite quickly, it was stored near the site, making the drive a lot quicker.

I quite enjoyed these weekends and holidays at the caravan which included country walks, trips on the river and picnics.

Prior to the caravan, other than going to Edinburgh or Leeds to see either grandmother, I don't really recall holidays being taken, except for going to a place in Devon called NALGO. Aged around six or seven at the time, possibly younger, we went twice to the NALGO holiday camp at Croyde Bay. This entailed a steam train journey from Birmingham New Street, with possible changes at both Bristol and Exeter, that lasted all of the day and was an adventure in itself.

NALGO of course wasn't a place in Devon but the National Association of Local Government Officers (now Unison, my union) retreat based on some no longer used military camp. This place must have been the prototype for the Joe Maplin's *Hi De Hi!* BBC comedy programme.

Campers were fed communally at breakfast and evening meal in two sittings. The fare was basic but wholesome. There were Ted Bovis and Spike-like sports, activities and entertainment organisers in abundance in some colour of blazer. The days seemed an incessant round of egg and spoon, sack and obstacle races for children and 'talent' shows for the grown-ups. Items were often misplaced by the happy campers and each feeding session concluded with missing items being returned to their grateful owners after paying a forfeit; a fine really. One time having been left in my dad's custody for 'safekeeping', a blazer-clad organiser held up my water bottle. Did my dad shoulder his responsibilities? No, he shirked them; it was my water bottle so I had to pay the fine. Up on the stage, in front of hundreds, my humiliating penance was to sing a song – with my mouth full of broken biscuits. Total ignominy!

Children had to be out of the communal areas and in bed by a specific and extremely early time. This meant that mums and dads could go for a drink or take in the show unencumbered. Again, this was very much pre-Child Protection and Safeguarding times. Parents put their children to bed and opened the top Crittall window of their ex-prefab chalet, hanging out a white hanky to indicate child left alone. The camp was patrolled at night and crying children listened out for. At the front of the entertainments theatre there was a sign stating 'Child crying'; where the identified chalet number could be chalked underneath.

We really enjoyed our week at NALGO but the second time we went I contracted one or other of the childhood diseases we all got; measles, I think. My parents explained this to British Railways, the outcome of which was us being allocated a quarantine compartment. We were isolated for our whole journey from all others. The compartment happened to be first class, something we'd never done before. As we got off (alighted) back at New Street my dad winked and said to me 'Mumps next time, lad'!

*   *   *

My primary school years were coming to their end, to be concluded by the mysteriously entitled 11+. This was an examination in three parts, maths, English, and some IQ (Intelligence Quotient?), its outcome, aka 'passing', determining whether you went to grammar school or not. Bright kids, in those days, went to grammar, the rest (with some intermediate bi-lateral, technical grammars or the newly established comprehensives) went to secondary modern schools.

Before the exams, I was bought a book from Midland Education which was, as it says on the tin, a massive education shop in the centre of Birmingham. The book was entitled something corny like *How to Pass your 11+*. The book included sample papers with the answers at the back. These were neatly razor-bladed out and the nightly routine of me being trained up began.

I don't really remember the actual exams, they must have come and gone. But we all knew the date that the outcomes would be communicated to us by a letter home. That day arrived as did the official-looking brown envelope. This was duly opened, the contents examined and the outcome announced by my dad. Initially he declared 'Sorry, son, you've failed' –

his inappropriate if not cruel attempt at humour. I instantly burst into inconsolable tears. He immediately but begrudgingly recanted. 'You've passed but not well enough to get to the grammar school. You've been allocated Sheldon Heath Comprehensive School.' It seemed as though there was an accusatory tone in his voice.

Around the City of Birmingham there were a series of King Edward's grammar schools. One of them had been placed as my first choice, my second choice had been the 'Comp'.

Later, my dad told me Keith Ginsberg had been admitted to the King Edward's school of his choice because his dad was a doctor. I didn't know if it was true and exactly what else was being inferred.

Anyway, Sheldon Heath it was and who knows what great adventures lay ahead. The long summer included the acquisition of the new uniform including a blazer that would fit me in about two years' time.

Chapter 5

The Sheldon Heath Comprehensive Years

My education hasn't hurt me none.

The summer came and went. My new school uniform was acquired but didn't include long pants as there was still 'some wear' in my short trousers. Neither did it include a bought jumper like those stacked tantalisingly high in former England rugby international winger, now schools' outfitter, Peter Jackson's shop. I was told we couldn't afford one. I think my dad felt an unreciprocated affinity with Peter as he played in the same position but for local 2nd or 3rd XV teams.

My first day at big school arrived. I was in no way prepared for the shocks to come. Sheldon Heath was a massive institution. I could only reach it by two buses or about a two-mile walk. And so, for the first morning at least, my dad drove me, an embarrassment-inducing act in itself.

I was put out of the car for inspection, a Royal Navy standard pavement parade. My cap was tugged forward, socks fully pulled up and turned over appropriately, belt on the gabardine fussed over. I felt sure that his pride, as well as his Navy days were factors in this very public process.

But where to go? I later discovered that there were at least four entry gates to choose from. The school itself was actually three schools, lower, middle and upper, each with its own assembly hall, dining room, school secretaries and several heads. There were over 2,000 pupils, a hundred-plus teachers, four gymnasia, a separate craft block and specialist rooms for sciences, cookery and needlework. To describe the vast network of buildings as labyrinthine wouldn't do the place justice.

But where to go? Neither of us had set foot in the school before so, embarrassingly, my dad waylaid a young male pupil. 'My son's a first year and this is his first day. Please will you show him where he is to report to.' The other guy and I were mutually embarrassed but, to his credit, he took me under his wing. On our walk I was shocked to find so many apparently fully grown men and women about. I later found out these were the sixth-formers, mature blokes with stubble on their chins and often a back-combed, en-bouffant, behived beauty on their arm. Some even held hands.

The lower school hall was our marshalling point. About 300 or more first years sat nervously waiting. Then a man wearing a black cape entered. It went quiet, pin-droppingly quiet, although he had said nothing. 'Good morning, children, and welcome to Sheldon Heath.' We later found out that this was Mr Ellis-Williams, the not-to-be-messed-with head of lower school in his academic gown.

This was our first morning school assembly. Mr Ellis-Williams nodded in the direction of the chap sitting at the piano, 'Mr Mapstone, if you please.' The piano thundered into life. All of a sudden, many children in the hall began to sing. I hadn't a clue as I had come from an 'All Things Bright and Beautiful' environment and now I was in 'Jerusalem'. Later we discovered that Mr Mapstone wasn't just Mr Mapstone, music teacher, he was also Cyril Raymond Mapstone, head organist at Birmingham Cathedral from 1961 until 1986.

What a day of change this first day became. In the assembly hall I was allocated 1PX, not having the foggiest what that meant. Then a rather spotty but apparently a grown-up stood up and said 'Will all 1PX people follow me, please.' This instruction we duly and dutifully obeyed. We snaked out through what we came to know as the foyer and made our way along a corridor to a classroom. This was to be our form room for the first year. We were sat down. The grown-up turned out to be not so grown-up at all. He was in fact our form teacher and fellow rookie, the brand new and newly qualified geography teacher, Mr Turner. He sported a camel-coloured duffel coat bedecked with what we later found to be his multicoloured university scarf. We found out later that this was his first day at Sheldon Heath too. That whole day was a complete blur. We had so many new people, both pupils and staff, and new procedures and places to discover, understand and assimilate.

Our first task was to copy down, with blue/black Quink in our compulsory fountain pens, our eight lessons a day, five days a week, forty--lesson timetable. We were given a small green pocket-sized, blank timetable card. Everything was emblazoned with the school emblem depicting some form of deer, or if not that, then the city crest with the motto 'Forward' featured centrally. Talk about corporate brand badging!

Our best handwriting was demanded when adding our names and Form 1PX to the front of the timetable card. Further, we were instructed not to lose our timetables and to carry them at all times. Was this our passport to education? But more strange practices were about to be revealed. In the forty boxes (Monday to Friday vertically and numbers 1 to 8 horizontally) we had to insert some very strange words. In the first box, top left we were instructed to add in 'Hymn Practice', 'Lower School Hall', 'Mr Mapstone'. So, we were to meet again. Indeed, the first lesson of every Monday morning we practised the four hymns to be sung in that week's school assemblies. I often wondered, why do we bother to sing them twice in the same week?

The morning went on, this process occupying most of it. For some reason, we were introduced to big words like Mathematics, English, Science, Religious Education, Physical Education, Games, History, Geography, French, Craft, Music (more Mr Mapstone?) and others. At primary school, topics seemed to merge during the day seamlessly. Little did we know that topics were now abandoned to be replaced by discrete subjects. But more change followed immediately. In each box, some of them doubles, a mixture of letters and numbers had to be inserted. But there was more to come. Someone's name, always Mr, Mrs, or Miss first then a surname, had to be included.

So each box, when painstakingly completed, displayed subject, location and teacher's name. Why, we didn't know, but we were soon to find out. We, innocent and brand-new converts both to secondary education generally and to Sheldon Heath Comprehensive specifically, were expected to get around the school, wherever and whenever, and find the right subject in the right room with the right teacher! This seemed like change overload to we bewildered eleven-year-olds, but it was soon clear that no change wasn't an option in our new educational institutionalised environment. Would we ever learn?

Just to recap what I'd experienced so far: fellow pupils, aged eighteen admittedly, in need of a shave, holding hands with women; strange men wearing capes; hymns sung without hymn books; the abandonment of the primary school practice of one teacher all day and the prospect of perpetually traipsing round the school in search of exotic and elusive subjects, locations and teachers. What more confusion could be laid at our door?

An electric bell reverberated from a small box on the classroom wall. I wondered what now redundant Gaston Ginsberg was doing and how he was adapting to grammar school. For the very first time, but with thousands more to come, our form teacher announced 'That bell is there for my information, not yours. No one move'. No one had. 'Right, now that you're all still and silent, you may proceed to break'. We had been still and silent but what were we going to break? Like the ever mysterious question I sometimes ponder at airport arrivals – how does the first person off the plane know where to go and why do we always follow them? My new classmates stood and filed out in some form of unison. Lemming-like we found ourselves in a playground, known eventually as the yard. We stood around, over-large blazers chafing our necks. Some attempted small talk with their new classmates, others with some relief spotted old primary school chums with whom they could compare notes and seek the solace of their familiarity.

And then another bell, sonorously signalling the end of break. What more could they throw at us? We filed back into our form room, our only safe haven in our new world. 'Right, dinner money now. You've all had a letter telling you to bring exactly five shillings with you. Line up, please.' We duly queued up, most of us clasping two half-crown coins, to pay for our five lunches (to remind people, each two-course midday meal cost 5p in today's currency). Some poorer youngsters qualified for free school meals. They were set apart from the rest of us by having different coloured tickets.

The process of paying dinner money took quite a while but we still had timetable cards to complete. Another bell announced that it was dinner time.

Some sixth sense led us to form another queue. We were learning to like them. But then I recognised the room we arrived at had been the foyer some hours before. Now, Formica-topped tables and many chairs transformed the foyer into the dining hall and what a din there was. Another grown-up split the queue into boys and girls. 'One, two, three, four, five, six, seven, eight,' he counted, each numeral necessitating poking each enumerated child. 'Right, you lot next table.' Everyone did as instructed. Silence was shrilly demanded by the banging of a spoon on a table and quickly achieved. 'Right, these are the rules, listen on'. This yet to be identified teacher stood at one end of a table. 'The boy or girl at this end of the table is known as the server, the person to his right is the assistant server. The person sitting at the other end of the table is the mucker upper, the person to his right is the assistant mucker upper. Any questions?' He continued without pause. 'Right, when I indicate, the server and assistant server will go to the serving hatch and get the tray of food for their table. On returning to their table they will find the food is already scored into eight portions. These will be dished up carefully and distributed around the table. At the end of each course, when I indicate and only when I indicate, the two mucker uppers will have the plates passed down to them in an orderly fashion. After scraping any food waste into the empty serving dishes, they will then walk, and I mean walk, to place the tray at the slops hatch. Any questions? No! Good, right, Table One!' What ensued was state-condoned anarchy, servers and/or their friends made sure they had the biggest portions. Mucker uppers were treated abominably. Lessons about your own personal queue position management were quickly learned. I'd already felt like I'd featured in the nascent *Hi De Hi!*, now perhaps I'd met a potential screentest candidate for the teacher part played by actor (and slightly balding) Brian Glover in the 1969 film *Kes*.

Back to our form room and those blessed timetables. Once they were completed and checked that we had subject, room (and some rooms were called labs and others called workshops) and teacher's name totally correct, there was a further level of detail required. This was a detailed list of what additional requisite uniform was necessary for specific and specialised lessons, such as PE, games, cookery or craft. Our form teacher then reeled off a litany of what was needed and when. We had to make further note of all this detail. We gathered that PE was conducted in a gym and needed one set of strip whereas games was conducted out of doors and needed a different specific strip. Further, some lessons, cookery and craft for example, required that an apron was worn. I meekly asked if boys could do cookery and was immediately and abruptly told 'No'. Whatever, it was repetitively stressed and then repeated, that all items of school uniform clothing must include the attachment of an embroidered name tag. I think the brand was 'Cash's Names'. Don't worry, we'd already got ours from Peter Jackson!

I think as first years, none of this new-fangled year seven malarkey, we'd been blindfolded, spun round and dizzyingly mesmerised by this first day at the new, big, comprehensive, secondary school! Little did we know that the second day, indeed the whole of the first new week and beyond would be a cocktail of change and challenge. The main trap of day two that malevolently awaited us was crystal clear to the cognoscenti but not us innocents! We were to find out that lower school alone had three staircases over three or four floors with three or so classrooms on each landing. Should we throw in the towel, with name tag duly attached, now?

Day two dawned. We started to muster together in the yard, perhaps as 1PX Against Adversity? We had our timetables zipped up inside our inside blazer pockets so removed and consulted them. We knew what subject we were intended to go to, clear where each classroom was and who would be our teacher. We hoped! We hadn't really had a phased introduction to our biggest transition yet; more a baptism of fire!

Our new teachers, appearing not to be operating as a team (or were they operating Double Bluff?), employed different tactics which metaphorically either wrong-footed us or kept us on our toes. When we arrived at the new venue, for a new subject, with the new teacher, the induction process of being allocated a never-to-be-varied seat was Item

Two in this psychological war. Waiting outside for the teacher's permission to enter was Item One. The instructions began with 'Enter' and then could be bespokenly punctuated by normally monosyllabic utterances such as, 'jumper, tie, socks, or go to the back of the queue and try again'. Where we got to sit was a bit of a lottery too. One adopted a system whereby those who rushed to the back of the classroom, i.e. the troublemakers, had to swap seats wholesale with those preferring the front stalls, i.e. the creeps. Another tactic employed was to sit people generally by house. By far the worse, especially for testosterone and other hormone-free eleven-year-olds, was sitting a boy and a girl next to each other. Sitting people in birthday order was novel and where I learned, quite uselessly, that I was born on the 100th day of the year. One teacher, I think it was in maths, sat us in alphabetical order of surname. It was by this quirk of fate that I was placed next to Roderick Charles Weatherhead, formerly of Blakenhale Primary School, date of birth 10 March, member of Kingsley House and St Thomas's Scouts. We remain the closest of friends, warts 'n all, over sixty years later. I went on to be Rod's best man twice, to Heather, then Yvonne. He had three children: Chloe, Robert and Jamie.

We'd been in houses in primary school, just colours then. At Sheldon, we had people's names: Slessor (the best, of course, I was in it), Lister, Kingsley and Bray (not because they were all donkeys!). We Slessorites soon knew our onions about our materfamilias. Mary Slessor was born in Aberdeen in the mid-1850s in some poverty. Mary worked in Aberdeen's jute industry and at the age of fourteen worked a twelve-hour day. She was a member of the United Presbyterian Church, later to become the United Free Church of Scotland. She sensed a calling to become a missionary and aged twenty-eight went to Africa to fulfil this sense of mission. Her work was mainly with children, the sick, hungry, homeless, orphaned and uneducated. Mary Slessor of Calabar died from and of the consequences of her calling, aged sixty-seven in 1915. Lister was so named after Joseph Lister, a surgeon and pioneer in the use of surgical antiseptics. I believe Kingsley was named after another great Victorian social pioneer, Charles. He was multi-disciplined – a minister of the church, academic, and novelist inter alia. Thomas Bray came a century before the other three. He also was a man of the cloth, an academic and a campaigner opposing slavery and the poor treatment of native Americans. I've often wondered how this quartet was chosen and by whom and what the process and outcome would be today, fifty years on? Mandela, Teresa of Calcutta (she's actually Albanian), Bob Geldorf, Alan Turing? Any others come to mind?

But over our first weeks things got better, or had we just got inured to them? Much continued to be new to us individually and collectively. Each subject had its own text books that were issued to us to further burden our load physically as well as cerebrally. Each subject gave us an exercise book; not sure we'd had those before either. Light blue for science, red for English, maths green; a proper rainbow in our ever-bulging satchels and bags. But one good thing back then, inside your form room, your allocated but unlocked desk was yours. They were capacious and anything left there by you was safe and secure: books, PE or any other equipment, sandwiches, personal stuff. They would not be touched by any other of the multiple users of that desk that day. The same for your coat. Hung up at 8.30, it would remain there safe throughout and beyond the school day. I don't think that that would happen these days, and I don't know why there seems to be so much less respect now for other people's property. Most people today have many of the trappings of a crazy consumer society: several cars in every family, flat-screen TVs in many rooms, TV satellites on walls and roofs, up-to-date, change-every-year mobile phones, tablets and laptops galore, expensive trainers, designer clothes, foreign holidays, you name it. Back in the fifties and sixties, it seemed like nobody had very much, with the corollary that no one coveted others' possessions.

Looking back, the strangest thing about our new school was getting used to pupils moving round to lessons with teachers staying put. Some lessons and subjects were better than others, some teachers more captivating or inspiring than others, some days were better than others, but there was a lot to learn and a lot to enjoy.

Just as we got used to slouchingly dawdling around the school from lesson to lesson, they threw an unexpected curved ball at us. This came in the shape of sometimes turning up at the right classroom for the right subject lesson, only to find the wrong teacher there. One time when this happened, we found ourselves in a non-music lesson with the ubiquitous Mr Mapstone. 'Right, children,' he began, 'I only know about music, so I'm going to set a music test.' Groans all around the class. 'Question one, name four Beatles, question two, what river flows through Liverpool?' And so on... My desk neighbour and I answered as best we could – black beetle, brown beetle, red beetle and then, inspiringly, ladybird. I wrote the answer Severn to the river question and then we petered out. Mr Mapstone, rather impishly for the head organist at Birmingham Cathedral, asked the class for hands up if you knew the answer. 'John, Paul, George and Ringo, sir.' We sniggered at this obvious ignorance. 'Correct, four points and the river's name?' he continued. 'The River Mersey, sir.' We were totally flummoxed. Perhaps the Swinging Sixties and Beatlemania had set off without us!?

I particularly took to PE and games. PE was normally conducted in the gym. This was crammed to the ceiling with apparatus and equipment: beams, benches, wall bars, ropes, horses, mats. In the double games period in the winter, some lads played football, some played rugby; I think the girls played netball. In the summer, boys played cricket and did athletics. The girls played rounders, some athletics and a little bit of tennis. Boys weren't allowed to play tennis for some reason. That first year I definitely played rugby and possibly cricket for school. Playing rugby on a Saturday morning meant up early, get to school by 9.30/10.00 then either a game at home or a coach trip to an away game. After the game, back home and off out again either shopping or watching my dad play rugby at the city council's vast sports ground, not so far away. The rugby team was rather grandiosely named Birmingham City Officials and was a team disproportionately populated by Welsh-playing and speaking teachers.

I preferred the rugby-watching as, at the conclusion of the game, I'd be given two shillings (also known as a florin) to go and get myself a bag of crisps and a Woodpecker cider. Eventually my dad would emerge from his post-match bath, and buy me another Woodpecker (or two) then I'd sit listening to him and his team mates analyse their match. Finally, we'd go home for tea and watch *Juke Box Jury*, then *Dixon of Dock Green*.

Really, that first year flashed by. New friendships were forged and new things tried. Around about Christmas that year, the idea of the school camp was mooted. It sounded fantastic. There was the mandatory letter home followed by a meeting. The idea was two ten-day camps, one after the other, on the Isle of Wight. I fancied it and was allowed to sign up to go. I think we had to take in so much money every week to lighten the load of the cost of the venture.

The summer soon came. We had our list of items to bring to the Isle of Wight camp. We seasoned Wolf Cubs felt we had a slight advantage, knowing the ropes of camping. The list included taking with us a pre-addressed and pre-stamped postcard to post home advising we had arrived safely. We had to assemble at New Street Station in Birmingham. The train trip included at least one change before we arrived for the Isle of Wight ferry and crossed the Solent. A coach met us on arrival on the island. The teacher, Mr Edwards I believe, pulled his rightful rank and stood in the door-well using the driver's microphone. 'Please hand me your postcards for home as you get off the bus.' The lad in front of me no longer had the requisite postcard. 'Don't worry, sir, I posted it at New Street so they'd get it sooner'!

There was great adventure on the Isle of Wight. Filling test tube-like glass phials from the multicoloured beach sands (Alum Bay?), visits to Carisbrooke Castle (where Charles I was once imprisoned, prior to his execution in 1649 and which houses a 160-foot-deep well, the water all being drawn up by braying donkey-power) and Albert and Victoria's Vectian summer retreat, Osborne House, were interspersed with more tourist-like excursions to resorts like Ryde, Shanklin, Sandown or Ventnor (where did they have trains on the pier?). Where was Blackgang Chine? What was it? I think we went by boat between the Needles? Returning back to the camp (Freshwater Bay?) in the evenings meant eating in the mess tent and then either a game of rounders or football or board games later. We thoroughly enjoyed ourselves and I went for two years on the trot.

*　*　*

This talk of camping reminds me, evokes much nostalgia, of my happy Scouting years. 1963 saw me turning eleven years old. In the world of Scouting this meant progressing from the Wolf Cubs to the Boy Scouts and of course, this was via a ritualised ceremony entitled the Going-Up

Parade. My now tiny Wolf Cub woolly jumper and cap festooned with progression and proficiency badges, stars and rank stripes were discarded as a thing of the past. I went up into the Scouts, joined the Kestrel patrol and settled down to learn the Scout's promise and laws, by way of induction. I have no hesitation in telling people how much I enjoyed those times and those years. This was mainly to do with the comradeship, the regular troop night, new skills to learn, badges and awards to tackle and gain. The weekends sometimes brought trips here or there, swimming at Green Lane baths a regular early Sunday morning feature. My time in Scouting got me around the City of Birmingham and other parts of England and Wales, it taught me not only the value of acquiring skills but also the positive cumulative impact that gaining recognition for these skills has. It also gave me opportunities to practise being in charge of things but more importantly, other people.

My new Scout shirt totally bereft of any adornments, was two sizes too big. It was supposed to last me to the age of sixteen. Over those years I became a standard Scout, Second Class and then First Class. I gained various specific badges such as Cook, Backwoodsman, First Aid, Firefighter inter alia. I even gained the Interpreters badge, which proved quite elusive to assess. There was no one in Birmingham Scouts who could *parlez* the old *Français*, so I was sent across town to find an old retired head teacher who could. Those acquiring this esteemed, rare but not coveted insignia got a double whammy, the standard badge for wearing on the arm and a further oblong badge that said something like *'Je parle Français'*. *Malheureusement*, some years later having failed O level French (*trois fois*) three times, this proved to be my first and only linguistic success. I stayed in the Kestrel patrol throughout my time in the 261st, making Seconder then Patrol Leader.

I was about fourteen when Skip asked me to pop along to the Cub pack night to speak to Akela. As by then I'd twigged that Akela was Mrs Dadd, married to Skip, aka Mr Dadd, it seemed a bit odd. However, I dutifully did as instructed and was pleased and proud to be invited by Akela to help out with the eight to eleven-year-olds. My first bit of youth work?

I don't think we were too hot on the now much maligned health and safety stuff. The annual weeklong Scout camp, which meant our Scoutmasters taking a week's holiday from work, were much loved. I can recall two, one in the Welsh borders somewhere and the other near Walesby, in the Nottinghamshire area. These trips were accomplished in a huge furniture removal van that somebody borrowed, and into which went tents, mess tents, latrine tents, mess tables, benches, campfire and other camping equipment, the kitchen sink... and thirty or so excited and expectant adolescent boys. I think we got stopped once by the local constabulary, but we seemed able to bluff our way out of any suggestion of any moving traffic transgressions.

In Wales our week-long stay included a trip to the Machynlleth and District Agricultural Show. We Brummie city boys had never experienced any such thing before. There were many marquees hosting exhibitions, competitions, demonstrations and various other examples of rural and Welsh life. Outside, there were numerous opportunities to try and buy all shapes and sizes of agricultural paraphernalia from tractors and combine harvesters downwards. There was much livestock on show and, of course, sheep dog and other displays. Many of the competitions were for the biggest and best fruits and vegetables, home-made hats, cakes and jams, the whole gamut of things associated with rural life. There were physical activities too: fell running, wrestling, and a number of more athletics-oriented competitions. This included the 100-yard dash for schoolboys. I entered the competition, removing my beret and neckerchief. The finishing line was a tape stretched out in the distance. The starter raised his gun: BANG! We were off!

I was nifty in those days playing lots of sports and games. I breezed it. An easy winner. The locals didn't seem too happy. I didn't realise there were prizes for first, second and third and a podium. Last to be announced over the PA system 'and the Machynlleth and District schoolboy sprint champion this year, is Bill Taylor of Birmingham Scouts'. There was little applause, but to make up for it, a cash prize of 3/6d, 17.5p in decimal terms. To this day I've always maintained that my usurious acceptance of this prize purse rendered me a professional and therefore debarred me from any future Olympics in the amateur era.

We returned to our campsite and got back on with chores like digging fresh latrines, soaping the outside of billycans, chopping wood and spud bashing.

*   *   *

But back to Birmingham and following the return from the Isle of Wight there were even greater transitional events set to happen but only of great importance to yours truly. The 'wear' was adjudged to have been had out of my short school trousers, so a trip to Foster Brothers, including the fascinating use of their pneumatic or hydraulic flying change tubes, resulted in me progressing to long school pants. But there was greater breaking sartorial news. After twelve years of hand-knitted home-made woollies, it had been further decided that the family coffers could stretch to a shop-bought school jumper. Previously my jumpers had been knitted by hand by my mum or gran gran, sometimes with rewound wool from an earlier incarnation, reknitted with an extra ounce of wool to accommodate the next size up. My socks too were often home knitted and that used to flummox the recipient, being basically a knitted tube that needed four needles but always seemed to have one spare! I can remember the agony of holding skeins of wool on my outstretched arms whilst the ball of wool was created by my mother or grandmother.

Not all women worked in the 1950s and sixties. My mum would have left school in Edinburgh aged thirteen or fourteen, starting work as a tea packer in Melrose's tea warehouse. Whilst in Leeds, there was Mrs Wagstaff's wool shop but she didn't work initially in Birmingham. As I got older, she returned to working in shops, first of all in C&A, a multi-floored clothes shop in the centre of the city, and then as an assistant in more nearby chemist shops. At C&A, Mum's work pal was Mrs Potter, wife of Ray Potter, West Bromwich Albion's first team goalie in the fifties and sixties! No WAGs in those days! This must have meant we had a little bit more money. It wasn't enough, as I recollect, to pay for our groceries one time. When it came time to pay, the checkout lady announced 'That's three pounds and….'. Whatever amount that came next didn't matter, we'd had three pound notes with us! Mum had the ignominy of returning something to the shelves and we sheepishly skulked out of the store.

*   *   *

This humiliation in front of a store load of staff and customers must have been hard to bear for my mum, probably in her mid/late thirties! Her housekeeping and budgeting was meticulously planned. How on earth then did this misjudgement happen?

In Mum and Dad's wardrobe they had an old shoebox containing numerous old pay envelopes. On a Thursday I think, from memory, my dad's weekly pay would come home in a pay packet containing cash, around £15-20. The envelope would have a 'window' and the pound notes would be stapled in place. All this to try to prevent any financial skullduggery either at source or on the breadwinner's homeward journey.

On Thursday teatime the household budgeting process took place, which I occasionally witnessed. The shoebox held a range of used pay packet envelopes designated as rent (originally 28/- (£1.40) back in 1955), gas, electric, groceries, milk, bread, etc. Each envelope would have had adequate funds dropped into it to cover that element's costs. At times handwritten notes would appear, 'Dear Gas, I owe you two bob, Milk'. Publicly accountable honesty gone mad! Obviously, groceries needed a few extra pence allocating to it to avoid further public mortification!

*   *   *

The school holidays were coming to an end and the second year loomed large.

It was around then that my dad and I, sometimes in cahoots with his fellow Yorkshire émigrés, started to attend sporting events more frequently, first of all Leeds United away games in the Midlands. These began with a visit to Walsall FC. I was intrigued and fascinated that the ground was called Fellows Park. For some reason the ground boasted a Laundry End, which I assumed was where the players' mums washed the kit after matches. I was further confused when the home team fielded a player called Colin Taylor. I kept checking during the game that my dad was still stood near me. I was bought the matchday programme, I assume to stop me asking questions. Unfortunately for my adult travelling companions, it caused me to raise more annoying little-boy questions than it resolved. Dad, Uncle X, why would you call a football team the Saddlers? This was around 1962. My dad used to call the team Leeds Urinals and then chuckle. The names in the team included a Charlton and a Collins, but I called the wrong player Bobby. There was also a Hunter and a Reaney. Leeds also had, unusually for then, a mercurial, but much kicked, black player called Albert Johanneson from South Africa.

In the early sixties, I was taken along to quite a few notable sporting occasions, including the 1965 FA Cup Final where ten-man Liverpool (still no subs at all back then) beat my now beloved Leeds 2-1 in extra time. This was also a managerial clash between Bill Shankly and Don Revie. I don't recall but I would imagine Hunter and Bremner for Leeds and Ron Yeats and Tommy Smith for Liverpool enjoyed a very creative ball-playing tussle that afternoon.

Also in 1965, I attended and witnessed one of the greatest displays of flamboyant, assertive, buccaneering batting that ever 'graced' Lords, the home of cricket. Aficionados of the willow-on-leather sport would know immediately that I am talking about the inspired performance of one Geoffrey Boycott (Yorkshire and England) in the sixty-over-per-innings Gillette Cup Final versus the favourites Surrey. I 'scored' every ball, over by over, in my green Acme scorebook. Surrey's captain Micky Stewart (Alec's Dad) won the toss and ill-advisedly inserted Yorkshire in to bat. Bad decision. Surrey had a vastly experienced opening bowling attack. Losing one Yorkshire opener cheaply, Boycott was joined at the crease by his captain Brian Close. They added nearly 200 runs for the second wicket, Yorkshire ending on 317/4, a seriously elusive target. The Surrey batting line-up included Stewart, Edrich, Barrington and other stars. Only forty overs later, Yorkshire, spearheaded by the bowling of Ray Illingworth and Fred Trueman, Surrey were all bowled out with a 175 deficit score 142. What a day!

After the second year and into the third year, we were moved up into middle school. The pace of learning and volume of homework intensified. But for me aged thirteen and fourteen, the biggest changes and challenges to confront me were at home. The relationship between my mum and dad deteriorated, imperceptibly to begin with but then it got so bad it was hard to ignore or deny. The atmosphere at home worsened. My dad had taken on a second job that entailed working some evenings and weekends. He had to make home visits to people who had borrowed money for them to pay back in instalments. The chicken and the egg here was that staying away from home made the return more fractious and that made staying away longer and later more attractive. There were many arguments and quarrels and I witnessed lots of pushing and shoving. I never saw anything over aggressive or violent but there was enough shouting, name calling and arguing to distress a youngster. My single-bedded room was directly adjacent to my parents' room, so there was little chance of not hearing everything. Quite a lot of what could be heard was really quite disturbing. At times I had to physically intervene between my mum and dad, actually separating them on occasions. This meant many nights for me never actually quite properly dropping off to sleep, waiting for dad to return at eleven o'clock or later, and then listening, waiting for hostilities to break out. My strategy was to hope that they didn't, that I didn't hear them, or that I'd drop off to sleep. That became increasingly less and less the case. The odd incidence of this behaviour became less infrequent, more regular and then the norm. Weeks of this became months.

The impact on my home life soon affected my school days. I'd manage at home on a few hours' sleep, four perhaps five. Then there was the two-mile walk to school and back, register, then assembly, I was straight into a packed and intensive six-plus-hour academic day. In lessons, it wasn't long before I was nodding off and not much longer after that came the flying piece of chalk. If that minor missile didn't rouse me, the wood-backed blackboard rubber soon followed. 'Taylor, wake up BOY!' I often wondered why I was frequently told to wake up, but never asked why I was falling asleep.

This was a dark period in my life that had impact upon me then and for decades to come. I felt guilt that perhaps I was an instrumental cause of what was happening before my eyes, and I was angry about it too. Add to this that I felt isolated and alone; isolated in that I thought I was the only person going through all this, and alone, because I didn't feel like I could share both what I was going through and more importantly how I was feeling about it all. This affected my journey through adolescence, it influenced my career choice, many of my relationships with people, how I viewed and conducted myself with them and also developed a sense of mission for me to work for them.

After a year of these episodes, possibly longer, things came to a head. I was sat down and told they were going to split up, my dad moving out. Although probably expected and the right thing to do, the legitimising saying of it was still a devastating bombshell for me.

However, there was worse to come in that I was told to decide who I wanted to live with, one or the other. It didn't seem too fair then or even now. I drew up a two-column list, one headed Mum, the other Dad, as to their qualities and what they did for me. Miraculously, the outcome was a draw. 'Sorry, you can't split up, I can't decide between you.' But that wasn't in the rules, my listings went to both extra time and penalties, before these were sporting norms. If I'd have known the phrase then, I might have declared that I'd been put in an invidious position. In the end, I can't recall how or why, it was decided I was stopping at 563 with my mum. The rest of the day I settled down and, as a fourteen-year-old, watched the 1966 World Cup Final. England versus West Germany again, but this time we won! It wasn't a great day for me.

Quite a lot of the ensuing period I remember little about. I'd instantly become a member of a single-parent family twenty years before the phrase came into common parlance. My mum swore me to secrecy; no friends, no one at school, teachers or pupils, no neighbours, no one was to know our business. I complied as instructed, telling no one whilst 563 was my home and I accepted home's rules. I'm not sure, by a long chalk, that bottling this up would be common developmental practice these days. But back then what mum says goes. I stayed mum.

Divorce was quite unusual in those days. About 25,000 occurred annually back then, that figure is sixfold these days.

Sometime later there were some legal processes entered into and resolved. My mum was given custody of me, but that's all I really know. The issues around maintenance and any other financial matters, I know nothing about. This was the 1960s and these processes were not informed or conducted through things like the CSA, the Child Support Agency.

*   *   *

In our third year at Sheldon Heath we were physically moved up to middle school at the other end of all the buildings. Our stay there was for a single year as we were moving up to upper school for fourth year and the beginning of our two-year O level period of study. Other third years would stay in middle school for their fourth year if they were taking no exams. At this time exams taken at the end of the fifth year were split into O levels or CSEs (Certificates in Secondary Education). At O level, both the curriculum and the exam content were controlled by universities and less academic youngsters did CSEs or nothing. Some pupils who took no exams at all left at the age of fifteen, some left at Easter time if they'd reached that age.

I did particularly well in geography already spotting a potential theory that British rivers were numbered. I'd already got the Forth and the Severn located but was yet to discover others. Perhaps if only I'd waited until algebra came along, I would have spotted the Dee, the Exe and the Wye.

Tipping you the wink or confirming what you've already rumbled, this story has woven into it a journey during which I was exposed to experiences, emotions or skill acquisition that built up into a portfolio of great life skills. The world and more especially Britain needs what seems to be in scarce supply. In my mind, these are organisational skills, leadership qualities and communication abilities. Understanding what makes you and others 'tick', how to get the best out of one another, how best to lead an organisation are vital attributes and I began to realise that I was amassing them incrementally.

Nowadays, this bundle of things in terms of leadership skills have become conceptualised and vocalised as *emotional intelligence*. Being able to pick up one's own and others' emotions makes organisations, interactions and communications easier to understand and engage with.

This means that the poor 'shell-shocked' World War One soldiers after months of artillery bombardment, gas attacks, 'going over the top', lack of sleep, death and mutilation would not be automatically court-martialled for the military crime of 'lack of moral fibre' but seen as experiencing PTSD or Post Traumatic Stress Disorder. The battle, the war, still has to be fought, of course but a good military leader realises that understanding and enhancing the morale of the army could pay military dividends.

I joined the Middle School Debating Society, becoming its secretary. This involved liaising with the teacher responsible, sorting out the practicalities such as dates and venues, deciding a programme of topics to be debated, securing a proposer and seconder both for and against the opposition, taking the minutes of each meeting and repeating that cycle. Every organisation always has a secretary, done well, it is not purely a bureaucratic function. A good secretary is central and essential to the smooth running and general direction of a good organisation. Some people in every organisation never want to take on any responsibility, some people want to be seen to be involved but don't want to actually do anything. That's where the secretary can make or break any organisation. The secretary gets to know all the members, what the organisation is up to and deals with the outside world, often including the media. The secretary keeps all the organisation's information, keeps all the records and sends and receives all communications. This was my first dabble at a secretaryship. I did quite well at it but didn't initially realise the skills I had collected in doing so, or how much these budding skills would be called upon fifteen or so years later.

The third year (aged fourteen) became important as it was during this year that pupils really decided their academic and even possibly career path. In those days we sat eight O levels: two different English papers, language and literature, and maths were obligatory, the other five selected from options that basically determined almost irretrievably if you were to follow a science or arts-based future. I think possibly French might have been a standard choice, making a fourth compulsory so-called choice. It really meant that a pupil did physics, chemistry and biology or history, geography and commerce. There was some assumption by the teachers that I was going to university and going to university to study history. That meant I had to study Latin as the eighth subject. Pals following the science route and expected to go on to university, had to do German.

So, 1966 was quite a year of change. Upset at home and school decisions taken that seemed almost set in concrete, would appear to be shaping the direction I would take for at least the next four to eight years.

*   *   *

Looking back to 1966, for the next four years I created a busy life for myself. Was this a distraction, a deliberate ploy? I had school that occupied all my weekdays from getting up till 4 p.m., with some homework too. Scouts and now helping at the Cubs two or three nights a week, and then lots of different sports during but also after school, meant it could be six o'clock or later before I arrived home. These included practising and playing rugby, basketball, badminton and volleyball for school, and even tennis after 5 p.m., after the girls quit the tennis courts. Add a school rugby game on Saturday morning and my week was chock-a-block. My mum must have gone full-time working at the local chemist shop around this time and I gained another, then socially stigmatising, status as a latchkey kid. But this gave me the freedom to come and go as I pleased. But still no one knew what I presumed was a guilty secret that stayed behind the front door at 563.

I'd created a good set of friends at school and in school's sport; the Scouts and Cubs similarly were the source of a different set of friends, and the teachers at school and leaders in the Scouts were a set of reliable adults too.

I also acquired a schoolboy nickname. Goon Michael Bentine had a really zany BAFTA Award-winning TV programme called *It's a Square World*. It included a sketch about intrepid explorers seeking the source of the Thames. Finding a tap dripping in a field, they turned it off, resulting in the Thames, all the way to the sea, draining away, with cataclysmic results. Bentine's Goonish humour appealed to me. In the show, he invented a nonsense pastime that required participants to boggle, nurd or drat to advance. I became Boggler!

The summer of 1968 found me sitting my O level exams. The school had eventually decided that trying to get me to learn Latin was a waste of everybody's time and there's my three times' failure at O level French not to talk about. This meant I had achieved six reasonably good results and could proceed into the sixth form to study history, geography and economics at A level.

It must be around this time that we said *adieu* to our musical mentor,

Mr Mapstone. But there was some notion of music being compulsory at Sheldon Heath and we were introduced to Mrs Faultless, Mr Mapstone's assistant, we presumed. With ¼-inch skinhead haircuts, many of us wearing highly polished Doc Martens, we sauntered into her music suite. She sat us all down, distributed some books. When we opened them, we were shocked, awestruck, to find there was line after line of a variety of different blobs and other indecipherable squiggles, known to others as a musical score. The title page read Mendelssohn's *Elijah*. Mrs Faultless set her gramophone revolving to play some classical music. She closed her eyes in appreciation. We didn't really know what to do and then she circulated the room. I was asked why I was on the page I was when the music was on another page. She inspected the progress we boys were making (the girls must have been in cookery or something). Mrs Faultless lifted the stylus from the LP. 'How many of you can read music, please?' Not one arm reached for the sky. 'What is the significance of this music to our city?' This question was met with stony silence. What we didn't know, but soon did, was that this oratorio was first performed in Birmingham Town Hall in 1846, conducted by the composer. It may well have been commissioned by the city council. Mrs Faultless despaired and collected in the books. Our next lesson with her we sat down quietly. Then from her storeroom she produced cellos enough for one each. She then appeared to slip into talking algebra… C, D, A, etc. 'Stop, stop. How many of you can't play a musical instrument?' This time every hand was raised. What was she going to do with us? I don't really know what she expected. The compromise was for the rest of that course we brought in an LP that we liked, mine being Simon and Garfunkel. What we found out later was that Mrs Faultless was something like the resident harpsichordist on the BBC classical music station. We had given her a rude awakening!

Sadly, in some ways, at about sixteen or seventeen years of age the Scouts and I parted company. To be in the Scouts you had to believe in God and be loyal to the Queen, both things I had increasingly begun to question. I spoke with Skip, the outcome being, with some sadness, that we went our own separate ways. Great times, great memories.

*   *   *

But other things were happening across the world of which we couldn't help but be aware. The Sixties had swung but other things were happening too. The Beatles (yes, I'd found out who they were now), were in the vanguard but not on their own, of a music-driven social change; I steer short of describing it as a revolution, but it may well have been. They led, or had attributed to them, the idea of turning the previous intergenerational order on its head. Young people, it seemed, not only ignored or challenged the social mores established by their elders, they began to establish their own.

I suppose the pace was set in 1966 when John Lennon asserted 'we're more popular than Jesus now'. Once these comments sailed the Atlantic, there was furore. Starting with WAQY (as in wacky) in Alabama, some radio stations stopped playing any Beatles songs; the records were publicly burned, especially in the Deep South conservative Bible Belt. Rolling Stone magazine reported that the Beatles' tour of the USA saw some concerts picketed by the Ku Klux Klan. Was this a challenge to the established theological order or a publicity stunt? The Beatles were very marketable and marketed. For what seemed like the first time ever, young people began to have disposable income and this fuelled a period of conspicuous consumerism – youth culture had arrived; it was there to be exploited. The Beatles and others experimented with recreational and hallucinogenic drugs and transcendental meditation under the Maharishi Mahesh Yogi. Sgt. Pepper's came along in 1967, reporting there were 4,000 holes in Blackburn, Lancashire. In a very few years, the Fab Four had come from 'She Loves You' to 'All You Need Is Love'. It wasn't just the Beatles, many other groups emerged on both sides of the Atlantic, both challenging the status quo and promulgating different values and different ways of life. The Byrds, The Rolling Stones, Dylan, The Who and others were all talking about my generation. Young people possibly listened but most certainly they got caught up in this maelstrom of change. It wasn't cool to conform. Youth found and developed its own culture, with its own music, its own fashions, its own vocabulary, possibly even language. As Canadian singer-songwriter Joni Mitchell said, 'we were trying to understand ourselves in our world'. There was nothing that you can do that can't be done.

Just think of all these changes. National Service by conscription came to an end finally in 1963. That meant, that for better or worse, all of our young men were no longer immersed in and inculcated by a top-down, no questions asked, relatively brutal military discipline. Hang on a minute, young people thinking, speaking and acting for themselves? What is going on here? Things were happening to young people en masse and individually.

During the Sixties, most homes owning a television became commonplace and with more televisions, came more news. Not dedicated 24/7 news channels as we have today, but world events being broadcast right there into the corner of people's living rooms must have had immense impact on what we knew and began to think. 1963 saw moving, in both senses, images of the assassination of US President Jack Kennedy in Dallas, Texas, being beamed across the world.

Dr Martin Luther King Jnr was a civil rights leader throughout the fifties and sixties. A committed and devoted Christian in the Baptist movement, his faith caused him to speak out against social injustice. King saw issues such as racial segregation on buses, discriminatory racial bias in employment and career opportunities, the increasingly opposed war in Vietnam, amongst many others, as issues he must address; as he did in his hugely moving, iconoclastic 'I have a dream' speech delivered from the steps of the Lincoln Memorial in August 1963. 250,000 people in attendance heard King's speech, many millions more around the world on TV. April 1968 saw the murder of Dr King in Memphis, Tennessee.

Two months after King's slaying, JFK's younger brother Bobby, and likely Democrat presidential nomination, was murdered in June 1968 at the Democrat primary in Los Angeles, having just won that vote.

In August 1968, the Democrat Party Convention, to decide their presidential candidate, was to be held in Chicago. At the time, Democrat Lyndon B Johnson was the increasingly unpopular president, having taken over after the assassinated JF Kennedy. In March 1968, Johnson, seeing the writing on the wall, announced his withdrawal from seeking the (his second term) candidature, backing Hubert Humphrey instead. With Bobby Kennedy dead, Humphrey became the likely favourite. All this uncertainty and the growing disaffection with the war in Vietnam mixed a heady cocktail in Illinois' major city. Intended to be peaceful, students and other protestors gathered. The police and national guard, akin to a stood-down Territorial Army reserve, were deployed, bayonets fixed on M1 rifles. The resultant scuffles became exchanges of rocks and bottles from one side and baton charges and tear gas from the other. Scuffles broke out on the floor of the conference hall too. America and then the rest of the world, in their own living rooms, had never witnessed such domestic conflict, insurrection even. The Establishment's response seemed disproportionate. The cry 'the whole world is watching us', very much brought home, literally, that the general public were now, irredeemably informed about world events, almost as they happened. This was especially true for the world's younger people.

Richard Nixon subsequently won the November 1968 election for the Republicans, and the rest of that is truly very much history.

These events and their instantaneous global broadcasting were not restricted to the United States. Our televisions brought to us the exploits of Fidel Castro in Cuba and Ho Chi Minh in Vietnam, all challenging the old world order.

The continued military intervention of the United States in Vietnam galvanised opposition opinion, first of all within the US and then globally. Those opposed to the war were initially dismissed as hippies, students and other leftist subversives. The US finally pulled out all its troops in 1973. However, the road to that final evacuation caused much disquiet and dissent at home, including, in 1970, the national guard being again deployed at Kent University, Ohio, to quell protesting students, resulting in nine students being injured and four being killed.

Anti-Vietnam War protests had also been seen on the streets of London when in 1968 there was a stand-off and conflict between protesters and the police outside the US Embassy in Grosvenor Square. In Britain again, but a couple of years later, demonstrations occurred led by the anti-apartheid movement's Peter, now Lord, Hain against rugby tours to Britain by apartheid-stricken South Africa.

Right across Africa, much of it attributable to the colonial carve up of the continent during the Europeans' scramble for minerals and other resources during the eighteenth and nineteenth centuries, there was growing demand for independence from Britain, France, Holland

and other colonial powers. As so-called national borders had been decided taking little or no cogniscance of a centuries' old tribal or other delineations, that process was never going to be easy and much blood was spilt. Botswana, Gambia, Kenya, Lesotho, Nigeria, Sierra Leone, Tanzania, Uganda and Zambia were amongst those countries to gain independence from Britain during the 1960s.

Of course, in China throughout the 1960s, Chairman Mao Tse Tung (as we knew him then) and his Red Guards, little red books and Cultural Revolution was one interpretation of communist reform.

Europe was in transitional foment too. During the Prague spring of 1968 the communist government of the then Czechoslovakia attempted change within their country resulting in a military invasion by the USSR and other Warsaw Pact troops to get these miscreants back in line. I remember the name Jan Palach so well from these times; the local student committing suicide by fire in protest at the Soviet intervention.

Paris 1968 also saw conflict on its streets and in other French cities when students and workers protested about how things were. At one point, President de Gaulle fled France for his own safety. Again, police and the much-feared anti-riot CRS (Compagnies Républicaines de Sécurité) were deployed on the streets to suppress social unrest.

The sixties also brought conflict during the Troubles in Northern Ireland. These were unresolved issues ostensibly between the Protestant majority and the Catholic minority. Sectarian paramilitary groups on both sides proliferated, resulting in many casualties and fatalities, the deployment of British troops on the nation's streets and internment without trial.

The story I tell, the picture I paint as the 1960s draws to its end, is one of challenge and change. I know it now to be hegemony, having studied the Italian philosopher Antonio Gramsci many years later. One dominant class or societal group had controlled the rest for a long time. Things were about to change politically, economically, socially, sexually and in many other ways, we thought and hoped. Ideas had their proponents or potential leaders:

+ Andy ('Art is what you can get away with') Warhol and his Factory;

+ Jerry ('Just do it') Rubin who infuriatingly blew bubbles when he appeared before the House UnAmerican Activities Committee;
+ Abbie Hoffman, co-founder of the Youth International Party or Yippies (the FBI had a 13,000-page dossier on Hoffman) became one of the Chicago Seven eventually convicted for crossing the state line to demonstrate at the 1968 Democrat Convention in Chicago;
+ Tariq Ali, a Pakistan-born, British, Oxford-educated leftist activist, now writer and broadcaster;
+ Allen Ginsberg prominent in the Beat Generation of writers and other poets, painters, writers and other artists offering their interpretation of events.

*   *   *

It was around about this time I started to do a bit of part-time work. My first job was at the weekend as a petrol pump attendant very close to Yardley Parish Church at Charter's Garage. If serving petrol was slack, the two brothers got me doing a bit of basic motor mechanics. I liked working there. I had a crash apprenticeship in industrial language. Every tool was prefixed by the adjective 'fucking'! There were 'fucking' spanners, 'fucking' wheel braces, 'fucking' jacks. I wondered if this was taught at college, and although not qualified to do so and remember being a failure at languages, I felt compelled to join in.

I was given a one-size-doesn't-fit-all boiler suit and after any fiddling with engines I could clean my oily hands from the huge tin of oil and grease-dispersing Swarfega. I went home with my hands but especially my fingernails blackened not just because of oil but because I felt inducted into the Midlands manly world of engineering. Nearly every bloke I knew or came across always had grubby fingernails. I'd now joined them and could speak their lingo a bit.

The garage paid me the princely sum of half a crown an hour. So eight hours work clocked me up a quid. But I was destined for greater things.

Greater things for me at that time meant a pay increase and the career change. My wages rocketed up 40 per cent from 2/6 to 3/6 an hour and

I went to work at the supermarket near the Yew Tree area. Yes, the very same one my underfunded mother had had to leave in disgrace a few years earlier. I believe that the building is now a Wetherspoons outlet, ironically and paradoxically possibly named after me, The William Tyler.

I worked there either in the evenings or weekends. There were female shop assistants for me to fantasise about and, befitting of my station in the staffing hierarchy, they allocated me a role. It was unofficial, but I was appointed biscuit breaker. My job, when so directed, was to get clumsy in the storeroom, bash some biscuits, rendering them unsellable and thus destined for the staffroom. I was expected to bash to order, biscuit specific. The only problem with that I didn't particularly like custard creams, although I grew to do so.

I had other transferable skills to master, mopping apparently being one of them and identified by management as being high up my skills acquisition list. This wasn't discussed and agreed by any sort of staff development process. The manager just told me. I was absolutely useless at it and left more soapy suds on the floor than got returned to the bucket. The manager's office was high up above the shop floor and had a large window from which he could survey his demesne. 'Excuse me, lad, it doesn't seem like you've been taught how to mop properly, let me give you a lesson.' My manager grabbed the mop, immersed it in the bucket, twisted it between his outstretched palms, scrunched the mop head into that strainer thing and again twisted this cleaning apparatus barely moist. He then adopted a slight stoop and with one hand high on the handle and the other lower, he continued quite vigorously with a side-to-side action. I was quite impressed; he was good at it. Fortuitously, I chose not to praise him and his obvious skill attributes. I was told to get on with it and that he'd be back in twenty minutes. I didn't know if he knew, but I knew he watched all that time from his inspection eyrie.

He obviously had his eagle eye on me. One time I had no tasks allocated to me. Even the staffroom biscuit tin was full. I was alone on the shop floor near the refrigerated display cabinets for margarine and butter. The Lurpak and other leading proprietary brands (the stuff Mrs Paine would have applied) were neatly displayed in lines like guards at Trooping the Colour. Our own brand seemed haphazardly dumped in willy-nilly. I didn't think that was very fair or nice. So, I then painstakingly embarked upon rectifying this discernible dairy goods injustice and eyesore.

I got completely engrossed in this self-identified process; it took me ages. When complete, I stood back and admired the order I had brought to anarchy. All of a sudden, I felt the manager's presence and omnipotence bearing down very close to me. 'Son, I've been watching you for an hour or more very carefully and patiently reorganising that fridge. Now, can you please take out all of our own-brand butter and chuck it all back in randomly and higgledy-piggledy?' Being a bright (spark) kind of a lad, I misguidedly ask the question, the obvious question, why?

I got the impression I'd angered my superior. I suddenly got the inkling of irksome wrath. However, he remained serenely calm and composed on the outside at least. 'Son, you have the balls to ask me a question. I reward that by paying you the compliment of replying. One,' he tapped on imaginary military epaulettes on his shoulder, 'Cos I'm your 'fucking' boss and you'll do as I tell you.' I was taken aback, astounded. Had he worked in the motor industry too? 'And two, and only because you've asked, here's the other reason. We're trying to create a merchandising or marketing atmosphere. We want customers to feel quality in our leading proprietary brands and be prepared to pay a bit more, with a bit more profit for us. We have our own brand, however, and we want them to buy those because they're value for money, a cheaper option. So we present them as a 'stack them high, sell them cheap' alternative.'

So, a for-free lesson in comparative power structures within an organisation and an introduction to basic marketing in the retail trade. I felt the whole incident to have been one of instructive learning. I also felt, well I'm pretty sure I did, the hot breath of ire on my neck as I walked away to find another task from which I could learn.

*   *   *

Whilst all these values and opinion shaping events were taking place globally and my introduction to the world of work was going so well, I was still waiting to start my sixth-form, A level education.

As it turned out I had to wait a little longer because on the first

Saturday of both the rugby season and the autumn school term, I broke my leg playing rugby. Somehow and somewhere or other I had found a scrum cap. This lent itself quite obviously, I'm sure you'll accept and understand, to me switching position to wing forward to emulate and then hopefully replace the then England (and Bedford and British Lion) star Budge Rogers.

That morning the opposition kicked off, the ball heading towards me. I assertively claimed 'MINE', caught the ball cleanly and ran forward. An opposition player headed for me, making to tackle. In true RFU training manual fashion, I took the tackle, holding on to the ball for long enough to ensure my tackler was fully committed before I smoothly distributed the ball to my teammate. 'Ouch' I cried, no room for my newly learned industrial or retail language in schoolboy rugby. My leg hurt and I walked off after twenty seconds of the game. No ambulance was called, no medical attention offered. After the final whistle our teacher commandeered a car from somewhere and took me to casualty. We had to be quick as he was playing himself in the afternoon. X-rayed and plastered, I basically spent the next six weeks at home alone as my mum carried on working.

So, six weeks later I belatedly started my sixth-form life. Halfway to school that morning I called for a female sixth-form colleague; her name was Gail. She sported an incessantly stroked pageboy-like haircut and a very, very short skirt, more of a pelmet really. It really was an ego boost to walk to and into school with her. The 1968 intake of first years had already been inducted six weeks previously so sadly I couldn't even make it appear that we were 'an item' like I'd gawped at admiringly way back in 1963. Sometime later I did indeed have the gall to ask Gail out. She enquired enigmatically 'Have you got a car?' The much hoped for date never happened.

Anyway, as I basked in the triumph of Gail's company, she briefed me on the ropes of sixth-form life and its privileges. Sadly, these were the only ropes she was to teach me. Exclusive use, along with staff, of the sixth-form corridor was the first perk I discovered. Whilst walking along it with Gail, an older, rather well-suited man walked towards us. I didn't know him. 'Young man, may I have a word with you please?' It wasn't really put as a question. My companion whispered to me, 'That's God.' She sauntered on.

So, there I was, face to face, with a divine deity. This earthly manifestation came as a shock, as I'm sure you could imagine. What would happen next?

'Young man, I couldn't help but notice that your hair is rather long. Will you please rectify this.?' That was that; no real on the road to Damascus cathartic revelatory experience.

Gail had waited around the corner for me, eager to know about the encounter. 'He only told you to get your haircut?' 'Yup, I don't think he knew that I'd broken my leg the first day of term playing rugby for school. I've had no time.'

'That's Joe Smith, THE headmaster. His nickname amongst both pupils and staff is God. You never see him, but he's always there,' she said rather enigmatically.

I put this to the back of my mind and after school jumped on the number 17 bus to the Yew Tree and Vic Kent's Hair Stylist. I used to be taken to Mr Vaughan's, such an olde worlde barbers that when his outmoded skill with the scissors petered out, he turned the shop into one selling antiques. When I was taken into Vaughan's a carpet-covered plank was produced to straddle the arms of the proper barber's chair, swiftly removed when an adult was incumbent. Just as Mr Vaughan finished every man's short back and sides he would whisper something almost inaudibly in the customer's ear. Eventually, and a little older, I picked up what was being said. 'Anything for the weekend, sir?' I was never asked.

Eventually, when a bit bigger, as I arrived at the shop, the plank remained stowed away. But whatever was needed for the weekend was never offered to me. Whatever men might need – I didn't?

Becoming more and more a Mod I had switched to Vic Kent, a much more modern hair stylist. When it was my turn, I eased myself into the height-adjustable leather chair. 'Quarter inch Perry Como with a Boston squared back please.' I had no real idea who Perry Como was, whether quarter of an inch was the ideal length or what a Boston squared back actually was. But then again, I always did what my mates told me.

The very next day at school was my second encounter with Sheldon's supernatural being. The door to our classroom opened quietly and Mr Smith entered. The class, to a boy and girl (well perhaps we were near enough men and women by then) stood, and the teacher stood too. Mr Smith spoke. 'I'd like a word with William Taylor, please.' We went outside of the classroom, and he waited till the door closed. 'I see you've had your hair cut, young man. Good. But I've come to find you, because I feel I owe you an apology. Since our first encounter yesterday I've ascertained that you've been off school for six weeks with a sports injury sustained representing the school. I wasn't aware of this and so I do apologise and also thank you for getting your hair cut.' He sashayed off.

I returned to the class and to my seat, my colleagues anxious to know what I had done wrong. My reply, rather sangfroid, 'the headmaster just wanted a word with me'. Two rather contrasting first engagements with Mr Smith, but I thought well of him to come and seek me out as he had.

I'd better explain. Joe Smith, aka God (with apologies to my friends of faith), was indeed actually JE Smith CBE. CBE, eh!

Smith must have been a huge educational cheese. There is news reel footage with him welcoming Hugh Gaitskill, the leader of the opposition Labour Party and aspirant prime minister, as Gaitskill performed the local, national and educational high-profile official opening of the school in June 1959. Joe must have had some 'clout' nationally?

According to Hansard, in 1961 JE Smith was appointed to sit on the Central Advisory Council for Education in England. In 1963 Conservative Minister of Education (and local Birmingham MP) Edward Boyle appointed JE Smith to the Newsom Committee. Their report, entitled 'Half Our Future', was a root and branch investigation with recommendations into secondary education for all eleven to sixteen-year-olds in England. It was ground-breaking and set the pattern for decades to come. It embraced how schools should be built, their organisational structure, issues of the curriculum and the thorny issue of testing and other assessments. Joe Smith was a high-profile educationalist of national repute. No wonder he had such a sanctified soubriquet. Even more, he parked his imposing and shiny grey Rover not only directly outside the school's imposing main entrance, his own personal portal, but also his prestigious vehicle was parked half on and half off the pavement. Big Kahuna or what?

JE Smith was no slouch when it came to choosing high-quality teachers either, and we became increasingly aware of this as we went through our sixth-form life.

I suppose the glittering star in this firmament, for me, was Celia Gaskin. Miss Gaskin, whose dad was headmaster at Moseley Grammar School for Boys, had everything; well, we seventeen-year-old boys thought so. She wore short skirts and slightly tinted specs. I think she came mainly to teach French (not my metier, you'll recall), the language of love. She tried her best. She also tempted us with a holiday, with her, to Italy in the summer of 1969. We readily agreed. She then introduced the caveat that it was dependent upon us signing up to study Italian in the breadth subject period in the lower sixth. We fell for it. But she had more to offer. She would come to our desks saying 'you owe me 3/6 (17.5p in modern lolly)'. Why? Because we were going to the performing arts venue known as the town hall. This got us an introduction to and the taste for going to see performances of the classical CBSO, Simon and Garfunkel (15/- a seat in 1967), French mime artist, Marcel Marceau, the Spencer Davis Group, guitar virtuosos John Williams and Manitas de Plata and jazz's world-renowned Dave Brubeck Quartet, amongst others.

*   *   *

It was the concert, only in their mid-twenties, of Simon and Garfunkel that captivated me. I have had a lifelong infatuation with Simon, his poetry and music, and managed to see him three more times (once in duet with Sting), Garfunkel too, disappointingly recently, just the once. Each chapter of this book begins with a Paul Simon song lyric, my homage to the poet. We were glad to immerse ourselves recently in one of Simon's farewell concerts, such that I concluded my review of it, published in our local *Telegraph*, pensively pondering 'Who'll be my role model, now that my role model's gone?'. I think my favourite musical genre remains the introspection and somewhat melancholy of the singer-songwriter. My list would include Joni Mitchell, Judy Collins, Crosby, Stills, Nash (and Young) and Joan Baez. Honesty and hope were weft and warp for Carol King as she wove the tapestry backdrop of our transition from adolescence to adulthood.

* * *

But our favourite beatnik didn't stop at music. One time she said to three or four of us, 'meet me after school next Monday, bring some jeans to wear. You'll be home about 7.30'.

The appointed day arrived, and we assembled by her Hillman Husky. 'I'll be back in ten minutes, try and look as little like school kids as possible'. She returned and we set off. 'Right, guys, you're gonna have a taste of university life'. She drove us across town to Edgbaston, where the university was located. She parked up, instructing us to follow her, pointing out the campanile, an exact replica of that situated in the Italian city of Siena. We followed her into a smoke-filled and shabbily decorated room. 'This is the student's common room,' she announced. 'I'll go and get the coffees'. She returned with a tray of drinks and explained, 'This is all you really do at university. Hang around, drink coffee, meet new people, have a few arguments, Friday and Saturday have a few drinks, it's a doddle. But just for now we're going to go and see a university standard lecture by a professor, AJP Taylor,' adding, 'he's an historian'.

Coffee consumed, we entered a steeply tiered lecture theatre. The professor entered, stood at the front and began. He wore wellies on his feet and sported a dickie bow. His enthralling, hour-long lecture was on the subject of Adolf Hitler. It was fascinating.

Mr Knight, Cecil I think, was head of RE. In the summer of 1968, he led a group that took us camping in Germany and Austria. Around about the same time, fellow sixth-former, Ken Wilby and I produced two half hour programmes on a reel-to-reel tape recorder for his use in the RE curriculum illustrating key human qualities with sound clips from Beatles songs.

Maggie Fells was a history teacher. Her medium-long ginger hair and the huge purple shoulder bag she toted everywhere made her stand out. It was from this bag that she would randomly distribute extracurricular history books that she'd bought herself. What made her stand out even more was that she was eccentric too. At the end of our time with her as sixth-formers she invited us to a drinks party at her flat.

One day in school, a rather hairy teacher called Stewart Trainor (his daughter Jess Phillips went on to become the MP for Yardley) approached me. 'You're Bill Taylor, aren't you? Have you ever had a curry?' I hadn't which resulted in me being collected by him early one Friday evening in his VW Beetle and taken to Moseley where his wife had prepared my first encounter with Indian food, poppadums included! I was deposited home about 9 p.m. I can't imagine some of these things being allowed and taking place these days.

I got on well with all of the PE staff. The head of department was Norman Eve. There were two Daves, Francis and Fisher. Francis once took me to the schoolhouse on the shores of Lake Bala in North Wales in his VW Beetle. That was cool. Fisher was good himself at both basketball and volleyball.

Our team became good at volleyball, beating most schools and some colleges and universities. One day I suggested to Dave Fisher that an all-Birmingham schools and colleges volleyball competition could be organised. 'Great idea, follow me.' He strode off towards the school offices. We entered the school secretary's room. 'This is Bill Taylor, he's going to be organising a volleyball competition for all schools and colleges in the city. Please do any typing, postage and any other administrative tasks he might ask of you.' Some weeks and several letters later the multi-teamed tournament was hosted at our school. I don't think we won but I picked up further organisational skills from my role. I also gained recognition for all the hard, successful work, and putting Sheldon Heath on the map once again.

I also did a stint in a fledgling editorial capacity in the school magazine *Microcosm* and the wonderfully named school newspaper (I can take no credit for this title) *Miniscule*.

During our time as sixth-formers we seemed to congregate in the library or library stock room. This became a bit of a club, a talking shop. Some of the teachers mentioned here and others came along for a coffee and chatted away about world events and things closer to home too. Was this a mini Brummie Bloomsbury Set? Self-appointed and self-important? These members of staff were not demobbed army educators. Fellow Baby Boomers, perhaps five or so years our senior, they had gone to university and attained academic qualifications, just as we wanted to do. We listened attentively, milked what they were saying. 'Imitation is the most sincere form of flattery.'

One topic that persistently arose was the pupils' voice and how it could be heard better. We'd seen students and other people across the world gaining confidence and speaking up for themselves and we fancied a slice of this action too. The commonly held view amongst our little group was don't just talk about it here, go and see the powers that be. We drew up a list of things we'd like to see happen. A less religious school assembly, different religions discussed in RE, encouraging outside speakers in on a range of different topics, allowing girls not to wear collars and ties, an elected sixth-form council to work with staff on ideas, and, most of all, a sixth-form common room. But where to go and who to see with them? No reason not to and nothing to lose in not going straight to the top. JE Smith, CBE, his very self.

So, one Monday afternoon directly after the lunch break, four of us turned up unannounced in the almost taboo headmaster's area, that's the headmaster, JE Smith, CBE, deity on earth. We timidly tapped on his office door and almost instantaneously, his secretary appeared from her room. 'What do you four want?' she emitted shrilly. 'We'd like to see the headmaster, please.' 'Mr Holmes, you mean?' 'No, he's head of upper school. We want to see Mr JE Smith, the headmaster of all school.' 'But Mr Smith doesn't deal with children!' During this exchange, Mr Smith's door opened. It was him. 'Gentlemen, please can you explain yourselves?' 'There are some things we'd like to discuss with you, sir!' 'Then you had better come in.' We entered his study; a clock tick-tocked imperiously. 'Please sit down and explain yourselves.' Before we did, Mr Smith depressed a button on his intercom ordering five coffees.

'Mr Smith, there are some things Bill Taylor wants to raise with you,' one of my colleagues-turned-accomplices volunteered. In for a penny, in for a pound, sharing the list with Mr Smith I went through it point by point.

To be fair we all chipped in during our discussions and Mr Smith raised questions of clarification and challenge. At times he agreed to some things, said some weren't possible, identified others for further discussion. The session went on for the best part of two hours. At its conclusion we were thanked very much and shown out as all guests would be. As we left, sat patiently on chairs arranged in the reception area were all the high-ranking heads, deputy heads and senior teachers from across all the school – twenty-plus top brass. Their jaws dropped in disbelief. We weren't to know but Monday afternoons were sacrosanct, reserved exclusively for a senior staff strategic meeting, which we'd gate-crashed. One of the assembled scrambled-egg wearers, whispering, enquired as to what we had done.'We've just been talking through a few ideas to improve the school with Mr Smith, that's all.'

I reflected that all of us, all five of us, had conducted ourselves well. Win-win.

The things that Mr Smith had agreed to started to happen quickly, those he wasn't too happy with, didn't. The others took a bit of time.

I became the inaugural chairman of the Sheldon Heath Sixth-Form Society.

Just outside the upper school library the corridor broadened. The walrus-moustached Mr Baggs, head of woodwork, came to see me. He had taken some measurements and had a few design ideas to screen off the corridor alcove to give us a little bit of seclusion, but not too much, as he put it. He offered to come in during the next holidays as long as we joined him. This happened, resulting in a wood and plastic screen that was a reasonable compromise and that did the job. Result.

I was to have one final run-in with Mr Smith. As captain of school rugby First XV it was my duty every Wednesday in upper school assembly to read out all five rugby results from the previous weekend. One Wednesday, on reaching the first team result, I prefaced my remarks stating that once again the first team had had to train itself, select itself and get itself to and from the match with no teacher supervision. Mr Smith was on the stage, over 500 pupils in the hall were in total silence, enrapt in this drama. Nothing was said. In dismissing the school Mr Smith simply said 'I would like to see the head of boys PE and captain of school rugby in my room now, please.' What had I done? The senior teacher was seen first. It took a while. Then it was my turn. I was in and out in a trice, my presence only required to receive an assurance that there would be teacher supervision in future.

Miss Gaskin stuck to her word and in the summer of 1969, experiencing my first air flight, we went off to Italy. We were accompanied by Mr Gaskin, the head teacher from Moseley, known to his mates, as I rather presumptuously assumed I was, as Bruce. We both got ourselves in trouble with Miss on an extended confection bender in the celebrated ice cream parlour 'Perche No!'

I had a chance to check out the real authentic appendage of Michelangelo's David whilst there in Florence. Seven years earlier Miss Cawley hadn't seemed too happy with my scaling of the sculpture. But it seemed authentically life-sized to me.

It must have spurred me on as during the same two weeks I managed to lose my virginity in Florence; Florence being the name of the city. With less than sixth months of them left, I just about joined in with the Swinging Sixties!

*　*　*

As we settled down to revise and prepare for our A level exams, all the teachers in Birmingham, on behalf of teachers nationally, went on strike for a better and deserved pay deal.

The exams sat, we awaited the results. What could be a better distraction from our anxious wait than the Isle of Wight Festival 1970. Four of us, Rod Weatherhead and me along with Paul Carpenter and John Burton had got ourselves organised enough to book a large caravan on the island for two weeks. The plan was to attend the rock music event over the middle weekend. It was quite enjoyable in the caravan with decent facilities, a bar on site and some girls to chat up. At the appointed time we set off for the festival venue, initially by the Southern Vectis service bus. The traffic became increasingly horrendous as camper vans and other ramshackle vehicles headed in the same direction. Passengers on the bus were advised that we'd be quicker walking, so we did. We arrived at the festival fields, not so far from where school camp had been six or seven years earlier, which really was highly disorganised chaos. We pitched our tents in an already crowded field and went off to the performing arena, i.e. another field. I really don't recall who we did see and didn't see over three days. The main arena was good for seeing the bands and climbing a nearby hill meant you could both see and hear what was going on. The bill included: Chicago, Procul Harum, Melanie, The Doors, The Who, Joni Mitchell, Emerson, Lake and Palmer. Rod and Paul had their rendezvous with their Birmingham girlfriends Heather and Sue, so they were happy enough. John and I, whilst happy with the music, were not happy with all other aspects of our stay.

I needed to go to the toilet, simple enough. The gents was a set aside area the size of a football pitch. For discretion this had been surrounded by a six-foot-high corrugated iron fence. The fence was no longer there, having been removed by fellow festival-goers to construct makeshift shelters. To have a pee, a trench several feet wide and deep had been dug directly next to the no-longer-there fence. For those who needed more than a pee, there were cubicles, built back-to-back stretching for a hundred yards or so. These would have been fine if only all the plywood backs, sides and doors had not been similarly removed for ad hoc shelter construction. So our only choice was a communal one, sat back to back and side by side whilst we listened to the music and communed with nature. As it turned out, the band were the only Doors we saw! This process was a little bit too cheek by jowl for me, but needs must. Then came the tricky moment; no toilet paper, not even any from the City of Birmingham. I appealed to the other sitting tenants and fortunately provision was thankfully made.

I told the other guys I was heading back to our caravan and its comparatively lavish facilities. John Burton joined me and soon we'd had a hot shower, a cooked meal and a couple of beers. Was that the Summer of Love? We'd not really enjoyed the experience and had missed Free, Donovan, Pentangle, the Moody Blues, Jimi Hendrix, Leonard Cohen and Joan Baez amongst other great icons of the sixties and seventies! All-weekend ticket? £3!

I had been working in a jeans junction-style shop directly under the ill-fated Mulberry Bush pub. At the time, Wranglers were £3 3s and Levis 69/11.

But I moved for that summer to work as a car park attendant at the National Car Park directly over New Street Station. Here, I was to confirm that industrial language appertained to all aspects of things to do with motor cars. An old D-day veteran, Bill, was already working there. To ensure our colleagues didn't mistake us, I was called Bill and he was called Fucking Bill.

One day that August 1970 we received our A level results. I skipped work and we met in the pub to compare outcomes. Or was it the Kardomah Cafe, a haunt of ours in town?

I was off, as was Rod and Neil Coley, to study at the University of Lancaster, chosen because it was at the seaside, which it wasn't. So much for my grade A in geography.

That night we hit the town and celebrated with a few drinks and my first taste of Chinese food – sweet and sour pork and chips. I was obviously going places.

Chapter 6

The Seventies at University - Tyler is Innocent, 1970-73

A man walks down the street. It's a street in a strange world.

The 1970s were one massive never-ending transformation for me.

I began them still a schoolboy and living at home. Ten years later I'd been to university at Lancaster, taken a postgraduate qualification at Manchester Poly, left home, lived in several contrasting forms of student accommodation (including a year in Morecambe). I'd lived in a YMCA hostel, and bought two different houses, worked for years (in three different jobs in Blackburn as a detached youth worker, a youth centre worker and secondary school-based youth tutor), met and married my wife, become an elected councillor and we were expecting our first child.

I don't think I could have imagined surviving any of that change as I sat on the Midland Red bus waiting to take me, Rod and Neil to Lancaster. I travelled by bus to Digbeth Coach Station in the city centre with a heavily laden rucksack made to the same individually bespoke college design as PE teacher Dave Francis', my dad's Navy grip bag and a portable Olympia Traveller Deluxe typewriter from my dad. He'd rung my mum a few days earlier telling her he'd like to take me out for a meal as a gesture of congratulations for getting to university. I didn't really want to go but was coerced by my mum. The atmosphere that evening was strained. While we sat in his car, as I was dropped off at our house, he presented me with a typewriter. 'This is by way of a well done for getting to university. Now these are thirty-two quid to buy but, through my contacts, I've got it for you half price. Please don't send me the money until you get your grant through.' I couldn't believe what I was hearing.

My dad was renowned for his frugality. On one childhood visit to the very tip of Land's End, where the signpost points to New York (3147 miles), the Scillies (28) and John O'Groats (874) and there's a space for the duty photographer to slide in the name of your hometown (e.g. Blackburn 382), he conjured up a money-saving plan. It was simple. All he had to do was wait until a fellow holidaymaker from either Leeds (401) or Birmingham (280) came along and he could bootleg our family photograph without paying the five shillings' fee. What a Scrooge!

Back to the present-giving ceremony in my dad's car, I asked him to wait. I popped inside, wrote out a cheque to him for £16 (I'd been quite well paid at National Car Parks) and handed it to him with my thanks for his generosity. I was livid.

Returning to the journey from Birmingham to Lancaster, this entailed various changes of bus enroute, including Wolverhampton, Stafford, Crewe and finally Preston, all the legs of this journey conducted on ordinary A roads. No M6 motorway back then.

Some hours later we arrived at the entrance to Lancaster University on the A6. Those of you familiar with this area will know that it's a good three quarters of a mile or more up a steep meandering hill to get to the campus. We set off on our yomp. It was a warm day. I felt like a foreign legionnaire in a *Beau Geste* adventure film. First of all, the rucksack was discarded, then the grip bag. I arrived at the top carrying only the typewriter. I found reception and left the typewriter there for safekeeping, shuttling back and forth for the rest of my gear. This must have taken at least half an hour. We went through some formalities, were given our keys and shown to our rooms by an existing student. Neil had opted to be in Furness, accommodation in another college on campus, so we arranged to meet him later. Rod and I were allocated a double room in Bowland College tower (easily spotted when driving on the M6 and built in 1968 to hide the ventilation chimney for the university's heating system). We were excited. But I had something to disclose to my buddy.

When we got to our room, I told Rod I had something important to tell him. Four years of silence after the events, I explained about my mum and dad, including the reason why I had not told him before. It was like a weight had been lifted from me. He listened saying that made things fit that he had previously thought were strange.

We unpacked. We'd both been given a pair of pyjama trousers and produced them, both saying 'My mum made me bring them'. We hadn't really thought about eating, but we went off in search of food. We found a cafeteria-type place and studied what was on offer. When we saw what the day's special was, we gulped in disbelief. It was hash pie, as plain as plain could be. We chose things a little blander than that and then decided to find a bar. As everyone knows, regulars always seem to get served quicker. We just couldn't catch the eye of those serving. Then a voice behind us said 'Three pints of Scotch, please'. This time we couldn't believe our ears. We didn't know that McEwans sold such a beer, so we were thinking they drink whisky by the pint here. Marijuana-laced pie and huge helpings of spirits made us fear that university wasn't for us.

At this stage many people won't know or might have forgotten that not many people got to university in the 1970s; about 13 per cent compared to around 48 per cent today. Furthermore, there was no upfront burden of tuition fees on students or their families and also a means-tested and subsistence grant, not a loan, was available. So, the City of Birmingham paid my tuition fees directly to the university (I believe these are around £9,000 per year these days). On top of that, having our low family income assessed, I attracted the full maximum subsistence grant, the princely sum of £365 for the year. This was to cover my rent (about £3.00 a week), and other running costs, books, food, travel, beer, etc. It made me feel quite well off.

Our accommodation area was for ten guys and most of us became good friends at university and beyond. Pete Kiener (US based), Ken Langley (teacher and later married to Gill), John Brierley (council treasurer), Alan Bennett (teacher), Malcolm Smith (more later). We became *escrapeologists*, getting each other into, and out of, many a scrape. We discovered that our backgrounds were similar – council estate and state secondary school. We then found that we appeared to be socially engineered, amongst a very few who hailed from such modest upbringings. Most of the other people we met had attended grammar or private schools and most had professional parents who owned their own homes.

We encountered a myriad of different accents: north and south, posh and working class, quietly spoken and loud. But I had my own sociolinguistic problem. My relocation 120 miles north had resulted in a change of identity. Previously, of course, I'd had three years in Leeds and a further fifteen in Birmingham. These experiences can play havoc with your vocal cords.

The first few days and weeks at Lancaster meant an inordinate amount of queueing, form filling and other registration processes. Whenever it came to me disclosing my name I perpetually failed to communicate clearly.

'Name please.' I would tell them. 'Sorry, name please.' I'd try again. 'Please can you spell it?' 'Listen, my name is Bill Taylor.' 'Sorry. So, your first name is Bull, B-u-l-l, Bull?' 'No, it's Bill, B-i-l-l, Bill.' 'But you're saying Bull, B-u-l-l and your surname is Tyler, T-y-l-e-r, Tyler?' 'No, no, no, it's Taylor, T-a-y-l-o-r, Taylor.' The poor listener, not adeptly in tune to the Brummie accent would often then get me to write it. Then they'd study what I'd written and shake their head to read 'Bill Taylor'. As the Brummie reggae band UB40 sang 'Tyler is guilty, the white judge has said so'. I didn't mention the William Tyler pub!

* * *

Academically the first year was kind of doing three A levels at pace. I took economics, politics and a lower level maths course for people without A level, popularly known as maths for morons! Outside of the lecture theatre and tutorial room I got on with the other extracurricular activities on offer. We had a good time, met new people, sank a few too many beers and I caught up a little in the girlfriend quest.

The first year came and went. I'd done the requisite Christmas post job in Birmingham and that summer I also became an assistant youth hostel warden in Troutbeck in the Lakes. It sounds glamorous but it was hard work, a six-day week, eleven hours a day, for £6.00 wages. We were always busy, up early around 6.30, making porridge, cooking bacon, frying eggs, making mountains of toast, all well received by voracious walkers and cyclists. Next was the supervision of chores allocated to the visiting members, mainly cleaning (I was a highly qualified mopper!) and some food preparation. We finished about noon but were back on shift again by 4.30 or 5 p.m. This was mainly in the kitchen or serving in the shop. I did it for a couple of months, picking up many practical and management skills.

Soon it was time to return to university for what was known as our Part IIs. I hadn't enjoyed the economics and found even the watered-down maths difficult. The courses framework was good at Lancaster. In years two and three students took nine units or courses, and so I went for politics major, education minor and my FNU (free ninth unit) was in trade union studies.

My courses included foreign policy analysis led by Professor Philip Reynolds, pro vice-chancellor, head of department and author of a number of books. He introduced us during his ten-week course to some highfalutin notions: overarching parameters, irreducible minima and conceptual frameworks. These could also be found in his books. He refused to call the Middle East, the Middle East, because it wasn't the middle of the east of anywhere. His moniker for the Middle East was the Levant. This name has its origins in French, Italian and Arabic, meaning 'the east, where the sun rises'! Not much better really than the Middle East. Professor Reynolds took questions at the end of his talks, my friend asking if the learned professor thought that a pelvis was a conceptual framework? He moved on quickly.

Another course was about voting records, patterns and analysis in British elections and was quite interesting. It was led for decades by Dave Denver, a really nice, informative Scottish fellow. Ironically, later, from 1979 till 2010, I was recipient and responder as Labour agent to his regular post-general election psephological surveys. Other politics units taken from a dimming memory include: concepts of force, violence and aggression, strategic studies, civil-military relationships and finally, possibly revolutions. These don't look on the face of it very marketable or employable areas of study. I would contend however that they, along with extracurricular acquired skills, equipped me well, preparing me for the future, but as yet neither identified nor designated tasks and challenges in my life.

Once every term, each student was expected to present a researched 'paper' to their tutorial colleagues. These put you well on the spot. The most memorable being from a guy who was destined to go on to a hugely successful career in radio, his tutorial topic, the foreign policy of Joseph Stalin. Our tutor invited our fellow student to begin his paper, customarily delivered in uninspiring monotones. A cassette tape recorder was produced from a bag and plugged in and the play button was pressed. We were immediately informed and entertained by a stentorian voice-over, with martial music in the background, announcing 'the foreign policy of Joseph Stalin'. Our aspirant broadcaster must have had access to some sound archives and sound effects and his paper, aka a programme, ran for about half an hour. It was really, really good and out of the ordinary. Sadly, the tutor didn't share our admiration for this input and scored it poorly for being non-academic.

To be fair, I didn't really get the academic/social/extracurricular balance of my days at university quite right (by a very long chalk). I got involved in student politics, accidentally and with some hindsight, almost certainly stupidly. We ascertained one evening that the university provided standard, Birminghamesque toilet paper in the male toilets but more luxurious soft tissue in the ladies. I was nominated for the next elections requiring a student rep, stood on this tissue issue and surprisingly won; my first step on the 'bottom' rung of university student politics.

In the second year we had to move out of university residences, and we found a hovel for ten or twelve of us in the west end of Morecambe. The bus journey from the campus followed a looping route taking in much of the city of Lancaster and then on to the dingy down-at-heel almost seaside town of Morecambe. It took about an hour and the passengers' mood was determined by whether the bus followed the library's closure or the bars' chucking out time. The names of the buses were prefixed by the letter U for university and the terminus conclusion was a pub near Heysham called the Battery. When the front of the bus displayed U2 Battery I always chuckled.

One night a group of us were travelling on the last bus from the campus through Lancaster to Morecambe. We'd had a *couple* of beers. When we reached Lancaster bus station, more students got on including the very ebullient Denis Wolinski, a really nice guy, and a bit of a Cockney wide boy! For some reason, Denis would often scatter throughout things he said with his catchphrase, which was 'shit the bed!' (no one knows why!). It appeared Denis had had more than a couple of beers and was eating a bag of fish and chips. The bus left the station. The lady conductor came up the stairs to collect our fares. 'What the hell do you think you're doing?' she screamed at Denis. 'Trying to pay you my fare, missus,' said Denis with a few examples of his favourite catchphrase scattered liberally. 'And what do you think that is in your hand?' 'I know what it is, missus, it's a bag of fish and chips.' 'But surely you must know the consumption of any food or drink on a corporation bus at any time of the day or night contravenes the bylaws of this borough?' 'Sorry, missus , I actually didn't know that. Would you like a chip?' Everyone on the crowded top deck, bar one unfortunate innocent more academically-focussed passenger who had inadvertently missed the penultimate library leavers' bus, chuckled as the conductress stormed down the stairs. The bus had continued on its way but then suddenly stopped. The male driver appeared at the top of the steps. 'What's going on, lads, she's giving me a right earful.' Denis explained, meaning to be helpful. 'The lady came up for my fare, which I offered her. She then related to me the current bylaws about the consumption of food or drink on a corporation 'bus at any time of the day or night. Would you like a chip, mate?' The driver prudently declined. 'OK, I'll tell her it's all sorted.' He returned downstairs and the bus set off again. Straightaway we were joined once again by the conductress. 'Has he not told you to stop eating those fish and chips?' 'No, missus, but I did offer him a chip like I did you.' Once again, she stormed down the stairs and the 'bus stopped again. Our conductress, obviously a stickler for the rules, joined us once again, by which time Denis had consumed his supper. She suddenly turned on the one poor guy who had sat quietly throughout this farrago reading his book. 'Right, you're the ringleader here. Get off my bus immediately,' she ordered, storming downstairs yet again. We were actually in the east end of Morecambe by now and it was approaching midnight. One of the guys on the top deck had a loaf of bread with him. This was hurriedly distributed amongst all fellow travellers. Coming upstairs, once again, was our bête noire in this little panto. Everyone bar one was now chomping away on a slice of Wonderloaf; we were all Spartacus. 'Right,' she said, 'I've got the lot of you, you're all banged to rights. Get off MY bus, NOW!' We all complied with her instructions, including the innocent party, and happily marched along the Prom to our various billets.

I kept my hand in as a poor man's or aspirant journalist with articles in many of the student titles that proliferated on campus. I became editor of Bowland College magazine entitled *Bumf*, which I found was public-school parlance for toilet paper. This reincarnated itself under my imaginative leadership as *Bogrole*! One of our editorial board was Rick Dunning. Rick was a funny guy, but quite shy. To guarantee his journalistic anonymity, he wrote under a rather cleverly spoonerised version of his name. Using this heavily coded nom de plume I don't think his true identity was ever rumbled. At Rick's graduation ceremony he was secretly awarded asterisk status. This meant Princess Alexandra, officiating at the event, was deemed to be safe talking to Rick. She congratulated him on attaining such a good degree, asking to what use he was going to put it. 'I'm hoping to become a postman in Suffolk, Princess.' In fact, Rick went on to be hugely instrumental in the establishment and development of the Quay Theatre complex in Sudbury. Sadly Rick died young, only thirty-nine. I didn't make the funeral, but I'm told that singer-songwriter Labi Siffre, actress Sheila Steafel and rock's Tom Robinson's band performed at his celebration.

Later Neil, Rod and me volunteered to edit the 1,500-print run Freshers' handbook in 1971 and made a good job of it. We worked on securing so much advertising revenue (nascent entrepreneurial skills?) that the venture cost the student union almost nothing.

My communication skills were not only in written form as I turned them to broadcasting. Radio Bailrigg, still going today and on which I recently appeared, was a pretty Heath Robinson campus-only radio station, broadcasting from deep in the bowels of the still being constructed campus. Wearing some headphones and speaking to the mike, actual vinyl records were teed up using a piece of paper. My programme included bits of interviews with people and music. One show I took a couple of bottles of Newcastle Brown with me. All well and good till I needed to relieve myself. The nearest toilets were some distance away. Solution? Play actor Richard Harris' 1968 version of 'MacArthur Park'. Not at all my kind of music, but at over seven minutes long absolutely fitted my immediate needs.

Friday nights at Lancaster were routinely sacrosanct. A few beers then a wander up the central Spine walkway into the Great Hall to see a band. The ents programme at Lancaster was second to none and led by Barry Lucas. His more gobby pal, Gaz Taylor, was the on-stage front man in the early days. Gaz had the ability not only to swear most of the time but in the middle of words. 'And don't forget, next week it's Pentangle and they are su-fucking-perb!' I think, Rolling Stones excepted, and Elton John who didn't show, every band who was anyone appeared at Lancaster. Barry's work really put the university on young people's radar and fleets of buses full of youngsters came from all over the north-west to attend our gigs. Barry later went on to produce his encyclopaedic A-Z account of the rock years 1969-85 in his 400-plus-page *When Rock Went to College*. This 2017 work, in which I had a tiny role, is absolutely worth a purchase and a read (Carnegie ISBN 1910837115 – 2nd Edition).

So, with a little bit of studying, a little bit more learning about the opposite sex and quite a lot more beer, I continued to pick up key organising, leadership and social skills. Contributing to publications, speaking at public meetings, organising agendas and minutes of organisations, hanging around then listening to others with different skills and experiences were all valuable acquired attributes. I also managed to have my first immersion in falling in love. She was an intelligent, witty, engaging and pretty girl, a little younger than me. It lasted six months, then ran its course. That hurt but that's what love and life teaches!

In between second and third year I returned home to Brum and worked in the nearby hospital laundry. It could be quite a nasty job especially when dealing with the orange laundry bags (I'm sure you can imagine) but the money was good and my workmate colleagues, rich in experiences, were a great source of learning. One once said to me 'Bloody students, if there's a right and a wrong way to do something, they'll find a third way!' With there still only being a black and white telly at home and me having earned quite a lot with the NHS, I treated myself and hitchhiked back up to Lancaster to watch the ill-fated Munich Olympics on campus in colour.

*　　*　　*

I then entered the most complex, challenging and developmentally educative episode in my university life. I had thought an underlying principle of universities was to question and challenge. With hindsight, I got it very wrong. Lancaster's motto, in Latin of course, reads 'The truth lies open to all'. Trouble is, I'm not entirely sure where and when this episode started or where and when I should start recounting it.

Although the students' union structure was different at Lancaster, I was effectively vice president of our students' union. The de facto president was Mick Murray, a member of the Communist Party of Great Britain (CPGB). To describe Mick as a takes-no-nonsense firebrand would be understating his charismatic presence, forcefulness and determination.

The early part of 1972 saw the National Union of Miners going on strike across Britain for the first time since the 1926 General Strike. Events of note included the creation by the strikers of flying-picket squads and the Battle of Saltley Gate (a massive coke works in Birmingham). Prime Minister Edward Heath didn't really offer either sensible or strong leadership leading to six to nine-hour-long power cuts and a three-day working week across Britain. We were told that there were only enough reserves of power left to last the country a week. At Lancaster, under Mick's leadership, the students 'twinned' with an NUM branch in nearby Wigan, raising funds, and sending clothes and food to help during the seven-week-long industrial dispute. We got well involved with this and learned more about organising things, others and ourselves.

It was to be another thirteen years, in 1985, when I renewed my engagement with the National Union of Mineworkers. This time, accompanied by John Roberts, a local Labour Party member and future councillor, and Jack Straw, we attended the official NUM picket line at Golborne colliery near Wigan. I have to say the experience was frightening. We left Blackburn very early one morning, got to the picket buses, joined in the infamous strikers versus police tussles, had a quick hard-boiled egg breakfast in the local miners' welfare and got back to Blackburn. I was there in time for our 9.30 a.m. scheduled work meeting. Coal had been mined there since the 1860s. About a thousand miners worked there. By 1989, like many, many others the pit closed for good.

But going back to 1972, I hired a band from Preston to do a fundraising gig for the NUM. For students to financially support such organisations directly had been ruled *ultra vires*, but there were legal ways round that. I'd booked this band, probably with Barry Lucas' help. We paid the band, students paid to watch, all profits to the NUM was the plan. On the teatime of the planned event I bumped into Barry walking through one of the cafeterias. 'You coming to see Wings tonight?' My reply was short and monosyllabic.

Barry went on to explain that MY band had arrived and were setting up. One of their members had taken half a day off work, hired a van, loaded up their equipment and set off as the advance party. The driver of this van didn't know exactly where he had to report. Driving up on to the campus he saw a group of men, women and children playing an informal game of football on one of the university's many grassy areas. He enquired of them the whereabouts of the students' union offices, explaining that they were a band hired to play at the university that night. 'It's a big breakthrough for us,' he proudly told the footballers. 'I've taken half a day off work, we've hired this van and we're being paid £30!' 'Brilliant,' said one of the guys. 'We're a bit the same really. That's our furniture van over there. We were driving along a motorway, saw this university on the hill and thought why don't we try and get a gig there tonight? But we're playing football with the kids first.' The other guy interrupted, 'Hang on a minute, mate, it doesn't quite work like that. We've been waiting months for a break like this. I've taken half a day off work, hired this van, driven up all the way from Preston (twenty miles?) and we're appearing tonight. And we're getting £30! Thirty bloody quid! What's your band called anyway?' he asked. Their apparent spokesman said, 'Denny, what have we called ourselves?' Denny replied, informing their fellow but aspirant rock star, 'We've called ourselves Wings.' A very large penny dropped from a very great height very quickly. Our budding rock impresario from Preston promised, 'Right, Mr McCartney, I'll go and find out where the students' union is and come back and let you know.'

A few hours later, for 50p a head, Wings performed in the packed Great Hall, totally impromptu; indeed their tour was *ad hoc*. From memory they did four numbers, including 'Roll Over Beethoven' and 'Give Ireland Back to the Irish' and then repeated the same set. At the end Paul McCartney announced that everybody should go down to the other gig and support the lads from Preston. Win-win!

But back to the tension on campus. At our student executive meeting, Mick raised an issue of academic freedom. The department of English had Professor William Murray at its head. One of its staff was a Dr David Craig. Mick explained that Craig was a Marxist, known to be a Marxist and taught from that perspective. This focussed upon the course that he led entitled English Modern Literature from 1910.

Mick explained that Prof. Murray's contention was that Craig had shown bias towards students and their academic work who shared or were sympathetic to Craig's beliefs. Dr Craig was not particularly close to the student body politic. I think I met him once, perhaps twice, a quietly spoken Scotsman, going slightly bald and wearing a baggy jumper. This tension and conflict that had been simmering since the spring of 1971, came to a head, beyond the English department, over the ensuing year. It seemed like a mini version of the unrest and protests seen over the recent years in the United States, Paris and London and across the world. The shorthand title for this saga is the Craig Affair. But I think this a) put the modest, unassuming academic too much centre stage and b) distracted the real debate away from other dramatis personae.

Staff appeared divided, left and right, younger and older, prepared to compromise and entrenched. As an aside to vice-chancellor Charles Carter's second-in-command, eventual successor and conflictingly, my department's head, Professor Philip Reynolds, I once quipped that the university's motto had been mistranslated (I had studied Latin remember) and should read 'The truth lies open(ly) to all'. I don't think he appreciated the irony. It felt like the top didn't fit the bottom and the bottom didn't recognise the top as the top. There was little mutual respect.

Initially, the student exec's position was one of seeking some form of inquiry into all of this turmoil. The turmoil was not helped by the teaching staff either being in no staff association at all or split between the more establishment-like Association of University Teachers (AUT, now UCU) or the more union-like Association of Scientific, Technical and Managerial Staff (ASTMS, now part of Unite). Confidential university documents were frequently leaked and circulated widely. The university's 'top brass', an *ancien régime* in waiting, seemed unable to focus upon and address challenge and appeared to get further entrenched and didn't stop digging! The student exec's more conciliatory position seemed not to be working and really from then on, all hell let loose. Meetings open to all the student body, some 2,000 or so, were frequent and packed. The mood of students intensified. Meetings for students on a departmental basis were held and votes to go on strike taken. By and large most departments voted to strike. Students then chose to establish a parallel alternative curriculum, taught by themselves, to the official scheme of studies. This was known as the Free University Committee. I'm sure you get the acronym! (I think author Malcolm Bradbury may have shaped one of his novels inspired by these events). This anarchistic, but in many ways enlightening, empowering and invigorating time, went on for two terms. In alternative rooms, improvised classrooms, on patches of grass lectures mimicking the official lectures were prepared and delivered by students to their peers. It seemed to work quite well.

Despite meetings with the vice-chancellor and his team, the deadlock could not be broken. Previously, during the summer term 1971 students had voted to occupy the university admin HQ in support of poorly paid university cleaning staff and had been successful in securing for them a substantial pay rise. Had this miffed the powers that be? In February 1972 (only a few days after the disturbing Bloody Sunday shootings in Derry on 30 January) a mass student meeting was convened in the university's central Alexandra Square, attended by 2,000 students. There was much debate, motions were moved, and points of order raised. A motion to occupy the administrative University House was proposed, discussed, voted upon and overwhelmingly agreed. So that's what happened. Immediately we moved towards University House in the corner of the square. The place was empty and there was a sense of 'right, what do we do now?'.

To be frank it wasn't all that dramatic or exciting. Looking back now I can't recall what broke the deadlock. But after a while, a few days, the occupation was over.

Around this time the university appointed Councillor Tom Taylor (no relation), Labour leader of Blackburn Borough Council and pro-chancellor of the university to do a report on events. The terms of reference were: 'To consider the underlying causes of and predisposing conditions for recent disputes and disruption in the university, and to recommend any changes of policy which he [i.e. Councillor Taylor] may consider desirable'. The hearings took place between May and July 1972.

I was sent by train to Blackburn to meet with Councillor Taylor in his office as leader of the council in the town hall. I implored him to look at a bullying culture and other issues that I thought were clearly underlying causes of and predisposing conditions. He declined to include them.

The irony is that thirty years later, a different Councillor Taylor occupied the same office in the same room! A very different Councillor Taylor, although Tom and I became very good pals. I think he saw himself as my political 'dad'.

Forty-five years later in 2017 I was the only political speaker at Tom's funeral in a packed Blackburn Cathedral. I had never bothered recalling our first meeting to him. Tom was, inter alia, very old school!

In May 1972 I was attending the National Union of Students (NUS) Conference, ironically held in the main hall of Birmingham University, scene of my taster evening two or three years earlier. There would have been several hundred delegates in the room. The Craig Affair, Lancaster and academic freedom were on the agenda for debate. I was called out from my allocated delegate's seat. Two guys in suits identified themselves as police officers from Lancashire and told me I was now under caution under some arcane conspiracy to trespass law. This came completely out of the blue, lasted only a few moments and left me quite stunned. I returned to Lancaster, wondering what would happen next.

I found out that, along with others, I was now a member of the Lancaster Six or was it Seven or Nine? It appeared that of the 2,000 or so occupiers, a handful had been singled out as scapegoats. It looked like the powers that be had rather clumsily blown it, picking on a selected few from many, many hundreds. Within hours, over 300-plus students admitted signing witnessed documents that they too were co-conspirators in a mass act of 'I'm Spartacus'. Some staff resigned positions of university governance in protest.

Craig, a family man and by no way a political diehard, eventually acquiesced to an offer of personal compromise. This left many students and some of his colleagues, who had stuck up for him, feeling high and dry. A separate School of Independent Studies was established for him, with just one member of staff initially.

The Lancaster *x* were exonerated within weeks as the DPP found they had no case to answer. During these tense and intense months a lot of our energy seemed to have been put into rebuffing all attempts by Trotskyite far-left groups such as IS/SWP (International Socialists later the Socialist Workers Party), the Socialist Labour League later to become the Workers' Revolutionary Party (included in its membership were members of the Redgrave family) and others with their apparent obsession with diversionary transitional demands. In simple terms, their tactic was to link something practical or perhaps more short term with major more nebulous longer-term objectives. When the latter thwarted the former, the more left wing people then blame failure on those focussed on shorter-term more achievable goals. One illustrative example of this whilst we were trying to convince the students on campus of our case, the Trots wanted us to produce leaflets to be distributed on local council estates explaining what was happening at the university. No wonder Lenin dismissed them as an infantile disorder. I don't really know where the Labour Party was on campus at this time.

In the longer term, the influence that these experiences had on many of us for the rest of our lives, was deep and long-lasting. We'd effectively been radicalised. It gave us a for-real extracurricular insight into how the relatively powerless can be made to feel and hopefully taught us to be more engaging and less patronising in our use of authority and power. It instilled in many of us, future managers in all sectors, a default position of distrust in those in authority and a deep awareness of how apparent liberalism can be sinisterly cloaked in wafer-thin oppression, 'thus far *but no further*'. My studies at university included various popular risings around the world in the twentieth century, their causes, how the oppressor viewed and behaved towards their oppressed, how the oppressed responded and so on. There was an obvious cognitive dissonance between what was preached and what was practised. Within the curriculum, we were taught about the early twentieth-century Italian Marxist philosopher Antonio Gramsci and his concept of hegemony. Put simply, Gramsci's analysis was that ruling classes use cultural institutions to maintain their power. In 1926 Gramsci, although democratically elected as a regional deputy, fell foul of Mussolini's fascist repressive regime and was imprisoned. He remained in prison and suffering multiple ill health, was removed to hospital and died there in 1937. It felt like we learned theories within the curriculum but were subject to, albeit milder, forms of institutional control beyond it.

* * *

One thing this researching, pondering and writing has generated is to get the memory muscles moving again. I can recommend it. But not only that, I have now had e-conversations with both Mick Murray and Jerry Drew in advance of a meeting with Marion McClintock, the honorary archivist of the university. Between us, as three ex-students, all now in our late-sixties, we can remember some bits of this saga, but not the whole story nor necessarily the right chronology. John, we knew him as Jerry, Drew became student president 1974–5. After university he went into social work and youth justice where he excelled, became chief exec. of the Youth Justice Board, and gained a CBE in 2013. He holds a professorship. Mick tells me he spent some time with the CPGB as staff, then teaching in schools and adult education, including in the third sector. We three are all now in the Labour Party.

The consensus of our exchanges is that we think the Lancaster *x* makes *x* to be six, seven or nine! We cannot find any documented evidence that confirms this specifically and I wouldn't like to make it up. Neither am I going to name any of this band other than myself. I don't think that would be fair of me, or fair to my alleged co-conspirators, some of whom remain unidentified, some of whom cannot be confirmed and none of whom I have ever met collectively in any conspiratorial cabal. Many, many hundred had participated in trespass, a civil crime. A handful of us were investigated for the criminal crime of conspiracy which carried a lengthy prison sentence, if convicted.

Following the summer break, the return to campus was measured with a sense that things would never be quite the same again. Trust is hard to build but like all delicate things, easy to break.

It must have been around early 1973 that I decided to join the Communist Party of Great Britain; a few of us did. The impetuosity of youth. I wrote to my mum, close friends with Nikita Khrushchev I thought, to inform and explain what I'd done. I don't think she was over impressed. On my next visit to Birmingham it was never mentioned, but *Woman's Own* or *Woman's Realm* magazine's cut-out-and-keep all-colour souvenir poster of Prince Charles being invested as the Prince of Wales adorned my bedroom wall. I was to meet Prince Charles in person quite a few times, twenty to thirty years later.

I think I was surprised to find that most people in the CPGB were normal. One guy, Ian, from somewhere around Greater Manchester came back to university one time excited that he had earned a fiver (£5) for half a day's work. Although about my age, he always wore a flat cap. Walking through his local market doing his mum's shopping, he and his headgear had been spotted. He'd been sat down, plied with coffee and a bacon sandwich and introduced to the 1970s' folk group the Spinners led by Mick Groves. They'd been commissioned to do a TV advert for Jaffa Cakes. This entailed them walking through the market followed by an enthusiastic band of singers. They had to sing this song.

'Jaffa cakes, Jaffa cakes
Gimme, gimme, gimme some Jaffa cakes.
They're chocolate and spongy,
With a smashing middle bit
So orangey.'

We thought this was the business, learned the words and made it our local anthem. I'm no longer sure I renewed my party membership the next year, on leaving university.

We developed little idiosyncratic routines, for example, a simple Wednesday tea was always taken in a certain cafeteria. After which Neil Coley, Colin Hazelhurst and I went to Cartmel College bar, for some reason had three glasses of mead and played R5 and R7 on the jukebox. Neither of these choices were 'Telstar' by the Tornados. They were 'Without You' by Harry Nilsson and 'Half as Nice' by Amen Corner. I know not why.

It was in the third year that I had my second opportunity to visit the northern town of Blackburn. The far-right National Front had been agitating there against recently settled and comparatively small numbers of Asian immigrants and successfully fielded some candidates in the local council elections. Lancaster students hired two or three coaches and down we went, a journey of about an hour. We left our coaches and wandered around the small town but there didn't seem to be a plan. We skirted around what I now know to be the cathedral and suddenly I was linked in arms and lines and lines of anti-protesters were formed. There I was, arms linked, with someone who looked very much like Tariq Ali, in the front row as we started to walk and then trot (possibly an ill-chosen word) towards a police cordon. I think now this was along Jubilee Street, destined to be my place of work some years later. There was some scuffling, it was frightening and I managed to disentangle myself from my phalanx.

All being split up, I found myself on what I now know as the Town Moor. Gratefully I came across some Lancaster colleagues, we found our coaches and made our way back to the university. It hadn't been enjoyable and I'd felt quite frightened. On the other hand, I was glad I'd done it and I'd stood up and been counted.

I took my final exams and again waited for the results. I did badly, far worse than my submitted coursework. I managed the lowest form of honours degree, third class.

After spotting my result pinned for all to see on the politics department noticeboard, I sauntered along the corridor to find Professor Reynolds' room. I knocked on the door and was invited to 'Enter', which I did.

The professor was staring out of the window looking across the Lancashire Fells. 'Mr Taylor, tell me, did you manage to scrape an academic qualification from our institution?' His back remained turned towards me, still staring out of the window. 'That's why I've come to see you, Professor. I did, thank you very much. But I also came to thank you for a far more profound political education I've received whilst here. Sadly, little of it as a result of academic activity.' His back was still turned towards me and he remained silent. I left the room.

These guys were all extremely learned, recognised experts in their field. Oxbridge graduates, both Carter and Reynolds had been Conscientious Objectors. Carter, later, got knighted and Reynolds was awarded a CBE. It felt to me however, that when emotional intelligence was being handed out, these guys seemed quite a way to the back of the queue.

The academics at Lancaster taught political science. I learned the rudiments of the art of politics extracurricular in the world of student 'politics'. Successful applied politics, gaining power and doing 'things' with it, is a fusion of art and science.

A few days later it was Graduation Day. Most of my student colleagues' families proudly attended. I sat on my own in Bowland Bar and had a few beers.

Many of my immediate peers went off to work in the public sector, some into social work. By and large they went into teaching and did very well as classroom and head teachers. Neil Coley has written a number of highly recommended books, mainly focussed on his adopted city of Lichfield. (See *Lichfield Book of Days*, History Press 2014, *Lichfield Pubs* (thoroughly researched I'm told!), Amberly Publishing 2016, *Secret Lichfield*, *An Alien Autumn*, *The Cold Distance* and others.)

I didn't do much that summer, hopped around a few summer-vacated rooms, beds or floors. It was time to think about the world of work; getting an income generating job, I mean.

Chapter 7

The Early Blackburn Years, 1973-77

I'm on your side when times get rough.

Another summer came and went.

I had applied for a place on the Thomson's Newspapers' postgraduate journalist course and got to the final round but fell at that last hurdle.

I also despatched an inflated wildly beyond my abilities or experience letter to the ITV company based in Carlisle, Border TV I think, telling them that they should give me a job in TV journalism. It must have worked, as the top man responded by telling me to catch a specific train from Lancaster that got into Carlisle at a designated time where his company Rover car would collect me. I would then be taken to the studios where they would find out whether my audacity matched my potential. Sadly, the morning coincided with the one after our collective twenty-first birthday celebrations. I didn't make the journey, probably much to the benefit and relief of Jeremy Paxman I bet, had he known. When we met and chatted twenty-five or more years later on the main street in Blackburn, I didn't have the heart to tell him! Neither did I share with him the Taylor killer-diller question I had honed decades earlier in preparation for my illustrious journalistic career. My final interview question would have been: If I've not posed a question during this interview and you're relieved I haven't, what would it have been?

With a small legacy I bought a (£700) second-hand Hillman Imp, helped by Neil Coley's motor trade dad Fred. The registration number EOL 906L (always an O in the middle of a Brum registered vehicle, this Hillman was actually made in Birmingham too, back then). It made me more mobile for whatever my next steps were going to be. I applied to do a postgraduate teacher training course at Madeley College, somewhere near Crewe. I was interviewed and successful in securing a place. Then I got cold feet and on the morning that I was due to start I declined to attend. I wasn't a 100 per cent sure that working within the confines of the school as an institution would work for me.

So, now what? Paul Howard, a year ahead of me at Lancaster told me he had secured a job as a youth worker. He said it was good, gave you lots of freedom in how you worked and wasn't nine till five.

The places to look, Paul told me, were the *Times Educational Supplement* and the *Guardian*.

As I'd liked my time in the north-west, I restricted my scouring of the Situations Vacant column to that region. A few jobs stood out; one in Bolton and a number in Blackburn, which, under much contrasting circumstances, I had already visited twice. I applied and got interviews at both places. The Blackburn posts interviewed before the vacancy in Bolton.

I jumped into my Imp and went down to Blackburn for the interviews held, I think, at the YMCA. There were three, perhaps even four, jobs up for grabs. We were interviewed for them in a 'round robin' situation. One guy fell by the wayside when he candidly but possibly ill-advisedly disclosed he was divorced. This was October 1973.

My main drive was to get on the first rung of employment. I knew little about youth work or working for a local authority, which is what was on offer. Neither did I know that another episode of local government reorganisation was imminent, due to take effect on 1 April, 1974. This would mean that the Conservative shire county of Lancashire would be taking over the primary functions, including education, of which the youth service was a part, from the (normally Labour) county boroughs of Blackpool, Preston, Blackburn and Burnley. First of all, I didn't know that and secondly I was totally oblivious of it having any significance. I learned later that the borough principal youth officer wasn't hanging around to be, as he called it, 'Lancastrated'. He got himself a new job back 'home' down south, but it was his intention to leave his crew with a full complement, a full establishment of staff. We were interviewed in the early part of the week, I was offered a job and asked if I could start on the Thursday, that being 1 November. I apologised explaining I was travelling on the Friday to see some friends over the weekend. OK, I'll pay you from Thursday, but you can start on Monday. It all seemed very generous to me. I didn't realise my appointment was just a gambit in a bigger local government power game. I was told my starting salary would be £1648 per annum. I recall thinking that 1648 was a) a significant date in European history and b) quite a lot of money.

So, on Monday morning at 9.30 a.m. as instructed I duly reported for work as a detached youth worker for the young unemployed at Brookhouse Youth and Community Centre about half a mile from the town centre. These days a rookie public employee would expect a welcome as part of a supportive induction or probationary process, a welcome by the boss, the chair of education, meeting all the other staff, and a tour around the area perhaps? I arrived and bumped into the caretaker, Harold, who presented me with a cup of tea. It was horrible. The heaped teaspoon of tea leaves was chucked in a mug, then the boiling water. After brewing for five minutes, sterilised milk (known in Brum as bull's milk) was added, along with goodness only knows how much sugar. My work for that day seemed to centre around asking Harold not to put any sugar in my cuppa. I drove back to Lancaster late afternoon having only met Harold and achieved little else.

The next day was a little bit more exciting and comparatively action-packed. This was my first staff meeting. I learned that youth workers didn't start work till 9.30 a.m., mostly having worked till 10 p.m. the previous evening. There were about eighteen to twenty of us. At twenty-one, I was the baby of the group. I had faces, names, job titles and relationships to learn. The meeting concluded at 12.15 p.m. sharp when everybody disappeared. No one invited me to disappear with them. Not knowing where they'd gone, I think I tootled off back to Lancaster. Short days you're working, both my friends and I thought.

As soon as I got this, my first proper job, I joined a union. In the first place, I joined NUPE, the National Union of Public Employees that is now part of Unison. My membership didn't last long as it was pointed out to me that this wasn't a specialist union for youth and community workers, no seats on the JNC (Joint Negotiating Committee), so I joined the Community and Youth Services Association (CYSA), a central association of the teacher's NUT. CYSA later became the Community and Youth Workers Union that took itself under the Unison umbrella in the 1990s. Lancashire's CYSA held monthly meetings, which were totally relevant to our working issues. CYSA later morphed into Unison. I must try Croyde Bay again.

Things at work didn't really build up any head of steam. I was left to my own novice devices. I visited a few youth centres during the evening sessions, went and spoke to the local careers service and was taken one evening to visit the Duke of Edinburgh's Award Scheme executive. It all seemed very cliquey and pally. Some of the slightly older, family-based people like Tony and Pauline Parkinson and May Chadwick invited me round for tea occasionally, which helped me find my feet. I was also added to a regular Thursday night training course run by the youth officer's wife. They called the course Bessie, which I thought was rather nice. I later found out that the genesis for this low-key training was Gordon Bessey, previously the director of education for Cumbria. But the course, which ran until about 9-9.30 p.m., put me in touch with another dozen or so like-minded people, some of whom went for a quick beer before heading off home.

Was I to be in any doubt about Blackburn being a wise choice of settlement for me? Any such fears were soon allayed as I drove past local factories named Snap on Tools and Dick Bearings. My kind of town, I thought.

In the town centre the army surplus store, Famous Army Stores, had shed some letters from its title. In assumed Catalonian homage to George Orwell, it now declared itself to be Amos A Tores!

The round trip between Lancaster and Blackburn was about fifty or more miles and added an hour and a half to my working day, also preventing me from bedding into the Blackburn community. So, after two months of commuting I moved into Blackburn's YMCA hostel, staying there a couple of months. Hostel life was an experience in itself.

I was going nowhere with this job and I felt left on my own with little support or direction. I went to see the top guy. I'm wasting your money and you're wasting my time, I told him. I think I'm going to leave.

You're doing a great job, everybody thinks you're doing wonderful, we're going to promote you and here are the keys to your new youth centre. You start on 1 March. You're moving up from Grade 1 to Grade 2 (a few hundred quid!).

I was given a huge bunch of keys befitting to my newly endowed status as the centre/area worker of Accrington Road Youth Centre, Blackburn. I had no idea what my bosses, the young people or me had let ourselves in for.

I turned up, yes at 9.30 a.m., and the doors were already open. An old chap in overalls welcomed me, telling me he was the cleaner/caretaker, known as George. George Howarth told me he was approaching eighty. He was a totally reliable and great old chap.

My new place of work, perhaps one and a half miles to the east of the town centre, was housed in the undercroft of an old school. It was situated right slap bang in the middle of rows of terraced houses and two council estates, quite an established and stable community. Soon it would experience enormous ethnic transition, but for now it was solid white working class. Most people, men and women, were in work, many in cotton and other heavy industries. There were two local secondary schools nearby, one of them Roman Catholic.

The town of Blackburn was well described and discussed in Jeremy Seabrook's 1973 sociological book *City Close-up* (Penguin ISBN 0140037217).

I spent the morning getting familiar with the modest premises then went home to prepare for my first youth club night. Still no one had really spoken to me about the work and what was expected of me.

*   *   *

This new working environment coincided almost exactly with my purchasing my first home.

I hadn't seen much of my dad since he left home in 1966.

We'd shared a few notable national sporting events such as the 1968 Leeds United versus Arsenal League Cup Final (think that's all it was called back then) at Wembley in March. Both teams were star-studded: Cooper, Bremner, Charlton, Hunter, Giles and Gray pitted against the likes of McNab, McLintock, Ure, Graham and Armstrong. In a tight, hard-fought game, Terry Cooper scored the only goal for a Leeds' victory.

We also attended, two months later, the thrilling 'Watersplash' rugby league cup final again at Wembley, Leeds (a totally English thirteen) versus Wakefield Trinity (fielding one South African). Thirteen-man rugby followers will recall this momentous game played in monsoon-like conditions for the unforgettable under the posts last-minute conversion miss by Wakefield's legendary goal kicker, Don Fox, that made Leeds winners by 11 points to 10. He'd just been awarded the Man of the Match, Lance Todd Trophy.

My dad, being involved in housing, encouraged me, now I was working, to 'get on the property ladder'. He came up and we went around a few estate agents and viewed a couple of properties. He suggested a two up, two down, stone-built, recently renovated and extended terraced house in a town about four miles away known as Great Harwood. I put in an offer of £3,500, which was accepted. My dad offered me £500 towards the acquisition costs, which I thought was uncharacteristically generous. So, the process of purchasing my first little castle began. A few weeks later my dad notified me that there would be repayment responsibilities including notional interest on the £500. News to me! I went into a local building society, borrowed the said amount, and reimbursed my benefactor, paying off my debt to the Leeds Permanent monthly. I was never to see my dad again. He died, aged eighty-seven, in 2014. I learned much later that he remarried twice, both times to the same woman. The second time in Gretna Green.

It can't be long after this that I was approached by Pete Johnson and Dave Pendle, quite senior local youth officers, who also chaired national committees of our union and sat on the NEC (National Executive Committee) that met four times a year in London. They were looking for someone with committee secretarial experience and I told them I had it (middle school debating society circa 1965). So, aged barely twenty-two, I was on the National Executive Committee and secretary of the National Youth Work Committee of our union.

One incident sticks out in my memory. Most youth workers are, or were then, socialists or Christians. As secretary I had received a letter from an organisation called SAYS, Sexual Awareness in Youth Services. Their position was that gay youth workers should be treated reasonably and equal with others. I suggested we wrote back saying we agreed. Not for a moment did I anticipate any adverse response to this in a room full of youth workers. This initiated a tirade from a Christian-based colleague committee member in the room. 'Gay people should not be involved or even let near any young people.' There was a humdinger of a row, my original, I thought neutral, idea, eventually winning. How times have changed!

* * *

Returning to my first night in charge at Accy Road as it was and is known. (The old stone building was later replaced by a purpose-built youth and community centre as part of the council's developments. We were to build many of these, at my instigation.)

I arrived a little early for the 7 p.m. opening. There were twenty or more youngsters hanging around outside. Are you the new bloke? We miss Jill, we liked her!

I opened up, eventually selecting the right keys from my big bunch. A couple of grown-ups entered and introduced themselves as part-time members of my staff. So pretty damn quickly, I'd become responsible for some council premises, a few dozen young people and manager of a small team of staff.

A few moments later another slightly older grown-up appeared. He introduced himself as Bob Wilson, a student on the current Bessey course, who had been put with me as his placement. So now you can add youth work trainer to this rapidly expanding list of expected but unspecified skills.

The young people wandered in, by and large ignoring me and relating, quite understandably, to the existing staff members who they knew and had a relationship with.

The nightly fee to attend the session was 10p. The young people didn't seem to begrudge this modest charge; well, only the once. One lad wandered into the centre one evening with a cigar of Churchillian proportions gripped in his mouth. I asked for his 10p subs and he professed destitution, blowing smoke in my face. Like lightning, I snatched his cigar, threw it into and locked the subs cash tin. 'Give it me back!' he demanded. 'Sorry, mate, if you can afford that, you can afford 10p!' He coughed up; the 10p, that is, and got his cigar back. But they weren't too happy that the coffee bar wasn't very well stocked. Yet another new set of tasks for this innocent young man, accounting for and banking the income and visiting the local cash and carry to replenish coffee bar stocks.

The youth centre opened five nights a week, Monday to Friday. One night was run by Bhagvangiri Goswami and was aimed at a small number of Asian youngsters who lived around and about and across the town. This language mightn't even have existed in those days, but the only ethnic minority I'd come across had been in Birmingham, people from the West Indies, what we now know as the Windrush generation. I'd had no contact with Asian people whatsoever. The target youth club age was fourteen to twenty-one, but I soon learned that we also ran a junior club for under fourteens. A number of the older youth club members attended as volunteers to assist in running the under fourteens' activities. Another of my jobs was to devise and deliver alongside the older youngsters a curriculum, known as a programme, in youth work parlance, I learned. There was a lot to learn.

By and large the youth centre membership came from around five or six local Blackburn salt of the earth families: the Hudsons, Seeds, Derbyshires, Byrnes, Holmes, Uptons, amongst others. I slowly got to know them and they me.

In some ways, luckily, the previous post-holder Jill Kavanagh was still around, having left the service to have a baby. I say luckily because quite rightly she made it clear that a) she was going to be busy and b) I was the new captain of this little ship. Initially, I popped round reasonably frequently to Jill and her husband, Kav's, house.

The months rolled by. We had a small fleet of vehicles – two twelve-seater, four-wheel drive Land Rovers and a slightly larger Ford Transit. These were available for us to augment our programme with trips around the locality and beyond.

For my first induction into the use of these vehicles I was invited to move our flotilla of canoes off the water where they spent the summer, to be housed indoors. I accompanied one of the bosses and we picked up a couple of older youngsters to help shift the heavy and cumbersome canvas vessels. These were loaded, about a dozen or so of them, onto a hefty substantial trailer, designed for that very purpose. We set off for the other side of town. 'We'll just go through the middle of town,' I was told by my superior who was driving. 'Aha, here's the town centre and the town hall, I'll pop out here. Have you driven a Land Rover towing a trailer before?' 'No,' I replied, 'I have driven a Hillman Imp.' I don't think he even heard my reply. He hopped out of the driver's seat, leaving the engine running for me to negotiate the rest of the delivery journey. It was tricky, one of the late-teenaged passengers reminded me that I had to double declutch the Land Rover. His pal almost gleefully chipped in, 'You've not forgotten that towing a trailer more than doubles the length of the unit?' To be bloody frank, it had slipped my mind.

The main streets of Blackburn were narrow back then with many cars parked along the way. Given that driving in Blackburn invariably means negotiating either up or down often precipitously steep hills, my induction into what seemed an HGV proportion task was daunting.

Without any collisions, scratches or other incidents, we made it to the winter store, the lads unloaded and racked up the hibernating canoes. I dropped them off around town as required and returned the Land Rover to its base.

These days that would have involved at least two bits of training and testing. One would be, I think it's still called MiDAS, Minibus Drivers Awareness. There would be some other process if towing behind the vehicle and possibly one for the specialist Land Rover work. Police clearance for people working with young people was twenty years away!

The vehicles were stored at the massive flagship YMCA youth facility quite close to the centre of town. So, accessing them also gave me opportunities to meet and mix, professionally and socially, with other youth work colleagues based there.

Bob Beardsworth was employed by the Roman Catholic Diocese of Salford. His brief included working in the three Catholic schools in the borough, one of which, St John Rigby, was also in my locality. Bob was based at the other large youth facility in the town centre, namely the West End Roman Catholic Youth Centre. Father Michael Walsh was the chaplain there then, later succeeded by Leo Heakin. At the end of one of our monthly district team staff meetings Bob suggested that he and I met up to look at designing a school-leaver programme to be run at his centre. West End had originally been housed in a former town centre shop-like premise and then moved to a two-storey purpose-built centre that was totally surrounded by the now no longer there Thwaites' Brewery. It moved site again in the early/mid-seventies to another purpose-built building in the town centre. These moves put our ideas on ice.

*   *   *

Other ideas weren't. Youth unemployment was soaring in the late '70s, the Manpower Services Commission was established and based in Sheffield. It established Job Creation Programmes (JCP) paying the proper rate for the job. I moved quickly and set up a small scheme for trainee youth workers in the borough, collaborating with the borough council to take on the personnel, payroll and similar roles. We would appoint, train and support the team of eight or ten. It was a fabulous success, those appointed went on to become police officers, drugs, social and youth workers and kindred careers. Pete Haken, Bernie Huxley, Keith and Sue Owen, amongst others, are names that come to mind.

Our bosses from citadel county hall got wind of my plan and came to help. 'Have you thought of what pay scales to put these people on, how to pay them, tax, national insurance, pensions, liability insurance?' The questions rained down on me. I answered yes to everyone. 'I'm sorry. All the posts are filled and they start on Monday'.

In further collaboration with the borough, this scheme, that we appointed former Methodist minister Mitch Wyke to lead, grew and grew.

Eventually 200 people were employed in communities providing play and childcare, pre school and after school provision, youth work, sports and community development, family and older folk support. Communities flourished, the staff gained new opportunities, experiences, skills and qualifications.

* * *

At about the same time that I arrived at Accy Road a fresh wave of immigration occurred and the youth club was soon home to the Doyles, Burns, Hammells, McGurks and other Catholics who had fled the Troubles that beset Northern Ireland. As with most initial settlements of immigrants, these families congregated around a small enclave of streets ironically including Artillery, Woolwich and Ordnance Streets. I had occasion to visit one of the families' houses there. The front door was like a back gate with the handle and a sneck, no lock, just a bolt on the inside. I knocked and heard a faint invite to come in, which I did. Although daytime, the room was very dim; it may have been gas lit. I could just make out a slight figure laid on a bed. 'Be careful, Mr Taylor,' a female voice, the family's matriarch, warned, 'we've sold some of the flags from the floor. We had quite a nice house in Belfast but we had to leave it quickly.'

For one of my politics courses at university, only a couple of years before, I'd completed a dissertation on the catalogue of incidents in January 1972, that became known as Bloody Sunday. The Army had shot twenty-eight civilians, fourteen of them dead, all of them Catholic. Those old enough will never forget the image of Catholic priest Father Edward Daly waving his bloodstained white handkerchief as a makeshift flag of truce trying to get the wounded some urgent medical attention. The then government immediately convened an enquiry into the events led by the Lord Chief Justice of England and Wales, Baron Sir John Widgery QC. This was seen as a total whitewash, placing the blame almost entirely on the Catholic community. Over a quarter of a century later the government-appointed Saville Report totally discredited Widgery's conclusions, followed a few years ago, by Prime Minister David Cameron describing the events as 'unjustified and unjustifiable'. Others will remember the U2 anthem 'Sunday Bloody Sunday'.

So, stood in that dark, damp living room with a reasonable knowledge of the background to the difficulties in Northern Ireland I was able to engage with the lady with some basis of knowledge. She was quite surprised. I'd never really expected that piece of studying to be of any practical use whatsoever.

*　　*　　*

But once again (around 1976) there was a clash between my professional and political/moral positions. The area around Accrington Road, known as Audley, was starting to change. The demography of the area, unchanged for decades, first had the previously discussed influx of Northern Irish Roman Catholics and next came the Asian community, almost entirely Muslim.

This ethnic settlement, mainly encouraged to place people in employment in the cotton industry, began in the late 1960s in Blackburn. This was now the mid-seventies, as ironically King Cotton was in a process of global abdication. The Asian community started to occupy first the cheaper housing and then the bigger houses near the youth centre, a typical pattern for immigrant settlement.

There were a number of Christian places of worship in the vicinity: St Jude's, St Thomas', a non-conformist church on Audley Range, originally Congregational, which closed its doors in 1988. The minister serving from 1958-82 was Jim Watson, at the time a veteran Labour councillor and former mayor, amongst others (it always made me chuckle that Free Church Jim had JEW monogrammed on his briefcase). The Muslim community also wanted somewhere to pray, which seemed reasonable to me.

They had acquired a terrace house just off Accrington Road and sought to use it as a worship centre. The local population was not happy and ironically this caused an alliance between the indigenous population and the reasonably recently settled Northern Irish Catholics. They were united around a 'We don't want any Pakis here with their funny ways' platform. The National Front (later the National Party), led nationally and locally by John Kingsley Read, quite expectedly, stirred things up. There was an opposite reaction from anti-fascists. I became one.

This ended up with me on an anti-fascist march in Blackburn, again. This time 200 yards from my youth centre, which shared premises with the local English language centre for immigrant children. I was on the road with the march, quite paradoxically, my youth club members on the pavements jeeringly and vehemently heckling us. It wasn't an easy time.

This was my first engagement with any Asian folk. They'd come to Britain and more especially Lancashire at the specific invite and purpose of working in the textile industry. I don't think either the indigenous or immigrant communities could anticipate how this new wave of ethnic change would develop. It was mainly young men who came first to work, then wives or wives to be. A few youngsters came and started at schools.

Diet was an obvious difference with halal food being a requirement of the new settlers. When I went working at Shadsworth High School there were tins of Lucky Star Pilchards stored to the school kitchen ceilings and that was that. Some of the kids said 'Just how many Lucky Star Pilchards can we stomach, Mr Taylor?' In another well-meant culinary accommodation of this change, the ladies in the town hall staff canteen couldn't see why there was little take up of the pork vindaloo recipe they'd added to their repertoire!

It was about this time that I went to visit Rick Dunning and his partner Paul in Suffolk. Rick had already been a Labour Party member for a few years and whilst at university he'd been active delivering milk free to local schools at the time when Tory Education Minister Margaret Thatcher was demonised as the milk snatcher. Now back in his native Suffolk, Rick hadn't fulfilled his promise to Princess Alexandra to become a postman. He was creating and developing his dream of an arts and drama centre in Sudbury. At the same time he was also active in the Save Suffolk's Hedgerows campaign. On returning to Lancashire pondering that Rick was so tangibly involved made me think about what I was up to; what was I creating?

*   *   *

Once the West End new build was completed Bob Beardsworth and I put on a series of two-hour-long school-leaver sessions that lasted ten weeks each. Youngsters in their final year at secondary school came down to West End accompanied by some school staff. This included the head of final year, Mr Chesworth, aka Ches, who said 'We all like coming here, it's fun and the kids learn useful things'!

Bob and I fronted the input subjects which included: how to write a letter, how to make a phone call from a coin-operated phone box in those days, how to apply for a job, your first day at work, how to use the National Health Service, what to do if you cross paths with the police and things. Bob and I were self-taught role-play artists. For some reason he was always the senior and I was always the lad. In one session about the law, Bob, playing the lad's works foreman, asked, 'Have you tried Legal Aid?' Totally off the cuff, my unrehearsed response was 'I don't like fizzy drinks, mister'. This quip had me, Bob and our whole audience in stitches. They never forgot about Legal Aid after that. Some of our, actually groundbreaking, work was written up and replicated around Blackburn and Lancashire.

At some time during all this we had a change of senior manager. Ken Eccles became our district youth officer. Ken, like many of the other Blackburn staff, was home-grown, Blackburn through and through. He'd served in the Army Education Corps for his National Service and then went into school teaching, which he never really took to. Ken was an artist at heart, literally a fine artist. He drew beautiful line drawings for his folk music-inspired Christmas cards and had designed a few fantastic LP covers (one ironically entitled 'Bold Bill Taylor') for his folk-singer fraternity, especially Brian Dewhurst, later Preston. Ken smoked a pipe incessantly, always had one or two preloaded in the pocket of the artist's smock that he always wore. He had a succession of boxer dogs who accompanied him on youth work visits. Ken was completely laid back. This meant that he gave his staff, or they took, a great deal of scope to be both imaginative and creative.

There were some great characters amongst this home-grown team, not least Dave Walsh. Dave had been a junior school caretaker. He loved kids, they trusted and loved him. I'm told he'd stay around after the school closed to let the kids play in safety a bit longer till their mums and dads got home. He did this to the extent that he went away and did a year's training in play leadership under the aegis of the National Playing Fields Association. Having got the required qualification Dave came back and ran a hugely successful play facility, loved and adored by the kids, officially known as Daisyfield Play Centre, but known to everyone, kids, generations of them, their mums and dads, the whole community as 'the Rec'. It was in fact a huge wooden shed sat in the corner of the playground.

Dave, Bob, the Parkinsons, Ken Eccles, May Chadwick and Derek Ingham were the home-grown backbone of this team. In some ways it was a hard team for outsiders to assimilate into, especially if we were seen as clever dick arrivistes. This evolved more as time went on. Riaz Begum, Steve Butters, Bill Crook, Tony Doherty, Mark Hilton, Mick Huxley, Fiona Parr, Andrea Phillimore, John Poulson, Alison Ronan, Mike Waite, John Woodcock, amongst others, came from further afield and helped diversify our professional husbandry.

We had some great admin people: Julie Muldoon, Nannette Hogg, Denise Baron and Bernadette Gardiner who kept us on our toes.

We were totally white as a team, whilst the community we served was changing. As a well-intended response to this, I always assumed, Ram Lal Sharma was appointed to run Brookhouse Centre, very much in the middle of the main concentration of the Asian settlement (the main road through, Whalley Range, was known locally, by most, as the Khyber Pass). Ram was a lovely, highly qualified chap. Like his pal Bagu Goswami, another lovely man, he was a highest caste Brahmin Hindu. The growing Asian community was almost entirely Muslim.

It must have been quite early on in my time in Blackburn that I met Tim Mason. Tim was based at Shadsworth High School, where he had the role of teacher-community worker; Shadsworth was not far from Accy Road and where many of the youth club kids went to school. We hit it off straight away professionally, politically and as pals too. We remained strong personal and family friends until his untimely death some forty years later. At the time Tim was living at home with his mum and dad, Frances and Jim Mason, who, although I didn't know or appreciate it at that time, were big wheels mainly locally and regionally, both in the Labour Party and the Cooperative movement. Tim invited me to and met me at the local folk club, held every Thursday night at the Old Blacks. Again, something else I didn't know was that the Old Blacks was actually the Old Blackburnians, the old boys' sports and social club of Blackburn's Queen Elizabeth Grammar School. Most of the town's male lawyers, accountants, other professionals, senior public servants and all the other movers and shakers were former pupils. Thursday nights were good nights there especially if you worked until ten o'clock, like we did, as they were accommodatingly lenient with the 10.30 p.m. licensing rules. I got there around 10.15 p.m. and Tim was at the crowded bar. 'I've got four pints,' said Tim. 'Brill, pass me my two, I'll get them next time.' 'No, these are mine, you get your own four!' That's how it was from then on!

Tony Parkinson ran Kaleidoscope Youth Centre next door to Everton High School but not part of it. It always seemed like we were the Cinderella service of education. He said he heard about the leaver work Bob and I had more or less conjured up for the Catholic schools. Could we try the same at Everton? Why don't we give it a whirl?

We followed a similar format. The last two lessons on Friday morning leading into a youth club-type session, snacks on sale, table tennis and a disco as a reward for the youngsters who had studied without realising they were studying. The only tune I can remember was a seemingly repetitive playing of Adam and his Ants' 'Prince Charming'! It was here that Mike Davis, a hugely well-read and intelligent man, got involved in our work. He was head of English in an extremely challenging school. Our collaboration together brought added value much to the benefit of the youngsters. I've had people not much younger than me tell me, decades later, that the work we did was amongst their most memorable school experiences.

But still there seemed to be no theoretical basis to my work, to our work. Many youth workers were home-grown, had had real jobs in industry, were mainly Christian or left-leaning and had come into the trade from helping out, running their church's youth club. There were some one-year converter courses nationally run, for example by the YMCA. Teachers were automatically considered and classed as qualified (no longer the case). I walked into the job because I had a degree and that was viewed as being enough.

I was conscious of this gap in my skills and experience base and enrolled on an Advanced Certificate in Education course at Manchester Poly – one day a week for two years.

It was a revelation meeting other youth workers, some old school and others sharp cookies, from around the north of England. A number were employed in Sheffield Youth Service and seemed much slicker, better organised and focussed. So much so that I applied for a youth tutor's post at two massive secondary schools there. I did well at the interviews held over two days with a number of councillors participating. One of the guys off the Manchester course came out to see me after the selection process. I'd not been successful as the panel had decided I was too young (twenty-three) to get paid the comparatively high salary on offer – back I went to Blackburn.

I attended the course to its conclusion in 1975, really learning that there was only an emerging theoretical basis to youth work and its processes.

For my assessment dissertation I wrote up and evaluated our work around youth work and its complementary role in bridging adolescence, school and the world of work. I passed this Advanced Certificate in Education.

I started to form my own theoretical framework for youth work. What I saw is us, supposedly the grown-ups, guardians of the future, not really recognising, valuing, understanding and developing the main resource of our future, our young people. After being born, our babies become children, they then go through what we understand to be adolescence to become grown-ups themselves. From those teenage years young people emerge to become young adults accumulating many of the traits and qualities that that status confers upon them, whether or not they like it, whether or not they are ready. They experiment with and form relationships, they begin to make homes, they may marry and have babies, taking responsibility or not for their own offspring, they seek and gain employment and start careers, they become eligible to be voters, they become economically active consumers, they become decision makers, inter alia. Sometimes we, their assumed custodians, are surprised when youngsters don't quite get things right. I have no idea why we are surprised.

Most of the adult world with which young people come into contact will 'manage' them. Parents should lovingly steward their kids through to independence and beyond, doctors and other health workers should care for their health and wellbeing, the police are there to ensure that the law is upheld, teachers are there to teach, social workers to care for young people possibly outside the intended family situation and so on.

My embryonic take on youth work that was emerging was simple, short and sweet:

Good youth work practice enables and empowers young people to experience and experiment with responsibility and power.

My view is that unless young people have some practice goes at relationships, being responsible for money, taking decisions, homebuilding and family shaping and all the skills that entails, then why the hell should we be surprised if they don't get it right?

*　　*　　*

My daily working pattern was generally to work mornings and evenings, with afternoons to myself. I discovered where others disappeared to in the afternoons, to the boat workshop next door to Accrington Road Centre. It seemed like the fiefdom of the boat-sailing and owning clique of the service staff. But I tended to go home, go to the cinema or go for a walk. One afternoon on my return to Great Harwood a chap in a duffel coat knocked on my door. 'Hello, I'm Mike, I'm your new lodger. Did Rod not tell you?'

This was the first day of my still strong friendship with Michael V Turner. I am sworn to secrecy about what the V stands for, but he was born in mid-February. Mike had recently qualified from Poulton le Fylde teacher training college and was soon to start work teaching mainly history at the nearby Pleckgate High School in Blackburn.

A pal from Lancaster University, Malcolm Smith, had then gone off to Reading University to get an MSc in biology. He came up for a weekend. That meant a drinking weekend. Malcolm had been brought up in Shirebrook, a mining community near Mansfield. I visited him there once, a very strong working-class family who all worked in coal mining, but that day I collected him in my Hillman Imp from Blackburn Station. Passing a two-phase illuminated flashing advertisement for the local Thwaites' brewery Malcolm exclaimed loudly 'bloody 'ell, it's proper north country up 'ere, look at that sign. 'Thwaites' Ales, aye, Ales!''

Perplexed, I stopped the car to study the sign. 'I think you've misunderstood, mate. It's actually saying, 'Thwaites' Ales, A1 Ales'.' 'Oh yeah, sorry!'

After this idiomatic regional gaffe, Malcolm, Mike and I had a great weekend, if I remember rightly.

Malcolm must have done because a few days later a large trunk bearing his name at my address appeared in the backyard. At the front, through the letter box, the postie had delivered a letter. This was from Malcolm and explained that he'd enjoyed himself so much he decided to become my second lodger. So the dream team was assembling itself around me.

Mike started his professional teaching career. Malcolm started on the night shift as a battery filler in the weaving shed of a local cotton mill in nearby Rishton. His favourite part of the shift was when the other guys, mainly Asians, brought out curry and chapattis which they happily shared with him.

After a while, though, I think night shifts and him didn't agree with one another. Malcolm saw a job at a nearby secondary school as the science department's lab assistant. He applied for it and got called for interview.

It was a fair distance to what was known then as Billinge High School, six or seven miles with at least two steep climbs including over a nab. Undaunted Malcolm borrowed a pushbike I'd acquired and set off to get the job.

I met him sometime later, it being a Friday teatime, in our local. 'Well?' I asked. 'I didn't get that job. They looked at my application and asked if I had a degree in biology. No, I said, I've got two!' He went on to tell me that they'd explained they had a hard-to-fill vacancy on the teaching staff and offered it to him, to start on the Monday.

Mike was over the moon; Billinge was a mile or so from Pleckgate. Not only could Malcolm share petrol costs, but he could also give Mike's ailing Triumph a usually necessary shove every morning!

We settled down in Great Harwood. All bearded, local folk thought we were students; well, perhaps we were still behaving like that. Weekends were boozy dos, a pub crawl with a set routine culminating in the culinary climax of a sit-down fish and chip supper on Clayton Street. What more could you ask for?

We made some great pals over those four years. Philip Eddleston and his elder brother Pete, who owned a bakery, Dave Wally Walters, Pete Haken, the Sumners, but also the Greens, Reids and Bristoes and others. Several seemed to have ascribed work-related names: Jimmy Butcher, Jimmy Milk and Bob Mace, who ran the local Spar shop.

We also had some great adventures. We had a regular weekly folk night in the Plough pub, which was really well attended. Phil and Pete Eddleston were the driving forces behind it. This developed into rather boozy Saturday night trips to the Yorkshire Dales. We would drive up and pitch our tents in the back garden of the Helwith Bridge pub, just north of Settle. We'd then wander into the pub, have a bar snack and then settle down to an evening of supping and singing, all welcome, sometimes including the Rochdale Cowboy, Mike Harding, who lived nearby. However, a camping/drinking trip in Philip's VW Dormobile to the Scottish Isle of Arran was the highlight.

Philip got more involved in the youth club and encouraged some young people into taking up guitars and music generally.

* * *

I was really enjoying my time at Accy Road. I got to know the thirty or forty regular members and they me. I would describe it as being a trusting if sometimes challenging set of relationships. The part-time staff team changed over time to include some slightly younger people. I thought the balance of experience and ideas was good. We had quarterly staff meetings, where we discussed and decided things and planned a programme. We took this way of working responsibly.

Along with several colleagues at the time we chose to extend responsibilities and share them with some of the more responsible young people. A members' committee was established and this meant that every two months a meeting discussed matters to do with youth club. Items for discussion included finances, the programme, trips and visits and really anything thought relevant that the law and confidentiality would allow.

It is at this point with no real apology that I have to raise the issue of balls; yes, you heard right... balls. Balls and their valued safekeeping had featured in my life back to the junior school days of the cherished cherry.

Accy Road sported two rather high quality table tennis tables; they got a lot of use, every night. Some youngsters bought and brought their own much treasured bats (with apologies to the ping pong guy, Matthew Syed).

I bought, on official requisition, table tennis balls by the dozen. We always had plenty in, one star quality. We were then suddenly subjected to an outbreak of deliberate ball damage of epidemic proportions. My stocks were depleted very quickly. These things weren't cheap and were bought from club income. My solution? Not to buy any more; once damaged, table tennis stopped. There was an outcry: we want our table tennis back!

Solution two? If the evening ended with no balls intact, two members, usually from the committee, were dragooned into meeting me after school or work. We'd then drive into Blackburn to Mike Gibson's Sports to buy three loose balls, no stars. This process took an hour and lasted three evenings. The press-ganged, reluctant shoppers were well peeved with 'wasting' an hour of their time, no thought of mine, but I was on a crusade. The informally established ping pong ball protection league was vigilant to the point of being vigilante about policing the preservation of the ping pong balls. This wasn't really about those blessed balls, more about the issue of resource wasting, from their own generated resources. I'd like to think that this lesson was transferred then, and in later life, to the wider community not to mar or vandalise its own resources.

One thing we introduced, and in some ways it really shouldn't be rocket science, was to listen to what young people were saying. But not only to listen but to hear as well. But not only to hear but also to try and understand how and why they were saying what they were.

At this time Blackburn had a concentration of a few very large industrial factories: three breweries (Thwaites', Whitbreads and Matthew Brown), Philips, an electronics company or Mullards as it was known locally, the ROF (Royal Ordnance Factory, known locally as the Fuse), the NHS including Blackburn Royal Infirmary, a large power station and everyone employed by the local council. On top of that there were dozens of cotton mills with the associated support industries such as shuttle making. There were still numerous heavy-metal engineering plants with roaring furnaces and sparks flying, concentrated in an area served by the Foundry pub. Many of these were family businesses going back decades, some like Walkers Steel more successful than others.

The cotton industry had been King in Blackburn and the surrounding towns, to the extent that Mohandas K Gandhi came to Darwen in 1931. According to the Cotton Town website, there were over fifty cotton mills in Blackburn in 1950, employing 11,000 weavers. By 1967, only twenty-six mills were still going, employing 5,000, perhaps 6,000, weavers. Four years later, six more mills had closed. There is little cotton production now.

It was in places like these that many local people found employment as their parents often had before them. I listened to these youngsters talk about their aspirations. Frequently their parents, uncles or aunties got these soon to be school leavers (the school leaving age went up from fifteen to sixteen around then) jobs where they themselves worked.

I listened to one sixteen-year-old. He'd started an apprenticeship his uncle had got him. I asked him an apprentice what? Not sure yet was his reply. 'So what do you do all day?'

'We clock on at eight and I go round all the blokes to see if they want anything from the shop, fags, sweets, bacon butties and stuff. I make a note of what they want and how much money they've given me and then go to the shop. When I come back, I hand out their stuff and quite often they say 'keep the change, lad'. Then at half ten, I do the same again. Then it's dinner time and I go around getting the orders for chips, pies, fish, John Bulls (a John Bull was a locally delicacy, with two layers of potatoes either side of a mince filling, battered then deep fried), peas, barm cakes (a large bread roll) and the like. I then walk down to the chippy and give the lady the order which she carefully places in a box, ticking off each order as she goes along. When that's done the boss is outside waiting in his car to take me back so people's dinners don't get cold. I then go round the factory giving out their wrapped-up meals. By then, it's time for the last visit to the shop so it's another round of taking orders, money and distributing what's been ordered.'

'I didn't get paid the first week; it's called working a week in hand. But at the end of the second week, I got my first wage packet in a see-through envelope with a staple through the pound notes. It wasn't very much, nowhere near as much as my going to the shop money and I didn't get to keep it. I went home, handed it over to Mum, who opened it, took quite a lot out and handed me the rest.'

A few months later, our apprentice something or other triumphantly came into the youth centre. 'I found out what I do! I'm an apprentice caster pouring hot metal into moulds.'

How did you find out? 'The new lad started today. We send him to the shop and I started my training.'

This exchange, interesting in itself, had two effects. Firstly, we acquired an A4 hardback notebook kept securely in the safe where members of staff could confidentially enter any occurrences or observations they thought worthy of note. Secondly, we decided to work on broadening the horizons and hopefully raising the aspirations of our young people by increasing the range of options, across all kind of issues, that might be available to them.

It is important to understand that youth workers are generalists, not specialists. But not only that, good youth work aspires to take a long-term view of the development of the individual, but not just about the individual, their family, friends and community. Teachers teach, social workers care, the police police and so on. Youth workers should have unconditional positive regard for their young people as a vital starting point.

One particular set of issues that regularly recurred centred around these adolescents' bodies and the changes they were going through and sex education. We were aware of specialist agencies around us with whom we met to seek their input and advice about how much we needed to know as youth workers and when to call upon more expert advice.

But there were other things we wanted young people to experience, some simple, some more complex.

By and large our young people didn't move much beyond their own backyard.

Three or four times a year we would take eight or ten youngsters to Kentmere Cottage, a set of ramshackle former mining buildings, well off the beaten track, in the southern approaches to the Lake District. It would have been easier for the youth workers to decide which young people came along, buy all the food and so on, but that's not how we did things.

A week or two before the event a meeting open to all youngsters was convened. This was first of all to choose who was going. Not an easy task in itself. Those who attended had to elect a chair and someone to record decisions. Some came only to promote their own case for inclusion, others advocated sharing the opportunity over the occasions available to us, others promoted the case for others to participate if they hadn't been before or were going through tough times. There were all sorts of things said. These were real issues for them to tussle with and resolve. Perhaps without really noticing it these youngsters developed skills in organising meetings, public speaking, sticking up for themselves and others, allocating tasks and recording decisions?

This process didn't go too well one time. One young man, fifteen or so, came late to the meeting and hadn't secured a place to go to Kentmere. He wasn't happy but rules were rules. He left the premises very angry. Some other members wandered in. 'You're not going to be happy with what's been done to your car.' I wandered out to the parked Hillman. According to the freshly coined or knifed down to bare metal slogan, I was a ****. I'll leave you to work out the unpleasant word.

The likely culprit was fifty yards away giving me plenty. I gave chase, I was still fleet of foot then and caught him after a good mile pursuit. I clunked him one; pure outrage at what he'd done to my prized possession.

That done I was still very upset at his actions and still was the next day. It weighed on my mind and clouded my day. What to do?

When I thought his people would be at home, around teatime, I went around. His mum came to the door. 'What do you want, you ****?' (using the same rudimentary biological language that adorned my car's bonnet). Several other members of the family came to the door and were equally as welcoming. Eventually the lad himself arrived and lo and behold was no more amenable. I handed him an official looking brown envelope addressed to him. 'What the **** is this?'

'It could be the repair bill for the criminal damage that you did to my car last night?'

He opened the envelope and read the brief letter. 'Why would you do that for me?' he asked.

'Because I've spent all day thinking about what the best thing to do is, and this is it. I might be the last person ever to give you one last chance.'

The letter was inviting him to join the group going to Kentmere. That day I'd chatted with many people and was taking a risk. Did I do the right thing? What would others have done? These questions still linger in my mind.

The lad came along, was no trouble at all, couldn't do more for me. I used to see him occasionally over the next forty years and he'd just wink at me.

Who would attend Kentmere eventually got decided and, from those people, certain jobs had to be allocated. Someone had to ring the town hall to book the vehicle, there were menus to be argued over and agreed and a shopping expedition to take place.

Knowing how quickly demands were made and bookings diarised for our vehicles, I had already booked one sometime in advance. But the allocated young person didn't know that and was tasked with ringing the already briefed office in the town hall to sort.

Perhaps the night before, I would collect a couple of youngsters from school or work and, with the menus translated into a shopping list we would make a trip to the local cash and carry. Everything was ready and the next evening we would set off on the hour and a half trip.

Kentmere Cottage was by no means four-star accommodation. The roofs leaked, the building was cold, there was one chemical toilet. The youngsters loved it. Nobody got very much sleep the first night, not much more the night after. Duties were allocated without much fuss; well, perhaps toilet duties weren't a favourite. The fayre was simple, but still had to be prepared and washing up to be done.

Even after only two nights away, the vehicle home carried many weary travellers. Back at Accy Road there might be soaking wet cagoules and similar to be hung up to dry prior to their return to the stores.

Little did I know and found out only very, very recently, that these youngsters loved Kentmere and couldn't get enough of it. So much so that when we didn't have an official trip and they had a) some money and b) some means to get there, off they would go. Over time they acquired their own rucksacks, tents, sleeping bags and a stove and they'd be there at the drop of a (woolly) hat. Even now, as they approach sixty plus years of age. They've also planned and prepared their own bespoke holidays – no package deals here! No slouches, eh?

Visits to other places included more recreational day trip events but others were far more substantial. One week-long trip was to Lancaster University's centre in the Yorkshire Dales, another to the Duke of Edinburgh's Award Scheme near Bron y Gader in North Wales. Far more ambitious and hugely loved were the two annual canal narrowboat trips, one out of Rugby, another along the Llangollen Canal. As pieces of youth work these were all about the planning and the doing and getting young people to see and experience other parts of Britain.

There were other, more educational, residentials on offer to these youngsters, notably at Borwick Hall, a youth service training centre an hour away near Carnforth. Sometimes these forty-eight-hour experiences were midweek and designed for young people on the brink of leaving school. Others scheduled at the weekend were designed by youth workers and other colleagues to fit identified needs of the specific group of young people. Topics or issues could include me and my community; living in a more multicultural world; the media and young people; giving young women more of a say and using drama techniques to enable young people to better express themselves. If we could, on the Friday-Sunday events, we tried to take the whole group to see a play on the Friday evening. I recall everyone (including the staff) being bemused at the Brewery Arts, Kendal by the *Threepenny Opera* by Bertolt Brecht. On another occasion, this time at the Dukes Playhouse, Lancaster, I think we all found *Stags and Hens* by Willy Russell easier to digest. It's a play about two groups of young people on a night out in a nightclub. At the play's conclusion one seventeen/eighteen-year-old from our group asked 'Was that a drama or a documentary? It was just like what we do most Friday nights'. These courses went down well and once again, I can still bump into former participants from four decades ago who reminisce fondly about their experiences.

I also recollect one fifteen/sixteen-year-old lad. On our coach journey back to Blackburn, we included a guided tour around the Shire Hall, Crown Court and prison cells of Lancaster's medieval castle. We found ourselves near the cells of the gaol with massive thick walls, huge doors and bolts the size of a man's arm. To be frank, the youngster had been a bit of a pain in the arse during our forty-eight-hour period away. The usual script: late for everything; not listening; pratting about; usual adolescent behaviour when feeling out of their comfort zone. He asked me if he could go in the cell to see what it was like. I said 'Why not? I'll draw the bolts to make your experience more authentic.' 'Brilliant,' he said on entering the cell. The bolts were not easy to draw but I managed to waggle and squeak them well and truly shut. I then remained silent. After a minute or two our intrepid volunteer captive asked, 'Can I come out now?' His request was met with literally stony silence. A few moments later, 'Mr Taylor, can I come out now? Please, Mr Taylor, can you let me out? Please. Mr Taylor are you still there, please, undo the bolts. It's not very nice in here now'.

The bolts were released, after perhaps two or three minutes in total, and our pitifully incarcerated captive freed. 'It was great in there, I really enjoyed it,' he bravely lied.

Next week, back in school in a lesson that he'd missed the previous week whilst away with me, the class were tasked with writing a report of their time away.

The teacher made a point of seeking me out later. The lad's report included 'Definitely the best time for me was when Mr Taylor took me to a medieval fortress somewhere where hundreds of people had been hanged, and he locked me in a dungeon alone for hours'. My teacher colleague mused, 'You should have left him there!'

*   *   *

All in all my life was work hard, play hard during what became known as the Great Harwood Years. And I nearly fell foul of this heady cocktail.

One weekend my schedule was to be: Friday to Sunday away with a group of young people followed by the union National Executive meeting in London immediately after on the Monday, a gruelling, if not plain daft set of commitments. There would be little guarantee of any sleep over the weekend, followed by the need to get up at 5 a.m. to catch the 6 a.m. London train from Preston.

The weekend happened and the young people were their normal energy and patience-sapping selves. I went to bed exhausted on the Sunday evening.

The next morning, presumably having slept through my alarm, I woke up around half past five. I didn't have enough time to make my scheduled train. I'd booked a day off work, so rolled over to catch up on some obviously necessary sleep.

I woke up when I woke up, feeling much better, comparatively refreshed. But what now to do with my free day?

I took a leisurely start, enjoyed a lengthy soak in the bath, jumped in my Hillman and drove up to Lancaster hoping to bump into some friends.

This happened and we planned how to spend the gift of an evening together. These guys were still on modest grants and my salary was four or five times their incomes. A few beers and my treating my pals to a curry was mooted and agreed. I parked up outside where I'd be sleeping and walked into town. We had a few beers and set off to the curry house. Quite soon into the meal, I didn't feel too good. I told my pals I might be better outside in the fresh air. This I did, sitting on a nearby bench. The next thing I knew, a torch was being shone in my face. The voice behind the torch told me 'I'm a police officer and believe you to be in possession of illegal drugs'. That was certainly a rude awakening. I was escorted to the nearby police station (I'd been there three or four years earlier as an alleged member of the Craig Affair's Lancaster x) and ended up in a cell until I could produce the required urine sample. This accomplished, I was allowed to leave and rejoined my friends, who'd wondered where I'd got to.

I realise that going outside when I felt ill wasn't my best move but it felt right at the time. Possibly more disturbing was the speed with which one of my bosses, who was also a JP, contacted me and said he'd been advised that the police were investigating me for the use of illegal drugs. This was the very next day when I'd returned from Lancaster.

Some weeks later I was advised that there would be no further action taken. But it all seemed quite an odd cycle of events, an addition to my experiences and an insight into how the police perceive and treat young people.

Meanwhile, back at work we focussed on breaking this cycle of only seeking out and securing a job within the realms of what the young people knew. I think we called it 'Different Worlds of Work'. Intermittently I would arrange visits to: a brewery, a hospital, the local sewage plant, a local newspaper, where they produced articles that appeared in real time and ditto at the local radio station. We went further afield including to Manchester to see a live TV pop show being broadcast, with Mudd topping the bill.

Another midweek daytime trip to Manchester, to an almost no-seater Old Trafford Stadium, was a highlight for the mainly Irish Catholic lads including sitting in the home changing room, imagining it was five to three, running down the tunnel and emerging to the chants of adulation of tens of thousands of Reds fans. One of our group was beside himself with excitement and just couldn't contain himself on the way to the ground some thirty miles away. He just couldn't shut up. On the return journey, his mates suddenly announced he was being sick everywhere. I had to stop, tidy him and the minibus as best we could. Why didn't you tell me you were going to chuck up? You told me I had to shut up and not talk to you again till we got home! The first time ever he'd 100 per cent complied with anything I'd told him.

Those three to four years at Accy Road were fantastic. A great group of youngsters, challenging but responsive, a great team of staff prepared to try things, other full-time colleagues thirsty to be imaginative and creative with an amenable, encouraging boss.

And the music… wall to wall Gary Glitter, Suzi Quatro, Slade, Queen, Mudd, Bay City Rollers (many of the youngsters wore those yellow-on-green starry jumpers and had tartan trimmed baggy pants).

And to end the evening? The last tune? Everyone left the centre on the stroke of ten, happily singing The Monkees' 'Day Dream Believer'.

Chapter 8

The Lucky Break Years, 1977–79

I got nothing to do today but smile.

In 1977 I reached the highly unripe old age of twenty-five!

Lots of things happened and changed during the year. Some of these breaks proved to be luckier than others.

In the April, we had a joint twenty-fifth birthday party, always quite raucous affairs, at our house. The product of which was that the next day I started going out with Anne Charles, who taught biology at Pleckgate where Mike Turner worked – the poor girl. I'd often get dragooned into playing for the Pleckgate staff footie team, so I'd known her a little via that august sporting body. She wore an Afghan coat and university scarf.

The Pleckgate team's main renown was that it included PE teacher Rick Grogan, and his claim to fame was that whilst at teacher training college he played football, quite well, for Alvechurch in the West Midlands. Alvechurch's claim to fame was playing the longest ever FA Cup tie versus Oxford City in 1971. No namby pampy penalty shootouts in those days. Ties were played and replayed and replayed until a victor emerged. There were six full matches played in seventeen days until there was a winner, 1-0 to Alvechurch, played at the mighty Villa Park. The matches were reported in the *Oxford Mail* by a youthful Jim Rosenthal. Alvechurch was the first Midlands Combination club to make it to the first round proper, where they were beaten 4-2 at Aldershot.

We were all still living in St Edmund Street in Great Harwood. Our group of friends had diversified our social repertoire to include playing football in a team. I think the terms playing football and team must be used with the lightest possible interpretation. We were to all and every intent and purpose just a group of guys in their mid- to late-twenties who enjoyed their own company especially if it was mixed with a few beers, perhaps a curry, a few girls as friends and the occasional sing-song.

I think our football team had a set of shirts but no name. We played other teams of this ad hoc and haphazard nature, although I do recall that we once went on tour to Poulton Le Fylde, not far from Blackpool. Indeed I actually scored a goal there, my one and only ever goal on a proper pitch with real goal nets.

Matches were arranged, if you pardon both expressions, usually on a Sunday morning. Whoever was in charge of us would designate a rendezvous point usually scheduled for 10 a.m. We would congregate and be given instructions as to our destination. But it was never that simple and straightforward.

We never booked a pitch anywhere and in a convoy of a dozen cars or so would wander round until we found one unused. I don't recollect us having any authentic match officials, referees, goal nets, corner flags and things. The duration of the game was calculated by the time between kick off and around 11.50 a.m., so we could get to a pub for its midday opening and a pint.

One Sunday we played a match, pirating a pitch about ten miles away in Blackburn; Feniscliffe, I think. We kicked off around 10.45 a.m., so, about half an hour each way.

Quite close to the end of the game, I think I had the ball, there was a loud crack and I was immediately in very severe pain. I'd either twisted or been tackled and to be frank it was not a pretty sight. Mike ran over to see how I was but he felt faint. It looked like I'd broken bones and dislocated my ankle too. I felt more than faint.

The match was abandoned and someone kindly and (after)thoughtfully offered to ring for an ambulance from the pub. A couple of people hung on with me till the ambulance arrived. The ambulance men sauntered over, hands in pockets, whistling. I was screaming in pain. 'What have you done, lad?' As though it wasn't patently obvious. They enquired as to if it was OK to cut my sock off. My response was 'Just now, I don't care if you cut my fucking leg off'. They chuckled, applied a temporary inflatable splint which helped and gave me gas and air, which didn't.

I got to A&E and my pals disappeared, presumably to the pub and presumably to ring Anne. Poor Anne, my girlfriend of some two weeks, suddenly appeared with her teaching pal, Josie Ashton (now Smith). Next to me was a trolley with sterilised hammers, chisels, hand drills, etc. Josie kindly lifted up some of these tools of torture to show me. She didn't do what I abruptly recommended she did with them.

The medics got to work on me and I woke up sometime later on the orthopaedic ward.

The consultant came to see me and following X-rays and other considerations, he advised that surgery to insert any ironmongery wasn't going to be necessary. I thought he was joking but he wasn't. I had suffered a Pott's fracture, the tibia and fibula had fractured and the ankle dislocated; quite messy really. I was to stay in hospital for three days and in plaster for six weeks.

I wasn't really looking forward to the prospect of Mike or Malcolm acting as reluctant inattentive nurses and this is where this break proved to be lucky. Anne had visited me each evening and on one of them, told me I was to be staying with her. So in a matter of a fortnight, she had not only become my girlfriend but my nurse and carer too. I have to say a) I feel some sympathy for her, b) I'm sure I'm not alone in thinking that, c) not much has changed and then d) please reapply clause b) as above.

We loved each other right from the start and forty-plus years later that's still the case, of course with the ups and downs of married life and other challenges, when normally I was in the wrong.

The six weeks sped by. I was on crutches but the physiotherapy was gruelling, an at pace half-mile yomp to the nearby canal side Thwaites pub, the Navigation, and back, at a more sedate but less stable pace.

Those six weeks brought us quite close to Anne's school holidays and I tentatively asked what we might be doing during them. She suggested a spot of camping. More or less straightaway we were in the Outdoor

Action camping shop acquiring a tent you could stand up in, a table, two chairs, Gaz stove, etc.

We loaded up my recently acquired Vauxhall Chevette to spend a couple of weeks under canvas in Wales. One morning, just before eleven, I wandered out of the tent, clutching my transistor radio. Anne gave me an enquiring look. 'It's nearly eleven,' I said. 'Time for *Test Match Special*.' She looked at me with bemused incredulity. There was no play, RSP, so Freddie Trueman, Brian Johnson and I think Yorkshire's Tony Nicholson prattled on about pipes, the ones that you smoke. FS Trueman held forth about pipes he'd lost, pipes he'd found, his favourite pipe-smoking characters, different tobaccos. His cameo vignette was about an acquaintance who smoked a very small bowled pipe, except when he was sampling a fellow smoker's favourite tobacco. It was then, Fiery recounted, that a pipe the size of a saxophone would be produced! By the end of the holiday, it was Anne who was ready in time for *TMS*. I think she'd preferred listening to the cricket better when there wasn't any.

Derek Ingham, who previously had been the West End youth worker, was the youth tutor at Shadsworth, working alongside Tim. Derek got promoted to become youth officer in Pendle District, leaving a vacancy at Shad.

Coming back off holiday in Wales, I had applied for, was interviewed and offered the job of youth tutor at Shadsworth High School. The panel included the head teacher, Ken Bretherton, the youth adviser, Denis Lewis and Ken Eccles, who'd taught there. He and the head teacher had no time for one another. Leaving Accy Road to go to Shadsworth was a youth work practice mistake. Denis told me so emphatically. This ain't ever going to work, he advised.

This was because of the 1974 local government reorganisation. Previously Blackburn Borough (Labour) Council had had ambitious plans to develop six community schools with comprehensive leisure facilities across the town. Shadsworth was the first and the physical infrastructure had been put in place. Next to the former secondary modern school for around 1,200 pupils a leisure centre was built. This included outdoor all-weather and grass sports pitches, a massive sports hall, swimming pool, squash courts, library, community rooms, cafe and bar. The concept was that these facilities would run seamlessly from eight o'clock in the morning till ten at night, seven days a week, under the overall direction of a super head. That was the theory. But as I learned later, in theory there is no difference between theory and practice, but in practice there is. In April 1974 Lancashire County Council took control of their school and library, leaving the Borough of Blackburn as the minor authority to run the sports and leisure facilities. Both Tom Taylor (later Lord Tom) and Jim Mason (later CBE) were the architects of these ideas and facilities in the 1960s; changes in local government structures put the kibosh on them.

Leaving Accy Road was quite an emotional wrench, more than I'd anticipated. I missed everything about it but these bridges were burnt behind me.

My first day at Shadsworth was literally a rude awakening, the school day began quite early. I was the new boy and sat quietly in an almost deserted staffroom. There was an older lady, leather coat, fag in gob, wandering around. She'd made sure that the urn was full and on, offering folk a welcoming cuppa as they rolled in. The meeting began, Mr Bretherton, the head, doing most of the speaking. Then the tea lady chipped in and I was relieved at this sense of democratic inclusion. I later discovered that she was the deputy headmistress. When the meeting ended, the staff went off to begin their autumn term, leaving me in the staffroom alone. I hung around for a bit, but whatever I thought was going to happen, didn't. So I went and found Tim to talk over my feelings. Tim was soon to leave Shadsworth to take over at Brookhouse Community Centre from Ram Sharma.

It took me some time, quite a few months, to realise that nobody really wanted Shadsworth as an integrated concept to be successful. I think other people began to realise that the new appointee, whoever they may have been, was invidiously on a hiding to nothing. I had no real role, no office, not even a desk or a phone. Shambles?

I asked where the youth club might meet. 'Well, we've not really thought about that, not even sure we want one.' I was offered a covered way, no real access, no access to facilities, no toilets, that had been a paved outside area and had had a corrugated plastic roof put over it. I rejected it and nothing else was offered. I ended up piecemealing myself a role, by no means ideal, by working alongside Kedric Thomson, head of PE, Brian Simms, head of drama, Peter Street in careers and eventually within the RE department under head of department, Anne Jones.

I really did have to make my own way on Shadsworth, a huge sprawling 1950s council estate, much bigger but not dissimilar to where I'd been *brung up* in *Brummagem*. One idea was a multi-agency group of professionals based there, before the idea was conceived or the term coined. The school and community centre were totally disconnected from people's homes, by a good half mile, and some parts were a mile or two away. There was a shop and a pub slap bang in the middle, where some twenty years later inspired thinking (mine) put a purpose-built community centre. We convened a meeting for staff working or providing services on Shadsworth: police, social workers, careers people, and the like. The police officer present reminisced that there used to be half a dozen police houses on the estate. That's six serving officers and their families living, working, shopping, drinking, going to school, etc., on everyone's doorstep – how's that for community policing? We met in the pub, the Rovers Return. A guy in a dog collar came along, the Reverend Geoff Pearson, who lived on and was the vicar for Shadsworth. We became quite close. What bonded us was that I was the youth worker without a youth club and he was the vicar without a church. As an aside, over a cuppa at his house, he was really angry about his lack of the basic tools. He said we needed to think bigger. He would get higher up in the Church of England and agitate for a different, more community-focussed approach and his role for me was to get on the council and fight for better community-based facilities. Geoff did eventually get a church built, The Redeemer. It was built in the wrong place, opposite the already ill-located school and community 'centre'. He lost the battle NOT to have fixed pews, no chance of offering what he knew his flock needed; youth club, playgroups, older folks meeting, adult education, parties and other events. Later, after Geoff with his charisma and drive left, the building was burned down.

Anne and I were getting on fine, very nicely thank you, and we decided to get married quite early on. Met in April, broke leg in May, holiday in July, new job in September, engaged and wedding date set for the following February. Quite a lot going on!

*   *   *

It was around this time that my mum remarried. Her new husband was Alf or sometimes Jim (Alfred James). They'd met a few years before, I think at a Wednesday afternoon dancing club a mile or two away. I didn't attend as I suffered a neck injury at work and couldn't drive.

Our wedding date was set for the beginning of the February half term 1978.

I'd moved in with Anne after breaking my leg, never really going back to Great Harwood except really to try and do it up, preselling it for £2,500, a £1,000 loss in four years, to the local Asian community leader, Mr Rehman. Mike and Malc moved on; both of them were seeing local lasses.

We decided to buy our first married home together, a brand new three-bedded semi about a ten-minute walk across the field from Anne's school. It cost us £10,165, upped a bit as we decided, for the first time in either of our lives, to have central heating installed.

Bob Beardsworth had been promoted to being the Salford (RC) diocesan youth officer. John Russell Fletcher aka John, Russell or Fleckie became in charge of West End. We too became pals and remain so today.

Where would we hold the wedding? I didn't really feel much about faith, though, like many of us, had been brought up in a generally Christian-imbued environment. Still today I think I'm probably agnostic. I understand people's desire to believe and follow a religion. I find those world religions that I know a bit about, mainly the Abrahamic ones, quite interesting. I also feel that these religions or perhaps those who follow them or even perhaps those who profess to follow them have been at the root of aggression, conflict and murderous wars throughout history. But I also recognise that should they all disappear, some things quite like them would soon invent themselves. It's the apparent cognitive dissonance of those who purport to practise a faith that gets to me. Sermon over.

I explained to my wife to be that I wasn't too keen on a church do and she agreed. The Registry Office then? Yeh, that's fine but I'd better tell my mum. Ah, she's a church goer, I thought, I wouldn't want to offend. I'd met my potential in-laws, Fred and Mary, a few times in not so far away

Bolton. There'd never been any mention of church going, because they didn't. They were both well over seventy. Fred had been sent down the pit aged twelve in 1917 as a *hewer* and (aged seventy-three) had only recently finished working as a factory production worker and Mary, a carder in a cotton mill when Anne was a child as well as a cleaner in pubs, offices and the like, respectively. They'd wanted Our Anne to get to university and worked themselves hard and long not to accept the full grant. Anne told her mum and dad about our intended wedding venue and they were fine.

West End was almost brand new and nicely presented so we booked with Fleckie and his then Mrs, Marilyn, to hold the after-wedding do there. As they could sell alcohol in the bar from 11 a.m., we booked the Registry Office, only a hundred yards away for 10.40 a.m.

The Eddlestons were to produce a buffet and Philip (known as Philips), generous as always, offered to do the cake. Things were shaping up nicely. My best mate Rod was invited to be best man as I had for him in late 1976.

Everything was looking hunky-dory for 11 February, our wedding day.

I had a member of staff at Accy Road called Eleanor, perhaps twenty-plus years senior to me. Her 'boyfriend' Kevin drove taxis. She said, as her present to us, would it be OK if he used the firm's white limo, trimmed it up and took Anne to the Registry in it. Brilliant.

I'd clocked Kevin was a bit disorganised so booked Tony and Pauline Parkinson to drive past Anne's place to check she had indeed been collected; just insurance, you'll appreciate.

To describe these arrangements as impromptu wouldn't be fair; they were on the makeshift side of Heath Robinson. We'd not had a contribution of any kind beyond our own and we were skint, saving up for our first home.

The day came, I'd been despatched back to Great Harwood the night before with my best man for the sake of appearances and had an onerous list of tasks: keep best shirt pressed and clean, get some flowers, comb hair, don't be late; all high order stuff. Anne had girlie things to do: her hair, make up, dress, etc., make trifles, etc. But she had Kevin to collect her. Sorted.

Rod and I soon whittled our way down our list. Anne was on the hindered side of helped by the fact that as we'd not told folk travelling from all over where the wedding venue was (we knew), they all turned up at the only address they had, her house. So, from 8 a.m. onwards, people she'd never met, including now US-based Dr Pete Kiener and his to be wife (and later not to be – he has a different Cath now), Cath, turned up on her doorstep, were introduced and welcomed, offered tea and toast, etc.

Rod and I were soon ready, flowers obtained and the like and got ourselves to the Registry Office. Others arrived, all in their best. No sign of the blushing bride.

To be both fair and frank, I've never made a hoo-hah of this uncharacteristic tardiness; she was only a matter of minutes late. She looked lovely. I think she used a phrase along the lines of 'No ******* sign of Kevin' but extremely sotto voce as befitting the event. The ceremony commenced.

It went well until came the time to cough up the fee; £6.25, from memory. Beer being around 25-30p a pint, everyone had a fiver or two in their pockets. The registrar decreed that the fee had to be proffered exactly. The audience all began rummaging, corners of pockets and handbags were turned out, sticky pennies and tuppences, any loose change was passed forward until the requisite amount could be handed over. One could argue that everyone had a stake in this marriage.

It was a nice sunny day. I'd overlooked to arrange a photographer. Housemate Malcolm had brought his camera, so he was hurriedly appointed. The photos he took ranged in quality from not over professional to rubbish. Everyone wanted to take some with their own camera which meant that on absolutely none of them were all the subjects looking at the same snapping camera. Ah well.

The reception went well, the buffet went well, old acquaintances, some five years after leaving university, were renewed. Mine and Rod's speeches came and went. There was a bit of an incident when Anne's Auntie Annie was caught nicking Eddleston's highly nickable meat pies and stashing them in her capacious handbag for Ron, later on.

There was further incident when Kevin arrived mid-afternoon.

Eleanor had no idea as to his whereabouts, making my getting Tony and Pauline as backup inspired. 'Hi Kevin, is everything OK as you didn't collect Anne as agreed?' 'Yeah, fine thanks. I got a run to the airport which is worth a few quid, so I did that. But I was whacked so had to have a kip.' 'But what about Anne, though?' 'Did she not ring through for a taxi? They'd have sorted her out, no trouble.' I left it there.

People were starting to ask what's next? The bar would be closing at 3 p.m. Next? We'd not planned a next.

People piled back to Anne's rented terraced house expectant, of what, it wasn't clear. Evening meal? What?

My wife of but a few hours intervened, issued her first Tsarina-like ukase. Get your homebrew pan down off the shelf. Within about an hour spuds and carrots had been peeled and diced, onions chopped, gravy made. I think it was a corned beef hash. No matter, people's appetites were assuaged.

And now the question of the evening do was raised. Evening do? How far did folk think our budget of £150, including bride's dress and the cake, would stretch?

Well, I was just thinking about wandering down to the Navvy! That's it then, lead the way. We set off. The Navigation wasn't the most salubrious of hostelries, the tap room had seen a few fights and the best room wasn't really. I told Norma behind the bar I was thinking of having our night do there. Great, when? In about five minutes. Those already sat in there were told to 'hutch up', it's a wedding, just as thirty, forty or more revellers arrived in their best apparel, already fairly pissed. The juke box was turned up, still no 'Telstar', and a good time was had. Although I'd been gone nearly a year a big group of the older Accy Road eighteen to nineteen-year-olds turned up too. We're not missing this!

I've no real idea what time we were kicked out, if we were, but we had now been drinking since 11 a.m. It was snowing, a white wedding, when we wandered home, along with the rest of the folk from the Navvy.

Something to play music on was produced and more beer. As there had been no plans for any celebrations after say 3 p.m., we'd neither warned or invited any neighbours. They were OK about it the next day when we apologised.

I'd had enough, needed to be asleep. Anne tells me that she and eighteen-year-old Jimmy Byrnes put me to bed and just as I dropped off to sleep, both gave me a wedding night peck. I understand that Anne and the other revellers went on well into the wee hours. I slept on through like a baby.

We had a lot to do those early months in 1978: sell St Edmund St, get married, buy Penshaw Close and move house. And most importantly, worry about money. We had no budget that could stretch to any form of honeymoon.

We then settled down to married life: getting the garden straight, a spot of decorating, getting on with work, getting to know the neighbours (all very much like us, mainly; recently married, first new home). On either side were Stuart and Sue Lamonby and Tommy and Chandra Nair with their lovely, funny daughter Cindy. Other neighbours were Bill and Sue Robertson and Pete and Marjorie Niemeyer. It was a small close, around fifteen homes, all little box starter homes. We were there for around nine years.

We acquired a dog, a Guide dog in fact. Well, he came from the local dog rescue centre situated in the area of Blackburn called Guide. He was a border-collie cross, a lovely dog. We were never sure how old he was when we got him, nor was the vet. We had him, as a real member of the family, for fourteen or more years, Danny, as in Daniel Thwaites.

I was called upon to act as best man again in 1978, this time for Malcolm Smith. Malc put me in charge of the stag evening, the typed-up itinerary for which I still sadly possess. Friday evening licensing hours back then were 6-11 p.m. We had thirteen pubs to visit along Accrington Road from the Toll Bar opposite the youth centre, a mile and a half into town, ending with the White Bull. This was at a pace of twenty-five minutes per pint. There were fifteen of us. Entry fee a fiver to buy thirteen pints, about 35p a pint? The order was twelve pints of bitter, two of mild and one lager. The pace was gruelling and Malcolm and I set it. Stragglers began to spread out and could be seen bobbing in and out of these hostelries along the route. In each pub the designated drinks were set out on trays, paid for and designated as Bill's and Malc's beers to be consumed on arrival. Unluckily we didn't all make the thirteenth pub, terminating at the Veteran, which we found had become a gay pub. No matter to us but I'm sure though that those already imbibing there might have thought that all their Christmases had come along at once. After the pub crawl, I'm not entirely sure what happened next but it would have almost definitely included a massive late-night curry session. Suffice to say and sadly as a footnote, every one of these dozen or so fantastic pubs except for the Toll Bar (just about) is now, forty-plus years or so on, no longer either licensed premises or in some cases even a building.

Malcolm's wedding day to local lass Barbara Smith came along in September 1978.

It went nicely bar a few incidents. Malcolm had eventually moved out of my place pending its sale, to a nearby and shall we call it modest flat not so very far away. It presented many charming and traditional features; an outside lavatory was its most quaint, quirky even. Had Malcolm to brave either nocturnal or winter conditions or worse still both, he was well prepared. Was it to prove prudent or necessary, toilet paper was stored in the kitchen by the back door for fear of becoming susceptible to the damp conditions. Once inside his Victorian feature midden, Malcolm had a woolly hat on a hook behind the door ready for longer stays and also a wax night light. The purpose of this was threefold: light, marginal additional warmth and somewhere to light his cigarettes.

Another incident worthy of more discreet note was that both sets of future in-laws had never met until they did so immediately before the ceremony at the Registry Office. I cannot break any confidences here when they did meet dressed up to the nines. One pairing was able to say to the other, 'It's a good job we got to Malcolm's bachelor pad first, it was a right tip. We gave it a right good bottoming before you turned up!' They both had!

After the formalities at the Registry Office, we repaired to the Plough Inn, one of our (many) regular haunts. Here we relaxed and celebrated the occasion with a modest buffet and more liquid refreshments. Well, we were relaxed until around 7 p.m. when Malcolm got increasingly agitated about the night do to be held in a big pub four miles away on the outskirts of Accrington. 'Make sure they're all already for 7.20 p.m.' urged the groom to his best man. I commended a calmer approach. Malcom got more and more het up; a cattle prod would not have looked out of place. 'Right, the lot of you, outside now, the bus will be waiting, but not for long!'

We all wandered out, shocked at the starkness of his demands. The awaiting charabanc was not the expected private hire coach but the scheduled 7.23 to Accrington. We filed aboard, Malcolm counting each person. 'That's forty-three adults to Accrington, please'. He popped back into the pub, collected the wedding flowers and trimmed up the Ribble service bus for our twenty-minute journey.

*   *   *

It was around then that I engaged in what I thought to be harmless that became a seminal moment for me. Out in Great Harwood late one night in a mixed group of mid-twenty-year-olds I espied a flashing roadworks traffic light. Like most university students that I'd known, these held some mesmerising magnetic attraction. I lifted it and then pretended to be a spaceman or something; it was after 11 p.m. on a Friday night. We all thought it was funny but unfortunately the beat bobby observing these antics didn't. I apologised to the bobby and offered to put it back but he was having none of it. I was separated from my pals and taken to the police station. I was released later but warned that in Great Harwood they took a dim view of such behaviour. I was subsequently charged with something like unauthorised movement of a traffic signal but it was later dropped. But it, perhaps at last, taught me a lesson: less tomfoolery.

And so precipitated by my perceived adolescent stupid prankster behaviour, sometime in the mid-seventies, either between the two 1974 General Elections or a touch later, I joined the Labour Party. Rick Dunning had laid down the gauntlet in many ways; although the causes he championed weren't my cup of tea, at least he was doing something. So I joined, expecting something to happen. Guess what? Nothing did!

Still nothing had resulted from me actually joining the Labour Party. One Sunday afternoon round at Tim's mum and dad's (Tim by this time had married Audrey), I was whingeing about lack of involvement/activity. Their advice was the Labour Party here doesn't come to you, you've got to go to the Labour Party.

I'd attended a handful of meetings. It seemed very staid, procedural, uninspiring. It seemed to be run by quite old blokes, all with receding hair, most of whom smoked incessantly, who spoke in very administrative parlance.

It was coming up to the 1979 General Election scheduled for the same day in May as the local elections. I came home one night to be told that Councillor Ernest Gorton had rung and I was to ring him back. I did do and he told me to come down to the office on Saturday morning.

Anne drove and parked up outside as 'it wouldn't take long'. I had no idea what it was. I was in and out in five, perhaps ten minutes?

Well? she enquired. 'Um, I've just been appointed local government candidate for Pleckgate Ward, signed up and everything. I've got to meet someone at the end of Briar Road (a five-minute walk away) at six pm on Monday with a pencil.'

So, that April Monday evening came and I wandered down to the rendezvous point. There was a man hanging around on the corner.

'Hello,' he said, 'I'm Jack.'

Chapter 9

Starting Out in the Labour Party, 1979-81

One man's ceiling is another man's floor.

This was our first man to man, face to face meeting. My encounter, semi shrouded in mystery, was with none other than Jack Straw, the Labour Party prospective parliamentary candidate, who was selected to succeed the then sixty-nine-year-old Barbara Castle, who had been the town's MP since the post-war 1945 Labour landslide victory – thirty-four years. Mrs Castle had held three Cabinet posts in the 1964-70 Harold Wilson Labour Government and one more during his 1974-76 premiership. Although anti the Common Market, as it was then commonly known, as many of us were during the 1975 confirmatory referendum (yes, won by 67 per cent to 33 per cent), Mrs Castle was elected to the European Parliament immediately on departing her Blackburn constituency seat and served in Europe for a further ten years, until she retired from public office aged seventy-nine.

I knew of Jack from his NUS president student days but with him being five or so years older, our paths had never crossed. CPGB (Communist Party of Great Britain) member Digby Jacks as NUS president and Jack's younger brother Ed were more my era.

Back to our first night working together, Jack whipped out what I learned to be canvass cards and some pencils. 'Very kind of you but Ernie pre warned me to provide my own. But could I ask exactly what we're going to do?'

'Canvass. Have you not done it before?' 'No, but I'll accompany you for a while and I'm sure I'll get the hang of it.'

Now to slightly digress it's probably worth a brief explanation of what canvassing is and isn't. It is not an opportunity to have a rant and rave at someone who dares to proclaim opposing political views to your own or for you to pontificate at length about yours, as I wrote in a very simple paper a few years later entitled 'Canvassing IS, I stands for Identify and S for Secure'. What the caller at a home should be trying to do is a) make 'soft' contact with all residents but MAINLY b) assess 'hard' information as to the resident's and all other voters in the properties, voting intentions. You're really trying to identify who is a firm, in our case, Labour voter. Back in the pencil and paper days any Labour promise was then manually written up onto a three or four sheet, no carbon required, street by street list. This system was known as the Reading or Mikardo system after Ian Mikardo the Labour MP for Reading, who perfected it. (This will all be computerised these days.) On polling day youngsters sat outside polling stations asking for a voter's number. These numbers were ferried back regularly to the nearest party HQ known as a committee room. Here all Labour promises were crossed off when they had voted – no further action required. Most people vote on their way to work or when they dropped the kids off at school, then there's a lull until the reverse of these trips, just before the soap operas or as part of an evening walk. The party workers role as the close of poll approaches is, hopefully without haranguing, to get those who've promised to vote Labour to go and do so. That's the I and the S explained.

Party workers spend weeks canvassing in the evenings, but now as life patterns change, weekends and daytimes as well. On election day they're up before dawn and, if the count is straight after the close of poll, they'll probably see the next dawn too! Party workers can become zealots at election time. 'I can't go voting till I know if Zac Dingle's going to the Woolpack for a pint' could be perceived as inflammatory.

So back to my first canvassing experience. Jack and I went on for a couple of hours, then he suggested a drink. The Farthings was only a hundred yards away and about 200 yards from our house. It was also my local. 'What about in here?' Labour's PPC suggested. 'Let's try it,' said the local government candidate.

We wandered into a chorus of 'Hiya Billys'. It then went immediately quiet as my companion followed me in. Drinks ordered, we sat in a corner and a number of people came over to say hello, but I guessed not really to me.

We got talking, sharing stories about our upbringings which were remarkably similar. But not before, and I learned that Jack could tuck his food away, he'd enquired what I was doing about tea, which he called dinner. Now I knew what was happening about my tea; Anne had told me that she would prepare a stew to sit in the oven until I got home. 'I don't know,' I lied. 'Anne will have made something.' 'Could I be rude and ask to join you?' 'Of course you can but let me just advise Anne.'

No mobile phones back in 1979 so I used the pub's pay phone. Anne told me that was fine but to give her at least another half an hour. More drinks. Jack, as was his lifetime habit, was on halves, usually of mild. We then wandered up the road to our house.

I got totally and unexpectedly berated on our arrival: 'Why didn't you give me notice what time you'd be turning up and who with!' We sat down to eat and the stew for my tea had been transformed into a steak pie for Jack's no longer dinner, he declared it to be supper. We scoffed the lot and Jack set off into the night.

When alone I asked what all the kerfuffle about food had been, whilst praising the unexpected pie. Anne explained, 'I couldn't just give that lad stew, he's going places!'

After that I went out canvassing a few times mainly on my own which wasn't a particularly stimulating experience.

3 May election day, came along. I wandered down to the dismally lacklustre constituency party HQ in a dismal, unwelcoming tiny terrace a five-minute walk from the town centre. There was some altercation between who I recognised as Lord Tom Taylor and who I found out later to be Ted, Mr (later Lord) Castle. I left them to it.

Polls close at 10 p.m. at general elections. I'd been invited to the count and made my way to King George's Hall, a 1700-capacity main hall in Blackburn's massive public hall complex opened in 1921. I didn't really understand nor did anybody explain what was going on. Lots of people in different party colours, milling around the periphery of the frantically busy hall and lots of others quietly counting ballot papers, bundling them together and then placing them in racks. At two or perhaps three o'clock in the morning it was announced that the said Jack Straw was duly elected with a majority of 5,500, slightly reduced from Barbara Castle's last showing. Those in the hall wearing red rosettes seemed pleased. Across Britain, Margaret Thatcher's Tories had given Labour a good post-Winter of Discontent drubbing. Labour, and Jack would have to be content with the Opposition benches for eighteen years.

So that was that. I went home to bed and off to work the next day. Not long after that and out of the blue, I received an official letter from Councillor EW Gorton, the Labour Party secretary/agent, appointing me to become a member of the General Management Committee of the Constituency Labour Party. Ernest had a brother Frank, also a councillor, a male nurse and a big cheese in the COHSE union (Confederation of Health Service Employees). It raised a wry smile that these two hard-working guys were Frank and Ernest. I had no idea who had appointed me or why or what it entailed but duly went along to my first smoke-filled Labour Party meeting.

Ernie was on the top table along with another guy, County Councillor Eric Smith of the AEUW (Amalgamated Union of Engineering Workers). The meeting was conducted under a fug of cigarette smoke and in a shroud of mystery. Letters received were read out and sometimes responsive action to them was decided; many points of order were raised often with the chair ruling them out; resolutions received were moved, seconded and discussed. Some of the speakers were extremely eloquent; I remember the Rev. Douglas Cave and Welshman Clive Edwards, a trade union studies lecturer at the college, especially. Standing orders required that the meeting concluded at 9.30 p.m. It never seemed to and someone would move an additional ten minutes be added, and that was never long enough either. I didn't know what was going on, not a clue, as none was given. Don't get me wrong, these guys, and it was a very male environment, were the salt of the earth, many World War II veterans. They approached things in a very procedural/administrative fashion with no eye or flair for policy development, campaigning or membership recruiting.

I'd had goes at prematurely starting school aged barely three, challenging the induction of my eventual infant school, making a stance against artistic repression with Michelangelo's work at junior school, challenging the Boy Scout's Law, changing power structures and increasing the student voice at secondary school, experiencing and enduring very traumatic domestic circumstances, standing up to perceived academic repression at university, changing with colleagues the way the youth service positioned itself and operated at both local and national levels, all to varying degrees of success. I'd worked in some great teams in different positions, including leadership and being the secretary. I'd written for and edited various examples of the newsprint and broadcasting media. I'd been a manager, organiser, curriculum developer trainer, public speaker, had various roles that had developed me professionally, politically and personally. So, what next?

Well, lo and behold, my next incursion into change for improvement would be Blackburn Labour Party. Probably unchanged for some forty to fifty years under the municipal and party leadership of Sir George Eddie, was it fit for the new politics of Thatcher's Britain? Scotsman and Christian Evangelist, Eddie had come to Blackburn in the 1920s. He was interviewed by Radio Blackburn (later Radio Lancashire) in June 1971 about his long career. It's to be found on the cottontown.org website. Sir George became so in 1966 having been conferred a Freeman of the Borough in 1960. He did hint at needing to be far more consultative, more engaging with Blackburn residents on matters such as housing, health and education and also to rejuvenate the local party both in approach and personnel.

Ironically and coincidently, I did have one brief encounter with Sir George. It must've been in 1979. I went canvassing on my own on Willow Trees Drive, a lovely cul de sac in the north of the town, originally council housing. I knocked on the door and an old, small chap answered. I went into my spiel. I didn't get very far; he must've spotted my red rosette. And in a very strong Scottish accent he said 'Dinna you worry, laddie, you're alright here'. As instructed, I pressed the point, to confirm and seal the deal. 'I've told you, laddie, go back and tell them you've met George Eddie, Sir George Eddie,' gently closing the door. Feeling I'd made some horrendous gaffe, I chose not to report this encounter any further.

I'd acquired an eye and ear for discerning what makes people and their organisations tick. In the few months I had been involved in the local Labour Party I'd spotted things that could be done that would improve it. I distilled this into a twenty-point list entitled 'Ideas for the Future'. (Hadn't VI Lenin put pen to paper in 1901 in his pamphlet, 'What is to be Done?')

This list was a mixture of improved organisation and improved engagement both internal and external to the local party. Amongst them:

+ The establishment of a massive imaginative and exciting recruitment campaign. Focusing more on recruitment and membership. Encourage new members to participate more.
+ Making the party HQ more accessible, clean and more inviting and welcoming.
+ Communicating better with regular bulletins, more books and pamphlets and open political education meetings.
+ Focus upon engaging with young people and other hard to reach groups.
+ The central collation of the issues raised whilst canvassing for analysis and action.
+ Make the party locally less of an elections-only machine by including social events and other gatherings. Set up a Labour social club.
+ Be more media savvy and have greater presence and profile.
+ Campaign and support the weaker, more marginal, non-Labour areas.

I typed these ideas up on my £16 Olympia typewriter and circulated it to all GMC members.

Almost immediately after it was circulated, my ideas were overtaken by events. The current Labour agent, Councillor Ernie Gorton, was not a well man and fell more ill. I was approached, I think by Jack Straw, to act as honorary (i.e. unpaid, as Ernie also had been) temporary secretary/agent until such time as Ernie got better. This was around September 1979. My temporary incumbency in post was to stretch over five decades till the spring of 2010. So, I had chirped up and chipped in with a wide-ranging and comprehensive agenda for improvement and change and as Kismet would have it, was now placed in the driving seat to implement it. Did I never think 'me and my big mouth'?

Once again, without really fully understanding the organisation, I was cast at its very hub. I'd put up, so, once again, this wasn't the time to shut up. It was jacket off and roll sleeves up time.

The General Management Committee (GMC) of the constituency party (CLP), acronyms in their own right, consisted mainly of a litany of even more acronyms: The AUEW (Amalgamated Union of Engineering Workers), TGWU (Transport and General Workers), GMBTU (General, Municipal and Boilermakers Trade Union that had earlier been ASBSBSW – Amalgamated Society of Boilermakers, Shipwrights, Blacksmiths and Structural Workers), USDAW (Union of Shop, Distributive and Allied Workers), ASTMS (Association of Scientific, Technical and Managerial Staffs), UCATT (Union of Construction, Allied Trades and Technician), EETPU (Electrical, Electronic, Telecommunications & Plumbing Union), SOGAT (Society of Graphical and Allied Trades), NUR (National Union of Railwaymen), COHSE (Confederation of Health Service Employees), NUPE (National Union of Public Employees).

Sleepy yet? Need I continue? I was effectively simply thrown in at a very deep end to understand, embrace and organise this Alphabetti Spaghetti of trade unions, affiliated and ward organisations. But mock not, these men and women and their antecedents fought collectively for votes for all, parliamentary democracy, our National Health Service. They are societal heroes. I really didn't see very much of Ernie again and was left almost totally to my own devices.

The simple servicing of the GMC was a gargantuan task in itself, the way I did it. The GMC met every month, preceded by a half-hour-long Executive Committee. Previously there had been a standard agenda and the minutes were read out, taking up much of the time of the meeting. It really was plain daft.

My new broom approach instigated a written agenda with items specified upon it and written-up minutes being circulated by post to all delegates. This entailed quite a few hours of my two-fingered non-touch typing on to what I knew to be Gestetner 'skins'. This was very much a

1950s' way of duplicating the printed word. Once completed the 'skin' was then transferred to a large printing machine where ink oozed through where the typewriter had struck leaving the document duplicated onto the paper. That's hard to say, difficult to understand and almost impossible to do on Blackburn Labour Party's post-war printing paraphernalia. The process would take me three hours or more and then there was the stuffing of a hundred-plus envelopes, to be addressed, stamped and posted to all delegates, five hours in total every month? My wife, Anne, would sometimes accompany me and was a big help giving the offices a much needed once over, emptying the overfilled, rarely emptied ashtrays, washing up and vacuuming, making the place almost welcoming.

One time I assembled a small working party to totally spring clean what to many was the public face of the people's party. The back rooms were even more dingy than those at the front. These received a blinding light transformation when the security grills at the back were removed and years (at least) of thick accumulated grime on the windows were tackled allowing floods of natural sunshine into the rooms. I got a phone call from one of the office polluters the next week about a 'funny smell' in the offices. I suggested it was traces of lavender in the polish we'd used trying to neutralise years of nicotine and tar. If I remember rightly we got a similar team back later to roll some emulsion round the walls. Shame we couldn't get any nicotine-resistant paint. The painting party included a pair of relative newcomers to the party, Mike and Anne Higginson, who had eventually been allowed to join. Anne went on to become Jack's paid constituency PA and Mike, constituency treasurer, and county councillor and later a borough councillor. I say eventually because when they initially went to the offices to try and join, they were put off, being told that the party was full! Sadly, Mike died in the late 1990s.

With the offices squeaky clean and the organisation around meetings improved, things got a little better. Eric Smith was a big-hearted, dyed in the wool, committed trade unionist, in his late forties, but looking older perhaps, with his comb-over hair and incessant smoking. He would give of his time and his experientially amassed wisdom freely. I had a lot of time for him although he may well have been wary of the two newcomers that generally flanked him at meetings, namely Jack Straw and me.

Meetings became fairly understandable and to Eric's surprise and delight, easier to manage. They were still older male dominated, with few women, ethnic minority or younger people (i.e. under fifty?) attending.

Within a few weeks it was time to start the arrangements for the local elections due in a few months. As I was now the secretary/agent, all the organisation and electoral law responsibility fell on my shoulders. In the not uncustomary position of not knowing what I was doing and having no one really able or prepared to guide me, I had enrolled in the national Labour Party agent's year-long training programme. This entailed, all in my own time, weekend residential schools, a correspondence element and finally written and oral examinations held at the regional headquarters. When the training ran its course, I became one of the few qualified agents anywhere in the party.

Jack was now the sitting MP and didn't take long to change processes locally. He soon established regular, no appointment required, 'surgeries' right across the town. This he saw as a service to his constituents and over his thirty-six-year incumbency as a constituency MP it was almost irrefutable that we could claim everybody had been helped by Jack or knew somebody he had helped. It also enabled Jack to refute the often bandied around claim 'well, we never see you until election time'. But not only that, it gave Jack credibility and credence that he had his finger on the pulse of the things that were concerning or distressing his voters.

Jack's determination to get closer to the people of Blackburn didn't stop there. On my advice he bought a property quite close to the town centre and lived there whenever he was around. His predecessor had been more of a visiting MP. I helped convince Jack that this was a better way to be.

Jack also acquired at least three season tickets for Blackburn Rovers for himself, and children, William and Charlotte. They attended regularly as a threesome, having a pre or post-match drink in a little corner pub, the Ivy, halfway up Infirmary St.

*   *   *

I feel like I need to explain a little bit about how somebody can become a councillor or at least a local election candidate. We did a lot of improvement work on this locally in the eighties and nineties. We had quite a few long in the tooth perennial councillors, sitting for decades in the safe Labour wards but not really doing very much in or for that community. It really wasn't acceptable. We had to up our standard, quality and work rate. Some toes were going to be trod upon, feathers ruffled.

Anyway, aspirant councillors had to apply to be considered. Over the years the application form became increasingly comprehensive; sitting on x or y committee for z years wouldn't do. Campaigns, especially successful ones, were more important.

So, potential candidates applied and these applications were considered centrally. If agreed to, that person was then on the panel. Those on the agreed panel list could then be shortlisted, interviewed and voted upon to become the agreed local candidate for this or that ward.

As well as all that, each candidate had his or her limited words election address to compose, not an easy task or one that came naturally to all. Candidates also had to provide a warm, friendly, hair tidy, clothes acceptable black and white photograph of themselves, again, not always straightforward.

There appeared to be little cohesive or coherent connection between those senior councillors who controlled the Labour Group on the council and the rest of the party locally. There was minimal connection between policies pursued and a cogent manifesto to put before the electorate. Slowly but surely, this was improved, but to begin with I was more or less left to my own devices to draft the leaflets, arrange photographs and printing, again no mean set of tasks. Trying to get fifteen people of different backgrounds, literacy and organisational skills to get things to me at the right time was a bug bear so my skills developed as a youth and community worker and my amateur journalistic skills came in handy. As did schoolteacher Anne's grasp and insistence on good grammar and punctuation.

It was during this process that I was approached and asked to stand in a very winnable ward in 1980. The year before, Ernie Gorton alone had appointed me at the Labour Party rooms one Saturday morning. This time the process was more formal and resulted in me becoming the official Labour Party candidate in the Cathedral Ward. This, as the title suggests, was a very central ward comprising of many streets lined with terraced housing, much of which embraced where many of the young people that I had worked with and their families, lived.

I may well have been seen as some kind of rising star as I was also appointed the constituency delegate to the annual Labour Party Conference, which that year was held in Brighton. Little did I realise that the chosen delegate had to fund all of their own costs in relation to this; travel, accommodation and subsistence. I had to do this but vowed that never again would the ability to pay be a consideration and it never was. I didn't really enjoy the 1979 conference or the 1999 event twenty years on. Nothing really changed; people who speak to you whilst scanning over your shoulder to see if there was anyone more important that they could speak or be seen with. I could do without that.

Were all these new roles recognition and or reward for my new responsibilities, or did I hear sighs of relief that some unsuspecting dupe had been found?

So, with Jim and Frances Mason's advice ringing in my ears that the Labour Party in Blackburn didn't come to you, you had to go to it, a lot had happened to me. In a matter of weeks I became the secretary/agent, enrolled myself in a national course specifically designed for that role, got selected as a local government candidate and was the delegate to the conference. This was as well as both Anne and me having full-time jobs. What more could the world throw at us?

Talking of Jim and Frances Mason reminds me that in the summer of 1979 we had ventured forth on our first foreign camping holiday. We carefully packed all our camping gear into our Vauxhall Chevette and set off driving, using a cross-channel ferry for the first time. Our target was the south of France near Millau on the River Tarn. Those familiar with the area will know it as the place where a mile-and-a-half-long suspension bridge, opened in 2004, carries the A75 autoroute soaring 1,100 feet above the river below. The not-long-married Tim and Audrey had accompanied Tim's mum and dad with their close teacher friends Cliff and Brenda Gillam in their caravans. We spent about ten days with these good people. It entailed quite a lot of wine drinking, some nice meals out, a little bit of sightseeing along the river system and down the caves, limestone in one case and home to the Roquefort cheese in another. Around about five o'clock was the young fellas versus the old fellas French game of boules or pétanque.

On our way home we stopped off in the outskirts of Paris to spend a few days with Chris Berry. Chris had gone out for his third year of four studying French but I don't think he ever returned to complete the course. He had a good job working for Aérospatiale, the French equivalent of BAE. It would appear that he was actually employed by Colonel Gaddafi's Libyan Government. Gaddafi's personal guard flew helicopters and it was Chris' job to translate for them. It was quite a weird few days and we saw bits of Paris perhaps we would have preferred not to. Our gastronomic highlight was eating in Le English Pub on the Champs-Élysées, presumably as guests of the good colonel. It was whilst in Paris that we heard the news of Lord Louis Mountbatten's murder off the coast of County Sligo.

In May 1980 I won the seat for Cathedral ward on Blackburn Borough Council, assisted by the voluntary campaigning efforts of two similar-aged guys, Bill Pickup and Phil Dagger. My sitting ward councillor colleagues Frank Hulme and Jack Yates, both union official diehards, didn't canvass *like that*. They took cards off me to do round *their end* and returned them later. Seeing the ruled-edged, neatly lined returns, Eric Smith quipped 'He's done them sat in his club with a pint!'

The chief executive then was Clifford Singleton, Blackburn born and bred and an accountant by qualification. Clifford, not Cliff, took the (Manchester) *Guardian* every day; well, in fact, it was delivered to his house overlooking the QEGS and Old Blacks sports fields. Near the paper's slimmed down title on the front page, Clifford's newsagent pencilled in not the address or name but simply and somewhat yearningly it stated 'Town Clerk'. I was invited into his office where I met Miss Kenyon, his personal assistant and was ushered through to swear in as a councillor. The official business concluded, he went on to explain my role. It was to be his customer-based market research unit. He would get on with running the council with me feeding back on how he was doing. I interrupted audaciously to suggest that I was thinking of operating checks and balances, financial and otherwise and also developing policies, submitted to the electorate, that best suited the differing needs of our diverse communities. His response was, 'Oh dear'.

When I joined the council I was a relative baby aged twenty-eight.

So I had done what the Rev. Geoff Pearson had told me to do two or three years earlier, I had become a councillor. But I had no idea what it meant, what it entailed or what would be expected of me.

*   *   *

I think we all, including rookie Councillor Taylor in 1980, should know more about our local councils; what they are, what they do, how they are run and by whom, how they are funded and what they spend, what makes them tick; their serious side and some of their funnier moments.

Suffice for now, you may need to know a little more about councils and councillors. After all, there are many thousands of councillors (your neighbours, work colleagues, friends) that you can vote for or against (mostly people don't even vote), employing hundreds of thousands of staff (on your behalf) and spending billions of pounds (of your money).

In the UK, there are three levels of local councils. The picture across Europe is that there are far more councillors and even more complexity about their systems and procedures.

According to the annual census of councillors conducted by the Local Government Association, 59 per cent of councillors are male, 92 per cent white, although that is changing. The average age is sixty. There are more councillors that are aged seventy-plus than under forty-five.

40 per cent of councillors are retired, only a 1/3rd are in full or part-time employment. Only 3 per cent are bringing up a family. 64 per cent have a degree or equivalent qualification, 5 per cent have no recognised formal qualifications at all.

There are some 9,000 parish or town councils with 80,000 sitting councillors. They don't spend a great deal, around £25,000 a year per council?

At district or (all singing, all dancing) *upper tier* level, there are 20,000 elected members on the more than 395 local authorities in England. In England alone the total spend across all councils is well over £100bn pa. A councillor's term of office, once elected, is usually four years. The average number of years spent as a councillor is nine and a half. In the Local Government Association survey, councillors totted up their time, taking on average twenty-five hours a week attending to their duties. How many person working hours, days, weeks, years does all this activity represent? This is a massive secret army of folk, tens of thousands of well-meant, effective/ineffective, high profile/anonymous/faceless, hardworking/inactive individuals.

To be nominated (by ten local voters registered to vote), councillors must themselves be registered to vote in that council area and have lived, worked or owned property there for at least twelve months prior to the election. This means they may be your neighbour or work colleague, socialise or worship alongside you, send their kids to the same school as yours, shop or spend their leisure time like you do. None are from outer space. Some will hold regular 'surgeries' in a school or local hall. Councils hold elections nearly every year or at least every four. Councillors should be available and accessible generally and ultimately democratically accountable through elections. Collectively they make huge decisions that affect you, your family, friends and communities: schools, social, adult and elderly care, housing, planning, transport, sport and leisure, environmental matters such as refuse, recycling, food standards, pest control, issues with (and from) dogs. These are the things great and small that matter. And yet, paradoxically, usually barely a third of voters bother to vote in local elections. Why don't we? Why don't *you*?

* * *

I really hadn't got a clue about what was going on. At the end of that year I pondered how little help or support we'd been given. Nobody, not a soul, told me anything about how the council was run. But I didn't see getting on the council as being an end itself. You got on the council to do something with the position, power and influence that came with it. To me, being a councillor was a bit like being a youth and community worker. Part of my experience and skill development at work had been training and I saw there was a need for some induction and training for new councillors. Basing it upon what I hadn't been told, at the end of my first mesmerising year on the council, I jotted down and then constructed a two or three-page document called 'Guides and Hints for Newly Elected Labour councillors'. Nobody asked me to do it and nobody thanked me for it but once compiled, I shared it in a briefing session with the next year's rookies. They seemed to appreciate it and the chance to ask 'daft' questions which are always the most difficult to answer. Over the years, this document grew and grew to be in quite a few pages and from then on most new Labour councillors had it as part of their first few days. Somebody somewhere must have recognised the benefits of such a process as, by the end of my time on the council, a full half day's induction, with my original document bootlegged as being the council's, was common practice both locally and nationally.

But, to be frank, this really isn't any different from my first day at junior school or secondary school, joining the Cubs or going up into the Scouts, going to university or starting work. All these rites of passage/changes, assimilation of new cultures had come, been experienced, assimilated and moved on from. I think what I'd learned is not to be the Day One Dickhead, theory and practice I passed on to our two kids as they went through these rites of passage too. Day One Dickheads don't sit and watch but try and pick up the pace and style of the new organisation. And often make dicks of themselves on day one. This often became indelibly associated to them and stayed with them, usually unjustly, for the rest of their days in the organisation.

Quite soon I attended the formal ceremonial council AGM, better known as the Mayor Making, when Frank Gorton became the First Citizen as the mayor is known.

A few weeks later I attended my first full council business meeting. We were sat down on the arc-shaped green leather benches and the mayor entered following behind his officer bearing the municipal mace. The mace is part of the civic regalia and signifies, when in position, that the council is in session with the mayor presiding, gavel and all. The mayor invited us all to sit down and then immediately told us to stand up for prayers. It was customary for each mayor in their year of office to appoint a chaplain, at that time always a Christian cleric, to execute these religious formalities.

That's more or less all I really got the hang of during that first business meeting. I sat there for perhaps three or more hours not really knowing what on earth was going on. Various people stood up, some more often than others, and spoke at length on various matters. Some when standing to speak only did so, the thought crossed my mind often, so we could hear them better as usually they spoke 'out of their backsides'!

There was a very posh set of toilets but they were called something like Gentleman Members' Rest Room or some such other euphemistic title. The doors both to the rooms and to the WCs were highly polished real wood with brass fittings. The cisterns were huge and noisy and must've been ten or twelve-foot up in the air with a long chain and real wooden handle, again with brass fittings.

In a separate anteroom alcove were rows of coat and hat pegs, brass of course. Most of the members were men, most of them seemed old to me. They nearly all wore suits, jacket and tie as a minimum. Almost to a man they all wore hats of some style – flat caps or trilbies. One older councillor wore, as I quipped 'an imitation plastic trilby with feather in the headband'.

The meetings were conducted, as in chaired, by the mayor who had the chief executive sat next to him or her. A few days before the meeting a large envelope would be delivered to your house, containing a blue covered slide bound multipage document which was the agenda for the council meeting. To address the meeting you had to catch the eye of the mayor or perhaps the chief executive and wait to be called. It seemed overkill to me but if that happened, speeches would always begin with 'Thank you very much, Mr Mayor.'

When I got fed up, which didn't take long, I would go out to the male facilities and swap all the hats round from their designated habitual hooks just for a bit of sport. If my neighbour Keith Horsfield went out I would slide the spine off his order paper and re-shuffle his pages randomly. He sometimes said to me, tongue in cheek, that he really found the meetings hard to follow.

As well as sitting on the council, councillors were given seats on committees and being a new boy, I didn't get that much of a say on what I was allocated. It did include getting on the recreation committee with which I was pleased but also, at some stage and for some inexplicable reason, I was made vice chairman of the allotments committee with which I wasn't over enamoured. The highlight of the year for allotments committee members was the annual inspection visit.

The committee and key officers assembled at the town hall for a cuppa and a briefing on the day's events. We then mounted the awaiting coach to be transported around a couple of dozen midge-infested allotments. Before we alighted at one in particular, I was pre-warned that I might be surprised. It was a bit like inspecting the guardsmen at Trooping the Colour, every plant and vegetable regimentally lined up, row upon row. One proud allotment holder was sat with his wife, taking tea on the veranda of their summer house. It was looked after and presented with obvious tender loving care. Next to the proud couple was one of those plastic, polythene greenhousey things. Looking inside I saw lots of tomato plants growing from growbags. A cable travelled from the summer house into the adjacent polytunnel and was powering a small record player. 'So,' I asked, 'why are you playing Dean Martin songs to your tomatoes?' The reply came back instantly, 'Because they don't like Frank Sinatra, Mr Vice Chairman.' I moved swiftly on to the next plot.

1980 trundled along, our work keeping us busy, as did organising and servicing the local party and trying to understand as best I could, how the council worked. Nobody thought to tell me and I never thought to ask.

The acquisition of Danny the Dog had caused us to get the whole of the back garden fenced in and swap vehicles for a more dog-friendly Vauxhall hatchback. Then we were trying for a baby and in early 1981 Anne discovered she was expecting. All this meant after four happy years camping both at home and in France, we invested in a twelve-foot-long touring caravan.

It cost us, brand new, around £1600 with an awning and other bits of tackle. Caravans, these days, are very high tech: all electric, central heating, satellite TV, flushing toilets, running hot water including showers, fridges, freezers, microwaves; you name it! Our much cherished Monza 1200CT boasted two gas rings, a grill and one gas mantle that was the source of both light and heat. We loved it!

Our first caravanning expedition incorporated the Regional Labour

Party Conference held in Blackpool. Not knowing much about these events I drove off for the conference hall, leaving a noticeably pregnant wife to join me after walking the dog three miles along the Prom. Sometime later I was contacted by the event's officials to be advised that my wife, not having any official status and therefore no security clearance, was waiting for me outside. And there she stood, dog on lead, with only her slippers as footwear. New to caravanning, we novices really hadn't adopted foolproof routines. All of Anne's shoes and boots were safely locked away in the car. I don't think she was over impressed!

May 1981 saw the quadrennial elections for Lancashire County Council being held. Back in 1974 all the real spending power of Lancashire's four all singing, all dancing, and Labour, borough councils had been stripped from them and vested in the county council. Prime Minister Ted Heath told the shire county Tories in the early seventies that he would ensure that Lancashire, post 1974 would be Conservative for ever. He hadn't reckoned upon and calculated for Margaret Thatcher. Usually in British politics, usually, governments become unpopular and the party of government at local level gets punished. This is exactly what happened in 1981 in Lancashire. Mike Higginson was to stand for Labour in a ward where Tom Marsden, a local Conservative nice guy, had been the sitting councillor with a substantial majority for quite a long time. Still new as the election agent, I wanted to prove a point and win my spurs with a victory or two. We worked hard, it was the ward in which we lived and few, including Labour Party people, gave us little hope and even less support – just the incentive I thrive upon.

Enter Phil Riley. The unswerving feature for which I have a soft spot for Phil is that his birthday is on 29 February. He's turned eighteen. But above and beyond that, he turned up asking if he could help. Now this didn't happen too often. Phil had a degree in something classical and worked high up in the private sector, in the food industry as an IT guru. Eric Smith was immediately wary of Phil but they later became friendly and totally respectful of one another. Eric quite rightly had Phil down as a private sector guy and a university type. 'But I've been to university, Eric,' I said. 'Yeah, but you're alright. Give him some difficult things to do. That should see him off.' Phil came round to our semi, the stairs totally crammed with 'blocked off' leaflets to be delivered. The longest streets and therefore the tallest leaflet piles were for Lammack Road, Yew Tree Drive and Pleckgate Road. All of these roads had only 1930s detached and semis with the longish drives on both sides. A tough initiation for anyone, possibly a five-mile trek or more? Working to Eric Smith's direct instruction I set Phil off to do one of these three roads. Undeterred, he was back unexpectedly soon, taking the other two challenges very much in his stride. What I didn't realise till later is that in his leisure time and in a voluntary capacity Phil was a local moorland warden and used to walking miles and miles. After this election was over Phil became the assistant constituency secretary, taking over from me as secretary in 1986 after our daughter was born. We were by then a great double act, continuing to transform the party locally. I remained the agent until 2010, when Phil took over, now joined and supported by Damian Talbot, a member of the MP's full-time paid staff. When he retired from work Phil had the time, he'd always had the talent, to become a councillor. He has his own particular ways about him.

On one occasion in 1981, the two Annes, Higginson and Taylor, went out leafletting for Mike. The seasoned leafleteer will recognise that posher houses with longer drives are a challenge. Terraced housing streets especially without gardens have their advantages but also disadvantages. The height of letter boxes is crucial and can vary greatly on terraces. They can become a little bit like an aerobics class – stretch high, walk, bend low, walk, etc. It was during this routine that four or five-month pregnant Mrs T got a bit stuck, sat on the floor not able to get up. Mrs H to the rescue, but without ease or elegance. The inelegant pair managed to regain their stances but were in stitches of laughter.

On polling day, Tory Tom Marsden took up his customary position sat in the polling station next to the ballot box alongside the polling officials. When I saw this I complained directly to Clifford Singleton who at election time operated as the acting returning officer. Initially, Clifford said 'Tom's going to win by a mile, so don't worry about it!' I told Clifford that I would go and sit myself alongside Tom. Next time I went into the polling station, Tom was gone. At the close of polling and after the count, Tom was gone again. We beat him and under Louise Ellman's (later an

MP and a Dame), then others' leadership, the Conservatives did not regain power until 2009.

The next day, Mike's primary-aged girls, Joanne and Louise, were disappointed to find that all their dad had won was a seat. But even that was twelve miles away in County Hall!

Anne started her maternity leave at the end of the 1981 school summer holidays, not returning till after Easter the following year. As things fell, a good chunk of time; eight or nine months. I took my three days paternity leave allowance as Matthew William Taylor came into the world in September. Now that's what I'd call a seismic change in our lives, that no one can really prepare you for. Matt was born up at Queen's Park, actually in the former workhouse that dominated, threateningly and deliberately, the Blackburn skyline. He and his mum were soon moved to the local maternity nursing home. Babies took six days to be ready for the world in those days, often out the same day now. I had to bring a bonnet and scratch mittens with me or the midwives wouldn't allow us to escape with our little boy!

We had a lot to learn.

Chapter 10

Starting a Family

And what a time it was. It was a time of innocence.

There's a rule to having babies. People who have had them often say to people who are about to, things like, 'This is the biggest thing that will ever happen to you, life will never be the same again'. The yet to be initiated don't really take any notice of this wisdom/guidance. Then WHAM, it happens!

New mums and dads suddenly realise that this is the biggest thing that has ever happened to them and can't see life ever being the same again. The heady cocktail, laced with lack of sleep, of worries, doubts, fears, pride, love, practicalities, overwhelms. We've sensed a concomitant double whammy since latterly being admitted to the Ancient Order of Grandparentry. We both sensed how our 'kids' became better 'children' towards us, their parents, now they 'got' just how fucking complex, delicate, tough and rewarding becoming a parent is. When we return from visiting our families, we're sometimes expected to log in that we've got home safely. Lesson learned – tables turned!

To be frank there's never a day goes by where I don't think about the both of our 'children' or the pair of them, wondering what they're up to or how they're feeling. They are both doing well in their chosen working fields and have chosen two lovely people Siân and Gaz to whom they are now married, and have families of their own to love, care for and worry about. During my prolonged period of writing we have Joshua (born early 2016), Alfie (late 2016), Harper (early 2020) and Oliver (early 2021). We are conscious of how busy their working and family lives are, but we, especially grandma, aka Granny Annie, Covid days apart, love having them over for the day or overnight stay. Already grandma, aka Mamma Anna the Scientist, appears to be typecast as the go-to answerer of awkward questions, the normal babies and willies type, including recently polymorphonuclear granulocytes (again, don't ask, please).

* * *

I hadn't proved to be very supportive and definitely not stoic during the labour and birth of our firstborn, Matthew William Taylor, in September 1981. Indeed I panicked during the whole nocturnal experience and was asked to leave by our Great Harwood friend and midwife Lesley Briscoe to get some fresh air. The room I was banished to was already occupied by two quite spotty young lads a good ten years or more younger than me. I pushed past them, threw open the window and hungrily gulped in lungfuls of fresh air. 'What's it like, mate?' they asked. All three of us were novices. 'Nothing to it, nothing to worry about, it's a doddle, trust me.' I don't think I convinced them. I went home to catch some, as I described it, much needed sleep.

I crafted a poster declaring 'It's a boy' and proudly displayed it in the front window at home. Just over four years later a similar home-made poster announced 'It's a girl' after Katherine Mary (Anne's mum's name) Taylor was born in October 1985. I can't remember if there were strict visiting time regimes back in 1981, I can't expect that there weren't, but the quest to find our first child and his mother wasn't that easy. Not only had they quit Queen's Park maternity wing, aka the workhouse (no longer such an institution since 1929), they'd been transferred to Bramley Meade Maternity Home (closed and returned to being a private residence in 1989) ten miles away, near Whalley in the Ribble Valley. I tracked my prey down and wandered in with the requisite bunch of flowers. Anne was totally whacked, washed out, but happy with an ear to ear grin. She'd been transferred in some antiquated field ambulance to Bramley Meade but not before she was offered breakfast. She was ravishingly hungry but when she saw two greasy eggs sliding around on the plate, she declined them.

Back in those days babies took six days before they were released by the NHS. These days it's normal to be home on the same day as the birth. Modern mums and their babies don't hang around.

On day five I was briefed by the senior member of the nursing staff to ensure I brought with me a bonnet and a pair of scratch mitts. There was no chance of baby being set free without them I was instructed.

Excited as I think we both were I turned up at the appointed time with the necessary baby items and we prepared to return home. There was then another bit of ritualised rigmarole to perform. The nurse carried the baby to the threshold of the unit, I was instructed to stand in the open air and officially receive our first child in my arms.

We returned to our home with our wrinkled week-old bundle of joy. What now? Once again we were thrown into 'we don't know what we're doing' land. To be frank, our health visitor Sylvia Cullen was wonderful, listening, watching, suggesting, a real source of support. Thank you!

We got home, the three of us (oh, and 'Dan the Dog'), for the first time and sat in a sense of dazed amazement about the transformation we'd almost unwittingly imposed upon ourselves. This is back in the early 1980s: no Internet, no mobile phones, VHS video about to defeat Betamax and no reliably watertight disposable nappies.

Pioneer disposables were being developed when baby two, Katherine Mary Taylor, was born almost exactly four years later, again at Queens' Park and then transferred to Bramley Meade. Babies still took six days before they could be let out, still with the requisite hand and headgear. We both being only children, our family was complete and our children have been a source of great love and pride in their forties and late thirties with families of their own.

With both children being born in early autumn Anne was able to begin her maternity leave in mid-July at the end of the summer term and stay off until the end of the Easter holidays. Dads got three days' paternity leave and that's your lot.

Our lives were humdrum, helter-skelter, roller coaster, pell-mell and any other analogy you'd care to apply. Two full-time jobs, one baby and then another, was usually enough for most people to juggle.

*   *   *

But let me just remind you statistically I was in the preponderance of elected members by my gender and ethnicity. Then, nationally, two thirds of councillors were male, 92 per cent white. Over half were educated to degree level. Nearly half were retired and I was not even half the average age to be a councillor. Only 20 per cent were in full-time education and only 3 per cent were bringing up a family. Perhaps we were mad? We were, however, extremely lucky to have the support of a fantastic childminder 'Auntie' Cynthia Hayes, backed up at times by 'Uncle' Albert and her nearby neighbour and pal 'Auntie' Eileen.

One of my first tasks as party secretary was to arrange a thank you and goodbye event for the long-serving and outgoing MP, former Cabinet Minister Barbara Castle in the public halls. It was well attended and my highlight bizarrely was sitting in a little group with Barbara, Shirley Smith, Janet Anderson, my wife, Anne and a very old lady, Selina Raby, who had known and been active during the suffragette movement and told us stories about them. I think I realised I was sitting amidst history. We sat in a huddle ripping up the raffle tickets, folding and placing them in a bucket. In those days, a raffle was a constant presence at any and every Labour Party do.

I also became a fairly prolific, dare I say prosaic, contributor to the local newspaper's letters page, locking horns with local Tories! The subject matter of these missives ranged across topics such as inflation, the NHS, education, taxation, transport and local issues such as the quality of road surfaces, the state of the pavements and leisure facilities – so no change there really! Looking for something else entirely, I have found what I believe to be my first letter to the editor. It's dated 11/2/74, in the *Lancashire Evening Telegraph* (when it was exactly as it was then entitled!). I was still twenty-one years old.

Many people might not remember that the early eighties were witness, amongst young people, to quite an epidemic of glue and other solvent abuse. They could obtain such substances fairly easily, often from unscrupulous small retailers and an abandoned, soon to be cleared, house was an ideal place for groups of mainly teenagers to congregate, pour some solvent-based products into a used crisp wrapper and turn it into an improvised airtight face mask to get high; off their heads, in fact. Quite soon after I was elected, the local newspaper ran the front-page story 'Hoodlums go on terror rampage'. This wasn't good youth work practice and made for sensationalist journalism, which sells newspapers, but it was the first time that I was able to get youth issues in the public eye by dint of the fact I was now a local councillor. My youth work career had informed and influenced my new role as a local councillor. I'm not sure that it wasn't around then that I first sensed resentment/jealousy about what was going on, my council colleagues perhaps rationalising (or envying) that this young whipper-snapper was addressing issues left unaired for several years and my youth work colleagues seeing me as 'Flash Harry' using my new councillor status to highlight issues. This might be when my skin started to thicken. If it was right to do, then it was right to do. Don't worry over much about what people might say (often behind your back?). It got this dangerous practice of solvent abuse more in people's public minds and on the floor of the House of Commons, raised by Jack as an issue affecting his constituency and constituents.

As well as pressing for either a legal or a voluntarily imposed ban on the sale of these solvents under a certain age, I held a meeting in the ward for concerned residents, now called public engagement. About a dozen people attended including some people who were both residents and parents of youngsters indulging in this practice. They were pleased that at last somebody was taking an interest and pressing for some action. Jack was able to get a procedure known as an adjournment debate in the House of Commons with threefold purpose: to draw up a list of banned substances, to look at the categorisation of solvent misuse and to look at replacing solvent-based products with safer ones. Jack's involvement gave him something meaty to sink his teeth into and may well have contributed to the fantastic way he later handled being the Home Secretary.

Glue sniffing or other forms of solvent abuse seemed to quite energise many aspects of local life. The borough council and the county council within various different departments got involved, local religious groups, the local newly elected MP, the local chamber of trade, ironmonger retailers and the teacher unions locally were all united in the belief that there should be a debate and some resolution of what concerned many of us.

I continued to be determined that young people were put centre stage in the council's dealings, for example, advocating that there should be a live music festival held locally in one of our vast local parks. My soon-to-be Conservative nemesis Councillor Mrs Nen Bramley-Howarth accused me in full council of being irresponsible, stating 'I hope the committee will not recommend bringing all that muck and mess into Witton Park, an area where people are living. I can't think of anything worse.' I went on to speak up for council employee Mark Dunbar who had been chosen as a wrestler to represent Great Britain in the 1980 Moscow Olympics. A letter had been sent seeking financial support by the British Olympic Association which only got agreed to on the casting vote of Labour's committee chairman Councillor Henry Dickinson.

I found making things more attractive to younger generations quite an uphill climb. But I did manage to get Labour's Shadow Education Minister Neil Kinnock MP to visit the borough to look at local youth service provision. He visited my unit at Accrington Road, the very large Bangor Street community centre and Pleckgate School where we had some joint youth provision. So I was able to use some influence to inform national education policy. In the old Austin Maxi (LLU 85P) we had bought off Jack Straw, I collected Neil in Liverpool and we spent the day together and got on really well. Many of the councillors and council officers wanted to provide a service that appealed mainly to the older generations, i.e. themselves. I held, maintained and spoke up for the view that the younger generations deserved and should get services aimed at and tailored for them.

Other campaigns I initiated or supported included free bus services for all, and during a period of high unemployment more jobs especially for younger people. I also campaigned back in 1980 for greater focus and activity to reduce waste especially paper, glass, tin cans and plastics. That's now forty-plus years ago!

As was my involvement in the campaign in 1982 to get the M65 finished off. When built originally, it only stretched from a field SE of Blackburn to a set of traffic lights in the middle of the small town of Colne, with no much-needed link to the M6. Slightly further north (as I was quoted in the local press), the 'candy floss and kiss-me-quick hat' traveller-carrying M55 connected to the M6 near Preston and journeyed west all the way to Blackpool. In full council I went on to dub our motorway link the M64½, which is how it would have remained today had not Jack and Mike Higginson doggedly campaigned for the final western loop which Jack officially opened (Junctions 1 to 6) in 1997!

In my role as party secretary I established and encouraged regular Saturday morning 'talk to your local councillor' sessions in the Labour Party offices. These proved very popular in getting closer to people and hearing the issues that concern them first-hand. Again, forty years on, this doesn't really sound too groundbreaking. It was back then!

Another ground-breaking innovation was a civic newspaper delivered to every house in the borough to tell citizens what was going on including the leisure programme. Opposition parties were opposed to this on the grounds that it would be a propaganda sheet. *The Shuttle* as it was named still runs today albeit in an electronic format, as you might expect.

These ideas and innovations were just the beginning. The younger councillors, in their late twenties and thirties, were beginning to find their feet and voices and make changes. The first test of this came in Cathedral Ward when it was decided that veteran Labour councillor and trade union official Frank Hume would be deselected in favour of Maureen Bateson, thirty or forty years younger than Frank. The selection process ran its course and in the voting Maureen beat Frank. He wasn't happy about it and the headline in the newspaper read 'The Left has kicked me out'. He went on to speak about being stabbed in the back and knowing that these people had extreme left-wing views. He confirmed that he would not lower himself by going before the executive for reselection, as was the usual time immemorial custom and practice.

Locally the party continued to make itself better organised with more campaigning, and more accessible. This began with 'soft' canvassing, leafleting areas where we had never really been active before, and what became the regular institution of Jack's Saturday morning town centre 'soapbox' sessions. This wasn't planned/thought through entirely, so wasn't as comprehensive or connected as it became later. I devised the acronym ICE! Imaginative, creative, experimental.

* * *

As I've said before there is a cycle of events which is possibly not limited only to the Labour Party in that after a resounding defeat in the General Election the losing party flounders around for a while. It takes them time to select a new leader, new people, new positioning, new policies, new presentation.

It looked like 'Sunny' Jim Callaghan, the Prime Minister, had started his floundering before his defeat. Rather bizarrely he had sung an old music hall song, 'Waiting at the Church', to the TUC Conference in September 1978 and from there he wintered with discontent. Thatcher won the May 1979 election with a comfortable majority of forty-three seats.

Tony Benn appeared to emerge as the leading light in the changes being mooted for the Labour Party.

A group known as the Campaign for Labour Party Democracy developed three main demands:

a) All Labour MPs to face a mandatory reselection process during the lifetime of each Parliament.
b) The National Executive Committee to have the last word on the election manifesto.
c) The party leader and deputy leader to be appointed not by the parliamentary party alone but an electoral college including constituencies and trade unions.

I don't remember if I joined CLPD but I certainly had an affinity with their leftist aims. A special Labour Party Conference was set up for January 1981 to resolve these three issues.

Callaghan resigned in October 1980. This meant the new leader to replace him would be chosen under the old rules. In the second round of voting Michael Foot beat Dennis Healey but only by ten MP votes.

This was going on very much at a national level not really impacting on the renaissance of Blackburn Labour Party at all. Dennis Healey just about scraped in as deputy leader narrowly beating Tony Benn.

First time ballot loser Peter Shore was appointed as shadow chancellor and immediately brought Jack Straw into his front bench team. Jack from then on was to spend the whole of his parliamentary career deservedly, but at that time frustratingly, sitting on the front benches.

Then, a ticking time bomb that had been planted in many constituencies was unearthed here in Blackburn, in the guise of the so-called Militant Tendency.

Militant sold an eponymously named newspaper and that's all they claimed to be. However, their roots went quite a long way back to when they were known as the Revolutionary Socialist League, a Trotskyist 'entryist' organisation. A book entitled *Entryism* was published in 1959. I was thrown ten years back to my university days where adventurist and diversionary Trotskyites had been the bane of my students' union life. From my studies then I recalled that Lenin had dismissed these organisations and their members as 'an infantile disorder'! Militant became a proscribed, i.e. banned, organisation in late 1982. Their national 'editorial board' members were expelled from the party. The terms 'witch hunt' and 'McCarthyite' began to reverberate both locally and nationally.

Most people would associate and recall Militant more readily with Councillor Derek Hatton, Tony Mulhearn and others in Liverpool, and their dramatic 'run-in' and childish storm-out with the then party leader Neil Kinnock at the party's annual conference in 1985 when he passionately denounced them:

'I'll tell you what happens with impossible promises.'
    'You start with far-fetched resolutions. They are then pickled into a rigid dogma, a code, and you go through the years sticking to that, out-dated, misplaced, irrelevant to the real needs, and you end up in the grotesque chaos of a Labour council – a Labour council – hiring

*taxis to scuttle round a city handing out redundancy notices to its own
workers.'*

Two years earlier a youngish guy, Michael Gregory (then twenty-five)
had joined the party and appeared to be spending a lot of time with Jack.
To begin with all I thought was that it odd that Jack and Michael were
spending so much time together.

But the fruit of their meetings was a thirty-page-plus report that
became known as the Gregory Report. I insisted to Jack that Gregory
swore an affidavit, legally attesting his report to be the truth. It was
reported in the local press that Gregory had been a member of Militant
for five months but had then seen through them. Gregory had maintained
a dossier of notes of secret meetings he had attended, according to the
Guardian's front page in March 1983.

The main tactic of an entryist organisation was to seek and secure
membership and then operate as a party within a party. We tried to carry
on in a 'business as usual' way with Jack penning a twenty-page pamphlet
based on his experiences in Blackburn, 'Putting Blackburn back to work'.
Under Thatcher in four years, 6,000 jobs had been lost in Blackburn It
was a well-researched and crafted document that was well received both
locally and nationally.

One evening, as was my habit, I wandered into my ward on my way
home to have a mid-evening pint in a local pub known as the Florence.
It wasn't busy and I sat at the bar enjoying a quiet moment. This peace
and solitude was regularly broken however by random general Labour
Party members wandering down from the upstairs function room to get
themselves a fresh drink. There might have been twenty, perhaps thirty
of them and they were all pleasant with me. They candidly explained that
they had been invited here in a party within a party manner. They were
being told that the local party was too right wing (it was what it was and
I considered myself far from right wing) and not well organised (which
was most definitely not true). As in most organisations there is often
an inverse relationship between the sayers and the doers. For some in
attendance, 'trotting' up and down the stairs to get drinks was the most
active I'd seen some of them. Ask for volunteers to leaflet a dormant

ward, take on some 'soft' canvassing, attend our regular Saturday morning town centre 'soapbox' sessions and they'd be nowhere to be seen. It was very apparent though, that their open friendliness towards me wasn't particularly shared by the local Militant leadership.

Some strange things had started to happen in recent months. The Militant group were all affable and plausible people, yet they started to claim that as secretary I hadn't been sending them regular information and other communications. It simply wasn't true, but I took to sending those people their information by recorded delivery.

Then as Gregory's report hit the national press, I read in one morning's *Guardian* that one of their tactics was to 'destabilise Taylor a bit'. I was really upset by this and cuddled our baby boy. I'd gained new family-orientated priorities and values.

We had spent quite a lot of time during those couple of years making the local Labour Party much more organised and this paid dividends when it came to the quasi legal process of dealing with our Militant 'members'. I'm not sure two years earlier under a more bureaucratic style that the local Labour Party could have recognised and rebuffed these challenges.

A few weeks earlier during the Frank Hulme reselection many of us had been accused of being left wing. A few weeks later, we were now right wing accused of underhand manoeuvring in the local press. Left or right, we performed brilliantly in the local elections gaining seats to take full control of the council for the first time in nine years. We must have been getting most things right. That's 'right' as in correct!

The local newspaper and its local government reporter, the now sadly no longer with us Andrew Calvert, must have had a field day as the goings on in the Labour Party locally wrote his front page columns and headlines for him. Terms such as 'democratic purge' appeared in the newspaper. I was quoted as believing that the Labour Party's main task was 'to create an open democratic socialist society'. I went on to say that the economic and employment crisis that Britain faced was caused 'deliberately by the industrial, financial and political actions of capital as its class'. I didn't feel particularly right wing in saying such things.

A whole series of formal meetings, including rights of appeal, following due process and overseen by regional and national Labour

Party constitutional experts, were held with a view, as it turned out, to the expulsion of these people. They were interviewed individually when they had (paradoxically) doggedly tried to be seen and dealt with only as a group. Votes were taken and recommendations made from the executive to the full general management committee, over a hundred Labour Party members.

This whole saga must have occupied the time and energies of the Labour Party for something approaching a year. We did our upmost not to be distracted by this and continued to step up our campaigning style which had paid dividends at the local ballot box. It's a shame that the energies and loyalties of everyone were not put into pulling together and in the same direction.

So, by anybody's standards, 1983 was hectic to say the least: family life, a toddler son, off to study for a masters at Lancaster University, continuing to re-organise and re-motivate a more campaigning local Labour Party, taking control of the council and me taking a more prominent role on it, dealing with more democratic selections and deselections of sitting councillors, the post-Falklands Thatcher landslide and dealing in a reasonable and fair way with the Militant Tendency and general day-to-day life.

But probably the most significant history-shaping event locally and nationally was the 1983 General Election which potentially could have been a traumatic watershed in the political career of Jack Straw.

The odds were very much stacked against Labour, some self-imposed. Michael Foot was not designed nor had the taste for the combative bear pit of national campaigning. Margaret Thatcher was riding on the crest of waves caused by a patriotically well-received military campaign in the South Atlantic known as the Falklands War. Thatcher won a huge 144-seat majority. There was a 9.3 per cent swing away from Labour and a 11.6 per cent swing towards the fledgling Lib Dem alliance jointly led by David Steel and Roy Jenkins.

This scenario and the simple maths of the situation already bode badly for Jack seeking his first re-election with me, a rookie general election agent.

But even worse there had been a major re-drawing of the parliamentary boundaries upon which the 1983 General Election would be fought. In Jack's excellent and highly readable 2012 autobiography *Last Man Standing* (Macmillan ISBN 978-1-4472-2275-0 HB) he presents our daunting uphill task.

Openly and frankly, when Barbara Castle handed on what we hoped was the Labour baton to Jack in 1979, his electorate numbered around 53,000. The national constituency average was around 65,000 voters. The Boundary Commission in its infinite wisdom, decided not only to award Blackburn constituency a new total of some 76,000-plus voters, but also, as if that wasn't enough, all these new 22,000 additional voters were located in the west, in the more affluent owner occupier suburban belt of Blackburn which had previously been gerrymandered into a constituency called Darwen that had returned the Tory Charles Fletcher Fletcher-Cooke as Member of Parliament since 1951. 1979, in what turned out to be Fletcher-Cooke's final election, he was returned with a massive 13,000 majority, easily beating Labour's talented Louise Ellman who deservedly went on to bigger and better things. All in all Jack fought eight general elections during his incumbency in Blackburn, securing majorities usually ranging from around 5,000 to 14,000. In 1983, facing a more professional Tory candidate from the Institute of Directors, Ian Mather and a swing against him of 6 per cent, Jack clung on with the majority of just over 3,000.

That was the what but what was the how? Jack as I learned was naturally cautious, one might say pessimistic, about election outcomes, especially his own. If I recall rightly his overall expert analysis of the situation was 'we're going to have to work fucking hard to retain this seat'. He wasn't wrong. But how were we going to snatch victory from the perceived jaws of defeat?

Blackburn's motto translated from its Latin is 'By skill and hard work'. And that's *all* it took! And a stroke of fortuitous organisational skill, or was it good luck?

I took my usual three weeks' unpaid leave from work and we got around us an inner circle of trusted hard-working people, but we had to extend this inner circle to include as many people as possible who were diligent, perceptive and determined to win. But how did we do that?

As I discussed with Phil 'we need to get people in on a regular basis to find out what's going on, to motivate them and prioritise according to our resources how we are going to fight this general election'. But how? We came up with a solution, engaging and including as many party members and like-minded people – by skill and hard work! But how?

Enter Bill, the youth worker. I thought that we could invite people to a weekly gathering where everybody was welcome, everybody was valued, everybody could have their say and help make plans that were achievable and inclusively involve everyone. I made this idea up 'on the hoof' and those in attendance said okay.

I plumped for a Sunday morning. Not many people did much on a Sunday morning but I'm not sure Anne was impressed as one of our few family periods evaporated. I rang Eric, our party chairman. 'Hi Eric, we're going to have a meeting on Sundays to discuss the election campaign, everybody will be welcome.' 'Sundays are no good to me,' he replied.

We booked, I think, one of our community centres, and invited people to attend but we weren't really overconfident or sure what the response would be. Jack supported the idea and was quite enthused by it.

I think we started at 11 a.m., 10.30 a.m. perhaps, with a cup of tea and a chance for people to chat, to get to know each other. The 'barrack room lawyer', say a lot, do nowt, brigade of the party were AWOL. Other party members weren't interested or involved in party governance and sometimes general elections attracted enthusiasts who weren't bothered about the minutiae of party organisation but were bothered about the political hue of the government.

Quite a few people attended, not necessarily the ones you might have expected, which was quite refreshing. As it was a general election Jack circulated around those present and then began with a rabble rousing mini speech, just five or ten minutes. On the way to the meeting I'd gone to a 'quid shop' and bought some crappy trinkets: sweeties, toy sheriff's badges and princesses' tiaras – it didn't matter what. Then there was an awards ceremony with superb categories made up as I spoke, such as worst dressed, the latest to arrive, best party paraphernalia wearer. It mattered not what, nor were the categories the same every week. People clapped and cheered, award winners feigned pride in the modest accolade bestowed upon them.

Then it was down to business; my A1 flipchart easel was already divided into columns with the name of each ward listed down the left-hand side. Somebody from each ward reported in about activity in their area, both hard and soft information. Some wards did not attend initially, but soon sussed out their noted absence was a) a disappointment and b) conspicuous. What percentage of leaflets had been distributed, how much canvassing had taken place, how much 'enemy' activity had been spotted, what were the issues being brought up on the doorstep, who needed help/who could offer help? The meetings were conducted and I was the animator of them, using all my youth work motivational skills. Some chose not to attend to begin with. They were soon encouraged or shamed into being seen there.

We tried to conclude the meetings by noon or half past. Those who had leaflets to deliver or family commitments went off and attended to them. Those who fancied an hour in the pub could do that too. I got a sense that those in attendance felt engaged with, involved, valued and motivated to carry on or do more.

Eric rang me. 'How did that meeting go then?' 'Pretty good, actually Eric.' 'I heard it went quite well and people were laughing and joking?' 'I think I'm attending in future and I'd like to chair it.' Another convert won over, I thought. Eric attended and loved it, lapped it up. 'They're alright these meetings. Good idea.' Not faint praise, indeed.

These meetings were actually the social, motivational and political highlight of the campaign. Jack would always hang a press release around them to appear in the local papers. 'Jack told the regular weekly busy election campaign, attended by party members and others….'. More and more people attended. Some ideas were good, some ideas were indifferent. But they all got aired and considered.

Over a third of a century later I'm assured that these meetings still go ahead. In my personal opinion it is those meetings, organisational and motivational, and those meetings alone that made the biggest contribution and difference to the Labour Party's local performance at election times. For example, when the party's fortunes were buoyant, we identified places we were confident we might win. When the party's standing was low, we identified areas we really didn't want to lose. This determined what resources we had and where they would be deployed to the best effect. They were matchwinners! I most enjoyed our morale-sapping tactic where if we heard or suspected opposition campaigning was occurring, we'd send in a dozen or more 'shock troops' to send them scurrying for cover. More lessons learned from my university days!

Anyway, Jack won the election and his pre-prepared defeat speech, always carried on election night in his jacket pocket, remained exactly where it was.

Chapter 11

Getting a Chair – The Early/Mid 1980s Onwards

I must be what I must be.

They say, don't *they*, whoever *they* are, give a job to a busy (wo)man, because (s)he'll just do it. I think that's exactly how we were: demanding full-time jobs each, two children to raise, Labour Party and council duties to undertake. Anne taught at Pleckgate High School for thirty-six years from 1975 until her retirement in 2011 as head of sciences. By 1977, I'd moved to becoming a secondary school-based youth tutor, staying there for six or seven years until I went into a training post for the county, picking up an MA in Educational Research, and then various management posts in Blackburn and the Ribble Valley. Mostly, difficult intrusive/oppressive managers apart, I absolutely thoroughly enjoyed my time in the service, working with some great people, both youth and community staff, other public and voluntary sector staff and, of course, young people. What I valued most during my professional life were fantastic opportunities to be imaginative and creative, two attributes I think I brought to my family, party and council involvement. But you need to be uber organised. Uber!

As unemployment grew in the early 1980s especially amongst young people, the Labour Party locally organised a superbly well-attended and received march across Blackburn. I was only the man with the loudhailer, 'one of the organisers' as described by the local paper. I continued writing letters in local and national labour papers. I took up the case of the reduction in fire stations and fire safety cover across Lancashire. This was the beginning of the Thatcher years when much was to change, rarely for the better.

As is almost habitually normal in the Labour Party, a heavy defeat in the General Election leads to a cycle of internal dissent and division. The great writer and orator, Michael Foot, followed Jim Callaghan as party leader from 1980 till 1983. I met and spoke with Michael on a couple of occasions, a lovely man, intellectually sharp and very eloquent but not really keen or match fit for the cut and thrust of national political leadership.

As is often the case, a national landslide often 'brings through' local gains on the coat tails of the national surge. This was the case with Thatcher in 1979 and Blair in 1997. This cyclical 'surge' hadn't dissipated in 1980 leaving Labour locally in opposition to a Tory-led coalition with Liberals (who weren't really) in Darwen and 'rate payers' (which we all are) in the posher bits of Blackburn.

Locally the council was numerically split exactly fifty-fifty. For example, the recreation committee was charged with making £150,000 cuts to its budget. Roy Colling, the Conservative chair of the committee advocated one package of cuts, Labour's Henry Dickinson describing them as depressing and deplorable. Put to the vote, both sets of proposals resulted in a stalemate with the sole Liberal on the committee abstaining. No real way to run a rail road?

In the eighteen months or so that I'd been involved, we were in opposition and I (as usual) didn't really know what was going on, having to watch and learn. We made leaps and bounds in our campaigning activity and profile locally. People within the party and beyond seemed quite impressed and responsive to these breaths of fresh air. My received view of the 'fire brand' Barbara Castle from her local but also ageing party faithful was that she was a magnificent campaigner. I can't dispute that, only ever having seen her in action once or twice. Her successor, Jack Straw MP, grew in skill and stature locally and on the national and international stage. Dealing with an older person one-to-one in his regular and respected constituency surgeries, on our regular and renowned town centre soapbox sessions, in Parliament or on the global political stage, he developed and honed his talents and skills into a formidable repertoire.

Unemployment increased rapidly for school leavers: only one in seven got a job, another one in seven a training opportunity within the Youth Opportunities Programme. This meant 52 per cent of young people were without work and 20 per cent unaccounted for. At an employment 'summit' held in Blackburn I proposed a package of later-age school leaving (recently raised to sixteen then, now effectively set at eighteen), an earlier retirement age and a four-day working week. These ideas are still being kicked around forty years later.

In mid-1981 newly and unexpectedly elected Labour County Councillor Mike Higginson and me advocated a bold package that would open schools more within the community placing them at their hub. Schools would operate as children's education centres from say 8 a.m. in the morning until one or two in the afternoon. Then the buildings, possibly extended and with different staff to accommodate different activities, would be thrown open for all the community, preschool, school, post school-age, families, older folks, faith and community groups to use. This was aspirational, ambitious and both far-sighted and far-reaching and has met with different levels of implementation and success across the country. We still need to invest more in things like this. We under invest in our young people and communities at our peril.

But we were still in opposition locally and that meant having no real power with which to do things. Possibly inadvertently, we turned this to our advantage as this 'fallow' period enabled us to organise and campaign better.

In terms of housing and demography, Blackburn was very much in transition. Streets and streets of Coronation Street-type terraced housing, much of it built during the Industrial Revolution, were not really fit for late twentieth-century living. Anne said they reminded her of Hardy Street in Bolton where she was brought up as a child. Something had to be done. Most of the poor quality housing, in need of replacement, seemed to be in my Cathedral (central) Ward concentrated in three or four main tracts of really poor homes. I'm talking here of many hundreds of what was designated as pre-1919 housing.

Former residents wouldn't recognise these areas now. Eventually and resolutely the bulldozers moved in to flatten the existing housing to be replaced slowly but surely by a mixture of social and private housing for rent or purchase. Those neighbourhoods and communities that lived there were transformed.

It was around this time that national politics was turned on its head with the formation, by the 'gang of four', of the SDP Social Democratic Party. People may recall that four former Labour national politicians Roy Jenkins, David Owen, Bill Rogers and Shirley Williams defected and established this party in March 1981, partly as a response to Thatcher's Government and as a reaction to a perceived drift towards the left by the Labour Party. Their London launch was known as the Limehouse Declaration.

The local reaction to this national activity was that mixed long-standing and true liberals appeared to want nothing to do with this new grouping even resisting their adoption and incorporation of the newly coined brand name – the Lib Dems.

I also arranged a fact-finding trip to study the fantastic bus services available to the people of Sheffield and the surrounding South Yorkshire area. Looking back, given the current even more parlous state of our local bus services, we didn't do enough then or since to make environmentally sensible and affordable modes of transport more available to everyone.

Another campaign which I steered and for which I got the support of Jack Straw, was to avert the threatened closure of the YWCA hostel in the town. These facilities were much needed by young women threatened by the destitution of homelessness and all the perilous pitfalls associated with it.

*   *   *

Please bear with me as I feel the need now, some four decades distant from these events, to pause and ponder about power – its nature and use.

Up until this point I had only, in my analysis, experienced organisational power. In the Cubs and Scouts, as secretary of the debating society, as captain of the school rugby and various other teams, first chairman of the sixth-form society, whilst at university and in my very brief and fledgling time within both my union and the Labour Party, most of the power that I had, came from the positions I held within the various different groups, teams and organisations. Was it even actually power or was it more organisational responsibility – was that purely chicken and egg?? *De jure* not *de facto*. I suppose I'm asking with the benefit of hindsight, if that vision is in fact beneficial?

What I didn't yet know, understand or appreciate was that I'd never actually held any 'real life' political responsibility or power. But do you know what you don't know until you experience and learn it?

Yes, I had achieved the status of being a councillor but a councillor whilst only in opposition. I learned over the years that being in opposition quite suited some people within the Labour Party; they loved to be able to complain about things but asking them to be constructive and build things wasn't really their thing, not really their cup of tea. I didn't really understand this at the time but I'd seen them and heard them in action – often good orators, they would tear what exists to shreds with great eloquence and erudition. Ask them to take an idea, develop it, take it out into the world to see what others thought of it and they would run a mile.

So I didn't know I hadn't learnt this yet because being in opposition is simply that, being in opposition. I had yet to learn, understand and operate when I had political responsibility – not what can I *say* today but what must I *do* today.

As Polybius, born circa 200 BC, the Greek statesman and historian told us:

"Knowing how to win is the first step. We must also know how to make use of our victories."

There's a couple of apocryphal anecdotes to illustrate this point, both around seeking advice on how to get to our local football ground. Some visiting away fans stop their car seeing a little boy in Blackburn Rovers' colours: 'Excuse me, son, how do you get to Ewood Park from here?' Answer one: 'I wouldn't start from here, mister'; answer two: 'My uncle takes me'. In politics when you have political power you can only start from where you find yourself and you must take responsibility.

There is a natural default pessimism somewhere deep down in the psyche of Lancashire people. How are you today? 'Not as good as yesterday but better than tomorrow, thanks.' This *Jeremiahing* has either to be ignored, overcome or taken into consideration.

*   *   *

But this political limbo of opposition was soon to evaporate as we won back some seats in the local council elections putting Labour back in control as the majority party.

Once again I was thrust into a new set of unknown processes, the Labour Group AGM, not my first but the first when we found ourselves in power. As one of my veteran Labour colleagues, Councillor Frank Higham, put it: 'To the victor, the spoils.'

The AGM process, this would be my second or third, really was still something of a mystery to me. Because of its focus upon communities and young people, or indeed the lack of it, I had become interested in recreation. This at the time included our magnificent parks, sports centres and pitches, the public halls and their programme of events, the many allotment plots dotted around the borough and probably even cemeteries and the crematorium.

The outcome of the AGM was that Councillor Henry Dickinson became the chairman of recreation and me his vice-chairman. Henry was an interesting, private character in his mid-fifties, living on his own in a massive Victorian house near the centre of town. He taught English at a secondary school somewhere in Bolton and was well read and absolutely imbued in the world of classical music. His house was crammed packed full from floor to ceiling with shelving holding many, many books and twelve-inch long-playing records. He had many versions of the same piece of classical music played by different orchestras or conducted by different *maestri* which always seemed a bit of an indulgence to me. When he retired from both the council and teaching, he became an Anglican reverend, then turned Catholic over the ordination of women, eventually returning to the Church of England. A C of E bishop officiated at his sparsely attended unannounced funeral.

He seemed mainly interested in the classical music concert series that we promoted in King George's Hall, a fantastic auditorium holding about 1,700 people. The series was shared between the Halle Orchestra from Manchester and the Royal Liverpool Philharmonic. Henry knew so much about classical music that he personally wrote the programme notes for each of the concerts. Incongruously, our council massively subsidised the seats for these events, usually filled by residents from neighbouring councils.

My aspirations were to do more and differently with our recreation services. Less bourgeois, less formal, more diverse and more inclusive. I was soon to get my chance to bring my untested ideas into actual fruition.

During my initial year as vice-chairman to Henry's chairmanship, and quite early on in it, he took me to one side. Henry told me that it was his intention not to stand for election to the council again when his current term of office was up and that he also intended retiring from teaching. He told me he thought I had done a great job as his vice-chairman and that I was ready to take on the mantle of full chairmanship. He suggested that I took over at the group AGM to be held in the May of the following year and he tentatively suggested that we do the job swap – I became chair and he became vice-chair. This notion of succession planning was alien in both local government generally but in Labour politics locally especially. It seemed a good idea to me and I told him I was more than pleased with all aspects of his ideas.

And so at the next Labour Group AGM I became the chairman of the recreation committee with Henry supporting me as vice-chair, yet again plunging myself into the uncharted waters of being in charge of something I didn't fully understand. The budget for which I had responsibility was around £2.5 million (the equivalent of around £6 million today). There was going to be only one way to learn.

It must've been around this time the new chap became the director of recreation, a hard-working guy called Alun Llewellyn.

He invited me to his office to discuss policy development. 'Congratulations, chairman, and now we can get to work on developing thought through policies that fit together not only within the department but across the whole council.'

Although somewhat daunting, this was music to my ears. Developing and implementing policy, exactly what I wanted and had expected to do when I'd joined the council four or five years earlier.

Alun had been deputy director for some years and had to watch things as they did, or more usually, didn't develop. He went on to explain that we needed to get rid of policy by chairman speak and implementation by director do. So, let's work together on that. We agreed to give the responsibility for the drafting of a discussion document to Fred Cumpstey, an experienced officer within the department. I came up with its title: Working at Leisure.

Fred worked hard on this and it was wide-ranging and comprehensive. I found developing it imaginative, creative and stimulating.

We changed what it said on our 'tin' from the 'Recreation' Department to 'Community and Leisure'. But the change went wider and deeper than that, from why and how we did it through to what we did – process and product.

As Fred recently reminded me:

The headline outcomes from the delivery of the 'Working at Leisure' strategy.

COMMUNITY

Our communities were changing and some were fragmenting. We tackled community cohesion before the term became widely used.

+ Borough-wide development of purpose-built community centres in areas of social deprivation.
+ Development of new community bases and refurbishment of existing community centres.
+ Introduction of network of officer-supported community associations.

Ranging from large, old Edwardian-built former schools, through brand new 'off the peg' medium-sized neighbourhood centres to single former council houses, we developed in the region of thirty-five different neighbourhood hubs.

These were properly staffed, led by a youth and/or community development officer with some caretaking and other support staff. With these centres and the community associations that grew around them, communities were able to meet, grow and develop, to gain a voice. Sometimes they trained their feelings (and guns) fairly and squarely on the council. We saw this not as a matter of them biting the hand that feeds them but as opportunities for us all to learn and change together.

My public life and professional life took me far and wide looking at youth and community work provision definitely across Lancashire and across the north-west region too. There was nothing anywhere to compare with what we had established and developed in Blackburn with Darwen, giving all our diverse communities somewhere to convene, associate, interact, pursue their pastimes, old and new, learn new skills, some exercise, physical and otherwise. I was so proud of what we'd achieved. We always tried to get some celebrity to open our new facilities. These included local radio presenters, including the local BBC's Fletcher Richardson, Blackburn Rovers and Scotland defender Colin Hendry, Rovers' manager Don Mackay and me! The me came after we tried to get recent Olympic stars or rugby union players (as the 1980s developed these people were becoming increasingly professional). These guys were now starting to expect two or three or 4,000 quid to do the honours. I jokingly offered to do one event for two bottles of wine! I got the job but didn't get the wine!

ARTS
+ Development of South Asian Gallery (museum). The Asian community was growing both in number and voice. Children born and living here had no real idea how their grandparents, possibly even their parents and neighbours, had been brought up.
+ Establishing a bespoke display of the prestigious (Robert Edward) Hart Collection. Some 8,000 artefacts, mainly coins dating back to Roman times, were properly displayed in the museum.

PARKS and PARKLANDS
+ Transfer of service responsibility for cemeteries and crematorium to leisure services.

- Refurbishment of Victorian Corporation Park and enhancements of other borough parklands and open spaces.
- Partnership arrangements developed.
- Rolling programme of grass-pitch refurbishment and development principally at Pleasington, Witton, Blacksnape and Everton.
- Development of Witton Country Park – stables and coach house to provide an educational indoor and outdoor 'classroom' for local schools.

ENTERTAINMENTS

- Major £1 million (£3.25 million today) refurbishment scheme at King George's Hall, including the Windsor Suite and Blakeys Bistro Bar. The programme of totally refurbishing the 1700-seater main hall and other areas in this prestigious and well-located town centre venue brought great dividends. Artists such as Andy Williams, Don McLean, Mr and Mrs with Derek Batey, the *Antiques Roadshow* with Arthur Neagus, Culture Club, Gladys Knight, Vienna Boys' Choir, Val Doonican, symphony orchestras and many others, were regularly booked. Blakeys as a clean, tidy and welcoming café/bar was a haven for many of our older residents to take a breather, a cup of coffee, and a bite to eat. I showed the future London MP Tony Banks, my London counterpart, around our complex. His reaction was this can't be municipal – it's fantastic!
- New £3.5 million (£8.5 million today) build of the visionary and regional family magnet Waves Water Fun Centre; flumes, wave machines and all, now demolished after approaching thirty years of family use. In 2015, I officiated at the opening £13.5 million replacement Blackburn Sports and Leisure Centre along with Olympic double-gold medallist freestyle swimmer Rebecca Adlington OBE. She told me she hadn't been born when I'd opened Waves back in 1986.
- Re-modelling of Darwen Leisure Centre and refurbishment of Daisyfield Pools. Showing visitors around our developments we regularly used the phrase 'twenty-firstst-century facility'. It was true.

+ £300,000 (£900,000 today) Refurbishment of Witton Park all-weather Athletics Arena and changing upgrade. From recollection, the surface we laid back then was known as a 'Tartan' track. We invited and welcomed the 1984 Olympic silver-medal hurdler Shirley Strong to open this regional facility. The mayor at the time kept calling her 'Shelley Strang'. We worked her hard that evening doing the honours, meeting people and signing autographs. At one stage she pleaded with me for a quick fag break!

+ Development of two all-weather 'Sporturf' pitches with changing accommodation at Witton Park. These were opened by the World Cup legend Sir Bobby Charlton.

+ Development of kickabout areas in areas of social deprivation, one of which was opened by Kenny Dalglish.

+ Other 'celebrity' guests included *Bull's Eye*'s Jim Bowen, *Question of Sport*'s Emlyn Hughes, *Coronation Street*'s Curly Watts and Reg Houldsworth. Some of these paid 'celebritites' were not all as eager to hang around as others!

+ Re-formation of the Blackburn and District Sports Council, bringing all the different sports and their officials together. This was a brilliant 'sounding board' but also a campaigning group to get key partners to enable doubting elected members to support our proposals.

+ For several years we hosted, and I'm not quite sure why, an annual motor show in Darwen Leisure Centre. I'm told this was the brainchild, that means a passion, of the director Alun Llewellyn. We always had a star attraction: year one was a vintage car, year two was James Bond's Aston Martin. Year three we were looking for something bigger than that and we did it!

Somebody knew somebody, who knew somebody, who knew Richard Noble. Richard had broken the world land-speed record, at 633.468 mph in Nevada, in his jet-propelled car *Thrust Two*. To secure such a feather in our cap was beyond reasonable expectation, but Noble's team came back with a message from the man himself saying that he was so impressed by our ambition and 'bloody cheek and enterprise' that he couldn't say no!

That really was only the beginning of a problem. Noble's car was massive and extremely heavy, it took a huge crane to lift it into the centre and then had to be pushed through the doors with millimetres to spare on the other side. This was achieved and Richard went away happy as he was able to sell signed copies of his memorabilia. He was an interesting, quite eccentric character; well, you'd have to be, wouldn't you? The queues to see *Thrust* were amongst the biggest ever witnessed in the small town of Darwen.

*   *   *

We nurtured and developed key funding partners including Sport England, Urban Programme, Arts Council, Heritage Lottery Fund and SRB Challenge Fund. It was because we always had ambitious schemes ready, on the shelf, ready to go, that such organisations wanted to fund us. We were the 'go to' organisation, again before that phrase had been coined, having a reputation for getting funding spent and spent well.

Other social participation schemes included 'Passport to Leisure', 'Fitness for Life', 'Action Sports' and 'Play and Recreation'.

The department would also act as 'honest brokers', go-betweens where necessary, e.g. for 'Active Communities Programme', 'Sports College' status.

These things didn't happen by accident. Ten or twenty years before their time, we made two key appointments.

The council didn't have any PR (public relations) function, the local media ran rings round us. So, in community and leisure we appointed our own. Lindsey MacDonald was our first designated press officer. Andrew Kidson was our first designated marketing manager. These were visionary appointments, proactively getting our message out to people.

But in saying that, we needed to reinforce that the 'Working at Leisure' document wasn't purely or simply a dreamed up 'wish list' but a policy document which drove and informed the recreation/leisure services revenue and, more importantly, capital budgets. Other than major town centre redevelopment projects, the combined package was unprecedented within the council. Another significant point to make is that the outcomes from the policy document, initially resisted, started to fire up the imagination of members across all parties and was seen as something of a 'revolution'. This general acceptance enabled officers to frame service budgets (capital and revenue) in such a way that officers were able to pursue grant funding from statutory bodies and other streams. Conversely, any applications for external funding, particular capital projects, were further enhanced by the content and detail of the policy document. The most important aspect was that the outcomes were not only deliverable but were delivered mostly in a timely fashion. They were heady days for members, officers and the public alike.

Two departmental characters stand out during this process, deputy director Brian Smith and his partner in crime, Ged Baldwin. One way or another these two guys would get things sorted; really they should have sported *spivvy* tiny moustaches on their top lips. During a full recreation committee meeting I spotted that Brian had stripped his pipe down and was giving it the equivalent of a full annual service, pipe cleaners and other gadgets engaged. He was miles away. Tory Councillor Mrs Kasia Malowana-Murphy was 'on one' with a massively complex, multi-facetted, hard to follow question. I kept facing Kasia hoping I appeared like I was following her drift. When she'd finished and without turning my head I said in an interrogative intonation, 'Mr Smith?' Brian lowered his pipe paraphernalia to the table, buying himself some thinking time. 'Chairman, the councillor's question is so thoughtful and complex I do feel it deserves a full written response, which I will organise in the morning, if that's OK?' Ged, his pal, sat next to him, nodded knowingly, agreeing with his mate's ploy. Inaudibly and with a smile Brian mouthed what I took to be a two-syllable phrase towards me. In the pub after, over a pint, we chuckled with each other.

And we'd also, unwittingly, set a new style and atmosphere for the design, delivery and development of public services. Involving and engaging with the public, not seeing them only as customers but stakeholders too. People with young families, young people, older folk, the Asian community, people with disabilities, the voluntary sector were all approached, embraced and involved. It was, after all, their money we were spending!

* * *

There was a lot going on. Lower Audley, bounded to the south by the Leeds and Liverpool Canal and not too far from the town centre, had been identified in the 1981 census as the 'bleakest' in the borough, including an actual 'Coronation Street'! This resulted in the clearance of 550 houses. We three ward councillors, Maureen, Peter Greenwood and I campaigned hard for their eradication. As we did for a pelican crossing located half a mile further up the road. We worked well as a team taking up issues that threatened well-being, health and accident safety.

One issue was the apparent neglectful management of the relatively new Higher Audley council estate. Residents were regularly ringing to complain about litter and roaming dogs related to council bin emptying. We decided to get the top people out of the town hall and onto the streets in the community.

The group of experts, from various different council departments, was led by the borough engineer, Leo Seed. The estate had been rather nicely planned and laid out and the residents quite liked it. There were a number of really nice grassed areas. But why, we asked, were there three different standards of grass cutting and area tidying? Our experts consulted their departmental maps. This grass is owned by the environmental services department said the man from environmental services pointing to his grass. This grass is owned by the housing department said a man from housing pointing to his grass. And this grass said the man from recreation belongs to us in recreation. Get the idea? So, said we simple folk, these bits of grass adjoin each other? Do we have different grounds maintenance teams, all with their own staff and equipment, doing different things at different times in different ways to what normal people would say are the same areas of grass? Yes, councillors.

The interrogation continued. We've got the situation, said I, where it would appear the street cleansing team with men and machines visit the area and leave it spotless. The dog warden service patrols either randomly or responsively to calls made to them. The lads pulling out the plastic bin bags from residents' dustbins (this is long before multi-binned recycling) do so very early in the morning, putting all the bin bags in one place to make it easier much later in the day for the bin wagon to come and chuck all the bin bags in the back. That makes the dogs roaming on this estate brighter than you guys because they know once a week they've got a few hours where they can rip the bin bags to shreds and feast on all the contents. Could it not be arranged that the bags are pulled out, got into the bin wagon as soon as possible with the dog warden patrolling and then as soon as possible afterwards the streets are swept? I think we'd better look at that, Councillors.

We were a fairly new team of councillors in Cathedral Ward, I'd say eager and inventive. Peter especially had advocated that there should be a small community centre set up in the pretty large Higher Audley estate. Apparently there was no funding for something so modest but there was funding for a £660,000 sports hall known as a SASH – a standardised approach to sports halls! We arranged a trip for some of the residents to see a similar project in Colne about fifteen miles away. A SASH was pretty big, housing a four badminton court-sized multisports area, activity room and weights room. Residents weren't over impressed, all they wanted really was somewhere to meet, have a cuppa and have a game of dominoes or something. The shiny tin and brick edifice was constructed and pretty well used by everybody, other than local residents. Some years later a much more modest extension was added with a coffee bar area and a meeting room; ideal really.

*   *   *

So summarising but not concluding this was a fantastic period in our lives. Our two children were born. They were and remain a great source of love, responsibility, fun and pride and alongside that came our fulfilling professional lives.

Politically we'd accomplished a lot: Regaining control of the council, returning Jack in that very precarious 1983 General Election and dealing with Militant Tendency in a way which I thought was fair and right.

Perhaps our best sustained high-profile political campaigning in the local community came in late 1985 when we hosted right across the borough and every night of the week, a series of meetings entitled Jobs and Industry. These were chaired and addressed by a whole range of well-known local and national Labour Party and trade union speakers.

These included TGWU, NUT, NUPE, AUEW officials, MEP Michael Hindley and shadow ministers Jack Straw, Joan Lestor and John Prescott. A few weeks earlier I had invited the Greater London council leader and future MP Ken Livingstone to address a packed meeting held in the library lecture theatre. We were getting Blackburn very much on the local and national political map.

In 1986 Phil Riley took over, from being assistant, as local Labour Party secretary, although I retained the duties of agent I'd had since 1979 (on a temporary basis, remember!). Eric Smith's twelve-year stint as chairman came to an end as he was replaced by Martin Guinan. At the AGM Jack Straw very kindly praised me, saying 'if there is one individual responsible for our local success it is Bill'.

Indeed it is indicative of our burgeoning success that quite often the Conservatives (the national government) couldn't muster a full team of candidates locally and the new 'centre ground' Lib Dems appeared to collude with them by not fielding candidates to compete with one another in most wards.

Our team of councillors in Cathedral Ward were more active and proactive and we got things done.

From bread-and-butter-type issues such as roaming dogs and reducing litter at ward level right through to council flagship projects such as the transformation of the public halls, the total restoration and exhibiting of the world-famous Hart Collection of manuscripts, printed books and coins and the establishment of the Waves Water Fun Centre, we'd also done very well. Small things if well received, can be welcomed. The council's £30,000, five-year sponsorship deal of then Darwen, subsequently to be rebranded Blackburn and Darwen Band is an example of that. It seemed pretty well received and attracted public acclaim all round.

The Waves project was ambitious and high profile. It absorbed a lot of behind-the-scenes time by our council officers. It was never reported to me that the project was going to be concluded sooner rather than later and cheaper rather than more expensive. A small group of officers and members took a whistlestop tour of similar projects in places like Swindon, Kingston-upon-Thames, Fulham, Leicester and Newport in

Wales. I made it my business to get my cossie on and get into the water at each venue.

You have to be of a certain age to remember Live Aid way back in the summer of 1985. I have the whole concert recorded on both VHS video tape and DVDs, somewhere. This was the Bob Geldof-inspired fundraising mega concert staged at Wembley Stadium and in Philadelphia, USA, raising over £100 million. Prior to that, Geldof and Midge Ure had assembled every available world-renowned pop star to join together and sing 'Do They Know it's Christmas' which was the previous year's Christmas number one. It raised millions and was regularly re-released. Still today Christmas wouldn't be Christmas without hearing that tune – or Noddy Holder.

But in 1987 Geldof challenged us all 'to run the world'. This was in the shape of a ten-kilometre fun run. I was most definitely not in particularly good shape so at the same time I dropped a stone or two or three of weight and took up jogging; to call it running might contravene the Trade Description Act. However, I announced that I would be participating, most certainly not competing, in the event. The fairly new director of community and leisure, a great guy called Eddie Runswick, and Peter Butterfield, the editor of the local paper, offered to participate too. I would be around thirty-five then and these two guys perhaps four, five or more years older. We got into training. At the same time, around our communities, in churches and mosques, pubs, etc., less gruelling but equally participatory ways of fundraising were accomplished.

The day of the big run came. In our dreams we had hoped for perhaps a maximum of 1,000 participants. But our reality was even better; over 2,000 people of all age groups, shapes and sizes, cultures and abilities congregated in the public space in front of the town hall. The route took us away up Preston New Road, a main route in and out of Blackburn, through our Billinge Wood and Witton parklands, past Ewood Park and back to the town hall. How brilliant! I think the official total raised was around £40,000 but I'm sure with everybody's individual fundraising efforts that will have been easily exceeded. How and however quickly people got round didn't really matter. The fastest time of just over thirty minutes was achieved by Commonwealth Games local athlete Jason

Lobo. I was personally quite pleased with my time of around forty-eight minutes but it was the sense of togetherness and comradeship that was the real winner.

After the razzmatazz and hullabaloo of the hugely successful and well-received 'I ran the world' fun run, the next big event would be the opening of our flagship project, Waves. Coordinated by officers Andrew Kidson and Lindsey MacDonald, we mounted a really high-profile 'sell' of this project by going into most schools, and communities right across the borough. A double-decker bus liveried with 'Waves Water Fun Centre' emblazoned across was our most expensive mobile advertising. We invited every primary school in the borough to select a boy and a girl and their families to attend the big opening day.

Unfortunately, things didn't go quite as we'd hoped on this highly planned, high-profile opening day. Excited kiddies queued on the spiral staircase to get to the top of the 200-foot flume. Once on the flume, it was intended that they would whizz down, water assisted, at some speed, outside of the building, twisting and turning, re-entering it then flying into the splash pool at the bottom. Some youngsters emerged with bloody noses. I was absolutely livid. The flume was closed indefinitely pending safety checks. I was quoted in the local paper stating categorically that the flume 'would not open again until those responsible for its design and construction have made it right.'

The next day, still livid, I went back to the building. The manager was down at the bottom of this room with a guy I didn't recognise, wearing an RAF-type World War II sheepskin leather jacket. The manager gesticulated for me to join him. I got down to join these two guys and the manager introduced me as the chairman, Councillor Taylor, the senior member and lead on this high-profile project. In a posh southern accent the chap told me he was pleased to meet me. I don't think his pleasure lasted too long.

'Hi,' said I. 'May I call you Bill?' my new acquaintance asked. Uncharacteristically my reply was 'No, Councillor Taylor will do.'

I began, 'I went to university and got a degree in social sciences. I've just been back, to achieve a masters in educational research. These, of course, aren't really exact sciences. I would imagine in your job your training and qualifications would be very exact, physics and engineering based.' My interviewee was nodding.

I continued. 'I imagine this might include the dynamics of inclines and acceleration assuming average stats of the likely users of this flume, say an average height and weight of an eight-year-old?'

'Yes, that sort of thing,' he confirmed.

'And I assume you have graduate qualifications and then postgraduate qualifications, membership of institutes and things?' He nodded.

'Brilliant. What I'd like you to do now is go back to London and ask your chairman this one simple question. Why didn't this fucking flume work?' I left. I was still livid.

The rumour had it that I'd given this guy an unceremonious beating up. I didn't really care what people said or thought.

Quite soon after, the chairman of the Waves construction company arrived in Blackburn and asked to meet me in person, which I did. He assured me that they were working on the answer to my precise question and that everything would be redesigned and carefully checked before the public were allowed back on the flume. I think I left him in no doubt as to what was expected of his organisation and him as its leader.

Some weeks later, after a redesign and re-engineering, the flume was assured as being safe. It had been rigorously tested by a whole variety of different shapes and sizes of users. The message got back to the chairman that I 'bloody well hoped so' because it would be me taking the very first public ride down the flume.

The dreaded day came and I was quite apprehensive. I'd put a lot of political energy and reputation into Waves as a project. I was determined that it would work. The human guinea pig set off down the flume.

The next day, on the front page I think, was a picture of me hurtling down the flume about to enter the plunge pool with thumbs up from both hands. On either side of me was Eddie Runswick, the director of community and leisure and Peter Butterfield, the editor of the local paper. I appreciated their endorsement in being there.

Once again, we took to the streets one Saturday morning as cognoscenti, gifted amateurs in street theatre, drawing on more of my youth work skills and experience. Our Labour Party production was a thinly veiled parody of *Robin Hood*, but this time the poor were robbed to pay the already rich! Our five- or six-man troupe including four-year-old Matthew Taylor and Councillor Tony Cross, later to become barrister then Judge Anthony Cross QC, enacted our self-penned *Not so Merrie England* and it was critically received locally as a right performance!

* * *

All this was extremely hard work, difficult to fit in to busy lives but also totally rewarding. And, of course, the letter-writing carried on. Talking of courses, I had been awarded my master's degree, an MA in educational research in 1985.

In the summer of 1985, Anne was expecting our second child. Our caravan holiday that year was taken in the UK, in Devon. These three- to four-week-long holidays were really very important as battery chargers but mainly for family bonding. Katherine was born in October and so in 1986 we chose to share a gîte in Brittany along with our friends Neil and Sue Coley who had by then had their first child, Tom. I can't tell you how much we looked forward to, enjoyed and treasured these brilliant holidays in the sun in the summer and weekends away in the caravan. Matt would quip later that he didn't think there was a British castle we'd not been traipsed around. This didn't include Edinburgh however as when we got to Auld Reekie the winds were unprecedentedly so strong they closed the castle! Matt recalls still, aged four or five, chasing our washing-up bowl across the campsite as it soared away in the gales like an enlarged Frisbee.

Kit, as she chose to become known, carried on coming away with us, or more properly to us, until her Manchester University days. She would fly into a nearby airport, Nice or Nîmes, spend ten days or so with us, more correctly with Sarah and Amy Graham from Morpeth and Michaels Gordon and Taylor, her holiday friends since the age of four or five.

Matt did a similar kind of thing dipping in and dipping out of the south of France holidays as he switched from his three-year LLB (law degree) at Newcastle to a one-year law course in York.

And what did we do on holiday? Mainly laughed. As we reminisce about them over a randomly chosen photo album; sometimes now with spouses and grandchildren observing.

Chapter 12

Juggling Home, Work and Everything Else, 1986-89

Someone could walk into this room and say your life is on fire.

So, after a fantastic summer break in the gîte, it was back to work.

Anne had progressed to being head of biology at school as David Bacon went off to Blackburn College which had assumed responsibility for A levels across the borough as many of the schools found it increasingly difficult to sustain A level class sizes. I had been appointed to sit on the college governing body in 1981 and different governors were appointed to oversee different specialisms in sixth-form provision. I was rather grandly put in charge of humanity, quite some responsibility!

After some seven years trying to operate as an effective youth tutor I found a way to escape. I successfully applied to be the first secondment from the youth service and for a year studied for an MA. With the pupils and some of the staff, I had had a great time at Shadsworth. I had seen the role successfully working in Sheffield where the youth tutor was a senior post, responsible for everything in the secondary school that wasn't eleven to sixteen schoolwork based. In my time in the role in Blackburn there had never been any collaboration, negotiating or planning to make the post work. I was not replaced. As the saying goes, if there's a will, there's a way. At the end of that year I didn't achieve my masters, because I didn't conclude the requisite dissertation. This was achieved the following year.

In some small way, my dissertation study added to trying to sort out the confused situation with regard to the training of youth workers who were employed on a part-time basis but who very much took the lion's share of face-to-face youth work delivery. The support and training of this vital group of staff was very much a curate's egg. There was no national or regional awarding body with any sense of training towards qualifications. There was no agreed common curriculum. What did a youth worker do? What did a youth worker need to know?

There were some colleges (formerly of education, training teachers) and some universities (often formerly polytechnics) offering full-time courses for people wanting to become full-time youth workers, but that didn't meet our service needs. There were pockets of fairly decent training across the country but no equivalence, so somebody qualifying in one place had to go and do the training course in another place were they to move. Once again I was seconded, this time for two years, based at our training centre at Borwick Hall to the north of Carnforth, my identified task being 'to sort out part-time youth worker training'.

We had some real talent in terms of training part-time youth workers. Our staff team was still a mishmash of different people from different backgrounds, some of whom had been responsible for training in different organisations, in the forces, in industry. Don't get me wrong, I like the diversity of mishmash. Why surround yourself with people who all think the same?

We started from my semi-conjured up (Manchester Poly 1976) definition of youth work going back to the mid-seventies: *Good Youth Work practice enables and empowers young people to experience and experiment with power and responsibility.*

For my master's dissertation I'd taken a study by Professor Paul Willis in the mid-seventies called 'Learning to Labour' and revisited it. His work and its findings struck a chord with my experiences as a rookie youth worker at Accrington Road Youth Centre. The lads there mainly came from low aspiration working-class backgrounds. Their dads may well have had the same manual jobs as their dads and so on. The cycle perpetuates itself and to be fair, there was little driving change whilst there was relatively full employment.

My reassessment of Paul Willis's work led me to conclude that during childhood children need and seek out three things: a) supportive adults, b) peer friendships and c) a secure routine.

These are by and large provided by a) teachers, parents or other close adults, b) school or neighbourhood pals and c) the routine that home, school and leisure provides.

When they make it to adulthood, these same needs are then provided by a) the boss or supervisor or other adults at work, b) new workmates or social friends from different sources and c) the new routines of work, things outside of work and the beginning of family forming.

It was my contention that the transition period that we call adolescence would be better navigated if youth workers provided for those same needs for those three or four vital, potentially volatile, years.

So here were some foundations, homegrown, not really tested, from which we could develop. We got to work and hard work it was. We tended to meet once a week to consider progress, who had done what, what was next to be done and who was going to do it and by when. We were both imaginative and hard-working.

Without going into too much more detail the result was an introductory course that acted both as a taster and a recruiter to youth work, a qualifying course for those ready to become qualified part-time youth workers and a third level course for those people who although working part-time were responsible for units or areas of work. We're talking here of several hundreds of people; this was no mean task.

But we also had to face other issues such as the quality of tutors for these courses, dozens of the more experienced staff. That meant designing and delivering tutor-training courses delivered by ourselves to ourselves. External scrutiny, moderation, did come but later.

We had a lot to do, a lot to think through, write up, argue over and resolve. In my opinion, what we designed and published was absolutely excellent and setting the tone for youth work training locally, regionally and nationally for decades. It was designed by the field to be delivered by the field in the field. Simple but brilliant?

But that wasn't enough either, we had to give this training some academic credence, not just for its own sake but to give it some currency, at first at least regionally and hopefully eventually nationally.

We had battles to fight. Initially we aligned ourselves with St Martin's College, later to become the University of Cumbria. That gave the work that we produced academic validity. It could now stand and compete in the academic marketplace as something of value to be sought after. We then joined battle with the regional youth work unit and with the National Youth Agency based at Leicester to get some national comparability and compatibility, not only for our work but also for the work of other colleagues across the north-west and across England.

I'm confident that we led the field in much of this work. We produced two or three lever-arch folders of course content, tutors guides, students guides and tasks to be performed either in training groups or on the job. We left nothing to chance, no one could be in any doubt as to what their role was, that of their colleagues and others around them. We had moved the work on leaps and bounds. Of course, there were those 'self-employed' youth workers who tried to 'swim against this tide of change' but we made it almost impossible to corrupt the high standards we'd set for ourselves. After all it was young people that were our focus, young people who we had to help have better lives.

One brainwave that's worthy of specific mention was the birth of NAOMIE, a very useful woman. NAOMIE stood for needs, aim, objectives, method, implementation, and then evaluation. She was a very simple tool to develop some framework of commonality that was very soon embedded into youth work practice. It got to the point where our youth workers spoke about no one else. Working in Lancashire we knew that she was from Accrington, not acronym.

This is not to say that youth work operates in a rigid structure, quite the opposite. Working with young people is not always a predictable science. Therefore, both the management and the training of youth work needs to build in a flexibility of approach. Is this any different to any other setting?

At the end of my secondment I returned to my substantive management role having had a whale of a time working with great imaginative and creative colleagues. John Cowgill, Margaret Blake, Pete Francis, Bren Cook, Pam Hickin are amongst those who come to mind, having taken training on to new heights and having learned a great deal.

*   *   *

Not so long after Katherine was born, it was time for Matt to go off on the next stage of his adventures, that is, starting primary school. I walked him down the two miles or so to Lammack County Primary School that first day. At first it seemed a bit strange a) letting go and b) passing him on to someone else.

Just a little later in 1987 we decided that our small semi wasn't really big enough and we moved perhaps a mile and a half to a house called Foxlease on Mollington Road. The house was a four-bedroomed detached and was our favourite family home in that it was where we spent the formative years of our two children where they went from toddlers and early primary school children through to them fleeing the nest in the early part of the next millennium. We didn't know at the time of purchase, but Mollington Road was so named after the cotton family, the Feildens, who had made vast fortunes. They purchased Mollington Hall in the village of Mollington just to the north of Chester around 1796. And why Foxlease? Well, we didn't know that either but did notice that all the iron 'manhole' covers had 'Livesey Brothers' as part of their casting. We were later to find out that Miss Livesey had lived in Foxlease and her brothers had built it for her interwar. She had been a very early Girl-Guider and Foxlease is actually the name of the Baden-Powell family house in Hampshire, now a Guide leaders and Guides' residential training centre. Ladies quite a bit older than us would say I took my housewife badge, cookery badge or needlework badge in your living room. Just a little bit of serendipitous local history.

There was a strange series of events witnessed by our new home, Foxlease, not so long after we moved in. I received three separate visitations from senior local Labour Party members. I think in the Tory Party they would be called grandees. These aren't people who would normally pop round to see me for a cup of tea, but that's what happened. Some are still with us, so it's not reasonable for me to reveal their names here. That is up to them, in my opinion.

These folk rang up, asked if I had half an hour and then popped round. We met sitting opposite each other at our dining table. It was all a bit awkward but after some social niceties, they all three got down to asking me the same bombshell question. Would I stand against Jack Straw in the next selection process for Blackburn's Labour candidate? Not something I was expecting to be asked and certainly not something, as Jack's agent, I had entertained, not for a moment.

But ask they did and in all three cases I just sat quietly, to start with. But I'm Jack's agent, he relies on me, in my opinion, to be loyal to him. I have no idea if these three people had coordinated their approaches to me; they weren't particularly like-minded political bed fellows. Once I declined, our afternoon cuppa didn't last too much longer.

The Satanic Verses, was Bombay-born in a Kashmiri Muslim family, Salman Rushdie's fourth novel, first published in 1988 and inspired in part by the life of the prophet Muhammad. It caused massive controversy around the world as it was said to be blasphemous towards the teachings of Islam. The global outrage against Rushdie and his book reverberated around the Muslim community in Lancashire. No less so than in the Whalley Range area of Blackburn with a high concentration Asian settlement. County Councillor Len Proos (ex-Communist Party) was the local Labour councillor for the area and had been for a long time. He also did a massively successful job in and for that community in his professional role as the town's community relations officer. Len was vice-chairman of the county council and chairman of their finance committee; he got things to happen.

I would imagine Len was atheist; what religion anybody was didn't matter to him, he treated everybody with equal respect. Some of the Asian elders called for Rushdie's book to be banned and to be removed from all public libraries, then the responsibility of the county council. A meeting was convened in Bangor Street Community Centre where I had started my professional life fifteen or so years earlier. Tim Mason was the warden of the centre and asked me to attend with him thinking Len should not be there on his own. The atmosphere in the hall of this former Edwardian secondary modern school was highly charged. The meeting happened sometimes, as it would normally have been, in English and sometimes not. The mood was tense and agitated. After a while Len asked for some calm and quiet so he could speak. He explained that he wasn't in favour of any form of censorship and that people had the right to express their opinions and other people had the right to read or listen to them or not. That wasn't what the atmosphere of the meeting was in any state to listen to or understand. I asked what was in the book that was so offensive when read. The answer to that was that nobody had read it as they were against it. It was at this point that a copy of the book was produced, hanging on a six-foot pole. The book was set alight and burned in front of us. The meeting ended.

At the next local elections Len Proos was beaten by an Asian guy standing as a Conservative. Len was defeated but the Asian community lost a champion who fought their corner loud and hard. I don't think his victor was ever very active on the county council. I thought the process was purposeless and the outcome cruel.

*　*　*

Over my years working at county level I had spent two hours a day travelling up and down the M6 so now I had a little bit more time to myself. Of course I didn't. It meant I could work on some more projects within my council brief.

One of the most exciting and rewarding developments began quite humbly in a terraced house not all that far from the town centre. I was invited to a meeting of the Ewood Ward residents' association. I had been pre-briefed that they wanted a community centre and had been given all the reasons why that just wasn't possible. I turned up and the meeting was led by Christine Connell, a local resident. She's a canny operator and we grew to respect and like each other over the years. 'We want a community centre but we've been told you won't be able to provide it, so we've already bought one.' Quite an opening gambit. They had bought a very large multi-roomed wooden hut used by the golf pro at the nearby Wilpshire Golf Club. They took me outside and walked me down the backstreet. They had taken the structure to pieces and had them stacked up in different residents' backyards – wall section here, roof there. To call this edifice a hut was much to malign it, it was quite a big, quite snazzy construction. Their plan was to reassemble it and run it as a community hub. You have to admire their determination and ingenuity. This meeting took place sometime in 1985. About a year later I was able to promise them that they would have a purpose-designed proper brick-built centre by 1988.

My second general election as agent came along in 1987. With a similar percentage turn out to that of the potential knife-edge election of 1983, we improved Jack's majority from barely 3,000 to 5,500. Nationally, Thatcher lost seats with her majority dropping from 144 to 102 and the threatened Lib Dem surge never happened; although gaining 22 per cent of the vote, they only got twenty-two MPs elected compared to Labour's 229.

The education authority function was still with Lancashire County Council and as a sop to the district councils they had created fourteen district liaison committees for education with little powers; talking shops. I was made chair in Blackburn in the late 1980s. It seemed pretty pointless at the time, but I didn't know what was to come ten years later.

*   *   *

In response to some Monty Pythonesque 'what has the Labour Party ever done for us' letters in the press, I was able to recap.

- A campaign to provide allotments in Darwen, where there had been none previously.
- Various initiatives to encourage and develop children's reading and greater use of libraries by families.
- Activity to increase and diversify use of our museums.
- The issuing of over 20,000 passports to leisure, opening up services to lower income citizens and their families.
- The diversification of all of our services to be more inclusive for
- all members and sectors of our communities.
- Facilitating, in partnership with a local newspaper, an annual community charity fun day.
- Opening up our all-weather sports facilities to more school groups.

The list was extensive. What we didn't realise at the time was that we were sowing seeds for things in the future that we had not yet anticipated. We were still only a comparatively low-budget modest lower tier district council. Collaborative service design, dealing with groups at the time that were known as hard to reach, getting into our schools and getting them to know and trust us, offering things that made schools', children's and their parents' lives easier and better. These would pay dividends in the future, but we didn't know so then.

*   *   *

Most people's lives are pretty run of the mill, aren't they? And so it was for us, up early, get things prepared at home, take the children where they have to go, get to work. And then towards the end of the working day, the reverse process. It always quite shocked me (although perhaps was I simply jealous?) that there were people around who had no kids of school age and simply went home-work-home. We were particularly assiduous not to miss things. I ran my training courses in the evenings and sometimes the weekend. Between us, we never missed any of our children's parents' evenings and Anne never any of her work parents' evenings and even included taking her pupils away on camp.

I can almost hear some of you saying 'what's he on about, nobody is forcing him to do any of this'. I can almost hear myself saying it too. But to be honest I did feel compelled to be involved in this; going back to my childhood in the early 1950s, where better housing, decent state education and the national health service had made a massive difference to my life and others like me. We were socially mobile before the phrase was coined. I have always felt two things a) my sense of needing to repay for those advantages I felt I've been given and b) to make sure future generations could have similar advantages. I can't work it out of my system.

A review of things that were happening at the time included my taking the initiative and setting up an exploratory meeting with the North-West Arts Association to look into establishing a regional arts and craft heritage centre. This was a period when our officers had the confidence to be imaginative and creative. We had a culture and atmosphere where no idea was too small, too big, or too zany not to be shared and aired.

A prime example of this was St John's Church, only a few yards from the town centre but seen only as a problem. The 1789 Georgian building, magnificent both externally and internally, had stood empty for more than ten years, so what could we do with it? This was the town's oldest church and grade II listed. The council had bought it in the late seventies and spent more than £100,000 renovating it but then not doing anything with it.

My idea, coming to me one weekend, was to turn it into a voluntary sector bureau-style base. We could relocate some 'anchor' tenants already using other council premises into the property. For example, the Citizens' Advice Bureau (CAB), the Council for Voluntary Service (CVS), the Community Relations Council and the welfare benefits advice service. On top of that we could offer small office and meeting space to all the hundreds of voluntary organisations in the borough. My ideas were rebuffed very early on from within, by elected members, but I was not to be thwarted. I'd be back!

The total population of the borough was around 140,000 people, around 25,000 of whom lived in Darwen. Still having their own newspaper at the time, the *Darwen Advertiser* and vociferous, say a lot, do nowt councillors, I always kept my eye out to steal a march on them in the south of the borough. With this in mind we found £25,000 to invest in a total refurbishment and refit of the town's leisure centre's fitness studio. The Darwen councillors were conspicuously absent from the grand opening.

Really nothing had been done in recent years around play, play provision and play development. I had learned, raising our family, that children learned a lot through play, it helped family units and supported working families during the long school holidays.

I also learned that if you're proud of something, other people will be interested too. This resulted in Waves becoming very much on a local government tourist trail. We were visited by groups from all over the UK and Ireland. We were happy to show people round and answer questions. This also hones up your presentation skills. Which is how you learn best, in my opinion.

Waves had gone from strength to strength after its rocky launch and during its first year, attendances went up 27 per cent. We developed a mutual promotion linking a trip to Waves and a visit to the Witton Visitors' Centre for schools – a mix of fun and curriculum studies. A press cutting from the time shows me presenting then eleven-year-old Sharon Rushton a momento of her being the millionth flume rider! From nearby Nelson, she'll be in her forties now!

The name Christine Connell should ring a bell, mentioned earlier and very much a community activist in the Ewood area of Blackburn. Christine had gone ahead with her committee to obtain a former golf professional's hut because she'd heard we had no intentions of building her community centre. But I promised her. As I learned in life generally, most certainly in my professional work and definitely in political life, never overpromise and underdeliver.

So there we were, Christine and me, along with fellow councillor Gail Barton, perhaps eighteen months to two years later, photographed in the local paper laying the foundation stone on Ivy Street in Ewood Ward. It was a purpose-built neighbourhood centre, not a quarter of a mile from where Christine lived. The design was fantastic: a large multi-use main hall for a youth club, playgroup, tea dance and meetings, a kitchen area, some smaller meeting rooms, toilets and offices (N.B. always plenty of storage!). At the time these cost £215,000 (£1/2 million today). A second, its 'twin sister' was being built a mile or so away, in the Bank Top area. We intended to build several fully staffed with a manager, caretaker and other staff as required. The running costs including heating, lighting, etc., would be around £50,000 a year (about £120,000 today) per unit. We were determined not to skimp on this. These neglected, unseen, unlistened to communities deserved better and working alongside them, we were determined to give it to them.

Four or more years after leaving Shadsworth School, I was able to announce that the borough council had refurbished and/or improved the pool, the changing facilities, squash courts and activity rooms at Shadsworth. £150,000 well spent!?

* * *

To say I'm not recognised for my sartorial elegance would be a grave understatement. The highest profile example of this came in early 1988. PE teacher Pete Briggs, a school colleague of Anne's, had provided me with several hundred large posters for the forthcoming England versus Holland under-eighteen football match to be staged at Ewood Park. Pete knew I had something to do with our network of sports and community centres and other settings The task wasn't onerous and meant moving these posters from his car boot to hers, her boot to mine and my boot to somebody in the department. Pete was a great bloke, a champion for Pleckgate and for school sports and it was no trouble. As the day got nearer I received an invite to attend. But this was erroneously addressed to Lord Taylor, my friend Tom. I asked Anne to have a quiet word with Pete to explain the mistake. Anne came back with the message that Pete rather sheepishly meant it for me, for all the 'hard work I'd put in', which in fact had been negligible.

It was a bit of a rush that cold winter's night. I'd toyed with the idea of taking six-year-old Matthew with me, but it would have made for quite a late finish for a boy of that age. We decided we'd eat on my return, 9 p.m. or so.

I wrapped up warm that night, big trainers to ward off cold feet, my fleecy jogging pants, a big jumper, Rovers' bob hat and my scarlet ski jacket – normal spectating garb. I got down to the ground and presented myself at the main stand, as instructed. I went to the first turnstile. Sorry mate, try further down. I tried a little further down. No, mate, club officials entrance, that's where you need to go. There I gained entrance and got pointed up a flight of then wooden steps of the then wooden main stand. This led out to the director's box where I had been invited on a few occasions before. I sat down amongst the others, recognising a few people.

To be fair the match was unremarkable, uneventful. At half-time we were welcomed down to the boardroom for the traditional and well-renowned cup of tea from a Russian samovar, and a warm meat pie. I'd been a few times and it was really enjoyable. The local PE fraternity was there from all the local secondary schools. Are you stopping behind after, Billy, they asked. Aye, I'm always up for a pint, you know that.

The mayor at the time was Sylvia Liddle, a highly presentable swimming instructor in the borough, perhaps just turning forty, who was magnificently civically clad, up to the nines, if not beyond.

I commented upon how wonderful she looked, which she always liked, but mentioning that she looked quite cold. Yes, Bill, she said, don't forget this year I am the mayor and I'm attending the do afterwards.

Wandering off for the second half I wished Sylvia a lovely evening.

At the final whistle I wandered down to find my pals in the bar and we organised a beer.

We exchanged a few pleasantries regarding the game, from recollection not much of note happened. Someone said to me 'I'm looking forward to the grub, Billy, are you?' 'What grub?' I asked (I'd agreed with Anne that we'd have some supper when I got home). 'You'd better check the seating plan for each table.' Given the company I was in, I rather gruffly enquired about what seating plan and what tables. 'Over there on that easel, check it out.'

I did so only to find B Taylor with T1 next to it. I found Peter to report my discovery.

'No, that's not you, Bill, you're not on the first table. You'll be under W Taylor.'

I returned to the table plan. W Taylor TT.

'Pete, what does TT stand for?' He replied, 'As you well know, Bill, and rightfully deserved for all the work that you've done, TT stands for top table.'

I could imagine Anne could've heard my jaw drop three or four miles away. 'But nobody's discussed or pointed this out to me, Peter.'

At the same moment Peter took up a spoon, bashed the table, he'd have done that a few times at school, and asked the top table group to assemble in the anteroom. I felt myself descending from being in the shit to being in deep shit; no chance to wriggle out of this now, even for an arch wriggler.

To be fair, to this obviously inappropriately dressed sore thumb, I had already removed my woolly bobble hat out of a sense of occasion. I was in this ante room with Sylvia the mayor, stunningly coiffed and clad, chains and all, Bill Fox, the chairman of the club, everybody else wearing colours and ties and blazers with the crest on the pocket announcing them to be executives of the ESSFA, The English Secondary Schools' football Association, and me. Now, I'd like to pride myself on not being easily visibly embarrassed. Luckily, my bright scarlet ski jacket complemented the colour of my face.

That stupid slow marching handclap began and I took my appointed place in the line of dignitaries. As we entered the room where everybody else was stood up, someone said Grace cursorily and invited people to sit down. If only the ground could swallow me up.

In front of me there was a place card and a lovely printed menu embossed and bearing the same coat of arms as was displayed on the executives' blazers. I read something along the lines of the ESSFA welcomes Councillor WG Taylor as their guest of honour at this banquet.

I was sat next to Bill Fox, the chairman and I tried to explain the inappropriateness of my dress. What seemed worse was, it didn't seem to matter to him. We chatted away and the courses, most beautiful food, wonderfully served, came along.

During the breaks between the courses was a great opportunity for my pals to approach the top table and basically take the piss out of me. Few missed the opportunity.

I was conscious that Anne was at home expecting some form of supper and that I was driving. The wine list was fantastic; I stuck to plain water.

I felt like I needed the opportunity to escape. This came in the form, as it used to in those days, of the fag break. I explained to Bill Fox I was going to have to go. Again, he didn't really say much. I didn't make any further excuses, but I most definitely left.

Rather than it being perhaps around 9 p.m., I got home nearer to 10.30 p.m. 'You've been a while?' my wife considerately asked.

'I'll make you a spot of supper,' I offered. 'Nothing too much now at this time of night.' I came back with a plate adorned by two slices of cheese on toast. 'What about you?' 'I don't really need to have anything to eat, I've just been to a banquet with the mayor.'

I had quite a lot of explaining to do. *Luckily*, I could back up my alibi with my place card and the beautifully produced menu. Regardless I don't think she was very impressed with me. I wasn't, to be truthful. My cheese on toast was consumed without any comment or compliment!

*   *   *

Poll tax first got mooted by the Thatcherites in the mid-eighties. It was an ill-fated replacement for the existing rates system, that part funded local government services. Rather than incorporating some element of means testing, it appeared to be a flat-rate charge. Ultimately it contributed towards and cost Margaret Thatcher her eleven-year premiership. This ended acrimoniously and in tears in late 1990, when John Major became Prime Minister. The spectre of poll tax very much clouded national and local politics for years.

We tried to just get on with things in Blackburn. We opened two neighbourhood centres in the summer of 1988. We called them that to differentiate between the county's youth or youth and community centres.

Where it was fruitful to collaborate with the county, which after all was by far the Goliath in terms of local government, we did so. And this began, in terms of community and leisure, with summer playschemes. These were really important as they gave children aged five to fourteen somewhere exciting but safe during the long school summer holidays but also their parents knew they were safe too.

We really got into the development of this network of centres. They were extremely well received in communities. They opened up opportunities for people to meet together, very much in an old-fashioned and much-missed way. Our next planned centre was in the deprived community of Green Lane to the south-west of Blackburn.

After that we wanted to move into the southern part of the borough, that is Darwen. We had just agreed and embarked upon a complete refit of the sauna suite at Darwen Leisure Centre costing £140,000 (around £375,000 today).

But my foray into Darwen didn't stop there! They were to get a neighbourhood centre too. I set up and chaired an initial consultative process to establish a community association for a deprived area of the town known as Sudellside. This was to whet the residents' appetites about the shape of things to come. These neighbourhood centres were now costing £300,000 to build (over £800,000 today). The meeting didn't get off to a very good start as the sixty people who attended had to wait after a mix-up as to the whereabouts of the keys for the meeting venue.

I took any and every opportunity to get our borough on the map including writing to the recently appointed chief executive of the FA Graham Kelly about why international football matches could not be taken away from Wembley and staged regionally. I got support from Gordon Taylor, the chief executive of the professional footballers' association but locally based. Later, I did get a reply explaining that the long-term contract with Wembley Stadium meant matches had to be hosted there, but eventually, years later, international games were played in different parts of the country.

The plan to bring the neglected St John's Church back into use might have gone away in the minds and eyes of doubting Thomas' but I was not easily fobbed off. It was announced that the department of the environment and other national organisations had given the go-ahead for a £110,000 conversion plan to give the building a new lease of life housing various different diverse community groups. I was dead pleased that my doggedness had paid off. The CVS made it clear that they were very excited about the project, and I felt quietly vindicated. (Sadly, in 2019 the much used building was razed to the ground by fire. It was totally devastated. Hopefully the £3.75 million insurance settlement will enable an intended reconstruction of the landmark building to be 'repurposed and refurbished to create a high-quality flexible workspace'.)

*   *   *

I'd had four fantastic years in my first chair post.

As 1988 came towards its close, other events were going to overtake me and my family.

Chapter 13

The Mayor! Who? Me? 1989-90

It's very difficult to make something simple and good.

How does one become the mayor? To be frank, up until late 1988 I'd never really given it a thought. I hadn't got a clue about the detail of how it worked.

Then there is the fairly recent advent of directly elected mayors, a phenomenon exported from the US? Batman's Gotham City has had various mayors. Even the long-running cult cartoon programme, *The Simpsons*, had the mayor of Springfield, Mayor Quimby, nicknamed Diamond Joe. Didn't he seem a little like Ted Kennedy? Ken Livingstone became the first directly elected London mayor in the year 2000. He was followed by, yes that's right, Boris Johnson, who took the post for a similar period of eight years, to be replaced in 2016 by Sadiq Khan. To further complicate matters, London has its own Lord Mayor who is the head of the City of London Corporation. I would imagine for most of us Dick Whittington in the early 1400s is the most famous Lord Mayor of London.

Outside of London, directly elected mayors seemed to be established in the more urban conurbation areas, Greater Manchester and the Liverpool City Region, for example. These were established by an Act of Parliament and/or a local referendum. There are several dozen now across England. I believe it was Hartlepool, after a very tight referendum result, that opted for a mayor, then elected the town's football mascot, a monkey, H'Angus!

Blackburn had a ceremonial civic leader, the mayor. To me, they always seemed like quite old people, in their sixties and seventies. They tended to be married and if they were a bloke, their wife or daughter became the mayoress. When a lady was installed as mayor she tended to appoint a daughter or husband to be the mayor's consort.

In late 1988 I was thirty-six, I'd been on the council nine years and during that time, we'd had both children and learned to juggle all those duties plus two full-time jobs as best we could. I'd become the chair of recreation aged thirty-three. Under my leadership it was modernised and transformed into being the community and leisure department, which better fitted the changing needs of Blackburn with Darwen's rapidly transforming communities. We had totally refurbished and revamped our public halls, making them a fit and welcoming place for the more modern and changing programme of events that took place there. We had updated many of our tired sports facilities both indoor and outdoor. Our multi-million-pound, hugely innovative and popular Waves Water Fun Centre went from a dream to reality with many travelling quite long distances across the north-west to enjoy the exciting experience with their families and friends. We had consulted upon, planned and put in place many changes and the service was twenty-first century, if a little bit early.

As chair of the community and leisure committee, I automatically sat on the very powerful, all service leads, policy and resources committee. In late December 1988 I was a few moments late for the Labour Party caucus meeting always held prior to the full committee to discuss and consider things on the agenda. Councillor Frank Higham, who plied his trade as manager of the Co-op grocery department in the centre of town and was a leading member of the shopworkers' USDAW union, was leader of the council and therefore chaired P and R. As I walked into the committee room Frank was explaining to my fellow Labour councillors present that Labour, out of political necessity, would be taking the mayoralty again that year and that it had been agreed that Bill Taylor would be our nomination. I think back then and still now I am the borough's youngest mayor.

The *real politik* of our situation was that for many years the council was numerically split fifty-fifty with no one with a clear majority. Labour consistently had thirty councillors out of the sixty and Labour had six mayors on the trot: Cliff West (an instructor at the Remploy), Eric Smith (engineer), Mike Madigan (H Samuels jewellery manager), Sylvia Liddle (swimming teacher) and Gordon Toole (mental health worker) had all taken the position and Labour needed to do so again.

It was actually Jim Blackburn's turn. Jim had been in engineering all his life and having been elected the year before me, it was his turn on seniority of time served on the council. There are possibly four or five long-serving Labour councillors who for some reason of their own have never wanted to serve as the mayor and Jim was one of them. I would guess many people would think being the mayor wasn't really our cup of tea but I had the attitude that if it was your turn, it was your turn.

At the full council meeting to decide who would be the mayor for the following year, the Liberals nominated Paul Browne, who got their five votes. The Tories nominated George Bramley-Howarth, who got twenty-nine votes. I was then nominated by my ward colleagues, Peter Greenwood and Maureen Bateson and I got the requisite thirty votes. George got his due turn two years after me in 1991/2 and Paul two years later, 1993/4.

The next day the phone began to ring. This was only early January and officers of the council and the mayor's office wanted to start to fill up my diary going well into my soon to be mayoral year. I also got lobbied! Charities including the Red Cross and SPUC requested that I made their charity my charity for my year. The idea for my charity was totally my own and focussed as you'd expect it to be, upon young people. I was going to call it Youtheme 90. I suppose it had a two-fold aim, wanting to raise young people's profile especially with older people and also to raise funds to buy equipment to enable youth groups to widen their programmes. We eventually raised, with lots of help, £30,000 which helped many youth groups acquire equipment for their work. The residual balance, a fair wedge, went a long way towards a much-needed modernisation of Kentmere Cottage, our Lakeland facility near Ambleside.

I was also advised that the mayoralty had some financial allowance attached to it; from memory, around £4,000 for the year. Perhaps uncharacteristically, Anne's eyes lit up. I bought two new suits (my first in fifteen-plus years) and some shirts, about 300 quid, which is I think all I saw of my allowance.

I was invited to come and see the draft of my official letterhead for the year. I was quite taken aback and a little bit proud on seeing it in black and white.

I'd spent four years as chair of what was now community and leisure and the director Eddie Runswick told me I was to be taken out by the senior officer group for being such a supportive and imaginative chairman. Again, a little bit of recognition and praise goes a long way. I wondered if I would be back to that position after my year, as Jack Fairless filled it.

The annual council meeting for 1989 also known as the mayor-making was fixed for 13 May. I had a set number of people – family, friends and colleagues I would be allowed to invite. The number I had hoped to invite hugely exceeded my limit. A chance meeting with Brian Nicholson, a technician at the college and very accommodating chum of mine, solved my problem. Seats for the mayor's invitees were limited after key people from the community had their allocations made and really rightly so. Brian came up with the idea of videoing proceedings and relaying them to committee room number one, next door. That room would easily seat 150 or more people and solved the problem. Brian also turned this into a project for a group of students to give it some real-time learning application. It worked very well. I have a (VHS) copy of the video somewhere. Something else in my archive treasure trove for me to search for.

The appointed day duly arrived and was packed with appointments and allocated tasks. Into the town hall to check arrangements, attend my word-processing course at the college, across to King George's Hall where the post-ceremony reception was due to be held, met Eddie Runswick and Jack Fairless to debrief them on departmental matters. I then travelled to a local pub to drop a bunch of house keys off for my visiting mum and her husband, Alf. For some reason I then had or took the time to go for a sauna at Darwen Leisure Centre, although this wasn't relaxing as Colin Brindle from the local football referees' association was there and badgered me about matters to do with football. I dashed to John Slater's hairdressers where Alison gave me a quick coif. Then off to pick up children from Auntie Cynthia, our irreplaceable childminder.

I'd requested and introduced an innovation to the mayor-making, a non-dress rehearsal of proceedings to make sure they'd run smoothly on the night.

The mayoral car driven by one of the mayor's team, Ted Connolly, arrived (there's only one officer in the team now, I believe). We four set off in the mayor's car followed by my mum and Alf, and our close friends, Rod and Yvonne, in a Silverline private hire car.

Our immediate guests took their seats and it was time for the event to start. I was nominated and seconded, the mayor asked if there were any further nominations and the council chamber fell silent, thank goodness.

The next bit of the proceedings always seems clumsy to me, having witnessed the event over some ten or so years. The retiring mayor goes out of the chamber to collect the mock reluctant new first citizen. They are supposed to re-enter the chamber holding hands, fine by me. Then there is a whole episode of de-robing and robing, removal and swapping of chains between the six active participants in the ceremony. I take the mayor's seat then stand to read aloud and sign the declaration. Peter Greenwood and then Maureen Bateson make nice speeches by way of a nomination of me. They take around twenty minutes and it gives me the chance to scan the room to see who I can recognise in the crowd. My boss, John Goffee, Emily Parker with her mum, Ann, my wife, Anne's, head teacher Heather Jameson, my mum and Alf and children Katherine and Matthew wanting to go to the toilets as usual. At aged only eight and four, I hoped they'd be OK with this, this year; in fact as 99 per cent always, they were sources of great pride to us, the assets that they proved to be! Looking further round I saw people all from the business in the community partnership, their chairman Mike Murray, Peter Butterfield, editor of the local newspaper, and Eric Smith's wife, Shirley.

I've retained the notes of my speech in the two-volume diary I kept of this year. Highlights included beginning with the phrase 'This is the time to be grateful' with various specific people and organisations to thank, many of who were present. Reading it now it was quite a left-wing speech, not normal at a mayor-making. I referred to my cherished life gifts: better quality post-war housing, the national health service, well-resourced comprehensive school provision, a publicly provided university education including adequate subsistence support and the LEA where we both worked enabling us to repay the debt that we felt towards society. I concluded that we wanted the year to be a celebration of these deep-felt gratitudes. I sat down to a tumult of applause I didn't expect! It rang out from committee room one next door, too!

*   *   *

Speeches!
How to write, build and deliver a good speech?
How does anyone/how did I develop such key skills?

The honest truth is, no one really helps you. Sink or swim!

But we all do it, we all learn to speak in public. Watching our grandchildren develop recently from no apparent verbal communication skills to becoming communicators with widening vocabularies and other ways of expressing themselves bears witness to that. Many books and other www.-based training media now exist to help with these processes. Thank goodness, haven't we all had to endure excruciatingly atrocious speeches at events over the years?

Looking back, in school, sports, Cubs and Scouts I'd had to speak in public. Had to and learned from it.

Over the years, decades, I've put myself or been placed into different situations where speaking in public was a must. Harold Heys, a semi-retired local journalist, author, quiz-setter, local heritage aficionado and Benedictine liqueur imbiber, has witnessed and reported on meetings held in the council chamber and local government generally since the 1960s/70s. I met up with Harold a year or two back in neutral Tockholes, in the Bell family excellently run Black Bull pub/Three Bees Brewery where he presented me with a copy of his recent book, Harold Heys' *Darren and Darreners, People and Places*. Harold's fee was a bottle of Benny. Harold inscribed my copy, 'One of the best local government orators I have ever heard and I've heard a lot!'

Thinking about speeches I think that perhaps there are four 'house' styles.

1. The pre-prepared keynote point speech

I've delivered and witnessed many, many of these in council chambers, academic institutions, government departments and other 'theatres'. I chose that collective noun wisely as good speeches, well delivered, must include a sense of drama, in my opinion.

Know your topic and your audience. Switching jobs back in 1995, I got my new staff team, thirty or so folk, upstairs in a pub in the small Lancashire village of Ribchester. Many of the assembled were unknown to me and each other. I introduced myself and spoke for fifteen to twenty minutes or so. Had the talk had a title it might have been 'Developing and Delivering Effective Youth Work Within a Rural Setting'. As I finished, I welcomed thoughts and questions. There had been an older chap sat uncomfortably on the front row displaying anguish and anxiety throughout. He immediately piped up in a booming stentorian local accent, 'This isn't the Ribble Valley Rare Dog Breed Society meeting, is it?' and stormed out, presumably to an adjoining and more germane room. He probably thought we were all barking.

There's a traditional format to keynote speaking: tell them what you're going to tell them, tell them, then tell them what you've told them. Using 'trade jargon' should be OK. 'Warm' your audience up a little, but not too much humour. And not too many key messages; three or four is plenty enough.

2. 'Warm' speaking

Here you aren't trying to convince anyone over much or, on the other hand, confront the obdurate to change their minds.

During our mayoral year and don't forget my wife, Anne, thirty-six years a secondary school teacher, was a professional public speaker, we adopted a loose formula of a) thanking people for the invite, b) finding a link between that group of folk (sports clubs, charity fundraisers, community-based volunteers) and yourselves and c) thanking them all, especially the committee for all of their Herculean and often thankless work. And never, never talk for too long. Never. Think 'buffet'!

3. Dealing with the press and media. Appearing on TV or radio, often the local scene

These 'guys' are a busy crowd, under deadline pressure and sadly a dying breed. I think the erosion of proper trained journalists with local nous is truly lamentable. Local councils and councillors get away with murder these days. They employ, often their former local journalist colleagues, as 'comms' or PR staff who put the council 'spin' on often really serious, life and death issues and email it across to a less-experienced, worse-paid, novice/newcomer 'reporter' who hasn't the knowledge or energy to do much more than cut and paste the story. There is little or no scrutiny or accountability of whatever yarn the council, school, hospital, utility is being spun. Dreadful. This can cut both ways.

The twenty-first-century digital reporter doesn't want too much background info. 'You're not letting the local swimming club use the council pool early on Sunday mornings'. 'No, we've had to endure 35 per cent cuts to our staffing budget, Sunday pay rates are double time, the government now insists on additionally trained and equipped water safety staff following recent drowning tragedies, we offered to fund the safety training of swimming club volunteers and new increased standards of water quality was going to add £250,000 to running costs.' Headline? 'Swimming club condemns council closing pool'.

If the press contact you when you're genuinely busy or catch you on the hop, apologise, promise to ring back and do so very, very asap!

When talking to the press don't use too much council speak, acronyms or professional jargon. Don't talk like a doctor, accountant or architect would. Use easy, acceptable 'man in the street' language. And don't slip into politically correct language. People will understand who the 'man in the street' is. People won't know what the various funding or inspection regimes are and won't use Latin-based medical talk. Describing something as the council's equivalent of a big MOT or major operation will cut the mustard.

4. Combative hard-hitting taking-no-prisoners summarising

This is the toughest on-the-hoof speech to design and deliver. I used to love them. These were mainly at full council meetings, mayor presiding, chief executive, with legal, financial and all other service chiefs present, time-keeping device, mayor's chaplain there for prayers, all and any members of the public and the press welcome to attend and latterly ask questions and expect answers. All councillors expected to attend, but there were a small band of sloper-offers, around 9.15/30 p.m., for a frame of snooker, beer, who knows?

The agenda for a full council meeting was massive. Motions to be debated on almost any topic, summaries of all the business that committees and subcommittees had conducted in quite some detail – a hundred pages of A4, more? Committees and subcommittees had opposition spokes-(wo)men, who would tend to fire the shots, but anyone else could give covering fire. It was the job of the committee chair, executive member or the council leader to answer any questions, legitimate or otherwise, or deal with anything chucked at them. Some members would disingenuously raise issues, possibly playing to a specific gallery or lobby, that mattered not.

The man or woman in each specific role should know their agenda like the backs of theirs hands, or do their homework prior to the meeting, including getting any useful facts and figures from their relevant senior officer, e.g. it might be nice to prune the encroaching foliage along Acacia Avenue but to offer such a service across the whole borough would cost £3.5 million, money we just haven't got.

As council leader I was alert all the time. I pre-highlighted potential points of ambush. During any debate that was engendered I concentrated on who had raised that issue (and why) and who had joined in. But it wasn't just what, who and why; how and when may matter too.

As soon as a debate on an issue began, my ears were pricked. I made notes all on the council agenda paper, either the gist of what John, Jenny or Junaid had said or verbatim. If something was said that was ludicrous (I called it B&B, work it out) I might have a taking-the-piss riposte. More serious comments needed and deserved a more serious, measured response.

As the debate developed and seemed to be heading to its conclusion, I would check my annotations, who had said what. I would then number them, 1 to however many, to give my response/rebuttal the appearance of a logical natural flow, pruning distracting bits. Depending on the subject matter, if it did have more light-hearted facets, I might make a couple of such comments to get the audience listening. If humour isn't appropriate, don't even try to use it.

As you go through your response to what has been said from 1 to x, attribute who said what, but not always.

Don't speak too quickly, try not to read from your notes, look up and speak up. If you're trying to 'see off' a strong speaker, mention them by name, not too often and look directly at them.

End on a high spot that accentuates the tenor of your case: indignation, anger, frustration, whatever mood you're looking for. Then sit down.

*   *   *

Press photographers spent quite a while getting the photos they wanted. Then I wanted to walk the 150 yards or so to the public halls but we weren't allowed to by Ted and Francis Massey, the mayor's main drivers. Again, it felt like a kaleidoscopic photomontage in my mind of people's faces, Anne's mum, Mary, Bill and Sue Robertson, Tommy, Chandra and Cindy Nair, the Dog Inn set, my colleagues from Borwick Hall and Henry Dickinson. From work, I spotted Margaret Blake, Sylvia Crook, John Woolf and his wife, Betty, John Clark and Chris Reeve. John and Joyce Mason were there along with Ken and Mavis Eccles and Greg and Kate Pope.

People started to drift away from the post-ceremony reception around 8.30 p.m. and it was time perhaps to pop into the Dog Inn. I think my mum and Alf too enjoyed their ride in the mayor's car. I was pleased to spot John Radcliffe and Pete and Dot Haken joining us. We left the pub around 10.30 p.m. to another post 'Lord Mayor's' show gathering at our house. This was a bad idea because Anne told me it was. Our guests left around 1.30 in the morning! Anne, Rod and Yvonne then stayed up even later, putting the world to rights! It was ever thus!

Next morning I have various press calls to visit. First of all the *Lancashire Evening Telegraph* and then Radio Lancashire where Stuart Whaley did a good live interview. Jenny Billingsley, later to teach at the college for thirty years also puts an interview 'in the can'.

For some reason I totted up mayoral hours 'worked'. Thirty-four in the first week. My employers had agreed to me having seven and a half hours allowed off each week.

I also kept the weekly engagements sheet that was circulated to the mayor and staff and have two A4 hardback exercise books in which I kept a diary of the year. I'm not sure if that's normal behaviour, not only for me or anyone?

Being able to refer to it now enables me to tot up that over the year we attended over 420 separate engagements and that's not including chairing full council meetings or attending committee meetings, making the total nearer 600. I also kept a rough running total of the hours spent each week: I would suggest never less than twenty each week, usually thirty and sometimes well above forty-plus.

Like most roles in life, there is not just one way to be a teacher, nurse, cleric, bus driver, shop keeper, parent or sibling. Every role has as many ways of interpreting and playing it as people occupy them. This applies equally to how to be an MP, councillor or mayor. People will have a view of me; I've heard some of them. What I always tried to do during our year is compromise between how I am, like to be and the civic office we occupied for that very short year. It flashed by in a trice, I can assure you.

Although the year was very stressful in the sense of juggling this additional layer of commitment into our already busy lives, having been the mayor was a great, humbling, exciting and rewarding experience. A complete and utter privilege. The warmth and the depth of the welcome we received wherever and everywhere we went was fantastic. People opened up to us, opened a brief window for us into their world. We found out a great deal about people's working lives, something that perhaps we never think about. We saw at first hand the hours, weeks and years of dedicated service that people give, for no financial reward, to the hundreds of voluntary organisations where people work tirelessly for the benefit of others.

So from those 420 or more engagements, I've picked out only five to give a sample, a flavour of what a year as the first citizen is like.

Chapter 14

Five Notable Mayoral Engagements

You know life is what you make it – so beautiful or so what.

Blind to Misfortune

In August 2012 the local paper, the *Lancashire Evening Telegraph*, carried the sad news that Bill Griffiths had died aged ninety-two.

Bill Griffiths fought with the RAF in Java in 1942 and, aged only twenty-one, was taken prisoner of war. Bill was ordered by the Japanese to uncover a booby-trapped ammunition dump, which left him with horrific injuries. He was totally blinded and lost both hands. In adverse clinical conditions, Bill was operated upon by Australian surgeon Colonel Sir Edward 'Weary' Dunlop and didn't return back home till the war ended, four or more years later. I took the opportunity to visit the statue commemorating the colonel at the Australian War Memorial, Canberra, perhaps ten to fifteen years ago.

Bill, despite everything, went on to be a leading light in the St Dunstan's charity for blinded ex-servicemen and women, raising funds to enable their work to develop. He was named as disabled athlete of the year in 1969, having won many sporting events. In 1972 he was guest of honour on *This is Your Life*, presented by Eamonn Andrews. In 1977 he was awarded an MBE. In 1995 he was honoured by Blackburn when he was given the civic medal in recognition of his inspiration and example to others. Councillor Maureen Bateson, who presented Bill with the civic medal as mayor, was quoted as saying it had been an honour to know such a 'wonderful gentleman'. She said: 'Bill was a really kind and gentle man'.

He was very brave for what he went through. How he survived the war in a prisoner of war camp is just incredible. He told such wonderful stories and he was so proud of being honoured by the council. Bill was an example of what you can do with courage and how through adversity, you can still do something positive with your life. He and his wife are an inspiration to everybody. William Griffiths Court, in Mill Hill, which cares for ex-service people and their families, was also named after him.

We were privileged to meet Bill Griffiths too.

Bill and his wife, Alice, had moved to the much flatter-terrained Blackpool some years earlier. He'd written a book about his life, its challenges and successes. The book was called *Blind to Misfortune* (Publisher: Pen & Sword Books Ltd; 1st ed edition (1 Mar. 1989) ISBN-10: 0850526027 or ISBN-13: 978-0850526028) and we were invited, as mayor and mayoress, to the launch of it in Blackpool. The mayors of Blackpool, the Wyre and the Fylde were there as well. We'd got Emily Parker to babysit and then collected Anne from school and rushed straight down the M55, for a 6 p.m. start. One of the other mayoresses appeared to have had a few already and confided to Anne that she had eased her upper underwear, to make herself 'a bit more comfortable'.

We spent a bit of time with the mayor of Blackpool, a former guesthouse proprietor and her daughter Patricia, the mayoress. Mayor Mary's husband, Harold, had been a Liberal councillor in the town from 1954 till his untimely death in 1968, just as he'd been nominated to be the next mayor. A bit like Florence Oldfield in Blackburn, Mary Barnes stood and won the by-election caused by her husband's sad death, promising that one day she would be mayor, an honour snatched from Harold. I've learned recently that Mary herself passed away, aged eighty-four in 1996. She'd resigned from the council in 1991.

The mayor's attendant for Blackpool lined us up. Blackpool as host mayor then alphabetically Blackburn, Fylde then Wyre. The musical quartet struck up 'Oh I Do Like to be Beside the Seaside'.

The four mayors with their mayoresses or consorts set off to walk, you could even call it march, in time with the music to their designated seats identified by their officer by standing next to them. But the planning for this part of the ceremony had not been completely thought through.

The mayor of the host borough, Blackpool, was an old lady forty years my senior, and was not fleet of foot. She moved quite slowly across what must have been the dance floor. When I say quite slowly I think I really mean very slowly. I bumped into her a couple of times as we paraded in front of the assembled guests. They were doing the normal welcoming hand clap but in time with the music, not the less than pedestrian pace of the marchers. We weren't really sure what to do then, so I improvised and said to Anne, swing your arms in time with the music but walk slowly. It was indeed so slow that by the end of the tune, signalled by four drumbeats and a cymbal, we'd only got halfway across the floor. Now what?

The leader of the band then improvised; perhaps he'd come across this before? He went 'A 1,2,3,4' and we plunged into an encore of what must be Blackpool's most famous tune. This time we made it!

We sat at a table which included Bill's son Bob and family. It was a cracking evening. We bought a copy of his book which Bill signed, with his wife Alice's help.

Maureen is right, Bill was a true gent. Our paths were to cross once again when we visited William Griffiths' Court. But residents there are far more likely to recall our four-year-old daughter Katherine during the visit. She was a star and lit up many faces.

For me, the poignancy of Bill Griffiths' story is the incongruity between the inhumane treatment meted out to him (and many others) and the determined resolve and humility he displayed in conquering those ordeals.

Sunday at the Polish Club

Blackburn, like many, is an ethnically diverse community. The 'indigenous' population is enriched by Irish, Scottish and Asian community groups and a Polish community who initially settled here after the Second World War. Many got here during the war and fought from here, others walked here after the pogroms. In the late 1980s, there were two Polish clubs in the town, one was Catholic, the other for ex-combatants. As a teenager, inadvertently, I played for KS POGOŃ, a Polish community volleyball team in Small Heath, Birmingham.

It was a very hot summer's day in Blackburn and Francis collected me around 10.30 a.m. to attend the Catholic Polish Club, which is now an Indian restaurant. We were made to feel very welcome by the community and there was a church service outdoors on the car park; I would imagine 300 people were there. I was to wear the mayor's formal robes, fur trimmed and decorative jabot or ruff at the neck. The service went on for a very long time as the hot sun beat down on the congregation. Eventually it was over. I was asked if I'd enjoyed it. I didn't really want to say that I didn't know which I understood the least, a full Catholic mass or that it was conducted entirely in Polish!

We went inside the club and I was glad that mayor's officer Francis Massey disrobed the mayor so now I'm only wearing the lounge suit that I'd had on under the civic regalia. 'I need a drink,' and that was the worst possible thing I could have said. It felt like every one of the guests was anxious to get the mayor a pint of *Okocim*; it's about 6.2 per cent strength. To be fair I did down the first one with enthusiasm. This seemed to accelerate the generously meant offer of further 'refreshments'. 'No thank you,' said I. 'If you want me to speak, I'm afraid I won't do so if I have any more than one or perhaps two drinks.' The second seemed to appear immediately in my hand.

The secretary, the lovely warm, welcoming and friendly Romuald Foks, quickly convened his committee members and there was a conversation I presume in Polish. The president banged the table. I'm told he said 'the mayor will speak now, so please be quiet'. He'd rearranged the order of proceedings, in the interests of hospitality.

I said a few unrehearsed words concluding with 'na zdrowie' or cheers! The assembled audience clapped and cheered. Michael Hindley, then Lancashire East's MEP, married to Ewa, a Polish lady and college lecturer, said that that went down very well, as did the Okocim!

Anne left promptly with the children to go and see her mum in Bolton and I didn't stay too long.

I made my farewells to our hosts having thoroughly enjoyed, after the service, a convivial hour also in good company. As I walked down the steep stairs to be met by my driver he said, 'By Jove, Mr Mayor, you've walked down the stairs. We've had to carry mayors down before now.'

Yet another ecclesiastical/multi-cultural event under my belt and appreciated. The Polish/ex-Poles/Polish heritage folks there confided in me that their community and culture seemed to be both being diluted and was disappearing. Few youngsters wanted to learn Polish folk dance, which the elders loved and missed. Some years later, for different reasons, there is a much stronger Polish presence here.

I was dropped off at home, we had something to eat and I spent an hour in my local with my mates.

Our First Civic Funeral

Chris Oldfield had been a councillor for a few years, in Ewood Ward. He'd not been very well for a while and sadly died. His widow, Florence, in her late fifties, had worked in cotton mills for most of her life. Naturally upset by her experience, Florence asked me if I would support her on the day of Chris' funeral, which of course I said I would.

I collected Florence from her house in the mayor's car and proceeded to the crematorium. The turnout was good and nice things were said about a nice guy.

We got back in the car and Florence told me she'd arranged a simple buffet at a local pub, not far from Ewood Park.

The mayoral car parked directly outside the door to the pub. It was about 10.30 a.m. or so in the morning, before pubs used to open. The pub's door looked well and truly shut. Florence was upset by this. 'I told them to make sure the door is open,' she said.

'Leave it to me, I'll knock on the door.' I was, of course, wearing a suit and the mayoral chains.

I tapped on the door lightly. From some distance away from behind a most definitely locked and bolted front door I heard somebody shout 'Fuck off, we aren't open!'

Florence asked from the car what was going on. I didn't feel like it was appropriate to tell her verbatim.

I tapped once again on the door, this time a little bit louder, a little bit more persistent, perhaps.

'I've told you to fuck off, we are not open.' I bent down, pushed open the letterbox saying, 'Sorry, I've been told there is a buffet in here for Chris Oldfield's wake.'

My unknown conversation partner dropped his voice a little. 'For fuck's sake, I've just told the mayor to fuck off,' he stage-whispered to a companion, real or imagined.

Bolts were drawn, locks unlocked. Our host stood at the portal to the pub. 'Good morning, Mr Mayor, lovely to meet you, we've been expecting you all. Do come in.'

I stayed for half an hour, had a sandwich and a cup of tea and then went back to work.

Chris' sad death caused a by-election in the Ewood Ward. Florence was the Labour candidate and won. She sat on the council for twenty-five years and was mayor in 1998/99. As a former mayor, she had her funeral service in the cathedral.

A New Bishop

Saturday, 3 June was the date set for the enthronement of the seventh Bishop of Blackburn, the Right Reverend Alan Chesters. As mayor of the borough of Blackburn where Blackburn Cathedral is situated, but for some reason does not qualify us for city status, I had a key role to play in any enthronement, I was to learn.

We were up and off early by 9.15 a.m. Jonathan Parker was in charge of our two kids at home. Many of the mayors of Lancashire with their chief executive in attendance made the mayor's parlour busy. The soon-to-be bishop arrived with the Reverend Paul Warren, his chaplain. Paul had been the chaplain at Lancaster University during my time there. Our lives were to cross a few times in the future too. The mayor's officer Francis and I argued about whether I must wear the mayor's hat or not. As it's only a size 6 5/8^{ths}, it's never going to fit my 8 1/3rd head (I hear you say!). 'I know that, Mr Mayor,' said Francis, 'but it'd cost 131 quid to replace it.' We pre-assembled in the town hall foyer making sure we were in the right order. 'Mr Mayor, please can you hold the mace, I've lost my top hat now!'

The officer in charge announces that the procession will now set off. I'm right at the procession head with mayoral hat in one hand and the civic mace over my shoulder. Francis catches us up, slightly out of puff (he was near to his retirement), freshly reunited with his top hat and relieves me of the mace. The procession is lengthy and makes its way along the half mile or so to the cathedral. The streets are very busy, thronged with people. As the bishop-elect arrives at the cathedral west door, it's flung shut in his face a bit like for Black Rod. Simon Townley, aka Sir Simon Peter Edmund Cosmo William Townley, aka the Lord Lieutenant of Lancashire, and I have to feign reluctantly allowing him to enter.

It's a very long communion service during which I have a speaking role. Two hours later, the process is complete. The beautiful building was absolutely packed! People from every one of the x parishes and y C of E church schools were present to witness this splendent pageant.

Around 1 p.m. I've done my civic duties and am rewarded by being given the weekend shopping list. After that, we hear that Rovers are defeated 0-3 away at Crystal Palace. They'd won the second division play-off final home leg 3-1. I get a teatime pint with Bill Robertson; no real compensation for a) missing the match b) not being promoted!

Another quite long, enjoyable ecclesiastical day for someone who's probably an agnostic. Probably.

If I appear ambivalent about my understanding and relationship with formalised religions and faiths, that's because I am just that, ambivalent.

I defend everyone's right to follow any faith, religion or denomination they wish or none as long as that doesn't impinge in any way on anyone else or the way they want to run their lives.

If all the great world religions disappeared, they or something very much like them, would very soon be reinvented. Every civilisation or culture has striven through the history of time to understand or explain who they are, why we are here, where we will go. On my travels I found listening about Zulu, Aboriginal and Maori spiritual beliefs very interesting and as plausible as any.

Dr Bashar Hafez al-Assad has been president of Syria for twenty or so years, his father before him, thirty. He studied and qualified in medicine at Damascus University and then ophthalmology in London. So, as a qualified doctor bound by the Hippocratic Oath, how does he reconcile barrel bombing his compatriots in places like Aleppo? Don't they follow the same god but perhaps in a slightly different way?

That's the genocidal atrocity pole of the cognitive dissonance that formal religions seem to produce.

There are day to day manifestations of the same phenomenon that I can't square. This is the practice of people who suddenly get religious and having never darkened the door of a church in decades, become regular church goers. This, miraculously, coincides with their children attaining the ages of four and ten, just before junior and secondary school applications are to be submitted. Churches, mainly Christian, with centuries of great tradition of providing good education, are complicitous in this unprincipled recruitment blip, desperate to keep their admissions numbers up.

Rant over.

The Garden Party

Sometime in May at my regular mayoral meeting with Steve Jones the chief executive, he raised the issue of the annual invitation to the mayor to attend a royal garden party at Buckingham Palace. As an immediate there and then reaction, I declined. Steve suggested I discussed this at home before making a final decision.

So in mid-July the four of us made the trip to London. From recollection the town hall covered the expenses of the civic couple. We wanted to take the children to London, paying for them ourselves.

They'd never flown before, so it was a real adventure. My contemporaneous notes record that although we weren't leaving the house till 8.30 a.m., nearly eight-year-old Matthew was ready and dressed by 6.30 a.m. We got to the airport by 9.45 a.m. Matt indulged in taking photographs of planes close up, nearly four-year-old Katherine just enjoyed visiting toilets. I think the flight only took twenty-five minutes in the air.

The aircraft went into descent flying over the twin towers at Wembley and then actually over Buckingham Palace. My notes add 'massive grounds, lakes and woods at the back – something I've never realised before'. Flying over the Thames, we pass over a football stadium that had 'Next time fly KLM' painted on its main stand roof.

We landed with a bump and it was very hot, excellent garden party weather, it being mid-July. We took a taxi and arrived at St Stephen's entrance of the Houses of Parliament where a full security search nicely filled the time whilst Janet Anderson arrived. At the time Janet was still Jack's London-based PA and had bravely volunteered to look after Matthew and Katherine whilst we attended the palace. We followed her around the labyrinthine corridors, staircases and passageways with which she was well familiar, popping into her office before getting something to eat in the staff cafeteria. It only cost us £8 for the five of us (I noted). After that Janet took us out onto the terrace overlooking the Thames where we sat next to Tony Benn, Bernie Grant and Tony Banks then influential left-wing Labour MPs. It was time to dress up, to give Anne's palace hat its first major airing. Janet very kindly took photographs of us dressed up to the nines, no selfies or selfie sticks in those days. We jumped in a London cab, Janet advising us that the London protocol was to share a taxi if it was appropriate. As fate would have it, another couple jumped in once we established we shared the same intended destination. The ladies sat facing forward on the proper seats already adjusting and fiddling with their headgear, whilst we chaps sat facing backwards on those flip-down seats.

Knowing Anne as I do, I was given the eye to initiate a conversation. As I opened my mouth it became one of those occasions when even you don't know what your brain is going to instruct your mouth to say, a bit like the Numbskulls comic strip (from memory, in the *Beezer*, *Topper* or *Beano*?).

'Been before?' I enquired. Not having heard our fellow passengers speak before, the most perfect cut crystal glass, public-school-accented reply was quite a shock in both content and delivery.

'Not this year.' That hopefully not intended put-down reply stumped the Yorkshireman with a Brummie accent. Anne silently but clearly encouraged me to continue this forlorn interrogation.

'Have you come far today?' I was quite impressed with my improvised line of questioning.

'Oh no, we live in Town.' I'm thinking to myself, 'so do we' but I remembered and deciphered that, to Home Counties types, 'Town' is code to the metro cognoscenti for London. A very loud silence descended again.

'Have you come down today?'

'Yes, we've flown down on the Shuttle.' That failed to impress.

'Are you local authority?'

'Yes, my wife and I are mayor and mayoress of our town this year.'

'Oh, which town?'

'Blackburn.'

'Oh.' My travelling companion's voice became more awkward and perplexed even with monosyllables.

'Do you know to go to the back gate?'

'No.'

'Right then, follow us.'

We got to wherever we had to get to and I paid the £2.20 fare. My new and far more knowledgeable chum then argued about who was going to pay, suddenly handing me a pound and a 10p coin.

At the back gate we were security-checked by soldiers and then my mayoress and I promenaded through the grounds. The grounds seemed the size of Blackburn's Corporation Park, one of the biggest urban parks in Blackburn.

We were entertained by a couple of military bands that took it in turns to play. I remember one of them doing a selection from Simon and Garfunkel. I was wearing my best lounge suit, most of the other chaps wearing top hats and morning suits. It has always seemed to me that posh people talk louder than ordinary people. And also that morning suits were actually upper-class boiler suits, things to be seen and get drunk in. We spotted one guy with a yellow crossover waistcoat, a purple shirt and a green tie.

Spotting an acquaintance this guy bombastically boomed out, 'Philip, old chap, congrats indeed!'

We sat quietly in some directors chairs with a cup of tea from a samovar, a little plate of cakes and savouries and a glass of lemonade (the real stuff, not R Whites!).

Two pairs of morning suits and two hats approached and bumped into each other. Top hats were doffed and cheeks offered for pecks. One top hat said to the other, 'Congrats, did you have any idea of the impending elevation?'

'Well, I must admit, a pretty good intimation was given.'

'Good show, well done. Mind you, after all you've done, you thoroughly deserve it.'

We knew nothing of this world. We recognised James Anderton, then chief of Manchester police and John Smith the Labour MP. That's all.

I was sweltering hot and removed my jacket only to be immediately told off by the mayoress. One of the army of waitresses went busily past and I asked how many were in attendance. She told me that 8,000 people had been catered for. The Scottish Yorkshireman in me hurriedly tried to assess the cost of the event in terms of travel, hotels, hire of clothes, etc., and I reckoned not less than 3 million quid, if not loads more than that, as we were doing it economy style.

Then it happened. A loose scrum, or perhaps more aptly an Eton Wall Game manoeuvre began, obscuring something or other from view. 'It's them. They're here.' We missed it!

Seemingly it was the emergence from the palace of Her Majesty the Queen, Prince Charles, Princess Diana, the Princess Royal, Mark Phillips, the Duke of Edinburgh and Sarah Ferguson.

I was sent to see if I could see at five-foot-eight what my mayoress at around five-foot couldn't see. The answer was: not much more.

I'm starting to formulate a theory that not only do posh people talk more audibly than the rest of us but also they are taller too.

I invited my mayoress to accompany me on a promenade of the grounds, which she graciously accepted. We'd been there around an hour and a half, we'd seen everything that we were likely to see including Anne stretching possibly to five-foot-two on tippy toes to catch a glimpse of Princess Diana.

As we'd parted company from the 'Back-Gates', they'd recommended that we could leave via the palace. We mounted some steps and entering through some French windows we found ourselves actually inside Buckingham Palace. Were we allowed in, I wondered?

Still referring to my notes of the occasion, it was cool and comparatively dark inside. Every room had massive display cabinets in every corner crammed with what I thought was horrible but inevitably priceless china. Invitees, I thought perhaps not wishing to look like they were anxious to dash away from the event, nodded knowingly at the exhibits. Little cards leant against each piece described what it was. I thought I'd take a punt at it and said in my best booming voice, 'I told you it was a Mecklenburg, dear.'

We continued to saunter around and then left the building by what I thought was the front door. But it wasn't the front door, as Buckingham Palace is a square of buildings and we found ourselves under the canopy of that middle bit where really important people are greeted upon their arrival.

Then we found ourselves going through the real front doors and out onto the front where the guards march up and down. Anne spotted that one of the marching guardsmen, though still marching in formation, had split his pants from bottom to thigh.

We thought our visit to the palace was over and relaxed our stifling apparel, but we were suddenly aware that various Nikons, Canons and various other makes of (pre-digital) cameras with telephoto lens were trained on us, presumably in case we were important. Tie hurriedly readjusted for our global tourists!

As we quit through those gates behind the Queen Victoria Memorial facing The Mall, spivs took our photos presumably at a price as in those days no cameras were allowed at the garden party. I wonder if that is still the case in today's digital smartphone world?

The Back-Gates had recommended a stroll through St James's Park so that's what we did. We reflected upon our experience as we walked along past people sitting, kissing, Walkmanning and skateboarding. We did feel like we were being unduly stared at, but I put that down to Anne's millinery. I think we decided we'd quite enjoyed it, an experience, a chance to visit Buckingham Palace. Our first and only visit, we thought, never likely to be repeated. I quote from my notes at the time: 'The chance of a garden party shouldn't be turned down – not a lot happened and it may not be worth going twice – but it's certainly very interesting and worth being able to say you've been and seen.'

We were reunited with Janet and our two children. Janet had taken them on an open-top tourist bus. Matthew had quite enjoyed it and so had Katherine in her own way, crashed out, fast asleep, across two seats.

We got back to Janet and her then husband Vince's house in Lewisham and the nine of us sat down to a lovely family meal including their children James, David and Katie.

Early the next morning we were up, Vince dropped us next to Tower Bridge from where we visited the Tower of London, saw the Crown Jewels, then took a boat trip on the Thames and walked past the usual tourism sites of Horse Guards Parade, Trafalgar Square, Carnaby Street, Leicester Square, inter alia.

It was then time to taxi to Heathrow in time for the Shuttle home. We were all fatigued. A number of the businessmen on the flight home were the worse for wear; my notes say very. Our little quartet got back to our house around 10.30 p.m. I noted 'great adventure but everyone very tired'.

Chapter 15

Reflections on our Mayoral Year and What Next?

I would not be convicted by a jury of my peers.

So many wanted to attend the mayor-making in 1989, that there was no chance they were going to fit in the usual venue, the council chamber. Problem? Yes! Solution? The college, in the guise this time of the IT-savvy technician Brian Nicholson. That's Brian the unflappable, Brian the let me have a little think about that there must be an answer, Nicholson. The solution was a video camera in the main room and the largest possible TV screen, at the time, in the adjoining and formerly named committee room number one. So, the college could show off its adaptability and skills to around 350 key people from the borough and beyond.

I recall a former government minister when asked 'What is it like when you stop being a minister?' saying 'You get wet'. In a way that's what it was like twelve months later when we stopped being mayor and mayoress and became deputies to Malcolm and Joan Doherty, our successors. Just as we had taken over from Gordon and Joan Toole in 1989. After the civic formalities, we walked across to the reception in the public halls.

I think we thoroughly enjoyed our year as first citizens. 'Think' because it was demanding and tiring, we were 'on show' a great deal and on our mettle too. But that fleeting concern soon melts away. We met so many interesting, hard-working, committed people, across so many different walks of life. The whole experience had been a privilege, a humbling privilege. Both of us with full-time jobs (county allowed me, on top of my forty-two half days for my civic duties, a further forty-two half days) and with two children now aged eight and four, our time management had to be the best. Our number one babysitter Jane Hopwood, whose mum and dad, Helen and Peter, were both teachers locally, living just a bit further down the road, did very well for us that year.

I think that the dichotomy of both the commonality and the diversity of the people of the borough is the one that will remain with us for the rest of our lives; thousands of people doing their best, working their socks off, in all manner of different ways, in different settings, for different purposes. We got the sense that, at times, these people felt on their own: running that one night a week voluntary organisation, working hard to raise desperately needed funds (rarely a fortune) to keep that work going, feeling responsibility towards somebody, often a family member, neighbour or friend with a medical condition or other needs that would benefit from a little bit more. If only we all gave an hour or a tenner a week to help!

The previous chapter related to only five engagements out of over 420 in our mayoral year. Flipping through the list, I've not even touched on the youth, sports and other organisations, prizes and award-givings, the additional hours put in by many of our teachers and other hard-pressed employees (and employers!), charity events put on in our local pubs, churches and other faith organisations, music and other heritage, cultural and arts events, health and disability groups, hosting the town-twinning weekend with our friends from France and Germany, welcoming HRH Prince Charles on one of his fairly regular visits to Blackburn.

So, I've picked out a handful of engagements and snippets from other moments from this great year. I couldn't include them all. For another time, perhaps?

If you only take one message away from all this, then it is this: It was a great opportunity, honour and humbling privilege to serve our borough and its people, during a year we will never forget. We still talk about it and people will come over and talk to us about it and the part they played.

I went into Boots the Chemist. One lady assistant suddenly said, 'Thank you so very much for what you did for our daughter and our family.'

She'd lost me but went on to explain. Apparently on a recent mayoral visit to a junior school I had encountered her daughter. I'd recently, after a few years trying to be persuaded, agreed to let our long-standing dentist, Chris Lees, remove several of my jumbled-up teeth and use braces and wires to slowly draw them into better place. This little girl, like me, didn't like wearing her braces. I told her she must, showing mine in place. When she went home she told them the mayor had said that she must. Job done!

*   *   *

I do recall attending the Christmas party at some old folks venue. The lady in charge somewhat accusatorily told me 'I understand you're a vegetarian'. This isn't true but I did at the time have such a preference during the long banqueting mayoral year. As we dined, I was sat on the top table munching my way through a large bowl of beetroot which she kindly provided.

It would be around halfway through our mayoral year when Francis Massey reached retirement age. He'd put many years in and knew the job inside out. Francis wasn't a particularly tall guy, diminutive, you might say. But why does this matter, you might ask? His successor was Graham Brunton, previously a military policeman in the RAF, therefore quite different in build and stature, most definitely, compared to Francis.

The job description did not include the clause 'must be able to fit Francis Massey's returned uniform'. So we were a bit stuck, Graham was a good six to nine inches taller than Francis, much longer in the leg and larger in the chest. He simply didn't fit the vacated outfits.

The handover day between Francis and Graham coincided with Children in Need day, of which I'm not a particular fan but I threw myself at it. My take on such charity efforts is that quite a few tax evaders get involved in charity fund raising to fund things that we as tax payers should fund.

Our day starting with the bog-eyed jog at a Witton Park's fabulous running track at around 6.30 in the morning and going through without a break till midnight, well beyond. That 'without a break' only appertained to my good self: jogging, serving at stalls on the market, drawing various raffles, pulling pints in pubs, appearing in a rock band (tambourine player!), playing badminton. It was a non-stop, no break, really enjoyable, energy-sapping day.

It was in between the gig and playing badminton that I got Graham to park up near a cash machine; dear dos these charity days. When I returned to the car, dressed in my track suit, Graham had acquired a pretty gorgeous young woman, well presented, sitting in the passenger seat and obviously ready for a Friday night on the town. 'Come on, hurry up, keep up with the taxi in front with my mates in it!' she instructed the poor guy. 'She won't believe I'm the mayor's driver taking him to his next engagement,' Graham explained. 'Of course, he's not the fucking mayor, dressed like that! Put your foot down, he'll have to come too!' Graham got out of the car, got the chains from the boot and only then did the girl accept our highly implausible alibi!

It was followed, of course, by Remembrance weekend in which the mayoral party plays a very active role. The events on Sunday were mainly focussed on Blackburn, at the cathedral and at the war memorial in the park. On the Saturday we attended a wreath-laying at Darwen war memorial. It was a cold November day. I was dressed in the full robes of my office which kept me as warm as toast but next to me, my officer, new to the job and not entirely adequately kitted out, was shivering. I asked 'Why haven't you got your coat on?' I paraphrase a little in that the reply was 'Because you haven't given me one.' 'Why not?' 'Because we've run out of budget for this year,' I was told. 'But I've been promised one in April in the new financial year.'

At the end of the event we jumped in the car and we went to the gents outfitters that I knew the mayor's office dealt with, probably with a Masonic connection. It was obvious who I was as we walked in, and I got greeted with a 'Good morning, Mr Mayor, how can I help?' Gesturing at Graham I said 'Give this guy a coat.' Graham was quickly issued with a coat that would've drowned Francis. 'And the payment, Mr Mayor?' I was asked. 'I'll just sign for it now and hand it into the administrator on Monday.'

On the Monday I walked into Clive Palmerley's admin office. 'Morning Clive, I had to buy Graham a coat on Saturday before he froze to death. I went to the normal outfitters and here's the chit. There is no problem with that, is there?' The answer came back 'No, not at all, that's fine.'

The mayor, of course, also chairs the full meeting of council, with the mace in front of him and the gavel (little hammer) at his right hand. These were normally quite pedestrian affairs. But this was the year of poll tax and the council meeting to discuss this was tumultuously stormy. From the usual handful of people attending in the public gallery there were many, many dozens of really angry poll-tax protesters from all sorts of political perspectives, some neighbours of mine. They carried placards and chanting slogans and threw things across the council chamber. I had the best seat in the house but not a passive role. To be frank, at times, things got out of hand, I bashed the gavel craving for order. I hit it so hard one time that the gavel head flew off and hit a councillor on the head in the front row of the benches. Those in attendance were getting angrier and angrier. On several occasions, I suspended business which meant the mace had to be removed by the mayor's officer and I went behind the mayoral screen back into the mayor's parlour.

Every time I did so I was joined by a veteran Labour Councillor Len Proos, a good friend of mine. Every time he did so, he helped himself to a scoop of whisky from the drinks cabinet. We generally waited five minutes hoping for tempers to calm. This must've happened at least half a dozen occasions until it got so completely out of hand that the chief executive called for police support. We suspended business again and returned to the mayor's parlour with Len still accompanying me. 'I think it was a good idea calling for the police.' 'Why is that?' I asked. 'Because I'm getting ratted here,' was his reply. The police arrived, about half dozen of them; I know not from where they came. That seemed to calm everything down and the meeting was eventually conducted to a conclusion.

We also became frequent invitees and therefore guests at am-dram plays staged at the nearby arts club. The theatre club put on plays perhaps once a month and we attended a few that year. I understand that former Blackburn mayoress (and *Coronation Street* actress who played corner-shop owning Renee Roberts) Madge Hindle 'trod' the Gibraltar St boards in the 1960s. There is a name for the genre that they were, in that the plot (thin) had to be fit to the given scenery layout with both French windows in the middle at the back and a door on either side. The mainstay of the organisation was a lady called Ethnie, Ethnie Best. Her daughters Harriet and Victoria, and one of their husbands were usually in the cast, the other was self-appointed custodian of the bar and took his duties personally.

Usually we arrived half an hour before curtain up (was there a curtain?), tried to refuse a welcoming drink and settle down for the first half. At the intermission, we would have been presented with a drink and then back for the second half. A quick drink in the bar at the end of the performance and we'd be home by ten or ten thirty or so.

For one of the Thursday to Saturday 'runs' we happened to be there on the final night. Ethnie, a little bit coyly, invited us to the post-production-run buffet party. We really didn't like to say no, so we removed our chains and sent Graham home.

The performance concluded to a round of applause. We descended the steep steps and sat in the bar awaiting the buffet. A few drinks later the buffet duly arrived. It was a massive box of wrapped-up portions of chips pre-salt and vinegared. They were rather good and I wondered if this was the sort of thing Dame Judi Dench, Sir Larry, Sir John, Dame Helen and co would have indulged in after their West End run came to an end?

Of course, some of you may not realise that during my mayoral year, I held the highest office in the land. Believe me. There was a very serious bunch of runners who mainly worked for the council, who included now Corfu resident Chris Hughes and now novelist Paul Wilson with John Almond, Jeff Randles and Geoff Oldfield. I'd got to know some of these guys quite well and Chris approached me to tell me they were going to run Britain's three peaks for the mayor's charity, the three peaks being Ben Nevis, Scafell Pike and Snowden. I said 'Brilliant, I'll meet you halfway.' I was shocked at what I said and Chris appeared even more incredulous. I went on to explain 'I'll meet you at the top of Scafell Pike.'

I did have some reasonable mountain walking boots and had had them for a decade or two. I pulled them out of the cupboard. They were in a lamentable, unloved, very unloved condition. What should I do? Buying new would mean 'breaking them in' and I didn't have the time. There was a proper cobblers just down Dukes Brow from where we lived. I took them and it was totally old-fashioned just as cobblers used to be. I'd never been in before. 'Hello, Mr Mayor, I'm Ernie Smith. How can I help you?' I put the uncared-for footwear on his counter. 'You've not looked after those very well, what do you want them for?' I explained. He told me to come back the same time tomorrow, which I did.

'Aha, Mr Mayor, I've done my best with these.' On the counter he placed the most magnificently transformed footwear: New soles, new heels, new laces and wonderfully dubbined, ready for action. They looked absolutely brilliant. I enquired as to how much I owed him. 'You know, if you're daft enough to go up high mountains for your charity, I'm generous enough to contribute that you will be decently booted. All the very best.' I made sure the local paper carried a little piece about this. Thank you, Ernie.

The day of our ascent duly came and these intrepid fell runners were to address the gruelling challenge they had set themselves. Twenty-six miles to run, nearly 10,000 feet to ascend. Participants usually aim to do this within twenty-four hours, thirteen hours on foot and the remainder for travelling by road, a drive of almost 500 miles (cue for a song?). Despite sustaining a time-consuming puncture between Ben Nevis and Scafell Pike, there is an excellent press picture of me in cagoule and mayoral chains with five successful fell runners. These guys performed very, very well and I was proud of them. Actually, quietly to myself, I was proud of me too – Scafell Pike in the dark is no mean feat. About eight or ten people (thanks all) joined me on the ascent of England's highest peak, led by John Ratcliffe, the borough play coordinator. After descending, we found a very welcome hot breakfast at the Little Chef near Penrith, during which I was interviewed live by Jenny Billingsley on BBC Radio Lancashire's breakfast programme. She chuckled on air at my quip about mine being the highest office in the land. People who know me won't be surprised I've used it perhaps once or twice since.

I also got to look years younger, almost instantly! Encouraged, egged on or goaded by Eric Leaver and other journalists at the local *Telegraph* I accepted the challenge of a mayor's charity public shave-off of my seventeen-year-old beard! I'd been going, along with 1985 World Snooker Champion Dennis Taylor and others, to John Slater's Hairdressers at

Bastwell for years. John and his omnipresent wife, Josie, did the deed and the Dog Inn-supping Silverline taxi driver Peter O'Hare joined me in this close shave! It was all great fun until John produced an antique cut-throat razor. Just for the press photos, he didn't assure me! Dennis and I had recently done a double act opening St Phillip's Court housing accommodation and I'd played golf with him and golf driving-range owner (and local character) Jimmy Gornall. Dennis came into John's salon just as four-year-old son Matt had had his hair cut and was waiting for me. Dennis read to Matt whilst they both waited. On leaving, I asked freshly coiffed Matt if he knew the chap who'd read to him? 'Dad, he's the best snooker player in the world!' 'How do you know?' 'He told me!'

Once the dust had settled on our mayoral year, I was approached by Councillor the Reverend Jim Watson, a United Reformed Church minister and Scout district commissioner. Jim was getting on a bit by then, in his early seventies but he had been chair of the ambivalently titled civic affairs committee. Yes, I always wondered too. Jim assumed the role of the council's sagacious elder statesman. He died in 2013 aged ninety-five.

'Bill, I wanted a word with you.' That made me feel quite worried. Jim and I couldn't be further apart, probably further than poles! He went on to say to me that he'd been cautious to the point of being apprehensive when I accepted my turn to be first citizen. I expected you to make a right pig's ear of it and I waited and watched for you to stumble, to make some horrendous gaff. To be frank, you've totally astounded me; you've done a fantastic job as incumbent in the post, you didn't put a foot wrong and translated your character, personality and family situation perfectly. All I can say to you is very, very well done.' This was indeed no faint praise from the dour cleric.

It was time to return to the ranks on the council, possibly even the back benches.

But where might I end up? I was on my fifth council leader in only ten years.

When I got on the council, the leader was Tom Ellis, a nice older guy, a Catholic who owned Gillibrands, a large vehicle body repair shop. He was superseded by Christine Ryden, perhaps a little older than me, maybe early thirties? Christine was by trade a schoolteacher and in close order she'd had four quite challenging boys. She took on the leadership, though perhaps a tricky idea with four kids. She resigned after perhaps eighteen months and was replaced by another schoolteacher, Rod Martin. Rod was a decent guy but I'm sure his life was quite complex. Rod taught in a secondary school in Mytholmroyd in Yorkshire near Hebden Bridge, about an hour's drive away. Rod would get up early, drive for an hour or more to get to school by 7.30 a.m. and then leave around 3.30 p.m., to return to the town hall for about 4.30 p.m. He tried to finish his council business by around 9.30 p.m. in the evening and got home about 11 p.m. or perhaps half past. Rod retired early from teaching, a smidge older than his mid-fifties, in the summer of 1985. This was to enable him to concentrate more on the role of council leader. Sadly and suddenly, Rod died three months later in October. He was then succeeded by Frank Higham, who had worked in retail for the Co-op in the grocery department, eventually as manager, all of his life. Frank's party piece (not the Labour Party) was his ability to add up pounds, shillings, pence and part pence (i.e. ha'pennies and farthings) as he went down columns of figures, totting them all up. So, post decimalisation, he found pounds and pennies a total doddle.

Frank must have been the leader for three, perhaps four years before retiring from that role in his early seventies. He wasn't particularly well with arthritis and lived on his own, which I think was quite difficult.

So the fifth council leader in only seven or eight years was Peter Greenwood, my ward colleague. Like many of us, Peter was a complex character, who had married quite young. With his wonderful wife, Dot, who ran sheltered accommodation for older people, he'd had three kids, again all lads. Peter had been a time-served engineer and a member of the AUEW. When I first knew him he was travelling back and forth from Ruskin College, the trade union training centre in Oxford, where he was studying. Peter was a bright and genial character with a brilliant sense of humour. By and large, we got on very well but not 100 per cent of the time. Peter was fantastic, very insightful and gregarious but not 100 per cent of the time.

Looking back, perhaps I was a problem for Peter. At the time I had no inklings or aspirations for any leadership within the group. I was quite content and most certainly had my hands full with full-time job, two young kids and a little bit of time to be a ward councillor and hold some committee chairmanship. I had also taken up the game of golf, having during my mayoral year attended a hotpot supper at the nearby Blackburn Golf Club. At the do, loads of my friends from teaching, working in industry or tradesmen were all there. I'd had a jaundiced stereotypical view of golf clubs being full of knobs. (I joined in 1990, wasn't particularly good at it, but enjoyed the first eighteen holes and the subsequent nineteenth too. This made some 'Bill time' at the weekend.) I wonder if Peter saw me as a threat and I think he thought it best to give Taylor something to do in case the Devil made work for idle hands.

So, immediately after finishing as the mayor of the borough in May 1990, I became the chairman of the urban programme committee. That's four years prior to becoming mayor as chairman of recreation/community and leisure, with a service/'doing' function and then four years after in this new, more of an enabling/facilitating role. They proved to be great groundings a) to effectively engage my existing skills and b) enabling me to accrue and improve new ones.

The urban programme (UP) was under the control of government minister Sir Michael Heseltine. Having made his fortune as a property developer and then publisher, Heseltine got elected as an MP in 1966, becoming Lord Heseltine of Thenford in 2001.

In Margaret Thatcher's Cabinet he held various offices, including environment (mainly dealing with councils and local government). 'Tarzan' also became Deputy Prime Minister, tackling issues such as urban riots in the inner cities including Liverpool. He was sometimes the darling of the Tories and sometimes a thorn in their side.

He came to Blackburn once and had a private meeting with Peter Greenwood and me at Eanam Wharf, a transformed set of buildings, part funded by urban programme, European Union money and other funding streams. Set on the tow path of the Leeds and Liverpool Canal, it housed a prestigious 'flag ship' project, a canal-side pub, restaurant, business starter units and was very close to where Thwaites' Brewery's famous and nationally renowned shire show and dray horses were stabled. Peter and I, though determined not to, both took to Heseltine, an interesting, engaging and not suffering fools gladly kind of a guy.

*   *   *

In a way, from my perspective, the urban programme was rather clever. Council rates or poll tax or council tax, whatever you want to call it, is raised locally but in no way funds all of what councils spend. These days roughly 52 per cent of councils' spending is paid by local council tax, 17 per cent via (locally levied) business rates and 31 per cent by central government. During the 'austere' 2010s, central government contribution to local councils' spending fell by 38 per cent – £10bn in real cash terms.

Central government, regardless of which party is in power, rarely actually trust councils, so they want to control local council spending. This always seemed a conundrum to me. Many MPs/ministers had cut their teeth serving as councillors in local government. Once in 'other places' they mistrusted their former colleagues almost with a passion.

So using devices, and the urban programme is only one example of many of these, central government removes, one might say starves, local councils of funds and then gives them a little bit back with strictly stipulated parameters about how it can be spent. Somewhere between clever and devious, eh?

When I became chairman of the urban programme committee, the overall council spend was around £20 million a year. On top of that and in some ways separate, was the urban programme funding, which totalled around 4 million quid.

I'd been given a considerable amount of money to spend with a heavy responsibility to spend it in conjunction with the chairs of the other major spending committees, but also to use it in the most visibly effective manner. This was music to my imaginative and creative ears.

I think, going back some years before, Roman Road Neighbourhood Centre, our first 'go' at community provision, had been partially UP funded, Waves too. Ewood and Bank Top neighbourhood centres followed. We developed a winning design and build model and community consultation process. I'm not sure of the chronological order of these buildings but soon we had them at Little Harwood, Accrington Road, Shadsworth, Sudellside in Darwen, Green Lane, Mill Hill as well. That's nine in total, well designed and built, with a lot of local resident and ward councillor involvement, well-staffed with a varying programme developed for all age groups and interests. Simply brilliant and very well received by all.

By this time Steve Jones, the chief exec, had moved on to the bigger and better post at Wigan Council, a greater Manchester Metropolitan Unitary. He was due a move and ready for bigger things. As Steve left, I, as mayor, presented him with a tray, decanter and glasses as requested, in front of the full council. He said to me in private, go back to community and leisure after this year, you were really good at it. Steve was replaced as top officer by a guy called Gerald Davies, whose background was in housing. Long gone now was the tradition that the chief executive always had a legal background, i.e. had been the borough solicitor or, at a push, the borough treasurer.

Sadly, in my opinion, another trend gained its grip around the late 1980s. Earlier many council staff mainly lived within the borough, but this became decreasingly the case. Residents of course lived here, as did their elected councillors. But many teachers and head teachers, council and voluntary sector staff and senior officers lived and travelled in fifty miles or more: Manchester, the Peak District, on and across the Pennines, into Cheshire and Merseyside, the Lakes. I didn't like it. These folk were good, hardworking, talented staff but didn't 'get the edges knocked off them' by rubbing shoulders in pubs, shops, places of worship and so on.

Not actually running a service department with its own dedicated 'officer corps', I appeared to have some up-and-coming officers allocated to me. Phil Watson, who is a Blackburn man through and through, born and bred in the town, educated in the town, went away to university in Sheffield for the five years it took to train as an architect and returned in 1968 to begin his architectural career. He'd had some considerable responsibility for the design of a number of the council estates and other schemes that were built during the 1960s and after. Phil was totally committed to his hometown and had some determined and definite ideas on how it should develop. He moved from being purely an architect into a more generalist role within the council which included overseeing the urban programme. He became assistant chief executive, then deputy and eventually the big cheese of being the chief executive where he conducted himself with vision and commitment. His 'wing man' for many years was Steve Weaver, quite a complex guy. Steve had trained as a teacher, went working at a geography fieldwork centre and then changed career to become a planning officer. Both of these guys had vision, drive and could be ruthless. Steve moved on from being purely in planning and similarly became deputy chief executive when Phil became chief executive. Later, Steve was to move on and become chief executive at Blackpool Council, another unitary with huge social challenges. Sadly, Steve died in 2014 in a mystery 'hit and run' collision with a never found motorist whilst cycling in Provence. Steve was sixty-four years old.

We became a successful team of officers and me as the lead elected member. We knew how much we had to spend, where and how we could spend it. And more creatively, how to bring additionality to that spending by matching it with other internal and external funds, such as north-west funding agencies and *euro-funding*, involved in different spheres. We always had 'ready to go' schemes 'on the shelf' as it were. If other organisations had money to spend especially towards the end of the financial year, they could always rely on us a) to spend it and b) to give them credit for our partnership arrangements. We were quite clever about what and how we did things, sometimes quietly, sometimes not so quietly.

Although frenetically busy ones, we continued to enjoy our lives as parents, husband and wife, employees, caravanners, party agent, being on the council, and as an aspirant, but non-achieving golfer.

Chapter 16

I'm the Urban Programme, Baby, 1990-94

The thought that life could be better is woven indelibly on our hearts and our brains

I recall, after the global broadcasting of some aviation near miss, the passengers complaining about not being kept informed immediately it was obvious there was some problem.

The pilot had probably worked miracles in getting the plane down from the sky with all passengers and crew safe and sound.

He told the world's press there was a three-stage procedure when faced with such circumstances, namely: 'aviate, navigate, communicate'. I can still hear his message and tone.

I think I was learning a different mantra as we developed our interaction skills with our local citizens.

To start with we had to identify our ultimate goal in the delivery of our services to our citizens. Councils, like our schools, colleges, the NHS and many others in the public sector are people-to-people organisations. They are not usually producing things to sell to customers. In fact, I feel sure that all three sectors, public, private and the third sector, have learned from each other and now have different and more effective approaches to embracing their citizens, customers or clients. Some are still left behind or catching up.

So what was our ultimate goal? The simple answer is to achieve excellence. But how do you do that? By seeking small incremental improvements. In every walk of life unless you make small improvements, you'll never reach that goal of attaining excellence. Now quite clearly that isn't easy and there will be setbacks but you mustn't let those deter you. You'll get knocked down but get up again! I've spoken here about service delivery but, before that, services have to be designed and developed. None of this is in the slightest bit easy. You'll never please all of the people all of the time.

Did Confucius say every long journey is made up of small steps of which there is always a first one? If he didn't, he should have. If he didn't, I just have!

Where do you start? That seems straightforward to me. You get your staff on board. Let's take an organisation employing 5,000 people. They will have several thousand homes to go to, with husbands, wives, partners, children, family and neighbours. They will go shopping, pick up the kids to and from school, go to places of worship, the pub, have leisure activities. These people are your very first valued ambassadors, don't forget that. This doesn't mean silence critics or stifle different ideas, not in the slightest.

Please never forget, do not ignore or overlook children and young people as a key audience and conduit into families and their opinion forming. Many of our environmental orientated campaigns were best orchestrated by getting people's children and grandchildren on our side.

Within that first ring of ambassadors include people in other allied organisations, work alongside them. Do not forget the local and 'trade' media. They will never be fully on your side, just take that as a fact of life. These days, remember social media (and sadly keyboard Braveheart warriors) too.

After that, for local councils, the ultimate target audience is your citizens. Everyone over the age of eighteen is a voter and for everyone owning property or owning a business there is a council tax (or business rate) payer. The council is the third point of this triangle. You've got to get that design, development and delivery of services as right as possible and get your message across too.

The best way to do that is to get your interaction with all these players the best it possibly can be, seeking improvement then excellence there too.

Some fashionable management gurus emphasise change management as being the key to good management but in my opinion, in this field, it's not change management that's required but change leadership.

As we went along I worked out and embraced that information is the entry level process, consulting is better and engagement the best. At least tell, better to ask, best to effectively engage.

These would differ as to the degree of impact anything you were proposing might have on those who were affected or felt affected. The first judgement call is does the change you are seeking to implement require informing, consulting or engaging with the identified target groups? Getting that judgement wrong could cause all sorts of problems. Another ICE: inform, consult, engage.

In my opinion, born from experience, the acceptable minimum is to at least inform people. Informing people must be effective, and here I borrow some of Rudyard Kipling's honest serving men – how, where and when. Ideally people should be given reasonable notice and an outline of the issue and the process.

This also applies to the intermediate level of change implementation – consulting.

The most complex level in this trinity of process methods is engaging.

Something might be quite simple. In future, junior library books will have a blue sticker on the spine. That, hopefully, is simply information giving.

Moving around, within the library, where all the books may be located on shelves, may be more complex and perhaps a reasonable level consultation would be prudent. Change is best implemented when it's in the best interests of the service recipient, not the organisation. A staff member thinking, worse saying, 'But I've always gone to my mum's for my tea at 4 p.m. on Tuesdays,' doesn't cut it!

A total restructuring of the library service: How many libraries and where might they be placed? May some have to close? Days of opening and opening times; how many books may be borrowed and for how long; the vexatious question of fines for late returns. These are all the very issues that might benefit from a full engagement process, identifying those groups or individuals who may have constructive ideas on the best way forward. Putting some people from the community in charge of the process, with certain given parameters of timescales and finance, might expedite proceedings. Management gurus have dismissed these as the 'tent pissers' or 'skunks'. I say 'three cheers' to them. They don't have 'bees in their bonnets', they have passion, as yet unchannelled!

We also put some small pockets of finance, a few thousand pounds here and there into a community chest fund that enabled small groups to access exactly the small amount of funds that would facilitate them moving along. These small groups appreciated both these helpful levels of funding and the opportunity to participate in the decisions about their allocation.

Being the chair of urban programme and working alongside Phil Watson and Steve Weaver, all the other directors and chairs of the main service committees, was thoroughly enjoyable. I learned, indeed I think we all learned, a great deal during those three or four years. I think we perhaps didn't realise how valuable all these lessons and 'match practice' gained were or how soon they'd be brought into play and on a much, much bigger pitch.

* * *

I was perpetually centrally involved in significant new bits of this ambitious council's agenda. The waterside project was a key example of this – or should I say quay? I chaired that group and was disappointed when the post office rejected my proposal to give it the postcode BB1 H2O. The Leeds and Liverpool Canal, 126 miles long and completed in 1816, which opened up Yorkshire and much of Industrial Revolution Lancashire to the west-facing port of Liverpool, had seen better days. Much of its infrastructure and the canal-side buildings were in disrepair through disuse. This gave the council the opportunity to work alongside some of our local private sector 'big hitters'. Scotsman Jim McKinstry was one of those leading lights and his charismatic leadership brought in many key local business people who turned out to be not only eager to help but bloody good at it. The mutual reticence and reluctance to work together quickly faded as we found out these people were much like ourselves, wanting Blackburn to do well. The local paper volunteered Tony Watson, their marketing manager. Graham Threlfell of Tommy Ball's shoe emporium, Peter Robinson from Barclays, Alan Caster, the shopping centre manager and his deputy John Holt, and Canon Godfrey Hirst, the cathedral's industry chaplain, were amongst those with whom we struck up good friendships based on mutual objectives and respect.

1991 saw a change in the Labour Party's constituency chairman, when John Roberts took over from Martin Guinan who in his turn had succeeded Eric Smith. I was still election agent and Phil Riley party secretary, so in those key positions the party and most especially its campaigning style were in safe hands. Things were fine in Cathedral ward as we always got to see, address and reply to residents' issues within forty-eight hours. Nothing was too small an issue. I remember taking up driving instructors and their students only using the narrow streets of our ward to practise three-point turns. We eventually got them to share these manoeuvres around the town which residents felt was a fair compromise.

Modernising and 'youth focussing' aspects of our voluntary sector was important to us, especially me as a youth and community worker. My work colleagues John Mason, Eric Grindle and others fronted this work, and they established two fantastic organisations both of which still exist today. Action Factory was a superb community-based arts project initially run by Pete Aldridge but then by Julian Dunn and later Cath Ford. It ran workshops, processions and festivals centred mainly around community art and music, giving the often unheard a voice. These events were wonderful and wonderfully received.

Nightsafe was a little later but yet another brainwave. Many young people locally, for a variety of different reasons, became homeless. That homelessness then led to confidence and relationship problems, lack of education and employment, drugs, crime and various other resultant social problems. Nightsafe might start by giving a young person someone to talk with, access to a shower, clean clothes and some food in their bellies. They would then be moved on to emergency accommodation and eventually to a more stable housing situation that in turn enabled them to re-engage with all those things most of us take for granted. Various talented people shaped and steered this high-profile, highly regarded organisation. These included Kathy now Ashworth, Linda now Sharratt and the gently indefatigable Paula Kaniuk, both now sadly taken from us. The BBC in 2019 did a Children in Need-funded transformation of an old St Silas' church hall into six self-contained flats. *DIY SOS* Nick Knowles and his purple-shirted team, an uber team of volunteer trades people and other helpers, Pudsey, ex-Rovers and Scotland Colin Hendry all got stuck alongside Jan Larkin chief executive and chair Julie now Thomas.

Along the road of establishing these two organisations that transformed people's lives, we found a star to champion them and all the things they confronted and challenged. This was in the shape, all four-foot-ten of her, of Councillor Edna Arnold. Like all the best local councillors Edna was a little eccentric and wouldn't take no for an answer, ever. Oh and by the way, she was a Conservative councillor, something that we had to keep reminding her of as she battled along as our pint-sized young person's champion. Edna, once a nursing sister, died in her early eighties in 2019. No one can find anyone who knows anyone else having two funerals! She had one in the cathedral as she had been mayor in 1994/95 and one the next day in Pleasington Priory as she had been, very quietly, a lifelong Catholic.

That these organisations are still in existence and flourishing today is to do with the sound foundations upon which they were built and the dogged commitment of everybody who has helped run them over the last twenty-five or thirty years. Thank you to you all. You changed many hundreds if not thousands of local young people's lives.

I recall there seemed to be an annual ding dong about the provision and funding of the central bonfire and firework night. Even to this day, when organised and supervised events such as these are the norm, local Conservative councillors moaned about the £500 grant given to the Lions. They still run the event today I think, or at least Norman Walker did (he sadly died quite recently), without any strapped for cash council support at all.

I continued to press for what I saw as the right way to run our schools and education service locally. Something I'd been vocal about for at least ten years back then. My belief is that there should be no faith schools but that all youngsters should go to their local community school, say from eight o'clock in the morning until 2 p.m. to receive formal education. After that, different staff, paid or voluntary, would offer sports, arts, culture, faith, you name it opportunities, leaving the evenings by and large to general youth clubs or activities for older folk. Anyone disagree? The answer here, I'm afraid, is Yes! It's often less imaginative teachers, heads and their governing bodies who see their school as exactly that, often only 9 a.m. till 4 p.m. and term time too. Schools are public buildings and community assets, they don't have to 'breathe' after the end of the school day as the bell goes.

I think my love of youth work has never really left me and is woven weft and warp through my life. I'm not even sure there are many youth work jobs any more but I did campaign to increase and improve the quality of youth work in colleges and universities in 1999 as I started my second year as national chairman of the education and training committee of the Community and Youth Workers Union. Then, fifty-four higher education institutions trained 900 yet to be qualified youth workers a year. I wonder how much the cost, financial and in other ways, to education, schools and colleges, the NHS, the police, community safety and criminal justice service, individuals, families and local communities, the nation and its young people, has been adversely affected by the defunding of this vital service?

Jack Straw, although still in opposition, was doing a fantastic job both as a constituency MP and nationally in Parliament. Since his first general election in 1979, it did look as though the quality of the opposition chosen to face him deteriorated.

From the Tory Party, Jack had faced Ian McGaw in 1979, a half-decent candidate, lawyer Graham Mather from the Institute of Directors, Westminster councillor and yet to be MEP in 1983, Anne Cheetham in 1987 and Ross Coates in 1992. From half decent, that fraction plummeted.

That really quite suited us as we had other things more local that we had to concentrate upon.

There must have been an element of paradox in our being awarded and assigning Tory Government urban programme monies. As I wrote in one of my letters to the local paper, during the first ten years of the Thatcher Government the Retail Price Index (RPI) had increased by 201 per cent but the monies allocated by her government to Blackburn Council only increased by 150 per cent. In 1989 local councils controlled 61 per cent of their spending but two short years later this had dropped dramatically to 18 per cent. Tough but we just got on with it.

Some of the higher profile schemes included:

+ Improvements to the market halls both in Blackburn and Darwen
+ Continued work that transformed the canal around Eanam Wharf with business starter units and training facilities
+ Providing childcare facilities to enable parents to seek and secure work
+ The provision and improvement of all-weather sports pitches based on local schools and community centres
+ Bringing the disused and dilapidated Queen's Park lake back into use as an urban water recreation facility
+ Voluntary organisations such as Nightsafe, Action Factory, the new women's refuge under the stewardship of Pauline Gerraghty MBE, the family support charity Home Start as well as the CAB, benefitted from monies awarded to their applications.

These economic, environmental and social projects and schemes proved very popular both in neighbourhoods and across the borough.

What wasn't too palatable came late in 1992; the Conservative Government suddenly froze large chunks of previously agreed but now withdrawn urban programme funding. At the time we were one of fifty-seven urban programme authorities. It was announced that it was likely that would be reduced to twenty-four, so less money for fewer areas.

Similar to the urban programme and running around the same time, was another government initiative, City Challenge. Twenty councils, Blackburn included, benefitted from this funding. Fifty-five councils had bid in to benefit from it, aimed at inner city areas. Around thirty-five of them failed to convince Michael Howard that their schemes were good enough during his brief twelve-month stint as Secretary of State for the Environment. (Howard had taken over from Michael Heseltine but didn't stay long before John Gummer started his five-year incumbency.)

Blackburn had a rigorous approach with a good track record and reputation with these governmental external funding regimes. We had a sound set of policies and an overall strategy when it came to this kind of spending. We wouldn't bid in for or spend this funding if it didn't match our overall plans and intentions. There was always a danger of being seduced by extra funding and embarking on a supermarket sweep approach to it. The danger there was ending up where you didn't intend or want to be. The national pot of £750 million meant £37.5 million to each successful council, spread over five years, in our case 1993-98.

Our local paper reported that the £37.5 million attracted a further £129 million of private investment to the hundred or so schemes involved. These were mainly in housing but also designed to create jobs and training and crime reduction schemes. It was estimated that unemployment in the designated zone fell by 26 per cent and reported crime by 30 per cent during the five years. We were also able to match this funding with additional European monies that enhanced spending power. Officials at regional, national and European levels liked doing business with Blackburn Council; we always had 'shovel ready' schemes on the shelf, could always spend any surplus left unspent by other councils and always gave good publicity to the way the money had been well spent.

We did very well out of EU funding. Schemes had odd names: Erasmus, Archimedes, Civitas, but they all had good intentions. A youth work colleague got drawn into this vocabulary when applying for European funding for a massive summer playscheme in their area. Calling it GOYA, the people in Brussels didn't twig that the acronym stood for 'Get Off Your Arse!'.

In my opinion, the result of the 2016 referendum was all wrong; Boris Johnson being opportunistic simply to fulfil his personal egotistical ambitions – remember the £350 million bus claim? Were you duped? People had an irrational fear stirred up about people they'd never even met. Not sure if we got Brexit done or it 'done' us!

* * *

After thirteen years Margaret Thatcher was removed by her own MPs and John Major became the Prime Minister. He called a general election in 1992 and returned a Conservative Government. The main local attraction of that general election was the continued electoral success of both Barbara Castle's and Jack's former PA Janet Anderson in Rossendale and Darwen and former Blackburn councillor Greg Pope in Hyndburn. Jack had a further five years to wait before he could join a Labour Government.

We had been rather hoping to win the 1992 General Election but it wasn't to be. Neil Kinnock had provided good leadership, determined to make Labour more electable. The high point of his campaign was the final week Sunday night rally which the national Labour Party chose to be held in Blackburn's King George's Hall. This was a huge feather in our cap and was a very good, uplifting event, but obviously it didn't swing the mood of the nation sufficiently.

A day or two before the actual event we had a final run-through preparation/briefing session. Given the high-status security risk that the event could be, nothing was left to chance. With sniffer dogs doing their job amongst the rows of seats at the sealed-down and armed police-guarding venue, the Gold Command-style meeting began. In attendance were Special Branch from both Scotland Yard and Lancashire Constabulary, high-ranking uniformed officers, the army, fire and ambulance, numerous senior officers of the council, the Labour Party press office and spin doctors from national and regional HQ. Oh, and me.

The meeting had hardly started when my brick-sized mobile phone rang. The display showed 'Home'. Anne wasn't in the habit of ringing me without any good reason and anyway it might have been one of the children. 'Please excuse me, I'll have to take this,' I told the assembled top brass.

The noise in my earpiece was high-pitched and cacophonic, I could hardly hear Anne's shrill voice over the 'background' noise. The noise was a mixture of a very, very loud shrill claxon and two screaming children. On entering our home the burglar alarm had been triggered and Anne could not deactivate it. She was obviously distressed and reasonably so. Missing out the odd and unladylike word, she tried to communicate with me that she couldn't turn the alarm off. My sangfroid response didn't help matters. 'Hello, Anne love, I'm a bit busy just now. I'm afraid you'll have to deal with this yourself,' and turned the phone off with a further torrent of abuse ringing in my ear. I knew I'd 'cop' for it later. 'Sorry,' I said, 'it's my wife asking me something, please carry on.' We did and all business was continued and concluded.

Several hours later, I returned home and to be fair, Anne had calmed down, even able to see the funny side of her version of events. Having set the alarm off and it being deactivated by a key, she had attempted to do so, unsuccessfully. It simply wouldn't turn off. Not having had any support whatsoever from me, she recalled that our next door neighbour Jim Crawley was the director of Atlas alarms, the company who had installed it. Very helpfully Jim came round immediately. Well, the whole of the street had been alerted to the alarm. Jim spotted the problem instantaneously: 'That's not the right key, Anne love.' Anne had been trying to deactivate the alarm with the key to her petrol cap for her Austin Maestro. Selecting the appropriate key instantly worked a treat!

Labour lost and it happened to be on the day before my fortieth birthday. I was hoping my family and friends might organise some form of celebration or at least commiseration.

At lunchtime my chums Jack Fairless and Joe King took me to the Corporation pub near where we lived. Aha, the beginning of my birthday celebrations, thought I. That wasn't to be. After a couple of pints and a cold meat pie with mustard, they said bye bye and went their separate ways.

Later, Janet Anderson rang me and said she and her family were going to Tiggis, a local Italian restaurant in town and would we like to join them? Aha, thought I, it's going to be a birthday meal. Anne and I walked into town, entered the restaurant and there were the Andersons sat waiting for us. So, this wasn't the big shindig either.

After a lovely meal we set off walking back up to our house again. En route Anne took me slightly off piste to the Alexandra, a large pub we didn't often go to. Twigged it. We went in and the pub was almost totally deserted; still not got it. We only stayed for one and Anne said let's get home, it wasn't too late.

The house was in darkness; this must be it, a surprise party at home. I entered the house with a mixture of anticipation and trepidation but I'd got it totally wrong. We got home, had a final glass of wine, and went to bed. Another Labour defeat one day and a miserable birthday the next. That's life, I suppose.

Chapter 17

Getting Gout and Getting On

It's really not my habit to intrude. Furthermore, I hope my meaning won't be lost or misconstrued

I was expecting the years immediately after finishing as mayor to be anticlimactic and pretty much the 'same old, same old'. The twist came unexpectedly and almost indiscernibly about four or so years later.

Son Matt had transferred to big school, starting at Pleckgate High School in 1992 and Kit was enjoying herself at Lammack Juniors. They both still thoroughly enjoyed sports and that took up a lot of their time as did the Cubs, Rainbows and Brownies. They both seemed to 'outgrow' these organisations, as many do, aged about eleven or twelve. We both had busy working lives still and looking after our two kids and ferrying them around kept us busy. The caravan still provided us with gratefully received distractions travelling around Britain and still taking three-plus weeks in France in the summer. I enjoyed the urban programme aspect of my council life.

Sadly, our much-loved family pet, almost a member of the family, Dan, the border-collie cross, had to be put down. We'd had him before we'd had kids, since 1978. That's fourteen years. He wasn't a puppy when we got him so goodness only knows how old he was, seventeen perhaps. Danny (aka Daniel Thwaites) never spent one single night in kennels and except for his three-week summer holidays to his 'grandma's', was with us all the time. We all loved him, especially the kids. But he became doubly incontinent, deaf, his eyesight was poor and he was generally unwell. I took him to the vets and that was that. I think the fact that we never had another family pet is a measure of how much we were upset by his departure.

*   *   *

Don't ever get gout. This pernicious blood-borne form of arthritis is one of the most painful things you can have. It happened to me in 1994. In the middle of one night the pain was so immense we had to call out Dr Dorothea Privonitz our GP, to administer a pain-killing injection. Colchicine, derived from the autumn crocus, got rid of the deposits of uric acid crystals initially. After that and ever since, I have taken allopurinol and have never had another attack. I would never wish gout on anyone. The only people who joke about it are those who have never had it. It set me off work and out of touch with everything for several weeks, if not months.

But it was during this protracted period of illness that things changed on the local council. Anne went shopping at our local supermarket and bumped into the other Anne, Anne Higginson, coming back with some hot and totally unexpected news. Peter Greenwood, my ward councillor colleague and leader of the council for quite a few years, had resigned as leader. At the time I knew nothing of this, what caused it to happen or what led up to it. A quarter of a century later I am still none the wiser. I have quite recently asked both senior elected members and senior council officers of that time and none of them profess to know what caused this to happen. That they don't know and/or won't say, then and now, seems very odd. However, Peter resigned and that was that.

A new leader was duly elected by the Labour Group, Malcolm Doherty, who had previous been a local government trade union official. Malcolm was a strong churchgoing Christian, very active in his local Anglican church.

Malcolm telephoned me, which was quite unusual. He rang me to see how I was and how long it might be before I was back in circulation. He told me he needed a new strong team for the challenges ahead. Would I consider standing for the post of deputy leader? He told me I had done so well in the urban programme role that many people saw this as the natural transition for me. My response was that I would consider it. But he went on, I need a strong, well-qualified and experienced person to take on the role of chair of the finance committee. He told me he had somebody in mind, somebody with an economics background at both A level and university degree standard, somebody who was good at resisting officers who tried to dominate their chair and who was good at explaining things simply to other members of the Labour Group. That person seems ideal, I responded, it looks like you found the right person. I'm glad you agree said Malcolm because I'm talking to him now. Sometime later I was elected chair of finance and deputy leader.

*   *   *

Few will have heard of or know who Sir John Banham is. He was born in 1940. He worked in the Foreign Office, moved into the private sector then moved onto the Audit Commission, the Local Government Commission and had periods as chairman of massive companies such as Whitbread, Tarmac and Kingfisher. He will, without any doubt, have made a few bob in the world. But it is his time, in the early 1990s, at the Local Government Commission that is of most local significance to the people of Blackburn and Darwen. It was at this time that it was decided to create forty-five to fifty new unitary councils. For some, U-Day would be April 1998.

I need to present another *dramatis persona* to this unravelling plot, John Selwyn Gummer. As well as being legendarily infamous for force feeding his then four-year-old daughter Cordelia a burger in 1990 during the BSE crisis, we should be indebted to him locally. He had served in Ted Heath's, Margaret Thatcher's and John Major's governments. From 1993 till 1997 he was Secretary of State for the Environment with responsibility for many things including local government. Readers should note that between 1992 and 1994 Jack Straw was the shadow environment secretary under the then Labour leader John Smith. I can hear pennies dropping and plots thickening. As most people know, politics is often the art of the possible.

Blackburn, with quite a small population of around 150,000, perhaps shouldn't really have been on the list to become a unitary. Indeed, originally the Local Government Commission had recommended no change to Lancashire. I feel sure Jack had one of his persuasive words in an ear, this time the ear belonging to John Selwyn Gummer. Job done! This drama will have to be returned to later.

There are many examples of how Jack Straw always looked out for his constituency and its people. Jack was resolutely dogged over many years about completing the M65, finally succeeding in 1997. As he was campaigning for and creating a new twenty-first century hospital now called 'Royal Blackburn' to replace the Victorian buildings of the old infirmary, Jack's critics, pot-half-empty people who have never tried or achieved anything, would immediately dismiss this as PFI (Private Finance Initiative) funded. PFIs were the only game in town at the time. It was that or nothing.

*　*　*

It felt like we were always cleverer than the Tories locally, regularly out-campaigning them either in communities or in the local media.

Ten days or so before every election, as nominations were closing, we would assemble our full team of candidates for a press call photo opp, the subsequent photograph presenting us as a team. People like teams.

I would call a press conference and normally Cassandra Murray, the local *Telegraph's* local government reporter, would turn up. Cassandra was no slouch and knew her way around local journalism and local politics. She could give as good as she got. But with me orchestrating our Labour spokespeople, she would get a cracking opportunity to listen to the things that we wanted to tell her, on the understanding she could then probe us for any weak points in our political campaign platform.

In 1994 I recall having Andy Kay (housing), Ashley Whalley (economic development), Jack Fairless (community and leisure), Gail Barton talking about infrastructure issues and Maureen Bateson on matters financial. These were members of a strong team of well-experienced councillors who knew their brief and not only knew *what* they were doing but could express, in simple, easy to understand terms the *why* as well. Cassandra, for her benefit, in a one-hour slot, got many column inches of copy. I introduced this session quoting the government auditors stating 'Blackburn Council's service delivery is well managed, complying with best practice and without any major weaknesses in economy, efficiency and effectiveness.' The same message of success was repeated in the local media, in Labour's election material and by Labour Party workers on the doorstep in all of our communities. Outgunned, outflanked and almost unfair.

So, it was 'business as usual' working as a district council with a budget perhaps of around £22 million. I'm not even sure we knew what we were letting ourselves in for in wanting to become a unitary, the spend for which could be around £140 million. This is mainly because we would be taking on the very big spend functions of education and social services amongst others. 1995/6 turned out to be our last as district council only year. 1996/7 was earmarked as consultative. 1997/8 was like a 'dry run' year, leading to U-Day, 1 April 1998 and we were off. We committed ourselves from 1995 through to 1998/99 to four years of perpetual change in a row.

We had to think of a new name for this new soon-to-be-created 'all singing, all dancing' unitary authority. We didn't fancy that approach of calling it Riverside or Four Mountains or Twin Parks, that people never really understood and it was politically prudent to incorporate Darwen somehow. But Blackburn and Darwen was a bad idea, a very, very *B.A.D.* idea. So we came up with the idea of replacing *and* by *with*, making it Blackburn with Darwen. So, the idea of BwD or 'Bee double U Dee' was born. I'm not sure who thought of it but it fitted the bill and is now seen as normal.

So, two busy jobs, two busy and energy-sapping children, now adding the duties of deputy leader to those of being a ward councillor and chair of finance, what other duties could I seek out or have bestowed upon me? My most cherished area of council activity was of course education. Education was the main 'door opener' to social mobility at individual, family and community level.

And you shouldn't need three guesses to work out who became the first shadow chairman of the education committee? With nursery, primary, secondary, and special schools we had around ninety in total. Around 1,500 teachers plus other staff were employed in these schools. The education budget was around £100 million, half of the new council's spend. I was the outgoing but still in post chair of finance and the chair of education designate. I welcomed and relished those twin challenges. I anticipated I was going to be even busier in my already busy life.

This meant, for us elected members especially, we had a lot more on our plates, and we had more plates to spin.

A great local government gauntlet had been thrown down in front of us and every one of us, not just the Labour councillors, was well up for it.

We 'seconded' two of our most talented, experienced and honorary rottweiler councillors, Gail Barton and Sue Reid, to lead and coordinate all the work that had to be done. They pulled in key officers that they respected to get on with these jobs. Phil Watson and Steve Weaver were in charge from the officer's side.

To say the response to all this from the county council, county councillors and especially Labour county councillors was hostile gets nowhere near how they felt and how they acted and that's understandable. It was clear right from the start that they would fight us tooth and nail, resist at all odds and do their damnedest not to lose not only Blackburn but also Blackpool. These two authorities by and large regularly returned Labour councillors, eroding the county's Labour seats majority and removing around 300,000-plus of the then Lancashire's 1.4 million population. The outgoing county council (my employer) were not over cooperative during the handover. At one stage they sought and gained a High Court judicial review against the government.

All this of course did not bode well for me, a lowly youth service employee of the county council's education department. A vulnerable place to be in but, as in any circumstance like this, I had to do what I thought was best. At the back of my mind, I did ponder that there may be acts or periods of retribution ahead for me.

The next problem I faced was that the remaining county council needed to restructure itself in terms of its new size and shape. If I remained in my job that was Blackburn based, that meant I would be employed by the new unitary and therefore not eligible to stand to sit on its council. In the restructuring process for the youth service I applied to be employed beyond the boundaries of BwB. This wasn't to be and I would have had to have chosen, in the interests of my family, to keep my job. This was a major impasse.

Our leader Malcolm Doherty had been a Unison full-time officer. Unison at county level were involved in the restructuring to ensure that it was fair. Quite often county Unison officers were employed in the county personnel department and they didn't always discern the difference in function. Malcolm picked up the phone and rang his former colleagues in County Hall to explain the situation. 'Listen,' he said. I overheard him talking to a Unison official ten miles away in Preston. 'Bill Taylor is a great servant to both the county council and this borough council and he needs to be out of this fix, not for his sake, but I need a damn good chair of finance and a damn good chair of education and he's the man I need.' That was more or less the end of the conversation of which I'd only heard the one side. 'That should sort it,' said Malcolm. Sometime later I received a letter confirming I was being redeployed to a post in nearby Ribble Valley. Twenty-two years, with three or four secondment years in the middle, working in Blackburn and now in 1995 I was off to the neighbouring but very rural Ribble Valley, the biggest town being Clitheroe with a population of around 13,000.

* * *

I can't enumerate how many different functions we were all performing. Take me for example: Ward councillor with all the duties appertaining to that role, constituency election agent for local and general elections, deputy leader, chair of finance and chair designate of education. Those all outside of my 'normal' family and working life. I don't expect violins to accompany my bleeding heart or self-pitying woe, this was just how it was. This is what I'd chosen for myself.

But I did wonder at times what our local opposition were doing, the Conservatives and the Liberal Democrats. Every year there is a special 'rate setting' budget full council meeting, around February/March time. But the process didn't and couldn't have only started then. How a council constructs its budget is often constrained by the rules or parameters of the government of the day. This information starts to emerge from Whitehall later in the previous year, around October or November. Once that information was provided and its clarity was often questionable, we could get to work locally shaping the budget for the following financial year.

This meant, four to six months prior, preliminary conversations with the Labour service committee members and their chairs about what their needs might be for the future year. It was normal practice, on our local council at least, to get departments to prioritise what they must have, what they might be able to see disappear and what they might like to see as growth. That would then be aggregated into the overall picture. There would then be a whole series of meetings held by the Labour members of service committees to work out what was the best way for them. Then there would be a whole load of horse trading between departments, chairs and across the council. I must have been in the finance department on an almost daily basis checking up on how things were going.

Then the chair of finance, in this case, me, would present a whole series of options to be finalised by the Labour Group, who would meet, decide its priorities, where it could and couldn't cut, where there was need for development, etc. There were two budgets to agree: revenue for the day-to-day costs, largely staffing, for the year and capital, things that needed acquiring or building; spreading that spend over two, three or many more years was prudent.

So, perhaps after four to six months hard detailed work, it would be time for the full council that was held in public.

One year (early spring 1996?) we got to this point and I moved our budget that would be submitted to full council. I prefaced my remarks at the high-powered policy and resources committee by reminding the other two parties that I had written to them in November to map out the process as it would be in front of us. We were responsibly ready but it appeared that our opposition wasn't.

It seemed to me, and I used the phrase in open debate, that the other parties had abrogated their responsibilities, not just towards the council but to their electorate too.

But that's for them to do and others to judge. It felt like we on the Labour benches took things seriously, in a professional manner. The workload of being a councillor within the comparatively limited context of a district council was nothing compared a) to that of a full unitary and b) especially during the run up and transitional period leading to that status.

Not taking their day-to-day responsibilities very assiduously seemed as bad to me as not actually standing candidates in the local elections. It was never the case, over decades, that there wasn't a Labour candidate fielded at every election and in every seat. My take on that was that not to do so was disrespectful of both the electorate and the democratic process. One of our local opposition parties was the national government of the day. Did that mean they didn't expect regular Tory voters to turn up to vote? And why was it that quite often local opposition Party A did field the candidates in a ward but not Party B and vice versa? If there hadn't been any inter-party collusion, which was repeatedly denied, it certainly looked like there had.

*   *   *

It was around this time, 1995, that the (Lord) Michael Nolan (QC) *Principles of Public Life* were published, the committee being set up by Prime Minister John Major's Government after the cash for questions affair.

The Seven Principles of Public Life are:

Selflessness Holders of public office should take decisions solely in terms of the public interest. They should not do so in order to gain financial or other material benefits for themselves, their family, or their friends.

Integrity Holders of public office should not place themselves under any financial or other obligation to outside individuals or organisations that might influence them in the performance of their official duties.

Objectivity In carrying out public business, including making public appointments, awarding contracts, or recommending individuals for rewards and benefits, holders of public office should make choices on merit.

Accountability Holders of public office are accountable for their decisions and actions to the public and must submit themselves to whatever scrutiny is appropriate to their office.

Openness Holders of public office should be as open as possible about all the decisions and actions that they take. They should give reasons for their decisions and restrict information only when the wider public interest clearly demands.

Honesty Holders of public office have a duty to declare any private interests relating to their public duties and to take steps to resolve any conflicts arising in a way that protects the public interest.

Leadership Holders of public office should promote and support these principles by leadership and example. These principles apply to all aspects of public life. The committee has set them out here for the benefit of all who serve the public in any way.

There are numerous good reference points regarding the *Nolan Principles*:

The Good Governance Institute is quite independent.

In their report they explain that the '*Nolan Principles* broke new ground when they were launched, due to their focus on behaviours and culture rather than process.'

The then chairman of the committee on standards in public life, Lord Jonathan Evans (Nolan died in 2007) marked the twenty-fifth anniversary of the *Nolan Principles* with a thoughtful blog post, in which he wrote: 'While organisations from local councils to NHS trusts and schools have published codes of conduct, the committee's reports in recent years have frequently identified weaknesses in scrutiny and insufficient education in organisations about the expected standards of behaviour. Good conduct is just as much about organisational culture as it is about formal rules and structures. Building and maintaining a strong ethical culture requires constant vigilance.'

Given subsequent and repeated events, one wonders if that vigilance was achieved and maintained.

* * *

Returning to the transformation of Blackburn with Darwen Council, the three-year endless change cycle continued. There was a great deal at stake, an awful lot to do. My continuing finance brief came with a number of shocks. In a meeting with the director of finance, a great bloke called Alan Cotton, I complained to him about the lack of detail in what happened to be the education budget. Over £100 million of expenditure confined to one side of A4. I'd had enough, I wanted more detail. Feigning mock indignation with my complaint, the director stormed out the room clutching his sheet of paper. He was back almost immediately. 'There you go, Chair,' as he always called me, with his rather nasal tones. 'That any better for you?'

The bugger had rather impishly gone to the nearest photocopier and blown the same information up from A4 to A3. We had a bloody good laugh.

But on the serious side, the education brief meant taking around ninety schools and over 1,500 teachers from the outgoing LEA. Being married to one, having worked in all of Blackburn secondary schools and a number in Lancashire and knowing many teachers as colleagues and friends both inside Blackburn and beyond, I knew that teachers individually and collectively weren't always the easiest people to get on with. I feel like it comes with the territory and the didactic processes in which they engage. They tell other people things – what to do.

We set up a whole series of different ways of consultatively creating and constructing our new education service. Even its name, education and lifelong learning, was important.

We split all the schools that we were to take responsibility for by sector. Blackburn, as well as having nursery provision within primary schools, had four stand-alone nursery schools, so I started with their heads.

These four ladies joined me in a room in the town hall along with a couple of officers. 'Before you start, Councillor Taylor, can we make it clear to you that we are not social services, we are educationalists; children are with us to learn.'

'Well, thanks for that. In fact, I wasn't going to start. I'd come here to listen to you. However, now you mention it, I don't see you as educationalists or social services. I see you as the very first economic development officers these children will see.'

I had quite a struggle with some of our head teachers but it was a struggle that had to be had and I think in the end they appreciated the rigour of it.

Mike Humphreys was a cracking bloke, another of life's characters. He was a Scouser and told me his favourite pastime was playing jazz piano sometimes in a pub or club. He was also, for fifteen years, the respected head teacher at Our Lady with Saint John Roman Catholic Secondary School in Blackburn. He retired in 2002, and attended Buckingham Palace the next year to receive his honour of being made CBE. Having been in post since the late 1980s he'd been head teacher whilst Lancashire had been the LEA. He was outspoken and well respected by his peers such that he was their spokesman as chair of the Lancashire Association of Secondary Heads, the acronym of which, LASH, always quite alarmed me. We developed a good relationship and when Prime Minister Tony Blair asked to visit Blackburn with the then education secretary David Blunkett, we approached Our Lady's to host the event.

Amidst tight security, I welcomed the PM to Blackburn and handed him on to a more than happy head teacher. Tony Blair was there for an hour, perhaps longer, and enjoyed the event. Mike was happy to share with the Prime Minister the fact that both of their wives (Cherie and Anne) had attended the same school in Crosby, near Liverpool, Seafield Convent Grammar.

When I heard Mike was retiring, I popped up to the school. He welcomed me and over a cup of tea we chatted. Mike told me that when it was mooted then confirmed that BwD was going to become the LEA he was totally opposed to it and after the transition did his damnedest to impede our progress. He said he'd be damned if a middle-ranking youth work manager was going tell him and his colleagues what to do (did he know we'd developed ground-breaking school-leaver work twenty-five years earlier in my work with diocesan officer Bob Beardsworth when the school was known as John Rigby?). But he went on that after a while he realised I was serious about this and determined to make improvements and it became an infectious educational atmosphere. He said he couldn't resist and joined in and he wanted me to know that the last five or so years of his career had been the most enjoyable, creative, productive and fun. On departing, we shook hands, enemies turned allies with the fullest of respect for one another.

Wandering down to the town hall one teatime I noticed some unattributed smoke wafting over a car park parapet and then a female voice presumably talking to others stating 'If fucking Taylor consults us any more, I'll go daft. Why the fuck does he not just get on with it?' Turning the corner I found two of our primary head teachers having a fag and a good moan. 'Good evening, ladies, I will do then. I'll just get on with things.'

We had various forums in education. Councillor Mary Leaver was the mayor of the borough in 1996/7, the last full-term first citizen for the old borough council. She was in her mid/late sixties. Mary had seven children and eleven grandchildren and had served on the council for around ten years. Her consort was son-in-law and *Emmerdale Farm*, *Coronation Street* and *Heartbeat* actor Keith Ladd. We called him 'Hey Up'! She was very much 'old school' having worked in cotton mills during her working life. She attended one of our primary education forums during her mayoral year unannounced, I believe. The youngsters already in the council chamber had turned to discipline in schools as the topic for discussion. Mary indicated she wished to intercede, and with a wink and the glint in her eye, she explained to the children that during her childhood it was quite normal to get caned for even the most minor misdemeanour. I'm not sure what astounded these children most, that children had got caned for the slightest breach of discipline, or that the mayor of the borough, chains and all, in the council chamber, had admitted that she'd been the victim of corporal punishment!

As an interim 'minder', we'd taken on Gordon Hainsworth, a former chief education officer and chief executive officer, to advise us. Gordon was brilliant. I think we could describe him as a character and we got on well. He helped me assemble my senior management team. We appointed Mark Pattison as director of education with three fantastic and able assistants Jill Baker, Peter Morgan and Steve Munby. These people had, by and large, been more junior officers in larger authorities and were wanting to spread their wings. We wanted great talent and it was likely that people like these four would be with us for a handful of years and then move on to bigger and better things, which is exactly what happened. Whilst they were with us, they made a great difference.

We had regular scheduled member/officer meetings, me, Mark and his team and my deputies, who included Kathy now Stephenson, later a senior lecturer in education at Sheffield Hallam University and Simon Danczuk, who, amongst other things, went on to serve as the MP for Rochdale from 2010 to 2017, and Mike Johnson, who taught at Blackburn College but is now sadly no longer with us. Topics ranged from the mundane but necessary to the imaginative and creative.

We had major concerns about the quality of our schools and from memory I believe fifteen of our schools were in special measures or serious weaknesses, the bottom two of Ofsted's inspected performance classifications. This meant that 20 per cent of our youngsters had a cruddy start in life. How a society views and treats its young people is a reasonable barometer of its social responsibility. We were determined to combat this and saw it as our first priority.

The outgoing LEA had teams of schools' advisers, which seemed a rather limp-wristed title to us. We decided to call our equivalent team school improvement officers; it had more of a cutting edge to it. At one of our meetings I asked how many we could afford and was told five. I then asked how many we needed and was told six. So six it was and we appointed a fantastic team, who I called my zealots, later under the leadership of Ian Kendrick. These folk were hardened professionals, mostly former head teachers. They were scary. They did the job. No stone was ever left unturned, no difficult question remained unasked, every bit of evidence required was sought. After the school had received the best attentions of their designated SIO, a very full report, warts and all, was submitted to the school improvement committee who would decide what was needed. It was really quite brutal but needs must.

As is often the case in matters like this, those involved and often others, knew things weren't right but often needed an objective hook to hang these subjective instinctive feelings on and the chutzpah, the determination to face up to them to a final resolution. These processes didn't come without their initial growing pains and hurt but we acted with determination and things got better including for those who had been struggling without any critical support.

* * *

I think there were about fifteen councils identified as going to become unitaries at the same time as us, April 1998. Nearby these included Blackpool and Warrington. As chairman designate of our education committee I wrote to all my fellow soon-to-be's, with a short bullet-pointed report on what we were up to and things we were strong at or could do with some help with. This candour seemed well received and some decent dialogues ensued.

Chapter 18

'A Northern Horde of Uncouth Garb and Strange Oaths' –
Home to 4,000 Holes

The stadium was old

As a teenager in Birmingham, one Saturday I'd take the number 11 bus to Villa Park and the next Saturday the number 53 to Saint Andrew's. Coming from Leeds, I didn't particularly support either Villa or the Blues but just liked attending football matches for the theatre and drama of it all.

Getting to West Brom's ground, the Hawthorns, involved crossing the city on at least two buses. West Brom were also known as the Baggies or the Throstles? I once went with my mum; yes, I know, embarrassing. She worked in a store in the centre of town called C&As, mainly clothing, I think. Her work pal was a Mrs Potter. Mrs Potter was married to Mr Potter. Mr Potter was better known as Ray Potter, the Baggies goalie in the fifties and sixties (217 appearances). One Saturday home game, adolescent Bill had to accompany his forty-ish-year-old mum to the match. Why? So she could stand behind the home team warm-up end, right behind the goal. Why? Ray didn't know my mum from Adam (or Eve). As Ray trotted out he was greeted by 'Co-ee, Ray, Co-ee'. Embarrassing or what? Decades later it did make me ponder the likelihood of Mrs Beckham, Rooney or Vardy working in a department store for a pittance?

Later I took another trip to the Hawthorns with the sole purpose of seeing the young George Best play. A momentous and mesmeric experience.

On another occasion, in my later teenage years, I quit the ground early to beat the crowds. I noticed something under the feet of the scurrying spectators. It was a pound note. Who amongst the thousands on the ground could it belong to? I got home a few hours later. With a pint only costing a few pennies then, I wasn't in tip-top condition. I got a right rocket off my not-too-impressed mother!

Add to that taking the number 11 bus to watch (and painstakingly annotate in my Acme score book) a full day's county cricket at Edgbaston, Warwickshire's ground. There was a great Pakistan test cricketer Khalid Ibadulla, who played for them for nearly twenty years from 1954. I winced even back then as Brummies decided they couldn't say Khalid. Calling him Billy had to do! What must his German-born wife, Gertrude, have thought of this linguistic impasse?

And again using the number 11 bus, back in the days when top rugby union was an amateur game, I went to watch Moseley RUFC, including internationals, who played (but now no longer) at Reddings Lane. I recall attending a packed ground when Moseley hosted the top Argentinian club team, Belgrano, probably in the late 1960s.

There was also a banked cycle track and an athletics stadium, both somewhere near Villa Park, yes, on the number 11 bus route. I saw Olympic cyclist Trevor Bull, a former pupil from our school, race there and the nearby athletics track was home to Birchfield Harriers, a great and successful club.

*   *   *

I must've started going to Ewood Park, home of Blackburn Rovers, in my bachelor days of the mid-seventies and alone. I had neither a routine nor any rituals, so had to create my own. Football goers will understand: a set time to set off, 'your' route to the ground including customary route 'shimmies', 'your' place to park, a pint before the game or not (I tend not to), 'your' turnstile, 'your spot' to stand, yes, stand, to watch the game, have 'your' view of the game, who played well, who was a tosser, opinions on the officials, the manager's team selection and tactics, etc, etc. Almost by osmosis, a collective analytical opinion of the game emerges, mostly totally untutored. But no one cares!

Then a post-match post-mortem over a pint in a pub, the win or the loss tending to shape the mood of the assembled self-appointed and opinionated 'pundits'. All that settled, it was time to go home perhaps with a bag of fish and chips and to get ready for a few more pints in a few more pubs. Job done.

In 1975 Rovers gained promotion from the then third division into the second. These terms are long gone but still used in secret by the nostalgic cognoscenti. What a night of celebration that was! After our traditional, very blokish wander around Blackburn town centre pubs in an area known as the Barbary Coast, we ended up in the local nightclub known then as the Cavendish. But so did the team; all the players. Also playing that night were Gerry Marsden and his Pacemakers. Goodness only knows how many times 'You'll Never Walk Alone' was played. Who cares? Rovers midfielder and Ewood legend and servant Tony Parkes and I were embraced, our arms intertwined, singing our hearts and throats out!

*　　*　　*

Please don't think this chapter is about football or sport intrinsically! It's about the people that embrace sport within their family lives and routines.

I've loved, in a very absorbed way, Botham, Willis or Stokes and Leach tenaciously turning a definite test cricket defeat to a victory, especially if it's against the Aussies. I'm still not really over Sunderland beating Leeds in the 1973 Cup Final. I'm still relieved that Wakefield's man of the match Don Fox missed the last-minute, under the posts kick at the 1968 'water splash' Rugby League Cup Final that Leeds won 11-10.

I know not if or why Clough, Wenger, Sir Alex, Pep, whoever, is the best football manager or what it takes. I've been blessed to see the skill, determination and luck of Best, the Charltons, Hunter, Francis, Banks, Shilton, Dalglish, Shearer, Gascoigne, Beckham and the Nevilles. As to who is/was the best is, in my opinion (such as it is) in the subjective eye of the beholder.

The nuances of team selection or tactics go straight over my head. I don't understand or often recognise 5-4-1, 4-3-3, 3-4-2-1, 3-4-1-2 as formations or variants thereof. I rarely see players swapping wings, dropping into midfield, creating an offside trap. I'm not there for that. I'm there to be with my family, benefit from the collective therapeutic experience of sitting with 10,000-20,000, 90,000 others at Ewood, Wembley, Cleethorpes, Burslem, Anfield, Celtic Park, wherever.

*   *   *

Then I started seeing Anne who happened to rent a terraced house in Mill Hill less than a ten-minute walk to the ground. That meant new routines and rituals. The post-match verdict was discussed and agreed after a walk along the Leeds-Liverpool Canal towpath back to the aptly named Navigation pub. That meant new people to agree or fall out with over the observation and opinion of exactly the same match we'd all watched collectively. But hey ho, that's what it's all about! Don't let any factual reality get in the way of a spot of light-hearted banter!

We chose not to stand on a terrace but to sit in a stand; this apparent contradiction confused me as a boy! We sat in the Riverside stand, so called as it backed onto the river. In this case the River Darwen. When son, Matthew, started to accompany his dad, I tried to convince him that it was the same river that circumnavigated every football ground we visited.

Anyway, Anne and I grew accustomed to the Riverside as our vantage point and to this day, approaching forty-five years later, it is where she, our son and his son, Joshua, still sit, just above the O in ROVERS, picked out in white seats amongst all the other blue seats. The wooden benches are long gone and the stadium, thanks to our much-loved homegrown benefactor, steel magnet Jack Walker is now all-seater. It holds 31,000 spectators but rarely does these days, more like 10 to 12,000.

It must've been 1979 or 1980 when we had to induct someone new into the Masonic-like rituals of match day, the prospective parliamentary candidate/new MP Jack Straw. I don't think football had been part of Jack's growing up but he rightly sensed that the club and match day in particular were inextricably woven into the fabric of a cotton town, indeed the club's blue and white colours are cotton trade related. We took him to quite a few games where he learned people did quite openly question the sexual practices of the referee and the parentage of some opposition players. To this day, Jack, and fair play to him no longer our MP, does try and get to matches when he can be seen sitting in the home supporters' main stand, the Blackburn end, aka the Ronnie Clayton Stand, as he has for approaching forty years or so! There's even a Jack Straw trademark chant, pretty derogatory about our nearby local rivals, Burnley. The chant goes 'Burnley fans eat bananas with their feet'. Well done, Jack.

*   *   *

Back in 1966 England, of course, won the World Cup at Wembley but it wasn't a good year for Blackburn Rovers who left the top-flight of English football never to return for decades, even on occasions dropping into the third tier, still known then as the Third Division.

They, and I still didn't think of them as we, climbed out of the third tier in 1975 after which Parksie and I had celebrated in the nightclub. They spent one more season down there then settled in the Second Division for the next dozen or so years of the 1980s and early 1990s. I think it was the late 1970s that Rovers became 'us' with Anne and I being regular home supporters sitting in the wooden seats on the Riverside.

There was one frisson of success in 1987 when Rovers went to Wembley and won the short-lived Full (or Associate) Members Cup, where a measly 40,000 saw First Division Charlton beaten 1-0. The Rovers team was almost completely English with two Scottish players making up the XI.

Soon after there was a civic reception held in the town hall to which I took my neighbour and pal Bill Robertson. The main photo with Mayor Mike Madigan with the trophy, the chairman, manager and captain included me who performed possibly the first recorded photo bomb, bobbing up as flashguns popped! A lot of wine was served in the reception that night. Bill got in a spot (a lot) of bother with his wife, Sue. He'd only been allowed to accompany me, we both enjoyed a beer or six, on the promise he'd return with some fish and chips for her. Being a steady cove and man of his word, he duly bought her supper, returning dutifully home with it. Sadly, the package went astray, presumably en route from the chippy. Sue unluckily for the still asleep Bill, found it early the next morning as she set off to work. She stood in the stone-cold offering which Bill had momentarily positioned on the front doorstep as he'd searched and found his keys and entered the house.

*   *   *

The Rovers' board back then comprised of successful self-made local businessmen. David Brown of wallpaper company Graham and Brown, Terry Ibbotson a local solicitor, Rob Coar (director of local building firm Caton and Duckworth), wholesale greengrocer Bill Fox, Dr Milton Jefferies, manufacturer Iain Stanners, George Root and art dealer Keith Lee.

In 1989/90 I became the mayor. These days most things are only transacted financially; people know the price of things but not always their value. Back then the council had its own horticultural nursery with vast greenhouses, etc., in Witton Park. The Rovers had the most wonderful boardroom under the main stand known as the Nuttall Street stand, because it stood on Nuttall Street! This oak-panelled luxurious room, before and after the match and at half-time, hosted VIPs who enjoyed cups of tea from highly polished samovars that washed down the most plentiful and succulent meat pies probably obtained just across the main road at the local Leavers bakery. The borough provided and created the most wonderful, elaborate and sweet-smelling floral displays that adorned the boardroom on match days. The mayor got two seats in the directors' box for every match by way of a quid(less) pro quo!

Eight-year-old Matthew Taylor got a whiff of this largesse and put a marker down to benefit from it. Pulling very thin wool over his mum's eyes, he told her 'Our Katherine, aged only four, is probably too young to attend and appreciate a match, so I'd better go.'

This meant a different routine and different rituals and Matthew Taylor, combing his gelled hair 'sticky-up' fashion, acquired a pair of long pants, a couple of decent shirts, a blue sweater and blue tie. To be truthful, he scrubbed up well, quite a Bobby Dazzler! He also had little shame and would quite happily wander around the boardroom at half-time and chat to the great and the good. Kenny Dalglish comes to mind, before he became the club manager. Matt used to chat regularly with home-grown club legend and England international Brian Douglas (then in his mid-fifties) who would give the little boy his scratch cards to see if there were any winnings. I never asked what happened if there was!

So the 1989/90 season meant that Graham Brunton, the mayor's officer, would collect us in the car and take us down to the ground. This isn't the large and lavish stadium that people are accustomed to these days; the stands were wooden and there was almost no car parking. Most spectators travelled to and from the game in fleets of double-decker buses, dozens of them, that worked rather well. There was a very small car park behind the main stand, probably the footprint of two terraced houses that appeared to have been demolished. This was supervised on match days by a smashing old chap, whose name I think was Alan. Graham had negotiated that we would arrive just before kick-off and depart quite quickly after the final whistle. Alan made it his business to shuffle the cars up a little so there was just enough space for the mayoral vehicle which appeared and disappeared before most people could spot it.

One day Alan seemed a little preoccupied. I always spent five minutes chatting with him. 'Mr Mayor, I'm eighty on the day of the next home match and they told me I've got to finish. It's a bit sad really.' It was.

At the next home game I arrived and approached Alan presenting him with four cans of beer and a borough crested tie. This brought tears to Alan's eyes and then mine. 'Thank you so much, Mr Mayor, this is the nicest present I've ever had.' It never ceases to surprise me that small gestures can mean so much to people.

At every home game I invited the mayor of the borough of the away team to attend, putting our Matthew's company in jeopardy. I thought it was a small way of building bridges between clubs, teams, supporters and communities. I think two mayors took up my offer. I recall attending away games at Leeds and Port Vale by way of reciprocity.

At the end of that mayoral year, Matt asked if we could become pukka season ticket holders, which we did. When our Katherine was old enough to speak up for herself, i.e. quite soon, she demanded equal rights with her big brother. That immediately meant Mum quite reasonably wanted a season ticket too. So, from quite early in the nineties Dad, Mum, son and daughter attended all home and quite a few away games until Kit started her own family, twenty-five or more years perhaps?

The walk to the ground was in fact a fortnightly family catch-up opportunity. Mum annotated the match day programme (weather conditions, ends chosen, teams, substitutions) and supervised the distribution of the two quarter (lbs) of Everton Mints, blackcurrant and liquorice, Chocolate Limes or Chocolate Eclairs chosen with great deliberation at one of the three corner sweet shops that used to be along the route to the ground. To make this transaction go more smoothly, the confection proprietor usually had pre-weighed 1/4s pre-bagged at the top of the glass jars of sweets on the shelves. My job was to make the flask of hot chocolate. Hot chocolate as the compromise beverage – not tea, not coffee. Then the pre-match chat with your stadium 'mates', names never known, but who's fealty was by dint of their seating proximity. The Wag in the crowd and the Dick!

Back to the pub. The outrage of someone sitting in your place, yours because once a fortnight you occupied it for an hour! Phil Riley's one-word summary of the match: Marvellous, Mesmeric, Atrocious, Appalling would always be both accurate and succinct. Then home.

*   *   *

Rovers were mediocre until Jack Walker (the crowd still chant there's only one, he died in 2000), a self-made multi-millionaire steel magnet took the club over in 1991. Uncle Jack rebuilt the stadium costing some £20 million and in October 1991 brought the legendary Kenneth Mathieson Dalglish to the club as manager. Rovers were still in the then Second Division. Jack told Granada TV 'I'm only interested in putting Rovers where they should be. Blackburn Rovers is one of the greatest football teams in England. They are one of the founder members and we want them right back on top.' Over the next three years £25 million were spent on transfers in, including record signing Alan Shearer for £3.5 million and again record-breaking signing Chris Sutton for £5 million. With Walker's money Dalglish built a marvellous team. See *The Club that Jack Built*, Charles Lambert, ISBN-101903854032, 10th Aug 2001.

Matt and I saw both legs of the Second Division play-off semi-final versus Derby County. The final end of the 1991/2 season saw all four us at Wembley in the Second Division play-off final versus Leicester City, sat alongside the Carr family of Jim, Pauline, Matthew and Paul. Rovers won 1-0. Late in the first half, David Speedie was brought down and Mike Newell scored from a penalty spot. Job done. The Rovers team included: Bobby Mimms, David May, Alan Wright, Gordon Cowans, Kevin Moran, Colin Hendry, David Speedie, Chris Price, Mark Atkins, Mike Newell and Scott Sellars.

That close victory saw Rovers, although finishing only sixth in the division, join the new inaugural elite of the Premier League.

*　*　*

The football season 1994/5 was massive for Blackburn Rovers, our town and communities, the council and us as a family. Being pipped to the title by Manchester United in the previous season Walker, Dalglish, assistant Ray Harford and the team were determined to win the championship.

The final game in which we had to do better than the nearest challengers, once again Manchester United, was to be at Liverpool's ground, Anfield.

This would be an all-ticket match for Rovers' supporters who were given the opposite end to the Kop. We had to queue at Ewood Park to get the tickets and I arranged that we would meet Jim and Pauline Carr around 6.30 a.m. to join the queue. Matt couldn't stand it, didn't sleep and had us up and out of the house by 5 a.m. The queues were already massive with the ticket office not due to open until 9 a.m. I believe. It was very cold and the snake-like queue very anxious. The Carrs arrived and I offered to join them further back in the queue but they declined the offer.

Eventually the office opened about five kiosks and the anxiety heightened. I approached our allocated kiosk and got the four tickets we required. Almost immediately the tickets were sold out.

That was a relief but the next few pre-match days were tense, very tense.

The Sunday of the game came, none of us had really slept too well. We set off for Liverpool stopping halfway to have some pub grub. None of us really felt like eating. We parked up and walked through Stanley Park bumping into Phil Riley and partner Ann Parker on the way.

We got to the ground and got to our seats right behind the goal. I was equipped with my quite pricey Panasonic Lumix compact SLR camera and a small pocket radio. The game commenced. I don't really remember too much about it. Manchester United were away to West Ham.

To remind readers of the Rovers' team that day: Flowers, Kenna, Berg, Pearce, Hendry(the only Wembley 1992 survivor), Le Saux, Ripley, Batty, Sherwood, Sutton and Shearer.

My intention was to watch the match in front of me but, at the same time, listen on my headphones to the game at Upton Park. My fellow Rovers fans around me had a different role for me, their constant public address update system. 'What's happening? What's the score? How long's left?' My 'Quiet, I'll let you know. I'm concentrating', soon became 'For fuck's sake (with apologies to our nine-year-old daughter), shut up. I'll tell you if anything happens!'

In the twentieth minute Shearer scores and at half-time it's 0-1. West Ham are 1 up at half-time. Going well! But then Manchester equalise. 'Are you sure?' I was asked repeatedly. 'Of course, I'm fucking sure! Leave me be!'

Sixty-fourth minute Liverpool equalise, then take the lead in what was the last minute. Ten yards away, our goalie, Tim Flowers, shouts at me asking the score in London. I say I think things are OK. As long as the Manks don't win, we'll be OK.

Then the BBC commentator at West Ham tells me that 'That's the final whistle here. Blackburn Rovers are the champions!'

I can't believe my ears! I shout out 'We are the champions!' My neighbours ask if I'm sure! 'Of course I'm fucking sure!' I'm hugged and kissed by all and sundry as though the result was my achievement. The Kop at the opposite end of the ground resounded with chants of 'Champions'. As long as the Manks didn't win!

I jumped up in delight, catching my (not cheap) Panasonic camera on the seat in front and broke the lens! Who cares? Rovers had eighty-nine points, Manchester United eighty-eight. We **were** the champions!

Elation wasn't the word about how we all felt as we made it back to the car. Champions! Champions! It didn't really sink in! It felt like years of purgatory were being repaid – BIG style.

We got totally lost on the drive back. I couldn't tell you where (because we were lost) but we eventually found ourselves coming off the M6 and heading along Preston New Road just like I'd seen the 1928 FA Cup-winning team do in stuttering black and white Pathé newsreel images some years before at Peter Worden's house.

But what a reception there was for us, like we were the returning conquering heroes. For hundreds of yards the pavements were thronged with flag-waving, hooter-hooting, cheering, proud Blackburn Rovers fans. We were the champions!

We parked up. 'Let's get to the pub.' So off we all went to the Dog Inn, my regular local 200 yards away. The pub was cram packed and operating a one-way system.

To get a drink you went into the pub by the front door, bought what you wanted then left by the rear door to stand outside in the car park. No one cared. We were the champions! There must've been some beer supped that evening. Blackburn is topographically a natural bowl and the cheering resonated around our proud little town. We found Jim and Pauline Carr and they joined us in a celebratory bottle of bubbles at our house; although we'd probably had quite enough to drink for one evening, probably several evenings.

I'd had the foresight to take the next day off from work, not knowing how I was going to feel or what I was going to do. BBC Radio Lancashire only had one phone-in topic for discussion that morning. Behind the Blackburn end of the ground there was a, no longer there, factory with a very tall chimney. Some guys had scaled the chimney and were painting vertically down it the word 'Champions!' People didn't know what to do, where to congregate. Some in the main town square, some down at Ewood Park.

Someone from the council's chief executive's office contacted me telling me I was invited as a guest of the club to the celebrations to be held that evening. Ewood Park was to be opened to allow 31,000 fans to witness the parading of the trophy around the ground. Mine was a VIP invite.

I entered the directors' entrance in the main stand and was thrust amongst many footballing and local dignitaries and the atmosphere was totally electric. People milled ecstatically around the communal hospitality areas. I bumped into Sue Bell, wife of Norman Bell (ex-Blackburn Rovers) and their two boys, Norman and Andrew. Then we noticed we were stood directly in front of the Premiership Trophy sat on a table in front of us. Spotting my camera Sue asked me to take a picture of the two lads with the trophy, which I did. I had no idea if my camera would work, it having had the lens end disconnected the day before.

Then I said, 'Right, Sue, your turn, take one of me please with the trophy.'

Sue began to protest that she didn't know anything about posh cameras or taking photos. But this wasn't the time to make limp excuses or for me to be polite.

It wasn't a straightforward camera but I said 'Sue, don't bugger about, point the bloody thing and press the button.' I handed her the camera.

I lifted the trophy and told Sue to press the button. But just as I did, an older male voice from behind me said 'Excuse me, mate, do you mind if I come in your photo?' Looking round it was none other than the club's multi-millionaire benefactor and hero Jack Walker. Who was I to say no!

We lifted the trophy between us, arms around each other and I told Sue to snap away, not knowing if her efforts were going to be successful or not. We'd have to wait and see. We then regrouped as a family and made our way home.

The next morning I was up bright and breezy and quickly got to the nearest and fastest photo development shop. I ordered the express service and slightly larger prints that would be ready in the afternoon. I could hardly wait.

I anxiously went down to the shop and the results were absolutely fantastic: Jack Walker and I holding the Premiership trophy between us, arms around each other with big beaming grins. I ordered larger prints and a T-shirt emblazoned with the photograph and the words 'We are' above it and 'the Champions' below. I think I wore it for most of that summer. I think, outside of family photos, it's my proudest impromptu, momentous, might not even work photo ever! Thank you, Sue.

Outside of our support of the Rovers, at the family level, after years and years of watching from the touchline, along with other multifarious duties, it was great to see the smiles of success on Matt and his mates and Katherine and hers. Matt's team Revidge Youth won the under-16s Stanley Cup at Great Harwood FC. Kit had to wait a little longer, into her mid-twenties perhaps, to win her Caley Cup Final with Witton Warriors hockey team at Stanley Park in Blackpool. Decades of striving, great lasting comradeships made, thousands of pounds raised, miles travelled and sets of kit washed for a few sweet and cherished moments of victory. Kipling's twin imposters are bittersweet bed fellows.

*   *   *

So, nightclub camaraderie, the Full Members Cup and allowing Jack Walker onto my photo opportunity with the much-coveted Premiership trophy witnessed highlights that brought us to be playing in the top flight and in the European Champions League, albeit very, very fleetingly!

For the next twenty or thirty years we have bobbed up and down between the top two flights, now known as the Premiership and the Championship. We endured the ignominy of two short spells in the third tier, now known as League 1!

Other than these promotions, our only other success came in 2002, when we beat Spurs 2-1 in the League Cup Final, Matt Jansen and Andy Cole scoring for us.

Our attendance in 2002 was an unbelievable experience, probably unrepeatable. Of course, we all wanted to go to the match.

Rovers had done very well to reach the final, of what I still call the League Cup, playing Spurs, to be staged at the Millennium Stadium, Cardiff, as Wembley was still being remodelled. The club very kindly invited the mayor John Williams and his wife, Sheila, Phil with his wife, Shirley Watson and Anne and me to attend as their guests. But it just got better as the club's benefactor Jack Walker had owned an airline, based as he had been on the Channel Island of Jersey, later to become Flybe. This charter flight took the players, officials and others to and from the game in Cardiff via Blackpool Airport.

It was actually very exciting. The day started early and Phil had arranged, at our own personal cost, a car to collect and take us to Blackpool. We landed at Cardiff, where we were collected by coach and taken to a hotel in the city for a bite to eat. I presume that the players and coaching staff under manager Graeme Souness were elsewhere preparing and discussing tactics for the game. We made our way on foot to the stadium and took our seats. The game entertained a 72,000 crowd.

The team that day was: Friedel, Martin Taylor, Berg, Johannson, Bjornebye, Gillespie, Mark Hughes, Dunn, Duff, Cole, Matt Jansen.

When the former Manchester United and England footballer Andy Cole scored Rovers' winner in the sixty-eighth minute, the rest of the game seemed to take forever but as the final whistle sounded, we had won the Cup.

With the trophy presented and paraded around the stadium, we made our way back to the same hotel. This time we were joined by the players, their families and the team management, led by the manager Graham Souness, jubilant with their success. There was quite a lot to drink. Uncharacteristically Anne plucked up sufficient courage to circulate amongst the players getting their autographs – 'for the kids'!

After a great celebratory event, coaches came to take us back to the airport. The atmosphere was boisterous on the plane, a few more corks popped and some of the effervescing liquid filled the cup, which made its way down the aircraft and eventually arrived with me. There wasn't much champagne left in the trophy and I didn't really know what to do about being its temporary guardian. It sat with me, on the adjacent empty seat for the duration of the flight all the way back to Lancashire. We got home in good time. Happy days.

We were home by mid-evening but Matt, Katherine and their pals Keith Frankish and Si Harrison had travelled in Anne's Peugeot 106 in horrendous traffic jams, not returning until the wee small hours. I'm not sure that all those autographs compensated them for the peach of the day that we had had, compared to their onerous marathon.

* * *

Sadly 'Uncle' Jack wasn't in Wales to witness this cup victory as he had died in 2000 aged seventy-one. His nine-year 'reign' made him respected and revered within the club, the team and the town. I was surprised how much his passing had an upsetting impact our 'kids', then aged nineteen and fifteen. They went with their mum and a bunch of flowers down to the ground where at least hundreds if not thousands of subdued mourners congregated to pay homage and their last respects. This was the club that Jack built. The only town team to win the Premier League in its thirty-year existence.

Since Souness's departure to Newcastle in 2004, Rovers has had fifteen or so different managers, some very short-lived and ill fated. In 2009 Indian entrepreneurs the Rao family also known as the Venkys bought Rovers for a reported £43m. The purchase very much divided fans' opinions. The club gained promotion back into the Championship, previously the Second Division in 2018 having spent a season in the next league down. I was central in trying to broker a rapprochement between the fans and the club but those are stories for another time.

A 'northern horde of uncouth garb and strange oaths' was how the *Pall Mall Gazette* described the Rovers' fans arrival in London for the 1884 FA Cup. Rovers defeated the Scottish team, Queens Park (don't ask me) 2-1 in front of a crowd of 12,000 at Kennington Oval.

Some eighty years later, on the Beatles LP, 'Sergeant Pepper's Lonely Hearts Club Band', in the concluding song 'A Day in the Life' they sang:

'I read the news today, oh boy
Four thousand holes in Blackburn, Lancashire
And though the holes were rather small
They had to count them all
Now they know how many holes it takes to fill the Albert Hall
I'd love to turn you on'

My now departed journalist acquaintance Ron Kennedy, often seen reporting matches from the press box at Ewood Park, spotted the Holes story in the then *Lancashire Evening Telegraph*. It emanated from a report by the council that there were 4,000 identified potholes in the borough's roads. *4,000 Holes* is the title of the supporters' fanzine.

I quite like the serendipity of these Rovers' related legendary stories. There are many, many more. Everyone will have their own stories, their own routines, rituals and recollections.

It's not about sport or football. It's about people, families, communities, being together, striving, laughing and crying, failing and succeeding.

Matt and I, when he was mid-primary school age, went to watch Rovers play at Anfield. 'Dad, can we go through those (Shankly) gates?' Yes. 'Dad, please can we hold hands as we do?' Yes. As we did so, he said 'Dad, we'll never walk alone.'

Cherished, if some enigmatic, memories.

Toddler Taylor in Scotland. My mum (aged 28), Auntie Betty's son Drew (?), Auntie Betty (Lewis, mum's cousin) and Gran-Gran (aged 66) in front of the Forth Bridge.

Me, on my trike, with my rabbit on Tinshill estate, Leeds. 1953/4 (?).

On a beach, wrapped up! Probably Bridlington.

Outside 563 Bordesley Green East, Birmingham.

NALGO holiday camp, Croyde Bay. Outside chalet in fancy dress – as a knight!

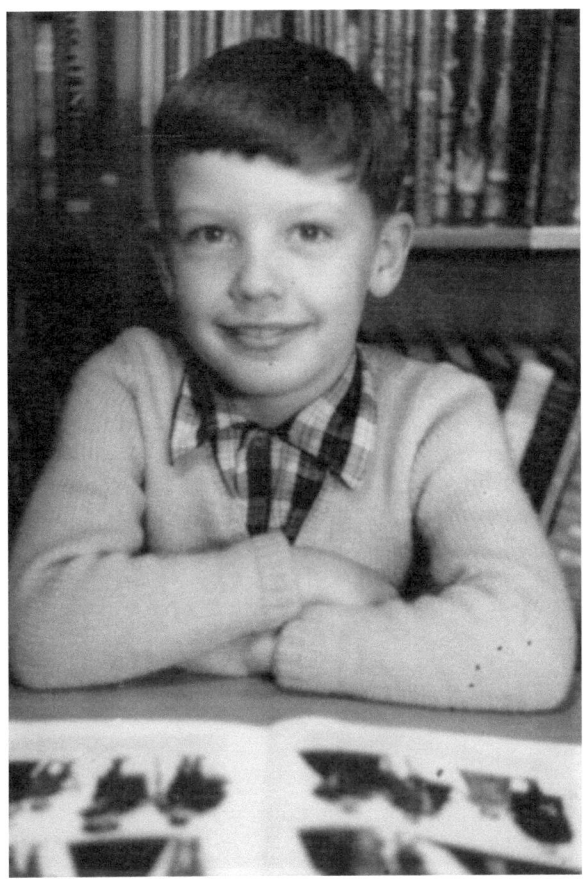

At Church Road/ Yardley Primary, in the school library. I went to the council library, 10 minutes' walk away – three books, twice a week.

This is me on the left, temporarily not patrol leader of the Kestrels patrol, but I am reliably informed the Squirrels, on 261st Birmingham St. Edburgha's annual scout camp 1966 at Walesby Forest near Newark. Tracking down June and Bob Dadd on their recent European motor caravan trek they tell me the left to right is:-Ewart Williams, Steve Small, Dave Shaw and Brian Urch. 'I got you babe' might have been No 1?

My first passport photograph 1969.

At Lancaster University, with student handbook co-editors, Neil and Rod.

At university, in Alexandra Square.

Working at Accrington Road Youth Centre, Blackburn.

On the road to Kentmere Cottage, near Staveley. Danny Burns, Ant Upton, Johnny Doyle.

Showing young people different places to work. We went to a radio station, a local newspaper, a TV studio (featuring Mudd), a sewage farm and this football ground (before they did tours!).

We took young people away on the canal. Rob Crompton, Ant Upton, Jimmy Byrne, Jackie Geddes.

Meet a girl.

My first letter to the editor. I was still 21.

We get married.

The Labour Party find me plenty to do, just as an "Organiser".

I organise Barbara's farewell for 500 people.

Neil Kinnock visits Blackburn as my guest. Early 80s?

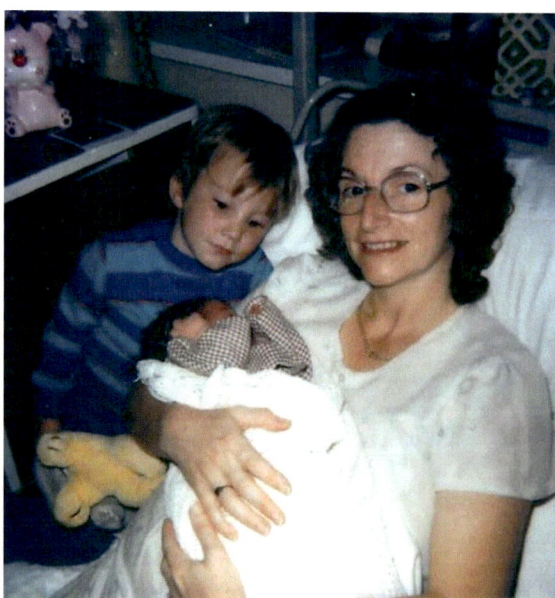

Matt(hew) 1981, then Katherine (Kit) 1985 came along.

Caravanning – note perm!

I present Christine Connell, her sister Doreen Mitchell and others with the keys to our first purpose built Neighbour Centre on Ivy Street, Ewood.

Youth Work street theatre skills employed. Robin Dad with Merrie Matt.

Mummy's got a necklace, so Grandma Mary found one for granddaughter Katherine.

Opening Peter Hobkirk's company's sewing machine factory extension.

Mayor Bill Taylor tries out a machine watched by Peter Hobkirk (centre le[ft] [st]**aff and guests.**

Wait a minute Mr Postman.

Go to Blazes Mr Mayor!

The highest office in the land! Scafell Pike.

Didn't they all do well?

■ THE Mayor of Blackburn, Coun Bill Taylor, said a big thank-you to
people who raised money for the Children in Need Appeal. Coun Tayl
reception for more than 25 different groups of fundraisers in t

*Thanking all Children in
Need participants.
I nearly went 24 hours
round the clock!*

28   LANCASHIRE EVENING TELEGRAPH, Friday, October 6, 1989

ALL THE LATEST ON THE NON-LEAGUE SCEN

■ The Mayor of Blackburn, Councillor Bill Taylor, (front left) is welcomed to the club's
annual meeting at Blackburn Town Hall by Blackburn Rovers chairman William Fox
watched by, from the left: Ian Stanners, Don Mackay, Ken Beamish, John Howarth, Terry
Ibbotson, Robert Coar and George Root

After chairing the Rovers AGM.

THWAITES

*It's a shame you weren't there,
Mr Mayor.*

Encouraging diversity in sport.

LANCASHIRE EVENING TELEGRAPH, Friday, September 15, 1989   31

■ Northern Sunday League Summer 7-a-side presentation night at Cob Wall
WMC Blackburn. The winning captain's show off their trophies with, from from
left Amjad Mahood, captain of Harwood Street, receiving the sprotsmanship
shield from the Mayor of Blackburn Coun Bill Taylor.

Scholarships for scholars

NINE teenagers are heading for an African experience of a lifetime in Nigeria after being awarded Thwaites scholarships.

The nine have all been nominated by mayors from Lancashire towns and will be setting off for Nigeria in July for a three-week stay.

But one of the teenagers, Rossendale student Melody Chapman, is still waiting for final visa clearance from the Nigerians for the trip when her nominations caused a hiccup after it was revealed she had lived in South Africa as a child.

Thwaites Scholarships were introduced by brewery chairman Mr John Yerburgh to promote international harmony 31 years ago.

The young people are ambassadors for the Western world and will play their part in breaking down the barriers between different cultures.

This year's group is made up of five boys and four girls and will be led by Mr Carl Robertson of the minority ethnic group support service based at Preston.

The successful scholars are: Toby Lister, Gisburn, from Clitheroe Royal Grammar School; Melody Chapman, Helmshore, of Accrington and Rossendale College; Joel Francis Wood, Todmorden, of St Theodore's Sixth Form Centre, Burnley; Claire Elizabeth Babbitt, Radcliffe, of Holy Cross Sixth Form College, Bury.

Gillian Mary Staziker, Langho, Blackburn, of St Wilfrid's CE School, Blackburn; Simon Prodip Chatterjee, Blackburn, of Queen Elizabeth's Grammar School, Blackburn; Matthew Iain Brook, Lancaster, of Morecambe County High School.

Lisa Ann Holden Blackpool, of Blackpool and Fylde College, and Timothy Jackson, Fulwood, Preston, of Preston College.

■ The mayor of Blackburn, Coun Bill Taylor, centre, with Mr David Kay, director and general manager of Thwaites, left, congratulating Gillian Staziker, watched by Simon Prodip Chatterjee, left, and Melody Chapman, far right. Mr Robertson is pictured back row, top right.

LGT 30/4/92

Many young people saw more of the world with the Thwaites scholarship, over many decades.

LANCASHIRE EVENING TELEGRAPH, Monday, September 25, 1989   5

Golden oldies help young

THE Mayor of Blackburn's youth fund received a welcome boost of £345 from staff and elderly residents of a residential home.

Coun Bill Taylor visited Magdalene House, Shear Bank Road, to collect the cheque from resident Mrs Mary Rothwell.

The money was raised at an August garden party and will go towards Youth Aid '90.

Care assistant Mrs Brenda Braddock said: "We have a charity fund-raising event at the home every year, and this is the second time we have organised one for the Mayor's charity."

Visiting Magdalene House. Where my mum spent her last days 30 years later.

Dear Mr Mayor . .

Visiting Saint Paul's primary in the village of Hoddlesden.

Installing the new Bishop, Alan Chesters.

Bells sound for new Bishop

Welcome your grace LFT 3/6/89

THE bells of Blackburn Cathedral were ringing out today to mark the enthronement of the Rt Rev Alan Chesters as the seventh Bishop of the Blackburn Diocese.

A procession of hundreds of academics, readers and clergy from all over the country were walking from King George's Hall to the steps of the town hall and then to the cathedral.

Civic dignitaries, including the new Mayor of Blackburn, Coun Bill Taylor, who was making his first official appearance, were to watch as the Bishop went through the tradition of knocking on the cathedral doors with a stone-age Saxon hammer to gain admission.

The Bishop is pictured with the mayor at the town hall before the service at the cathedral.

Check the date.

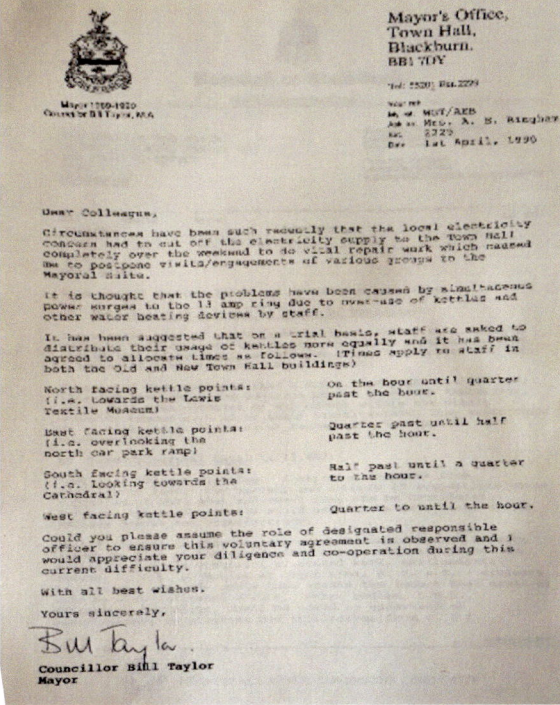

Mayor's Office,
Town Hall,
Blackburn.
BB1 7DY

Mayor 1989-1990
Councillor Bill Taylor, M.A.

Dear Colleague,

Circumstances have been such recently that the local electricity concern had to cut off the electricity supply to the Town Hall completely over the weekend to do vital repair work which caused me to postpone visits/engagements of various groups to the Mayoral suite.

It is thought that the problems have been caused by simultaneous power surges to the 13 amp ring due to over-use of kettles and other water heating devices by staff.

It has been suggested that on a trial basis, staff are asked to distribute their usage of kettles more equally and it has been agreed to allocate times as follows. (Times apply to staff in both the Old and New Town Hall buildings)

North facing kettle points: (i.e. towards the Lewis Textile Museum) — On the hour until quarter past the hour.

East facing kettle points: (i.e. overlooking the north car park ramp) — Quarter past until half past the hour.

South facing kettle points: (i.e. looking towards the Cathedral) — Half past until a quarter to the hour.

West facing kettle points: — Quarter to until the hour.

Could you please assume the role of designated responsible officer to ensure this voluntary agreement is observed and I would appreciate your diligence and co-operation during this current difficulty.

With all best wishes.

Yours sincerely,

Bill Taylor.

Councillor Bill Taylor
Mayor

Welcoming the Prime Minister Tony Blair to Our Lady and St. John's.

About hidden history. This led to greater things.

A caricature.

Winning our first Council of the Year award.

Sat with Jack Straw at the awards ceremony.

The guys out in the cold.

Full Members Cup 1987. Manager Don Mackay and Mayor Mike Madigan

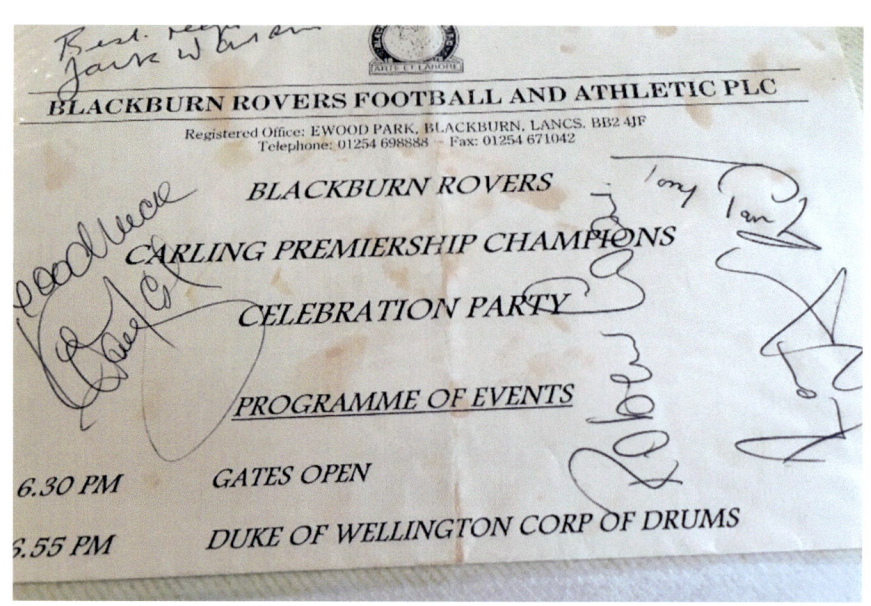

Signed on the night by Jack Walker, Rob Coar, Kenny Dalglish,
Ray Hartford and Tony Parkes.

We are the Champions.

Flying home from Cardiff on Club 'plane with League Cup 2002.

National recognition.

In a similar successful vein.

Early 2000s. One of three invitations Anne and I got to visit the Foreign Secretary's house Chevening. Jack and Alice in the middle of fellow invitees: Mo Khan, Ibby Master, Akhtar Hussain, the Batesons, Annette and Paul Murphy and Damian Talbot

Building a £68m 21st campus alongside Principal Ian Clinton. Jane McCann led the project for the College.

www.clitheroetoday.co.uk   Clitheroe 422324 (Editorial), 422323 (Advertising), Burnley 422331 (Classified)

Valley Matters

a weekly look at local issues, people and places

Clitheroe Advertiser & Times, Thursday, October 19th, 2006   6

Love, respect and trust your children!

As I see it . . . by Sir Bill Taylor

WHETHER we are parents, grandparents, aunties or uncles or "more senior" members of the community, we all love, respect and trust our children, our children's children, the younger members of our families and our communities – don't we?

Love, respect and trust. Simple words and surely something our young people, whether related to us or not, can and must expect from us.

During what is commonly accepted as the transitional period known as adolescence, young people change – physically, emotionally and in many other ways.

Quite suddenly and not in any particular order – and certainly not in an order we adults would like (or recognise from our own adolescence?) – our young people gain, perceive or have thrust upon them:- becoming a householder, worker, voter, parent, trade union member. Why are we surprised when they don't quite get things 100% right – did or do we ever?

One of my own children, when aged around 17, came to me admitting that they had made a mistake.

My response? "You're supposed to make mistakes – you're 17!"

"OK, thanks dad."

"But you're supposed to do something else too! Learn from them."

There is a lot of talk these days about parenting, effective parenting and parenting skills. What is it? What are they?

I have had two "shots" at this parenting myself and 33 years as a youth and community worker with other people's adolescents as my main client group.

Young people do make mistakes – don't we all? They have the same hopes and fears that we all have. They, by and large, are good, honest, law-abiding people.

Sadly a few, a very small minority, give the majority a bad name – or enable or allow many, if not most "adults" to dismiss all young people as lazy, good for nothing wasters – good old-fashioned words – suggesting it's an old-fashioned phenomenon?

That simply isn't good enough from us – the adults, grown-ups, whatever.

How did/are you doing your parenting? How well are you doing it? Could you do it better?

Lack of time, consistency, resolve –

whatever the qualities or characteristics that are required – may have happened or not during toddlerhood or early childhood, but may not manifest themselves until all the other challenges of adolescence present themselves relentlessly.

So, it is we as the adult members of the family and other communities who have a responsibility to shape our young people.

● Do we listen to them?

● Do we afford them our richest gift – time?

● Do we give them opportunities to experiment with responsibility and participation – real ones? Real ones that they can learn from?

● Do we know where our kids are – all of the time?

● Have we asked young people many times what bugs them about their mums and dads, what do they argue over most. It's always the same.

● What we wear/how they look.

● Who we hang around with.

● What time we have got to be in.

Those three things recur again and again. It's just the fashion, names and times that change. But we, you, me have a responsibility to take an active interest in the young people we love or know.

Take that responsibility to heart. It's a matter of love, respect and trust.

Banging the young people drum – a press cutting from the Clitheroe Advertiser.

Arise Sir Bill.

Anne and me at the Palace.

Matt(hew), me and Katherine (Kit) at the Palace.

Red Nose Day. The College Board welcomes His Excellency Ünal Çeviköz, Turkey's UK Ambassador, guest of our Foreign Secretary.

Launching Cotton Town in 2003 – a great resource. As was the Talbot Collection, saving the Mitchell and Kenyon moving images archive, amongst others.

Blackburn Youth Worker colleagues. 1992, I'm told.

Elections 2004.

My portrait by Mariam Iqbal.

The Taylor/Rogan Ten at Steve Smith's wonderful Wiswell Freemasons.
Good job Geoff Duxbury was there to take this photo!

Chapter 19

New Labour, New Council

Time it was and what a time it was, it was.

As U-Day, April 1, 1998 came nearer and nearer our trepidation increased. We didn't want to mess it up. To be fair, the conditions could never have been more favourable.

*   *   *

The year before, in May 1997, the Labour Party, including our local MP Jack Straw, as an 18 per cent opinion poll lead suggested, came out of the political wilderness of opposition and the new PM and his family gleefully walked to Downing Street.

I had had advance intimation that Major's Government was uneasy about their prospect of electoral success. It was in the run-up to the election that I got a lovely but begging letter through the post asking me to contribute to campaign funds. The only problem with it was it came from Brian Mawhinney MP, the national chairman of the Conservative Party.

At the time, the national news seemed dominated more by BSE, bovine spongiform encephalopathy. As the general election was to be held on the same day as the local elections I told our Sunday morning election campaign meetings BSE was important to us. We needed to make sure that our priorities were Blair, Straw, then – everything else.

We sent supportive canvassing teams into the neighbouring constituencies of Rossendale and Darwen and Hyndburn to help Janet and Greg win again. Locally our campaign focussed on our main priority, to re-elect Jack and get him into government. He won with a massive majority of over 14,000 against a sad-looking field of eight other candidates; the most notable of which could well have been local personality Margo Carmichael-Grimshaw, then we guessed, in her mid-sixties. Margo has been described, in speaker notes, as 'an entrepreneur businesswoman and self-styled Baroness, who has led a colourful life'. She'd run many pubs and clubs in the area, bringing the Boomtown Rats, the Sex Pistols and others locally in the seventies. It was claimed she was Blackburn's first topless barmaid when younger. She denies the claim's authenticity. A few years ago I shared a local radio programme with Margo and she's a *trouper*. To mark our broadcast she gave me a signed copy of her autobiography, *A Licence to Live* (Scopecrest 2004 ASIN B00189ZX9K) from her capacious handbag.

Jack had spent the previous five years, still on the opposition benches, as Shadow Home Secretary with Michael Howard as his Conservative adversary. So, we all hoped that Jack would be Labour's Home Secretary, something which he merited and deserved.

As usual at a general election, the count took place immediately after the polls closed at 10 p.m. and seemed to take an awfully long time. Jack, his wife, Alice, their two children and his mum, Joan (in her mid-seventies) were all anticipatorily present in King George's Hall. The exit polls were predicting a massive Labour landslide as the results came in from far and wide about seats being gained by Labour almost literally left, right and centre. This evening of course included what became known as the 'Portillo moment', when, in the Enfield Southgate constituency, Stephen Twigg beat defence secretary Michael Portillo by some 1400 votes. We had to be patient in Blackburn but eventually in the traditional manner the said John Whitaker Straw was duly elected. The roar of Labour's cheer in the hall was tumultuous.

But what now? What time was it and frankly who cared? Around four or five o'clock in the morning, coming light, we walked the quarter mile or so back to Jack's house. But we'd gained some new companions. As we went down the stairs of King George's Jack was met by his new police protection officers, something he'd have to get used to.

We got to Jack's and all sat around. Satisfaction, elation, no sleep for twenty-four hours and a quick few slurps was quite a heady cocktail. Jack's best pal from Brentwood School, Patrick, later to be Lord Carter, was with us. Jack produced a bottle of champagne, which I guessed would be a rather good one. He'd acquired it eighteen years earlier when he'd first become our local MP, saving it for the time when a Labour government was elected. It had, all on its own, become quite a vintage. It tasted good but that seemed enhanced by the sweet but tardy taste of success. I felt sure Patrick fell asleep next to me. Alice instructed son William, then aged sixteen, to take some of the cans and bottles to the bins outside. He came back a little distraught; his innocent housekeeping activity had aroused the attention of Jack's personal protection team outside the back door.

It was light when we got home. I fell asleep and eventually later that day, it was announced that Jack had been appointed Home Secretary. It had been twenty-one years, 1976 since Blackburn's MP had been in the cabinet, Barbara Castle, as the Secretary of State for Health and Social Services. Jack sustained a Cabinet role throughout the Blair/Brown governments, thirteen years in total. We quickly learned locally that having your MP right at the heart of government was a very useful bonus.

Government ministers are in the driving seat and they take decisions, there's no doubt about that. As many years later Jack told *The Times'* political journalist Peter Riddell: 'The thing that I believe that no one can know until they are faced with it is whether they can make decisions. And not just one decision, with the luxury of a day to think about it, but a box full of decisions and another box full. I'm sure there are ways of testing that, but certainly in the British system prospective ministers are not tested for that. And that leads to there being an assumption that if you've been good in opposition, you're likely to be good in government. Whereas the skills needed for the two are often very different.'

It must've been within days of Jack becoming the Home Secretary that I happened to be down in London on education matters with director Mark Pattison and my deputy Kathy (then) Ramsden. He got wind of our visit and invited us for a cuppa at the Home Office. Jack was in his very early ministerial days, and after eighteen years, who could blame him showing off a little.

We duly arrived and were shown up, after security checks, to his office. Office? It was massive! The size of a school classroom? Bigger? It was situated on the top floor, I believe at an address on Petty France, a cock stride (?) across Bird Cage Walk from St James's Park, at the time. Jack was very relaxed, enjoying his honeymoon period telling stories about his first day at his new 'school' and the reaction of the civil servants there after having been used to Conservatives for eighteen years (Willie Whitelaw, Leon Brittan, Douglas Hurd, David Waddington, Kenneth Baker, Ken Clarke and Michael Howard). He was on great form with stories to match. I had been to Buckingham Palace to a garden party when we were the mayor. Big Chief of the *i-SPY* book of famous London buildings (if there is one) wasn't yet to know that I would add to this: No 10, Somerset House, the Dept of Education, the Dept of Communities and Local Government House, The Treasury, the Cabinet Office, various parts of the Commons offices and meeting rooms, the BMA, Church House, St James's Palace. Well over a hundred-plus points there, I bet.

In my opinion, looking over Jack's time in the Blair/Brown governments, holding four of the great Cabinet posts, his greatest, most effective piece of legislation was the Crime and Disorder Act 1998. Jack's legal background, a qualified and practising barrister and his political background in his constituency work, suggested that the reason why people ended up in court was not actually their wrongdoing. Their wrongdoings were being badly parented, being ineffective parents themselves, mental health issues, poor education, being or having been in care or straightforward poverty. This legislation and its comprehensive nature was not the work of a namby-pamby do-gooder, much of it crafted by Jack in Blackburn with the collaboration of Eddie Walsh, the local police chief superintendent since 1987. On his retirement in 2000 Eddie said of the 1998 Act 'It has the potential to make massive improvements in community safety particularly where all the agencies and communities work together closely to tackle the problems rather than it just being the responsibility of the police.' In the twin adage 'tough on crime, tough on the causes of crime', they were equal partners. I became operationally active in community safety as part of my work, so I'll return to the act and its bearing later.

* * *

I say in the most favourable conditions for us as a local council because we had the treble bonus of a talented, hardworking, well thought of, high-profile Labour MP, sitting in the cabinet, an ambitious Labour council, and senior members and officers of that council who, I believe, were similarly well attributed. Could we fail? Of course. Were we determined not to fail? Of course.

But there were bound to be bumpy bits and, of course, people for a variety of reasons, were determined to undermine us.

One such issue was that of allowances for councillors, financial recompense, for performing their duties. It has always been and probably always will be a bit of a hot potato. So, an independent review body was set up. This included Rev. Mike Wedgeworth from the cathedral, Brenda Rudge the MD of the local paper, Mike Murray and Anne Edwina Forrest both local businesspeople, Sheena Ewing from the college, Ian Woolley from the health service board and Ian Gallagher from the local trades council. We agreed at the outset that we would accept their proposals without alteration.

It was also around this time that we produced, after a great deal of hard work and (pre the openly accessible www) expense, specific *green papers* on eleven key areas of the new unitary councils' activities. These were for wide distribution and open to comment and responses from within and across the community. This process was coordinated and collated by the local government reorganisation group. At the time, its chair Councillor Gail Barton said 'For all the service areas, we are anxious to consult widely and get as many views as possible before we formulate our ideas for the new authority.' With regard to the education-specific *green paper* I was quoted as saying 'Education is a very important ingredient of our aim to improve the life chances of our young people and others in the community.' I urged parents, governors, pupils and others to join professionals in offering their views. I much preferred this 'bottom-up' approach to service design. We had eight different meetings with heads, governing bodies, teachers associations and other groups.

We also set up a school improvement forum which was a fairly informal group made up in equal proportion of pupils and students, teachers and head teachers, governors and education officers. Mark Pattison, bless him, whispered to me just as we were about to start that he felt sure I was the best man to run this consultative group. But how would we initiate the notion of equality of opinion amongst this diverse set of people? This was left to Bill the youth worker, experienced and skilled as an animator of group work. The group was aged from pupils aged elevenish right the way through to quite senior people, in terms of age and perceived stature.

What ground rules did we need? How should they be established? I needed to ensure that big jargonistic words and acronyms were ruled out, including words like jargonistic and acronyms. After a cup of tea, we got down to business. I think apprehension was a direct function of increasing age. OK, I blagged Rule 1, 'Can you please go round the room making the noise of your favourite farmyard animal?' What a menagerie! What a ruckus! I doubt that such goings-on had ever before been witnessed in committee room number one of the Victorian town hall. What would the burghers of the borough whose portraits bedecked the walls be thinking?

'Right,' I said moving on, 'if anyone, regardless of who or what they are, uses a word or a set of initials you don't understand, you are within your rights, indeed it is your responsibility, to make your favourite farmyard animal noise as loudly as possible.' It didn't take many outbursts of audible animal impersonations to get that practice embedded in our informal rules of engagement.

The forty or so people in the room still seemed to be congregating within their peer group. Not healthy. Solution? 'Please can you line up in the order of the first record or' (hastily added for those younger) 'CD you ever bought.' That process took quite a long time as it necessitated people talking to one another, breaking the ice. My next trick was going to get people to sing that tune but I ran out of courage. After all that, the group was fantastic and people shared lots of different experiences and opinions and listened to the same.

*   *   *

Even before we were operating as an education authority, I was appointed as the north-west rep on the national Local Government Association's education committee. This was quite a surprise and a speedy elevation.

I was also invited to join a national working group looking at better ways of consulting young people which was set up in collaboration between the Local Government Information Unit (LGIU), the Children's Rights Office, the National Children's Bureau and the Joseph Rowntree Foundation. I must have been doing something right?

Again, even before we were actually legally the educational authority, we had bid to become active as one of the Labour Government's new initiatives – Education Action Zones (EAZ). David Blunkett had become the new Secretary of State for Education and Employment. This was another external funding regime, worth £3.5m, specifically targeted at improving educational standards in targeted schools in a designated area. We planned to bring together local business, police and health organisations to improve a group of schools including three secondarys, fifteen primaries, three nurseries and one special school. Our EAZ ran so well during its intended three-year lifetime and was used by central government as a test bed so that, after three years, we were given an additional £2 million to run the zone for a further two years. Few councils were awarded such an opportunity.

We had been promised a one-off grant from government to fund the transitional costs of becoming a unitary; £5.2 million would be required. Only being allocated £2.5 million effectively meant we had to make cuts to our budget before we were actually in charge of it.

As U-day became increasingly imminent we guessed that the waters ahead were choppy and likely to get even more choppy. That didn't dull or dilute our anticipation.

Chapter 20

Going Live as a Unitary!

Hear my words that I might teach you.

I'd got in the habit of taking our daughter, Katherine, aka Kit, and a car full of her friends to some performance or other around Christmas time. I loved doing it. It had started with a trip, when they were nine/ten-ish, to see the 1911 novel turned drama *The Secret Garden* by Frances Hodgson Burnett at the Library Theatre in Manchester. The rigmarole was always quite a palaver, as it should be with excitable young girls.

It entailed the chosen quartet or quintet assembling at our house. They were then given the same set amount of money with a plastic bag with their name on. As they were nearly all called Katherine it did become quite complicated, until, between themselves, fate morphed this name into derivatives such as Katy, Kit or in Catherine Duckworth's case, CD. Girls jumped in the car and we went down to the local sweet shop where they would spend a disproportionately long time choosing from the penny tray.

Grasping their sweeties, the next stage of the journey was often to park up in Bury, have a sit-down fish and chip lunch and then jump on the Metro tram into the centre of Manchester. The whole thing was such an adventure that the chattering was deafening but it was great fun to be around.

Another quintet was taking the pop world by storm, the Spice Girls, formed in 1994. About three years later, *Spice World*, mimicking The Beatle's *A Hard Day's Night* 1964 film, was released in December 1997, showcasing the girls' dramatic skills. This was chosen by the twelve-year-olds, going on seventeen, as Billy's (no due respect here?) Christmas treat.

We jumped in the car, bought the traditional sweeties, ate fish and chips and headed for one of those multi-screen cinemas, in nearby Preston. Watching the film was total purgatory for me. But that wasn't the point. The girls, several hundreds of them, were cock-a-hoop. The din both from the Dolby surround sound and the pre-teen-aged audience was deafening. Was I glad to get out?

Was I glad to get out? It remains a reasonable and possibly unanswered question.

A day or two prior Jack had tipped me off that there could be some unexpected press interest in the Straw family. Their son Will, seventeen and exactly to the day one year older than our son, had been set up to acquire a small amount of cannabis by a young female undercover journalist from the *Daily Mirror* in a pub somewhere in London. More can be read about this in Jack's autobiography.

I didn't expect to have much of a role in this until we were driving away from the cinema and my in-car fitted phone with microphone and speakers went berserk. I couldn't tell you how many phone calls I took during the half-hour journey back to Blackburn, up to half a dozen, from BBC, World Service, Sky News and the like.

I was told that they were setting up outside broadcast cameras at the only location they knew in Blackburn, Ewood Park. There was no game on.

The girls in the back were still giddy from their *Spice World* experience. Catherine Duckworth, aka CD, was uncharacteristically completely silent in the passenger seat next to me. 'Billy, something serious is happening, isn't it?' she inquired. Catherine screamed at her travelling companions 'Be quiet, there's something really big happening.'

I tried ringing Jack but no doubt his number was jammed with calls too. I rang Anne, asking her to get my suit ready, making sure I had a clean and ironed shirt.

The process seemed to take moments. In the house, brief Anne to take over returning the girls to their homes, shave, brush hair, quick wash and change of clothes, back in the car and off to Ewood Park, fifteen minutes away.

There appeared to be several hundreds of yards of cables, numerous cameras and operatives, sound people, whole outside broadcast crews for several broadcast companies. And me.

The questions were repetitive. What sort of young man was Will? 'Friendly, warm, funny, thoughtful and hugely intelligent.'

Did I know why he had done what he'd done? Is it the sort of thing he frequently did?

My replies were consistent and truthful. We had a son of a similar age, as did many thousands of others, parents of older teenagers, going on into adulthood. Parents who could say exactly where their children were and exactly what they were doing at any one and every time, would be completely few and far between. Again, parents of 'children' that age who knew absolutely categorically that their children had not been exposed in some way to the world of drugs were fooling themselves. I could speak not only as a parent but as a youth worker, that drugs were available in local pubs, shopping centres and on school playgrounds. This could have happened to any family at any time. The Straw family faced up to events and handled them completely appropriately, in my opinion. I was resolute, this had been an unprincipled tabloid set-up.

I set off back for home. There seemed to be total dissonance between the early part of my afternoon and the latter.

*   *   *

We'd experienced an unprecedented four different years of multiple distinct varieties of change: 1) a normal district borough employing 1,600 staff, 2) consultative year, 3) a dry-run year and 4) finally in April 1998, the real McCoy Blackburn with Darwen, the unitary council with some 6,500 employees.

U-Day loomed ever nearer. We set up an NFU unit. NFU almost stood for no foul ups! Well actually, it was only Steve Weaver! Steve sacrificially volunteered that if anything went wrong, major or minor, first of all it was his fault and then he had to solve the problem there and then. If a school bus didn't arrive to collect and take a child to school, if meals weren't served to a group of old folks, if a traffic signal stopped working it just wasn't going to be allowed to happen. Luckily, the day ran smoothly, glitch free.

The front-page headline on our local paper, still then called the *Lancashire Evening Telegraph*, heralded the change – 'Flying the Flag'. The new borough flag was held proudly by Malcolm Doherty the leader of the council, chief executive Phil Watson, chair of the reorganisation committee Gail Barton, the Conservative John Williams and Lib Dem Paul Browne. Perhaps there was one person missing off that historic photo but I thought it was prudent for me not to be around for that particular photo shoot so as to not further aggravate my professional and political colleagues at the county council. Don't get me wrong, since 1981 I was committed to everyone being inside an 'all singing-all dancing' unitary authority of an appropriate and effective size. That size, in my opinion, was between a population of a third to half a million. BwD and Blackpool becoming unitaries only accounted for 300,000. But in my mind, this represented an easing of the tectonic plates, the art of the possible. Perhaps, at a later date, Lancashire established as two or perhaps three unitary authorities would become a reality. I thought that not to gloat in public about this not insubstantial achievement, but not the full victory, was the better part of valour.

A special victory celebration breakfast was held in our public halls attended by over 400 guests, including school children of course. The appropriately named George Campling (a council director) had composed a special peal of bells which rang out from the cathedral loud and clear. Malcolm Doherty added 'This is a big day and exciting time for all of us. I really feel as though we are at the start of something big.'

In education we did have some mountains to climb. For example, too many schools were in Ofsted categories special measures or serious weaknesses, capacity needed to be increased for three and four-year-olds in nurseries, work was necessary to improve the quality of our governors and enhance their role.

The new Labour Government was as committed to improvement and innovation as we were, things couldn't have happened at a better time. David Blunkett had the role of education secretary for the first four years of Blair's Government. He had a great thirst for both the function and role and was probably Labour's best during their thirteen years in government. I got to know David quite well. He visited Blackburn at least twice and we spoke with each other at conferences and things to the extent that he recognised my voice when I spoke. Blunkett handed over the education brief to Estelle Morris who was a lovely and talented woman. Estelle visited Blackburn on at least one occasion I think to launch our education plan – 'Aiming high, including all'. She also happened to be my mum's MP for Yardley, Birmingham constituency. Sadly Estelle, who I got on with well, didn't last very long, which was disappointing. When she stood down from the House of Commons in 2005 she became Baroness Morris of Yardley in 'another place'. Ironically, from 2015, the Yardley seat has been held by Jess Phillips, the daughter of Stewart Trainor one of my teachers from Sheldon Heath Comprehensive.

People may recall Prime Minister Tony Blair's mantra of 'education, education, education'. I think the incoming government very much meant what they said and delivered on it too. On Labour's 1997 pledge card the very first bullet point was to cut class sizes to thirty or under for all five, six and seven-year-olds. No fault of the outgoing LEA, but I had visited schools with leaking roofs dripping into buckets that seemed to be fitted as standard. It simply wasn't good enough to expect teachers to teach and pupils to learn in such a non-conducive educational environment. Blunkett immediately established an emergency repair programme of which we got nearly £1m. Additional new classrooms and other extensions to schools soon followed. Both the government and the local council had committed themselves to reducing class sizes and they got on with the job.

A little time later the government launched another initiative, City Learning Centres. These were to be IT based and a hub for pupils, staff and the community generally to develop their IT skills. We fancied having one and so applied. Not too long later we were advised that our bid had been disqualified by civil servants as we weren't a city and so therefore couldn't have a CLC. I was uncharacteristically livid and told Mark Pattison to ring the department in Whitehall and find out which civil servant had done this to us and tell them I was going to take this up directly with David Blunkett. Mark reported back a few days later, to confirm he had done as instructed and that the outcome was that we weren't going to get a single CLC. We have since been allocated two and to this day they sit proudly in front of Witton Park and Pleckgate high schools. I was dead chuffed – still am when I drive past the premises and have a wry smile to myself. Being told we couldn't have one CLC because we weren't a city resulted in us being the only place in the country to have two! Proof that having friends in high places who knew, respected and trusted us often helped.

But just improving bricks and mortar, although important, wasn't the be all and end all. We sought to enhance the vital trinity of pupil-school-home. I staged regular specialist surgeries for parents, especially so they could ask about what was happening in them; after all, they were paying for them.

We got an indication that we were edging closer to establishing our Education Action Zone. It depended upon a visit by the department and then a final process to select the chosen twenty-five. We were confident our bid was of the highest quality and that ultimately we'd be successful pushing on for more resources to improve education in our borough and to keep our borough firmly on the map. Fingers crossed, for now.

As I had said previously, we had far too many schools and therefore their pupils, in the two lowest of the then seven Ofsted grades, namely serious weakness or special measures. We needed them all to be at least grade 4, i.e. satisfactory. (I had suggested in some conference or other that the seven Ofsted gradings were too complicated and might be better known as right, might, tight and shite. They met my proposal halfway trimming the grades down to number only four but rejected my more accessible nomenclature.) Within two years of becoming the educational authority, with a lot of carrot and a little bit of stick, all of our schools were out of serious weaknesses or special measures. Our hard-working and both voracious and ferocious team of school improvement officers were at the heart of this vast improvement. Around 10 per cent of our weakest heads were encouraged, incentivised to leave their posts during this time.

Our plan for the Education Action Zone was to increase the percentage of our youngsters getting five grade Cs at GCSE from 26 per cent to 40 per cent. This is why we had strengthened both the capacity and quality of our school improvement officer team. We planned to get many more interactive whiteboards into all of our schools and train up teachers to use them effectively. Promethean, a local company with Tony Cann at its helm, were world leaders in the development of this twenty-first-century educational wizardry. But we didn't just rely on state-of-the-art gizmos. We intended to get key local partner agencies on board: parents, the police, the health service, the Rovers, the local training and enterprise council, the careers service, the Duke of Edinburgh's Award Scheme, local FE colleges, community and faith groups as well as the private sector, including ICI and Whitbreads. All these had much to offer and much to gain from closer and better collaboration. The other thing that we shared was determination – to confront the issues that challenged us and win.

So much so that although a very young educational authority, we found ourselves invited to explain our story, our mission. Our director Mark Pattison and me were invited to the highly prestigious Local Government Association Education Conference held in Torquay in 1998 to talk about our experience.

As long as it didn't distract us or divert us from our main aim, we were happy to participate in any educational innovation. Junior Education Minister Steve Byers announced £810k additional funds for us to repair school buildings, so we invited him up to come and see how well the money was spent. Blackburn on the map again. He came and we hung quite a sizeable regional event around his visit.

Not long after, David Blunkett announced around £0.5 million funding for schemes planned to cut schools' truancy and exclusions. Well, as is said around here, we 'chucked our caps' at that as well. Both senior Whitehall officials and politicians at the department knew to trust us here in BwD. A child not in school is not learning and susceptible to other temptations. I went out on the streets with a truancy team comprising of social workers, educational welfare officers and police officers. We got a lot of press coverage (local and in education national 'trade' publications) and got the issue aired. Whilst out in the shopping centre, I was shocked that some grandparents thought taking their grandchildren to buy some new footwear was regularly cited as a justifiable excuse for 'nicking off'.

Both ministers and their mandarins liked the way we operated in cooperation with them. If they had a scheme they wanted to trial and it fitted our needs, we'd give it a go. That often meant a high-ranking and high-profile visit which convinced our local education family we meant business and our visitors went away and talked up BwD. Win win; always a good result.

Our local MP and Home Secretary Jack Straw also used his constituency as a test bed, for example with a pioneering project aimed at tackling youth crime. The Audit Commission backed this shake-up, criticising existing agencies and telling them they needed to collaborate together to improve their collective performance.

With Jack's regular constituency surgeries, his Saturday morning town centre soapbox sessions and all the other ways he had developed to ensure engagement with the community, he knew that crime and anti-social behaviour was very much to the forefront of local people's minds, Jack's Crime and Disorder Act 1998 introducing specialist multi-disciplinary Youth Offending Teams (YOTs), measures ensuring collaboration between the different public agencies, ASBOs or anti-social behaviour orders, parenting orders, updating and streamlining the youth criminal justice system, to name but a few, interrelated and comprehensively covered in the legislation. It felt like Jack had eighteen years of crafted ideas to implement and felt he had much he wanted to get on with. They made a difference to young people's lives and to their homes, schools and communities.

It wasn't just in my political life that I was involved in crime and disorder/community safety. In my working life in the Ribble Valley, very much contrasting as a rural community, I worked alongside Dave Morris and Bill Alker from the borough council and the local police inspectors Les Martin, Bob Ford and Jenny Coulston. As things developed, my expertise in matters of crime grew.

I was regularly invited to present prizes and open things for all types of different people in all types of different places. I usually accepted, urged on by our PR people, who told me Brand Taylor was a strong one.

I'm not actually sure what people think of me but I have a tendency to believe that most people are quite shy but have different coping strategies to deal with that. In some ways when in the public arena I disassociated myself from the inner me and projected a different person. As to who is the real Bill Taylor, this is a question I have raised with myself but never resolved.

*   *   *

The pace of change in Blair's Government was fast and accelerating. But to be fair, we didn't mind that in BwD, we could keep up.

A group of highly experienced, high-powered and high-achieving local government officers from across the country descended upon Blackburn in late 1998. We had volunteered to be the first in the country to be surveyed and assessed. The leader of the review team Andrew Kilburn then the chief executive of Redcar and Cleveland Council commented 'we have been impressed in particular with the extensive partnership work in the borough'. Little did we know that this process was the portent of a future where all councils were subjected to a Comprehensive Performance Assessment. When asked sometime later in a radio interview, I likened a CPA to being a mega-municipal MOT. That's another thing we learned to judge, when to jump in and participate in new things and when not. The advantage to being quick off the mark was that the process was yet to be set in concrete, which meant you could influence its development and also you could advise others on how to do it.

In the run-up to Christmas 1998 I had to travel to London, a fairly frequent occurrence, for various reasons. I bumped into our leader Malcolm in the town hall before setting off. When I told him where I was going, he asked me if I'd read today's *Daily Mirror*, which I hadn't. He recommended that I read it on the train.

The headline in the *Mirror* that day was 'Minister leaves husband for whip'. And, as only red tops could, featured Janet Anderson MP for Darwen and her marriage breakup. I had arranged to spend an hour with Jack Straw whilst in London. I passed through what comparative little security there was in those days and sought Jack out along one of the many long corridors in the House of Commons. Jack, seated on the top table, gave me a thumbs up. He'd been addressing something like the National Association of Shopping Centre Managers. They were giving him a vote of thanks at the end of their meeting with him.

We left what must have been a committee room and found his office somewhere nearby. He removed his jacket and relaxed, feet on table. 'Have you seen Janet today?' I asked. 'No, I've been really, really busy. Oh no, I did, I saw her this morning.' 'What did she say?' I pressed. 'Well, Bill, from memory, I said good morning, Janet, and her reply was, Hi Jack, yep, good morning. But why, Bill, do you ask?'

'That's easy,' I replied. 'Because the front page of today's *Mirror* reports that her and Vince have split up.'

'Good grief, I knew nothing about that and she gave no indication of it either.'

'So, what's been keeping you busy, then?' I asked our Home Secretary.

Pointing to several capacious lever-arch folders on his table, he said 'I've been spending most of the last few days reading this lot; as I decide about the extradition of General Pinochet.'

*   *   *

General Pinochet had been the President of Chile. His dictatorship lasted from 1973 to 1990. He came to power after a military coup deposed the democratically elected socialist President Dr Salvador Allende. Allende was elected in 1970 and embarked upon social reforms in housing, health, education and employment. Ironically and incidentally, I'd taken part in a huge pro-Allende, pro-democracy demo in London in 1972. The military coup took place on 11 September 1973. Allende died the same day committing suicide.

After the coup, the national sports stadium was used by the junta to jail, torture and murder thousands of political opponents of the regime. Pinochet stood accused of human rights violations, embezzlement of millions and other crimes.

In October 1998, the British branch of Amnesty International spotted that Pinochet was heading for Europe including coming to the United Kingdom.

Legal proceedings against Pinochet had been commenced both in Spain and in Chile. He was arrested in London in October. A huge international legal wrangle ensued. *Hansard* for 9 December records:

'Mr Straw: 'I signed an authority to proceed in respect of Senator Pinochet today. The Spanish request for his extradition will now be considered by the courts. The reasons for my decision were sent to all the parties concerned in a letter from one of my officials.'

*　*　*

So comparatively Jack had quite a lot on his plate that day, a fair few plates full. Much more and in much more detail can be read about this in Jack's autobiography. I continue with my take, my minimal experience, in what at the time was a massive international issue with the international legal and public eye very much on the British home secretary.

In quite a small room at the Palace of Westminster I asked Jack what the folders were. It seemed there were briefings from an intense legal perspective about the situation. I continued, 'Jack, you're a trained, qualified and practised barrister. Do you think you could do this job and tackle these tasks without those attributes?' Jack reflected and then replied 'no'. 'What's Blair and the Cabinet's take on all this?' 'Not a lot really, it's more or less being left to me.'

It was my turn to reflect and weigh up the profundity and the responsibility that Jack's decisions and actions had. My eyes were opened to a world beyond my scope and responsibility. Jack was very much the man in the arena: '*the man who is actually in the arena, whose face is marred by dust and sweat and blood; who strives valiantly.*' The arena was massive and the audience global.

The room fell quiet but the silence was broken as the telephone rang. Jack answered it. The conversation was brief. 'Billy, I'm really sorry but that was Tony and he wants a word with me.' I made to put my jacket on. 'Where are you going, Billy?' 'Listen, Jack, if you're going to get the sack, you're not going on your own.' My quip lightened what had been quite an intense few moments and we went our separate ways.

I don't think what was perhaps four or five minutes will ever leave me as I got an insight into being in government and having Cabinet responsibility. I remembered the tale about the man shaving in the morning. Not in power he said to himself, 'What should I say today?' and in power he said, 'What shall I do today?'.

*   *   *

Back to the 'day job', I chaired a national education conference in London, the main speaker at which was Schools Minister Estelle Morris.

Later we hosted a number of national education conferences in Blackburn, rather than everybody traipsing down to London. We got a reputation for great hospitality and good organisation. Why should the capital always be the focus for important events and why shouldn't little old Blackburn, 4,000 holes and all, not get itself on the map every now and again and again?

We enjoyed several days of a family Christmas break. Reflecting on the first few months of being a unitary council, I thought our team of both officers and elected members had done really quite well. Nine out of ten?

1999 began with quite a bang as Prime Minister Tony Blair and Education Minister David Blunkett came to Blackburn, accompanied of course, by the Home Secretary and our MP Jack Straw. I welcomed them to a rainswept Our Lady and Saint John RC High School and handed them over to headmaster Mike Humphreys and his head boy Alastair Eccles and girl Lisa Grogan. Dog lover and trusted pupil Lucy was entrusted to care for David Blunkett's then guide dog and namesake, Lucy.

The three ministers toured the school looking at the innovation the Education Action Zone had created and then told the packed and enthralled school hall things about themselves and the future. The whole event went down very well with the staff but more especially with the pupils. Many of our private sector partners, British Aerospace, United Utilities, Whitbreads, Lloyds TSB, Promethean and the Rovers were there as active participants too with EAZ chair and local entrepreneur Mike Murray orchestrating their presence to optimum impact.

Quite early on in our life as an LEA, we were identified as a source of support for struggling LEAs. We were 'twinned' by the Department of Education with a weaker LEA nearby. Mark Pattison, Phil Watson and me travelled to them for an initial conversation and assessment of their needs. We planned the 'return leg', their chair to 'shadow' me as I visited Shadsworth, one of our local primary schools.

We arranged that my opposite number would be welcomed by the head boy and girl, which our visitor seemed to think strange. I just thought it was nice and quite empowering.

Brian Peacock, the head, a friend who I'd known for many years, and I, had arranged the afternoon.

Our guest was shown to the head teacher's room. We had been joined by the chair of the governors, a local woman with kids in the school. Cups of tea drained, Brian said he'd leave us three to have a natter. The chair spoke very well in a relaxed manner about the priorities of the school and their performance. We spent half to three-quarters of a very productive hour with her, she left and Brian joined us to speak similarly in a very candid way about the school and its relationship with the LEA. He then announced, and this was prearranged, that the children were ready for me in the hall.

It was literacy hour and I had prepared a little bit of a speech but mainly to recite to them Spike Milligan's 'On the Ning Nang Nong'.

The children all loved it, their faces beaming and a teacher took over, I presume, to facilitate some further curricular activity.

We left them to it and congregated in the school foyer to say our farewells. Before our visitor left us, he said he was incredulous as to the afternoon, its format and fun, simply saying it's not the sort of thing we could ever do. Oh dear, I thought, as I drove back to work. We didn't realise that what was normal for us was special and unreachable to others.

*   *   *

The afternoon at Brian Peacock's school seemed to exemplify issues of culture. We seemed to have a 'can do, let's get on with it' approach.

Brian Peacock must have moved schools because on another occasion, after a brilliant Ofsted inspection report, we turned up to celebrate his new school's achievement. Intack Primary this time, I think. A really talented and locally based at the time photographer, Jason Broadhurst, had been booked to do the snapping. (Jason is pretty high flying these days and based at Salford Quays.) Jason lined us up, head teacher at one end, me at the other, children in between and school in the background. I had a little lad stationed next to me, let's call him Wayne. Wayne couldn't settle. To describe him as fidgety would be an understatement. My mother would have enquired directly, 'Have you got St Vitus Dance?' I engaged my full repertoire of encouraging or diversionary tactics on the poor infant. 'Please, Wayne, this is a really big day for you and your school.' 'Not bothered, mister.' 'That photographer is called Jason and he's come here especially to take your photograph, please try a smile.' In a rather Casperesque fashion Wayne replied, 'Don't care'. The old adage about never work with children or animals came to mind. 'Why not, Wayne?' I said as encouragingly as I could. 'Cause I've just trod in some dog muck and it stinks.' Wayne's slightly happier face appeared in the paper the next day wearing a pair of borrowed pumps.

In education our top team of officers and elected members seemed to get on very well. We had regular policy development discussion meetings sometimes inviting key experts in an area of council activity to brief us in more detail. But we also had what they might call up in Lancashire 'bits and bobs' of housekeeping to tidy up as well.

We had to address the schools' music service. At the point of takeover from Lancashire we had retained our relationship with their service but we wanted to establish and develop our own, which we were able to do by attracting a government grant. Music brings so much to children as individuals and groups; new skills, the discipline of cooperating with one another and the joy(?) of performing in public.

The youth worker in me can't perceive the development of a child to be purely around the school and the school curriculum. What was labelled as extra-curricular is really all part and parcel of a child growing up. So, we actively involved organisations such as the Prince's Trust, designed to offer a supportive bridge for older teenagers after they had left school.

The Duke of Edinburgh's Award Scheme is similarly focussed. Young people could start their bronze, silver or gold journey at secondary school and complete it later. The national director of the scheme, former Vice Admiral Mike Gretton came to Blackburn to see the work we did here, talk to participants and award their accomplishments in front of their peers and proud parents. Another big hitter in Blackburn.

As we came towards the first full year as an LEA, there was much of which we could be proud. But none of us was complacent, none of us ready to rest on our laurels.

We'd set off on this voyage, we were out of the harbour and heading for the open sea. Little did we know how choppy the water was going to get. A storm was brewing.

Chapter 21

Our First Real Challenge

Time hurries on and the leaves that are green turn to brown.

We had become used to change and challenge, we were 'battle hardened' to them, without losing our passion and compassion. But what seemed like a real challenge came along quite soon and was actually one we chose to face up to. Not facing up to things wasn't the way we operated.

At one of our regular policy conversations, I think it was Jill Baker who raised the issue of special education and special schools in the borough. They were described as 'just not working'. My vice chairman, Kathy Ramsden at the time (now Stephenson) and I listened attentively. I'd listened to my teacher wife, Anne, talk about change in education and how sometimes it feels like, as you sense there's a new cycle of change beginning, you often realise it's the same cycle but perhaps third or fourth time round. We were told:

Numbers of children attending our special schools were dwindling as parents wanted their children to be in mainstream schools with special provision. The special schools were in danger of becoming non-viable.

Special school provision had been developed on a total county basis. Lancashire was reorganising its provision which had a knock-on effect on how we needed to structure ours.

Doing nothing would mean the eventual need to close schools. It was better to be proactive and manage the situation than let it happen to us.

We developed a consultative document which was widely distributed amongst parents, staff, governors, the health sector and other key players.

There were several reactions to this mainly by parents and staff comfortable with the status quo. We'd floated two or three possible options in the discussion document, some quarters accusing us of not being clear which one we supported, and on the other hand, others saying we had an undeclared hidden agenda. We promised that there would be at least an eighteen-month lead-in time to any agreed change. We further undertook that each child would be considered individually.

I personally didn't have an axe to grind one way or the other in all this, but I did get a sense that some parents were opposed to change per se and some teachers were speaking not from a professional point of view but with the intention of ensuring that their own job was retained.

Letters began to appear in the local press. One took the history of 'open-air schools' back to pre-war years. As we stood on the threshold of the twenty-first century, the 1930s seemed like a far country.

We established a whole series of public consultation meetings, mainly held in the special schools themselves and usually scheduled to start towards the end of the normal working day. On the front row at every one of these meetings it seemed, there were a couple of parents, unrelated to each other, who had kids or had had kids at different special schools for different reasons over quite a long period of time. To them any change was not good, not an option. They sat there taking copious notes of everything that was said and had on their knees various different bits of the legislation and case law appertaining to special education. I got to quite like them; they seemed rather well informed and doggedly determined.

This was an intense process. The meetings became heated. It felt like those attending were only of the status quo camp and the atmosphere inside the room fed off that and they off each other. An innate quality of mine never to show anger or any other extreme emotion paid dividends. Those already committed to change or precipitating its need weren't present. They were the happy customers.

More letters appeared in the press. They claimed I had a fixed agenda and that the decisions were already made. Nothing could have been further from the truth but there's no greater barrier to change than intractable tenacity. This wasn't a cost-cutting exercise but trying to convince people of that, in some cases, proved impossible. Many of the parents of kids in our special schools had been pupils there themselves; it was almost like a family tradition. Our hands were tied, as, if a child chose to move to a mainstream school, the funding attached to that individual (several thousands of pounds) went with them. We were trying to design our way out of this impasse but there were those who just wanted things to stay as they had always been. Common sense versus nostalgia, that's always quite a battle. Jill Baker, a very warm, reasonable and approachable woman, patiently and clearly explained that pupil numbers at two of our four special schools in the borough were shrinking and that the vast majority of our pupils with special needs were already in mainstream provision.

The consultations about how we might structure and fund the education of special needs pupils went on for several months. It was tricky, as is often the case when making political decisions, because most of the people who were happy with the proposals were just that – happy with the proposals. Those who weren't happy were omnipresent and the most active and vociferous.

The process came to a public head one Saturday morning in Blackburn town hall. We couldn't carry on not making a decision so I convened a final consultative meeting. The room was full and there were a number of young people there in wheelchairs. As I entered the room, prompted I believe, they told me 'Please don't close our school, Mr Taylor.'

I opened the meeting and immediately addressed the concerns of that group of young people. I couldn't help feeling some councillors from other parties had prompted these youngsters to think and speak as they had, not in the pupils' best interests but perhaps for political motives.

I invited Jill Baker to specifically explain how things would be for these youngsters and I think she was able to allay the fears of both the children and their parents. The meeting was lengthy and wide ranging and as it came towards an end, after perhaps three hours, I asked if there were any further questions or concerns. There weren't.

Two days later when meeting with both Mark and his assistant Jill, we discussed the way forward. They started by praising me for my courage during the whole process. But I told them I hadn't felt particularly brave. I asked them had we done the right thing in terms of both process and outcome? Were we going to improve special needs education across the borough? They concurred and so I said we hadn't been brave, we'd just done the right thing. Although, I had to admit, at times things had been pretty tricky.

We developed and presented a plan with proposals that included merging two of our special schools and closing the primary department at another. Further proposals included investing more money in our secondary schools to make them more accessible and adapting two of our primary schools for children with moderate learning difficulties. We hadn't rushed the consultative process and didn't intend rushing implementation. The whole process would take three full years but that didn't lessen our determination to resolve things that had been left for too long.

Visiting one of our local large supermarkets around this time I bumped into a senior teacher at one of our special schools. She said to me with her Scottish intonation, 'Dinna wobble'. Having been brought up amongst people with Scottish accents, I knew what she meant. I'd been told that previously the restructuring of special needs education had almost been accomplished before. But people had 'wobbled' at the last moment. I didna!

Having, courageously or otherwise, stewarded the consultation process to a conclusion, I left the leadership of change passing it on to those who were going to manage it. I actually heard little about it ever again.

Some years later I happened to 'bump into' one of the two main front row protagonists from that fraught consultative process. We said hello in a friendly manner and asked each other how we were. I was told 'you were right in what you did and in the way that you did it'. I replied that you had no necessity to say that, that we had done what we had done and that was all now behind us. But I thought their words then were both magnanimous and courageous.

* * *

Whilst we addressed and resolved the issue of special education across the borough there were other things that had to be addressed and accomplished.

David Blunkett announced a major investment programme doubling the money the government spent on repair and renewal of our schools. This really was wonderful time for education, making for a land flowing with milk and honey.

A whole primary school in Darwen, Holy Trinity, described as crumbling, was to be totally replaced and extended costing some £1.5 million. As always, we had schemes properly costed and ready to go. Civil servants and politicians at a national level loved us for that and that 'trick' gained us a lot of additional funding.

It was also in early 1999 that I was approached by the Labour Party nationally to contribute towards drawing up the manifesto for the next general election, which eventually occurred in June 2001. To be honest this approach came as a surprise as I'd only been involved really for less than two years. But it kept Blackburn on various metaphorical maps, in the inner realms of education but also in developing education policies responsive and attractive to people electorally. The local paper quoted me as saying 'This is a great achievement and compliment for Blackburn with Darwen. Things we have faced, achieved and learned here may help inform and influence national education thinking well into the Millennium.'

The director, Mark Pattison, was similarly having his track record in education recognised as he was invited to join the government assessment panel that would select future rounds of applications to be participants in the Education Action Zones as that process got further rolled out nationally.

I remained as chair of the Prince's Trust locally, having taken on that role from Malcolm Doherty a few years earlier. Although I sometimes worried about some people's motives for their participation, it did fill gaps in moving post-school-aged young people along.

We also developed a programme called Parents as Educators. This was a scheme designed mainly for parents of primary-aged kids so they knew more about what and how their children were being taught in schools, so they could support that process. Initially, around seventeen primaries in the Education Action Zone participated. Those completing the course based at the college gained Open College certificates. After presenting a hundred, mainly mums, with their certificates, it was great to talk to them afterwards. For many of them, this was their first foray into further education and, because of that, they were going on to take qualifications in childcare and similar kinds of work. Fantastic!

Some of these successful students found work in the summer school schemes that we ran throughout the long school summer holidays. Utilising substantial government financial support, we were able, especially with pupils with special needs, to involve some 400 pupils in a whole range of activities.

We had addressed and resolved an important issue that I'd been told had been left unresolved for a long time, far too long. But, as in life generally, leaving something unsolved not only means it doesn't go away, it gets worse. Also facing up to the difficult issues means you can then spend more time on the more positive, productive ones and we were certainly doing that as well. I think we also learned that tackling these issues showed that we had the strength not to duck but to face up to our responsibilities. We were no pushover.

Chapter 22

Say Hello, Wave Goodbye – Our Soft Sell, 1998-99

Making love with Cecilia.

We invested a lot of time and effort building strong, effective teams and celebrating and sharing success in whatever form it expressed itself.

As my own experience had taught me, teachers are extremely important agents of social mobility and social change especially if they'd travelled that road, as I had. We wanted to welcome every new member of each year's intake to the borough into the team.

We employed something around 1,500 schoolteachers when we went unitary, so I would estimate that's about fifty brand new, brand new both to teaching and Blackburn with Darwen, every year. They used to be called probationers (with little or no supervision or support during their initial year), now known as NQTs, newly qualified teachers. School improvement officer Maxine Froggatt oversaw this group of fledgling professionals. Maxine had taught in and led schools so knew her stuff. Like many of the staff we recruited to BwD, she went on later to become an assistant director and beyond.

Director Mark Pattison and I attended the NQTs' first induction day held in the upmarket conference setting of Blackburn Rovers' Ewood Park. Maxine began in her warm and disarming manner. But don't be fooled by that. A few years later I saw her in action in London at the department (of Education), locking antlers and winning against her adversary; her adversary being none other than Mike Tomlinson (later CBE) then chief inspector of schools having taken over from (later Sir) Chris Woodhead.

'Good morning, everyone, and welcome to Ewood Park but more importantly to Blackburn with Darwen's education team. I have some introductions to make, first of all these two guys next to me. One is Councillor Bill Taylor, the executive member or perhaps you might know it as, chairman of education here. And next to him Mark Pattison, the director of education. This is your first day as both a member of the teaching profession and the Blackburn with Darwen team. Whilst you're here it won't be unusual for you to meet Bill or Mark 'cause that's the way they do things. I had been a teacher and a head teacher for many years before I met the chairman or the director where I'd been working. But these guys are around and about. You can expect to see them quite a lot, because they take leadership very seriously. We used to call our director of education Mr Rubber Stamp because we never actually saw him unless you were in a great deal of trouble, and the chairman sat isolated in the town hall and issued instructions via the 'office'. We never actually saw either of them. They've asked to say a few words and I don't know how long they'll be able to stay but it's a mark of the men and this organisation that they are here to share in the first day of the great journey you're embarking upon.' We did and I stayed and later shared a cup of coffee before heading back to work.

That was saying hello to new teachers but also we wanted to celebrate every learner in the borough who made some progress, achieved a qualification or moved on to bigger and better things. Not quietly, but in front of their peers, their parents and all the professionals who had worked with them.

Let's book King George's Hall for an evening, I suggested. Our main public hall was used to staging big events, orchestral concerts, rock bands, local private schools' prize-givings. As it was planned, the afternoon was given over to displays of pupils' work whatever it might be, and then from around 6 p.m., the main event. Mark took me through the running order and the list of invitees. These included the mayor (that first year my ward colleague Councillor Salas Kiani), the leader of the council, the principals of our two FE colleges, Peter Butterfield, editor of our local newspaper and other people, leaders from local industry and commerce. Mark went on to explain that the events of the evening would be a mixture of music, dance, a little bit of drama, some poetry, all the different sorts of things that young people enjoyed doing. On the stage would be children from all walks of life and all different types of ability very much 'aiming high, including all'. I was enthused both by the hard work already put into the evening and the prospect of it too.

'Just one thing though, Mark, we need somebody to hold this together, somebody who can keep the evening "zinging" along. Someone who can engage both with the learners on the stage and everybody in the audience too.'

He came back at me immediately and not for the first time volunteered me, 'Totally right, Bill, you've talked yourself right into the job!'

The evening came along and I equipped myself with a prop, a clipboard. I'd seen TV presenter Johnny Vaughan use one as he presented Channel 4's *Big Breakfast* for four years.

We started off and I introduced each act or turn as we went along. I was linked up to a lapel mike and Howard Alderson-Perkins, the sound engineer, looked after me as he always did from somewhere up in the gods. I started by setting the scene, warming the audience up, like a poor man's Ted Robbins, the maestro of mirth and champion of chuckle as I called him on his Radio Lancashire programme. I split the audience, some on the ground floor stalls, the rest in the tiered circle, into under eighteens and over eighteens. 'I've been asked by Howard on the mixing desk to check out sound levels.' I urged the younger end of the audience to make as much commotion as they could by clapping, cheering, whistling and then it was their older counterparts' turn. No competition; you'll all know exactly who won that one. It took two or three goes for the oldies, many former 'yuffs' of mine themselves, to get anywhere near as raucous as their younger rivals.

I think the evening started with a drum and percussion band from our special schools. The boys (and girls, of course) in the band thoroughly, thoroughly enjoyed it and them being centre stage. Their joyous elation lit up their faces, the stage and the whole auditorium.

I could go on but the whole evening was a complete and utter wow, nearly 2,000 people in the building enthralled and enraptured. We made some 250 presentations, not just the normal kind of things, but for pupils who'd contributed positively to school life or their local community, helped by volunteering somewhere, that sort of off-curriculum stuff.

What an evening. My shirt dripping with sweat, I finished with my normal few little words that I think mean so much. 'Well done and thank you.'

The evening had run for two, perhaps three hours and everybody left happy and proud, either of themselves or the young people who had performed or been presented to or who were simply happy.

The directors' team surrounded me just off the stage and said well done, it was brilliant, we loved it and that I'd done very well. One commented that the clipboard had been an excellent idea and had kept the evening flowing. I showed them exactly what was attached to it. The running order, a list of who came next, the people I had to mention or thank?

The reverse side of my prop was completely and utterly blank. I'd 'winged it' for the best part of three hours. Was it why it had gone so well? I slurped a couple of pints on the way home and felt like it was a good night well done. For about the next week or so, people in schools and colleges or just going about our everyday lives commented on how fantastic it all had been.

A lengthy comment column in the *Lancashire Evening Telegraph* stated 'How heartening that our children and so many of them are being inspired and encouraged like this. This bold and excellently executed concept of the educational authority not only deserves praise for this but also for setting a standard that is bound to raise standards and which reflects the true meaning of education'. No faint praise at all from what often is a more cynical and critical direction.

But we didn't leave enjoying, celebrating and showcasing the successful work of our youngsters and their fantastic teachers there. We also felt we had a story to tell and a message to spread about our experiences during our first year. I was asked to address a national conference by the Education Network, which was attended by thirty chairmen of education committees, as they were mainly still called. I told my assembled colleagues 'the key aspects of what helps an educational authority be effective are things that include consulting and evolving, providing leadership, being creative and productive and empowering people. Another key asset is stamina'.

We ended our first year as stewards of the education of our children and all other learners with a massive musical event at Ewood Park. 2,800 children from fifty or so of our schools assembled in the massive Blackburn end of the stadium. Tina Wilkinson, previously a teacher at a primary school in Blackburn, had recently been appointed as our music advisor. Tina did us proud. Putting in the finishing touches during the morning, the children performed in front of the picnic hamper-bearing parents and others, with an orchestra and mass choir. Kathy Ashworth, my colleague at work and mother herself, came and was captivated by the unique goings-on. We were regaled by the 200-strong orchestra to 'The Saints Go Marching In', 'No Matter What' and 'The Bare Necessities' amongst other favourite tunes. Sponsors, including Crown Paints, the Music Cellar, Midland Bank, Blackburn Transport and McDonald's were all happy to help make the day a wonderful and enjoyable experience. I said a brief few words of welcome and appreciation slipping on my clown's multicoloured wig in the spirit of the event. I was quoted in our paper as saying 'this is exactly the right note on which to end our first full academic year as a local education authority'.

We'd worked hard in this first year (1998/99), got the children, their parents and communities, staff and governing bodies, the local private sector and other key partners on board with us. In terms of getting our name known in the regional and national education world, I don't think we could have done more.

*   *   *

Back at work for the Youth and Community Service in the Ribble Valley, our team had expanded such that our original make-do premises in the centre of Clitheroe were nowhere near big enough. In collaboration with Kathy Ashworth and her What Now team, providing youth information services across Lancashire and selling it on to other youth services nationally, we collaborated with local entrepreneur Andrew Ronnan who built and rented back to us a purpose-built two-storey set of premises near the railway station in the neighbouring village of Whalley. The premises included a general office, outdoor pursuits equipment store, parking for our mini buses, an IT suite, a meeting room and specific offices for key staff. It was an excellent facility and put us clearly on the Ribble Valley map. Some called it 'mini County Hall'.

When I moved to become the manager of the Ribble Valley, it had not had its own discrete focussed management. There were only two full-time members of staff: Geoff Jackson based in Clitheroe (population 13,000) managed from eight miles away in Great Harwood and Shelagh Richardson based in Longridge (population 7,000) managed a different eight miles away in Preston. The very rural Ribble Valley was 20 per cent of Lancashire's land area but was home to only 4 per cent of its population.

By attracting external and other funding, I was able to increase the team to include John Kirkham, Phil Evans, Lisa Harvey, Louise Neville, Stuart Lambley and later Gaja Gannon and Katrina Wilkinson and additional part-time staff. We also had Pino Pozzi in charge of the building, the vehicles and all the outdoor pursuits equipment, at times assisted by ex-publican Steve Fairclough.

We had an absolutely fantastic relationship with all of the six secondary schools in the Ribble Valley, many of the primary schools, the borough council, some of the more active parish councils (I think there were nearly forty!) and local police inspectors Les Martin, Bob Ford and Jennifer Coulston. Above them at chief super was John Thompson and Dave Mallaby who I also dealt with, wearing a variety of different metaphorical hats, in BwD.

The gem in all this was the general factotum of the borough council Bill Alker. Bill was like a Peter Sellers omnipresent film character; he was always there, totally reliable, knew everybody and everything. We loved him to bits. Dave Morris amiably led the little district council as chief executive with other key borough staff Chris(topher) Hughes, John Heap and the hugely talented staff at the Platform Gallery, Heather (now Chapman-)Fox, Elaine Sagar now Walsh, Katherine Shoesmith now Rodgers. Another key character and supporter was former district Scout commissioner Len Dickinson who loved the way we mutually looked after each other. I was so proud a little later to be appointed an honorary vice president for the district Scouts, unprecedented in the county. If Akela could see me now! At that AGM I produced my fitted-me-aged-fourteen and badge-bedecked Kestrel patrol Scout shirt. Quizzed, the district commissioner could not recognise or name all of my 1960s' badges!

The local Press frequently carried stories about our work, showcasing the county council. My grounding in PR in BwD had taught me media tricks which I passed on to my staff. We appeared in the two local weekly papers, the *Clitheroe Advertiser* and *Longridge News* most weeks, giving them spoon-fed copy mainly of young people doing things. We had an advisory committee that met three times a year. Appended to my report were the press cuttings from recent weeks and months. The members of our committee (mostly Conservatives) appreciated the press coverage as it demonstrated how well public funds were being spent. Our report also got to the borough and parish councils where it was widely read, well received and commented upon.

* * *

Back at BwD Council, 'why don't we take our foot off the accelerator?' was a phrase never bandied around because we just weren't like that.

An opportunity presented itself once again for us to become a city. To this day, I do not know what the benefits are of being declared a city, but we seemed up for it and tackled the application with our usual gusto. Bookmakers William Hill rated us as 33-1 outsiders to be successful.

The Right Rev. Alan Chesters, our bishop, reminded me that Blackburn was only one of two places in the country that had a cathedral but wasn't a city, the other one being Chelmsford. The tradition, linking city status to having a cathedral, goes back to Henry VIII issuing *letters patent* in the 1540s. St Asaph in Denbighshire, North Wales, also has a cathedral in a community of less than 3,500 people. St Asaph had city status confirmed upon it in 2012 to celebrate the Queen's Diamond Jubilee along with Chelmsford and Perth in Scotland. There are currently sixty-nine cities in the United Kingdom, fifty-five of them being in England.

Blackburn unsuccessfully applied to become a city in 1977 as part of the Queen's Silver Jubilee. In 1992 despite Blackburn bidding again, this time to celebrate the Queen's fortieth anniversary, only Sunderland was successful.

For the millennium year 2000, Blackburn made a bid once again. Brighton and Hove and Wolverhampton succeeded in that year. For the Queen's Golden Jubilee (2002) Preston and Newport (Wales) were successful. Platinum winners in 2022 were: Bangor (Northern Ireland), Colchester, Doncaster, Douglas (IoM), Dunfermline, Milton Keynes, Stanley (Falkland Is.) and Wrexham. We are doomed?

This is a pretty abysmal record of (five) failures and perhaps city status will prove eternally elusive to us. Or perhaps we could call ourselves the Cathedral Borough of Blackburn with Darwen?

Chapter 23

Business as Usual, Into the New Millennium, 1999-2001

When something goes wrong, I'm the first to admit it.

As the pages on the desk calendar counted down to the dawning of the new millennium, we heard the news that we had been shortlisted to be awarded beacon status for our work in education.

300 educational authorities had applied to be judged, so getting to the shortlisting was a feather in the cap of such a brand-new authority. Mark Pattison was quoted 'Our team of school improvement officers have forged excellent relationships with our schools and the recent test results (for children aged eleven) have shown tremendous improvement in performance'. He was right, we'd worked hard to establish sets of superb teams, starting with his top team of education directors which dovetailed well into the overall corporate management team and linked well with my team of chairs and vice chairs. Our best schools functioned and flourished around teamwork. Strong leadership from the head down, a good leadership team, a clear school ethos with rules where needed and strong, challenging but not intrusive governance and healthy relationships with the PTA (parent-teachers association) and other community linkages are all in the recipe for a good school.

Only two years into our time as an educational authority it was gratifying to see that the blood, sweat and tears of many dozens if not hundreds of professionals had worked wonders. As our eleven-year-olds moved from primary to secondary schools, in one year alone, their English results improved from 69 to 73.5 per cent, maths from 64 to 68 per cent and science from 70 to 82 per cent. There's no point striving for political power, achieving it, and then not harnessing it to the best effect.

Very close to Christmas we learned that we had been successful in winning beacon status and the local newspaper carried a small comment piece of praise. Two years earlier we had languished in the bottom five authorities in the country; we had moved up that league table significantly. Anne Connor, head at St Antony's RC Primary, kindly hosted our celebration event in her school. It went very well until, on leaving, my car got well and truly stuck in a muddy patch in the school. It took direct action by Peter Hunt's borough engineers to tow me out of the quagmire by Land Rover! Again, having awards and accolades bestowed upon you is all fine and good, but only if the lessons learned are bedded into practice.

Further proof that we didn't always get things 100 per cent right occurred when we hosted a national conference on educational improvement at Darwen's Astley Bank Conference Centre. Fifty education officers from all over the country assembled to hear our experience and discuss it more widely. As usual, I was the warm-up act, welcoming people, explaining a little about Blackburn with Darwen and some of our significant factors. Director Mark took over and dug a little deeper into the detail of the process. Much of this was delivered by our old friend the PowerPoint presentation. Deputy director Steve Munby, who later went on to be an author, professor, CBE and chief executive of the National College for School Leadership, was the main act. His was to be the major input for the day. It came to his turn and I think, to be fair, we'd given him a great build-up. What everyone had overlooked to ensure was that the laptop, that connected to the projector that delivered the presentation, had been switched on and was powering Steve's treatise. Almost at the moment he delivered his first words, the laptop ran out of steam and the overhead screen went blank. Steve's language was most unprofessorial having been honed in front of his beloved Toon in the Leazes end at St James's Park, Newcastle. Note to self: always keep the battery charged and take a spare and sufficiently lengthy power cable with you. After this minor setback, the day was a huge success in which Steve played the starring role.

It was also great to be present when Mark Price, the chief executive of our local TEC (Training and Enterprise Council) presented our education director Mark Pattison with the Investor in People national benchmark, the department being judged to be a best-practice employer. Mark Pattison told the local paper 'it reflects our striving for excellence and our commitment to continuous development'.

But it wasn't all plain sailing and it was disappointing to hear that our infant-aged children were taught in the biggest class sizes in the north-west. The government had set us ambitious targets to meet by 2001 and we were up to that challenge. We had recently opened three extra classrooms and funded fourteen extra teachers. Recruiting twenty-three additional teachers and building eight further classrooms was also on our drawing board. The new New Labour Government set an exacting pace, but we were up for it. We were up for it because it would transform our schools, our children, their families and their communities.

We had to change mindsets in some schools. I was asked to visit a junior school where the head teacher told me there were problems at the weekend with 'outsiders'. He took me into the playground. The school was set with housing surrounding it, surely not that unusual. 'Our problem is,' I was told, 'the outsiders use the playground at the weekend and in the school holidays. I need the fence to be higher.' 'Aren't the children safer playing here than on the surrounding roads?' Yes. 'These outsiders, do they live in these houses near to the school?' I pointed at the houses less than fifty yards away. Yes. 'Can't their mums and dads see that their children are safe?' Yes. 'Aren't the majority of the kids who play here your pupils here during the week, and not really outsiders?' Yes. 'Where do you live?' The answer was the best part of forty to fifty miles away. I wondered who the outsider was.

We must have been thought of quite highly locally. I was regularly asked to present the prizes at our local secondary schools' awards evenings. I always got a buzz from doing this as it's great to see young people and their families having a sense of success and pride. I had done a complete U-turn on this issue. The youth work culture was success, achievement and awards-averse, phobic even and I must admit I swallowed all that. Given that the top drawer in my mum's sideboard was crammed with certificates and badges, from my national cycling proficiency badge, badge-bedecked Cub and Scout uniforms, onwards, all mine, my position was hypocritical. I had to shift it and shift it I did. It's easy to eschew qualifications and certificates when you've a glut of them. Public life isn't a personal beauty parade, doing what's best for your public is the mission. As I told a not very receptive, indeed hostile, audience of my professional colleagues but realistically 'inertiavik' youth officers as a speaker at a national conference in London, 'The days of the issue-obsessed, self-possessed, self-employed youth worker are numbered.' They, displaying unheeded stubbornness, wouldn't shift from wallowing in some form of entrenched purist dogma, a bit like Labour's 'Corbynistas' in the 2015-19 period. In Lancashire, urged on by me, the Youth and Community Service snatched the opportunity using the Crime and Disorder brief handed to us, to work with schools, district councils and the police. We took some high ground left in a void. Within this Trojan horse of opportunity, we got the 'youth agenda' into mainstream policy and practice.

Back in BwD we did the little things that people liked. Little but important things. Child safety sadly became and remains increasingly important in schools and we funded extra security measures which were well received especially by schools and parents.

Mark Pattison and I tried to get round as many of the schools as we could. One day we booked ourselves in to visit Belmont Primary School. The school is more or less the last building before you cross the boundary from BwD going into Bolton Council/Greater Manchester territory. It would appear that the school is still confused about where it is situated. Even now on its website www.belmontprimarybolton.co.uk, it lists its email address as office@turtonbelmont.blackburn.sch.uk. Whilst acknowledging the school (with ninety or so pupils) is in BwD, its website goes on to explain 'Many of our children live outside Blackburn with Darwen, in the Bolton, Horwich and Bury areas.'

If you're confused, you're not alone.

Mark and I turned up and were met by the head, a very cheery, welcoming youngish guy from memory. Over a cuppa in his office he said 'Please can you tell me why are you here?' in a mildly worried tone. Bright and breezily I explained. 'Well, as chair of the education committee and

Mark here is the director, we like to get out of the town hall (a half hour drive away) and into our schools to find out how they are and how you're doing.' The school was built in 1898 and had been in the education remit of BwD, Lancashire, Bolton, possibly Manchester Councils' responsibility. No wonder they were confused.

'So, would you like a look round?' We followed his lead and he showed us around a few classrooms. The children were wonderful, extremely polite and bright-eyed and bushy-tailed. We spent about half an hour looking around, talking briefly to classes and their teachers. Then we were offered another cuppa, which we graciously accepted. I chipped in, asking if he was OK with our visit.

'To be frank,' he said, 'I was a little confused if not apprehensive. I've checked the school diary for the last hundred years and never in that time has the director or chairman of education ever set foot in this school. I was expecting the worst.'

'Is there anything we could help you with?' I asked.

He went on to explain that there was a little room at the top of the school which, with a little bit of creative refurbishment, could be made into the staffroom, releasing the current space for an additional teaching area.

'Could you look into that, Mark, please?' I asked my fellow educational intrepid explorer. 'Of course, Chair, it sounds a totally laudable project. I'll get back to the head later this week.'

As we left having made our first 'one small step' and then becoming quite pally, I undertook that Mark and I would try and return before the year 2098 – we never did.

When I became the chair of education we 'passported' onto schools about 55 per cent of the total schools' budget. Later this figure was around 90 per cent. To begin with the LEA retained responsibility for practical issues such as school transport, cleaning, grounds maintenance, etc. Schools increasingly and possibly rightly seemed to want to take on more responsibility for more of their budget. But as is said locally, you can't have your cake and ha'penny, it seemed rich that they then blamed the LEA if the school buses didn't run. I have no idea where the responsibility and the funding lies these days especially with regard to two key issues, admissions and schools' standards. These were retained within the ambit of the LEA for reasons of impartiality, equivalence, effectiveness and economy. I fear these days that strong schools flourish, leaving weaker schools, their children, parents, staff and communities, to flounder. Who is there to champion the cause of the little guys?

After initial reticence I got the sense that most of our head teachers came on board with us, team players in a winning team. It was great to see so many rewarded with honours. In early 2000 Barbara Booth, head of Shadsworth Infants, was recognised with an MBE. My youth work colleague Riaz Begum similarly was awarded an MBE. Ian Clinton, college principal an OBE. Chief executive Phil Watson, head teacher Mike Humphreys and later education deputy director Prof Steve Munby all got CBEs. Similarly, Donna Hall, previously the deputy chief executive in BwD later got awarded a CBE and also a professorship from Manchester University. Margaret Nowell, superb with the most difficult to teach children, retired in 2013. Margaret received an OBE for her work as head of St Thomas's Centre, our PRU (pupil referral unit). Being a former PE teacher, Margaret was particularly pleased to share her day at Buckingham Palace with Olympian Jessica Ennis. Former council leader Malcolm Doherty also got awarded an OBE as did one of his successors, Conservative Colin Rigby. Another council leader Councillor Mohammed Khan was awarded an OBE, later a CBE. A former ward colleague of mine and hugely dedicated Councillor Maureen Bateson gained an MBE.

* * *

With all these honours and other awards being gained I got a few invitations with which I was very pleased.

Our invitation to St James's Palace by Prince Philip, for our hugely successful work with his Duke of Edinburgh's Award Scheme (begun way back in 1956) produced its own little 'moments'. My Ribble Valley colleague John Kirkham and his wife, Brenda, had been invited too. I'm not sure anyone else from Lancashire Youth and Community Service has ever been invited.

St James's is a Tudor building commissioned by Henry VIII, going back to the sixteenth century, situated between The Mall and Pall Mall. Various different royals have lived there over the years, most recently the Princess Royal, Princesses Beatrice and Eugenie and Princess Alexandra (ex-chancellor of Lancaster University 1964-2004), the Honourable Lady Ogilvy. Little did I know, and why would anyone, that the palace also housed the Central Chancery of the Orders of Knighthood.

Anne (with stipulated hat) and I presented ourselves as directed. Every time, when required, I showed our tickets to the ushers they went 'Oh, purple tickets,' (don't hold me to a specific colour) and directed us on. All the ushers were well presented and very polite, Gold Award holders themselves.

Getting to our appointed positions was quite a trip through a catacomb of wonderfully decorated chambers known, I've learned, as the state apartments. These were a long line of interconnecting rooms.

We eventually arrived at our allocated room. The very grand fireplace was monogrammed H and A for Henry and Anne (Boleyn). Anne wasn't destined to stay over long! She would be-heading for the chop!

Both sides of this main room were cordoned off, allowing mums and dads and other relatives and my wife and I to sit and watch the proceedings. At the head of the room four chairs were positioned and, much to my surprise, that's where I was invited to be seated.

The quartet of what turned out to be the day's VIPs sat quietly and introduced themselves to each other. On one side of me there was a chap who was a furniture remover and wherever he plied his trade, he always moved anything that the Duke of Edinburgh's Award Scheme locally wanted shifting. I explained to him where I had come from and our role in the award scheme. He said that's a great idea, I've never heard of the youth service before, they should have one everywhere.

To the other side of me was a tall, athletic and very ginger-haired chap. 'Hi, I'm Bill,' I offered.

'Hello,' he said, 'my name is John Gallagher.' My mind quickly processed these little snippets of information, visual and spoken.

'You aren't John Gallagher, the famous Leeds rugby league full back?'

'Well, yes I am, but more people might remember me better for being an All Black rugby union World Cup winner.'

'Oh I don't remember that, but well done! Your accent isn't particularly Antipodean?' I observed and asked him.

'That's right,' he said. 'I was brought up in the Blackheath area of Lewisham.'

Gallagher went on to explain quietly that he had been brought up by his Irish parents in London (he was born in 1964) and what happened next was a bit of a jumble. I think he'd attended school in Blackheath and then as quite a young man had occasion, perhaps to see grandparents, to visit New Zealand. There, in Wellington, he continued his rugby union career being picked to play for the national team in his early twenties. It was a really interesting story.

'The trickiest bit,' he volunteered, 'was when I first ran out to play for the mighty All Blacks and we assembled to do the traditional and customary Haka. I'd never done it before, only having watched it and done pretend Hakas as a schoolboy' (hadn't we all?). 'I got myself hidden as much as possible in the middle of the formation. I did my best, which wasn't very good. The guy next to me said have you done this before and in best rugby language I explained I hadn't.' Gallagher told me he redressed this deficiency by taking a crash Haka course.

Unbeknown to me, whilst this exchange was taking place, proceedings began.

Everyone stood as Prince Philip, Duke of Edinburgh, entered the room. He made his way towards us four.

He spoke to the furniture remover first and thanked him very much for his logistical support. Then it was my turn. I happened to be wearing my Princes' Trust lapel badge in my role as chairman of the Lancashire Princes' Trust set up by Prince Charles. Prince Phillip pointed to it and in mock indignation asked me why I was sporting that badge. 'Well, Prince Phillip, it keeps it in the family, surely.' I thought the duke appreciated a bit of spirited repartee.

The prince quickly moved on to my rugby 1987 World Cup (held in Auckland) winner neighbour. At this point some may need reminding that Prince Philip (he would be aged around eighty when we met) had retired from polo-playing aged around fifty. But being a committed horseman, he had taken up horse-carriage riding, representing Great Britain around the world. The sport was big in New Zealand and Prince Philip had a sense of affinity and familiarity with that member nation of the Commonwealth.

Gallagher was introduced as the famous All Black World Cup winning rugby player (Gallagher was a volunteer ambassador for the DofE and he'd gone on to teach, becoming head at Colfe's Preparatory School after his joint code rugby playing career).

'So, whereabouts in New Zealand are you from?' the prince asked. There was then one of those silences that goes on longer than anticipated and the longer it goes on, the longer it's going to take to break! I found those few seconds unbearable.

'John's from Lewisham, Prince Philip. But his mum and dad are Irish,' I eventually interjected with a misdirected attempt to be helpful.

The prince tried again. 'So, what were you doing in New Zealand?' It happened again, that painfully extended uncomfortable silence. I felt the urge to try and be helpful again. I don't think my brain had processed the ineffectiveness of my first attempt! Do you know when your brain and voice disconnect from one another, but they don't tell one another that they have done?

'He was there taking Haka lessons, Prince Philip.'

I quickly discovered that, for an older chap, the prince was quite spritely on his feet. He had a quick word with the final member of our VIP quartet and then got on with the presentation of awards to the assembled younger people and their rightly proud families.

As we left the palace Anne asked what the conversations were about. I told her I'd tell her later. Much later.

*   *   *

We continued to work on improving services for the people of BwD. Nursery education had grown a little bit like Topsy (whoever Topsy is?). There were fourteen nurseries attached to primary schools, nine separate education nursery units, five social services-run nurseries and twenty-three private providers in the borough, something of a mixed bag. Working alongside Councillor Sue Reid, the exec member for social services, we set about streamlining services and provision, involving both the NHS and the voluntary sector. What I don't think we realised at the time is that we were pre-empting a future national Labour triumph, in the shape of Sure Start centres. Which like many great innovations, was abandoned due to 'austerity'.

* * *

It was at the same time as we were preparing for and undergoing a full LEA Ofsted inspection, that we started to consider entering into a public/private partnership with Capita.

It was originally mooted to me at a meeting with Malcolm Doherty, Gail Barton and Phil Watson. My initial reaction there and then was no; as had, they told me, Malcolm's and Gail's. A private sector company meddling in our affairs? Bah humbug! They told me a further discussion document was due.

At the next meeting, having received and digested this document, the meeting had more 'meat' to it. It explained that Capita were going to do this somewhere or other, that Unison, the main union whose membership could be affected, were on board with the process, that a £5 million new landmark building at the town's 'gateway' would be built by Capita but revert to council ownership at the end of the proposed fifteen-year deal. The final aspect of the proposals, that swung it for me, was the promise of several hundred new jobs coming to the borough, taking over the massively impressive Victorian India Mill in Darwen. The development of India Mill would also include serviced starter units for fledgling businesses that would be created. Any misgivings I had were fading as I read the document. The deal was costed at £205 million over its life, with opportunities to negotiate changes along the road.

This process of initial reticence was repeated as the ideas were floated past the Labour Group, then the council, until we moved towards a full and final contractual agreement with Capita.

* * *

A major systemic change in how councils functioned and were structured was offered to them in the shape of moving from the 150-year-old committee structure to a more modern executive and cabinet style. As was our common practice, we circulated our possible blueprint out far and wide beyond the town hall for a period of general consultation. Much of the work of a council goes on with little political disagreement but often when it came to council meetings, it was the empty vessels that made the most noise.

The proposals had been first mooted by Hilary Armstrong, MP for a Durham constituency and minister for local government. It really was a thinly veiled micro-mimicking of how Parliament had developed into working. There was merit in having a small number of senior councillors making all the major decisions which was indeed already the de facto situation. But for the dynamics of political group management, there were too many people outside the tent. The eight executive members with specialisms such as education, social services, economic regeneration, etc., created and allocated roles for two or three additional councillors known as executive assistant or lead members. I think I had three, one for early years and primary, another for secondary and a third for further education, training and the youth service. This certainly spread the workload around more councillors but also, to be frank, gave a broader spread and the majority of the ruling group's numbers in positions of responsibility – that is being inside the enlarged tent.

There were several models to choose from the cabinet system, an elected mayor appointing his/her own people, or an elected council leader ruling alongside a chief executive officer. Retaining the status quo seemed to be reserved for the smaller and smaller-minded councils.

To begin with it was the local media who seemed strongly against the change. Were they becoming lazy as we seemed more and more to take on the role of their copy writers? Two decades later, local papers are dim shadows of themselves as is the interaction between local people and their councils and the rigour of journalists reporting. That third party scrutiny spotlight with the associated accountability has suffered, more or less disappeared.

The business of the council was to be published six months before any major decisions. This was done totally publicly and so no member of the public, the press, or the council could claim they had no prior knowledge. All minor or major decisions were again matters of public information. Any decision could be 'called in' and subjected to further scrutiny and consideration. Each area of council activity, take education as an example, had a dedicated scrutiny committee at which any officer or councillor could be required to attend and explain or defend any decision. From my perspective, it seemed that the small 'c' conservative councils and councillors were more opposed to this streamlining. My Labour colleague Councillor Dave Smith made a good point when he said 'people are not interested in how we go about doing things on the council, they are interested in the results'. Ironically the committee system, which we were about to replace, had open access by the public to the meetings. Almost without exception, it was rare for any member of the public to attend these meetings, except perhaps for the planning committee.

Having said all this I'm not entirely sure, with the benefit of hindsight, that we got this right. We appeared to be ambivalent about how open this new form of democracy would be. Now, that ambivalence could have come from not really understanding it ourselves. We should have done better. It was late in the process that we appeared to get to grips with it. Odd really when we'd been so well prepared and open during the run-up to becoming a unitary only a couple of years earlier. Perhaps it was one major change too many, or had we become tired or even complacent? At the very least we had some remedial work to do.

To be fair to ourselves, notions of secret cloaks hadn't been our style and certainly didn't feel very comfortable. I no longer remember why it was me not council leader Malcolm Doherty who chaired the first meeting of the executive style cabinet held in June 2000. It was held in private. I issued some obfuscating smoke and mirrors statement in the local paper claiming that the meeting was to clarify procedures, not to make any decisions and placed the blame on the *Telegraph* for misleading the public.

I'm not sure I wasn't sticking my own neck out, but the metaphor works as I stuck my chin out too explaining that all future cabinet meetings would be held in public. But we also went further because for the first time members of the public could ask questions in the full council meeting. We chose to allocate time at the beginning of the meeting where previously submitted questions could be asked and answers given by the relevant person. I also argued that the eight executive members would be more accountable because people would know exactly who was responsible for making vital decisions. I went on to clarify that at least one seat for the senior opposition party would be allocated on the executive, giving them full access to all information and the right to speak and ask questions. I can't remember if I made some of this up on the hoof, but it seemed to clarify our determination to be publicly accountable.

As we got into these new procedures people got used to them and I thought they worked rather well. I don't think there's a murmur of dissent any more twenty years on. But we, on the Labour benches, at the time could have and should have done a lot, lot better.

*   *   *

Amongst all this brouhaha, Tony Blair declared a general election to be held on 7 June 2001.

It wasn't BSE that dominated the headlines in the run up to the 2001 General Election but the outbreak of foot and mouth disease which resulted in 6 million cows and sheep being slaughtered in the UK. Ironically the Cheltenham (horse racing) Festival was cancelled that year for fear of spreading the disease but not during Covid.

Jack was now firmly established, after four years as home secretary, as a Labour Party big-hitter. This meant he spent a lot of time nationwide supporting other Labour candidates in potentially weaker Labour seats. It also meant that our time in Blackburn was less frenetic. I took my usual three weeks' unpaid leave and set about all the tasks involved in being the constituency agent with, as always, a great team around me.

I always tried to get out and listen to what people were saying 'on the streets' and this normally took the shape of half an hour in Mark Smith's wonderful Coffee Exchange in the town centre. His mainly female waitressing staff always look after me still to this day. It's both decorated and furnished in an olde-worlde style and is a haunt for the boulevardier types who lecture at the college a couple of hundred yards away. I still don't really understand the barista coffee culture and leave what I'm given to drink to the girls. Whilst waiting for my drink my phone rang and a lady spoke to me. She told me she was David Hare's personal assistant and that he wanted to speak to Jack Straw as soon as possible. I explained that Jack wasn't in town but that around about the same time tomorrow might be a good time to ring. She said she would.

The next day it just so happened that around about the same time I was in the Coffee Exchange and Jack was with me. The phone rang and it was the same lady asking to speak to Jack. I asked her to hang on. Muting my phone, I told the candidate that David Hare's PA was on the line. I asked her if she could give me some idea of what it was about and she did. I asked her to hold. I told Jack pretty much verbatim what she'd said, that David Hare was interested in writing a play about candidates in this election and wanted to speak to Jack. Jack took my phone off me, went outside the coffee shop and had a ten-minute conversation.

On his return he was full of praise for me. 'Bill, that was absolutely deadpan fantastic, the way that you pretended not to know who David Hare was.' I never really knew any of the detail of the phone call but I did make it my business to find out who David Hare (knighted in 1998), playwright, screenwriter, theatre and film director was. I'm still not sure whether Jack believed that I'd never actually heard of him.

There were two difficult local election results announced. Both my former ward colleague Peter Greenwood and fellow former mayor Edna Arnold had been deselected by their respective parties in their respective wards and both chose to contest them as independents. They were both defeated after many years' loyal service to their electorates.

In the early hours of 8 June 2001 Jack won his sixth general election with a comfortable majority of over 9,000. This was my fifth general election as constituency agent.

Jack won and returned down to London, I thought still expecting to be the Home Secretary.

Chapter 24

Change Out of the Blue, 2001-02

I've waited such a long time.

We had inspection regimes, external funding applications and awards coming out of our ears. This was no less the case when it was announced, only two years into our being an LEA in 2,000, that Ofsted had determined we would have a full LEA inspection. All schools were subjected to these, so why should we expect any different? A great deal of preparation went into what was, in those days, a no-stone-unturned five-day inspection visit by a high-profile team of men and women from the ministry and the field. I got a good grilling as expected and I think gave a good account of myself. The inspection team picked out several key local schools where they wanted to test the water to a greater depth, involving governors, head teachers and other staff, including classroom observations.

Published in January 2001, comments about the LEA included: 'is very challenging and not being afraid to tackle difficult issues... has been able to establish a mutually trusting relationship with its schools... has engendered a climate of excitement and a feeling of collegiality... very high standards from the elected member leadership'. I could go on and probably on and on.

However, leaping out of the forty or so pages at me came 'a remarkable unique record that is not paralleled elsewhere in the country'. We'd worked very, very hard and I was hugely proud of everyone involved. Perhaps, quietly to myself, I uttered a word or two of self-praise. We hosted what was becoming our customary celebratory breakfast morning in our public halls including pupils, school and LEA staff, governors, private sector partners, the whole kit and caboodle.

These successes got me around the country, spreading our word. At one event I first met Mick Groves, for thirty years the lead singer with the then vastly popular folk group The Spinners ('My Liverpool Home', 'Dirty Old Town', 'The Twelve Days of Christmas', etc.). But thirty years on, Mick Groves was now Councillor Mick Groves, chair of education on the Wirral Council. Stood next to him at the event reception I started:

'Jaffa cakes, Jaffa cakes
Gimme, gimme, gimme some Jaffa cakes…'

'Good grief, are you the lad from Stockport Market with the flat cap?'
'No, I was his mate.' We reminisced, never having met before. It's worth listening to people and storing stories. They make people feel valued and break the ice.

*   *   *

I don't think most of us really understand national politics and the Houses of Parliament; it might be better that we don't. I don't think I would particularly like it and although approached, never fancied it. Another factor was I would only have been interested in being Blackburn's MP, and the incumbent and my friend, Jack, was so particularly good at it, it never crossed my mind. Also, locally is where things happen. Working locally alongside local residents to design, develop and deliver local services, aimed at local people is what floats my boat. I had never aligned myself or openly associated with any particular clique in the Labour Group. I wanted to resolve issues not join clannish factional teams. As Tory MP and former Cabinet Minister Ken Clarke put it in his autobiography 'don't play the man, play the ball'. (*Kind of Blue* Macmillan 2016 ASIN B01HBR2MIC.)

Early on the day after the June 2001 General Election our re-elected MP was on the train back down to London and Parliament. Jack's autobiography talks of him fancying a change away from the Home Office to the much broader (local government-focussed) brief that was then currently held by the Deputy Prime Minister John Prescott. But it was the job of the Prime Minister to build his team. Senior ministers had been instructed to be available in London by 11 a.m. that morning.

Robin Cook had been an MP in and around Edinburgh since 1974. From 1987 under Neil Kinnock, John Smith and Tony Blair he held four or five different 'shadow portfolios' until, in 1997, he became the Secretary of State for Foreign and Commonwealth Affairs. This was a post, according to political commentators, that Cook was adamantly reluctant to relinquish in 2001. Hence Jack's lengthy wait on the day after the General Election. Cook was shifted to another Cabinet post, Leader of the House of Commons, which was seen by many, especially him, to be a demotion. Unable to support British military intervention in Iraq, Cook quit the Cabinet in March 2003. His resignation speech in the Commons chamber, with Jeremy Corbyn sat nodding right (or is it left) behind him, has been described as amongst the most effective and brilliant in modern British politics. Sitting down, close to tears, he received a standing ovation from all sides of the house and the public gallery, entranced and captivated by it. Robin Cook died in August 2005 aged only fifty-nine, on a walking holiday in Scotland.

Jack's book explains that it got to 5 p.m. and nothing had happened, no phone call, no summons to Number 10. I'd gone for a teatime pint in the Dog Inn, my local, sitting for while with my Tory councillor pal Ian Forrest. Two-hundred and fifty yards away on Revidge Rd. I'd rung Jack at least a couple of times to find out 'what was going on' and his reply *entre nous* was short and sharp. We can read in Jack's book that it was 6 p.m. before Blair spoke with him. Totally out of the blue, he was offered the post of Foreign Secretary. Robin Cook had been in that role but now it was handed on to Jack Straw. From memory, Jack sent me a text letting me know and my wife, Anne, joined me for a quick celebratory drink.

*   *   *

But there was more unexpected change to come. This time much nearer to home.

Malcolm Doherty had been council leader seven or eight years, having taken over from Peter Greenwood. They were quite different characters. Malcolm's period of leadership had brought massive change as we moved to becoming a unitary authority. I don't think he and his two deputies Gail Barton and I could have been more different to one another, but we got things done. The transition to becoming unitary with all the squabbles along the way, mainly with LCC, adjusting after eighteen years to actually having a Labour Government to work alongside and all the transformation brought by the move towards an executive style council leadership were amongst the major changes that we faced.

In 2001 Malcolm would have been in his early sixties, not particularly old in local government terms. He'd repeatedly made it clear to both Gail and me that if ever there were rumblings that he should retire as leader he'd like to know about them. Well, there seemed to be and we spoke with him and he said he'd like to take the opportunity to retire. It was as low key as that.

There were three or four days, including a weekend, between the local elections (held on the same day as the General Election) and the Labour Group AGM. I decided to stand for the leadership. I'd been instrumental in transforming the Labour Party locally. I'd done well as chair of community and leisure, during my year as mayor, my initially reluctant three or four-year spell as finance chair and in both the transition to becoming a unitary and an LEA. Our son, Matt, was happily off at university, with Katherine about to start her A level studies.

Gail chose not to stand. Her colleague from the stewardship of the re-organisation process and now holding down the complex social services brief, Sue Reid, did. Sue and I have always got on well, to this day.

The evening of the AGM came and the votes for new leader were cast, the outcome being that I became the leader, aged forty-nine and in the council's 150th year, by a narrow margin. There appeared to be no kerfuffle or rancour. Sue Reid and Kate Hollern were elected to be the two new deputies and then executive portfolios and lead members had to be determined.

Malcolm and I had a quick word at the end of the AGM. I asked him if there was anything he would like to continue with and there was. He'd been the chairman of the county police committee for a while, had enjoyed it and was good at it. I promised that I would ensure he retained his seat on that committee. At the next group meeting, I presented Malcolm with an engraved rose bowl to thank him for all his work. Ironically, as I shifted from education to being the leader, my counterpart at County Hall, Hazel Harding, made the same portfolio move.

The opinion column in our *Lancashire Evening Telegraph* certainly threw the gauntlet down to me. Stating that I was following 'one of the most popular leaders of recent times' it went on to conclude 'Politicians both local and national need to do far more to engage the public. Open government is the key'. They didn't add that the developing digital age was transforming both journalism and the media, changing things for them imminently and irrevocably.

I got to work as a priority on three new citizen engagement projects. The first, a dedicated telephone hotline number to which residents could ring in. The second, a more modern media dedicated email address: council.leader@. And the third, regular monthly council leader-only Saturday morning surgeries, again where residents could come along with any issues they wished, directly face to face with me, accompanied by the chief executive or one of his assistants. Prior to these, residents could, if they so wished, be more specific and detail what they were going to ask. That way we might get the most relevant officer of the council to attend. This wasn't a one-way process at all because we learned first-hand what our residents were most concerned about. I can think of at least three occasions when tears were shed on all sides.

As far as the senior/executive members were concerned there were two small but key departments that were vital to our work, its development and success. We had a small policy unit originally led by Alison Milner that trawled all new initiatives policy or financial and made sure we were totally briefed and always in the 'get set' position ready to go.

That was backed up by again a small democratic services unit originally led by but including, over the years, excellent supportive officers including Carol Russell, Ben Aspinall, Phil Llewellyn, Paul Conlon, Marjorie

Waddicor, Diane Hill, Tara Duce, Cathryn Barrett, Christine Wood, Bev Wood and Wendy Johnson now Bridson. These officers were always at hand to support members in all the ways that were helpful.

Our citizens had a broad range of different means to communicate with their elected representatives. The above were complemented by the things which Jack had introduced as our MP. To regular drop-in constituency surgeries, he had added the Saturday morning town centre soapbox sessions for which I was the warm-up man. People could also visit his excellently staffed town centre-based offices, if they needed advice or support. We had a massive emphasis on getting off *our* home territory, getting out of *our* institutions, town halls, meeting rooms, offices – getting out into *our* communities – where people work or worship, shop or socialise.

We continued seeing education and employment as key council issues and I was invited to open a new classroom at Edgworth Church of England/Methodist Primary School not too far away from Belmont, near our boundary with Bolton Council. Later that same week I was on another of our frontiers with Lancashire County Council, this time opening a brand new Key Stage One extension to St Paul's RC Primary with classrooms, an IT suite and library. I was accompanied by council officer Helen Olive and the new building was blessed by the fantastic, long serving and much-loved Father Kevin Kenny of Pleasington Priory.

Three months into my time as leader the September 9/11 attack on the World Trade Centre's twin towers occurred. I'd been in work in Clitheroe and our son, Matt, rang to say something massive had happened in New York. We had no access to television in the office and I was due to move to the leader's office in Blackburn town hall a half-hour drive away. I must have got there later that Tuesday afternoon. Back then fast and adequate broadband wasn't the norm and I couldn't get to see a screen. People were very shocked. I didn't actually see footage of the events until late the next evening, catching a pint in the Dog Inn and watching their TV. It was truly shocking.

We arranged that we would hold three minutes' silence conducted from the steps of the town hall on that Friday at eleven o'clock. I stood alongside the mayor, John Williams, as shoppers, shop assistants and office workers stood with other citizens in complete silence. Those there came from every part of our community, regardless of age or ethnicity. All flags were flown at half-mast. At the time, people weren't to know that the events in New York would have national and local implications.

* * *

The Blair Government continued to assist places like Blackburn and we were awarded nearly £10 million from their Working with Towns and Cities fund. Phil Watson and I, along with private sector guys, Peter Robinson and Mike Murray, were invited down to the Cabinet Office in London to discuss this with Lord Charlie Falconer in charge of this work as Minister for Housing, Planning and Regeneration.

We also continued to contribute to the national innovation and improvement debate and activity with a joint submission by Phil and me to a parliamentary select committee on public administration.

Again, soon after I left the education brief behind and became leader, we got the news that Mark Pattison who had been our director of education for four years had found pastures new. Mark had been identified as being amongst the top ten education bosses in the country, the local paper told us. It was almost inevitable that he would be a target for private sector companies hoping to cherry-pick top talent. And so it was reported that he was moving on from his £80k a year job with us to work for Serco running Bradford's outsourced education for a reported £130k. Looking back, I often wondered if Mark was ever sure he made the right choice in leaving. The dust had hardly settled on Mark's departure when his senior assistant and acting director, Jill Baker, announced she was bound back to Salford to take up the post as head of their education service. But that's history and we went about recruiting replacements and were first of all pleased to offer the top job to one of our deputies, Peter Morgan, sadly an Everton fan. Then we learned that Steve Gallagher, one of Phil Watson's senior exec directors, had secured the role of chief executive at Knowsley Council on Merseyside. Losing these key staff to bigger and better jobs in larger councils didn't come as a surprise. For it to happen in such quick succession was an organisational blow but one we'd expected and had to face up to. Replacing them meant examining the vacancy so created re-evaluating and reshaping the job description, recruiting, reading all the application forms and going through the shortlisting and selection process to making an appointment. That could easily total five full 'working' days for each elected member involved, on top of all the other things in their lives. I think we mainly got these things right.

*   *   *

Something we got particularly wrong, and this is because of poor leadership, information and consultation, was the rerouting of the triangular orbital route just south of the town centre (known locally as Town's Moor). Twenty plus years on, nobody will really recall this but the town centre ground to a halt, drivers were totally incensed as gridlock came to town. We'd just beaten West Ham 7-1 at Ewood Park but yours truly and his family carload soon swapped their victory-pumped elation for static driver's road rage. This had been mismanaged. Council staff and senior councillors responsible should have been out there weeks before with leaflets explaining what was going to happen and why things would be better. Leader's lesson learned – make sure you know what's going on and where things could go wrong.

But, by and large, we had done very well, managed massive change, introduced creative innovation and improvement and made a number of things much better in less than four years, to the extent that chief executive Phil Watson advocated and encouraged us to compete for the leading local government trade magazine, the *Local Government Chronicle*'s annual showcase event. We were to be considered for the prestigious Council of the Year award.

This was a rigorous process, the outcome not to be announced until March 2002. Our 3,500-word submission brochure accentuated the positive.

Several our innovative improvements were in the area of education, school improvement being the most prominent. Sue Reid, with her deputy Jack Bury OBE, supported by director Ken Foote, had worked hard to get our social services department into the top twenty most improved in the country.

We also moved our 9,500 previously council homes into a new arm's length social housing provider then known as Twin Valley Homes (now, as Together Housing, their portfolio of 38,000 properties stretches coast to coast across northern England). Proud to have been brought up in council housing, this didn't sit comfortably with me. But the move gained access to millions of pounds that would be spent on improvements such as double glazing, central heating, new kitchens and bathrooms, better insulation, the domestic features we all desired.

We'd also negotiated and agreed a public/private partnership with Capita. Similarly, the deal with Capita was initially not really my cup of tea but I became convinced as the negotiating process progressed. This was ground-breaking at the time, moving 500 'back office' council jobs across and attracting 700 new jobs locally including BBC TV licencing.

Our thirteen-point public service agreement with the government also meant the prospect of a reward of £275k for every target met by 2004. Minister Nick Raynsford visited us to hear our good progress towards being successful in securing the £4 million additional funding. The way we had tackled the new governance arrangements with an executive making decisions and scrutiny committees examining them was hailed as a national benchmark of good practice. It also seemed like we were on a local government tourist trail with national (including ministers Stephen Byers, Phil Hope, Alan Johnson, Chris Leslie and leader of the Labour Group in the European Parliament, Gary Titley MEP et al) and regional bodies as well as other local councils, visiting us to look at how we did things. Our local citizens satisfaction rate had gone up from 49 per cent to 59 per cent; not bad for 'that bloody council'.

The council did of course have its dissenters and, stepping outside of what should be a non-political role, the mayor that year Councillor John Williams was particularly politically vociferous. After a trial period of some eighteen months where we dealt with some of the teething problems, we formally adopted our new system as tried and tested. Paradoxically, some years later, when the then critical Tories and Lib Dems had a brief period of power, they chose not to change the 'undemocratic' system they'd inherited. MMMmmmmmmm?

We went through a disruptive period of losing senior staff who'd cut their teeth in Blackburn. After Mark Pattison and others, Steve Weaver, deputy chief executive, who had been a key man over twenty-seven years especially in the reorganisation of the council and difficult inspection regimes, went to be chief executive for Blackpool Council. Director of social services Ken Foote's departure to Hull followed. That we promoted another deputy to that vacant post, Stephen Sloss, was testament to our strength in depth 'squad approach'.

As well as the beacon status already awarded for education, we had also gained the same prestigious national award for community legal services, fostering business growth and our library service.

But still as a comparatively new council were we not 'punching well above our weight'? Well, that's what we normally did.

The Oscars-style Council of the Year Award celebration was to be held in London in the middle of March 2002 at the Savoy Hotel, four or more months after despatching our submission. The group that travelled down to the capital included Phil Watson, me, former leader Malcolm Doherty, Tory Group leader Colin Rigby, Sue Reid and Steve Weaver. Our MPs Jack and Janet joined us later.

The evening progressed with awards in different categories, e.g. best HR department, finance department, etc. It was compered by actor Richard Wilson who played Victor Meldrew in TV's *One Foot in the Grave*. The climax of the evening, of course, was the result announcing the Council of the Year. Our table fell quiet in expectation. When it was announced 'I didn't believe it!' We had won, we were elated. I really don't remember the next few minutes, the walk down to mount the dais, the pats on the back and the handshakes. This year it was a joint award with the London Borough of Camden. Their leader, whose day job was as a consultant child psychiatrist, didn't seem over comfortable with me putting my arm round her as the triumphant photographs were being taken. Well, perhaps, you can't win 'em all? It must have been a night to remember but to be honest there's quite a lot of the evening, especially later, that I didn't.

I was up early and interviewed by BBC Radio Lancashire on their breakfast programme as I crossed that 'boingy' footbridge that traverses the Thames somewhere between St Paul's Cathedral and the Globe Theatre. Its springy nature did nothing for my fragile state.

Achieving this award was no mean feat but we couldn't have done it without the talent, hard work and cooperation of our 7,000 staff. I was quoted as saying 'today is a new day and it's back to work. We will not be complacent. We know there is room to improve and we continue doing so'.

*   *   *

But back to routine council matters it was. We had things to get on with, especially the new dynamics of having outsourced some of our services and staff to Capita in a public/private partnership. This was ground-breaking at the time and took a while to negotiate and agree. Their then chief executive Rod Aldridge (later Sir) took a very much hands-on approach to this supported by key senior staff such as Tony Lubman, Terry Boynes, John Tizard and Graham Cowley.

The agreed implementation date in the summer of 2001 coincided with me taking over from Malcolm as leader. I'm not even sure it wasn't on my first day in the leader's office. My youth work union had begun life as CYSA (Community and Youth) then CYWU (from association to workers' union; Trotskyist influences).

I'd had experience of being a union member whilst employed by the county council and had never felt particularly valued. So, as a demonstration of how I felt, meeting Unison members on my first day seemed like a must.

The town hall official for the union was a younger woman and I invited her in for a cup of tea. I'd not met her before. After a spot of 'getting to know you' chit chat, I asked her what was on her agenda. I said I assumed the deal with Capita would be high up. 'Not at all,' she replied. 'Everything is being dealt with, everybody is happy and we just want to get on with things.' I was genuinely surprised. 'OK, please always contact me, if there's any way we can help. Is there anything else right now?'

Back then 'facilities agreements' were designed to enable the staff side to conduct their roles within the organisation and she went on to explain that she felt she'd been allocated insufficient time to fulfil her union role. Being the recipient of half a day a week allowance by the county council, I knew this was a tricky balance to strike and maintain. I invited the union official to go away, think about it and produce a paper for the next personnel committee and in the meantime, I would also think about it and chat to the committee chair. The issue must have been resolved as it was never raised again.

So, talking of time, how long does it take to be leader of the council? I monitored this during my first week as leader and then in the final week, before we went on our annual family summer holidays. I didn't dare tot them up again. My at-work working week was 36 1/4 hours, and I added to that the hours I spent on council matters. The first total was seventy-four hours, the second ninety-four. Perhaps you can see why I never kept a running total again?

To know what was going on and never face any surprises, I established a series of regular Friday teatime meetings. I would go and shop on Blackburn market, buying meats or fish and other stuff. Anne would drive past to collect my secret bag of ingredients, like an episode of *Ready, Steady, Cook.*

I would then wander over to my office in the town hall. These Friday meetings were on a four-week cycle. Week one, just Chief Executive Phil and me. Two, was with his deputies included. Three, my deputies were participants and four, the other party leaders, usually Colin Rigby from the Tories and Paul Browne for the Lib Dems.

Why that format and sequence? Well, first of all, it gave me and Phil a chance to chat things through, then for his deputies to report back, so we could all discuss right across the council in more detail. Then the council leader and his deputies got engaged in an informed debate with the senior council officers. Finally, the Lib Dems who had whinged about the new council system, but then never really participated in it. This was an in front of witnesses briefing, mainly by the chief executive to explain to those who didn't want to hear what was going to happen and why, over the next month, three months, six months. The regular full council forum was usually a whingeing session by the Lib Dems that they hadn't been told what was going on and were being kept in the dark. This process stopped them having such an alibi.

These meetings started about 4.30 p.m. and went on perhaps till 6.30 p.m. or a little later. Anne would drive to the old town hall, collect me and then we'd have an hour in a local pub together. After, it was home to see what she'd concocted from her given bag of market-fresh produce, often fish. We know how to party!

Some of the Friday teatime meetings were big dos and some were little dos, a mixed bag. What was to become known as the Capita building was quite a big do, six storeys and £5 million of investment, in a way the manifestation of this public/private partnership. What we'd undertaken was indeed cutting-edge local government services provision. Once again, we were on the public services tourism trail and were regularly the main speakers around the country on what we'd done, why and the lessons that we had learned.

Mistakes were made and lessons learned early on in our relationship with Capita and their performance in delivering our services. The first of any significance was dealing with housing benefit claims where it would appear the delay and the backlog were spiralling out of control. This became headline news in the local paper and it wasn't photos of the staff responsible at Capita splashed across the front page – it was me! It was reported that the length of delay had increased to three months and in some cases, people had been evicted. I was livid. I didn't mind taking the rap for things I'd got wrong but not for things that other people had. A meeting of all the senior people concerned, aka the accused, was convened. I would chair it.

Uncharacteristically, I think most people would agree, normally having a very long fuse, I went into the meeting in a 'take no prisoners' mood. The Capita side began rather limp-wristedly, not a good tactic. There was quite a bit of swearing, all of it from me. I didn't want to hear what had gone wrong. I made it clear I wanted to know who was going to put it right and by when; it seemed straightforward to me. Then I must have mellowed from my red mist moment, as I apologised for my language but made it clear to the private sector professionals who had made these mistakes that had they been made by our council officers they would have been similarly the focus of my ire. Terry Boynes, a good bloke, undertook to lead both the rectifying of the crisis and report back. I learned that displaying a loss of your temper sometimes helps but can't be your default demeanour.

The outcome of this benefits backlog fiasco was some serious increased investment in staffing to tackle it after direct intervention by Capita big cheese Rod Aldridge, harried by exec member Councillor Frank Connor, after which 92 per cent of claims were processed within the target thirty-five days.

People, including some councillors, like to have hobbyhorses, often for them to swankily ride about on to make the maximum noise and nil impact. Gritting the roads is one such cause célèbre. Sometimes it was those who didn't submit any ideas for the council annual budget who bellyached that we should spend more on this, or that, or the other. Freezing weather results in icy roads, icy roads cause chaos. We all get that. But when it does happen and it's not all that frequent, everybody expects every road, country lane and pavement to be treated with grit and salt. In a very cold spell in February 2002, it happened here in Blackburn with Darwen. One of our least responsible scrutiny committees, it was reported, called for all of the roads in the borough to be gritted. The local paper reported that the committee did not discuss the cost of such a process. I got only a little bit livid about this. We spent at the time £330,000 on gritting. I got officers to cost up how much it would cost to have an all-roads, all-weathers gritting service. The answer was an additional 143 per cent, a rise of £6.50 a year on every resident's council tax. More new vehicles would have to be purchased that would be mainly mothballed for large chunks of the year, more salt and grit would have to be bought and stored, usually without being used, more staff would have to be put on unsocial hours standby to load and drive the gritters. We actually gritted 25 per cent more roads than was nationally recommended. We conducted a random-sampled phone opinion poll about residents' preparedness to buy into paying extra for more gritting. 64 per cent thought it was a bad idea. I was starting to get a taste for this 'put up or shut up' approach. It made sense and had a curbing impact on the stupid, inane, empty vessel gobbing-off by certain councillors and, in some cases, journalists. Officers also saw that having the arguments prepared and costed was a good approach and minimised having to tilt at windmills. I think this would be called 'on the job' training for me at least. As Jack Straw had said in his interview with *Times*' journalist Peter Riddell, 'there's no real training for being in charge, for being where the buck stops'.

We had many things as an executive to discuss, decide and get on with. One excellent forum that we introduced was our fortnightly policy development sessions starting about 6 p.m. and going on till around eight or nine. These were open and honest, no holds barred sessions with the eight elected members of the executive and Phil, with his team of exec directors. Sometimes, for bigger issues, this might be a full day in a seminar room somewhere. If an exec member or one of the senior officers had an idea or an issue they wanted to be resolved, that was the place to bring it. There was a huge amount of imaginative and creative energy amongst that talented and committed group of people. And we had fun too. It was in this setting that we would tease out the problems, the strengths, weaknesses, the opportunities and threats. Tease maybe too soft a word; sometimes these were thrashed out with some rather heated arguments and colourful language. Parallel processes also took place within each executive member's specific portfolio area where the lead members for education, social services, whatever would similarly thrash things out solving problems or generating policy.

*   *   *

People put unrealistic, not really relevant, expectations on local councils. 'They' should do 'something' about 'it'?

We were entering what must have been the heyday for citizen/voter engagement in Blackburn.

Jack had his nine to five, Monday to Friday offices slap bang in the middle of town. His staff built up great knowledge and expertise in dealing with the myriad of different issues presented to them. He held constituency surgeries, half a dozen of them a month, in numerous different parts of his constituency. He handled and solved issues presented to him so successfully that he quite rightly restricted taking up cases from actual Blackburn constituents only. It appears that his Saturday morning outside Marks and Sparks soapbox sessions had been running forever. He drew 'rolling' crowds of possibly a hundred or more. People and Jack lapped it up, interactive banter, some serious, some not, Jack always including in his repertoire a light-hearted dig at nearby local football rivals Burnley, known locally as the Dingles.

Jack's session was so nationally renowned, visited by many news crews, that when I hosted Deputy Prime Minister John Prescott on a visit to Blackburn he wanted to see and stand on the very spot. The photograph I sent was used to tease Jack at the next cabinet meeting. Even Jeremy Paxman heard of and was interested in this activity. He came to Blackburn to experience it. It was interesting to talk to him about the different *tactilities* of the modern politician. His field trip to our town warranted a mention in his 2007 book, *The Political Animal: An Anatomy*. Jack and the processes around the soapbox and our other engagement media gained Paxman's praise.

After the soapbox Jack would nearly always pop over to the market to buy some fish, often kippers, some potato cakes and stuff like that. The main thing was to be seen, to chat affably with stall holders and their customers. Then it was back to his flat just off the town centre for a bite to eat. Often William and/or Charlotte would arrive and off they'd go via the little street corner Ivy pub on Infirmary St to the match at Ewood; a lot of visibility and interaction with all different segments of his community of voters.

On one occasion whilst in the Premier League, late nineties I think, Blackburn Rovers were hosting Newcastle United. My pal and the chairman of the education committee for Gateshead Ian Mearns was an avid Toon fan. Ian contacted me to say he was in town to watch his beloved Magpies and for me to name a pub for us to meet around about midday, far too early for me. I told him that my friends would be in the Ivy before the kick-off but I probably wouldn't. 'Howay Man,' he responded.

Feeling guilty, we did pop into the pub just before two. It was packed with away fans. I found Ian. 'Well, you never told me that the Home Secretary was going to be in the boozer.' I found Jack at his usual table sat with the usual people, often Bob Hogg and his two sons. In public, I don't think I ever saw Jack drink very much, a half of mild, perhaps two. There was hardly any room on the table it being absolutely laden with multiple half pints of mild. Jack said, 'I'm not sure who they are but people keep putting halves of mild down in front of me.' I asked Ian what was going on. He said 'It's just so the lads when they get home tonight can boast that they bought the Home Secretary a beer!' Most of the beers remained not drunk as we set off for the kick-off. In 2010 Ian became the MP for his hometown.

On another occasion, at one town centre soapbox session, some younger guy was giving Jack some grief. He never minded this, a bit of mild heckling, which added to the street theatre. He nearly always got the better of these exchanges and anyway he had the microphone and PA system. After the game, Anne and I usually bobbed into the Ivy for Phil Riley's one-word analysis of the match. His repertoire wasn't extensive, marvellous or atrocious spring to mind. One time as we were watching the results and highlights on the TV, this young lad started. 'I bloody gave Jack Straw what for today on his soapbox session. Wiped the bloody floor with him!' he swaggered to his assembled audience. It was indeed the same lad from the morning's events. He caught me out of the corner of his eye, smiling. He recognised me, winked and returned to the usual bar room match post-mortem.

The council also developed a suite of different ways the public could engage with us. Gone were the days when a previous leader, a lovely guy called Frank Higham, told me 'Nah, they vote for us once a year and then we get on with it.'

Most ward councillors held monthly surgeries in their communities. We posted the Labour arrangements in the council paper *The Shuttle*. Opposition members complained their surgeries weren't published, the reason for that being they didn't always hold them. They soon did or at least published that they did.

As leader of the council, I offered people a dedicated telephone number, an email address and the Saturday morning talk to the leader surgery session.

We also didn't only hold our meetings in the town hall in Blackburn. Our 'exec on the road' initiative moved the meeting of senior councillors to being sometimes in Darwen and sometimes in community centres dotted around different communities.

The icing on the cake, the jewel in the crown of all this activity in my opinion were our Friday night meetings held in different communities. I don't think we actually coined a term for them, but I called them community accountability engagements. Different venues, mainly community centres, were chosen and Jack's staff by and large would leaflet 1,000 of the properties nearest to the location. Meetings were always on a Friday night and began promptly at 6 p.m. with the promise of lasting no more than an hour and a half to two hours.

The top table comprised Jack the MP, me as the leader of the council, the chief executive of the council, the senior police officer, usually the chief superintendent and the senior member of the local NHS staff, at the very least.

Someone would always start the meeting with a welcome and introductions. People on the top table might sometimes do a brief input. But it was mainly for local residents to raise local issues or points of view. It was very rare that less than 150-200 people were in attendance. Issues were raised and if they were slightly personal, people would be asked to hang on till the end of the public session. At the end of that, the audience would be told the date and place of the report back meeting, usually six or eight weeks later.

Residents appreciated these opportunities but also enjoyed them. At the end of one meeting, an older guy, one of those that always held the elbow of your jacket when he was telling you something, told me he'd told the wife as he took his hat and coat off the back of the door 'I'm just popping out to listen to the Foreign Secretary for a while. I might have a pint on the way back. I'll see you later.' Pure gold!

At the report back meeting, the top table would give an update on tasks they'd undertaken to follow up. Police Chief Superintendent Dave Mallaby, another really good bloke, was asked about something quite detailed. Dave checked his notes of the earlier meeting; he had made note of whatever it was. 'I've got to hold my hand up here,' he told the audience. 'The reason why I've not done anything about this, is because I forgot.' 'Fair dos,' said his interrogator. Dave then offered that, if he had the resident's address, a reply would be with him in person within forty-eight hours. In my book, that's Rolls Royce standard community accountability. Dave's fallibility and honesty endeared him to those present.

I think by and large our residents appreciated all the different ways they could engage with local public servants. One guy wasn't too happy with me one Friday evening whilst I was out having a drink and conversation with my wife – he came over and said, 'I've got this problem and I want to talk about it now'. I apologised to him saying not now but I was more than happy to listen to him the next day, Saturday morning, at my regular talk to the council leader spot, starting at half nine. 'You expect me to get up that early on a Saturday morning? Stuff it!' Not really a satisfied customer.

Chapter 25

Moving Things On

I'm following the river down the highway.

I've been in leadership roles, in a number of different environments, over many decades, before I became leader of the council.

This seemed to come with even greater scrutiny. There is of course the old adage that the opposition's in front of you and your enemies are behind you. But it didn't feel like that to me and I hoped a team spirit had been engendered in the Labour Group. I involved the opposition parties as much as possible, perhaps sometimes more than they wanted. Most of the officers seemed to understand some sense of newness with my approach. As far as the local media were concerned, I always replied to any inquiry they made as soon as possible. Even if they rang me in the middle of some major issue at work, I tried to reply promptly and with a proper answer. I think they respected that and understood I had no problems with the critical but had little time for the cynical.

One time an article appeared in the local paper with a photograph of some horrendous fly tipping in a neighbourhood back street. I rang them straight away and asked them to tell me exactly where this stuff had been dumped and I would ensure it was removed ASAP. The answer? The photograph had just been lifted off the Internet as an example of how the fly tipping might have looked. Poor, lazy journalism and I told them so and they didn't repeat that kind of unprofessional behaviour again.

There was another 'episode' that annoyed me which I took up in writing with the perpetrators. Namely, actor Kevin Kennedy who played Curly Watts in *Coronation Street*. Curly Watts annoyed you, Councillor Taylor? I tried my best to take being a councillor seriously as did most of my colleagues. But Granada ran several storylines about how Curly, a former bin man, now the manager of Freshco, having beaten poor old Audrey Roberts, was behaving badly as a councillor. The things they had the character doing were well beyond the rules that appertained to councillors. Granada's written response included, 'Curly is one of our best-loved characters, mainly for the comedic side of his personality' and that all viewers knew what was fact and what was fiction.

Two lessons for me to learn early on were that people would approach me apparently amicably, only wanting to use my position and also that my thinking was and really had to be three to six months ahead of everybody else, including some in the ruling council group. In the first case, I learned to weigh up not only what people were saying, and indeed at times weren't saying and also why. Always feeling like the pathfinder and pacemaker but also having an overall comprehensive and comprehensible view of things, not just one particular issue, was just a fact of life of leadership.

Going back a century or so, councils really were 'all singing, all dancing', responsible for gas, water and electricity, road fund licencing, running (literally) baths for dirty citizens to wash in. You still hear older folks calling water 'corporation pop'. But a lot of this is no longer the case and it's often the citizen that hasn't kept up with the times, or adopts the approach that, when I run out of people to blame, just pin the fault on the local council. How many hours these days do we waste on a customer 'care' line or 'help' desk trying to get a utility or other service matter resolved, change a payment, get a tradesman to call or even talk to a human being? Councils, councillors and town halls are accessible and easier to target to moan about or at, even when it's nothing to do with them.

* * *

The main shopping centre in Blackburn was tired, looking like the 1960s construction which indeed it was. It needed significant investment, which was mainly the responsibility of the private sector, quite often using massive insurance companies' investment funds. The main role of the council was as an honest broker, bringing together those who could actually make change happen. This is exactly what we did and I think for a medium-sized town in northern England, our current shopping mall is now state of the art.

In the early seventies when I first came to Blackburn there was one main artery, King William St., through the centre of the town with shops, offices and other facilities loosely congregated around it.

Now, after many years and many people's skill and hard work, traffic, that doesn't have to enter the town centre, flows well around it and the footprint of the town centre stretches much further afield. The cathedral seems part of the town centre, next to it a pedestrianised Church Street has five public art statues in bronze, granite, steel, water and light as a metaphorical depiction of the growth of cotton. When I first showed these to Red or Dead brand designer Wayne Hemingway, he was over the moon about the imagination shown in the centre of his hometown. I'd met Wayne for the first time at some conference or other staged at the Dunkenhalgh, a Mercure group hotel facility a few miles from Blackburn. We got talking and got on well. He was straightforwardly adversely critical of councils and the public sector. We exchanged some ideas and parted company, with him assuring me that he didn't expect to hear from me or for us to meet again. Three days later we met again in Phil Watson's office (for reasons of probity) and much better relations and reputations were built from then on.

The cathedral quarter with its much-loved mother, child and teddy bear statue, now has restaurants, office blocks and a hotel. There's one large supermarket, with aspirations for at least one more. King George's Hall sits in the middle of the next development area of the town centre. Nearby with some £60 million-plus worth of new build investment, all except the original Victoria Building, of course, sits the very twenty-first-century Blackburn College. The college stretches the town centre by several hundred yards. It is here where thousands of students, taught and supported by hundreds of staff, can study from community education through to university degree standard.

But not just in Blackburn the main town, but in neighbouring Darwen, things were happening although their Jeremiah gloom and doom merchants would have you think otherwise. India Mill is an iconic Industrial Revolution-born building, its chimney dominating the Lowry-like skyline. It was built in the 1860s resembling an Italian campanile. It is 303 feet high and spans twenty-four feet across in both directions. Working alongside our partners in Capita, they brought in 230 new jobs including the BBC TV licence and Criminal Records functions. It was intended to bring 200 more jobs and also to open up the mill for additional job start-up units covering some 37,500 square feet at a cost of £2 million.

A list of some of these achievements in a June 2001 *Telegraph* opinion column ended stating 'today our unitary authority can feel rightly proud of what it has achieved'.

I very much wanted to get this positive message and a sense of pride in our borough out into the community and my next scheme was a tour of our secondary schools in the borough, to speak to our fifteen to sixteen-year-olds there – Year 11?

First stop was Pleckgate High School where head of year and celebrated church organist Mike Emery welcomed me as guest speaker to his year eleven assembly. I'm not quite sure which one of us was Morecambe with the other one Wise, but we performed a superb double act which Mike later described as one of the best assemblies ever. I developed an agenda to this input including offering a £10 voucher if anybody could get the question right at the end of my input. It made for very attentive listening. I began by asking the 200 or so young people in the hall had the council done anything for them already that day? No. And if they thought it was money well spent to cheer. No. Right, well, we've paid Mr Emery's salary for today already. One person cheered. We've made sure the roads and pavements on your way here were safe and well maintained. We've made sure there's no vermin in the sewers by the sides of the roads. The parks where you might go to play after school, that's the council's responsibility too. And on and on.

The $64,000 question? Well, a tenner! That was how many bins a year did the council empty? I, of course, knew the answer then but no longer remember and certainly it will be many fold more now we have multiple bins to deal with. The winner of the prize was always dead chuffed. Mike Emery told a local paper 'the presentation was an excellent introduction to citizenship which received positive feedback from the pupils'.

My exploits in the school hall must have won national notice because when I addressed Year eleven at St Wilfrid's C of E School a reporter from BBC Radio 4 was dispatched to witness and report on it.

The assembly took place in St Luke's Church just up the road from St Wilfrid's. The acoustics enhanced my lapel mike and speaker system, and I was quickly into the full swing of my routine.

At the end of my performance the young southern journalist asked if he could ask me some questions but before doing so there was something he'd like to say. 'I'd just like to say, Councillor Taylor, how wonderfully eloquent you were just now.'

I retorted 'Thank you very much. I don't know whether to blush or curtsy at that, but I can see the headline already. Man in north strings sentence together.'

If necessary, we would string a few more sentences together in public criticism of our own Labour Government and this was particularly true as we were pathfinder status for housing market renewal funding. It was slow in coming and later than expected so we made representations to the responsible minister John Prescott. This I did in conjunction with local Labour MPs including Peter Pike in Burnley, Janet Anderson in Rossendale and Darwen, Greg Pope in Hyndburn and Gordon Prentice in Pendle.

Whatever the case was we were always prepared to fight our corner, the council that is. Opposition councillors disingenuously joined in a hoo-hah about school transport, providing buses to get kids to and from schools. Our schools had lobbied hard to have more of their budget devolved directly to them and we had acceded. Lib Dem Paul Browne told the local paper that 'the local Labour Group should be ashamed'. The Tory leader Colin Rigby urged that the decision should be revisited. Did these representatives of the people not understand or choose not to understand the implications of what they had previously discussed and voted for? A hundred parents turned up at the executive board to protest, not having, I assumed, all the facts. Some schools' buses were statutory, but not all. LEAs were also under increasing pressure from the government to devolve more funding directly for schools to make their own decisions about how it was spent (it moved in our first four years from 55 per cent to 90 per cent). Collectively schools also had £5 million stashed away in their coffers as reserves, more than the council (£4 million). I was disappointed in our schools being so 'economic with the truth' and made sure people knew. Schools had asked for and got more autonomy over their budgets, some schools' transport was mandatory but not all of it, schools had greater reserves than the council. As Sue Reid told parents via the local paper 'if people want the buses, they should talk to their schools. These aren't pleasant decisions, but we are doing what central government has told us to.' The reports ended 'no one from the affected schools was available for comment due to the summer holidays'. I think we demonstrated that we were no soft touch and wouldn't roll over to either the government, our schools, or the parents. People should make decisions based on the full facts and not emotive or petty party-political utterances.

We also had to stand up to central government, this time the new Home Secretary David Blunkett, as we felt we'd had a disproportionate allocation of asylum seekers being settled in Blackburn with Darwen, 894 when our target was some 700. Many of these poor folk had come from Kosovo and other places in war-torn Eastern Europe. I had gone to Manchester Airport to welcome these families. What shocked me about this plane-load of people, numbering 180, is that their collective entire worldly possessions would probably have fitted under and on most people's dining tables.

These wretched folk were ethnic Muslims, tending not to adhere to Islam as their Lancashire counterparts did. The representatives of the Lancashire Council of Mosques were wonderful and welcoming towards these refugees. But they drew the line at acceding to our guests' repeated requests for whisky!

It was in the August of 2001 when we got the news that the new inspection regime known as the comprehensive performance assessment or CPA had been agreed and that we were going to be one of the first beneficiaries or victims of it, however you saw things. I told the full council forum 'it's an opportunity for us to be tested on our strengths and weaknesses.'

Chapter 26

Beating the Boundaries, Again

Oh Congressman, won't you tell that Congressman.

When I first got involved in the Labour Party in Blackburn in 1978/9 the wards were mainly named after Anglican church parishes: St Michael's, St Jude's, St Stephen's, Cathedral, etc.

Things change and in moving from a district council to the new unitary arrangement, it did seem to make sense to restructure the wards to make things easier to understand and fairer. I don't think the wards had been restructured possibly for at least twenty years and many houses had either been cleared or built and families and communities had shifted and changed character.

This was a massive and complex process and there had to be some fundamental basics, the ground rules. In 1995/6, knowing the massive change (to unitary) was imminent, somebody had to take the initiative.

A small team of Labour people including me, Phil Riley and John Roberts met at our house to discuss what should be done. We plumped for a similar-ish number of councillors as there were currently, sixty. We thought wards with three councillors representing them made sense in terms of spreading the case workload constituents generated. So, from memory, that meant twenty-two wards; mostly the more urban situated had three councillors each (in outlying rural/less-populated areas, one ward had one councillor, two had two), each one with around 5,000 eighteen-plus voters, pro rata. That seemed to work as basic principles.

We decided to plough ahead with the process not being exactly sure how it should be conducted. Any submission would have to be agreed locally by the council and then sent to the Boundary Commission for them to consider, possibly amend and eventually approve.

The small team of us simply got on with it at our house with an 'old school' *Geographia* map and my computer, for which I had to learn spreadsheet skills. No mean feat in itself a) for me and b) for those times. We met often, starting early, going on late, arguing, agreeing, sometimes redoing. I wouldn't be surprised if the process didn't go on for two weekends, three or more.

Then there was the question of naming the proposed new wards. None of us was particularly religious and the religious makeup of the borough was on the move. We wanted names that people in those communities might understand and identify with, so names such as Shadsworth, Ewood, Mill Hill and Pleckgate were chosen. We finalised boundaries, using main roads or physical features such as the canal, voter numbers and finally ward names and put our exhaustive and exhausting endeavours to bed.

We submitted our ideas to the town hall. There was to be a full public consultation on any proposals and then a final council decision before the locally agreed document would be submitted to the civil servants based at the SW1A post code near Parliament.

The consultation document was based entirely and exactly on our efforts. When it came to the special one-item council meeting, we on the Labour benches were surprised that only our ideas were 'tabled'. For such a fundamental building block of the democratic process only to have ideas submitted by us, with no other party lifting a finger, seemed a total renunciation of responsibility. During our lengthy deliberations we had tried to act as impartially as possible. Had our generous objectivity been misdirected?

I think with little debate, the circulated proposals were agreed and sent off to London where they were rubber-stamped for implementation for the local elections scheduled for May 1997. This was the full year before we became unitary.

Lord Tom Taylor sent me a handwritten note congratulating me on my skulduggery and subterfuge. I thought it would be impolite of me to enlighten the noble lord with the truth. I did let the cat out of the bag some years later.

*   *   *

And so, to recap, probably from at least 1973/4 till 1997, there was one set of ward boundaries with anachronistically ecclesiastical names as possibly befitted the demographics of the borough in a previous time. Sixty council seats.

Then for the 1997 local (pre-unitary) elections we had another set of ward boundaries, with more apt geographical names. There was a little grumbling around this time that the new ward names didn't reflect the changing ethnography of Blackburn. I think I made people chuckle when I reminded them that there was now both a Sunnyhurst and a Shear Brow Ward. We expected these to be in situ as the previous set had, for some twenty-five or so years, until well into the 'Twenty-twenties'. Sixty-two council seats.

That wasn't to be so and the new wards, with one additional ward created, were reconsidered and adjusted in 2002 for 2004. Then, less than five years later, sixty-four council seats.

After that redrawing of the boundaries, they were left in place and in peace for around sixteen or so years until 2018, when further changes resulted in a reduction in the total numbers of councillors to fifty-one, sitting in seventeen wards with around 20 per cent more electors (6,200) each.

These apparently bureaucratic changes were actually the building blocks of local democracy and psephology. Things, perhaps unintended, would change because of them.

Chapter 27
Darkness Descends

Hello Darkness

Friday, 22 November 2002 was a dark day in our politics locally. For various reasons, I took it badly and personally.

Thirty-eight-year-old Robin Evans stood in a by-election in the ward of Mill Hill in Blackburn. Mill Hill is where Anne had rented her first property and I had moved in with her after breaking my leg way back in 1977. Mill Hill had become predominantly a white working-class area, a mixture of former council house properties and quite small terraced, often private, rental houses. My predecessor Malcolm Doherty had lived right in the middle of the ward for decades, bringing his family up there. Robin Evans was a member of and stood for the far-right British National Party (BNP). In quite a high turnout for a by-election, 40 per cent, Evans won by sixteen votes.

After two tense recounts he had taken the seat from the Lib Dems after their sitting councillor had moved to Sussex, and former council deputy leader, Labour's Gail Barton was runner-up. Her second defeat in that ward that year. Gail had been a local councillor, tackling some of the toughest issues and holding some of the most difficult portfolios for fifteen to twenty years, previously 'sitting' in neighbouring Moorgate Ward, before being selected in Mill Hill in the 'all out' pre-unitary elections of 1997.

Under a huge banner front page headline 'Shameful', reporter David Higgerson spoke of shock and dismay in Blackburn. Was it a shock? A question I've asked myself time and time again both then and even now.

Their campaign had taken political propaganda to a new extreme locally. It included peddling one story that Laneside, a sixty-roomed former old folks home in the ward was to be converted for the exclusive use of asylum seekers. The biggest lie which was 'photoshopped' onto their main election leaflet was that the council had agreed to allow a massive Saddam Husseinesque twin scimitar gateway to be erected at the entrance to Whalley Range, an area of high Asian settlement. Local people took both the small lie and the big lie to be true. I later learned not to blame the liars but those choosing to want them to be true. Refuting these claims on the doorstep proved very difficult especially with people who wanted to believe they were true. We were regularly told by voters that we needed to get rid of all the 'Pakis' who milk every system they could, for every penny they could. This response was regularly repeated, that the Asian community was disproportionately and unfairly in receipt of benefits and grants to which they weren't entitled.

I did take the result badly. There must be a variety of reasons for such a strong reaction. They may include the fact that my mum's blue-eyed boy, her brother and my Uncle George Selkirk, aka Marine, PLY/X 1550, had been blown to kingdom come fighting fascism on *HMS Spartan* off Anzio in 1944. I am William *George* Taylor, don't forget.

The first occasion I had gone to Blackburn was thirty years before, whilst still at university, to attend an anti-fascist rally. Two National Front candidates (including John Kingsley Read) had first won local council seats in 1976 when I was working in that very community as a youth worker. A former Conservative, Kingsley Read, was national chairman of the National Front for a time before leaving to help establish the National Party with John Tyndall. The National Party later became the BNP.

But the BNP had done electorally very well including high-profile visits of Cambridge law graduate and their national leader, Nick Griffin. Labour's approach to canvassing locally, right across the borough, was never to say different things to different people. We wouldn't say different things in a white working-class ward than we would in a mixed or predominantly Asian ward. The BNP had no need for such consistency of approach and in this election quite blatantly told the white working-class vote what they wanted to hear. Telling lies, the bigger the better and making unfulfillable promises was part of their style. But how would Evans fare as a councillor?

I vowed to myself I would do everything to ensure that the BNP's stay on the council would be as brief and unremarkable as possible.

Almost immediately and for a fair time on, the letters page of the local paper was flooded with opinions both pro and anti the BNP, from the usual suspects and much further afield. But there was also a strand of opinion telling the mainstream parties to waken up. And it was that that my thoughts concentrated upon. Was it the case that a whole tranche of what would normally be Labour voters, hadn't? The answer to that had to be yes but behind that the further questions were why and what can we do about it. No need to rush because Evans had at least eighteen months guaranteed on the council – rushing doesn't always mean getting things right and we had to be thoughtful.

Evans was on his own as a single representative of his party. What I didn't realise was that this didn't legally qualify him for any seats on any of the council's committees, so he would only sit on full council. There, if he wanted to propose something, he'd have to get somebody else to second it.

Having lost twice, Gail announced that she wouldn't be standing again, something I can understand. I invited her to attend a Labour Group meeting briefly at which I presented her with an engraved rose bowl to mark and thank her for her service. It also helped her with the process of closure, many appropriately kind things were said about Gail and she responded accordingly.

* * *

Almost immediately we had some fantastic news about our Comprehensive Performance Assessment, independently conducted by the Audit Commission. They had reviewed all 150 unitary and county councils. The best rating was Excellent and that is indeed what we got. Only twenty-two councils achieved that dizzy height, and we were told on the QT that nationally we had come second. Having only been in existence for just over four years and having much to ameliorate to begin with, this was a fantastic accolade for every member of our staff, all of our councillors, everyone in fact. Sir Brian Briscoe, professional head of the Local Government Association, had chosen to lead the big-hitting inspection team. At an informal debrief session, possibly his most interesting disclosure was that normally when conducting this kind of things he'd always found at least one section of the workforce, community or key partners who would slag the council off readily. But during his time in Blackburn everyone was in supportive unison about how good things were. Our overall score was 46 out of 48. As I told the now traditional celebration breakfast in King George's Hall 'I'm delighted. It can't be stressed how absolutely fantastic this result is but, of course, we'll see no room for complacency – onwards and upwards'. Lancashire, our predecessor top-tier authority, did quite well (33/48), achieving the second level, good categorisation.

The CPA assessment which I described on radio as a mega MOT (press officer Suzanne Halliwell praised me for that one!) was a reassuring signal of light and hope for us at the time when the BNP brought divisive darkness to our borough.

* * *

Three months after winning his seat on Blackburn with Darwen Council, but still yet, as far as I can remember, to make his maiden verbal input, there was a big announcement by Robin Evans on the front page of the local paper. He announced his intention to stand at the next general election against Jack Straw. It really didn't come as much of a surprise. (Checking the records of general elections in Blackburn in the last thirty or so years, there was no BNP candidate in or before 2001 or in 2015, 2017 or 2019, Nicholas Holt, 2,263 votes, stood for them in 2005 and Robin Evans 2,158 votes in 2010.)

After less than a year as a councillor, it was reported in the *Lancashire Evening Telegraph* that Evans had 'walked out on the BNP', due to 'organisational differences'. He chose to sit as an independent, vowing to continue backing far right policies. I was still not sure whether he'd actually ever spoken in the council chamber.

Two or three months later, and we have the *Sunday Mirror* to thank for this, they carried a headline: 'BNP bigot leaves wife and child for lover, 21'. The paper reported that Evans had met his new Nottingham-based lover whilst canvassing in the by-election, taking off to his new romantic dalliance 'in his distinctive red car with a Union Jack emblazoned on the hood'. His wife of ten years was quoted as saying 'the last time I saw Robin was last Wednesday when he came to the house to speak to a debt collector who was chasing him for money'. He certainly had plenty on his plate. He was reported to be living twenty-five miles away in the very rural village of Trawden near the Yorkshire border.

These goings-on appeared in our local paper the next day but far less salaciously. It was reported that the goings-on had been going on since the day after the by-election the year before. I was quoted as saying 'I do not want to comment on his personal circumstances.'

There were local elections held in a number of neighbouring councils in May 2003. Burnley found themselves with four BNP councillors. Luckily, the BNP having intended to stand in neighbouring Hyndburn, missed the date to submit nomination papers. I was quoted as saying 'We don't have elections until next year and our job is to make sure that our electors are not hoodwinked in the same way electors in Burnley have been'.

Councillor Evans dipped in and out of the civic and political life of the borough. He didn't attend prayers which were always held at the very beginning of each full council meeting. Although agnostic, I always ensured I was there out of respect for others of faith. He was also significant by his absence at the annual Remembrance Service in the cathedral, which is always followed by a march and brief service up to our war memorial in our nearby park. Again, the very event you might have thought he would ensure he attended.

But did I have a plan? Well, the answer is, yes, I did, to combat the BNP politically. In the Mill Hill by-election a major tactic in their campaign had been a) to tell lies and b) to cast doubt in Mill Hill about the Asian community living in other parts of Blackburn. They had been far more astute than we had, and we weren't armed with anything that would refute their claims. Sloppy work but lessons to be learned. We didn't have a clue about the proportionality of how public resources were distributed in different parts of the borough.

I envisioned and we embarked upon a lengthy and complex process that became known as community resource mapping. Later it became a national exemplar of good practice adopted by the Local Government Association and many councils.

What was it? Put simply and from memory, the borough council spent less than £200 million on its services delivered across the borough, but that was nowhere near the entire public purse. If added to by all the other things that got spent by the Department for Work and Pensions (Dept. Social Security as it was called at the time), Job Centre Plus, the NHS, police, ambulance and other similar services and much, much more, the total 'public purse' spend was many, many times what the council spent. Now what?

So, the council couldn't be accused of gathering, manipulating and presenting facts to support 'their position', we had employed independent auditors, analysts and report writers. They came up to BwD and at one point explained their methodology to me or at least tried to. One erratic conclusion they did come to was that there were a disproportionate number of deaths in the most westerly ward in the borough based around the small village of Pleasington. This is where a little bit of local knowledge comes in handy as Pleasington is the home of the borough crematorium and the main cemetery for its departed citizens!

They moved their work on and submitted a final report which concluded that the public purse was disproportionately allocated in the white working-class, former council house estate neighbourhoods, the very communities where the BNP hoped to spread their message. The Asian community didn't benefit as much as the indigenous areas. We got this message out amongst all key partner organisations especially their staff.

Our community resource mapping exercise and its final report, as is often the case for BwD, was ground-breaking and attracted the attention of Gordon Brown the then Chancellor of the Exchequer. It was published and publicised around four or five months before the scheduled 2004 local elections. I was quoted as saying that 'it would help people understand how the council works better and to combat myths about unequal funding and that I wanted to dispel myths that the council spent disproportionately on ethnic minorities'. It also helped with more precision being given on who spends how much. In this case, the council spent around £175 million a year, add in all other government departments and European funding and the public purse was around £700 million. So, the council spend of the total public budget was only 25 per cent.

Housing was a key issue for the borough. At the time, the national average house price was £140k, but locally only £60k. Much of our housing was pre-1919 and assessed as unfit for human habitation. We had a plan for prioritisation that embraced nearly 30,000 of the borough's 60,000 properties within the multi-million-pound housing market renewal scheme. It was our multi-pronged approach that was successful: condition reports on all areas of poor housing, costed-up schemes, good relations with government ministers and a track record of spending money wisely. In the first phase 450 homes would be face-lifted, 230 with major improvements, 939 demolished and 450 new houses built.

And so more or less exactly a year before Robin Evans' seat was up for re-election in Mill Hill, the headline appeared in the local paper 'Campaign starts now to oust BNP'. There had been no local elections in Blackburn during 2003 but the following year 'all out, every seat up for grabs' elections were scheduled. Blackburn Labour Party showed its hand early, honestly and openly. We would be prepared and fight the elections on factual information without trying to dupe the voters.

We kept a very strong local focus on the small matters, often the most important to citizens. We called it 'thrash the trash' and was about removing grot spots wherever they manifested themselves. Our message was clear and well received: it wasn't councils that by and large blighted areas but people, the neighbours of whom saw their council tax then being spent to clear up someone else's mess. We appointed a pair of town centre wardens, completely innovative at the time, with a dual fuel van, Phil McCartney and Tom Nelson, to get out in those particular areas keeping them clean and tidy. This included planting hanging baskets and other flower beds not only in the town centre but on some of our roundabouts on main thoroughfares. Our propaganda brainwave was to get to people in their homes, in their communities via children. We got into our schools and other places where children congregated with a strong message about civic pride. That group of people convinced, they would go home and tell off their mums, dads and grandparents. It was a strategy that worked very well indeed. £1 million well spent and we found that the areas where residents of all ages worked together to clean up their neighbourhood often stayed permanently spick and span, especially where complemented by a certificate of achievement and photo in the paper.

It was really all of the above that got Phil Watson and me invited to become members of central government's Innovation Forum. This was a high-powered think tank made up of senior government ministers and their civil servants and senior local government members and officials. I was appointed by my peers as the national lead for education and young people, a major feather in Blackburn's cap. I found myself locking antlers with Government School's Minister David Miliband in HM's Treasury building off Horse Guards Road. The purpose of the forum was very much to focus on legislation and how it helps or hinders innovation and improvement, also seeking to pull different funding streams together for maximum impact and how we can pool all of our expertise.

Chapter 28

Having Faith in our Schools

God bless the absentee. This country's changed so fast.

I respect religion although I'm not formally religious. I think I would best be described as agnostic, possibly areligious. But I'm also a realist. I'm sure that if all world religions were abolished, they would soon be reinvented and reinstated as something very similar. Many wars have been fought, much blood shed and many people killed ostensibly in the name of religion.

The three monotheistic Abrahamic religions, Christianity, Islam and Judaism have such common roots and rituals, but it would seem to me that it is humankind, abusing religion, that's at the core of all these paradoxes. It is estimated that over 55 per cent or 3.8 billion people are declared adherents of the three main Abrahamic religions.

There are numerous different places of and ways to worship and I see many 'attenders' demonstrating that they do not have the teachings of their faith as part and parcel of their core values or daily behaviours. Babies and children are often admitted into or 'signed up' to the religion of their parents before they can choose for themselves and that's that. I also think that many people are quite 'clubbable', like 'belonging' and like having parameters/rules pre-set for them? I feel that the lady who dutifully trudges round delivering our local parish church news (£10 pa) feels like she's 'doing some good', we 'pay into' something that doesn't really feel relevant to us, an article by me about road safety in the village is censored out for being 'political', the well-meant I'm sure, but never met, cleric signs off 'Your vicar and friend', but we've never met!

All my personal points of view aired in the open, locally there was another issue that wasn't going to go away and had to be addressed. Faith schools for all faiths.

Most of the primary schools (60-plus per cent) locally were Christian based, Anglican, Catholic, some Methodist. Of our nine secondary schools, two were Catholic and one Anglican. Demographically, however, the younger end of our communities were, and still are, preponderantly of Asian heritage. Am I talking here about Asian members of the community, or members of the Asian community? Am I guilty here of confusing ethnicity and religion?

I don't know much about the differences between Sunni Muslims and Shias. I've read that in Blackburn, 75 per cent of the Muslim population are Sunni and 8 per cent Shia. I'm assuming (and am I right in doing so?) that many people adopt affiliations, and the predilection to affiliate from their parents? But not in my case, religion or politics.

Similarly, for example in Scotland where I was baptised as a baby, I'm not too sure about the difference between the High Kirk, Calvinism or Presbyterianism. I never really understood why, in many of our major cities, Edinburgh, Glasgow, Manchester, Liverpool for example, the tribalistic support of a football team has its antecedents in whether you were brought up in Catholic or Protestant communities. Do we understand the influences that bear upon us? Do we know them, weigh them up, consider and judge them?

But back to the practicalities of everyday life here in Blackburn, many youngsters, after school, attended the madrassa affiliated to a mosque. At these teatime sessions young people were taught the Koran and Arabic. The nearest equivalent to madrassas for Christian youngsters is probably Sunday school. According to muslimsinbritain.org there are over forty-five mosques in Blackburn these days. Surely it wouldn't take an expert in ethnography to project what was likely to happen.

There were so many different pressures. 1. Christian organisations established and ran most of the primary schools and, to be fair, their significant contribution to the development of public education for the masses over several hundreds of years needs to be recognised. 2. If some faiths had their own schools, was it fair that all faiths didn't have them? (although most church schools had faith connections, e.g. governing body, admissions policy, appointment of staff, they were overwhelmingly (90 per cent) funded by the state). 3. The madrassas started to develop beyond their original religious dimension. These changes were by and large funded by substantial voluntary contributions from parents and others in the community. But it also meant that these *quasi* schools were not operating to LEA policies and procedures, creating various anomalies. 4. Many indigenous councillors, cutting across the political divide and many amongst the electorate professed to being opposed to faith schools, whilst in their next breath doing their best to get their children and grandchildren into them. Another duplicitous dilemma to vex both my heart and mind.

I was invited by Adam Patel to *his* school, based near *his* mosque originally and disingenuously called St John's. Adam was born in 1940 in a small rural village in the Gujarat in India known as Kamad (population around 2,500). When he came to Britain in 1965, as well as studying to become a qualified accountant, he initially had the classic immigrant lifestyle often working double shifts in cotton mills, living in poor, cramped conditions and sending money home. Adam had struck up a close relationship with Barbara Castle in the seventies, something that continued with Jack Straw. I'd known Adam and Akhtar Hussain since the early 1980s. I'd also got to know, Abdul Barlas, Yaqoob Dar, Noor Elahi, Ahmed Makda, Mohammed Khan, Ibby Master and Kam Kothia as good, respectable men.

I met up with Adam (who became Lord Patel in the year 2000) on the street corner in a very compact Victorian terraced housing area, near what many, across the communities, called the Khyber Pass. Adam liked to tell a story and he started by sharing one with me about his dad, who had always remained in their home village. Mr Patel Snr had been advised by the authorities there that perhaps the local drinking water was no longer safe for him. He'd replied politely that aged ninety-plus, the advice was somewhat 'too little – too late'.

There appeared to be nothing that looked vaguely like a school.'We'll start by meeting the head.' Adam turned around and was gone. He'd disappeared through the front door of a house. Timorously I tapped on the door and was invited in, to be met by a middle-aged white woman, who told me she was the head. I was invited to sit down and provided with a cup of tea. She explained the school to me. After half an hour or so I was offered the opportunity to look around the school. Back on the pavement, up a few doors and into another terraced house, aka the maths department. This process was repeated on several occasions until I'd been around English, geography, history, RE inter alia. The pupils were all girls, secondary age, all wearing head coverings that I later knew to be called hijabs and niqabs. Each room I entered, both the teacher, mainly white women, and the pupils stood up very politely and respectfully and it would appear that one of the youngsters had been nominated to welcome and tell me what they were up to. At the conclusion of this mini-input our spokesperson invited me to ask any questions I might have, as she would nominate somebody to respond. The girls all spoke eloquently with typical Blackburn accents.

I was shepherded back to the head's study for another cup of tea. I really had had my eyes opened but what was I going to do? I promised I'd speak to Mark Pattison, our director of education and we would both come back when our diaries allowed.

That took a few weeks to organise but soon we were back to be guests of honour, we were told, at a full school assembly. This was conducted in the assembly hall which appeared to be the front rooms of a few terraced houses knocked together. We were welcomed and introduced and said a few words. Then there was a short period of religious observation. An older student, the head girl perhaps, then stood up. She explained that half a dozen of the students had been designated to bring in a news cutting reporting a news event in which they had an interest. The junior news hounds spoke briefly and then invited questions on their chosen news topic and a brief discussion ensued; very enlightening.

Mark and I stayed for an hour or more and then left. Sitting in the car together we decided that doing nothing wasn't an option. What was going to be tricky was the what and the how of what needed to be done.

As you might expect, whatever we decided to do would be thoughtful and consultative from the outset, it was the BwD 'house style'. The inconsistent and incongruous conundrum of faith schools in a multi-faith borough had to be faced up to and resolved. Opinions were divided in all sorts of different ways both within the different faith communities and beyond, a very tangled web. There are numerous 'how do you feel, well, what would you do?' issues and moments here.

To begin with we discussed this within Labour's senior education councillors and the top officers. I think there was general agreement about what had to be done. How to do it was a more complex matter. The Labour Party in the borough had always traditionally been supported by the Catholic community who had originally settled here as economic migrants from Ireland in Victorian and more recent troubled times, many settling, as is often the case, in the poorer housing in the centre of Blackburn. Beautiful Catholic churches had been built; especially the magnificent St Albans overlooking the town, opulently rebuilt in 1901 with a 600-plus capacity in some expectation that it might eventually become a cathedral.

Over the decades (from the 1960s on), much of that neighbourhood became home to the Asian community, with its own mosques, madrassas and shops. This is where Lord Adam Patel had taken me. This school later became known and held in high local and national regard as Tauheedul. Already in the 1990s the not long-established school out performed others in the borough with 75 per cent of Year eleven pupils achieving the standard of five A-C grades at GCSE. Almost double that of some of their neighbouring LEA counterparts.

In November 2001, under my council leadership, we embarked upon a consultative process on the future of faith schools in our borough. Our document was entitled 'Faith schools, community cohesion and cultural diversity'. I think we expected quite a bumpy ride.

As you might anticipate, schooling for children in the Asian community had developed in an organic, demand-led approach. As well as 'Adam's' school, half a dozen other schools, initiated by other mosques, were beginning to spring up. Some of the premises being used were physically far from ideal and we had no idea about policies, procedures and standards. These schools were outside of the LEA 'family' and therefore didn't have to comply with things like admissions policy, teacher qualifications and standards, building regulations, health and safety considerations, discipline, adherence to a curriculum.

To recap, in the borough there were around 2,000 children in each year age group. There were three 'voluntary aided' Christian church and six 'state' secondary schools. The 'market' also now embraced seven 'private' Muslim schools, funded mainly by parental contributions of several hundreds, if not thousands of pounds a year. Of the existing secondary schools, one had 93 per cent Asian heritage youngsters on roll, one RC school but not both had 99 per cent Asian pupils on their roll. The CofE school, St Wilfrid's had a 98 per cent white enrolment.

Eventually the findings of the officers' and consultants' consultations were returned and processed. It felt like people were saying one thing but meaning another, saying the right things but for the wrong reasons. No longer being responsible for the education brief, I had no involvement in any of the discussions or the detail. The proposed plan, a classic compromise, was that one Muslim school would apply and be admitted into the LEA fold. That was to be the Tauheedul school, now a 700 girls-only secondary, 'voluntary aided' as were the other three faith secondary schools. For the other half dozen private Muslim schools there was an opportunity to twin with another secondary school in the borough. Most of the main players in the local world of faith-based education expressed support. Ibrahim Master, from the Lancashire Council of Mosques and Canon Peter Ballard, Anglican diocesan director of education gave the proposals their public approval. Lord Clark, author of the task force report following the recent riots in neighbouring Burnley gave it the thumbs-up. The NUT's fence-sitting position seemed ambivalent.

I am no great believer in exclusively faith-based education, but which is the higher concern, that or equality? Anyway, the first hurdle in the democratic process would be the Labour Group. A rumour was circulating that I'd made a deal with the Asian community given that a substantial minority of voters in my ward were Asian heritage. I'd never gone in for that Tammany Hall (a US 'boss-ist' and open to patronage and corruption) style of politics. Striking a deal, then another and another and, before you know where you are, you don't know where you are! I'd always tried to take on and judge issues on their own merits, playing the ball not the man.

The debate on this issue at the Labour Group was both lengthy and intense. It was described in the *Lancashire Evening Telegraph* as the first public split in the Labour Group since the new council format two years earlier. Little did they know! I suppose the leaks to top reporter David Higgerson could at best be described as mischievous. It looked like un or ill-defined battle lines within the Labour Group were being clandestinely drawn up. Were people not brave enough to pin their colours to masts in public? Higgerson reported one Labour councillor as unattributedly describing the meeting as a 'blood on the floor affair'. Normally in situations like this, elected members might be expected to declare an interest but none of the Labour members in the room, having themselves attended or sitting on governing bodies or with their children or family at faith schools saw it necessary to do so. Nor did anyone propose the absolute purist position on this vexed issue, that is, the total abolition of all church/faith schools. People needed to show some principle, some leadership here, some only demonstrated cognitive dissonance. I'm told one person at the meeting arguing strongly against the development of faith schools did so whilst filling in an application form for a member of their family to attend one. Four other educational authorities across the country had already taken this step. The Tory Group had decided to support the plan, the Lib Dems were against. I was quoted in the paper as saying 'I accept that some councillors have tough decisions to make and that not everyone agrees with me but many of them went to faith schools themselves'. Higgerson was able to report on who said what and who voted how in what was normally a private group discussion. Beyond mischief, I thought. There was a fortnight before the issue would be debated in full council.

So, the issue of faith schools was relegated to the back burner for a couple of weeks but no doubt some were busy trying to undermine the democratic decisions taken so far and yet to be taken. Couldn't some kitchen designer come up with a hob where there are only front burners as that's what life seemed like to me and a number of the other exec members.

*   *   *

Looking back on these times I seemed to have become a decision junkie. Most of us with executive portfolios had a lot to do, making big high-level decisions a lot of the time. I didn't feel the 'rush' of decision-making but perhaps it was there.

It was not only the pace of decision-making but its staccato nature. It was a heady cocktail of the routine, the proactive and the reactive. Just when all the plates appeared to be spinning very nicely thank you, something or someone else would come along for you to deal with. We had a great team of superb senior officers who understood their specific but also their corporate role, well led by Phil Watson.

As you might expect, the ruling Labour Group, 60 per cent of all councillors, was an amorphous group of people. The most consistent was a group of older ladies who'd had a very working-class, cotton mill life. They'd seen the inter-war poverty and knew that they wanted to combat it. I called them the grandmas and they were totally reliable. They asked me tough questions but once they were satisfied with the answers, they were on board. Some of the officers saw these ladies as having hobby horses, axes to grind. I describe it more as a passion. Between them they majored on housing, children and schools, public transport – the big bread and butter issues. Other members of the group were more complex having an eye on their future. One senior officer complimented me on my nimble management of the group, its positions and schisms. I'd never seen it like that but perhaps he was right. But back to the spinning plates.

In the middle of the faith schools' process, the fruition of yet another process came to be. This was one of my brighter ideas, even if I say so myself. It was the appointment of five neighbourhood coordinators allocated to the five neighbourhood areas into which the borough had been divided. The idea here was that in their allocated fifth of the borough, these officers could get on with either coordinating across council departments or liaising with other agencies with improving services to the local community at the heart of their mission. They had a licence to 'kick arse' of any feet-draggers if necessary. Joined-up thinking to ensure joined-up doing.

They were led by Tim Birch and the other four members were Tanya Gallagher, Elaine Gillibrand, Aziz Hafiz and Chris Waring. On their first day in post there was a press photo call including me and PCSO Emma Turner who later became a proper copper. They were all great folk who went on to do a great job and made an impact in the communities they served. This illustrates my point that there is no point in seeking political power unless you intend harnessing it for the better of the people that you represent and this was certainly the case here.

The scheme was so highly thought of it warranted two pages in the *Guardian Society*, headlined 'model partnership'.

The main picture was of PCSO Asif Malik, environmental works supervisor Adam Holt and neighbourhood coordinator Aziz Hafiz. Journalist Peter Hetherington, who spent a day with us, described our scheme as 'a pacesetter for other local partnerships and a model for the country'. My take on the strides we'd made to integrate and coordinate organisations and the way they deliver their services was to urge a touch of humility from councillors where there was a danger of them jealously guarding **their** services as I said 'we have to let go of things and it is hard for some'. The article comprehensively catalogued the journey from central control to devolved freedoms and flexibilities. BwD was in the vanguard of the merging of the NHS and the council locally. Service users often don't realise or understand divisions that organisations artificially imposed on service delivery to our citizens. It had to stop. Public service boards operating public service agreements had to relax councils and councillor involvement. At Whitehall, the civil servants are permanent secretaries often only ever in one department, **their's**. Ministers don't usually stay too long, five years at maximum. As I said to Hetherington 'we've had a lot of ministers up here looking at what we're doing, but when they get back to their department something seems to hold them up'. I concluded with the thought that locally 'we could push the democratic dynamic beyond social services and health moving into transport, skills training, higher education and housing regeneration'. I finished stating that 'the government first has to learn to let go and let local initiatives blossom'.

*   *   *

Around the same time, we had complaints from opposition councillors that the council wasn't run like it used to be. Well spotted, we'd gone through a long and open process consulting far and wide before we implemented this fitter, faster approach to decision-making. That they or the local media hadn't kept up with this was their problem.

The night of the full council meeting to discuss the outcomes of the rigorous faith school consultation process came along. When it came to the vote, four Labour members of the exec voted in favour of the plans and four abstained. Those opposed to the proposals suddenly got the hang of the new council procedures and voted to 'call' in the decision, effectively to review it. Ten members were required to vote in favour of this and five Lib Dems, four Conservatives and one Labour did so. The requisite education scrutiny committee was scheduled for the following week. My public view on the situation was expressed as 'we welcome input from scrutiny on any matter. The proposals are effectively frozen until scrutiny has considered them'.

An examination via the scrutiny function took place and then the issue was brought back to the next appropriate council meeting. I don't remember how the events ran their course. The right checks and balances produced the outcome that Tauheedul, as it became, was established as proposed within the LEA family. There were driving forces here, beyond Adam Patel: Ibby Master, Kam Kothia, Mo Isap, inter alia.

*   *   *

This school, its local counterparts and successors went on from strength to strength, growing steadily, organically.

Twenty or more years later, now under the 'banner' of Star Academies, their 'stable' runs around thirty schools, with around 20,000 pupils, from all backgrounds, attending, in Lancashire, West Yorkshire, Greater Manchester, the West Midlands (ironically not too far from my old schools) and London. Their website tells us:

'Star Academies is a mixed Multi-Academy Trust that runs a diverse network of primary and secondary schools. We are a values-based organisation, committed to enhancing social mobility. All our efforts are geared towards raising the aspirations of children and young people in areas of social and economic deprivation to improve their life chances and help them succeed at the highest levels of education, employment and the professions.

Star Academies is one of the country's leading education providers, and our schools promote excellence in everything they do. In every school, the entire staff team – working in partnership with parents and the local community – is committed to nurturing today's young people and inspiring tomorrow's leaders.'

They declare their vision to be:

'Nurturing Today's Young People, Inspiring Tomorrow's Leaders
Our vision is wide-ranging. It encompasses aspiration, educational excellence, system leadership, social mobility and cohesion.'

With these acronymic 'astral' values:

Service – Being a responsible citizen in our community.
Teamwork – Working together for excellence.
Ambition – Aspiring to be our best.
Respect – Treating others as we wish to be treated.

The Star Trust employs the full time equivalent of around 1,500 staff, teaching and support. Their total spend, all costs, is in excess of £100 million per annum.

Knowing some of and of some of the people, both in professional and governance roles, I believe the organisation is well and strongly managed and led.

Ofsted inspects these schools as it does with any other. Fourteen were assessed as 'outstanding'. External exam performance, GCSE and others, is always very high.

Mighty oaks from acorns! Good job I did 'something'!

*   *   *

Whilst this process was reaching its conclusion, it was announced that I had been named as being amongst the top fifteen council leaders in the country by the Local Government Chronicle. This is no mean recognition in the law of the jungle world of politics. I made it clear that 'the things we had achieved were not done by me but as a team. I want to make sure that all the other Bill Taylors out there have the same chances. That's my motivation'.

But our overarching ambition was for the towns and their residents. We came up with another imaginative scheme costing £1.3 million, for the inspirational rejuvenation of three dilapidated Georgian-era pavilions very close to the cathedral and on the main pedestrianised thoroughfare, Church Street. Out of character, the Conservative Group leader went on record as calling Blackburn 'a grotty mill town' in the paper. It haunted him for a long time. Regardless of that we pressed ahead with a further piece in our transformational jigsaw.

East Lancashire or its never-to-catch-on vogue name, Pennine Lancashire (a snazzy name and from memory, dreamt up and destined to fail after some paid for 'consultancy' from the Manchester, Factory Records and Haçienda nightclub-based and orientated Tony Wilson, aka Anthony H Wilson), was home to about half a million people. From Blackburn at the eastern gateway, it stretched across twelve to fifteen miles to Nelson and Colne, by and large following the M65 motorway. Half a million people but no institution of higher education where people got degrees; passports to a better future. As chairman of the East Lancashire partnership, made up of councils, the private sector and public organisations, I took the leadership of trying to secure a higher education study base somewhere in the sub-region. As you might imagine, there were some turf wars fought between the five or six councils and their MPs as to where this might be situated. Blackburn College principal Sheena Ewing was reported as saying 'At Blackburn College for example we have 4,000 students studying higher education, doing fifteen diplomas, eleven foundation degrees and twelve degrees including an MBA. Except for a Tory Government legislated break, I sat for some twenty-five years on Blackburn College board alongside Jack Straw and also for quite a chunk of time, Phil Watson. Our main interest was Blackburn College but as the prize was higher education for all, we might have to go 'softly softly catchee monkey'.

As senior councillors and especially as the leader even more so, our lives were helter-skelter or any other manic metaphor you might like to chuck in. I think we became inured to it all.

We didn't concentrate only upon the big headline-catching opportunities, we dealt with bread and butter matters too. We brought a fund together of £3/4 million to combat graffiti, chewing gum impregnated pavements and other general anti-social activities. This was generally very well received by the general public, Chamber of Trade, the cathedral and other movers and shakers.

It wasn't all good news. We had to make cuts in services to the tune of £3.8 million. We had a representative citizens' jury to air and discuss issues. This was a randomly selected and irregularly convened group of people with whom we tested opinions and ideas. As well as making cuts, we also invested in growth items with the involvement of this group, basically shifting the emphasis of council spending into areas with these citizens' involvement and approval.

Deputy Prime Minister John Prescott then unleashed a whole debate about devolving powers down to regional assemblies, for example, one for the north-west. I was quoted in the local and national council 'trade' papers as saying 'we have supported the principle of devolving power away from central government for a long time and we see a referendum as a step towards this'. I'm all in favour of anything that brings decision-making nearer to people and places where the money is going to be spent.

We had some more great news about one of our industrial and business parks on the fringe of the borough. £19 million was to be spent creating upwards of 1,500 jobs, as a result of our EU business development partnership with Tarnów in Poland. Mike Damms, chief executive of the Chamber of Commerce said 'Blackburn is certainly punching above its weight. It's using imaginative ways of bringing firms in and not just waiting to see what comes along.'

April 2003 meant we had reached our fifth birthday as a unitary authority. Time for a party and a cake with five candles? Chief exec Phil Watson and I shared the cake-cutting exercise with five-year-old Saima, born on the same day as the new council. We put Saima in charge of the candle blowing. Saima, of course, will be in her mid-twenties now.

We'd faced up to and dealt with unprecedented levels of change and by and large handled it successfully. We'd made a few enemies, but I believe many, many more friends. Change for the better and incremental improvements, moving towards excellence. I think we'd proved our intolerance to inertia, coasting along wasn't good enough, awards were nice but not if they led to complacency. In a major local article marking our fifth anniversary I was quoted as saying 'The challenges continue. It is hard to remain excellent when others are trying to compete. We need to keep striving forward and that is where staff play a key role. The challenge is to remain the best but in doing so improving services'. Colin Rigby, leader of the Tory Group, said, 'we now get to see where our money goes and things have improved service wise'. Lib Dem leader Paul Browne confessed 'I have no doubt we have done better as a unitary than we would have done if we had still had services from the county council'. We were one of only two unitaries created in 1998 that had been adjudged a CPA 'excellent' council. Phil Watson explained, noting that Lancashire had only achieved 'good' status, 'that proves that big isn't always best and that we were right to become a unitary'.

Of course, my 'day job' continued to be working for the county council which at times was difficult for me, leaving me vulnerable. Being involved in youth and community work totally suited me and I thoroughly enjoyed it enabling me to be imaginative and creative. I always had half an eye on those petty-minded envious people who might seek some form of retribution for BwD's success and my role in it. I was responsible for youth and community work and a team of fantastic staff that grew from two or three full-time workers to around ten or twelve. We worked superbly with the district council Ribble Valley and all their staff especially in crime and disorder, community safety, community development, and arts development. We worked in every secondary school in the borough and were well received there too, for both our curricular and extra-curricular inputs. Our work was regularly in the weekly *Clitheroe Advertiser* and *Longridge News*. We'd concentrated very much upon the Duke of Edinburgh's Award Scheme both in schools and out as a means for young people to develop themselves and attain highly CV-friendly accreditation. We must have contributed, although by far the numerically smallest district, a substantial proportion of the overall county's DofEs' success targets.

Success as a unitary council didn't come without any cost to those of us involved. Sue Reid as a local councillor and as executive member for social services had been a star. She was bright, hard-working, determined and successful in her roles, both with her portfolio and as deputy leader of the council. But that wouldn't put bread on the table forever. Sue had to choose between her own professional career and maintaining a sustainable decent income and the pros and cons, without a reliable income, of sitting on the council. I totally got her dilemma. I could have earned two or three times my salary had I not embraced a political career and that would have soon mounted up over two or three decades (hundreds of thousands) and also had an impact in my pensionable retired life (tens of thousands annually). I'm talking about a large amount of money not just for me but my family. Having said that, I wouldn't have changed the fraternity, excitement, sense of success and fun – for all the tea in China. Sadly, but understandably, Sue stood down from her executive role in BwD to pursue her professional career in nearby Bolton. But her career took another positive twist as she was soon 'snatched up' to work for central government in Whitehall, harnessing her experiences and skills gained at BwD.

At the next appropriate Labour Group meeting, I presented Sue with a rather large colourful framed caricature of herself to mark and celebrate her twelve to fifteen or so hugely productive years as a councillor.

Sue is now happily married and living in Hampshire, where she was tending various farm animals with her husband Tony.

Chapter 29

Not Such a Lovely War, 2001-03

Hear lunatics' and liars' wartime prayers.

The Iraq war by and large passed over my head. I was leader of the council, Jack's agent and friend. He was Blackburn's MP and Foreign Secretary. He rarely involved himself in council or Labour Group matters and never interfered. I think that that arm's-length position was correct and mutually observed.

The 9/11 attacks of September 2001 on the 110-storey twin towers and the Pentagon, US Defence HQ, left nearly 3,000 (from seventy-eight different nations) dead and 25,000 injured. It's not entirely clear whether the Islamist terrorist group al-Qaeda admitted they had perpetrated these attacks. It didn't really matter to the US. President George W Bush (son of President George HW Bush) addressed the nation by television that evening and a joint session of the US Congress nine days later. British Prime Minister Tony Blair attended Bush's Congress speech as a guest. Subsequent to that, Blair went off on a global round of diplomacy to garner support for military action. I didn't keep up with these events. I had a lot on my plate as leader of the council. Many pages in Jack's book are dedicated to this period and his role and take on it.

The Iraqi leader Saddam Hussain had invaded neighbouring Kuwait in 1990/1. George HW Bush Snr was the US President at that time, Margaret Thatcher was about to exit as British Prime Minister. The international military responses, Desert Shield and Desert Storm, backed by the UN Security Council saw a united coalition of some thirty-five nations. Intense bombardment from the sky and the sea was followed by a ground assault. The armed conflict lasted five or six weeks, then the US President ordered a ceasefire, choosing not to push on further into Iraq and crush the Hussain regime once and for all.

The terms of the ceasefire included Iraq recognising Kuwait's sovereignty and divesting itself of weapons of mass destruction. The second issue never seemed irrefutably resolved one way or the other.

A decade later massive public demonstrations against war in Iraq occurred around the world in hundreds of cities. Estimates of attendance in London on 15 February 2003 ranged from 3/4 to 1.5 million.

But didn't the foreboding shadow of 9/11 leave the US with no option other than to respond? As the US Secretary of Defence Donald Rumsfeld said on the evening of 9/11 'we need to bomb something else to prove that we're, you know, big and strong and not going to be pushed around by these kinds of attacks'. But how and against whom? And would the US act unilaterally or seek United Nations support. Twenty years later, the emphasis and interpretation put on the Security Council's unanimously adopted resolution 1441, is crucial. In early March 2003 Jack addressed a tense session of the Security Council, which I saw on TV. I described Jack's performance as his Finest Hour: 'thoughtful, considerate and passionate'.

Two weeks later the local *Lancashire Evening Telegraph* carried a front page headline 'Revolt in the ranks' stating that 'Ten Labour councillors threatened to quit if war starts without UN backing'. All ten of these councillors were from the Asian community with a variety of different levels of experience and seniority. The article confirmed that the protesters said their stance had nothing to do with religion. Mahfooz Hussain, executive member for education, explained 'we want to put pressure on Tony Blair and Jack Straw to finally listen. It is a matter of principle'. Salim Mulla was quoted as saying, 'there is a lot of opposition within the party and people are saying they will not vote for Mr Straw again'. I understand that Jack had a meeting with the ten men that evening, 14 March.

The invasion of Iraq began with an air bombardment on 19 March and ground attack the next day. Forces from the United States, the United

Kingdom, Australia and Poland were involved. The US President on radio stated the coalition's aim as being to 'disarm Iraq of weapons of mass destruction, to end Saddam Hussein's support for terrorism and to free the Iraqi people'. (Operation Iraqi Freedom – The White House).

News of the military conflict quickly galvanised public opinion, both for and against. In Blackburn town centre, hundreds assembled to make their opposition to the armed conflict clear. Students and lecturers from the college expressed why they thought it was wrong. They were joined by comments from the Bishop of Blackburn, the Rt Rev. Alan Chesters and Ibrahim Master from the council of mosques. Ibby said, 'Whilst we don't have any affinity for Saddam Hussein, my heart is filled with sorrow for the people of Iraq and for families of our British servicemen and women for whom this must be an extremely tormenting time'. I said, 'War is a very difficult and dangerous decision to make. We have to put our trust in decision-makers, such as our MP Jack Straw, and hope the conflict is as short and as bloodless as possible.'

* * *

On the same day as the protest, Peter Morgan, the director of education, accompanied me on a visit around the soon to be officially opened £13 million brand new replacement for the town's Church of England secondary St Wilfrid's. David Whyte, the head teacher, welcomed us and proudly showed us around the brand new 1,500-pupil school created by close cooperation between the LEA, instrumental in accessing grants and other financing and the diocese as a voluntary-aided school. Mr Whyte admitted 'the money was the most stressful part'. Not so many years later St Wilfrid's transferred to being a free-standing academy, shrugging off its ties with the LEA.

* * *

The armed conflict in Iraq lasted for around six weeks in early 2003. Few will forget the metaphorical iconography of the toppling of the Hussein statue in Baghdad. Saddam himself was captured later that year in December.

The initial fighting may not have lasted very long. Iraq seemed like another Vietnam. Barack Obama finally withdrew US forces in 2011. The numbers of casualties: estimates of Iraqis killed are 150,000-plus as a minimum, up to over 1 million, 4,500 US and 400-plus UK. The conflict, its antecedents and implications would resound locally and around the world for a long, long time. Twenty years of war in Vietnam cost an estimated 3 million total deaths (BMJ 2008).

There were those, on the periphery of active politics, who might seek to take advantage of Jack and the positions and decisions he had to take beyond our ken, as Foreign Secretary. Once every parliament, normally every five years, Labour Party MPs had to go through a reselection process in their constituency. Our local paper handled 'rumours' to their maximum journalistic impact. Councillor Maureen Bateson, now chairman of the constituency party, handled it rather well. Maureen stated, 'Jack has had to wrestle with decisions which I am sure he did not join the Labour Party to have to take.' The reselection process locally was put back several months.

Mulling it over, I'm not sure Jack and I ever had an in-depth conversation about the situation in Iraq, the build up to it and its implications. Perhaps we should have. I was most definitely busy enough; other people chose the luxury of having more time on their hands?

More metaphorical plates came our way in the shape of the notion of regional assemblies, with one being in the north-west. Within the proposals it was mooted that Blackburn with Darwen could be enlarged or a new East Lancashire-wide authority created. This certainly focussed the mouths of some of the 'big fish, small pool' elected members next door in nearby Ribble Valley where I worked. One councillor was quoted as saying 'It is a dreadful thought that we could end up in Blackburn with Darwen'. Good grief, man, the end of the world is nigh! There was already a quasi-regional assembly where seventy-eight councillors sat overseeing an annual budget of £7 billion. But this organisation was not democratically accountable, something I thought most people would want to rectify.

In BwD we were very pro-democracy and the encouragement of young people to participate within it, I could engage my youth work skills too. We ran processes for the youth parliament and held biennial elections to them. I was so proud of the elected representatives and the young people who worked with and around them. Rahima Patel did a fantastic ambassadorial job and I enjoyed watching her successfully tackling government minister Steve Byers on transport matters. Her successor, fifteen-year-old Declan McGuire, was equally good and a source of pride, I hope, for his community, school, family and self.

Chapter 30

Routine, Proactive, Reactive

Can you imagine us years from today?

The previous three chapters focussed on three episodes, about the BNP, faith schools and conflicts in the Middle East. I've also spoken about spinning plates and how things present themselves when in a leadership role – routine, proactive or reactive. Many things might be classed as routine or mundane, the normal things. Then there are things that you would like to get your teeth into in a proactive, imaginative, creative fashion. And finally, there are those unexpected, surprise or shock issues to which you need to react. Are these all interrelated? Not regularly keeping up with routine maintenance on your house could result in needing to totally replace something, not doing that might leave you severely susceptible to havoc during a storm. Then there are demands by others on what you should do, what your priorities should be. Ignore them and, if things do go awry, get ready for the 'I told you so' brigade. There are another two camps which you need to be aware of and alert to: the *inertiaviks* and the *changeaholics*. The *inertiaviks* would never move, not until all prevailing conditions, in every fine detail, were totally perfect to progress successfully. *Changeaholics* would set off, chop and change, not really having a clear strategy. Both sets of people or voices would rather give **you** advice on what **you** should do than take any decisions or action themselves. It's all rather irritating but I'm sure you can recognise all these factors from your own experience in any organisation.

Leadership, however, is a very complex set of skills; they sit on a very steep learning curve. Rarely does a leader have the luxury of only having one thing to concentrate upon. Whether you're a parent, in charge of a business, captain of a team, leader of a formal or informal group, the issues are multiple and the skills required infinite. Timescales and prioritisation can be in the eye of the beholder, not everyone shares the same priorities and priorities can clash with timescales; in both cases either yours, or somebody else's!

That is why these chapters are scattered, some might say littered, with other issues I faced that either confounded or appeared to confound my agenda as leader. If indeed you have an agenda or do you just roll over in a laissez-faire manner and let things happen to you? I suppose that is a leadership style. Later, I developed a leadership style and skills training module. My kind of leader. Using Kipling's 'Six Honest Serving Men', I ask:

When am I a Leader?
Why am I Leading?
What am I Leading?
Who am I Leading?
Where am I Leading?
How am I Leading?
Ask yourself!

I didn't want the BNP to retain or gain any further seats on our council. Putting great effort into achieving the highest ranking in our CPA (Comprehensive Performance Assessment) of Excellent was a high priority. This and sitting on the national Innovation Forum, within which I was appointed the national lead on children and young people, gave us both high-profile and direct access to and the ears of key government ministers and very senior civil servants. This is top of the super league stuff with me and Phil Watson key players, highflyers.

Working on the Housing Market Renewal Funding was a premium

sub-agenda, as was Thrashing the Trash. Eventually, after the Pathfinder process was refined and complex and comprehensive bids were honed and submitted, it was announced that Blackburn with Darwen benefitted by £22 million (plus an earlier £5 million) of the £68 million allocated across the Max Steinberg-led Elevate East Lancashire's territory. A great deal.

My being cited as being amongst the best council leaders in the country hopefully added to my currency and credence locally. Working in schools with sixteen to eighteen-year-olds, the youth parliament initiative and fighting for a higher education hub for East Lancashire all demonstrated that we meant business with our often overlooked younger people. Hopefully, they went home and told their mums and dads and grandparents about what was going on.

The five neighbourhood coordinator officers with a cross-cutting agenda and designated zones helped deliver our neighbourhood agenda. That, coupled with the community resource mapping process, provided us with good statistical information that enabled us to argue both about how resources were actually deployed and far more. Identifying, celebrating and sharing good practice such as the resource mapping, put our council on the national map as an exemplar of best practice.

The resolution of the issue of faith schools was one that was long overdue. Adopting the ostrich position only leaves one part of your anatomy exposed and vulnerable to a good kicking.

This wasn't just thrown together. It was a whole raft of measures that when presented and perceived coherently as a whole, put us in a stronger political position.

All this experience, lessons and success also enhanced my role at work. Perhaps these opportunities were unrecognised or despised by my bosses?

The BNP seat had been won at a by-election held in November 2002. The date for the re-run for that seat was predetermined as May 2004 (this was later pushed back a month, till 10 June, to coincide and facilitate the European elections). That was straightforward enough but 1) some Smart Alec sat behind a desk in London at the Boundary Commission decided that BwD needed to have its ward boundaries prematurely re-evaluated and possibly redrawn. Further to that, the same or more probably a different sage, also 2) decided that every seat would be up for grabs. And, in their infinite wisdom, there was a further electoral organisation shock 3) unbeknown to us locally, yet to be unveiled. But not quite yet?

*   *   *

In June 2003, the front page headline in the *Lancashire Evening Telegraph* was 'Vote rig probe: Six arrests', in relation to allegations made going back to May 2002 in the mainly Asian Bastwell Ward. Mohammed Hussain had first been elected to the council in 1997 but had lost the seat two years later. He was selected by his ward committee to re-fight the ward in 2002. As overall campaign coordinator across Blackburn constituency, at our regular Sunday morning campaign meetings I once again spelt it out crystal clear without fear of misunderstanding that the Labour Party must be seen to be squeaky clean about our conduct about postal votes. I issued a clear and unequivocal instruction that no Labour Party councillor, candidate or election helper should even as much as touch somebody else's postal vote. Not even as little as to take one completed and sealed postal vote envelope to a post box. Asking if everybody in the room of perhaps fifty people understood, the room fell in total compliant stony silence. In 2002 Bastwell Ward polled very high, 55 per cent, 10 or 15 per cent higher than most other comparable wards.

Asked to comment on the allegations and the arrests, I declined. In my opinion, the law must run its course.

The next day the front page news was 'Councillor arrested'. Their crime reporter Ian Singleton stated that there was an inquiry into alleged irregularities on hundreds of postal ballot papers in that ward. I was quoted as saying 'I am arranging a meeting with the councillor at the earliest convenience. I'm also taking advice at a regional and national level within the party to see what action should be taken at this stage. Apart from that, I cannot comment further'. The law must run its course.

I did meet with Mohamed Hussain, as a matter of urgency, the outcome of which was that he self-suspended himself as a Labour councillor. Whilst the law runs its course, people are assumed to be innocent until proven otherwise.

*   *   *

Our lives as family people and both working full-time, running the Labour Party and the council, continued to be jam-packed and humdrum. Jack's move from 'Home to Away' brought us a little bit of diversionary 'fun'. I'd never heard of Chevening, I had no idea what or where it was. I was to find out!

Chevening House is near Sevenoaks in Kent, over 250 miles and a good five hours' drive from Blackburn. A search around the Internet tells us that the current building is a large 115-roomed seventeenth-century country house, initially the seat of the Earls Stanhope. Chevening is the earliest known example of a compact double-pile house, traditionally attributed to Inigo Jones.

The estate consists of some 3,000 acres stretching between Sevenoaks and Biggin Hill in Kent. The gardens include a lake, maze, parterre and a double hexagonal walled kitchen garden amounting in all to some forty acres. Over 530 acres of mixed woodland surround the extensive park.

When the 7th Earl Stanhope (a former leader of the House of Lords) died in the mid-1960s, the house and over 3,000 acres of an estate were bequeathed to the nation and overseen by a trust. The incumbent of No 10 Downing St., the Prime Minister, has Chequers in Buckinghamshire as their country residence. It is the PM who decides who has first call upon Chevening. It was envisaged at one stage that Prince Charles, the Prince of Wales, would take residence there but, although he did make occasional private use of it, in 1980 HRH relinquished any claim to such a residency. Chevening then became mainly used by the Foreign Secretary.

So that's how it came to be that Anne and I got invited down for a weekend in October 2002. Something totally beyond our ken. We were to arrive on the Saturday afternoon and depart just before lunch the next day. I think we were both really excited.

Our fellow 'weekenders' included council chief executive Phil and Shirley Watson, Peter and Jackie Robinson of the Blackburn Partnership, Councillor Maureen Bateson, Lord and Lady Adam Patel.

On arrival we had a cup of tea and a piece of cake and then were shown to our rooms. Jack advised me he allocated us Prince Charles' rooms. Later we went down for pre-dinner drinks and then sat down to enjoy a really nice evening meal, known locally as dinner. We still have the menu cards: courgette and basil soup, salmon, new potatoes and veg, mixed fruit pavlova, not over lavish. I was placed with Adam Patel and his wife. Adam talked for England. At one point I said to him, 'Where have you come from Adam?'

'I've come from Ireland, do you know it?'

'Oh yes, I've been a few times; Belfast, Dublin, the Giant's Causeway and Donegal.'

'But they are all in Ireland,' asserted Adam. 'I told you I've just come from Mile End.'

After eating we all sat together for a while with a post-prandial drink. Luckily Peter Robinson was on his top raconteur/animateur form. After a good night's sleep, we went down to help ourselves at a buffet breakfast.

Jack invited me to follow him to a room overlooking the grounds of Chevening. On the table in front of him were at least two of those ministerial 'red' boxes. 'Billy, this is what you get up to when you're a minister. These boxes crammed full of stuff are the briefings or things I have to make a decision about.' I half wanted to but at the same time didn't want to take too close a glimpse at what these boxes contained. I didn't, I resisted the temptation. It seemed quite scary to me that massive decisions could be in the balance depending on how close a reader the minister was and how sharp his or her judgement was. Then, as they might say in an espionage film – the balloon went up!

Our bags were packed ready for departure, and Alice had led a stroll in the grounds, around the lake, well patrolled by armed police and then as people may recall, we, well, Jack, received news of the Bali bombings. Eight hours ahead of UK time, two bombs had exploded in the Kuta bars and nightclubs area. Over 200 people died: nationals from twenty-one different countries including eighty-eight Australians, thirty-eight Indian Asians, and twenty-eight British, and over 200 sustained injuries. Islamist groups were held responsible for these attacks. Jack went into a private room to receive high-level sensitive phone calls, I guess.

We were all brought together and briefly had what had happened explained to us. 'I'm sorry, you'll have to go as soon as possible,' Jack told us. As soon as we had loaded up, we set off. As we rolled through the security gate to leave Chevening, our little convoy of cars was being replaced by a fleet of those large outside-broadcast waggons, the size of horseboxes, from the BBC, Sky and many other news channels. They had come to interview the Foreign Secretary. Minutes before no one had known anything, then Jack had had to be briefed, weigh up what he was being told, briefly discuss this with senior Cabinet colleagues and civil servants. It really brought home to me the responsibilities of ministerial office and how things can suddenly change and develop. He would have to choose his words carefully, his demeanour too. Content and style mattered. People, the families of victims, those well-practised journalists, people across the world in government and not would be weighing up both what Jack Straw was saying and how he was saying it.

As we made our way home, we chatted about the contrasting set of experiences we had witnessed. It had been absolutely engaging, an insight into many things we had no real idea about.

In October 2004 Anne and I were invited again. The party included Labour MP Tessa Jowell and her husband David. Tessa was an MP in London from 1992 to 2015. People may remember that Tessa was elevated to the House of Lords but a brain tumour made her quite ill and she died in 2018. She was a very social being and made the weekend fun. Former local government minister but by then Chief Whip Hilary Armstrong MP (north-west Durham and a fellow former youth worker) and her academic and political health adviser husband Paul Corrigan were also there. Jack and Alice also hosted another couple whose names now escape me. The lady had represented Great Britain on the luge in a Winter Olympics.

A year later we were fortunate enough to be invited by Jack and Alice once more. This time we shared the time with Councillor Mohammed Khan (later CBE, mayor 2008-9 and leader of the council) and his son-in-law Quesir Mahmood (later a councillor and deputy leader), Councillor Akhtar Hussain (mayor 2016-17) and his son, Councillor Maureen Bateson (later MBE, mayor in 1995-6 and a leading councillor over many years) and her daughter Elaine, Ibby Master, Damian Talbot, Jack's constituency secretary, Annette Murphy, Jack's constituency PA and her husband Paul.

*   *   *

Sue Reid's earlier and out of the blue decision to quit, first of all as an exec member, and then totally as a councillor, weighed heavily on my mind. Had she done the right thing? Only she knows. At the time she was single and she was her only source of financial support. Her skill and expertise had been a great asset, but we knew and accepted the fickle capriciousness of our situation. Sue leaving raised questions in my mind about my own situation.

Over the years I'd delivered considerable inputs, writing and training for various local government and education-orientated organisations. I was on a circuit and was regularly called upon; this included peer reviews and inspections. A complex and rare set of experiences and skills. When this was coupled with my experiences of designing and delivering many different sorts of community-style training courses I had quite a unique and desirable CV: youth and community work with 'hard-to-reach' groups and individuals, curriculum design, training trainers, sustained successful stints as chair of three or four local government services, leadership across the council, political leadership, experience in governance across the whole range of education from nursery right through to FE and HE, public speaking, dealing with the media, appearing in the media, dealing with complex community issues and potentially hostile community reaction, local, regional, national and international experience in various different fields of public services, dealing with government ministers and civil servants, huge successes with LEAs, Council of the Year, Beacon awards, etc., vast experience of partnership especially in crime, housing, economic development and regeneration with the private and voluntary sectors and on and on.

Jobs were advertised to appoint regional field officers, ten of them I think, with the Improvement and Development Agency or I&DeA.

To quote their website around the time:

We enable councils to share good practice through the national Beacons scheme and regional local government networks. The best ideas are put on the I&DeA Knowledge website.

Our Leadership Academy programmes help councillors become

better leaders so they can balance the diverse demands of people living in the same community.

The I&DeA also promotes the development of local government's management and workforce. We advise councils on improving customer service and value for money. And we help councils work through local partnerships to tackle difficult problems such as crime and poor public health.

It was a job right up my street. I applied. The salary was around £100k a year, two or three times my current salary level and when the time came, potentially adding an additional £30k a year on my pension. This was a job I was eminently qualified for, would thoroughly enjoy and the money wasn't bad either.

I got to the interview stage and seemed to be doing well. The interviewing panel consisted of some pretty high-profile national figures. What I hadn't included on my application form and didn't divulge during the face-to-face processes, as I had been instructed to keep the information secret, was the extremely imminent announcement that I was going to become a knight.

At that point in the process where you are asked when you could start, I knew there was another skeleton in my career development cupboard. I had vowed to myself to do everything I could to ensure the BNP didn't retain the Mill Hill seat when it was due, ten months hence. So therefore, I asked if it could be held over for that length of time. The answer was no and reluctantly I withdrew my application. I must share with you that my heart was heavy on the train journey home from London.

Not too long later the issue of councillors' allowances was aired both in the council meeting and in the local press. The Lib Dems made public display of refusing to accept their increase recommended by the independent panel. I was reported, saying in a light-hearted way, 'I have always thought that performance-related pay was the best way and the Lib Dems have obviously felt the need to give theirs back as a result'. I concluded 'there are councillors who forsake career advancement to work as councillors. Nobody comes into it for the money'.

*   *   *

At the mayor-making in May 2003, Councillor Michael Barrett was installed as the mayor for 2003/4, with his relatively recently married wife Moira as his mayoress. One of their early civic duties was to walk the newly opened £2.5 million orbital route taking traffic round the town centre extending Barbara Castle Way across the main Manchester to Clitheroe railway line via the Wainwright Bridge. This was named after the Blackburn born and bred but nationally and internationally recognised Alfred Wainwright. Wainwright was born in Blackburn in 1907, he took himself through the night school route to become a qualified accountant and worked for the borough council. In 1930 he took a week's holiday and went walking in the Lake District. This began his love affair with the Lakes and he began exploring routes, making copious notes and fantastic line drawings of their key features. In 1940, he took a pay cut moving to a new job with the council in Kendal, fifty miles nearer to his beloved topography. Most walkers or visitors to the Lake District will be familiar and will have benefitted from his painstaking logging of the fells. Michael and Moira, who suited each other wonderfully, accompanied me and Jack Straw declaring the new stretch of road open. It wasn't the last time I would walk with Mike in public procession.

As you will read soon, on the day before Trooping the Colour 2003 there was quite a press hullabaloo as the news of my knighthood became public. I was the first Blackburn Council leader since Sir George Eddie in 1966 to become a knight of the realm. I had a few people I needed to tell about what had happened and that Friday evening ended up with us, Phil and Shirley Watson having a meal out in the town centre, later joined by Jack and some of his staff. Jack was quoted as saying 'it's very well deserved, he has dedicated himself to this town's welfare for twenty-five years'. Phil and Tory leader Colin Rigby also made nice comments about my honour. Birmingham's national morning paper, the *Birmingham Post* ran a few column inches on it: 'Sheldon Heath school gave me the opportunity and encouragement to speak my own mind and form my own opinions that have made me the man I am today.'

Chapter 31

Day Turns to Knight!

He's a poor boy, empty as a pocket.

It was a Thursday morning back sometime in May 2003 and I was in my office at home reading, considering and responding to several dozen emails, my usual daily traffic as leader of the council. I'd been up since about 6/6.30 a.m. Our daughter, Katherine, was on her way out to college where she was studying for her A levels.

As she stepped out, she picked up the morning's mail, another source of correspondence I had to deal with, always promptly delivered by our regular postie Martyn Thornber.

'Post, Dad, see you later,' she said as she handed me a considerable bundle of correspondence. Good time to stop and make a cuppa I thought, but then a rather posh envelope seemed to stand out from the others. I'll open that one first, I decided.

For some reason we have a silver letter opener, which for some other reason, I tend to use. I slit the envelope open as usual and removed its contents, for which I don't think anybody could ever have been prepared.

The enclosed letter was also printed on posh paper, that thick rich stuff. It was headed by a posh crest emblazoned with the maxim in French 'Honi soit qui mal y pense', decidedly out of the ordinary, I thought.

The address across the top of the paper simply said 10 Downing Street London SW1A 2AA. Hang on a minute, that's Downing Street,

Number 10, the Prime Minister's house. I'd been there once with our highly regarded local economic guru Steve Hoyle at the invite of Tony Blair.

The letter, in confidence, was from WE Chapman. I had at this moment no idea who WE Chapman was.

I read on: 'The Prime Minister has asked me to inform you, in strict confidence...' Then the odd word flew off the page such as 'the Queen', 'her Majesty', 'graciously' and then, yikes, the word 'Knighthood'.

I replaced the contents in its envelope and went and made that now much needed cuppa.

Returning with the bolstering beverage I opened the envelope again and now carefully studied each line, each word, such as:

'Her Majesty may be graciously pleased to approve that the honour of Knighthood be conferred upon you.'

'Before doing so, the Prime Minister would be glad to know that this would be agreeable to you.'

'If you agree that your name should go forward and The Queen accepts the Prime Minister's recommendation, the announcement will be made in the Birthday Honours List. You will receive no further communication before the List is published.'

I read and re-read what was a remarkably short letter. What the hell do I do now?

My wife, Anne, was teaching a mile or so away, so I rang her as a sense of panic began to engulf me. 'Hi Anne, could you pop back during your morning break? It's something I can't talk to you about over the phone, but I need to tell you. I think it's all good news.'

'Well, it had better be important because I'm really busy with exams and coursework and all those kinds of things,' she reminded me.

As she came through the door my instructions were to make her a cup of tea and tell her what was wrong. I wasn't sure I was actually going to be able to speak, just saying 'Please read this' and thrusting the envelope towards her.

Returning to the office with a cup of tea I'm afraid her response was short and unbefitting a Lady (in waiting). 'I'll see you later, I don't know what to think.'

Other than to confirm with one another that we were forbidden to tell anybody else of this impending news, I don't recall if we spoke very much about it over that weekend. I'm not sure we knew what to think and then what to say to one another.

Tuesday came or it could've been the Wednesday and I don't remember us talking much about it or making any decision. Inside the envelope presumably Mr Chapman's staff had kindly included a simple to complete return form. At its head the word Taylor and the letter K were displayed.

The next line read:

'I confirm that', then there were two tick boxes, one said I do and the other I do not and the sentence was concluded with 'wish my name to be considered for the proposed award.'

We decided to repair to a local pub, the Knowles Arms, equipped with the envelope, all of its contents and the nicest pen we could find. Over the acquired beverages we sat and chewed over what we were going to do.

I'd been brought up on a council estate by my mum and had attended the local comprehensive school. My dad had been a junior council employee and my mum served in shops. Anne had been brought up in a terraced house in Bolton (including an outside toilet in the backyard), moving later to a council house. Anne's dad, Fred, had started his working life as a *hewer* down a coal mine near Leigh in 1917 aged twelve and later after his war service was a factory worker. Her mum, Mary, was a *carder* in cotton mills or cleaned pubs, schools and offices. Without introducing strains of violins or re-rehearsing the old Monty Python 'You're lucky' sketch, these were not vainglorious beginnings. My view was that people like us don't become knights, it's not normal or natural. Anne's view was that it should be normal, should be natural and more people from humble beginnings, who worked hard especially for others, should be recognised in our society. And our decision was – Let's have another drink!

We can't just sit here not deciding, at least we both agreed on that. Yes or No, what on earth shall we do?

I reached for the best pen that we could find. I felt stared at by my companion.

In the forenames in full section, only the word William appeared, so I added George. The name of the house was omitted, so I added the word Foxlease in that section. The citation used the title Blackburn and Darwen for the name of the council, which we know is BAD, so I redacted the word and and replaced it with with. The only section I hadn't completed was Section 7, to be known as. It was here that we hesitated.

'Go on,' (I chuckled to myself recalling that 'Go on' was Sir Harry Secombe's chosen coat of arms motto) I was urged. It seemed like an automaton had taken over my bodily functions as I wrote in Section 7 for the first time: Sir Bill Taylor. It looked like the Rubicon had been crossed.

I think the original envelope included a stamped-addressed envelope to return our decision. Once we'd got so far, the decision was either easy or already made. I ticked the I do box, placed all the necessary documentation in the envelope and sealed it. There you are: job done.

There was a post box about fifty yards away, so we walked up with our envelope. As I put it in, through the slot, hovering at the top of the box, I called for silence. Letting go of the envelope, we both listened attentively to ensure it dropped all the way to the bottom. It would be a shame to miss out only because the letter had got stuck somewhere inside the post box! Our reply was dated 21 May 2003, a Wednesday. It had taken us nearly a week to decide what to do.

The Queen's official birthday in 2003 and Trooping the Colour (by the Grenadier Guards) fell on Saturday 14 June. This was only three weeks after we posted our return slip but it seemed like forever. We couldn't and didn't tell anyone and heard no more, not a proverbial dickie bird.

On the Friday morning, the day before Trooping the Colour, as we were preparing to go our separate ways for work purposes, Anne asked if I'd heard any more about the knighthood thing. I hadn't and said so. Perhaps we'd got it wrong. I think we briefly discussed and agreed to go out somewhere to eat and made some tentative plans for the evening.

I cycled the eight or so miles to work that summer's day and then mid-morning cycled on the further five or so miles for a meeting in Clitheroe. En route my mobile phone rang. It was David Higgerson, a nice guy from the local *Telegraph*. 'Hello,' he said, 'what are you doing?'

Mischievously I glanced down at the bike's minicomputer, 'About thirteen miles an hour,' I teased.

'No, no, no, I know you've had a letter from the big palace in London and now you're a knight.'

'Aha, so it is true, it's all been a bit mysterious.' I stopped and got off my bike at a convenient bench near Clitheroe Golf Club and we spoke for five or ten minutes.

I texted Anne, telling her that the knighthood thing was on and I'd see her later as vaguely agreed. I jumped back on my bike and reached Clitheroe for my regular Community Safety Partnership meeting with chief executive Dave Morris, Bill Alker and others. I stayed totally schtum, not telling anyone anything. Family first.

It being mainly uphill back from Clitheroe to Whalley I jumped on the train with my bike. I rang Matt. 'Hello, son, it's Trooping the Colour tomorrow when the Queen gives people honours.'

'Brilliant news, Dad. Have you got some letters after your name?'

'No Matt, completely the opposite. They're all at the front!'

'Fucking hell, Dad,' said Matt.

I retorted, 'That was your mum's reaction when she first found out!'

From the train, with a poor signal I rang my mum in Birmingham. 'Hi Mum, it's Bill.'

'Where are you? It's very noisy.'

'I'm on a train.'

'Don't be so stupid. Anyway, what's wrong?'

'It's Trooping the Colour tomorrow, Mum, you know, when the Queen inspects all the soldiers in London and she gives out Honours to people.'

'Is it? No, I didn't really know that, I'm not all that bothered. Why are you telling me?'

'Well, Mum, that's why I'm ringing you, because I've been awarded a knighthood. From now on, your little boy is Sir Bill Taylor.'

'This line isn't very good, Bill, and you're talking the usual nonsense about being a knight or being called Sir Bill or something. So, wait till you can talk to me properly. Bye-bye.' The phone went dead.

I then rang our daughter, Katherine. 'Hi Kit, there is something quite exciting and I can't tell you about it over the phone but can you be back home around four o'clock?'

'So, I'm not in trouble, good.'

The news must've got out. The phone never stopped ringing. I got home around about four and went straight into the house. Our Katherine was sat at the kitchen table.

'Dad, what's going on? The phone has never stopped ringing, there's journalists, some photographers and I'm not sure there's not a TV crew out there. What is going on?'

'I have no time to explain. The news is that I've been made a knight.'

She leapt up instantly. 'Dad, that's fantastic, I'm so proud of you, it's brilliant. I love you so much.' She gave me a huge cuddle and then drew back realising she'd got her eye make-up all over my shirt!

There were photographs to be taken, more interviews to be given, radio interviews to be recorded. It all was quite frenetically busy.

Later we went out with Phil and Shirley Watson if I remember rightly and had a nice meal in town.

I was up early the next morning because I was conducting a council leader's surgery in Darwen accompanied by two town hall officers Donna Hall (now CBE herself after a brilliant local government career) and Tara Duce.

On my arrival, Donna presented me with a bottle of bubbles and a lovely bouquet of flowers. I'm not sure Tara knew exactly what was going on.

My next task that day was to be interviewed by the local Labour Party as to my suitability to stand as a candidate in the all-out elections in June 2004.

I was early for the appointment and so Donna dropped me off near the cathedral with my two gifts, to sit there in the sunshine and wait my time. I wasn't the first person to sit in the cathedral grounds with a bottle!

Whilst sitting there, the Reverend Andrew Hindley emerged from the cathedral, where he was quite high up. Andrew is gay, openly so. I've known him for many years and he's a great bloke.

'Hi Bill, what are you up to?' Andrew asked.

'I'm a knight.' I repeated, 'I'm a knight.'

What I didn't know is that Ammonites were a religious sect, so I'm afraid I might have confused Andrew.

'You're an Ammonite?'

'No, I'm a bloody knight, as in of the realm.'

'Bloody hell, that's fantastic news, Bill.' Perhaps a few passing eyebrows were raised in incredulity as Andrew and I embraced and danced together in the cathedral grounds.

I then had to make my way to the town hall for my initial interview to secure a Labour Party candidacy. I must have done quite well as I was admitted onto the list

The next part of my day was a game of golf. My partners that day were Phil Watson and another guy Alan.

Blackburn Golf Club members are a pretty homogenous group of folk: a few lawyers and accountants but mainly guys who are engineers, painters and decorators, electricians, plumbers or work in the aerospace, brewing, and other local industries. Whilst, by and large, there is a competitive edge out on the course, once back in 'the nineteenth hole' its culture is light ribald ribbing.

We set off playing. It was a nice summer's day. As we walked up the fifth, a group of chaps going down the seventh removed their caps and applauded. What was going on? This happened again as we walk down the tenth and happened four or five other times. Phil explained it was in recognition of a member of the club becoming a knight. That's me, by the way!

It would be fair to say, with a handicap that hovered in the early twenties, I was never particularly good at golf. I knocked my drive reasonably well up the eighteenth fairway. I noticed a few folk out on the balcony overlooking the eighteenth green; no pressure there then on my second shot. Luckily, it landed miraculously on the green.

What happened next was a bit like the winner walking onto the eighteenth at a major golf tournament. The bar had emptied and around fifty members were stood on the balcony applauding. Peter Forrest came down the steps carrying a tray with a pint on it and a tea towel draped over his forearm, waiter style.

I quaffed the beer, wiped my frothy lips, acknowledged the gallery and finished off the game. As was normal we shook hands as a trio, signed and swapped our score cards. I went to put my clubs away in the car and glanced at my mobile phone. Goodness only knows how many text messages or voicemails there were. I sat in the boot of my estate car answering my texts or listening to the voicemails.

This must have taken a considerable length of time, half an hour or more. But eventually I got into the clubhouse. Phil chuckled, Alan couldn't stay, sends you his best. But he did explain that he couldn't understand why you'd had such a mediocre game but attracted such a fantastic reception. Phil went on to relate that he did explain to Alan that it was in response to me becoming a knight. 'Oh' Alan had said!

Then after that frenetic excitement of the weekend, it all went quite anti-climatical.

The Saturday after, for some reason, we were going by train to Manchester to meet up with our daughter, Kit. I was to set off and catch an earlier train, can't remember why, with Anne following on the train after.

My route took me past our bank, NatWest, and I thought I'd pop in and register my change of name.

I got an appointment with accounts manager Bernadette McHugh almost immediately and sat down with her. 'Right, Mr Taylor, how can we help you today?'

'Well! You've hit the nail right on its head. I need to change my name registered with you.' Not a problem whatsoever, have you brought some proof of change of name with you?'

'That's where my problem starts. There isn't any except for an entry in the most recent copy of the *London Gazette*.'

'I'm sorry, I don't really follow what you're telling me.'

'Please will you spin the screen round so we can both see it.'

This she did so we could both see the same computer screen. All the usual details: name, address, date of birth, etc., were all there. I've banked with NatWest since the 1960s – forty or so years.

'There it is,' I said pointing at the name blocks on the screen. 'My name has been changed.'

'You've changed your name?' she asked with an element of puzzlement in her voice.

'No, it's been changed for me. But it's not complicated, nothing like Engelbert Humperdinck. It's just there,' as I pointed to the Mr block on the screen. 'I'm no longer a Mr.'

To be frank the woman's face was a picture as she stutteringly enquired, 'So, you're no longer a Mr?'

'That's it, you've got it, I am no longer a Mr.'

There was quite a long gap; I don't think she had a clue what to say next. 'So please can you erase the Mr in that block there?'

'OK, so you want me to erase the word Mr here and replace it with what, might I ask?'

'That's it, I told you it was dead easy. Please insert the word Sir.'

A hugely relieved expression instantaneously manifested itself. 'It's you, Sir Bill Taylor, fantastic. I was just telling my husband last night we've got a Sir client in the branch.'

Immediately the M and the R disappeared to be replaced by Sir. Underneath the screen carried a category entitled something like documentary proof of change of name, e.g., deed poll, etc.

I didn't quite catch what was inserted here, something like I know the guy and it's true!

'Anything else I can help you with this morning, Sir Bill?' she asked rather extravagantly, with gusto even.

'Can we do the same for my wife as she has now become a Lady?'

'No, sorry. That's not possible. Lady Anne will have to come into the branch in person. It's the bank's rules.'

I left the branch having been told that my wife had to come in, as I wasn't allowed to do it for her due to either equal opps or data protection or something like that.

I rang Anne and reminded her she had to change her name at NatWest and told her the name of the member of staff she might be better asking for. Rather than tell her about the palaver I'd had, I told her the process was straightforward.

When we met an hour or two later somewhere near Manchester Victoria, I got a bit of an ear-bashing off Anne. She'd walked into the branch and asked specifically for the same accounts manager. To my usually quite quiet and unassuming wife's embarrassment, as she approached the lady in question, she dropped into a full curtsy in front of the other Lady in question, right in the middle of the bank foyer!

After that, not a lot happened. People around me generally fell into two camps. One lot who, sometimes openly to my face, said you weren't born a Sir, so don't expect me to call you it. However, the most vociferous advocate of this approach consistently calls me Sir Bill every single time. The other lot, never obsequiously, always call me Sir Bill. They explained that it made them feel proud, not of me, but the things that had probably contributed to the knighthood, in which they had played a part. Oh, and there was a third, creepier group who introduced me, eyeballs rolling to their peers, as their friend Sir Bill. After that they dropped it when talking to or about me.

I'd made it clear that people should call me whatever they were comfortable with.

Chapter 32

Carry on, Sir, June-December 2003

Half of the time we're gone, but we don't know where.

After the announcement of my knighthood things went back to normal. Normal manic, that is. I carried on absolutely loving most things I did and the decision to withdraw my application for the I&DeA job slowly diminished in importance.

Although most of the work was done outside the formal civic structures of the council, that is, the full council meeting, I enjoyed those events too, as a piece of theatre.

The four-cycle Friday teatime meetings with the chief exec, his senior officers, my deputies and then opposition councillors were thoroughly enjoyable. They were normally followed with a couple of drinks with my wife and then home for something nice cooked by her and wonderful unwind family time.

Once every six or eight weeks, we went on to different parts of our communities for a multi-agency community accountability event. Up to 200 people in a school or church hall all giving up of their Friday evening to listen and speak with their cabinet minister/MP, the leader of the council, the chief executive of the council, the head of police and NHS inter alia. The general demeanour at these events was warm, conducted appropriately either with a sense of humour or a due sense of responsibility.

One Friday evening meeting was held in Ewood neighbourhood centre, also known as Ivy St. *Telegraph* journalist, Sarah Warden, reported that Jack pledged to investigate how much public money was spent in different parts of the town. The underlying insinuation in this and most other white working-class communities being that people in the Asian communities got more than their fair share. The council was ahead of these communities and their MP. The report, following the community resource mapping exercise, was imminently to be published, for all to see. Jack was both a shrewd cookie and now twenty-plus years battle hardened. He was quoted as saying, 'When I go into the Ivy (pub – fifty yards away) people say in private that all the money is spent in the areas where there is a large Asian population. When I go there, the same complaint is raised against the white community'. I was determined that we would get to the bottom of these opposing and unsubstantiated views and the publication of the report would make it a matter open to public scrutiny.

It was at one of these sessions, this time across the town, in the more multicultural Corporation Park area, during a right good ratatatat about bins and road sweeping and the like, that I closed my eyes relying on my sense of hearing alone. The words and the accents were the same and one simply couldn't discern the ethnicity of whoever happened to be speaking at the time. That taught me many things, especially being more hopeful for the future.

Saturday mornings could mean either the council leader's surgery or one of Jack's town centre soapbox sessions, for which I was the warm-up act, setting in the audience's minds the potential agenda we may wish to discourse with our assembled citizens. I think they lapped it up and again there was a sense of street theatre about it; another skill I brought from my youth and community work repertoire.

Saturday afternoons were normally a game of golf, followed by a couple of beers and then home. We always had our Sunday lunch early on Saturday evening. Sundays, except for during election time, were quiet days, possibly a family pub lunch or a couple of beers or just a chill out.

* * *

Except, that was, during the football season. Matthew, Matt or Matty loved playing football. Playing in an organised team started in the Woodlands Cubs, perhaps even before that, in the (six to eight-year-olds) Beavers. Their managers then were dads Roy Breakell and Stuart Cawtherly, followed by Roy and former Wolves and Blackburn Rovers striker Norman Bell (dad to sons Norman and Andy) who took over the team. After that, Norman as a constant and informed influence, and Les Frankish, were managers of that oldest age-group team.

But things got silly! From a group of parents running a team for their lads, we became a club, running four teams! The original mums and dads, Taylors, Frankishs, Carrs, Harwoods, Beardsworths, Holmes and Collins became good friends with each other: parties, quiz nights, treasure hunts, drinks, theatre trips, etc. But most of all, fundraising. Each team needed two full strips (home and 2nd), numerous balls (match and training), goal nets, flags, training equipment, fees paying, thousands of pounds per team. With training nights, match days, fundraising and club and league committee meetings, disciplinaries and awards nights, Sunday afternoons washing fifteen or so sets of muddy, sodden strips, drying and folding them ready again, visits to A&E, police stations, etc., the commitment grew like topsy! But times four! Adrian Greenwood and his son Andrew took on a team to manage as did others. This father and son duo took FA coaching qualifications. Frank Barrett ran another, a great charities man with the Round Table. Eddie McGhee also ran one of the teams. Eddie was often late due to his work for our monthly club meetings, mainly held in the Hole I'th Wall pub on Shear Brow, but we didn't mind! As a baker, Eddie's box of savouries and confections brought to the meeting around 9.30 p.m. were well received!

Putting a gloss on it, some parents took on responsibility big style, others 'less so'! One asked if their kid could be collected from and returned home rather than them taking him to and from the match, so Mum and Dad could have a lie in (nudge, nudge?). Numerous parents attended nothing, raised nothing, did nothing! The work tended to fall on already busy people's shoulders. After many years' sterling work Mike Harwood relinquished being club secretary. My wife, Anne, offered to attend some meeting or other in his stead. She came back as the new duly elected secretary which made me chuckle. 'I shouldn't laugh too loud, too soon,' she advised! 'You're now chairman!'

We took on the posts for two or three seasons. As we came to the last year before all the boys would go off to university or into the world of work, we announced, giving a year's notice, that we would be giving up any involvement in the club at the end of that season. We repeated this on several occasions during the year inviting people to offer to take over the organisation. On the last evening a well-meant couple, David and Margaret Bateman, offered their services but we heard after that season, that the club folded. Sad really. We heard that thousands and thousands of pounds worth of equipment were taken to the next league meeting and other clubs helped themselves to the fruits of our extensive fundraising and organisational efforts. People, eh? Show some commitment to *your own* kids! Invest in them!

Over the ten or so years, the teams Matt played for morphed names from Woodlands to Beardwood Boys then Darwen Town and finally Revidge. Twenty-plus years later the names I can remember include Paul Carr, the two Bells, Norman Jnr (and Andy, a couple of age groups younger, pro footballer and a future England U16 international), Keith Frankish, Steve Harwood, Christian Clarkson, Stevie Holmes, Simon Harrison. Jonny Collins (who sadly died, very young), Danny Campbell, Anthony Harwood, Paul Jackson, Ross Harkness, Chris Ashton, Liam Lishman and the two Beardsworth lads, Garry and Andrew a couple of age groups younger. Almost the same lads played for Lammack Primary run by teacher Mike Jackman (Rovers pundit and author of authoritative reference books on the club) and Pleckgate High School with former semi-pro footballer Rick Grogan in charge. They all absolutely loved it and became good mates through all that period in their lives.

Our Katherine, also known as Kit, liked her sport too and I was still spending Saturday mornings watching her and another great gang of young women playing hockey as she went into her thirties, just prior to her becoming a mum herself. I was fundraising here too compiling and compering a couple of quizzes a year to boost the Witton Warriors' club kitty! The team was a mix of ex-Lammack, Pleckgate and St Mary's College pupils and students and somewhat oxymoronically Burnley

Ladies. All sound young women, hardworking, hard-playing and hard-drinking lasses! Ann-Marie Lambert, the Khansia sisters, Aysha (now Johnson) and Sophie (now Harrison), Catherine CD Duckworth (now Greathead), Karen 'Dottie' Dewhurst, Tara Leatherd (now Heys), Debbie 'Dobbie' Slater and Katherine (now Rogan).

*   *   *

Bank Holiday weeks with a school break, three French weeks in the summer and any non-earmarked weekend meant touring caravan loaded up, bikes, tents, toys, Dan the Dog, etc., and offski. Not too far, the Lancs coast, Lakes or Yorkshire Dales were all far enough away to mean a great family break. Long doggie walks on beaches or fells, bike rides, board games, barbecue, pub grub, anything to feel 'family' again.

Our favourite family holiday night-time pastime was a game of cards handed down from my mum's mum, Isabella. We called it 'Can I buy?'. It was basically rummy with a double pack. We would play for hours, outside, in the awning or in the caravan as the rain pitter-pattered on the roof. As the kids got bigger and better at it, the rules got more and more Taylorised and complex. The rule changes were often brought about by accusations of cheating or just for fun. The first card drop was adjudicated impartially by the temporarily appointed Decision Maker and the Nod God. If you got down to your last card you had to announce it in either an Irish or a pirate accent (don't ask me why or which). Humming was allowed during any lengthy break as someone with a fistful of a hand worked out their best drop, but only ABBA songs! Please don't ask why or try to understand. I think Katherine even handwrote the rules out once. Families, eh?

That meant it was Monday again. Back on the roller coaster, carousel and helter-skelter. Town hall, work, town hall or work, town hall or some combination of those with meetings interspersed with other agencies, other communities, citizens in neighbourhoods. Then, lo and behold, it was Friday again.

Eventually I'd managed to get round all of our secondary schools talking to their Year elevens about the council, democracy and civics. But guess what? Once I got around them all it was time to go round again, a little bit like the apocryphal painting of the Forth Bridge. I loved these sessions talking to around 150 to 200 fifteen to sixteen-year-olds and their teachers. The staff often commented after, that they hadn't known quite what to expect and found it accessible, informative, appropriate for that age group, and damn good fun – excellent.

It was in the middle of July 2003 that the *Telegraph* carried a short article explaining that the local police had passed the investigative file on the allegations of vote rigging to the Crown Prosecution Service. Independent Councillor Mohammed Hussain would have to wait to hear what might happen to him next.

*   *   *

We still had much more to do to transform our services to make them more appropriate and accessible to our service users. We continued to work closely with the council's education and social services departments alongside the NHS primary care trust to establish a children's trust. The idea here was to bring all these key services physically located together so that children and their families could benefit from a 'one-stop shop' approach to health and education alongside leisure, adult education, libraries, advice, pre-school education and creche facilities. Anticipating what became known as the much cherished, now lamented, Surestart centres, we understood that families, especially those with very small children and no access to a family vehicle, would benefit from the services they needed being located locally. Eventually we had thirteen centres right across the borough. This was going to cost around £15 million and create 150 new jobs and over 2,000 much needed new childcare places.

We had to ensure that educational provision in East Lancashire was truly from the cradle to the grave. As chairman of the East Lancashire Partnership focusing on improving education and employment across the sub-region and as a governor of Blackburn College, I was involved in the transformation of our degree teaching into the East Lancashire Institute of Higher Education. We were already in a degree generating partnership with my old stomping ground at Lancaster University and this was one further step towards degrees being able to be taught locally. At the time, about 2,000 local students studied for their degrees there. I think the university saw themselves as the senior partner but I was looking for an adult to adult relationship because effectively we provided them with a rich and almost continuous supply of students from more challenging, that is poorer, backgrounds. Stealth wasn't usually my default strategy, but it seemed to be working. We also had to be quite careful not to train up our local people to degree standard for there to be no 'big ticket' jobs for them. We didn't simply want to create a brain drain diaspora out of Lancashire. People attaining degrees should get better paid jobs, which should lead to people living in better quality housing, leading on to a healthier population. A complex chain of cause and effect.

Where could all this lead to next? The fame without the fortune of appearing on the silver screen. Our north-west regional ITV station Granada approached us to do a six-episode 'fly on the wall' documentary to be known as *Are You Being Serviced?* Phil Watson, as chief exec, had given permission for this behind-the-scenes filming. With their customary eye for entrepreneurial and publicity opportunities, the opposition parties didn't jump at the chance. Lib Dem leader Paul Browne said in the local paper 'It'll make us a laughing stock'. Tory leader Colin Rigby was enigmatically quoted as saying 'It could be good, but also be bad'. My reported view was 'This is a great opportunity for us to show the positive impact frontline public sector employees have on the lives of individual citizens'. That was the intended focus, to include the registrar's department dealing with births, marriages and deaths, our schools, summer playschemes, social services, what happens in our public halls and our bin men, amongst others. Did this mean that actor Kevin Kennedy, aka Curly Watts, would step off the hallowed cobbles and come and do a shift or two with our hard-working, target-driven local bin men? No, I doubted it too! But he did manage to make a few bob out of it for himself by doing the voiceover narration for the series.

Journalist Eric Leaver in his weekly 'Leaver at Large' feature in the local paper poured further cold water on the idea. When will people wake up to the importance, the accessible accountability and the multiplicity of services that councils deliver? Some journalists fall for their own lazy negativity where their cynicism dominates the critical.

Some weeks, possibly months later, the programme was televised. But who stole the show? Who became the stars? Not me, not the chief exec, not anybody in childcare – Peter and Derek did, of course. That's Peter Trueman and Derek Wilkinson, just in case you didn't know, two boiler-suited heroes. The heroics they performed included keeping our streets clean and power-jetting our drains to make sure they worked effectively. Phil and I did appear briefly and so did those running the summer playschemes, what goes on behind the scenes at our public halls known as King George's, our bin men grappling with a new fortnightly collection cycle, the registry office dealing with hatches, matches and despatches, work in schools, how the adoption process works and various and multiple other responsibilities and activities of the council. At the end of the show's successful run we invited everyone who had appeared in it to a modest afternoon tea in our public halls. Nothing over glitzy, or too Hollywood but, to a well-deserved standing ovation, Peter and Derek did get presented with an Oscar-type award for their work. I thought the series did our council, and other councils, a world of good. People delivering services to people is always a complex and often thankless process.

The six-episode Granada-only series was pitched directly in the 7.30 p.m. slot against the nationally broadcast BBC soap *EastEnders*; it had 1 million viewers. Chief executive Phil Watson said 'We have about 6,500 employees many of whom influence the lives of local residents on a daily basis. There are always risks in agreeing to programmes like this but I was determined that local residents should judge us on what we're actually like, not on some prejudice about what councils perhaps were like thirty years ago'. Good lad, Phil!

Whilst we were getting ready for all this excitement, we had another departure from the council with a councillor quitting Blackburn to go and live and work in Sheffield, a good two-hour drive away. Again, our local paper reported the Lib Dem councillor having a tirade in full council about councillors' allowances. Veteran Labour councillor Dorothy Walsh bided her time saying, 'It's particularly galling to hear you criticise what we get. Most of our work is volunteering; this money reflects the extra responsibility we have. You should get back to Sheffield'.

*   *   *

Something I'd been advocating for twenty years, a unitary council for the half a million people of East Lancashire, would, in my opinion, sit very nicely with regional assemblies. Deputy Prime Minister John Prescott announced there would be referenda to consider such bodies for the North West, Yorkshire and the Humber and the North East in the autumn of 2004. Once again, the 'big fish, little pond' brigade were alerted and stumbled into what they believed to be action. They saw the downside of these ideas, not the opportunities. One council means fewer councillors, fewer top-brass officers, less office space, less bureaucracy and more money to be spent on services, where the rubber hits the road.

Ribble Valley Council, the district in which I had worked since 1995, had as its boundaries what was left when everything else was taken in 1974. It stretched around twenty-five miles from very, very close to BwD's housing mass in the south to the beginning of the Yorkshire Dales in the north, east to west, thirty miles or so, from near Skipton in Yorkshire to the M6 and further west.

The rest of East Lancashire, using both the M65 and the railway line to Colne as its backbone, made more coherent sense: Darwen, Blackburn, Accrington and area, Rossendale, Burnley, Nelson and Colne. All of these five boroughs had sometimes been Labour and sometimes something else. To me it wasn't the party politics but the common identity that was important. I think the residents of Ribble Valley had both party politics and ethnographic reservations to what they saw or were told was a takeover. I went early, openly and publicly to say that probably the best bet was to let the Ribble Valley go wherever it wanted except the bits very close to northern Blackburn, possibly 10,000 residents, within 500,000 across East Lancs. What a kerfuffle that caused. Both the print media and the airways went mad in opposition to such an idea. I was quite clearly made the bête noire responsible for this outrageous suggestion.

Tanks and lawns may come to mind, I was publicly accused of being 'expansionist'. I preferred a more domestic analogy, being quoted as saying 'the status quo, although comfortable like an old pair of slippers, is too risky to move forward with. We don't see this as a takeover of any council, this is a merger'.

My vilification bordered on alarmist demonisation; I was cast as the Adolf Hitler of East Lancashire. The neighbouring council leader, Conservative Peter Britcliffe, was quoted as saying 'It's no coincidence that we are deciding this on 3 September because this is the day that war broke out. Bill Taylor would like to march his green and white buses right across Hyndburn, it is a doomsday scenario for Hyndburn' (pauses for a chuckle nearly twenty years later). Britcliffe continued, 'The last time I spoke to Bill Taylor was in Harrogate and he certainly didn't mention it then'. My riposte was, 'I was sat next to him in a conference room discussing this for two hours and there was a wide-ranging conversation about these matters. I've not been able to update him as he's been on holiday in Spain for a month'.

Deputy Prime Minister John Prescott went on a roadshow tour of the north-west to promote his ideas for regional assemblies. Regional assemblies offered opportunities for greater and closer to people democracy and a bigger say on how money (£2.6 billion at the time) was spent, especially European budgets, for the benefit of local people. These opportunities were immense but those who wanted to dabble in local village-pump politics refused to see that, preferring to apparently feed their own petty egos. At one of these roadshow events that was hosted in a conference suite at Ewood Park, John Prescott was the main turn, but I upstaged him. When introduced to the 200-plus assembled audience the boos for Bill the bête noire Taylor easily exceeded in volume those for the national politician. Infamy, infamy, I thought!

About the same time, I took the Deputy Prime Minister on a walkabout to see how European and other external funding regimes had been brought together to massively improve and regenerate Blackburn town centre, eventually, years later, to become known, because of its coherence, as the cathedral quarter. Much of this work was masterminded by the Reverend Andrew Hindley, a great ball of energy and an asset to both the borough and his ecclesiastical base.

It was during my two or three meetings with John Prescott that I lobbied hard with him. He announced that nearly 30,000 civil service jobs were going to be decanted away from London and the south-east. My case was 'we believe we are ideally placed to play a key part in this owing to our reputation as a successful, well-managed local authority. The council will put forward strong recommendations to encourage a relocation of civil service jobs to Blackburn with Darwen'. It seemed to me there was no point in regularly having the attention and the ear of senior national politicians without bending it occasionally.

The whole process of moving possibly towards regional assemblies and restructuring local government took its next teetering steps in early December, when the possible models for local government were circulated by the local government boundary committee. BwD were generally in favour of some form of pan East Lancashire unitary format. Everyone else seemed agin. I was quoted to say 'I don't have a particular preference. We need to consult people and find out what they want'. Blackburn has shown that unitary authorities are the way forward. The popes in their own parishes didn't want to lose their little bit of power, more likely their little bit of ego massaging limelight. If there are any inevitabilities in life, I predict that one day there will be a unitary council across the whole of East Lancashire. We'll all just have to wait and see how this epic saga unravels.

*　　*　　*

Councils are serious business. They face serious, literally life and death issues on a daily basis. No more so than in their dealings with vulnerable children who were or could be placed in council care. I didn't know about these youngsters individually in any detail, assuming that at the point of taking them into care, it had been assessed and adjudged that it was safer for them there than wherever they'd been before. A reasonable assumption I would have thought, in most people's opinion.

Without any warning the front-page headline in the local *Telegraph* was 'What the hell's going on?'. The allegations in the two-page article were quite dreadful.

I quickly convened a meeting of the senior officers and councillors involved. It was alleged in the press that one girl, aged twelve, had absconded from her care home thirty-six or more times, that she operated as a prostitute (as had her mother, the paper reported) and was pregnant. There were, of course, issues of client confidentiality and the danger of identifying specific at-risk individuals. I also learned that our complement of qualified and experienced social workers was down by some 20-25 per cent. I didn't know the exact figure of children in Blackburn with Darwen's care and was shocked to be told it was more than 350. That's the equivalent of a class full in every year age group. Today the cost of one child in council care could be in excess of £110k pa.

Usually, these youngsters were the vulnerable victims of abuse themselves, having experienced little love in their own upbringing, mistaking men's attention and gift-giving for love, not the unscrupulous grooming exploitation that it often was. They frequently displayed attention-seeking, extreme behavioural problems, often resorting to the use of threatening behaviour. Dealing with these youngsters was a very delicate issue. Sometimes the next port of call in their chaotic lives would be secure care. This could expose them to the next level of chaos and potentially, even more, to a life of crime.

Reporter Donna McKenzie spoke to the family of the girl, talking about how both the mother and stepfather were drug users and that when the girl was nine she'd seen her mum operating as a prostitute. They told the reporter that, aged less than ten, the girl was drinking, smoking cannabis, shoplifting, beating up other kids and was expelled from primary school. The paper spoke with the girl's auntie. The family had moved the girl to her grandmother's house, finding she was using crack cocaine. The aunt said 'We think the lads she keeps driving off with are pimping her. They are drug dealers and she is prostituting herself to pay them back'. Another aunt said, 'Her mother is definitely on crack, she started with drugs at the same age and it looks like history is repeating itself. Her mum started on cannabis then glue, whizz, acid, then heroin'.

There were other dreadful child neglect/abuse cases during my public lifetime, inter alia: Maria Coldwell in 1973, events in Cleveland in 1987 and Victoria Climbié (2002) with their associated enquiries by TG Field-

Fisher, Dame Elizabeth Butler-Sloss and Lord Laming. These may still be in many people's recollections. Cyril Smith, MP for Rochdale (died 2010), grooming gang cases across northern England, Saville (died 2011) and the others in Operation Yew Tree are more recent.

My friend and former council colleague, Simon Danczuk, himself a former MP for Rochdale, published the eerily entitled and well-researched book into Smith's not-so-secret life, *Smile for the Camera*. (ISBN-10: 1849548757 Biteback Publishing 16 April 2015)

The Laming Report (2002), after Climbié, states:

1.21. Having considered the response to Victoria from each of the agencies, I am forced to conclude that the principal failure to protect her was the result of widespread organisational malaise.

Following yet another child abuse case in 2009, this time Baby P, Minister Ed Balls asked Lord Laming to revisit his earlier report. It doesn't make for encouraging reading. Its first two recommendations:

The Home Secretary and the Secretaries of State for Children, Schools and Families, Health, and Justice must collaborate in the setting of explicit strategic priorities for the protection of children and young people and reflect these in the priorities of frontline services.

A National Safeguarding Delivery Unit be established to report directly to the Cabinet Subcommittee on Families, Children and Young People.

The meeting I established when the social services story broke in the local paper mapped out a 'who's doing what, when' approach. I was confident that Stephen Sloss, the director of social services and his team along with Councillor Maureen Bateson, relatively new to social services but a vastly experienced exec member, were clear, committed and united, to resolving these complex issues both in the immediate and longer term. It was agreed that we would reconvene this group weekly or more often if necessary.

Newspapers operate on different legal terrain. Councils have a legal duty of care right down to that of the individual, their family and their confidentiality. Those tensions got so fraught that the council took out an injunction to try and moderate both sensationalisation and the danger of revealing the main actors' identities.

Newspapers can move as fast as they like, be as sensational as they want, within certain parameters. Within days of printing the story initially, the *Lancashire Evening Telegraph* carried the front-page banner headline 'She's safe' adding 'Straw praises the *Evening Telegraph* as pregnant vice girl, twelve, is put in secure unit'. Not a very considered piece of journalism? The paper described the girl as 'out of control', describing the case now as being 'properly dealt with'. What had happened to her? She was placed in a secure unit forty miles away for an initial seventy-two hours that could be extended up to three months. Yes, she was removed from her family and other local adverse community influences, but was potentially being confined amongst a more hardened, institutionalised criminal fraternity, a move from the frying pan to the fire?

The girl's mum was quoted as saying that she thought 'social services had failed her since she put her into voluntary care two years ago'. Admitting she had a heroin problem and was a prostitute she said she was 'asking the council for a home where she and her daughter could be together again'.

Who is responsible? The girl herself, her family, the press, the council, schools, social services, the police, the law, government, predatorial grooming gangs who prey on girls? Who do you think? Whatever the solution is to this sad series of events and all the others, some yet to come, it doesn't appear that we have found it yet.

That was the end of that locally, for the time being at least. Crisis revealed, addressed and resolved in four or five days. The girl was in a secure unit. What happened to this girl in the longer term, I never knew the detail. I trusted Stephen Sloss and Maureen Bateson. The social service inspectorate were in Blackburn back then on a routine visit. They reviewed the events of those frenetic few days and were satisfied that appropriate procedures had been employed.

Later I read, given the far more concerning overall developing picture, a police-led but multi-agency group known as Operation Engage was established in 2005. This developed into Engage, a service made up of staff from children and social services, the police, health workers and the voluntary sector. There were three elements to their approach: prevention, protection and prosecution. The intention was to free vulnerable children and families from CSE, Child Sexual Exploitation. I know very little about their work as it developed over the next fifteen or more years. It was over this time that cases in Rochdale, Preston, Rotherham, Derby, Shropshire, Oxford, Telford and Middlesbrough of male Asian grooming gangs came increasingly to the attention of the press, police and public.

* * *

Knighthoods, packed 'working' weeks, inter-ethnic mistrust, keeping up visits to schools, allegations of voting irregularities, integrated pre-school services, local access to degree level study, our own TV series, a prospect of regionally devolved government, enlarged unitary councils, social services and vulnerable children in care crises, to name but a few. Some of these fell into the routine category of issues, some into the proactive and, most definitely, the final issue, the reactive.

Meanwhile, we had the general day to day needs of our public to improve. The world was changing, becoming more digital, whether we liked it or not. People were getting used to shopping, banking, getting their insurance cover, dealing with utility companies via the Internet and councils had to keep up with that. The local paper reported after a one-off 'mystery shopper' exercise, that only 59 per cent of people were happy with the council's services. 59 per cent!? That sounded good to me especially compared to many private sector client-focussed organisations with their 'customer care' departments. We listened, we learned and we implemented. Costing nearly £9 million, B-direct would make access to our services more digital and customer focussed, in that queries made by the public were not dependent on an exhaustive understanding of the apparently labyrinthine workings of the council. For the less IT savvy amongst our citizens, there would still be people to talk to both in Blackburn and in Darwen. It was a fact of life within our communities that there was a large minority of people who still not did not have bank accounts and lived in a cash only world. Both town halls still had 'collecting' halls with cashiers who handled citizens' cash on a daily basis.

The work to build our two city learning centres was coming to fruition. These were going to be digital IT hubs for use by our schools, community centres and voluntary groups, indeed anyone and everyone who wanted to enhance these increasingly 'must have' skills. With some robotic stunts, I was going to perform the opening of these two centres but don't worry, I had some primary and secondary-aged pupils to help. For once, I could almost cast-iron guarantee that my role was more ornamental than operational.

And with brain perpetually in active mode I thought of another constituent group of people to consult with – our local men and now also women of the cloth. We put an invitation out to all the Christian clerics whatever their denomination. Informed opinion amongst town hall officers was that this was a barmy idea and nobody would turn up. At the first meeting around thirty local clergy arrived. A lot of them had never met each other before and they were very pleased that the blessèd cathedral was not invited. Politics, eh? My perception of this group of public servants was that they might well touch a whole chunk of people in the community, older and more infirm. Jack heard about these meetings, thought they were 'a bloody good idea' and got himself invited. This, in turn, pleased the clerics. Issues raised ranged from a) why don't we invite all faiths including Islam and b) could they have a few more clothes hooks on the back of the cleric's door in the crematorium? I'm not sure which of these two tasks was the most taxing to implement.

* * *

Anne and I happened upon town twinning by chance. In 1979 we stopped briefly on the outskirts of Péronne, a small town on the Somme in Picardie. We've travelled and stayed there, either camping or in local hotels, on a number of occasions.

After World War I, Lawrence Cotton, the mayor of Blackburn from 1917-21, sent town hall officials to help rebuild the small war-torn town (population around 8,000). His son, 2nd Lieutenant John Cotton, died aged twenty-nine on 1 July 1916 during the murderous battles of the Somme. He is buried (Plot II B 24) at the Dive Copse British Cemetery, Sailly-le-Sec. The outcome of this was the building, by a public subscription of some £1,700 (around £200,000 today, Cotton began this with £250) from Blackburn town folk, of a replacement bridge, *Le Pont de Blackburn* (even I get that with my sparse French qualifications) and entering into one of the very first ever town twinning protocols in 1923.

I took town twinning seriously, on the philosophical basis that if everyone in the world knew just one person in every other country, the world would be a smaller and hopefully safer place.

I'm not sure this approach was fully taken seriously by all participants. Yes, there were ample opportunities to sample the other's gastronomic and viticultural delights, which I did, but we could and should go beyond that. Youth work colleague John Fletcher and I were substantial contributors to a BBC World Service radio programme about town twinning. This can be found by searching BBC World Service Twin Track Blackburn-Peronne.

Anne and I hosted two young women, Anke Wolzenburg from Altena and Valerie Fregard from Péronne, at our house for many months, a year. When our civic parties went abroad to our twin towns when I was responsible, we took young people with us to act as 'trainee translators'. One time we 'advertised' at our two colleges for a young man studying French at A level and a young woman studying German say at the other institution. Candidates had to formally apply and we interviewed them at the town hall, something they would have to do in later life. In the end we selected Becky and Luke to attend with us. They were also tasked with designing and delivering a twenty-minute audio-visual talk entitled 'Being Seventeen in Blackburn' in both French and German to be delivered to their foreign peers as well as the usual informal translation duties. These two were astounded; they had never spoken 'in foreign for real' before. 'It worked,' they shouted jubilantly and triumphantly, 'we spoke and others understood us!' They were a credit to themselves, their colleges, families and towns. It was a great boost to their confidence and career CVs!

Remembrance Day came round again, and somebody said something within my hearing, deliberately I think, in my local pub. I think the comment was intended to irk me but actually it got my creative mind thinking. The comment was 'You never see a Paki wearing a poppy, do you?'. On reflection his observation had some empirical validity. But I knew a different story. Since 1979, Anne and I, me sometimes with a civic twinning party or accompanying groups of young people, had visited Péronne on the River Somme a few times. We had been to the British Commonwealth Military Cemetery on the outskirts of the small French town. My reckoning was that around 540 military men were buried there. We found only one man, a lieutenant I think, over the age of thirty. Most of the other people buried had barely left their teens. 370 or more men, with names like Khan, Patel and Singh, had travelled thousands of miles to a war not of their making and laid down their lives on Flanders fields. Lest we forget. On a family visit to the cemetery, Anne wrote something in the Book of Remembrance safely inset in the wall. She wouldn't let me read what she had written. Years later, on a return visit, I remembered that incident and couldn't resist looking for what she had written. It said simply 'Please don't let this happen to my son'.

In the Great War, the war to end all wars, over a million people from what we now know to be India, Pakistan and Bangladesh served their 'mother' country overseas. 60,000 of them perished, nearly 10,000 won decorations including eleven VCs. Two decades later they answered the call to arms once again when the world's biggest ever volunteer army of 2.5 million men came from that same part of the world. 87,000 died, never to see their real home again.

I got a few remaining local veterans invited into the leader's office and about half a dozen old grey beards arrived, including Ali Khan, Jalal Din and Sardar Ali as well as Khadim Hussain and Fazal Hussain. They brought with them their army passbooks, some crumpled old photographs and other wartime memorabilia of which they were rightly proud. They told me a few stories as old soldiers like to do. They expressed frustration and sadness to me that their stories had never been told before, not in the wider community or even within the Asian community, and gratitude to me for helping them get their story out. One old soldier told me he often got called a 'silly old Paki'. I was instantly angry for this lovable, dignified, proud old guy. I asked him 'Who said that to you, white kids?' 'Sometimes,' he said, 'but usually our own Asian lads. I just say, listen, son, if it wasn't for me, you'd be speaking German now!' Not the first time I'd heard that but from a new direction.

I told all this to Amar Abass. Amar was around twenty or so at the time and was chief executive of Youth Action, a local organisation. This conversation took place at Radio Lancashire in Blackburn and was overheard by Greg Dyke, at the time BBC director general, who was visiting the station. Amar and his team, led by project manager Imran Master, worked hard, learned loads and informed many others when they later mounted a superb photos, words, press cuttings, audio and film footage exhibition entitled 'Mutual Respect' in the BBC Open Centre in Blackburn. At the time Imran said, 'This has been a massive learning chance for me and the youth group. We learnt this is the first of this kind of project ever to be done and we felt honoured to be doing it'.

One of these old grey beards, as I called them, was Fazal Hussain. Fazal had been born in 1918 and died at the ripe old age of ninety-five. He was a lovely, dignified, true gentleman. As a young man, in his twenties, he served in the Royal Army Medical Corps in the Middle East and Italy during the Second World War. Fazal, with his fellow veteran Khadim Hussain, eventually went into local secondary schools and told senior pupils about their experiences. Those who listened and learned from these two now frail old guys were captivated by their stories. Basically, whilst the battle continued to rage around them their job was to go onto the battlefield and remove the wounded and later the dead. Their bravery will have saved many lives and also enabled the bereaved to properly mourn their fallen loved ones.

Around 2011, this eventually resulted in the production of a half-hour documentary entitled *We Also Served*, much of it made by teenagers from Beardwood and St Bede's high schools in Blackburn in conjunction with the BBC. The film, used as a teaching aid to promote community cohesion, was eventually shown in many schools in Blackburn, across Lancashire and beyond. Fazal and Khadim were well into their eighties before they became film stars.

The film can be found by searching for 'Blackburn Muslim War Veterans.'

In 2016 I was proud to be able to promote Fazal's name to be chosen and used to identify households in the new Each Step purpose-built state-of-the-art dementia unit not so far from Ewood Park. This was a process driven by my ex-NHS chief executive Neil Matthewman, then in charge of New Step, who had 'got' my approach to public services. It was a proud, fitting and probably long overdue mark of recognition and respect for Fazal Hussain, a man of great humility and dignity.

*   *   *

Moving on relentlessly we submitted some of our town centre developments in Blackburn for national design awards. We had utilised six or seven different funding regimes to optimum effect. In the previous twelve years big cities like Manchester with the cathedral gardens and Urbis Museum had been the winner and Birmingham was tipped as favourite in 2003. So how pleased were we, along with local traders, that Blackburn with its pedestrianised transformation and street sculptures on Church Street and the beautiful new gardens in Fleming Square won? Local entrepreneur Mark Smith of the hugely successful Coffee Exchange company accompanied us down to the awards ceremony, I think in Birmingham. We had a great day. We had won the Best Heritage Project Award and the overall winner in the North-West Royal Town Planning Institute annual awards. What was all that about a grotty mill town?

We sought to regenerate Blackburn town centre further by concentrating on our market halls. Shopping habits had changed since the previous 1960s' refurbishment that brought them under cover, which is what shoppers expected and demanded. A five- to ten-year partnership with London-based building developers Bovis might cost around £50 million, but we had to keep up with the times. So much so that we engaged with primary school-aged children, shoppers and spenders of the future, about what they might like to see. We weren't hanging around, we had future generations to plan for.

But as well as looking forward, we needed opportunities and a vehicle to look into the past and this was wonderfully achieved when I was able to launch our digital museum charting the 200-year history of the borough on a website aptly entitled 'Cotton Town'. This has been a massive collaborative, participative process over several years. We had secured £200k of lottery funding and our local *Lancashire Evening Telegraph* donated thousands of its archived images into what was effectively an *e-exhibition*. Head of library services Susan Law said 'the project provides a historical overview of the communities of Blackburn with Darwen and provides a historically rich core base of digitised information which will form the platform for further developments of extended learning resources': www.cottontown.org From a little germ of an idea of mine this had been progressed with excellent work from town hall staff and volunteers from the civic and historical fraternity locally and has gone from strength to strength. Local heroes including Jim Halsall, Ray Smith and Mike Sumner hopefully have been congratulated for all that they have done.

In and amongst the nip and tuck of life, came more unexpected news from London. I supported voting by post for all who would qualify and benefit from it and thought it shouldn't be made difficult for any deserving citizen to access. It was decided that the whole borough should be rewarded for the 2004 local elections, moved to June to coincide with the European Parliamentary elections, and that every seat would be up for grabs in an 'all out' election. To that double whammy, a third component was being mooted, that the total electoral process would be fully and exclusively postal. This was unprecedented, unnecessary and unwanted.

Whoever decides whether votes will be totally postal or not appeared to be vacillating; I recall no local consultations whatsoever. I would have recommended YES to making it easier for appropriate citizens to go postal votes and a blanket NO to being totally postal. Compulsory postal voting was put on hold after a government defeat in the House of Lords. This seriously jeopardised the idea as it then had to be referred back to the House of Commons. The government seemed intent upon this as an experiment in the north-west. For some reason Tories and Lib Dems in the House of Lords wanted the scheme to be confined to the East Midlands and north-east England. I maintained my position stating, 'there needs to be a balance between making it easier for people without it being open to abuse'.

The government in the guise of Standards Board for England pitched in another curved ball – Freemasonry. Someone decided that membership of this secret society was a declarable 'interest' for councillors. From memory my declared interests included owning our property in the borough, trade union membership, my wife working as a teacher in the borough, membership of the golf club, Caravan Club and the Campaign for Real Ale. We were also compelled to declare if we were football club season ticket holders? But not cricket? Colleagues on the council who were in local lodges were quite indignant about this unveiling of their secrecy. Much ado about nothing really, but their outrage was quite amusing.

The investigation into alleged irregularities in Bastwell Ward in 2002 had yet to report its findings. I wasn't happy to have nothing but postal votes and our local political rivals were quick to link these two politically sensitive issues together and I don't blame them. I was quoted as saying 'we need to look at ways of encouraging and enabling more people to vote and postal voting is just one of those measures'. The police locally simply confirmed that there had been an investigation and the file was still with the Crown Prosecution Service.

My own date with the Crown was edging ever nearer.

Chapter 33

Bill and Ben (and Helen) go to the Palace

These days are ours, these tears are free.

On the knighthood front, nothing much happened after the initial excitement in June.

Then sometime later another slightly larger but no less posh envelope plopped through the letterbox. Opening it gingerly with the now celebrated silver letter opener, it proved to be THE invite. THE invite to the palace. Would somebody actually say, 'Arise Sir Bill'? We'd have to wait and see.

There was much excitement amongst the female wing of the Taylor family. New outfits were de rigueur and much spoken about. Indeed, there was little talk of anything else.

This turned out to be the parallel plan. Matt and I were to get kitted out with morning suits, top hats and all. Ours would be hired and we were tasked with getting on with it. For some reason, possibly a quirk of the female psyche, the girls had to have bought, top quality and expensive suits, headgear optional. This would entail a girly trip to Manchester, at least lunch, if not evening meal too included. I put my foot down when a night in a hotel was mooted. However, this proved to be a bargaining chip to be relinquished during negotiations, aka opening gambits!

Matt and I chose to shop local and decided on Ken and Steve Higginson's gents outfitters in Darwen, known as Sagars. The Higginsons were old-school proper tailors/gentlemen's outfitters. Ken had begun his bespoke career in the men's suits section in the large but now gone Co-op departmental store.

I went along one morning to be fitted up, which I was, in more than one sense of the phrase. I think the Higginsons had tipped them the wink/got themselves a bit of free publicity because, as I arrived at the double-fronted Aladdin's cave of men's clothing, so did one of the local papers' press photographers. Sadly, they don't have many or any staff photographers anymore. No Wally (or Howard) Talbot, Vincent Gormley, the husband, wife and son Barry trio, Roy Chatburn, John Napier, John Mills, Jason Broadhurst, Clive Lawrence or Neil Johnson.

The Higginsons were proper old-fashioned tailors, sporting proper tailors' tape measures draped around their necks, including that four-inch or so brass-ended 'stiff zone' for those more intimate measures. I always found four inches to be quite comforting, reassuring even.

The dad and son duo set about their business, tape measures flashing everywhere. As did the press photographer with his Nikon flashing everywhere. The press photographers at the *Telegraph* were always good guys, in fact exclusively guys (until Helen Brown). They liked working with me and I'd always try and go along with any of their zany ideas. They often pulled out or spotted bizarre 'props' to make something a little different of the photograph. I liked their professionalism and imaginative talent.

From memory the photograph that appeared in the edition next day was of me in top hat and tails with Steve and his measuring tape. All a bit stage-managed but it worked well, using a chevalier mirror to bounce the image back. I'd say it reflected well on all of our efforts and a local business was supported.

The girls' expedition to Manchester, planned like a military operation, took place and they came back giggly and laden with those posh carrier bags, broadcasting the chosen brand or shop. They most certainly hadn't had a parsimonious, frugal day.

The letter allocated a specific day, Friday, 3 December 2003. We had plans to make, it was like our family project for the rest of the year. Trains and times to research and book, accommodation too. We decided to push the boat out and include two trips to see shows, the night before and the same night as our trip to the palace.

Matt lobbied without much resistance or argument for *Les Misérables*. The others said, as it was MY day that I should choose the second night at the theatre. So, I went for the Ben Elton-penned, Rod Stewart-inspired musical, *Tonight's the Night*.

We booked into our favourite London accommodation, the Union Jack Club which I have used for many years, permitted due to my senior local government role. It was handily located opposite Waterloo Station. As a little girl, Anne had used the original Union Jack hostel, with her Uncle Jim and Auntie Annie. Uncle Jim had been a regular soldier attaining the rank of sergeant major. Although not having served in the armed forces and this being intended only for non-commissioned ex-members of HM forces, I've always been allowed to use what is an excellent quality, reasonably priced and conveniently placed accommodation for my quite regular trips down to the capital.

We booked a two-bedroomed family suite with kitchen and lounge for Thursday and the big day, the Friday. I think we were all excited. The day dawned and we made our way to Preston to join our train. We arrived at Euston and quickly got across London and settled into our accommodation.

The next two days were actually quite a blur. We got tidied up and made our way to the theatre staging *Les Misérables*. It's a cracking musical that Matt and I quite enjoy, not for the acting or story but I think preferring the complexity and yet the ease with which the stage and the set is transformed before your very eyes.

We must've had something to eat but I don't remember what or where or whether it was before or after the show. Tomorrow was a very big day.

We got up reasonably but not too early, hung around, had a spot of breakfast. Then both of our youngsters started to hassle me; come on, Dad, it's nearly time and you haven't even shaved! They were right, I'd underestimated the time and had to get a considerable wriggle on!

We did look a proper posh set as we assembled in the club foyer, waiting for a cab. I was so proud of my three loved ones, something that I think was reciprocated.

The cab came and I couldn't believe I was hearing myself right as I said 'Buckingham Palace, please'. We seemed to get there quickly. I never really understand distances or locations in London. The cabbie, of course, had done this dozens of times and knew where to drop us off. On paying, he probably even said 'Good luck, Gov'.

So, there we found ourselves, dressed up to the nines but still pretty much a simple working-class family, going down to the Smoke for a day. There were a lot of soldiers and quite a few police about and they started to tell us what to do, where to go.

I think we all stared up at the frontage of the palace in awe. Of course, we'd all seen it, the iconic balcony and all, on the TV and the news for state occasions, royal weddings and the like but here we were, the Taylor family, about to go into HRH's inner courtyard. It was also quite a person-spotting occasion.

As we moved across the central courtyard I spotted a pile of kiddies' bikes, just stacked in the corner. Not sure who's they were but it seemed quite a leveller; most family gardens would have those kinds of things stacked up in the corner.

We showed our passes. Mine was distinctly different to Anne's and our children's. I was ushered towards one carpeted staircase and they across the courtyard to another entrance. 'See you all later' didn't seem enough to say.

I climbed this first set of stairs that left the inner courtyard and followed the directions along a corridor. All the walls were lined either with paintings of earlier generations or great events or golden-coloured display cabinets full of things I'd never seen before and will never see again. They seemed mainly to be grand pieces of china and porcelain, serving dishes, sauceboats, plates and things used at state banquets. But who was I to know? I didn't feel like I had time to linger, to appreciate or learn any more.

I found myself at the portal of a very large heavy, oak door. The guy in charge or on guard there said something like 'Welcome, sir, I hope you have a good day'. Like I said, it seemed like I was in a surreal dream world and don't remember much of the detail.

Once inside this room, there weren't many people about. They looked like officials or attendants or something. I wondered what do you do when you go to Buckingham Palace, what do you expect, who would you meet? The honest answer is, I hadn't got a clue. I think I wandered over to the window and stared out of it, across the inner courtyard where there were a lot of people knocking about that day.

Another chap about my age or a little older, also in morning suit with a top hat wandered over.

'Hi, I'm Ben, Ben Gill. Pleased to meet you.' Quite a few filing cabinets and folders were metaphorically searched through in my mind and luckily I recalled the name.

'You're the NFU president, aren't you?' I just hoped I'd got it right. 'That's right, well remembered,' he said. Phew!

'And you are?'

'Councillor Bill Taylor, Leader of Blackburn with Darwen Council.'

'Nice to meet you, Bill.'

It was about then that the door opened again and in glided a brilliantly gowned, perfectly deported woman. I recognised her instantly, she having graced our TV and cinema screens for many decades. It was none other than the Shakespearean actress (they're called actors these days), star of *The Long Good Friday*, *The Calendar Girls*, *Prime Suspect*'s Jane Tennison, I can go on! Yes, Helen Mirren. I was determined not to be starstruck. Or do I mean, not to appear to be starstruck?

'Hello, I'm Bill and this is Ben.'

'Well, I'm sorry, but I refuse to be Weed,' she said in a mock coquettish, flirty manner.

We giggled. I don't think Ben quite got it.

But we were brought quickly to our senses by a rather tall, imposing chap who interjected. 'Well, now that you're all here, let me just show you the ropes.' I mused that the guy would have some antediluvian and highly embellished title 'The Gentleman Equerry to the Yeoman of the Royal Closet' or something like that. We'd better pay attention.

'Right, gentlemen, you two first, sorry ma'am.' A little kneeling stool with a steadying handle to one side was brought forward.

'Right, I will now demonstrate. At the appropriate moment, when invited so to do, you will approach the kneeling stool. You may use the handle to steady yourself for, as you are approached by his Royal Highness, he will expect you to kneel. His Royal Highness will then dub you with the sword and ask you to stand in the time-honoured traditional manner. He will then engage in an informal conversation with you. When your conversation is coming to its conclusion, he will shake your hand. Then you will walk backwards away from His Royal Highness, bow and turn to collect your badge from the table and return to your seat. Madame, the process for your good self is not dissimilar, however, rather than bow to His Royal Highness, you shall curtsy.'

Helen, winking at me, said, 'Something like this, do you mean?'

Now as a sovereign or a princess or a courtier or some form of period costume character, Helen Mirren must've curtsied hundreds if not thousands of times in her stage and screen life. She then dropped into a full curtsy, dropping towards the floor with an index finger under her chin.

'Ma'am, I don't think we need something quite so ostentatious. A simple dip at the knees will suffice.' She winked again.

Our time came and as impending knights and dames, we were first on. The ceremony is always conducted in the ballroom, where, as I understand it, state banquets are staged. It didn't seem to last very long. When my turn came, I moved forwards towards the kneeling stool. The heir to the throne came at me with a sword. I knelt in ritualised fealty before him. I then felt the weirdest of nostalgic sensations saying inwardly to myself 'this is not bad for a little boy who couldn't afford a bought jumper till he was twelve'.

Prince Charles then said 'Arise, Sir Bill'. Good grief, he did actually say that, I wasn't hearing things. There was no one within about ten yards from us, the line of Gurkhas behind Prince Charles were the nearest. In hushed tones he then asked me how the Blackburn Partnership was going and what regeneration had it achieved and questions like that. You may recall that he had visited Blackburn two or three times, had initiated some aspects of the Blackburn Public Private Partnership and I think it was his identified touching point with my life. The conversation lasted a minute or two and then his hand was outstretched, offering me the goodbye handshake. I collected my badge contained in a beautiful red leather box and sat down next to the newly damed Helen Mirren to watch the rest of the proceedings. I chuckled to myself, as I imagined it's not the first time, she'd played a dame. Oh yes, she has.

We sat quite near the front and observed the proceedings as various other ranks of others were awarded. All of a sudden, I spotted Riaz, Riaz Begum, approaching Prince Charles. Riaz had worked for me as the district youth worker for young Asian girls for twenty years and done a really, really good job. Of course, I'd been gone from Blackburn Youth Service for seven or eight years and didn't know she'd been awarded an MBE. Riaz, backing away from HRH, neither bowed nor curtsied but gave what was a Namaste salutation.

'There's Riaz!' I think my excitement was over audible, so I returned to sitting quietly. Looking up to the balcony at the back I saw the small military band who played before and after the ceremony, mainly (and rather aptly for me) a Simon and Garfunkel selection.

Then, all honours being awarded, the ceremony concluded. I really just wanted to find Anne and the kids. The family trio had observed the proceedings from seats for guests at the back of the ballroom. Outside they found me and we had hugs all round. Then the Press Association photographers found me. I don't know how that worked and they arranged and took several different photos of me, me and Anne, me, Anne and the kids, etc., etc. Quite a portfolio of different photographs appeared in the *Lancashire Evening Telegraph* the next day, the headline being 'Arise Sir Bill'!

I spotted England cricketer Alec Stewart. He's always been quite a sporting hero of mine. Should I bob over? Of course not, everyone was in their family moments. Stewart, newly retired after a fantastic thirteen-year test career as an accomplished wicket-keeper/batsman had been awarded an OBE to add to his earlier MBE.

What next? Jack had kindly invited us all to have a midday meal in the Commons. I'm not sure it wasn't called the Churchill Dining Room. What particularly touched me was that Jack's wife, Alice, attended too. Alice is a hugely intelligent, Oxford educated, and high-flying successful civil servant. It was because of the latter that she was not able to involve herself in the humdrum political life that Jack led. So, we were all dead pleased she came along.

It was nice to spend some time together, along with the Straws. The meal was lovely but soon it was time to go, still things to do. Matt went off to catch a train back to some event being held in Newcastle, where he was in his third and final law year.

We left, the three of us, to attend a meeting at the College of Arms. It's situated near the Thames just between Blackfriars and St Paul's Cathedral.

What is the College of Arms you might ask because I had never heard of it until two months before. The College of Arms is also known as Heralds' College. It consists of thirteen officers: three Kings of Arms, six Heralds of Arms and four Pursuivants of Arms, who are appointed directly by the Sovereign. Although it is not part of a government department, nor are the Officers of Arms civil servants, they are members of the Royal household and are subject to the general supervision of the Duke of Norfolk, in his capacity as Earl Marshal. The College of Arms is thus one of the few official heraldic authorities left in the world. It was founded by Royal Charter in 1484 by King Richard III. (He was the last king of England to die in battle, at Bosworth Field in 1485, although Shakespeare did start a rumour about Richard, his kingdom and a horse. After quite a gap, over 500 years, his remains now grace Leicester Cathedral.) Bet you're none the wiser now, as I certainly wasn't.

It's a three or four-storeyed, three-sided building that creates a courtyard in front of it, behind high wrought-iron railings and a double gate, all topped off with golden designs, presumably heraldic. I'd been invited to make an appointment there. It was only open to invitees and only between ten and four.

The three of us approached with some trepidation, rang the bell and we gained entry. Once inside it was like stepping into another world. I actually don't remember too much about it. But we soon realised it was to discuss my coat of arms for which I'd become eligible, a skant three or four hours earlier. There was a long discussion with a chap mainly couched in those words specific to the world of coats of arms, another name for which is Complete Achievement.

The only knights' heraldic shields I could remember were from black and white TV programmes of the 1950s and 1960s such as *Knights of the*

Round Table and *Ivanhoe*. The conversation seemed to be running away from me.

'How long will it take? How much would it cost?'

Those didn't really appear to be on our host's agenda. After a while I posed the questions again. After another while, I repeated myself.

Eventually my questions were answered. They were: about a year and somewhere between £3,000 and £4,000. Answer Two really made the rest of the conversation irrelevant. At that time in our lives, there was no way we could afford that much even if we wanted to. I did enquire recently and they are about £6,000 these days. I can only assume that that's small beer to most knights.

The girls watched me, I think wondering how I was going to wriggle out of this one. 'Gosh, is that the time? Right, I think I need a little bit more time to think about this. It's not the sort of decision you should rush.'

'I totally understand, sir. Please let me show you all out and I look forward to hearing from you.'

We walked down towards the Thames and sat on a riverside bench for a while. It had been a long day: up early, dressed in our finery, trip to the palace, two to three hours there, the House of Commons for lunch and then the College of Arms experience. I was still dressed as a toff with two Bond girlesque companions. And yet there was still more to come.

'What are we doing now, Dad?' asked Katherine.

'There's only one thing to do at times like this. It's beer time,' I announced to a duet of cheers.

We found a pub down some little very typically London riverside alleyway. It was still a crisp bright sunny winter's day, and entering the pub was a stark contrast, it being comparatively very pupil-adjusting dark.

Was I the beginning of a joke? That is, a knight walks into a pub in top hat and tails…

Walking up to the bar I asked the girls what they wanted; they hesitantly ummed and ahed.

'Yes, mate!' said the member of the bar staff.

'A pint of lager, please. Make that three in case they make their minds up.' I was stood at the bar in total preoccupation with my imminent refreshment.

The first pint was poured. It looked very, very inviting, condensation glistening on the outside of the glass. I could hardly wait and didn't. Boy, was I looking forward to this, I doubt it was going to touch the sides.

I didn't really know what to do with my top hat, which I was still wearing. I pushed it back on my head and grasped the pint glass.

Lifting the pint to my lips, the room was suddenly bathed in very bright electronic daylight. Unbeknown to me in the relative darkness, in a corner of the pub, there were eight or ten Far Eastern looking tourist people. They must've spotted me, a typical English toff having a teatime flyer in a London pub, top hat and tails and all. A proper British swell, a dandy even. He had just finished his day at the bank, the stock exchange, Lloyds or some other capital financial institution. It looked like he deserved his refreshing pint. What a photo opportunity I must've been for our visitors; little did they know how far from the truth they were. I wasn't just a name – I was a knight!

My girls came out of the darkness and quaffed their beers too. I think we had another beer after that and then departed. What a story our guests from overseas would have to tell when they got back home with their holiday snaps!

We made our way back to our overnight accommodation at the Union Jack Club. We got out of our formal outfits and freshened up. We were all knackered.

Off we went to watch that night's musical, *Tonight's the Night*. It was loud and we had good seats in the stalls. When I say loud, I mean really, really boomingly loud.

The performance started and then suddenly it was the half-time interval. I'd fallen totally fast asleep draped over a lady next to me and Katherine was slumbering slumped over me. So, it couldn't have been that loud, could it? The only other auditorium at which I have ever fallen fast asleep (and asked to leave as I was snoring) was at a ballet at the Bolshoi in Moscow on an NUS visit in 1973. So, Ben Elton was in good company.

I think our daughter and me perked up a little bit in the second half and managed to stay awake. Good grief, it was loud. Who could fall asleep with that din going on? Tonight was the knight!

We left the theatre and wandered back to the Union Jack Club. What a day it had been. What a series of experiences we'd had.

We got up the next morning, packed our bags and made our way home back up north.

We'd had a great time.

Chapter 34

Back to the Day Job – After the Palace

These are the days of miracle and wonder.

Our two days in London were fantastic, especially the day that included the palace, a once in a lifetime, never to be forgotten experience.

On the way back we went to Birmingham City's ground, St Andrews, to witness Rovers wallop the (other) Blues 0-4. Rover's man (and boy) David Dunn playing for Brum, during his four-year stay and multimillion pound transfer there, before he returned home to Ewood. I love reminding him when we occasionally bump into each other.

Travelling back on the Saturday evening meant we had some time to recover. Then back with a bump!

Conservative opposition leader Colin Rigby, usually a placid character, got quite uppity in the local paper accusing us of 'spin and scatter-gun spending'. He particularly pinpointed spending £150k on the five neighbourhood coordinators, who were funded via the Neighbourhood Renewal Fund. They were well received in their localities and acclaimed national exemplars of good practice. He went on to say we should focus on education, skills for life and jobs, especially the more skilled, and housing renewal, exactly what our priorities and our successes had been. The incumbent Labour Government was almost obsessed with target-driven performance-related activity, at which we were successful. We had a new agreed and comprehensive eighteen-point performance agreement in place to match funding to specific targets. We were not complacent, working hard to achieve these ambitious goals. A special comment column in the local paper stated 'The ferocity of his' (Colin Rigby's) 'attack may surprise some, particularly as his party and the Lib Dems have hardly distinguished themselves in recent years as credible opposition forces'. Dennis Healey's famous 'mauling by a dead sheep' analogy came in the next sentence.

I hit back in the local paper dismissing the accusation of 'spin' when indeed it was reacting to public demand locally for better information about the council. Citing the publication of our mapping of public resource allocations across the borough, I explained that 'everyone will be able to see how and where money is being spent and it just isn't the case that some areas get neglected'.

I tended to feel assured that we were heading in the right direction when the letters column in the local paper witnessed my arch nemeses putting metaphorical pen to paper. This cadre included: P Newton, L Lawes, D D'Arcy, D Smalley, Eddie Duxbury and of course, Roy Davies. Although these, I doubt card carrying Labour men, seemed to display Labour averse entrenched confirmatory bias, at least they got off their backsides and expressed an opinion.

It was about this time that the independent national Audit Commission published their findings about councils locally. The *Lancashire Evening Telegraph* reported that 'Blackburn with Darwen was assessed as an excellent top performing council for the second year running in its (Audit Commission) annual inspection of 150 councils'. We were one of only twelve councils awarded top marks in the comprehensive performance assessment. At individual service levels, with scores out of four, we were given: education 4, social services 3, environmental services 2, housing and use of resources 3 and libraries and leisure 3. The report continued: 'based on current plans the council is well placed to continue to improve the way it works and services it provides'. Chief executive Phil Watson echoed this saying, 'it highlighted the council's prominent position in local government'.

My take on all of these accolades and awards was that they were fine but should never be used to become complacent. They should in fact spur you on and on.

We continued to be asked to support poorer performing councils and this included Plymouth and Waltham Forest. The London borough's leader Clyde Loakes visited Blackburn saying 'we have been very impressed by what we have seen here. We hope we can learn some lessons from Blackburn and improve our performance as a result'. A few days later, local government minister Nick Raynsford and the Labour Party chairman Ian McCartney MP made similar fact-finding visits to our borough.

It was almost inevitable that the publication of the community resource mapping exercise would throw up some anomalies or glaring disparities. The harbingers of doom in Darwen were obvious prime suspects. The report specified that the population in the Blackburn wards in the borough was 77 per cent and received 79 per cent of the spend. The other wards, 23 per cent of the population, received nearly 21 per cent. Given the relative deprivation in the Blackburn wards, this miniscule difference was understandable. The two wards with a high proportion of former council housing attracted a spend per head of just over £6,000 and just under £5,500 a year. The ten most deprived wards in the borough were apportioned on average £5,750. I was quoted as stating 'if you compare the urban areas of the two towns, they have very similar funding levels. This was a unique and detailed exercise which shows that residents across the borough get value for money. A common myth peddled by extreme political groups is that money is constantly targeted at minority groups. This study dispels those claims'. Despite this factual proof, opposition parties kept using terms like 'not getting a fair crack of the whip'.

Our determination to improve got a serious jolt when Queen's Park High School got its latest Ofsted inspection report. I had worked there twenty years previously as the youth tutor, when it was still called Shadsworth. 'Special Measures' is not good. The *Lancashire Evening Telegraph* reported that this was the second school to hit Special Measures in a fortnight, the no longer there Moorland High School in Darwen being the other. I'd handed over the education portfolio nearly three years earlier to Councillor Mahfooz Hussain but this twin set of circumstances was a corporate disappointment. The LEA had taken the step of suspending Moorland's board of governors, a measure I'd not heard of before. The head there predicted that more schools could follow as Ofsted tightened its inspection criteria. The LET reported that Queen's Park was the worst performing school in East Lancashire with only 16 per cent of pupils attaining the A*-C standard, and Moorland similarly trailed in the 2003 league tables. A lot of hard work, blood, sweat and tears had been put in by a lot of people to raise educational standards in our schools. I was quoted stating 'this is still a really serious issue and we are letting the kids down. The worst thing we can do is not face up to it, the best thing we can do is to roll up our sleeves and tackle it'. At the time a new head teacher had been appointed only very recently at Queen's Park, and he certainly had a very full in tray. The LET carried stories of the opposition parties calling for Mahfooz Hussain's resignation as exec member for education. Former local school teacher Tory councillor Sheila Williams was quoted as saying 'now it is time to carry the brickbats'. The local NUT officer, Simon Jones, echoed their comments.

My style of leadership was predicated upon devolving responsibility to others, especially the two deputy leaders and the other five or six executive members with dedicated portfolios. They, in their turn, had a team of lead members who were allocated specialisms within that portfolio. That's how it worked on the political side of things. On the professional side of things, Phil Watson as chief executive was the head honcho, with three exec directors to support him. Below that came the departmental directors of education, social services, things like that. These people had their own assistant directors, specialists in specific areas, in education, for example, early years, primary, secondary, FE (further education) and youth service might be a logical configuration.

By way of coordinating all this, we held regular policy development sessions, the much vaunted 'joined-up' thinking and 'joined-up' doing. Every fortnight or so, for two or three hours, Phil with his senior colleagues including any appropriately required directors would meet alongside the parallel equivalent from the elected members. This really was a 'no holds barred' free exchange of ideas, proposals, criticism, things that were going well and things that were going badly. We had this paradigm of routine, proactive and reactive issues. Reactive was the 'red zone', surprises were bad things, to be avoided. Things that got to the press before they got to the leader were *bad medicine*. These things were bound to occur now and then because we were people delivering to people. More often than now and then was bad. Cockups with benefit payments, the children in care issue and schools' performance slippage were sloppy examples of problems that should have been anticipated and flagged up. Here endeth that lesson.

There were serious issues in the relationship between the management of a school and the diktats of the Ofsted regime. Opposition councillors picked up on this and I agreed with them. Any educational institution, especially a school, is not just an educational, conveyor-belt driven, sausage factory. They are environmentally organic organisations made up of people, the biggest imaginable and unimaginable variable. Conservative leader, Colin Rigby, made some really good points in the local paper about league tables not telling the full story about the end users – our children. I'm still not sure if schools consider the development of individual pupils' emotional intelligence. I maintain, and this is Billy the youth worker speaking, that how and what children think and say is important and we need our young people to nurture and develop imaginative and creative skills, tried and tested whilst they are young, so they can go on and develop organisational and leadership skills. To me, that's exactly what our nation is crying out for. Here endeth another lesson.

By the desire of both central government and many schools locally, the LEA had devolved more and more of the centrally held schools' budget, 'passporting' then standing at 93 per cent. Both the Blair/Brown Government and various of its predecessors were hell bent on 'freeing up' schools, leaving big decisions to the leadership of head teachers and their governing bodies. It's an old central government trick. Look like your devolving power and financial resources, reduce how much lolly is in that pot, then pass the buck on from central to local, obfuscating it as local choice. This meant that much of our *seed corn* money, used for the identification of individual schools' performance, schools' standards and improvement, the ability to support weaker schools and admissions policy was now salted away in schools' own individual budgets. This resulted in the ridiculous situation where the schools collectively were amassing and sitting on bigger financial reserves than the overall council. It made school bursars more powerful than the head! Knowing the price of everything is not the same as knowing its value!

There was another vagary of the Ofsted inspection system that didn't make any sense to me at least. By law, an LEA had to sit and watch as a school went into an Ofsted inspection unable to do anything until the report was published. I wrote as council leader, to David Blunkett, the education secretary telling him this needed to be changed.

Promoting what became known as social inclusion was high on our agenda here in BwD. I think it was Phil Watson's original idea or is it idea originally. He was proud to be born and bred in Blackburn and engaging with the sense of belonging, we came up with a campaign known as 'Belonging to Blackburn with Darwen', launched at Ewood Park. We got the initiative headed up by John Hawley, the archdeacon of Blackburn, who we are told is Venerable! We intended to get as many locally based citizens to sign up to the campaign objectives which included leadership and commitment, respect and pride, promoting equality, challenging prejudice and hatred and building positive and diverse relationships. We were told that Conservative councillors hadn't signed it, as they were awaiting advice from Conservative Central Office. One Tory councillor who had not been reselected to stand in his ward, who no one can recollect being a regular attender or ever having spoken at council meetings, resigned the Tory whip over this issue. Perhaps he thought he 'belonged' somewhere else. The leader of the Tory Group was quoted as saying 'his resignation is best for all involved'.

The campaign poster included many familiar faces from the locality, Lord Adam Patel, footballers Steven Reid and Gary Flitcroft, manager Graham Souness, community activist Nan Goodall, BBC's Graham Liver, World War II veteran Fazal Hussain, senior police officer Andy Pratt, Red or Dead's Wayne Hemingway, ninety-year-old Ron Ashmore, another World War veteran, window cleaner Paul Hargreaves, various young people, including Sarah, Bilal and Declan Maguire, town hall staff, amongst others. Phil Watson somehow slipped on in the final published poster, well deserved! About two or three years later our community resource mapping was 'revalued' – Council spend £333 million, overall 'public purse' £820 million.

* * *

April 2004 bore witness to the twenty-fifth anniversary of Jack Straw being our local MP. Quite appropriately we threw a party held at Ewood Park. This wasn't a Party party if you understand, invites were open to everybody who wanted to share in what was quite a landmark event. All of Jack's family were there including his mum, Joan. Over 400 guests were in attendance from a variety of different worlds: national and local politics, local schools and colleges, local and national companies including business, retail manufacturing, hospitality and various organisations from the public, private and voluntary sectors enjoyed the fantastic celebratory night. My 120-plus photo albums, very pre-digital, were plundered to compile a lengthy rolling PowerPoint presentation of images taken by me of Jack's career. On the night, I was promoted to act as MC and was more than happy to introduce the main speaker, veteran Manchester MP Sir Gerald Kaufman, knighted in 2004. After Gerald, Jack gave a superb, relaxed, wide-ranging, thoughtful speech that everybody enjoyed. The local party presented Jack with the almost traditional framed career caricature with Jack depicted wearing both the home and away strips of Blackburn Rovers – home for home and away for Foreign Secretary. Jack concluded saying his twenty-five years 'had been wonderful fun and Blackburn is special'.

The LET did a double spread over a couple of editions on Jack's Silver Jubilee featuring many of the highlights. There had been quite a reasonable chance at the peak of Thatcher's grip on Britain in 1983 that Jack may have lost his seat. But we, and Jack, survived. That said there were also many lighter moments in what had been and what continued to be a glittering career. In the article with Bill Jacobs, political correspondent, Jack listed facing up to the Militant Tendency, him becoming Home Secretary and introducing Anti-Social Behaviour Orders (known as ASBOs) in collaboration with Eddie Walsh, the then chief superintendent of police, Prince Charles going to town to promote the sense of partnership, getting the new £100 million-plus hospital, completing the M65, the council becoming unitary, the refurbishment of the borough bringing many new jobs along with it.

Sadly, earlier in February 2004, former mayor Mary Leaver died at home aged seventy-three after seventeen years on the council. Ironically, on my drive to her funeral at St. Joseph's RC church in Audley Ward, I chose to play 'Amazing Grace' sung by Judy Collins, a favourite of mine. The service in Mary's church began with a different version of the very same but no less haunting song. The valuable presence of the hard-working, throughout their lives, cadre of grandmas on the council was rapidly and irreplaceably declining. Mary would not be the last councillor to pass away during what little was left of that civic year.

The every seat up for grabs, local elections were drawing ever nearer and that meant every spare minute, of which there were few, was taken up with canvassing, on the knocker, on the doorstep, chatting with the electorate.

Whilst that was going on, there was some ironic pathos in a northern Labour controlled, 'ferret-keeping, pigeon-fancying' council being featured over a number of pages in *Lancashire Life*. As my friend Greg Pope might have said 'totally the wrong demographic, Guillaume'.

But there were still many positive, concrete things that needed doing and three years into the signed up public private partnership with Capita I was able to open the new building alongside their chairman (later Sir) Rod Aldridge. The new building sitting at a significant gateway (currently empty?) into the borough from the M6 Jct 31 cost £5 million. Despite my initial reticence, years back, this had become one of the first, biggest and most comprehensive and successful public private partnerships, had created something over 700 new jobs, driven down council costs and brought BBC Licencing and the Criminal Record Bureau to Darwen.

Chapter 35

The All-Out Local Elections, 2004

The next thing I remember I was walking down the street.

As leader of the council, constituency agent, campaign manager and candidate, my roles were complex, time-consuming and onerous. Just being a candidate meant you really had only one job to do, campaign to win your seat. On top of that and of course, on top of a full-time job and family duties, I had all the duties, and a sense of isolated loneliness of being leader of the council, which was another full-time job, dealing with all things routine and all the other things that get thrown at you, often suddenly without warning.

No one really knows the complexities of the role until you have it. I was stress on legs at election time not suffering anything or person who was a perceived disruption or distraction. Only Jack was a worse election worrier.

Ordering of canvass cards and Reading sheets, organising and printing posters, canvassing 'sorry you were out' cards, introductory leaflets, and finally, the main election address leaflet – these things don't organise themselves. Collating all the best 'voter-friendly' issues we had achieved and accomplished I would then travel around the borough looking for good images to photograph to illustrate our successes, adding further to my workload burden. Call me a control freak or perfectionist, I liked to show the things we'd worked so hard for and were rightly proud of, in the best possible light. This meant early-morning starts and late-night sessions, often on the computer, using desktop publishing packages to add text, images and design to our electoral publications. I was quite proud of the results.

This also meant umpteen trips to our printers. To begin with we used print firm Martin Nestor, then went to the Readett brothers, Gary and Neil, at the decade's-old local family company Linotype. A visit to these two guys was always a hoot, laughing as we, I mean they, crafted our raw material into something of a high-quality presentation.

Most electoral wards locally had about 3,000 homes, so a full print run would be 1500 A6 'sorry you were out' calling cards, and 3,500 A5 intro leaflets and finally 3,500 A4 'fanfold' main electoral addresses. On top of that, there were general Vote Labour or name-specific posters to acquire, some A2 or even A1 size. These had to be loaded into my estate car and I would inform candidates where and when they would be available for collection. It was normal for some of the candidates to say vexation-inducing things like 'could you drop the 'sorry you were out' cards at my auntie's house, leave the intro leaflets in the porch at the shop next door to where my brother lives and split the main leaflets into three and deliver them to three separate addresses?' That could be up to say half of the fifteen different wards for whom I had leaflets. I hope you're not a bit surprised that the answer was always negative. In fact, negative accompanied by a string of barbed invective!

In my opinion, and these have been maintained to the best of my knowledge, the Sunday morning campaign meetings which we established very early in the 1980s, made the real difference between Labour's campaign and those of the other parties.

At the outset, if it was a year we felt like we were defending seats, we would establish the two or three wards we most wanted not to lose. If it was a more hopeful, optimistic year, we would choose two or three wards we hoped to gain and allocate resources, mainly people, accordingly.

Party secretary Phil Riley and I were the main organisers, motivators and directors of the campaign and the Sunday morning meetings. During the intervening week, we would regularly ring each other, home landline to home landline. At the beginning of most of these calls we heard and commented to each other about clicking noises on the line. Were we being tapped?

On Sundays people were always punctual, meetings began with a cuppa, I would imagine up to fifty attended. I think they started at eleven and went on for an hour or two. There was a flipchart on a tripod at the front of the room. This listed all the twenty-plus wards across the borough or fifteen if it was a general election.

Meetings always began with a bit of fun, slapstick even. Something simple and stupid but it got people's juices flowing.

Then came the serious business as we went down the board ward by ward asking for a report, factual, not pie in the sky. We wanted to know what percentage of the electorate each ward a) intended to canvass and b) had accomplished so far. This was hard proper information that we wanted, not dreamt-up flights of fantasy. Our secret weapon here was Michael Poultney, a lovely bloke, slightly eccentric, former maths teacher and erstwhile record holder in the *Guinness Book* for his ability to recite pi – π from memory to a huge number of decimal places. His grasp of number and statistics is beyond belief.

After that, we asked if any issues were being brought up on the doorsteps, any we needed to address. These would be passed on to the relevant committee chair or executive member to address and also to 'get out' in the local media. There would always be a local press release issued after each meeting. There was always a meeting every Sunday during the month leading up to election day.

The meetings generated a sense of comradeship, an atmosphere of common purpose, of being together. I think they made all the difference to how we felt about each other and promoted working together.

At their conclusion, enthused, people would go off, buoyed. The most enthusiastic and regular Sunday 'award' recipient was Akhtar Hussain, a local greengrocer on Whalley Range and long-time Labour fanatic. Akhtar became a councillor and got his turn as mayor in 2016. I'm sure we caught him urging people to 'come on everyone, let's go convincing'! Akhtar's fervent convincing was better than most people's canvassing any day!

The proof of the pudding of Sunday meetings was our electoral success, sometimes against the odds, throughout the eighties, nineties and noughties. If things weren't going too well or were going very well in one particular ward, we would designate a mass canvassing night for that area. Winning one ward by hundreds of votes was not as good as narrowly winning two or three more. A team upwards of thirty would assemble around 6.15 p.m. and really make an impact not just on the canvassing workload but on the party's profile and our team's morale. Many a time I've seen the dejection of other parties' canvassers operating in ones and twos, compared to our little army.

*   *   *

It had been the practice locally over many years to elect to the council every year by thirds, that is one of the three council seats in each ward to be contested with one 'fallow' year with no elections. Other councils had 'all outs' every four years. That means every four years every council seat on that council was 'up for grabs'.

Locally, in Blackburn with Darwen, we quite preferred the 'thirds' option, especially in the Labour Party. Since the late seventies/early eighties when we got our election processes much better organised, it was better for us to go to the people regularly. This kept our campaigning machine well-oiled, kept our electorate in the habit of voting and obviated against erratic lurches in control that could occur if 100 per cent of the seats were contested at once. Neither the Conservatives locally nor the Lib Dem outposts were very organised or even united politically or socially.

Blackburn with Darwen became a unitary ('all singing-all dancing') council on 1 April 1998, returning to that status after twenty-four years as a district (lesser powers and lesser spend) council.

We'd got the green light in a hostile environment with the county council (aka my employers), with legal processes not only threatened but instigated by them to balk our 'takeover', around 1995.

As a result, we had a four-year cycle of total change in our format.

Year one was a business as usual year as a district council spending some £20 million per annum, during which we got the green light to proceed to become unitary.

Year two was a consultative year with a great deal of activity, producing draft structures, policies and practices. This was mainly led, on the political side by councillors Gail Barton and Sue Reid, who did a fantastic job although were rather Rottweiler in their approach.

As well as deputy leader, I was the chair of the management and finance committee responsible for the current finances of the district council. What I really wanted to do was lead on education and I was successful in being appointed to this pivotal role by the Labour group. I'd seen, experienced and knew at first-hand what social mobility (as it was now labelled) can be achieved collectively and individually by getting a good education. So that's why I wanted to put my efforts into improving our schools, relentlessly driving up standards and success rates and giving as many young people as possible the best possible start in life.

We engaged in many ways with lots of different groups central to the educational process: teachers and head teachers, governors and chairs of governors, parents and community and last but by no means least, learners, children and young people. It was very time and energy consuming, but the right approach.

Year three was a pilot year. In the run-up to becoming fully unitary, we tested what we had painstakingly put in place as carefully as we possibly could.

There was a local political side to all this because during 1996, there had to be a re-warding of the whole borough. This was a massive process where we had to start with a blank canvas and put in place electoral wards that were more sympathetic with natural local communities and had equality of numbers of voters.

This was achieved, consulted upon locally and agreed with the Boundary and Electoral Commissions.

So, following that process, we had already had all-out elections in 1997 with new wards with new boundaries and new, more twenty-first-century names getting rid of the wards named after Church of England parishes.

Then for some reason best only known to London-based civil servants, it was decided in 2002 to have another review of wards. This wasn't necessary or called for locally as four or five years is not long enough for any significant population shifts to impact.

However, mandarins in London (think they) know best. So, the review took place, changes, if any, were totally marginal but that wasn't enough. Somebody somewhere falteringly decided it was a good idea to have all-out elections in 2004 but not just that, these elections would be postal vote only, no polling stations on polling day whatsoever. Uncalled for madness.

This was a palpably bad time to consider extending voting by post right across the borough. In 2002 a successful Labour candidate in the local elections was charged with conspiracy to defraud (according to the *Guardian* newspaper). Mohammed Hussain pleaded guilty to irregularities in involvement in postal votes and was sentenced to over three years in jail. The BBC reported Judge Peter Openshaw saying the current postal voting system was 'wide open to fraud', adding 'The defendant has literally stolen votes'. And some bright spark 230 miles away had chosen not only to repeat the process but to extend it right across the borough?

Unnecessary all-out elections and a much-feared total postal vote were imposed by us from London. Our hands were tied. It was madness.

But what had happened to the wife-estranged, newly relocated Robin Evans, no longer a BNP, now independent councillor? I'm not entirely sure how much we'd seen or heard of the guy recently but the seat he'd won in a by-election in Mill Hill in 2002 was up for grabs again in 2004. As the time for nominations to close drew ever nearer the LET advised us that there would be five BNP candidates in the borough. The article advised us that the BNP would be fielding a candidate in Mill Hill but against the independent Evans. As well as the BNP slate, another nationalist party, the England First Party were to field a candidate in the neighbouring Meadowhead Ward. Robin Evans had intended to declare himself a Blackburn National Socialist but had failed to register that name with the Electoral Commission. A bit confused? That's fine.

* * *

Then, less than three weeks before the 'ghost' election day, a municipal bombshell landed.

Michael Barrett had been a councillor for a long time, in three separate stints, perhaps twenty years or more. He was a complicated guy, quite troubled, and had lived with his dad in a council flat as his carer for a long time, until his dad died. Michael had worked as a postman whilst at the same time studying for a first degree and went on to do a masters. After gaining these qualifications he worked for regional social housing organisations. He had a spell as chairman of the crucially important finance committee. He married quite late in life to Moira, a Labour Party member living in Darwen.

Mike had taken his turn to be mayor in May 2003. Towards the end of his year, his health deteriorated which led to a period in hospital. Phil Watson and I visited him there over the weekend. He was by no means very well. He died on Monday, 24 May, aged fifty-six, with less than a month left of his mayoral year.

His death threw the town hall into confusion. Immediately it was agreed amongst the three main parties that, out of respect, canvassing would be temporarily suspended. But that's not to say that informal cups of tea in people's living rooms were not being supped. No one could remember a sitting mayor passing away during his or her year of office (Mike was actually No 6 in 150 years). The mayor's officer, the redoubtable Graham Brunton, had to do some research, some ringing around. What had to happen? The last occasion this had happened was for Herbert Vaughan Dowdall nearly half a century before in 1957.

The Lancashire Telegraph reported on 9 June: 'Before the cathedral service, a procession, led by Blackburn with Darwen Council Leader Sir Bill Taylor carrying the borough's mayoral chains, moved quietly through the town.'

Shoppers stood in silence with their heads bowed and flags outside public buildings were flown at half-mast.

The Dean of Blackburn, the Very Rev Christopher Armstrong, said: 'Mike did not just preach the gospel, he lived it. He earned respect from everyone and his easy-going manner was greatly appreciated by everyone.'

Graham Brunton had researched the right things to do, in his normal thorough manner. My role as leader of the council was clear. A lengthy (more than 400 participants) procession including our local MPs, many of the mayors of Lancashire, local members of the House of Lords, local councillors and many, many others with family or civic connections made its way, on foot, the half mile or so from the town hall to the cathedral. I was at its head behind the mayor's officer carrying the civic mace on his shoulder. In front of me I carried the mayor's chain bedecked in black ribbons, sat on a very large black cushion. Out of respect to our friend, colleague and mayor I wore my knight's badge around my neck, its usual scarlet and gold ribbon being replaced by a black ribbon, the traditional colour of mourning. We were quite concerned that the procession, taken at a slow funereal pace, would be challenging for me walking with the cushion and chains on my outstretched arms. Our fallback position was that the senior democratic services officer Phil Llewellyn would shadow me in case I needed some respite. I didn't need to call upon that support, but was I glad to get to the cathedral west door. I stood there, still and silent, as hundreds of fellow mourners filed into the beautiful building. Job done!

All this happened two days before election day. Years later I ironically reflected that little did I realise then that I was walking metaphorically towards my own political funeral too.

* * *

Anyway, we set about addressing the electoral constraints and challenges imposed upon us.

Things seemed to be going pretty well in 2004, our main Achilles heel being the Iraq war and Labour's national position on it. Our local position on things, and there were very much divided views amongst local party members, was to urge people not to look at their televisions but look out of their windows to see the positive impact the changes Labour had introduced were making across all of our local communities. It didn't help, it really, really didn't help, especially amongst some Muslim voters, that our local MP Jack Straw also happened to be Foreign Secretary. I never, as Jack's agent for twenty-five years, either then or later, made my position on the war public.

In Audley ward Labour selected three candidates: me, who'd been there for nearly twenty-five years, a nice young guy called Tahir Mahmood and a fairly long-standing Labour councillor for a different part of town, where he lived, who chose to switch wards, Yusuf (aka Jan) Virmani. Other nominated candidates were two Conservatives and Zamir Khan for the Liberal Democrats, who I thought was or previously had been a Labour Party member. There had been a vacancy caused by a retirement in another safe Labour ward but putting personal opportunism above loyalty wasn't my way.

Usually, we worked as a team in Audley ward, the three ward councillors and any other canvassing support we attracted. We'd do our best to get round the whole of the ward which at the time was evenly split fifty-fifty indigenous and Asian community.

Canvassing in the Asian community was a bi-focal approach. One, drinking tea with perceived community leaders and two, getting round the younger Asian voters, knocking on their doors. It seemed to be that when the tea drinking was going on we worked as a trio. At other times, it was just me and Tahir knocking on doors, saying hello, asking for people's support and getting a very positive response. Increasingly less important was having an Urdu or other Asian language speaker with us but if need be Tahir was fluent. When we went into the indigenous community, we again worked as a trio. Sometimes if I went to a white voter's door I'd be met with 'oh yes, Bill, no problem here, we'll be voting for you. But we aren't voting for any Paki'. My stock reply was 'well, please don't bother voting for me either'. There were some instantly acrimonious exchanges with some older residents in the (Kathleen) Ferrier Court sheltered accommodation.

I'd seemed to have got a reputation amongst pockets of the white community for being and I apologise for the expression 'Blackburn's Number One Paki lover'. I heard this said about me on numerous occasions. Distasteful, really. I'd also been assaulted a couple of times in pubs in the same vein. Indeed, it was in the previous year 2003 that we had decided to put the house up for sale and move, after similar repugnant episodes in public. So, whilst I was campaigning during the election, in Audley ward and right across the borough, my wife was viewing potential new homes for us to move to.

Being in our early/mid-fifties and seeing retirement just over the horizon, we were hoping to downsize, a bungalow perhaps. (This aspiration we achieved some twelve years later.) I had promised both me and my wife that if re-elected and getting a four-year term, that would be that as far as sitting on the council was concerned. By then I'd be fifty-six or so, the kids would most definitely have flown the nest and hopefully set up their own lives, so it seemed like enough was going to be enough. I most definitely didn't want to be the doddery old geezer sat on the council and probably owed both me and my wife more time.

So, she was busy viewing and choosing our next home, which if I wanted to stay on the council had to be situated within the borough's boundaries, hugely restricting our choice. Limited for choice and pressed for time she chose a house bigger than anything we had ever had before. We had to apply for and secure a mortgage, having just finished paying it off. I think her strategy was to move the two of us into a property that would be easy to sell in our dotage, aka the future. Going from no mortgage to having a £100k-plus mortgage again irked, but *que sera sera*. I more or less left the whole process to her. I think we moved about two weeks after the election result was announced. Had we known, we could have widened our search beyond the borough and saved ourselves loads of money!

Our Sunday morning strategy meetings continued as normal and were well attended. With hindsight you might wonder if some people in that room were a) telling the truth and b) not taking back to others what they learned from our meetings. Did we have conspirators in our midst?

I don't think as a party we could have worked any harder, developed so many life-changing opportunities for individuals, families and communities; three brand new schools, two city learning centres, 40 per cent more investment in schools and education with more teachers and more classrooms, children centres, massive housing and other regeneration schemes, the list went on and on. But with still more to do and still more to come.

I worked hard in the ward during the three or four weeks of canvassing. I think I must've personally called upon over 1,500 of the 3,000 homes in the ward. At no stage did anyone, indigenous or Asian, tell me to my face that they weren't going to vote for me. Not one person. Council colleagues lent a hand including Kate Hollern and Jack Straw as we went canvassing together. I sensed people were worried.

In the immediate run up to (what wasn't a normal) election day, various accusations were made about alleged postal vote tampering and some fisticuffs in some Asian parts of the borough. The police were called out to intervene.

Election day came and of course what we would usually do is to be out in the ward and across the borough urging people to go out and vote Labour. As it was a total, all-out postal ballot, it was reasonable to expect most people had already voted, behind closed doors, well before polling day.

The atmosphere throughout the day was eerie.

Chapter 36

The Boot!

I ain't no fool for love songs.

In the late morning of Friday, 11 June 2004 I *lost my seat* on the council. Defeated.

The up-and-coming local government journalist on the local paper then still called the *Lancashire Evening Telegraph* (LET), Danny Brierley, another nice guy, crafted a brusque front-page headline 'Sir Bill gets the Boot!'.

Looking back, first of all that seat was never **my** seat, never to be taken for granted and also, was I defeated, or did somebody else just win?

That morning, as usual, I shaved, looking myself in the mirror, thinking, almost out loud, you may not be a councillor next time you look at yourself. And that was how it was to be.

I made my way to the public halls for the usual gathering and drama of the election count. At one time the count took place immediately at the close of polls, starting very late in the evening and going on into the early hours of the morning. Totally knackering.

This count started at 10 a.m. the next day and would take three, perhaps four hours. I was there early as constituency agent to make sure that everyone else was and that they knew their role in proceedings. The count proceeded as normal and results were declared on an electoral ward by ward basis.

One of the more junior electoral officials wandered over to me and whispered 'Bill, it's not looking good for you'. But by then there was nothing anyone could do. Whatever was the die, it was well and truly cast.

It then became more formal and theatrical. Candidates and their agents were summonsed into the centre of the hall under the apron of the stage. It was here that the chief executive/acting returning officer, Phil Watson, advised all in this little grouping of the result. In detail:

The three Labour candidates, including me. Yusuf Virmani polled 1476 (elected), Tahir Mahmood 1208 (elected) and (me) 1135 votes.

There were two token Tories who secured 604 and 542 votes.

The dark horse was the officially approved Lib Dem candidate Zamir Khan who polled 1542 votes (elected), similar to the top Labour winner. The Lib Dems rarely if ever fielded a candidate in Audley Ward. Something very strange appeared to have happened.

The audible reaction to this news as it was announced formally over the public address system by the acting returning officer was a cacophonic mixture of cheering and booing. Quite weird.

Press cameras were shooting and journalists with note pads, pencils poised, were hoping to grab some juicy quotes.

In a neighbouring white working-class ward, Highercroft, another drama was played out as my long-time friend Ashley Whalley lost a Labour seat there (two Labour wins, one Lib Dem). Ashley had been a councillor for many years and had earned the right to become the next mayor elect. At the time it was actually Ashley losing his civic opportunity that most upset me. I spent some time sat talking with him and his partner, Judith.

The news most gratifying for me was in Mill Hill Ward, where the former British National Party, turned Independent candidate, Robin Evans, had been given a sound drubbing, a message of rejection. Malcolm Doherty, the previous Labour leader topped the poll there, Lib Dem Alan Dean came next, Labour's Jim Smith, well known around the ward, came third. Of nine candidates standing in Mill Hill, Evans came bottom with 169 votes. Rather soberingly Evans' former BNP party colleague ran in seventh with 377 votes. Combining Evans' and the BNP vote to total 546, would have taken a seat-winning third place. Something still to remain aware of and vigilant about.

The balance of seats on the Council, thirty-three Labour, seventeen Conservative, twelve Lib Dems left Labour with a comfortable majority of four to carry on with our transformational, whole borough and beyond, programme.

The Comment column in the local paper could not have been more praiseworthy about me and my track record and there was strong enticement for me to return to the council chamber. 'Don't write off Sir Bill just yet' was their headline plea.

Jack Straw was quoted on the front page of the local paper that it was 'dreadful irony'. He went on 'Fate can be very cruel. The Labour Party's success in Blackburn owes more to Bill than anybody and yet he's the casualty. He's been a close friend for many years as well as a political colleague.'

The newly elected Councillor Zamir Khan poll winner's sole victory quote was 'mission accomplished'. People frequently pondered with me and one another what was the mission and what was accomplished. I struggle to blame the bloke, don't really know much about him. The systemic deceit of the 1,500 voters, many of whom I knew personally, many of whom had told me to my face that they were voting for me and then didn't, is another matter.

When the opportunity presented itself, I left the halls and wandered over to the nearest pub, the Ribblesdale, bought a pint as I watched other people leaving the count and set about texting my wife and children to tell them what had happened.

My wife, of course, was back in school on a full teaching day so we only managed a brief conversation. Our son, Matt, was in York at law school and immediately said he was catching the train home. Our daughter, Kit, was at sixth form college in the middle of her A level exams and she said she'd make her way home as soon as possible. I was asked to pop into BBC Radio Lancashire where I gave a live interview. I thought I spoke honestly and well and explained how I tried never to be complacent, arrogant or take anything or anyone for granted. The female interviewer concluded by praising me and saying she was sure that I'd be back. The Reverend Mike Wedgeworth emailed me to say how well I'd done to 'hold things together'. There's bound to be a name for this, as that evening it started to feel that what was happening was happening to somebody else and I was observing it. I've since found it might be called depersonalisation-derealisation disorder, DP/DR.

As soon as all our family had assembled at home we made our way for an early tea at a local pub, the Butlers in nearby Pleasington. Before that, however, Kit had thoughtfully bought me a card and wrote lovely things in it. They made me cry. It was the only time I did weep.

We had a nice family evening and I pondered what I should do immediately.

This turned out to be early the next morning, I went into the town hall. As it was a Saturday, I didn't expect many people would be about. I had my own set of keys so I could let myself in through the back door.

I'd only really gone to sneak in to get my personal effects, things that were in the desk drawers.

I opened the door to the leader of the council's office, expecting this morose activity would be done in private. I was wrong. Sat around the meeting table in no longer my room were a dozen or so of my former colleagues of twenty-four hours before, discussing and determining who might be allocated what in terms of leadership roles, portfolios, chairmanships and committee responsibilities. The starkly polarised nature of our two missions was not lost on any of us. I rummaged through the drawers removing toothpaste and brush, some eau de cologne, my nice pen and other effects. A family photo and also a print of Van Gogh's *Sunflowers*. I left my bunch of keys with my former colleagues and wandered down the stairs to my wife waiting in the car. Job done, I said. The process hadn't taken more than ten minutes, a very long, slow ten minutes.

That done it was time to be dropped off for a game of golf. I think I expected to be playing a lot more golf from then on.

The next day it started. With the news of my knighthood we received some 250 letters, cards, texts and emails, flowers. For this news we received not many fewer expressions but of many different sentiments. I know they were well meant, intended to make me feel better but they didn't. The sincere niceness of the sentiments expressed, really only made matters worse for me. I got messages from people, some I'd never met or even heard of, but also local folk, friends and neighbours, council staff, trades unions, members of opposition parties, local head teachers and chairs of governors, local business leaders, the voluntary sector, faith leaders, journalists from the media, local government colleagues nationally. Their sentiments came across as sincere and well meant.

It was only from the Labour Party that I heard little but silence; no sorry, goodbye, or thank you. Politics is a tough game; the ballot box is a blunt weapon; we know the rules. When other servants to the party locally lost or moved on, Malcolm, Gail, Sue, I made sure that they were publicly thanked, and some small token of our appreciation was made to them formally at an open presentation. I always thought it was important to say thank you and goodbye to people in front of their peers and also to give them some sense of closure whatever the reasons for their departure. Emotional intelligence.

I soon discovered that the practical processes for any councillor leaving the council were demeaning, unceremonious. Within a few days the IT people came and like bailiffs removed my loan computer. I went and bought my own. And a few days later my P60 arrived. I was so angry at this perfunctory dismissive behaviour; I ripped it up. It cost me £15 for the replacement required by the tax man!

I stopped going into town, shopping or any similar places where people could be 'bumped into'. The stock phrase was 'Hi Bill, sorry about what happened to you. After all you've done, it was wrong. I know exactly how you feel'. I didn't really want pity, anything judgemental or assumed empathy, I really just wanted leaving alone.

As my mind wandered, as it did frequently during this period of self-mourning, it lingered upon not the whys of what had happened, but what else could have happened. I could have taken my (successful) mission of defeating the BNP less to heart, I could have taken more time and spent less money on moving house, I could have gone for the fantastic and hugely well-paid job with I&DeA, perhaps letting slip to them that I was days off being publicly declared a knight.

But do you know, to this day, I wouldn't change a thing. I'd met fantastic people, had some fantastic experiences, felt like I'd achieved improvement and change for others in the world, stood up to prejudice and oppression and had a load of laughs along the way. Something I could do, that others couldn't or shouldn't, was walk tall, feel proud and not feel ashamed of myself.

Within weeks, days possibly, the by-election date caused by Michael Barrett's death was announced. I sought people's advice about whether I should seek to stand or not. I'd never been too keen on councillors who wandered around seeking different seats following defeat; I think some had served in three or four wards. I'd enjoyed, and been proud of, representing the ward where many of my youth work or school work clients and their families lived and with whom I'd worked. I didn't fancy carpet bagging. The advice around me, possibly for different reasons, was NOT to stand. Later I wondered was that for my sake or to clear the path for others' career ambitions.

We'll never know.

There was a field of twelve candidates in the two-seat Earcroft by-election. Moira, Michael Barrett's widow, stood for Labour alongside Frank Davis (in a vacancy caused by Mary Leaver's sad passing) in the by-election and they both won. A fitting legacy for both Michael and Moira. For the record, candidates seem to take paired placings; Labour, Lib Dem, Tory, BNP, Independent. Ex-councillor Robin Evans and his female British National Socialist Party fellow candidate came eleventh and twelfth with fourteen and ten votes respectively.

It also seemed weird that the experiences, relationships, skills and successes that I had accumulated and developed over twenty-five or thirty years were not only just suddenly left uncalled upon but seemed actively binned. It was this dichotomous dysfunction that was the hardest to understand and explain.

What I, probably no one, could have anticipated was the turmoil the Labour Party was thrown into within days of my departure. From spending hours and hours, most days, most weeks, over twenty-five years with communities, councillors, Labour Party folk and town hall staff, I was cast totally outside of all this, literally overnight. I don't know most of the story. Like most, I had to rely upon the local media. And, although I didn't fully realise it at the time, I was living in my own emotional fog.

Under the front page banner headline 'Town Hall Turmoil', an exclusive by reporter Danny Brierley explained 'Labour loses overall control of council as SIX quit party'. The article went on to explain that my successor in holding the education portfolio, Mahfooz Hussain, had lost that exalted and coveted Blue Riband role during the voting process of the Labour Group's AGM following the elections. The local paper stated that Councillor Hussain and the other five Muslim councillors were being made the scapegoats for the loss of former council leader Sir Bill Taylor. Whether or not some of the Six were actively involved in my demise or that they did nothing to help avoid it is almost irrelevant. Did it really matter ex-post facto?

The article goes on to quote me, 'I am certainly not responsible for any of this. However, the Labour Group has always chosen its best team based on track record, experience and availability. Only last night I was invited to visit a number of Asian residents in Audley who are profusely apologetic and concerned about what happened last week.' They spoke openly about the shame this had brought to the Asian community and the potential damage done to community relations.

Tory Group leader Councillor Colin Rigby was quoted, 'I'm surprised that the Six resigned, particularly Mahfooz Hussain. He hasn't done a particularly good job.'

No longer able to rely on those six votes removed Labour's twenty-one-year control, a lot of the credit for which was down to me, of the borough council. It really was quite a political pickle. My main contribution to it was giving Danny Brierley an ironic soubriquet for the new half dozen self-outcasted defectors: the Mahfia! I bet the young reporter felt that all of his Christmases had come at once, the local paper was almost writing itself with the intrigue of the crisis.

The paper recounted that the 'Mahfia' had, with an apparent lack of dignity or principle, touted themselves in talks with the Conservatives and Liberal Democrats on the council. I don't know, perhaps we'll never know, what wheeler-dealing went on. Foreign Secretary and Blackburn MP Jack Straw who prudently rarely involved himself in Labour Group matters worked alongside his future parliamentary successor but then new Labour Group leader, Kate Hollern, to try and resolve this can of worms. At one stage the local paper reported that Kate had tried to broker a power-sharing deal with both of the other political groups represented on the council. It was reported that those two groups had also met with the Six in an attempt to hammer out a deal with them. I only knew what we could all read in the local paper, and gladly I was very much out in the cold.

This was a proper baptism of fire for the newly elected Labour Group leader, and watching from a distance I didn't really envy her. She was juggling with the political realities of damaged egos, raw personal political ambition and easily led, weak individuals. Audley Ward councillor Yusuf (aka Jan) Virmani, the apparent spokesman for the Six, told the paper that the Six had met hundreds of the town's Asian community, saying 'we got the full backing of the community to the actions we have taken'. Really?

This democratic debacle was played out almost nightly on the front page of the local paper. One night the headline declared 'It's all over for Labour'. We were told that the Conservatives and Lib Dems had joined forces with the dirty half dozen to kick Labour onto the opposition benches. I was quoted as saying 'I am appalled and ashamed at the chaos that the council has been plunged into by this apparent unprincipled avarice of a small minority. It is not what our citizens expect or want.' Councillor Yusuf (aka Jan) Virmani, my former ward Labour colleague, did appear to emerge as the Mahfia leader. It left Labour with twenty-seven councillors and the mishmash with thirty-five. Again, I was quoted as saying, 'I have heard no one, but this minority themselves as a group, level or take the blame for my defeat. I would have thought under Kate Hollern's leadership or mine, that it was highly unlikely that Councillor Mahfooz Hussain would have retained his education portfolio. There had clearly been a perceived dip in the political management of the vital public service.'

Night after night the letters page in the local paper was jampacked full of views and opinions on this unfortunate episode. The six guys had done nothing to enhance the standing of themselves, the council or the Asian community, indeed, quite the opposite! Former Labour councillor Michael Madigan who acted as agent for two of the Six in Bastwell Ward quit his role stating, 'this action on the part of the gang of six has set back community relations as many in the indigenous community will view all Muslim councillors with suspicion.'

In a further edition of the local paper, Labour party secretary Phil Riley admitted that there were concerns about the way some Labour candidates had canvassed in the run-up to the local elections. He slammed the Six for having been an integral part of the two-/three-month election campaign for Labour and then disloyally reneging on their colleagues.

Every night in the paper there was a massive letters page and sometimes a 'Letters EXTRA' page!

The local paper reported or surmised that goings-on were going on behind closed doors between the three, possibly four, political groups on the council. I was as much in the dark as most people. I went back to work amongst good people most of who supported me well, and played more golf amongst more good people who equally supported me well. I remain indebted to them and their support to this day. Good comradeship!

The *Asian Image* newspaper (it is as it says on the tin) reported that the Six had had a private meeting attended by Jack Straw and Lord Adam Patel (who were close and long-standing political associates). A spokesman for the Six was enigmatically quoted as saying 'this is an internal problem within the Labour Group' (of which they were no longer members, having withdrawn themselves). 'We feel none of this would have come about if Sir Bill Taylor had not lost his seat.' This paper appears to have been the first to announce that Councillor Yusuf (aka Jan) Virmani had been given the Labour nomination for becoming deputy mayor meaning that the following year he would be mayor. This apparent trade-off raised quite a few eyebrows as there were a very strict set of successional protocols about how people achieved the civic office and honour of becoming mayor. Councillor Virmani had got the Labour Group's nomination when he wasn't a Labour Group member.

There must have been more behind-closed-doors horse trading as the council's Annual General Meeting drew ever closer. The Six had chosen to exclude themselves from the Labour Group for whatever reason. Did they belatedly realise their infantile actions were disproportionate to whatever wrong they sensed or cited? Political rabbits appeared to be being pulled from political hats. The local paper mooted that an independent enquiry might be a bargaining chip device to ease the potential return of the Six back into the Labour fold. The article went on to pose the question: 'It remains to be seen if they' (the Six) 'will use the balance of power to vote against Labour on key issues in the future?' There seemed to be a lot of smoke and mirrors in the arguments they were putting forward as to why they had chosen to exclude themselves. But it seemed to be the case that the potential loss of Labour's control of the council had been averted. Had principle been thrown out of the window and the adage that politics is the art of the possible been the victor?

The local paper continued to have a field day with all these shenanigans. They carried a front page with a banner headline 'Clown Hall' with a clown's hat, nose and bowtie airbrushed around an aerial photograph of the town hall. Further questions were posed, including 'another U-turn sees Labour in control – but for how long?' Five of the six exiles voted with the Labour Group. Lib Dem leader Paul Browne dubbed them 'the scum of the earth'. They had not formally returned to the Labour Group, remaining outside of it, still as Independents. The council AGM was described as a night of high political drama, a damaging farce making the council a laughing stock. The proceedings in the council chamber were conducted in a most undignified, unmunicipal manner. I attended and witnessed them along with my wife, Anne, in a defiant double act of *illegitimi non carborundum*. It made for a hard watch; a piece of theatre, tragedy, I guess. When asked I said, 'I am sure that the waters are not completely calm'.

It was further announced that the enquiry into the frenetic fortnight would be led by Trevor Phillips, a Labour Party member who had been national head of the Racial Equality Council. Being central to and repeatedly mentioned in events, might it have been expected that I would be called before that enquiry? That never happened.

A few days later I was able to thank people via the local paper: 'Thanks also to people in the street who have taken the trouble to approach me and say something, often just a few small words, they made a real impact.'

I expected and urged that the Labour Party should make its enquiry terms of reference and findings public but that didn't happen either. After the laundering of so much dirty washing in public you might have thought a conclusion to the affair in public might have been right and appropriate.

Who had anything to hide? I was later quoted in the paper saying, 'I will comply with the enquiries as much as I am called on to do so'. I didn't ever hear any more about it.

A few days later but unrelated to these local events, it was announced that the regional government referendum campaign was to be abandoned. Over quite a protracted period I had fronted meetings alongside Deputy Prime Minister John Prescott advocating this bold move and was disappointed when it was simply and meekly shelved. Was the Labour Party beginning to lose its bottle? There was quite a hoo-hah and much mudslinging about further possible widespread postal voting irregularities during the combined 10 June 2004 local and European elections. It was widely expected that the next general election would be scheduled for June 2005. The referenda on regional assemblies were scheduled for November 2004 and I think insightful political punditry identified that Tony Blair wouldn't risk at best shenanigans, at worst a rout so soon before his next general election. Regional assemblies simply edged off the national political stage, possibly for ever?

We learned sometime later that Trevor Phillips had approached a cross-bencher Lord Victor Adebowale to lead the promised but mysteriously clandestine enquiry.

The 'enquiry' must have taken place during August, September or October because at the end of October we learned via the pages of the local paper that it had been conducted and recommendations had been made. The local *Telegraph* divulged that it had seen the report, but to be frank the synopsis published seemed pretty much an asinine whitewash. I was never called to the enquiry, have no idea what its terms of reference were and have never seen the report or had any discussions about it, although I believe I was frequently mentioned in it.

Was a murine whiff detectable in the air?

It was around this time that one of my molar teeth simply dropped out. On visiting Chris Lees, our dentist for many years, he ground down the resultant remaining sharp edges. I asked him why this might have happened. 'Any number of reasons,' he said, 'being stressed or depressed included.' I quizzed him no further, deciding to make an appointment to see our doctor.

A few days later I walked into the surgery to be met by a barrage of indignation. The doctor was angry. 'You're the victim of bigotry,' he said with invective.

'Woah, steady up there,' I urged. 'You're my doctor and I'm your patient.' Some fifteen-plus years later I reminded the now-retired medic of this conversation.

'All I can tell you is that I don't feel totally emotionally right.'

'Tell me what else is going on in your life then.'

'OK. One, our son has gone off to start his working life. Two, our daughter has gone off to start her university life. Three, my wife has just started a new job. Four, we've just moved to a new house. And finally, five, the one to which you have alluded, I played a prominent part in a very media reported and examined drama in public life.'

'Good grief, man, any one of those episodes on their own can tip people over the edge. You've managed to notch up five of them! What do you want me to do? Do you want to consider a course of medications?'

There was a protracted silence between us. After a while he said, 'My advice would be, as you've been able to talk about these things, as hurtful as they are, not to resort to medications to start with. However, recovering from these things will take time, that great healer.'

I left determined not to resort to any medications, but my world was still pretty foggy.

When somebody becomes a newly elected councillor or council leader there are various courses, training and support available to them. Induction for newly elected councillors and newly elected council leaders is abundant. I'd designed and delivered many of them, locally and nationally. I know of no support processes for those who lose their seats. There will be those who will say tough luck, hard cheese, get over it.

A few years later two of my immediate former council leader peers experienced a fate similar to mine. I wrote to them both; I don't know if it helped. I told them it was not their personal fault and time would help heal. We are still pals today. United by a common experience and set of emotions?

Perhaps the Local Government Association or the political parties should look at this, but I doubt they will. Who cares about a loser? Whatever the personal cost.

How did I respond to something that can happen and does happen in politics? How should someone respond? There's an aphorism, attributed to Enoch Powell, that all political careers end in failure. What actually happened in the end, was it failure? I couldn't and wouldn't have done anything differently. Was I defeated by the wrong group of people, for the wrong reasons and does that matter?

It's now generally accepted that high-profile sports people, e.g. footballers George Best, Gary Speed, Paul Gascoigne, Tony Adams, Clarke Carlisle, cricketers Marcus Trescothick, Jonathon Trott, Graeme Fowler, rugby's Sam Warburton, tennis champion Andre Agassi and multi-Olympic gold-medalled rower Sir Steve Redgrave have all spoken or written about how they experienced depression and other emotional challenges during and as their careers concluded. High levels of skill and success, adulation, money, media-borne exposure, the attention of pretty women visit these magnets. Many of them have enough wealth or wealthy friends to seek and secure sources of support through therapy or clinics.

I've gone on in recent years to read some of these guys' and other's accounts of what happened and how they felt. The Professional Footballers' Association and the Professional Cricketers' Association have now, somewhat belatedly, responded more proactively to these needs of their members mid and post-career

Was any of that true for me? For others? In some ways I was lucky, I didn't attend what would have been my very emotionally charged final council meeting. What happened to me was very much in the public eye but how I, and my family around me, responded to it happened very much in private or inside my own head and heart. Had I been bitten by Churchill's Black Dog of Depression?

* * *

I tootled and pootled through my new normal life. Didn't have hundreds of extremely detailed emails every week to read, respond to and clear, no more dawn raids on the town hall, most nights were now our own, Saturday mornings joyously wide open free. My wife is clear that I wasn't right for eighteen months or more after the events leading up to, during and post June 2004, taking us at least through to 2006?

In late October 2004, the LET's chief reporter, David Higgerson, reported on its front page that there was seen to be a Labour power clique locally. He went on to say that the secret report led by Lord Victor Adebowale had revealed that a 'clique of non-elected Labour Party members influenced key decisions on Blackburn with Darwen Council', without naming who these mysterious people might be. I can only imagine there's an uninformed allusion here to locally elected, hard-working party officers, such as chairs and secretaries, who had places on various bodies and had done for decades. The Six remained outside of the Labour Group and we can only assume they were offered the opportunity to reapply to join the Labour Party. This must also indicate that they left the party at some stage and for some reason?

In November further revelations appeared in the LET when Queen's Park Ward (adjoining my former ward Audley) councillor Salim Mulla, a high-up in the Lancashire Council of Mosques and one of the Six, announced he wanted to rejoin the Labour Party. He said an apology from the Labour group had precipitated this. An apology for what, by whom? Had these Six in a peeved pique ripped up their party cards months earlier? When did they actually renew their membership? Were there any others due an apology?

Into February 2005 and David Higgerson revealed in the LET that of the Six, only Mahfooz Hussain had been told he could not reapply to rejoin Labour until he had served a six-month period of good behaviour, i.e. consistently voting with the Labour Group. We were told that three of the Six had rejoined in December and two more in February, leaving Mahfooz Hussain alone in the cold till after the summer, a year after the unprincipled events following my council departure. After years of expert and successful stewardship, could Labour's handling locally of this cloak and dagger saga be best described as inept?

It was around then that I was approached by a group of Asian private hire taxi drivers. 'Please, Bill, will you come back on the council? It's not the same without you. When we asked you things, you'd look into them and if you agreed and it was possible, it would happen. You always did what you promised. These guys aren't like that. We only got at you to give Jack a warning. Please come back.' I'm afraid my response to this serenade was short and sharp. I must have been starting to like getting my life back and didn't intend to put me and family back in the capricious perfidy of politics. Once bitten.

More important things loomed on the political horizon, the imminent general election scheduled for 5 May 2005. I was Jack's agent still, as he was still Foreign Secretary.

The *Mail on Sunday* did a four-page special about Jack in mid-March. Citing my experience, it went on to say 'There is no doubt that the vote (ousting me) was a protest against the Iraq war. With so many Asians in the constituency, a similar revolt at the General Election could destroy Mr Straw as it did Sir Bill.'

I vowed to myself that that would not happen!

Chapter 37

The General Election, 2005

The nearer your destination, the more you're slip sliding away.

A third general election victory for Tony Blair in 2005, only the second time this has been achieved by the Labour Party, was always going to be difficult, the causal difficulty summed up in one word, Iraq. Political reporter Bill Jacobs, under the headline 'Will Iraq flak bury Jack?', his well-crafted article began 'Jack Straw is clearly a worried man'.

During Tony Blair's ten-year premiership, the Tories had had William Haig, Ian Duncan Smith and Michael Howard as their leader. As was the Tory practice after defeat, Howard stood down in December 2005 after David Cameron was elected as Tory leader. Blair stood down in June 2007 to be replaced as Prime Minister by Gordon Brown.

As usual there was quite a lot of to-ing and fro-ing signifying the internal struggles in both major parties. Labour, as usual, between the left and the centre right, this time using the Iraq war as the football and the Tories having still not resolved their deep-rooted schisms over Europe. Charles Kennedy was at the helm for the Lib Dems.

Labour's 1997 landslide victory with the majority of 179 outshone even Clem Attlee's 1945 post-war victory (146). Blair's majority in 2001 held up well at 167.

I had become the constituency agent in late 1979, so the 2005 General Election would be the sixth for which I had held that honorary position, the dates of the others being 1983 (a tricky year for Labour with Thatcher at her zenith, the Falklands 'war' won and poor Michael Foot leading the party, pretty forlornly for such a nice, intellectual scholarly chap). In the intervening dates for the other general elections of 1987, 1992, 1997 and 2001, Jack's majority ranged relatively comfortably from around 3,000 to 14,000. 1983 could have spelt an early end to John Whitaker Straw's parliamentary career as the Tories were really riding high and Jack, a student of election history, knew that local Tory lad Tom Marsden had only been beaten in 1955 by Barbara Castle by 489 votes. In that year we worked very, very hard locally and the threat to Jack's seat was held off by a majority of 3055!

We went into the 2005 campaign knowing it wasn't going to be easy but that was never any reason for us to feel defeatist. We pulled out all the stops! There was a significant Asian vote in the constituency, a significant Asian membership of the party and within the overall party membership a real division of views both on Blair, Labour and Iraq and Jack Straw, Foreign Secretary and Iraq. The Labour Group on the borough council was divided in their views.

I was, to be candid, deep inside, still reeling from the events leading up to and after the local elections in June 2004. But I didn't want that to affect my performance as agent nor let it show on the outside, if I could help it.

We still had our Sunday morning Labour campaign meetings and I felt difficult inside at those most of the time. There was also a campaign public meeting at Audley community centre, right in the middle of my former Audley Ward. I felt duty bound to sit at the top table next to Jack at that meeting showing or appearing to possess the chutzpah to be there. Even during the meeting, facing some of the duplicitous faces who I thought had probably lied to me less than a year before, quite hurt me inside. I hoped I kept that to myself, and anyway nobody asked.

The main three or four weeks of the election campaign locally we were dogged by the Muslim Public Affairs Committee. These were a group of bright young Asian guys from London who had come to make Jack's life hell. They were comparatively active and vociferous but perceived to be uninvited and unwelcome outsiders, counterproductive.

Also during the campaign, Jack's parliamentary pal and former Foreign Secretary (1997-2001) Robin Cook, who had resigned over the Iraq war, came to speak up for his successor, Jack Straw, something we much appreciated locally. Sadly, Robin died whilst walking in his beloved Scottish Highlands a few weeks later.

The Conservatives brought in an Asian candidate from Yorkshire, Imtiaz Ameen. There was a Lib Dem, a UKIP and a British National Party candidate as well as a left-field, not left wing, candidate Craig Murray. Murray was a former Lib Dem and civil servant having served as British ambassador to Uzbekistan from 2002-2004. He left the post under a cloud either being a brave and principled whistle-blower or something at the other end of whatever that spectrum might be.

One of Murray's numerous election pranks was to park an actual ex-military Green Goddess fire appliance on the paved area outside Blackburn Town Hall, adorned with 'Vote Murray' posters.

I bumped into him one night during the election campaign, sitting on his own in a curry house in neighbouring Darwen. I was with a pal.

I didn't know him at all and I happened to say to him something typically Taylor-like such as, 'And what brings you up here?'

He went from nought to sixty in no time whatsoever. 'I'm here to stand against Jack Straw, the Foreign Secretary, to expose all that he and the Foreign Office and the government are trying to cover up. I'm going to give him a bloody nose.'

I invited Mr Murray to tell me his strategy and plans for his campaign. He obligingly over around half an hour spilled all his beans to me. Was I MI6 interrogation material?

My friend had sat there agog at proceedings. As we left to go I went over to Murray's table, shook his hand and wished him all that he deserved with his campaign. He said, 'I'm sorry, I didn't catch your name.' I enigmatically retorted that I was sure our paths would cross again and left!

Jack's majority held up well at over 8,000 leaving the Tory trailing in second and Mr Murray coming in fifth, losing his deposit. That was my 'mission accomplished'. On reflection, Jack's victory twelve months after my 'defeat' tidied things up. No one could accuse me of leaving anyone in the lurch or not honouring commitments and responsibilities, all of which may have only been in my head anyway.

The local paper noted that 4,000 fewer people voted for Jack than they did in 2001 but their analysis was that the backlash against the war in Iraq had split the opposition vote rather than toppling the Foreign Secretary.

In nearby Rossendale and Darwen, our friend and former secretary to both Barbara Castle and Jack Straw, Janet Anderson, with a reduced majority of 3,500 retained the Tory targeted seat. Her eighteen years in Parliament finished in 2010.

Similarly, in neighbouring Hyndburn, our friend Greg Pope won his fourth and final general election by over 5,500 votes. He similarly served 1992-2010 (and Labour's Graham Jones 2010-19). After seven successive Labour wins, the Tories won the seat in 2019, their first win in thirty-two years.

Tony Blair's third general election victory with a 5.5 per cent swing against, left Labour wounded but still with a generous Commons majority of sixty-six.

*   *   *

As all the election hullabaloo died down I went back to work after my three-week unpaid period of leave. I think the campaign had demonstrated to me I still had emotional wounds to lick, something, I thought, best done in private.

Having no political role or ambitions any more I became a little bit of a personality, presenting prizes and awards in schools and similar institutions and travelling to Australia to talk about our outsourcing partnership with Capita, all in a voluntary capacity.

I also continued to be on the board of Blackburn's magnificent college. I'd first gone on the board in 1981. I was later asked to become chair in 2008, another voluntary role that I enjoyed, working for young people, improving their opportunities, changing their lives and those of their families and communities, until 2016.

I did also pick up consultancy work with bodies like the Local

Government Association (LGA) and the Improvement and Development Agency (I&DeA), training and developing elected members and leaders engaging the experience, skills and successes I had gained over some thirty or more years. Picking up this small portfolio of work both 'kept my hand in' but also bought me some time whilst I pondered my future. I was also able to train various multi-agency teams across the country on the implications and opportunities presented by Jack's excellent Crime and Disorder Act introduced, based upon his experiences as a local MP, when he was Home Secretary in 1998. Jack was very much the architect of this brilliant piece of legislation, possibly his best work? If he was the architect, I'd like to think youth worker Bill was a minor draughtsman.

It was during this time whilst doing some community safety consultancy work, along with Paul Musgrave and others, in neighbouring Cumbria that I had the opportunity to meet Neil (Hughes) of Michael Apted's *7-Up* Granada TV fame. If I remember rightly Neil's ambition, aged seven, was to be an astronaut. Several units of seven years later, approaching fifty years of age, his feet were more firmly on the ground. He was born and brought up in Liverpool, did a brief stint at university, lived on the Shetlands, had been a Lib Dem councillor in London and in Cumbria and had served as a lay preacher. Fascinating.

I was also invited into the private sector by becoming a non-exec director of the Manchester-based social research company Vision 21 and the more local Community Business Partners.

Back at work I spent six months I suppose hoping to get back to pre-council 'normality', but what did that mean? Whatever happened in 2004 and why, had a run-up to it and an unprecedented series of events after it. This was all in the public eye, well documented by the local media. How I felt was a private matter, mainly between me and sometimes my immediate family, but not always. What had happened had rattled my confidence as my implicit trust in others had taken a severe bashing. There were parallels here with my mum and dad's split up? There were no catastrophic outcomes or implications to the events, most people wouldn't even recognise them having any significance. If I thought too much about it, I'd been beaten for the wrong reasons by the wrong set of people. I hadn't been and subsequently wasn't properly supported. Values and principles had been trampled upon in a pragmatic short-term dash to sort a 'fix'. The key characters in all this, I wasn't one of them, didn't apparently realise or care about that.

Some eighteen months after the events, however, the headline appeared in the local paper, 'Man who ousted Sir Bill quits Lib Dems.' David Higgerson's article continued that Councillor Zamir Khan had informed town hall officials that he was no longer a Liberal Democrat councillor. He was going to sit as an Independent, quoting 'personal reasons'. On being asked if he was going to apply to become a Labour councillor Khan was quoted to say 'I will not rule anything out. For the time being I need to work out what is best for me'. It must've crossed a few minds that surely what was best for his voters should have carried greater importance.

I was quoted as saying 'I have no personal animosity or qualms about my defeat to Councillor Khan, that's democracy.'

So, having thought the lid was safely secured, the can of worms was open again!

The washing of dirty linen in public escalated once more. The washing wasn't thoroughly washed in public, but I felt left out to dry. Councillor Mahfooz Hussain, the only one of the Six still in the political cold, applied for his suspension from the Labour Group to be lifted. This sparked another row in public, the threat of a rebellion by loyal long-standing Labour Group members if he was allowed to return. One unnamed senior Labour councillor was quoted as saying 'an all-out walkout is being talked about if Mahfooz is allowed back. It includes very senior members of the executive board. Many of us are still angry at the way he behaved'. Jack was reported to have been involved in trying to broker a deal. Neither Jack Straw nor Councillor Hussain chose to comment. The matter appeared to remain unresolved as far as we, the public, were to know.

As a minor distraction from all these shenanigans, Jack invited US Secretary of State, Condoleezza Rice to Blackburn. Given the mixed and polarised views on the intervention in Iraq that abounded throughout Blackburn, it engendered mainly anti-war activity. In April 2006, Dr Rice was welcomed on the town hall steps, amidst loud anti-war chants and booing, by the reported ex-Mahfia member Mayor Councillor Yusuf Virmani.

*   *   *

Some two years later, 2008 perhaps, the whole sad unfortunate series of events has still not been put to bed. I got a phone call from Jack Straw. 'Bill, what would your attitude be if Zamir Khan was allowed to become a Labour councillor?'

My immediate answer was that I wasn't particularly bothered. I wanted to be able to put the whole sorry, unethical and contemptible, mismanaged story behind me and this was prudent and best for me and my family. To let happen whatever others thought was the best to do. People's principles had long gone out of the window and pragmatism seemed the best course of action for me.

Some days later, a new *Telegraph* reporter, David Bartlett, posted the headline 'Labour rebel is back in the fold'. The article stated that Zamir Khan had been a Labour Party member for twenty years but he had quit over the war in Iraq. I don't recall Zamir being a very active party member or being present or vociferous at our numerous discussions about the military situation. Bartlett quoted Khan saying 'I had my differences with the party and decided to stand as an independent. I blamed the Labour Party for Iraq at the time. I was approached by the so-called Liberals and in my anger, I was persuaded to join them.'

Councillor Paul Browne, the Lib Dem leader was quoted as saying 'Good riddance to him. I am disgusted with the Labour Party for taking him back after he knocked Bill Taylor off the council.' The guy is still on the council, coming up for twenty years later. He took his buggins turn as mayor and later got awarded an MBE for his work for the Blackburn Muslim Burial Society.

In truth, I'd had enough of the whole three- or four-year farrago. Whatever the impact had been on me I judged the whole thing was best just putting to bed once and for all. Good night, sleep tight.

I was quoted in the paper with the noncommittal statement, 'This is a matter for the regional Labour Party and the local Labour Group.'

*   *   *

In May 2006, only a week after Mrs Rice's trip to Blackburn, Tony Blair moved Jack in a Cabinet reshuffle to become Leader of the House of Commons, ironically the same career path Robin Cook had travelled a few years earlier. After his five-year incumbency, his role as Secretary for Foreign and Commonwealth Affairs was taken on by Margaret Beckett but only for a year or so.

Jack's move was seen by national political pundits as a demotion. His well-meant reciprocal invitation to Condoleezza Rice to visit Blackburn was depicted by the media as having backfired on him.

Under my own steam I took the train down to London to see Jack in the House of Commons. I personally thought he had been shabbily treated and my visit was intended to let him know that and to offer my support. We sat in a corner of a House of Commons tearoom and he reflected upon events with me. Our conversation, like many others, remains private.

*   *   *

And besides it was nearly time for our annual family caravan holiday in France. Four months earlier in March perhaps, County Hall auditors arranged to come and see our local accounts. It happened every three or so years. We had nothing to hide, indeed we welcomed their intervention as they kept us on our toes. Almost immediately the district admin officer and I were asked about the 'rural account', which seemed strange.

We, in the Ribble Valley, had inherited this account ten years before, back in 1995. I had absolutely nothing to do with its creation or maintenance. I was told at the time that it was set up on the instruction of the county council leader, Louise Ellman and the chair of the county's arm's length economic development company Lancashire Enterprises, Jim Mason, to receive multi tens of thousands of European funding to develop an innovative and much-needed IT infrastructure in rural areas. Almost as soon as I got to the Ribble Valley there was a high-profile launch in West Bradford Village Hall, in which once again I had no involvement other than to attend. The VIPs on the front row included various County Hall dignitaries, many members of the press, Louise Ellman (who later served as a high-profile Labour MP in Liverpool for over twenty years. Louise was deservedly made a dame in 2018. She resigned from Labour (later re-joining) in 2019, after sixty or so years' membership, during the 'antisemitism' period that descended the party during the Corbyn years), Jim Mason (CBE since 1998) (both were known to me, Jim as a family friend) and Glenys Kinnock MEP.

We'd been audited two or three times since and had never once been asked about the 'rural account'. The account, like many other youth service accounts, was 'unofficial', outside the ambit of the county council. Generally, if a village had a youth club with funds, they would be managed by the village hall committee, the local vicar or parish councillor. We wouldn't usually involve ourselves in these. This account and our relationship with it had never changed. Generally, such funds could only be accessed by a couple of cheque signatories. I had no direct access to the monies, something I'd always tried to ensure. For four months or more we heard nothing further of the auditor's visit.

Anyway, off we went via the Hull-Zeebrugge ferry. The rest would do us the world of good. It had been a tough, emotionally scarring eighteen months.

Chapter 38

Back Off Our 2005 Summer Hols – Not Shy But Retiring 2005-2006

Hints and Allegations.

Usually, returning from our three weeks away in France entailed docking at Hull around 6 a.m., then Anne would drop me at my office around 9 a.m. to start work.

Our break had been interrupted, as we were having lunch in Le Grau-du-Roi, a small Mediterranean fishing village in France, by a phone call from my Ribble Valley second-in-command at work, John Kirkham. He told me following his receipt of a disciplinary letter from County Hall that he was required to attend a disciplinary interview about the 'rural account'. As we were a thousand miles away and were due home soon as a family, we agreed there was little we could do about this unexpected and surprise development.

As I returned to the office in Whalley and exchanged customary pleasantries about our hols, I went upstairs to my office, expecting hundreds of emails and many letters to be awaiting my attention.

What was awaiting me was totally unexpected; a devastating bombshell was dropped upon me. A two-page letter hand-delivered from County Hall by John Mason, my line manager, and son of family friend Jim and older brother of Tim. Words such as 'disciplinary action, serious areas of concern and gross misconduct' were phrases that leapt off the page. I struggled to take it all in.

Appended to the letter was a multi-paged advisory document entitled 'Disciplinary Procedure'. Halfway down the first page I scan read 'In many cases the right word at the right time and in the right way may be all that is needed and will often be a more satisfactory method of dealing with a breach of discipline or unsatisfactory conduct than taking action via a formal investigation'. This common sense informal approach hadn't been afforded to me after thirty-plus years' loyal service. Another appendix, entitled financial regulations, was one I had never been made familiar with or even seen before.

The serious areas of concern had numbered seven but were reduced to six by hand, prior to any hearing. I took it upon myself to contact my eleven district team manager colleagues across the county. They were shocked. We had been positively encouraged by Tim Mason, a close friend of ours of thirty years and a creative senior county officer, to be more 'entrepreneurial', to seek out, secure and utilise additional funding from the variety of different sources that were available to us to develop our work. This could include SRB (Single Regeneration Budget), the government office north-west, crime and disorder, the careers-orientated service ConneXions, the Lottery and other funds. Every other district manager told me they had such a fund, some far, far in excess of whatever we had generated. Many took proactive evasive measures anticipating getting on the receiving end of similar punitive action. No, it was only meted out to me.

Creatively using such funding, some neighbouring colleagues had even employed several staff on a full-time basis which could have long-term staffing legal and financial implications for the county council.

We had most definitely attracted additional funding and deployed it totally for the benefit of young people in the Ribble Valley. I immediately, fully and openly admitted our actions, apologised for them and undertook not to repeat them to our principal officer, John Goffee, by letter. What more can anyone do, encouraged on the one hand to be entrepreneurially creative whilst on the other, be threatened with extreme disciplinary treatment for contravening rules and regulations we'd never seen, my accusers weren't sure they'd ever drafted or distributed and they hadn't followed their own procedures. I understand that this letter was intercepted at County Hall, never reaching its intended recipient. My view is that had John Goffee got his letter as normally he would, the next year or so of extreme distress would have been avoided.

Some of the financial regulations documents that were cited against me were some ten to twelve years old and had never been seen by me, indeed most people. I was told that some preparatory work had been done on some draft new financial regulations, five or six years earlier in 1999. But there was no clear evidence or shared recollection that these were ever circulated, shared or discussed. Some newer ways of working though not necessarily distributed or implemented were depressingly described by the authority as 'better and quite good'. It was admitted that there was no consistency across the county, even down to which forms were used and accepted centrally at County Hall for the most simple of clerical procedures.

Reference was made on occasion to an admin handbook. No such document existed.

On several occasions money was moved in and out of the rural account following the advice given over the phone by the county senior admin officer and 'remotely' moved around by them at County Hall.

It was accepted by the authority that every penny was accounted for and that the Ribble Valley had not overspent its general budget, as had been previously alleged, in the financial year 02/03, 03/04 or 04/05.

Our 'sideways' acquisition of a rural youth work vehicle at the behest and involvement of County Hall 'high-ups' a) got the county out of a financial fix and b) was well received by the local media, the police, county councillors, the borough council and their thirty-five parish councils.

Much of this money was utilised to improve the take-up in the Ribble Valley of the Duke of Edinburgh's Award Scheme. Ribble Valley was the county's smallest district population wise with perhaps 4,000 young people in our fourteen to twenty-one-year-old target age group. Perhaps 500 youngsters in each year cohort? I think unlike any other district in the county (some easily treble our size) we facilitated the DofE in every one of our secondary schools. This is no mean feat and was staff intensive. All our schools, their teachers, head teachers and governors, mums and dads, regional and national DofE officials, even Prince Philip himself, loved and recognised us for offering this service. We brought in additional qualified experts and instructors in outdoor pursuits, music, drama, dance, the arts and various other disciplines. We rented various outdoor pursuits and other residential centres across the north-west. Our outdoor pursuits and equipment store was a brimming Aladdin's Cave of equipment (rucksacks, waterproofs, boots, ropes and other climbing equipment, tents, camping and water sports equipment, guitars, drums, PA systems, innovative video-making equipment, inter alia) quite often used by the voluntary sector and other districts who were grateful to have access to it. We contributed massively and most definitely disproportionately to the county's DofE 'take-up' figures, including youngsters with disabilities. I had been invited, accompanied by Anne, down to St James's Palace and was presented to Prince Philip himself, by way of an appreciative public thank you.

My life was a fog. It wasn't in my nature to 'fiddle' public funds, my public standing and reputation were hard won. The recommended initial informal pre-disciplinary route had been ignored, it would appear I alone was being singled out for this treatment, every penny piece was accounted for, we'd engaged with the most Duke of Edinburgh's Award young people in the county, we enhanced the service's standing locally and nationally. So, why?

The why question haunted me. I took time off work with stress, not my normal way. On a few occasions on the twenty-minute drive into work, I would stop in a lay-by, for an unknown length of time, then turn round and go home not being able to make any sense of what was being done to me or why? My confidence to trust others, long-term colleagues and family friends, took a severe, inexplicable bashing.

I think there were two or three 'hearings' and I am indebted to Carol Lukey, the county unison secretary, who stuck with me throughout. The process dragged on for almost exactly a year! Management's notes of meetings took weeks to be circulated, well after memories had had time to dim. There was no clarity about how much money was in question: £22k, £10k and £6.7k were all figures mooted. Never at any time was there any accusation made that, whichever was the actual modest amount, any monies had not been used to enhance our service to our young people and their communities.

At these 'hearings' the authority's side used phrases such as 'The service recognises it did not fully initiate… (we) think we did but can't find any record of this… (it was) felt the (previous) meeting was hard to follow… using the phrase 'gross misconduct' (specifically used in the initial letter), was never a likely outcome'. A targeted stich up – full stop.

I was summonsed to a further and final meeting where I think the word 'exonerated' was bandied around. For a year now I'd not felt anywhere near 100 per cent 'on top of my game'; I was emotionally shattered. On top of my electoral experience of 2004 and all its personal and political impact, this had inexplicable causes and imperceptible effects. Had my removal from the political scene enabled the opening of doors for others to level professional, political or personal scores against me? I tried to keep my thoughts above such low motives.

Much of this was detailed in a lengthy letter from our principal officer sent to my office in Whalley. This was the first and only time correspondence on this sensitive matter had not been sent, marked 'Private and Confidential', to my home. Luckily, although quite a junior member of staff, the admin worker who opened it twigged its sensitive nature and handed it to me. This could have easily fallen into others' hands and have been passed on to the local press and discredited me, harming my record and reputation. Perhaps that had been the intention of this whole process.

I got a written apology for this huge gaffe in March 2006. It really was the final straw. I wanted away.

* * *

When the opportunity to leave the youth and community service presented itself, I took it, in the shape of early retirement/voluntary redundancy. It could have been easily seen as constructive dismissal but the wind for any further prolonged fight had been knocked out of me.

I had really loved my time working first of all as a face-to-face worker, then trainer and then manager; thirty-three extremely imaginative and creative years mainly with like-minded colleagues passionate about enabling young people to benefit from the best possible start to their adult lives. This was marred occasionally by sporadic episodes of line managers who wanted to command and control how we operated. Luckily these people were few and far between as that style of management really is counterproductive. I call this captious or censorious management. Never praising the good work that people prevailingly try and succeed in doing but lying in predatorial wait for the smallest of failures to savagely pounce upon. Synonyms of censorious include: overcritical, condemnatory, deprecatory, reproachful, fault-finding, carping, cavilling. I'm sure you get and have had the style I'm taking about? I used to, every so often, self-manufacture a poster for my wall: 'If you think you've got problems, you should see your boss.' This manipulative style of control freakery demotivates and down-skills its victims. Inspiring and enabling staff, working alone, in teams and working alongside colleagues from other professions or agencies to be imaginative and creative produces the best youth work results. Of course, certain irreducible parameters – legal, financial, safety and other common-sense factors have to be recognised and observed.

As I left my career employment, the routine exit interview was conducted. Detailed notes were taken, pages and pages of them, as I went through how badly I felt I had been treated. I was told what I had to say was so incriminating that it would have to be reported to the county's senior personnel officers. They must have some pretty big carpets to sweep all that under. I never heard anything further.

My final eleven years were spent as district team manager in the nearby and relatively rural Ribble Valley, where I inherited only two full-time members of staff initially, Geoff Jackson and Shelagh Richardson. Our office to begin with was the ground floor of a former chapel in Clitheroe. However, we grew the team to the extent that we eventually moved to a purpose-built two-storey office block in the village of Whalley.

We must have had at least eight staff who were full-time including Lisa Harvey, Louise Neville and Phil Evans, and a great team of sessional workers too. With very rare exception, they were a fantastic group of younger workers who were a pleasure to lead.

We had four leaving dos for me. There was the official, i.e. dour, event where we travelled the fifteen or so miles to County Hall in Preston.

There was a local day do hosted by Shelagh Richardson and her team at her fantastic youth centre in Longridge, the second town of the Ribble Valley. This was actually a surprise do. When I arrived everybody was quite scarily wearing Bill Taylor face masks! At this event most of the staff, youth workers from the voluntary sector, LCC people, the police, colleagues from Ribble Valley Council, representatives from many of the local schools and local church people came along. The atmosphere was great and it made me feel like our work was recognised and appreciated.

The night do in the Ribble Valley started one Friday evening straight after work so, about five thirty/six o'clock kick-off. I'm not sure what the plan was, they kept me in the dark, but we convened at one of the local pubs, The Swan. I tried to buy the first round of drinks but wasn't allowed to pay for anything. I didn't for the rest of the night. We never moved from The Swan. Two of the younger female staff from the information service, What Now operation, offered to get me a drink. I said I'd get them. They told me you can't, the drinks are free.

At this point Andrew Ronnan, the landlord of our offices, came into the pub and wandered over. I explained that I had been trying to buy drinks but had been unable. He explained that that was correct and that everything, including a buffet later on, was on him.

He went on to explain that he'd never worked with public sector workers before, indeed initially when it was mooted, he was wary of us. But he grew to learn, much against his better nature, that we were a fantastic bunch of people, hard-working and fun to be around.

At the time his limited portfolio of properties alongside the railway station were just square-box incubator units; each uniformly with one large door for vehicle access and a normal door for people to get into the units. To accommodate us and the What Now service Andrew had to take the risk of a bank loan, £1/4 million for the first building. This had spooked him but not too much. Once he'd grasped that entrepreneurial nettle, he got the hang of and the taste for it. He built a number of high spec units on the site housing us, solicitors, playgroups, care workers, IT companies and various other mainly service organisations. He named our unit Lancashire House; amongst the cognoscenti it was irreverently known as mini County Hall. After my departure, many staff left but went on to work, mainly sadly lost to youth work, across the county and the country, one, Paul Wright, as far away as Australia. Our diminished presence soon no longer required the tenancy of Lancashire House. I believe several years later the estate was up for sale for several millions of pounds. Good luck to you, Andrew.

There was also a trip to Dublin for my closest working colleagues from the Ribble Valley. John Kirkham, Shelagh Richardson, Lisa Harvey, Louise Neville and John Fletcher came with me and we had a great few days in Dublin's fair city.

The local press were united in publishing quite nice end of career stories about me. The *Lancashire Telegraph*, the *Clitheroe Advertiser* and BBC Radio Lancashire all carried touching tributes.

So what now for me? My twenty-five-year council career and my thirty-three-year professional career were now both behind me. In 2006, son Matt was twenty-five. Having studied and qualified in law, he was now at the beginning of his career based in Manchester. Katherine, known by most as Kit, was twenty-one, about to graduate from Manchester University in business studies and on the threshold of her as yet to be chosen working life.

Anne or Mrs T as she was known with respect and affection, was thirty-one years into her secondary school teaching career at nearby Pleckgate High School where she was head of sciences. Her identified retirement target date was still five years off.

I'd been approached to be involved as a non-exec director in Simon Danczuk's Vision 21 and our local Community Business Partnership ably led by my now friend Mike Murray.

National organisations engaged to me to do what amounted to inspections of councils such as Gateshead and Bristol. I also did some training for the LGA and the I&DeA. Both are organisations designed to help councils improve.

I also did some youth work university level teaching at the Cumbria University campus in Lancaster.

I became an artefact in the history of local government, appearing in the Local Government Information Unit's publication on their 'Where are they now?' page.

Here, in 2007, three years after 'the boot', I was asked to list what made me proud during my time as a councillor.

They included:

+ Being a member, often in a leadership role, of some great teams of members and officers.
+ Establishing a network of some thirty-plus neighbourhood centres and community bases across the borough. Probably unrivalled elsewhere.
+ Enabling young people to have an effective voice. What we achieved in Blackburn was replicated across the country.
+ Beating off the transitory British National Party challenge but never being complacent about it.
+ Introducing community resourcing audit and analysis across the borough. This was in direct response to the British National Party surge when they claimed and made divisive political capital out of the repetitive assertion that most public resources went into BME communities. This process identified all resources of the council, police, fire and rescue, the NHS, the Department of Work and Pensions, etc. Pooled all together this amounted to a figure four or five times that of the council spend alone, nearly a billion pounds. This was then apportioned down to electoral ward level and even smaller enumeration areas. Its findings were that the most resources went into white working-class communities. The analysts, not locals, also highlighted a very high incidence of mortality in one of the more affluent wards in the borough which is at variance with the NHS statistics. During a debriefing session with them I pointed out that this ward was also the home of the borough's crematorium! Again, resource mapping was adopted as a national model of good practice for resource analysis.
+ Again, we were ahead of the field in what became known as community cohesion. Our 'Belonging to Blackburn' where we promoted the concept of diversity with unity, again became a national model.
+ Engaging with our communities whilst at the same time

empowering them, via things like Friday night community accountability meetings, the 'exec on the road' initiative and council leader's Saturday morning surgeries.

+ Again ground-breaking, our public private partnership with Capita brought extra flexibility to the way we provided services to our citizens. Other Capita jobs came into the borough too.

+ The recognition we gained for our achievements: winning Council of the Year, being awarded four beacon awards, an excellent Ofsted report for the LEA and being assessed as 'excellent' during our comprehensive performance assessment inspections.

+ And being knighted in 2003 not only for my time in public office but also in youth work.

The article went on to ask me what would I do differently if I was a councillor today? My reactive answer was 'nothing'.

Asked what did I do now? My first answer was 'sleep better'.

Leaving behind my council public life and my professional career both left big holes in my life. Did I miss them? I think initially the answer must be yes, however that dissipated with time. What I did miss was being in places and positions to affect positive improvement in people's lives. I had acquired from my experiences, skills, applicable skills in change, not change management as advocated in those 'management guru' textbooks but change leadership tried and tested as successful in the field. I was a public services polymath. I still bore the cuts and bruises (or as Theodore Roosevelt told students in the Sorbonne in 1910 'credit belongs to the man who is actually in the arena whose face is marred by dust and sweat and blood') sustained on the battlefield of politics.

What I did miss, which I believe secretly self-admitted but now confess publicly, was the limelight. There must be some payback for all those hours, months and years and to be openly honest, enjoying being in the public eye was part of that equation.

Nationally we (or was it becoming 'they', the Labour Party) were moving towards Tony Blair's (agreed or otherwise) handover of premiership to his long-term chancellor Gordon Brown. Jack Straw at the time was Leader of the House of Commons. Reporter David Bartlett of the *Lancashire Telegraph* rightly speculated that Jack who had become Brown's campaign manager would be moved to Justice Secretary which really did suit Jack's legal mind and background much better. In the local paper I was quoted as saying 'it's always good for a town like Blackburn to have the local MP in the middle of the cabinet'.

Chapter 39

Saving Heritage Things

Mama don't take my Kodachrome away.

'Tayles, what the hell are you doing next Friday evening?' boomed Councillor Jack Fairless, my successor as chairman of the community and leisure committee. I think Jack would be happy, were he still to be alive, to be described as a bon viveur. He'd been a secondary school teacher around town for decades, moving on to become a teacher trainer and had also studied and qualified as a barrister for fun. Like many of us, he had a very patient wife called Olwyn. It must have been 1994, 1995 perhaps. I was deputy leader and in charge of the council's purse strings.

'Just my normal Friday evening, Fally.' (I always called him that. It's a long story why.) 'I'll have two, perhaps three beers with my pals in the pub and then go home for a nice meal that Anne will have cooked.' 'Ah good, instead of beers at the pub, you're coming with me to Peter Worden's house.'

I thought to myself that I didn't really have much time for Peter Worden politically. Peter had been on the council for a few years representing the 'ratepayers' party. He was a bull-necked, ebullient sort of a character who'd had an optician's business in the centre of town for many a long decade. He was a neighbour of Fally's, both occupying huge Victorian brick-built semis in the north of the town.

I wondered why but I trusted Jack. He promised it would be no longer than an hour or so.

I wandered down the road to the Wordens' house. Peter opened the door, turning his head to a non-apparent person, saying 'Bill's here now' and I was ushered in to their high-ceilinged lounge.

'Beer!' It seemed like more of a statement than a question. There was a modest plate of sandwiches on the coffee table.

There was another person there, a senior council officer, I don't remember who. Indeed, like Jack and Peter, the fourth person may well have left us by now.

'Let me show you what I have to show you,' said Peter. The lights were turned down. I had no idea what I was going to be subjected to. There was an old-fashioned film projector on the coffee table, its beam trained on the wall.

The dated projector made a right din as it fluttered and spluttered into action. What transpired before our eyes was phenomenally striking. Old-fashioned film with blobs and scratches, burns and tears depicted life from nearly a century before. It was an indulgent feast of nostalgia of huge social historical significance. Peter Worden changed spool after spool with boyish glee, so pleased was he to display this fortuitous find.

During the interval (no ice creams served) Peter explained in the semidarkness of his front lounge that he had received a phone call a few days before. His story basically was that some guys clearing out the cellar of the former Mercers toy shop in the town centre had come across some milk churn-like containers. One of the workmen inadvertently pushed over one of these containers and out rolled examples of probably one of the greatest historical cinematographic finds of modern times. Rather than simply chuck the containers in the skip stationed outside the shop, the workmen had the insight to 'ask somebody' about them. That somebody happened to know Peter Worden and knew of his keen interest in local history. The first thing Peter assured was safe passage of this potentially unstable and volatile cargo to his home. He then went out and bought a second-hand fridge freezer in which to store the highly flammable material (nitrocellulose or celluloid) in his garage; some 800 films accidentally discovered and miraculously saved.

Soon after its 'completion' I shared a draft of this chapter with Mary Painter, a huge, huge asset to the borough, in charge of community history and ICT at Blackburn Library. I learned there was a potentially controversial alternative 'take' on the story of how the abandoned films were found and saved from extinction. I relate it here, directly from Nigel Garth Gregory and in his own words. Please judge for yourself where the truth lies. Does it matter? These pioneering moving images were saved.

Gregory Audio Visual
Mitchell and Kenyon Films (how they were found) by Nigel Gregory.
From: http://gregoryav.co.uk/the-mitchell-and-kenyon-film-collection/

So in a vain attempt to correct the facts, this is the real story about how Peter Worden came to acquire the films.

Back in 1994 my optician was Peter Worden and during an appointment one day he asked me what I did and I explained that I made videos of weddings and cine to video transfers. I remember to this day him saying to me if you ever get any footage of old Blackburn let me know!

Months went by and one day some old 9.5mm black and white film came in for transfer. I didn't have a projector to do this so Peter lent me his machine. It was then that Peter told me about his involvement with the North-West Film Archives in Manchester and how they restored cine film on to Betacam Video Tape to preserve history for the future generations.

Little did I know that within months the most important find of film history was about to land on my doorstep. In 1994 two Irish workmen were clearing out the basement of a shop called Mercers in Northgate, Blackburn. During the clear-out they came across three milk churns with aluminium tops on them. They looked inside and found hundreds of small spools of 35mm silver nitrate film. The milk churns were put on their wagon with other pieces of scrap metal ready to take to the scrap metal processors less than half a mile from my business. One of the workmen knew that on the way to the Lethbridges' Scrap Metal Processors in Mill Hill, Blackburn, he had seen my shop that advertised Cine Film to Video Conversion. That premise I own and is called Magic Moments Video in Shorrock

Lane, Mill Hill, Blackburn and one of the cine film signs still exists today in 2005.

The workmen stopped and dragged a very heavy churn into my shop and asked me to take a look inside asking, 'Are they any value to you?'

My heart stopped because the first thing I noticed was the strong smell from the 35mm nitrate film and just how much there was of it. I carefully removed a spool from the churn and found myself looking at film from the early 1900s. I was the very first person to look back in time. I was amazed at the quality of the film and quickly realised how important this find was.

What now, I asked myself? – What kind of value do we put on this lot? £50, £500, £5,000, £50,000, or even £5,000,000 or they could quite literally be priceless...

I thought, I know, I'll ask Peter Worden what I should do.

When I rang Peter (who was totally unaware at that time of the find or even where they had been found), the excitement in his voice was all to evident. He said to me that they were either going to be old films made by the Bancroft family or films made by Mitchell and Kenyon. He asked where they were found. I told him and I sensed he had to sit down. After a few seconds with a shaking voice he said, 'Right, listen to me and listen good, we don't want to get these workmen excited or they may realise that the films could be of value, so tell them I will give them £20 if they bring them down for me to look at.' I then made a stipulation with Peter that he must ensure that the films go to the North-West Films Archive for the public domain. He agreed to this and at that point the telephone conversation ended.

Now was the difficult bit; how do I convince the workmen to take it to Peter's? I told them the truth about the films. I told them that they were nitrate film and incredibly dangerous. I even showed them how dangerous it was by setting fire to a small piece of the film. The workmen said that £20 was not a lot to offer and that they couldn't be bothered and asked me for £50 to make it worth their while. I rang Peter again and told him that they wanted £50 and did he want me to pay them and he could settle up with me later. I also asked would the

NWFA pay him back? He said that really wouldn't be a problem, and told me to tell them that they would have to deliver them for £50. In the end the workmen agreed and that was the last I saw or heard about the films until 2004. During the six-year period my understanding is that Peter placed the films in a chest freezer and registered them as the finder with a solicitor. Apparently my understanding is that the law says that if you keep something for six years with no claim made to legally become the owner of the goods. My understanding is this was the only reason Peter kept them in the chest freezer.

In December 2004 (ten years later) an invitation arrived on my doorstep to a gala launch of the Mitchell & Kenyon Film collection at the King George's Hall Blackburn in January 2005. Reading the invitation I noticed the statement that the collection had been found by Peter Worden! – 'That's not right' I thought, and sent an email to the BFI (British Film Institute) telling them of my involvement and how I was saddened by the fact that due recognition owed to me wasn't mentioned. It got worse; the local evening papers wrote articles about the find and again it was 'the hero' Peter who found them…

I now resort to the power of the Internet in the hope that anyone who reads this story will read the true facts about the find of the film, and realise as the mayor of Blackburn said, 'if it wasn't for me the world would most surely have lost the most important piece of English film history forever!', 'the nation owes you a debt of gratitude'.

The BFI described the find as 'the film equivalent of Tutankhamun's treasure'.

Surely it's not too much for me to ask that they put the record straight and present the public with the true facts behind the find instead of the 'fairy story' expressed by others.

Finally: If you have had the opportunity to see what the BFI have painstakingly done with this film footage you along with myself will be in no doubt that they have done a absolutely fantastic job in preserving, restoring and presenting the most important film footage of our time.

Whilst I don't want to take away the fact that Peter Worden did uphold his agreement somewhat, ensuring that the films went in the public domain, I still feel badly let down by Peter Worden for not

*making the full facts of the film find more apparent and for the lack of
fair share in the massive financial benefits he obtained.*

*In short, if it wasn't for my professional knowledge and quick
thinking at the time of the find, these films would have indeed been
'The Lost World of Mitchell and Kenyon', forever.*

Nigel Garth Gregory

The Edwardian films we saw included children walking in a school
playground and women sporting their mill wearing clogs and shawls. The
capturing of these images was designed to encourage those appearing on
film to go and see it later that day at the local fair. Almost no one would
have seen themselves on moving pictures in those days.

There were more historic occasions including one of the unveiling of
the statue of Queen Victoria by her daughter Princess Louise in 1905
and also Blackburn Rovers returning with the 1928 (?) FA Cup.

Most clips of film began with somebody holding a white flag and
gyrating it in a figure of eight pattern. Why? The films were shot with
a hand-cranked camera and similarly projected by a hand-cranked
projector. To make sure that the films were shown at the same speed
they'd been taken, those involved got used to the synchronised timing of
the flag waving.

What we were learning about in Worden's front room was the so-
called lost world of Sagar Mitchell and James Kenyon. Great treasures
had been unearthed and luckily saved. The unspoken question that really
posed itself was what was next?

After our film feast, we briefly discussed what the best next steps
were. We all knew somebody or other. But what to do that was best was
really important. At least we knew (or was it hoped) that the artefacts
were safely stored for perpetuity.

The council officer was charged with ensuring that our treasure trove
was safely despatched into the right professional hands having weighed
up all the potential future avenues.

Mitchell and Kenyon's professional partnership was dissolved in
1922. Kenyon died three years later in 1925, but the business continued
to be based at 40, Northgate, Blackburn. Mitchell must have carefully

stored the films away in his business' cellar. He died, aged eighty-five in 1952 when his son John carried on the business until he retired in 1960. I originally met Terry Walkden on my first Bessey youth work training course in 1974. Terry's mum and dad ran a toy and sports shop at Number 40, probably not knowing of the treasure that had been stored in their cellar. I'm not sure how long they carried on running their business there.

But what happened after our Friday night film soirée? The provenance and painstaking preservation processes took many years and was done under the watchful eye of the British Film Institute and the University of Sheffield who were granted a three-year project to research, catalogue, identify and contextualise the films which appeared totally restored and preserved nearly ten years later. I feel pleased to have in my possession the 2004 176-minute BFI/BBC DVD entitled *The Lost World of Mitchell and Kenyon*. A three-part series similarly entitled *The Lost World of Mitchell and Kenyon* was shown on the BBC in January 2005.

Some years later, in 2014, we travelled to the Dukes Theatre in my old stomping ground of Lancaster to see the play *The Life and Times of Mitchell and Kenyon*. The drama depicted the story, the journey of those films. In the back of my mind there was, perhaps, a quarter of a hope that our Friday night clandestine gathering, some twenty years earlier, might have got some stage production time, but alas it didn't. What did make me really livid was that as well as Lancaster, the play was staged at the Coliseum Theatre in Oldham. But why not Blackburn, why on earth not Blackburn? The discovery, salvation, retention, preservation and final promotion of the discovery there had probably worldwide significance. Blackburn missed a massive opportunity!

*　*　*

We got our first touring caravan, a twelve-footer, in 1981. In 1984 we advanced to a fourteen-footer which seemed like comparative luxury. They were very simple without the frills and uber mod cons of today.

But what the ownership of the caravan gave us was the opportunity, or was it an excuse, to get away at the weekends, bank holidays and two or three weeks in the summer. Of course Anne's school summer holidays were six weeks long but I wasn't blessed with that freedom.

We always tried to include a little bit of 'culture' into our caravanning trips especially when in the UK. These included heritage places like the Ironbridge Gorge Museum, the Black Country Museum and the Beamish Living Museum up in County Durham, all fantastic and hands-on history places, all quite a distance from Blackburn.

But why haven't we got anything like it here in Lancashire, the home of the first Industrial Revolution where Britain's bread hung on Lancashire thread? There was a challenge!

I had an aspiration in my mind to establish the history of the working-class museum right here in Blackburn, my adopted hometown. But where, how, and probably most importantly how much?

There was in the centre of town a very modest textile museum but I was thinking bigger and better than that.

Blackburn was changing fast in many ways. Through my work as a youth worker but also spending so much time in our local schools listening to youngsters I realised that many, perhaps most of our children and young people had little understanding of how their grandparents lives must have been, especially for the Asian community whose ancestors came from 4,000 miles away in the 1960s and 1970s. In the late Victorian and Edwardian period at the turn of the twentieth century most people would have lived in terraced housing with poor heating, no electric, hot running water, or inside toilets, etc.

The Lancashire Saw Company had rehoused themselves in the massive Imperial Mill right on the Leeds-Lancashire Canal on the edge of town. Could we co-locate with them? The Victorian mill was the ideal sympathetic setting.

We tried. We failed. We couldn't assemble the right package to make this viable. So what was plan B?

So OK, what was your plan B, Bill Taylor?

The Internet was established and developing fast, its potential limitless. Could we harness the positive opportunities offered by the worldwide web. Could we create a virtual museum?

2001 saw a successful bid by the Library and Information Service to secure NOF (New Opportunities Fund) funding for digitisation of local history resources. In 2002 work started on building the Cotton Town website.

It was in 2003 that I was proud to publicly launch Cotton Town, using the cutting-edge technology then available.

The project continued after the funding ceased, with the library's Community History staff and volunteers having responsibility for maintenance and development of the site. The site proved to be very popular and well used. However, after ten years, technology had outgrown it and the site could no longer continue and had to be closed down.

A new Cotton Town site was needed in order to enable new developments whilst retaining the old content. The new site was launched in October 2013 and staff and volunteers continued to work on the transfer of articles and images which were held on the original site. In May 2017, a software update was applied which changed the look and feel of the website and vastly improved the efficiency of downloads and response times. (Some of the above text has been taken from the Cotton Town website.)

As the National Community Archives and Heritage Group explained about Cotton Town:

'If you're too young to remember the trams, if you never experienced the thrill of riding the clanging cars on their iron rails, then here's a chance for you to try it out. The site features a virtual reality tram ride to Darwen with an interactive quiz to test your local knowledge. For those of you who prefer a slower pace, there's a trip along the Leeds and Liverpool Canal in the company of a crew and their horse plying their trade along Blackburn's waterway in its early days.

If you have any information, recollections and photographs with reference to the area, or just a story to tell, you can contribute.'

I'm so grateful to those who supported my original idea, the council officers, including Norma Monks, and people in the community such as Ray Smith and Mike Sumner. There is a great team of voluntary workers possibly still called Blackburn Library's Community History section, stewarded by Mary Painter, to whom we are locally and globally indebted.

The Cotton Town website actually now includes audio and perhaps video artefacts including the speech made by Prime Minister Harold Wilson when he opened the town's new library in October 1975.

Although, like many things, Cotton Town had a rocky gestation and infancy, it is now a strong, much used and loved resource.

*   *   *

Soon after arriving in Blackburn, just before the first of the two general elections held in 1974, I was still only 21, I wrote a letter that appeared in the *Lancashire Evening Telegraph*. It was quite left wing in its tone. I cut it out and sent it to my mum. Over the next few years I must have had a dozen or more letters published there. I sent then all to my mum.

One time, when visiting her in Brum, I asked if she read and enjoyed them. 'No, you're just a communist and I'll not read them.' 'So, Mum, no well done, son, good for you for putting pen to paper?' No reply.

I took them off her and brought them home. I think I put them in a folder. I was upset by her response. What did it lead to?

Over the next thirty or forty years whenever I had something in the local or national papers, Labour Party, education, local government or youth work 'trade' publications, I would cut them out and save them. Result? Ten or so lever-arch folders stuffed with over 2,000 press cuttings, many of them from our mayoral year. This was first of all massively nostalgic then as it grew I started to see it as a comprehensive research resource archive. It logged the activity worthy of publication of one guy with many guises. The range of issues covered during the ensuing decades were many fold. Is it a unique catalogue?

I had been pressed, the Rev. Chris Chivers being my lead protagonist, to put pen to paper. 'Your stories are brilliant,' said the clerical thinker, writer and teacher of renown, 'you tell a story with some humour in it, but with a serious message there too, like a parable. You need to capture them. Write a book.'

That was around 2012/13, but I was busy with the college and the NHS. Then I remembered the lever-arch folder mountain. I could use those to stimulate my memory of all the things that had happened. But also I thought they were a rich resource in themselves, perhaps.

Not knowing really the size of the task or its complexity, I got the go ahead to explore this from the then principal Ian Clinton. This led to an initial exploratory meeting with the head of higher education IT (information technology) Katrina MacFarlane (now PhD and then successfully plying her trade teaching masters' students at the University of Sunderland and now Manchester). Katrina's transformation was totally due to the college. After fifteen years at a local computer firm, she studied and was successful, achieving a good BSc in 2004. She got some part-time hours at the college, took the teaching qualification known as the PGCE (Post Graduate Certificate of Education) and quite quickly made her way through the ranks. The beauty of Dr Katrina was like many others at the time at the college, she was a Blackburn person, had experienced personal adversity and beaten it.

I told her my ideas in her office. Later, after a two-hour meeting, her colleagues wanted to know what she'd done wrong to warrant such a lengthy meeting with the chair.

She came up with a plan and we met again. The plan was simple, using degree-level students to design an interactive website and incorporate my press cuttings into it.

But it wouldn't start immediately as in 2014-2016 we were moving house twice, refurbishing our hopefully final house and our first grandchildren were imminent. 'Oh dear, that's a lot on your plate as well as your college and NHS roles. Come back when you're a bit less committed.'

That was two years later when Katrina introduced me to Mick Seedall, a member of staff, local home-grown as was Katrina. Mick explained the plan and what was going to happen. I think it was at this point that I asked if I should make some financial contribution but was told this was a great opportunity for the college and any students who contributed to it. They would identify capable and trustworthy degree students to the work. This resulted in Sarah, later joined by fellow student Sean, cracking on with the work. We met every couple of months to discuss the project along with a new project leader Stuart Gregory. It looked really promising. Both Mick and Stuart had followed the same transformational road as Katrina. When she was going off to Sunderland we met to hand the reins over to her successor Caroline Bracewell. I think they were over halfway through when initially Covid put things on hold.

*   *   *

It will not come as any surprise to people who know me but one of my favourite things to do is while away time with people, old friends and new, and listen to their stories and perhaps occasionally impose one of mine on them, usually preferably over a pint.

One such character is Howard Talbot, who could tell a tale or two or three or… these were normally transacted sat at the bar in Blackburn Golf Club where Howard would meet up with his old sparring partner Tom Taylor. Tom has sadly left us now but I can see his likeness in his grandson Matt Taylor, the BBC weatherman.

So who is Howard Talbot (himself now sadly gone), son of Wally and husband of Nonny? Cotton Town tells us:

'Wally Talbot and his son, Howard, were Blackburn-based photographers working in the areas of press, sport and commercial photography from the 1930s through to the 1990s. Wally Talbot was born in 1914 and at the age of fourteen he started work as a "printer's devil" at the *Northern Daily Telegraph* (now *The Lancashire Telegraph*). He was to become one of the paper's first staff photographers. When the Second World War started he joined the RAF as an aircraftsman. He flew over enemy lines before and during bombing raids, identifying targets and taking photographs of the raids. He was also involved in taking public relations photographs which showed how the war was being won in order to send a positive message back home. He met celebrities such as George Formby who were entertaining the troops. Celebrities, military leaders and royalty alike were captured on film by Wally, and later, by Howard.'

After the war, Wally returned to the *Telegraph* for a few years before taking the decision to set up his own business. He worked from home using his son Howard's bedroom as a dark room, and the bathroom for developing. When the photographs were ready they were sent by train to Manchester for use in the major regional and national papers.

Howard continued with the business after Wally retired. When Wally died in 1994, Howard deposited their large collection of press and commercial negatives plus exhibition photographs in Blackburn Library.'

But it was during our lengthy bar discussions that I can offer you greater context and texture to these facts.

I think most people would say Taylor can talk a bit but to be frank in comparison to Howard I am virtually taciturn. Howard is one of those guys that for almost every random conversation topic he's got a story, always interesting, normally hilarious. They gave him a slot on BBC local Radio Lancashire to reminisce about himself and the family business. I think they filled three half-hour programmes crammed with anecdotes about sport, weddings, celebrities, photography tricks, poignant moments and deflating the more pompous.

I said to him one time, I think he was describing sending some cameras to auction at Sotheby's and Christie's in London, 'Tal, what are you gonna do with all the stories and all these photographs? They are unique. Since 1928, Wally, then you, have been snapping, depicting and reflecting East Lancashire. That's around eighty years worth of national, local and family events, history, characters. They simply can't be lost.'

'Well, I sometimes make a few bob out of a photograph I've still got, mainly of the footballers. I sometimes get twenty-five quid to let them use them in some book or other.'

I think he most enjoyed telling stories that included his dad in them. He told one where Wally turned up back at the pictures section in the offices of the local paper to find a young apprentice smashing some original glass negatives in the storeroom. The highly respected, revered and feared pro photographer enquired of the boy, in quite basic terms, as to what he was doing. The lad has been told to make space for 'new stuff' and to him this meant chucking out what he perceived to be the 'old stuff'.

We were told that Wally went crackers, gave the lad a clip round the ear and told him to leave. I paraphrase a little. Wally then boxed up the priceless images and took them home for safe storage. They presumably are still stored safe and sound.

Long before the digital era, Wally and Howard took photographs usually at Ewood Park where professional football matches were staged. Howard explained that time was tight and the negatives had to be on the train to Manchester for printing in the Saturday evening sports paper, so they had to quit the ground before the end of the game.

So it was, out of the ground, a quick drive to the studios and into the darkroom, do the processing and then another even quicker drive to Blackburn railway station. Sometimes the train had actually set off and the guard was hanging out the rear door waiting for Howard to sprint down the platform putting the negatives in safe hands. One time this was unsuccessful, so Howard had to spin round, race back to the car being driven by his dad and travel at speed to the next station down the line at Darwen some five miles away. Quite a different scenario to that of today when one send click of a JPEG will transport the images instantly around the world.

'Yes, but Howard, what are you going to do with all this?' I insisted.

'I don't bloody know. Have you got any bright ideas? You usually do.'

'Leave it with me. I'll have a think.'

At the time, of course, I was no longer on the council but was chairman of the board at the college. The college has IT students, photography students and history students. It made sense to try and combine all those talents and studies. I concocted a plan and shared it with Ian Clinton the college principal at the time. He more or less let me get on with it.

Like most good things this all took time and once again I am indebted to Cotton Town:

It was always the intention of Blackburn Library to digitise the collection but a partnership initiated in 2015 by Sir Bill Taylor with the Talbot family, The University Centre, Blackburn College and Blackburn Library introduced a dynamic, committed and talented combination of staff and students working on the BA (Hons) photography degree course who relished the opportunity to work on this singularly unique collection of images. Fate sometimes plays a deft hand and one person in particular deserves mention, Peter Graham. In his own words Peter recalls:

'I have grown up with photography really, my brother Paul Graham who is ten years older than me has been in the profession all his working life. Watching my brother working during the 1970s and 1980s, I met both Wally and Howard Talbot on many occasions, and I was lucky to see them both at work. A family portrait we have was taken by Wally. I was always amazed and watched in wonder as the films used to appear, as if by magic, in the darkroom. Since than I have had a fascination in photography and an even bigger fascination in local history, so once the Talbot Archive started to appear and I got a chance to work with it, it was a dream come true.'

I got to know and respect Peter well. He's a top guy.

What was the road that we took? After possibly a year or two of browbeating and badgering Howard we eventually convened a meeting in one of the rooms at the central library. Howard had no idea what I was going to say and frankly neither did I. But I do remember promising him tea and biscuits.

We spoke through the situation; how we got to where we were and what we should do next. The bones of a plan began to emerge. Like most ambitious and inspiring aspirations it would work best if we could take people with us engaging, inspiring and empowering them. Howard, eventually, got his biscuits (I sent someone with a fiver to Marks and Sparks nearby) and we left council and college staff to move the project on.

Three or four years after the meeting in the library with Peter Graham (having gained a first class honours and begun to study for a masters) at the helm, the W and H Talbot Archive was flourishing. My badgering and browbeating and the great hard-working creative people who are taking the project on is coming along just fine. I think there are 40,000 photographic images to process and taxonomise? What a loss that would that have been!

*   *   *

How poor would the world be if the Mitchell and Kenyon films had been skipped, Cotton Town hadn't been created and the Talbot images had been lost to the world? We've yet to see about my research resource archive entrusted to the college. At the moment, halfway through the process, the college first of all suspended this creative process and has currently terminated it, after the hundreds, thousands of hours I freely gave. Shortsighted, in my opinion. Similarly the Talbot Archive needs attention and some serious funding to get firmly established.

Chapter 40

Is it Something That You Said? New Challenges –
Transforming the College into a Twenty-First Century Powerhouse

Everything put together, sooner or later falls apart.

Things, perhaps only on the surface, moved along for me quite well during this (2006-2013) period. I'd finished on the council in 2004 and got 'retired' from work in 2006. I was then only fifty-four.

I began a regular article for the *Lancashire Telegraph* entitled 'Is it something that you said?'

What sparked off each column was something I overheard or witnessed as I wandered around. I wrote these for around eight or nine years and enjoyed doing them and the positive feedback I received. Topics included: my Uncle George and the role of Remembrance Sunday, a piece about a chair in Mark Smith's Coffee Exchange and about all the different people who sat on it during one day, one entitled 'Pomp and Circumstance' where I discussed great state occasions such as funerals and weddings and their role in modern British society, leadership and negotiating skills, Ramadan and the role of world religions and childhood holidays. I wrote about 200 or more, all for free.

I was also commissioned (for free, naturally) to review the odd play or concert that we visited. Ironically one starring Richard Wilson (aka Victor Meldrew) playing the government chief whip in a play at the Lowry Theatre entitled *Whipping It Up*. Not a great stage classic. I summarised the play as the plot being predictable and the pace pedestrian. I covered other plays around the north-west and gigs such as (25 per cent of) 10cc, The Police, Paul Simon. Things I'd go to anyway. I felt as though I was John Anson's (*Telegraph*'s Features Editor) understudy.

Mark Smith is an interesting character, a local entrepreneur, who cut his retail teeth as a teenager on Todmorden market, he told me. Hoping to have become an accountant he now owns a string of fantastic coffee shops, much better than the national chains, known as the Coffee Exchange. He also supplies a great deal of coffee across the region to hotels, restaurants and pubs.

The adage that there is no such thing as a free meal can be applied to cups of coffee too.

Around 2007, I was invited by the Rev. Mike Wedgeworth (later MBE) for a coffee in the Blackburn branch for a chat. I've known Mike for many years. Likeable and principled, he'd begun his local government life in Barnsley at the height of the miners' strike, then he came over the Pennines and his roles included being chief executive of neighbouring Hyndburn Council. He then also became a minister of the Church of England and progressed his post-career career within the church. He became a 'high-up' in the cathedral in Blackburn. At the time he was involved in the governance of the NHS and chairman of the board at Blackburn College.

Like most conversations it began with a bit of small talk. How are the kids? What are you up to? Have you had any holidays, etc.?

Then Mike explained that he was intending giving up the chairmanship of the board and that he'd taken soundings and they thought they had found the right person to take over. 'Great,' say I, 'I hope it all works well.'

'We hope so,' said Mike. Don't you wonder, as these conversations are being introduced, who the theys and the wes are?

'Because I'm currently talking to the guy we think is the best person for the job.' I felt I should look around for whoever Mike was intimating but then I realised the guy was me.

Like most things, I had never really thought about becoming the chair of the college. With a break caused by Tory legislation increasing private sector representation on college boards, I'd been on since 1981, at the time of talking with Mike that totalled around seventeen to eighteen years (twenty-six or so eventually). I had always taken my attendance at board meetings and subcommittee meetings seriously and participated fully in what were often very lengthy (two full days) senior staff recruitment processes. I tried to get myself actually around the college a bit, getting a sense of the feel of the place – how the students and all the staff were feeling. But my intentions or aspirations to get more heavily involved went little beyond that.

I told Mike I'd think about it, talk to key people and get back to him with a decision. The college was a big organisation spending over £40 million a year with 15,000 students in many different disciplines and over 1,000 staff. It needed somebody who would take the job seriously, throw themselves at it with commitment and application. There were those who thought attending some of the four or five board meetings a year was all that was required. They reminded me of an infamous pupil at Shadsworth High who travelled by bus to school, hopped off, got his mark and then hopped back on the same bus as it waited to set off on time at the terminus.

I made it my business to talk at home, to some of the senior staff but also people who I knew around the organisation – teachers, support staff and the blue-collar workers.

I got back to Mike within a couple of weeks. I told him I'd give it a whirl.

At the next board meeting I was proposed and voted in as chairman, a position I was to hold for the next eight years. The world of FE (Further Education) and HE (Higher Education), but more specifically its governance, was still pretty new to me. A familiar sounding story for me.

Governance in the world of education was quite different to that in local government. In local government, our actions as local councillors were both influenced and legitimised by the democratic endorsement of the ballot box. As chair of the college this process was influenced by more consensual processes. The principal and his or her staff held quite a lot of de jure and de facto power in that they were there all the time. As governors and as chair, our role was to try and bring positive influence to this heady cocktail. In local government there were apparent discernible lines drawn in that people were organised in political parties. But don't forget the old adage that in politics your opposition is in front of you but your enemies are behind you! On the governing body there were times when individuals' personal, sometimes covert, agendas shaped the way they spoke, acted and voted, although issues rarely came to actual vote. Some senior staff thought and acted like the college was theirs to run and governors a necessary evil to endure.

As chair of the college you don't always have any real say in the composition or complexion of its membership. There were people on the board who knew little about the ethnically diverse communities served by the college, knew little about state education, knew little about the vast range of educational and aspirational strata amongst the students. We had students from every ethnic background, of all sorts of different ages and abilities from those with severe literacy challenges through to those wanting to get to university and beyond. There were four, possibly five, full board meetings every year. Some board members barely managed a minimal degree of attendance. If you missed the meeting it would mean not knowing what was going on for a period of six months which is pretty critical in the life of a dynamic people-to-people organisation. Serving on the board shouldn't be designed to fill a line on a CV or satisfy egotistical needs.

There were some great board members: John Thomas, with decades of experience running NHS facilities locally; Jack Straw and Phil Watson; Lesley Wareing, academic registrar at our partner university at Lancaster; Garth Hodkinson, chief exec of the local voluntary organisation 'umbrella', the Council for Voluntary Service; Mo Isap a local successful entrepreneur, staff rep Gill Piper and Stephanie Anforth in charge of apprenticeships at BAE Systems.

In my eyes the college wasn't an educational establishment. It was probably the biggest engine of personal development and social mobility the borough had. We could offer people dreams and the capacity to fulfil them.

I tried to make Mondays my 'college day'. I would have an hour, more if needed, with the principal and any other people thought necessary.

The annual strategic seminar, an overnighter affair held at Astley

Bank, a local training centre, always began with a 'state of the college' input from the chairman. As is my way, my PowerPoint presentation was usually a mixture of serious and fun. I can recall quotes from Nelson Mandela, Mahatma Gandhi, Steve Jobs, Jagger and Richards, Heraclitus, General George Patton and Mickey Mouse being used.

At one event I launched my Paradigm of Governance. The graphic displayed a diagram split into three vertically. In the left-hand third, shaded red, governance wasn't assuring the minimum, that is that the basics, finance, legals, HR, health and safety, educational standards, etc., weren't being monitored and met. In the third on the right, again shaded red, was governance by micromanagement, over interference in those matters that were clearly the role of day-to-day and strategic management. The middle third in green, is where ideal governance operates, all the basics were covered, governors didn't stray into the role of management but did explore the imaginative/creative middle ground of retention and recruitment of both staff and students, driving up standards of teaching and the teaching environment (buildings, etc.), promoting the profile of the college; the things that make a real difference.

I told one seminar that good public services governance requires commitment, vision and stamina to which I think we now had to add courage and leadership. I must have been saying some of the right things in the right places because quite soon I was the regional governor rep on the Association of Colleges and soon after that was the rep at the National Association meetings held regularly in London. This got Blackburn College firmly on the regional and national college map. Our Ofsted rating was the top 'Outstanding'. Principal Ian Clinton ran a very tight ship, not always popular but people always knew where they stood with him. He had an excellent senior management team and his curriculum heads throughout the college were top-notch too. I very much appreciated Caroline Wilson's administrative support. Ian Clinton's PR/media team led by Claire Berry was good and maintained a high profile for the college. We played to each other's strengths intuitively.

I pretty soon worked out that the FE/HE terrain was a fairly hostile dog-eat-dog environment. We had to have the best possible staff, achieving the best possible results, in the best possible teaching/learning atmosphere.

Our estate, the buildings, were not of the highest quality. Listening to teachers who had been there a long time, they could remember teaching in the wooden huts scattered about the campus or old church halls in the locality.

We embarked upon a total transformation of the campus getting rid of old buildings, refurbishing some saveable buildings and building others brand new. Ian Barker and Derek Heap led much of this work with flair with the finances under close scrutiny by director of finance, Jane McCann.

The original Victoria Building was the first base of the college opened by the Prince of Wales in 1888. Around a hundred years later in 1986, I welcomed and hosted HRH Princess Anne in her capacity as president of the Save the Children fund to receive a fundraising cheque on behalf of the Sudan famine crisis. As I bade her farewell and saw her to her car, she commented on what a magnificent building the Victoria was and that it should be preserved. We did just that.

In March 1984 Labour's national education spokesman, Neil Kinnock, came to Blackburn and opened the new art and design building. This was later reconfigured as the central management building to be named the Harrison Centre. It was going to be called the Kathleen Ferrier Centre but some staff kicked off, not wanting to work in the KFC.

In 1970 when I wended my weary way up from the A6 to Lancaster University, their campus then played host to some 3,000 undergraduates. The degree courses with the qualifications being awarded by Lancaster University but taught on Blackburn campus gathered pace. And by the twenty-first century we also had 3,000 undergraduates being taught locally. The university centre was opened in 2009 when I invited Jack Straw, the then Blackburn Rovers manager Sam Allardyce and the North West Regional Development Agency chief exec, Steve Broomhead, to perform the opening ceremony. Two years previously Archbishop (of York) John Sentamu had opened our new sixth-form centre known as the St Paul's Centre.

The construction centre facing the main road, Montague Street, had been built a few years earlier but now we needed a centre to house all our FE students. I coined the phrase Beacon Centre, wanting it to attract students to it. I'd hoped to have a flickering real flame on its roof to send out a clear message to all of our townsfolk. I was told that the council put a planning consent kibosh on what I thought was rather imaginative symbolism. The Beacon Centre cost over £18 million and was opened by me in February 2012, assisted by Amelia Lily, a TV *X Factor* finalist. The young singer did an hour-long gig afterwards and enthralled a packed student audience, including a phenomenal version of 'Ain't No Mountain High Enough'!

Earlier that day I had had the privilege of welcoming the international, European and World medal-winning pole-vaulter and former Blackburn Harrier, Holly Bradshaw (nee Bleasdale) to both open the Everybody Young Person's Resource Centre just off Barbara Castle Way but also to talk with some of our aspiring athletes and sports workers about her lifestyle and career. Both Amelia and Holly were comparatively shy, self-effacing young people when chatting but when plying their chosen and contrasting careers, they were transformed into polished performers.

I had both hips replaced in 2012 and 2013 after enduring two years of excruciating pain, masked by Tramadol. I guess I was off the scene for at least six to nine months, during which time my new vice chairman and friend Phil Watson CBE had swung the demolition ball, aided and abetted by local man but regular contender for the World's Strongest Man, Mark Felix, on the 1960s-built and expensive to run Feilden Street building. Monday meetings were later temporarily transferred to my house where, in our living room, I was updated on the governance of the college.

When fully recovered, pain free and more mobile again, I returned to actually chair board meetings. It was during one that Phil Watson interceded to propose that the new STEM building (Science, Technology, Engineering and Maths) should be called the Sir Bill Taylor Futures Building. I was taken aback but also quietly pleased and proud.

Two more new buildings were yet to grace the campus. The RATH and the new sports centre.

RATH stands for Regional Automotive Technology Hub. It was designed to finish off the improvement of the frontage of Montague

Street, a major thoroughfare through the town which now links up with the Wainwright Bridge (named after the Blackburn resident, council employee and famous Lakeland walker and illustrated guidebook author) and Barbara Castle Way. Wikipedia incorrectly attributes the opening of the RATH to Blackburn lad Carl 'Foggy' Fogarty MBE, four-time World Superbike Champion. He was indeed there, but the building was officially opened by Phil Watson CBE, the college vice-chairman and former council chief executive. Phil is Blackburn born and bred. From humble beginnings, he attended Queen Elizabeth's Grammar School and then went off to university in Sheffield to study architecture. He then got a job back in the architect's department in the town hall where he worked for the rest of his working life. Phil is a good bloke, absolutely committed to his hometown. Whilst an architect, Phil was responsible, he tells us, for the design of many of the council houses in the borough. His career advanced until in around 1997 he became the chief executive seeing the council back to operating as an upper tier 'unitary' authority.

Phil's career was exemplary, he was a team player but knew when it was time to take leadership too. I don't think he got full recognition for the pivotal role he played both whilst working for the council, representing the council on the national stage and after his retirement assuming other roles; at the government office north-west, within the NHS and at the college too. Checking it out with the more prominent governors first, I then invited Phil to perform the opening ceremony accompanied by his wife, Shirley. I thought it was right and fitting.

When Phil decided, possibly prematurely, to retire as the council's chief exec, his shoes were more than adequately filled first by (Scouser and Evertonian) Graham Burgess who came to the post from a social work background. Graham, in his turn, was succeeded by accountancy qualified and experienced (Mancunian and Red fan) Harry Catherall. Although not local residents, these guys were also great for the council and the borough.

There's now a new person in post, Denise Park, again promoted through the ranks, finance this time. I don't really know her but I hear good things of her. BwD has been blessed, at the top and right across the council, with many, many great senior officers. Another top officer,

Andrew Lightfoot, got poached and has rightfully flourished working in Manchester.

The final new build proved to be more troublesome. Way back in the 1980s we were imaginative and bold enough to build a water fun centre in Blackburn. We called it Waves which I opened as chairman of the committee in 1987. With its slides, flumes and a massive wave-generating machine, it drew people from across the north-west of England.

For reasons never communicated to me but I think mainly based on cost, the council decided that Waves needed demolishing and replacing. That was the easy bit. More complex was what to replace it with and where.

With the demolition of the Feilden Street building came the demise of the college's sports hall. Being forty or fifty years old it really did need replacing. The council approached the college to see if a collaboration would work and could be negotiated. It started to feel like the Shadsworth syndrome from forty years before whereby two organisations, purportedly developing and delivering resourced services to the same people, that is local citizens, couldn't agree. The theory was that the college needed space to deliver its sports courses, mainly ten o'clock until 4 p.m. The council wanted mainly a new swimming pool with a toddler facility and some sports space for its many clubs and other sporting activities, mainly in the evenings and at weekends and in the school holidays. So a shared facility seemed to fit and make sense. Pro temps, I fronted the negotiations with Blackburn's brand-new town centre-based Youth Zone for interim shared use of their facilities for our students.

Witton Country Park, about a mile or so west of the town centre, is a massive 480-acre facility. It's home to an all-weather athletics track, cafe, various children's play areas, lots of football/cricket pitches, and two all-weather sports pitches; it's used by cyclists, horse riders, dog walkers, ramblers, the annual funfair, bonfire, fetes, model airplane flyers, you name it.

The council had an aspiration to locate the new facility right next to the running track. There was a lot of sense in this as it would enhance those facilities already there. They mooted with the senior management of the college to co-locate the intended facility in Witton Park.

There must have been months of behind-the-scenes meetings and negotiations, but nothing was being firmed up. They couldn't even agree on what the facility would be called; the college saw it as a sports facility, the council as a leisure facility. Senior college staff saw the distance, perhaps a mile between the main campus and Witton Park, as an irresolvable negative. Witton Park was council-owned land, the other proposed site was right in the middle of the college campus. The council was the planning authority. This was starting to look like a power tussle. As a board we were pretty much kept in the dark over the detail.

The council, having demolished Waves, now had a pretty extensive tract of land not far from the college or the town centre. I suggested to the principal and his senior staff team that we did a land swap with the council; the new facility could be built on what was college land if we were given the former Waves site (now another town centre multi-screen cinema) to build more college buildings. That seemed like a win-win to me. That didn't appear to have any traction and, looking back, I don't think the council invested sufficient senior council officers' or councillors' presence and profile on the Witton Park idea.

So it was that in 2014, the twin-logoed Blackburn Sports and Leisure Centre was opened by me as college chair and Kate Hollern as leader of the council. In attendance was the Olympic double-Gold-medal-winning swimmer Rebecca Adlington OBE. Chatting with her during the day I was astounded to find out that she was born (in 1989) two years after I had opened Waves!

Blackburn College certainly moved on with nine brand-new twenty-first-century buildings being planned, funded and constructed over about an eight-year period. By the end of this period of rapid expansion costing over £60 million there was only the original 1888 Victoria Building left and we still had plans for that.

What people need to understand and appreciate is that FE and HE colleges all begin with no income. All income is bums on seats generated. Every student comes with an income tariff that varies depending on what course they are following. All these students, in Blackburn's case some 15,000, had all their combined income tariffs aggregated together as the college income. A good college, and in Blackburn's case we were Ofsted

Outstanding, needs a good teaching environment that promotes both student and staff recruitment, the best possible teaching and management staff, a good, attractive broad curriculum, good student results, robust and resilient finances and the best possible governing body. To get all that in place, in the right order, with the right balance is a complex juggling process as all people-to-people organisations are.

Our ambitious and attractive new building programme had to be funded by borrowing money as would any other business. Here we were extremely foresighted to have Paul Levet on the board. Paul was a former assistant corporate director and relationship director with a big five (or is it four these days?) bank. This involved larger business financing including project finance and public company relationship management. From 2004 until 2011, he led the bank's education team in the north-west. His experience and guidance was invaluable.

So what of the old Victoria Building? It had had substantial structural and some cosmetic attention to make it safe and sound. But next door to it the fantastic training restaurant Scholars, the catering and baking departments and others such as hair and beauty were housed in a much more modern building known as the New Victoria Building. Rather unimaginative really. Until WGT had one of his inspirational brainwaves!

Queen Victoria reigned from 1837 until 1901, sixty-three years and 216 days in total. The reigning monarch, Elizabeth II, broke that longevity record. Indeed Elizabeth broke her great-great-grandmother's record on 9 September 2015. Elizabeth reigned for over two thirds of a century. Surely that had little to do with the college?

In an air of some secrecy, I took it upon myself to write to Buckingham Palace seeking royal permission so that on the reign record-busting day of 9 September 2015, the New Victoria Building would be no more.

Buckingham Palace kindly replied giving their consent that the new name for the building would be the Elizabeth Building.

On the very day, attended by every student and member of staff whose names included either Victoria or Elizabeth, I performed, in the presence of the current mayor and former Shadsworth pupil of mine Faryad Hussain and his mayoress wife, Parveen, the renaming ceremony which made the front page of FE and general education/local government trade magazines across the country. The PR coup brought a little smile of satisfaction to my face, a simple idea that hardly cost a penny and got us on the front pages with very positive publicity.

Having joined Blackburn College as principal in 2004, it had been early 2013 when Ian Clinton announced his intention to resign. Our five-plus-year mutually respectful partnership as principal and chair proved to be hugely beneficial and successful for the college in its entirety and beyond. I think he actually left us at Christmas. It seemed a long goodbye. Ian continued to be a principal, including stints in Shropshire and Northumbria. He gained an OBE very soon after his departure from Blackburn. We assessed how to use the opportunity of this vacancy in the best interests of the college. Various models of management structure were considered, a job description was drawn up and the process began. At the end of it, we appointed Dr Thomas Moore from a college in Scotland and he took up his post sometime in early 2014. There was quite a substantial 'interregnum' period and I felt it my responsibility to be around a little bit more to support those shouldering the interim arrangements. Existing staff, many of the most talented, visionary, long-standing and hard-working staff from senior management down through the college's curriculum leaders and key support staff started to leave, many following the excellent former vice principal Lisa O'Loughlin to Manchester College. I believe in total the number of émigrés exceeded sixty. The number and range of this institutional diaspora accelerated, many advancing their careers, seeking and gaining promotions to the very highest positions regionally and nationally.

From my time and observation locally in Blackburn and in the regional and national roles I performed, it was becoming obvious that the world of FE and colleges generally was going to get tougher as 'austerity' kicked in. I'd always thought that adopting the ostrich position left you vulnerable for a kick up the backside. I initiated protracted and delicate talks about collaboration with our neighbouring catholic college, St Mary's and across East (now badged as Pennine) Lancs with Accrington and Rossendale, Nelson and Colne and Burnley colleges. Blackburn is by far the biggest and most complex of these institutions and I feel progress was hampered as the others doubted our motives, assuming they were acquisitional. We aimed to be open and honest in our dealings. It became apparent that others were probably less so. Their fortunes have varied in the years since. St Mary's is to close all together, the other local colleges co-collaborated, Blackburn excluded.

I carried on in this strange atmosphere at the college. It was taking more and more of my voluntary time and getting increasingly difficult to lead. Some weeks I would be in the college every single weekday, sometimes for many hours. One Friday night I left the college around 7 p.m. and my car was the only one left in the car park. It was that stark realisation that made me start to question my role at the college. I'm afraid that once these doubts and questions were in my mind I started to seriously weigh up my options. I thought I would look for an appropriate lull in the college's cycle when I could take my chance to resign. My thoughts were that I really wasn't getting the support from some senior college staff that is important to foster good governance. The governing body wasn't unified with a common purpose, for which I must shoulder some responsibility. It felt like two or three of the governing body had some kind of personal vendetta against me, justified or not. I knew in my heart of hearts that it was time to go. I discussed things at home and then we went away for a week's break. I had already composed my letter of resignation.

I made all this clear to Phil Watson, the vice-chair, and he, to his credit, tried to convince me to stay. But I think once you're thinking about going, it's probably already time to go. So, one Friday afternoon in February 2016, from Spain I pushed the send button on my pre-prepared resignation email. That simple act seemed to lift a great burden from my shoulders.

I'm sure that those who hadn't fully supported the board's general direction probably felt victorious and vindicated. I had tried to bring my skills and experience to the college *pro bono* for over a quarter of a century. I think my emotional intelligence, or is it literacy, brought organisational and leadership benefits to what is a very complex and delicate organisation with policies, people and practices that all had to be juggled very carefully.

Jack Straw, no longer the MP but long-standing fellow board member, was quoted saying 'He has been chairman for some years and has fulfilled the role with great distinction. He has guided the college successfully through a period of great change and he is a great loss to the college'.

Hope Barnes, the president of the Students' Union, we still keep in touch years later (she went on to work for Shelter), wrote to me immediately my letter of resignation was circulated to the board. I have her permission to share her words here. My first read made me cry, the second smile:

> *Hi Bill,*
>
> *I'm regretfully writing this email to say you will be sorely missed by me and I'm sure the SU team when it becomes news; obviously right now it is to board members only and I won't be saying anything.*
>
> *A lot has gone on and I don't really want to get in to it or even care about it. You have done a lot for Blackburn College and I just want to thank you.*
>
> *I started in October and you were probably the person I was most nervous to meet. I had heard how lovely you were and all your other achievements. But I don't know why I was nervous because you made me feel at ease straightaway and you were so lovely to me.*
>
> *I hope you are having a lovely holiday, I'm sure it's much needed!*
>
> *I am very saddened by the news and knowing that you were in a students' union when you were younger. I will leave you with the promise to keep fighting for students' rights and work hard to make Blackburn College the place to be.*
>
> *You truly are an inspiration to me and many others*
> *Love with all my heart!*
> *Hope Barnes*

I'd, as usual, invested my full passion and emotion into the college, met so many fabulous students, staff, teaching, admin and management, the caretakers, catering and cleaning staff. I hope they fare well.

I got a letter of thanks from Phil Watson. He suggested a bit of a do. I declined. It would be too emotional for me and some who turned up may only do so to gloat?

I sent in a bottle of single malt and two huge bouquets of flowers for the principal and his two vice principals with a simple but heartfelt message, 'Best Wishes for the Future'. I never heard a thank you or anything further from them or the college. Lots of qualifications, no emotional intelligence?

Phil took over as chairman and at the end of his three-year incumbency saw through a further change in principal when Dr Fazal Dad took over during 2019. The former head of Westholme, a fee-paying school mainly for girls, Lilian Croston, became the chair. I wish them all well.

Chapter 41

2008 and Onwards, With NHS Too

Medicine is magical and magical is art.

After the council and finishing work I had quite a nice time picking and choosing what projects I fancied doing. I had set up a public service improvement consultancy company initially called Complete Achievement (a heraldic and slightly pompous choice by me?) which I changed to Improve your Council and it did well. This was a great opportunity to reinvest what I had learned back into other, sometimes struggling, councils, their public, members and officers and key stakeholders and partners but I think with all consultancy work there might be a time-limited shelf life, as after four or five years the phone stopped ringing. I enjoyed it especially seeing new ideas and approaches dawning on people's faces.

*   *   *

As you'll understand, initially I was only engaged very marginally on the college governors and picking up advisory consultative work with councils up and down the country.

The college had gone from strength to strength under Ian Clinton's leadership and that continued at pace with the new principal/chair partnership he and I forged. I never really discerned whether we liked each other, but that doesn't impact on establishing and developing good governance. A sense of 'professional' respect and also knowing that there is a line between professional and governance leadership are musts. We hosted a national conference at Blackburn College to celebrate but mainly to cascade to the forty colleges in attendance what we had done and what we had learned in becoming an OFSTED Outstanding Grade 1 assessed institution. I was also asked to provide support to weaker colleges, especially chairs and their governance. This developmental supportive role is one I've played across many aspects of public services.

We tried never to miss opportunities to promote the college to enhance its profile locally not just amongst potential students and their families but the wider community too. Any building opening, award ceremony or charity fundraising event would always get good coverage in either the local press or the general and trade media. One idea of mine was to invite all the half dozen mayors from East Lancashire, which we considered to be our student recruitment hinterland, to an evening meal in our fantastic training restaurant known as Scholars and 'fronted' by hospitality tutor Louise Ashworth. Here the six mayors were treated to a nice meal and given £500 to spend in their council area on young people's issues. They could choose. Three months later they were invited back to Scholars once again with the winners in their districts of the £500. Each mayor would report back on who they were and why and then the winning young people would explain how they were going to use the money to best effect. This gave several opportunities for us to show off the work of East Lancashire's biggest FE and HE institution and several bites of the cherry to broadcast our work via the pages of the more localised newspapers in each community. That's probably a double, treble or more whammy!

I organised a similar trick, this time involving our main local Members of Parliament. These included Jack Straw, who was on the board of the college, Janet Anderson, Greg Pope and Nigel Evans. Nigel had been the MP for neighbouring Ribble Valley since 1992 and we knew each other pretty well from my Ribble Valley professional connections. Janet and Greg were both parents and had their experience of their children's post-16 education. I think each of these MPs had their eyes opened to the diversity, quality and success of the provision that Blackburn College offered.

The format for our VIP guests was similar for each of them. A tour around bits of the college in action, a bite to eat with me and senior staff in our Scholars training restaurant and then a kind of mini question time where each specific MP addressed and was quizzed by some of their constituents or future constituents. Nigel Evans, with two stints as Deputy Speaker of the House of Commons, is an affable guy. As we finished eating, he thanked me for inviting him but asked me directly why we would meet students afterwards. When I told him we had many-fold the number of his constituents or potential constituents studying at the college as there were at Clitheroe Royal Grammar School sixth form, I think he was quite taken aback. The question and answer-style session usually lasted about an hour and I think to call the exchanges frank would be fair.

I left my 'Chairmans-hip' of the college board with the college in top condition:

+ Ofsted – Outstanding,
+ a fantastic £60 million-plus state of the art twenty-first-century campus,
+ being held in high regard for the training and educating thousands of local and beyond sixteen-plus-year-olds, by their families and communities, local schools, employers and other key players and partners,
+ awaiting a decision on FDAP (Foundation Degree Awarding Powers) – I put a lot of time and effort into supporting this lengthy and rigorous process of submission that would give the college the ability to offer flexible first stage higher education (I never heard of what fate it met),
+ a robust financial situation with rigorous accounting systems,
+ the college very much on the national scene and a high profile 'team' player regionally.

* * *

I'd been used to this approach of identifying, celebrating and disseminating good and best practice. We had hosted a similar meeting for local education authorities whilst I was chairman of the education committee and also when we got our Excellent Comprehensive Performance Assessment rating for the council. We had also been key players and I was the national lead on children and young people's issues on the National Improvement Forum where nationally prominent local government councillors and officers met and hammered out issues and policies with senior Whitehall civil servants and Cabinet Ministers. Rather than always traipsing down to London, I asked and got them to our town for once, to the fabulous conference facilities at Ewood Park. We were constantly on the local government improvement and excellence 'tourism' map, which Phil Watson described as punching above our weight. Being awarded Council of the Year in 2001 (and again in 2011 and 2018), along with other recognitions of our high-performing and outstanding work, put us on this map but also gave us freedom to experiment with other ways of working and also, thank you very much, some additional funding to explore new ideas.

In 2008, four years after leaving the council, I appeared in the *Local Government Chronicle* in another kind of 'Where are they now?' column. I was quoted as saying I had had a full-time job as well as being leader of the council and clocked up seventy to eighty hours every week. My wife told me I would leave the house at 6.30 a.m. in the morning to do my day job, then switch into council mode and probably not get home till 10.30 p.m. at night.

After I set up a company that became Improve your Council, which did as it said on the tin, I went on to mention the 'sitting by Nellie' approach to learning. It's a bit like how doctors learn: watch as somebody else does it, do it yourself with that person watching, do it on your own and then show others how to do it. I did observe in a magazine article 'I think the problem of local government is that it tries to be a mini national government. People are concerned that the bins are emptied and that our older folk are safe, not for some of the more political shenanigans.'

My reviewing portfolio in the local paper continued and extended to local pubs and the food they offered. Pubs, especially in Blackburn these days, are disappearing at an alarming rate. It disappoints me.

I love pubs (but frequent much less often, having chosen to give alcohol up in early 2023). Drinking a pint or three, having serious or silly conversations to help the day unwind. I guess the Farthings was my first Blackburn local, well hosted by Paul Waterfield. Then the Sportsman's with Frank Smith and his Mrs. From around 1987 till 2004, my regular 'watering hole' was the Dog Inn on Revidge Road, run by a succession of licensees, including Viv (then) Brown, Russell and Mike inter alia. Over the years the younger end staff included Katy, Niki, Anna the Viking, Russ Ford, Kieron Gavin et al. Nearby in the Lammack area, there is Ian Robertson who, possibly against the odds, has made a huge success of the Hare and Hounds.

After a game of golf, it was the bar at Blackburn Golf Club, again with a succession of stewards, the now departed Janet and John Spencer. But there have been others: John 'Geesh', the Coopers and some great youngsters who went on to become great adults.

And great characters that you find in pubs: Ken (mind the trams) Adcroft, Howard Ponsonby, Dave 'Craigie' Craig, Joe King, Dermot the Digger O'Reilly (and wife Sheila), Polish Rick the Drayman and Polish Rick the Breadman (who went on to drive private hire cars), Martin 'Southern Git' Wyeth, Fiona and 'Preston' Armstrong, Nick and Jane, Peter Hopwood, Steve Margerison, Zac Cole, Steve Catterall and many others to spend a silly, serendipitous or serious hour with.

We also went to see and I reviewed, the farewell gig of the rock band The Police, in Manchester. The four of us went. Way back in 1979 in the Roman amphitheatre in Nîmes, Anne and I hadn't gone to see The Police because I thought their name was daft. This was rectified thirty years later. We thoroughly enjoyed the evening with 'Bring on the Night', 'Message in a Bottle', 'Walking on the Moon', 'Don't Stand So Close', 'Every Little Thing' – all in their way family iconic anthems. Two lines of lyrics from them always seem to be a message (without a bottle) to me when they sing, '*Poets, priests and politicians. Have words to thank for their positions.*' I don't remember what the last song was that they played, as I didn't want the concert to finish. Last but two was 'Roxanne', the penultimate the wistful, 'So lonely', which within the family I sadly call Sue Lawley.

It was around this time that I re-established my connections with

Lancaster University and more specifically the students' union. I was approached to become a trustee to offer critical support and guidance to them. Was the poacher turning gamekeeper again?

In 2009, students' union newspaper *Scan*'s editor Dan Hogan interviewed me which resulted in a two-page spread.

Dan's piece began by talking about Sir Bill Taylor rejecting the label of politician. I went on to say politics doesn't exactly grab me. I wanted to improve people's lives, to do that you may have to get involved in some politics. Politics is only one of many vehicles that can improve people's lives. I reflected in the article that perhaps the events at Lancaster University of the early seventies had been a traumatic step towards the more collaborative learning environment of the twenty-first century. I'm quoted as saying it was a didactic experience coming here in the 1970s, a deferential thing – top down. I made an analogous link between my work of building stronger communities in Blackburn with the work of the students' union in creating better and stronger links between students, the university and the community. I was critical of the Blair Government at the time for not stretching working-class communities like we had been in the sixties and seventies.

The article concluded by quoting me: 'What we've got to do is look at social mobility. I'd experienced and achieved great strides of social mobility. I'd come from a working-class, single-parent background. I just wanted more people to have the chances I've had. And take them!'

I caught up with Dan recently. After university he worked for the Labour Party, helping to develop the party's 2015 manifesto, before joining the team responsible for upholding the party's rules and internal discipline. But in July 2019 Dan became a whistle-blower, appearing on a BBC *Panorama* documentary to dramatically expose how senior Labour bosses had undermined attempts to deal with antisemitism in the party. He now works as a public affairs consultant in London.

I worked alongside two outstanding presidents of the students' union. Michael Payne now a leading councillor in Nottinghamshire and on the national scene and George Gardiner, now teaching successfully in York. They've developed individually down the twin paths I had followed.

My position and profile as a knight and my successful track record across various different disciplines in the public sector often gave me chances to meet up with and learn from great personalities from all walks of life across East Lancashire. One such example being a *Question Time*-style event at Blackburn College which included Edwin Booth of Booth's supermarkets, former local paper editor Peter Butterfield and the then development director at Burnley FC and former Wembley Stadium chief executive Paul Fletcher – all great guys with great ideas, strong track records and high profiles allowing me to listen and learn from them and their experiences.

*   *   *

Almost by chance I came upon another opportunity that both harnessed my experiences and skills and which I thoroughly enjoyed. I applied and was appointed to the role of chairman of what we rebranded as 3rd Sector Lancashire, working in a leadership role with all the voluntary organisations across the county.

What is the third sector, you may be asking? It's what complements the public sector and the private sector, and is possibly better known as the voluntary sector. Without realising it I had had my first dabble with the voluntary sector as a teenager in the mid-sixties, when I became a volunteer helper with the Cubs, whilst still in the Scouts. Forty years later I was invited and appointed as chairman of the umbrella organisation of all voluntary organisations in the county of Lancashire.

So, what does that actually mean? I was soon to find out. A myriad of different organisations from very small to extremely large and complex, some with a national high profile, for example at the time Age Concern, and others very much at the other end of the scale. These were small often locality-based and single-issue organisations often serving a specific neighbourhood or a small village somewhere in the county. As I found my feet amongst this galaxy of groups I was disappointed that a village near Blackburn, Mellor, didn't have a dramatic society. Just as a village near Morecambe, Bare, didn't have a Women's Institute!

I asked exactly what the scale and extent of the third sector in the county with around 1.5 million people was. There were 4,500 separate registered voluntary groups, some that I called small V voluntary and others large V voluntary.

As an example, from the Wirral in the south to Barrow-in-Furness in the north there are nine lifeboat stations. The RNLI save thousands of lives in our treacherous coastal waters. It seems to me such a typically British institution, totally reliant on fundraising by the public and staffed by unpaid volunteer but highly skilled and brave crews. The same I feel can be said about the inland equivalent of RNLI, our network of mountain rescue teams. Five different teams can be called upon if ever rescues are required across Lancashire and beyond. In my experience voluntary organisations are run by extremely dedicated and hard-working people. Some are designed to address health or social care needs beyond that offered by the NHS and other statutory bodies.

Others offer sports opportunities to many often younger people and they are run by dedicated volunteers who rack up hundreds of hours freely given. I was so pleased when the new stand at our Witton Park athletics venue was named after George Kirby who sadly passed away quite recently having given decades of dedicated time to the local world of athletics. As did Nigel Dixon MBE, the driving force behind the Blackburn Community Sport Club. Nigel, a modest and determined guy, ran a team of mums and dads and others, coaches, officials, 'taxi' drivers for many, many teams of young males, females and disabled youngsters, including foreign sports trips. Every one of these folk is a hero, raising hundreds of thousands of pounds or 'donating' or investing hundreds of hours of their time. How many youngsters did their efforts keep on 'the straight and narrow', give positive opportunities to that opened up lifestyle and career choices?

Offering leadership to this disparate miscellany of organisations was at times a cross between treading on eggshells and herding cats and in many ways rightly so. Very often the well-meaning folk in these organisations felt neglected to the point of isolation, left to their own devices, without very much support. When asked, they said they wanted more money. What they actually needed was better organisation. You can do this in many different ways. Without appearing to, or making them feel that they were having their toes trodden on, we offered little bits of encouraging support, little bits of help to improve their organisation, increase recruitment to their cause to share the work and boost morale to make them feel a little better.

*　*　*

The period 2004 to 2006 and then on until 2009 or so was undeniably clouded by my emotionally distressed or depressed demeanour. I think I worked out that it was only me who was going to change things for myself.

In 2009 I was encouraged to apply for, was interviewed and offered the post of chair of a newly formed NHS organisation known as the Blackburn with Darwen NHS Care Trust Plus (CT+). Again, this was ground-breaking and an innovator for the effective future governance of the NHS in localities. Blackburn with Darwen was the only one of two such organisations in the country and I was proud and pleased to be selected to head it up.

Chairing the NHS CT+ was an exciting challenge, just my cup of tea. Nationally there was only one other CT+ over on the east coast, based in Cleethorpes from memory. I visited there once but I'm not too sure how it fared. We were in a bit of a mad dash to make as much headway as we could. We were established right at the end of the thirteen years of the Labour Government with Andy Burnham as Secretary of State. He and I got on well and he regaled publicly about our achievements whilst speaking in support of William Straw's unsuccessful bid for the Rossendale and Darwen seat at the 2015 General Election. There was a mini kerfuffle about who had stewarded our innovative CT+, my name escaping Andy in the heat of the moment. I sat quietly at the back of the packed audience.

The NHS is a great British, much-loved institution. Probably the envy of the world. We should respect and cherish it. It was, of course, the great reforming post-war Labour Government and firebrand Aneurin Bevan who introduced the NHS in 1948. Bevan, a huge champion of social reform, left one significant piece of the health service jigsaw unresolved (probably because it was irresolvable?): The role and power of doctors, then trained and paid from the public purse. Doctors were and still are self-employed free agents. They can work solely inside the NHS or private practice or a mix-and-match of the two. Bevan, understandably, compromised on this in the post-war period. It remains unresolved and a source of controversy within the NHS even today. Perhaps it's a lesson to us all to be a little braver?

In 1948 Bevan boasted that he was able to accomplish his goal 'by stuffing the doctors' mouths with gold.' What he meant by his famous and oft quoted statement is that he allowed some British doctors or consultants as they were called, to continue seeing lucratively private paying patients if they accepted NHS patients.

The CT+ concept was simple, as many of the best ideas are. I was the independent chair selected by a totally transparent process, conducted by the now lamentably defunct independent Appointments Commission. Under me was a tripartite group of people who made up my board. NHS professionals, local elected members, in this case the leaders of the three parties represented on the local council and three or four 'lay' people (Debbie Riley, Joe Slater and Viv King) who had applied, been interviewed and selected to sit on the board representing the local community. It was a brilliant idea and perfect, given my background, experiences and skills, for me to lead. It was a great and effective blend of professionals, local politicians and local key people.

I'd never really dabbled with the NHS before. Occasionally, whilst on the council, I would decide I'd better gird myself and try to understand how it was organised, but it seemed like every time I'd nearly got a handle on it, they'd just go and reorganise themselves. I also made the mistake of thinking the NHS was one unified organisation, all there to help the patient, to have the patient at the centre of all they did. It looked like I'd got that totally wrong. To the outsider, the person on the street, aka the taxpayer, wouldn't you all like to think that the doctors, the nurses, the accountants, directors of public health were all in it together united in one single cause, with a sense of common purpose, all agreeing what was the best to do and then just getting on and doing it? I'm afraid that, just like I was, anybody who thinks this is deluded. Everyone working within the NHS, whilst retaining and developing their clinical or other skills, must 'unlearn' their unswerving allegiance to those, and see and respectfully work in collaborative unison with all kindred disciplines. And I've yet to throw senior civil service mandarins, MPs and secretaries of state for health into this confused mix. All ministers want to dabble, leave some mark that they existed, made a difference. The only one I think many still recall is Kenneth Baker (1988) in education and his in-service training days (INSET), where the children don't attend school which annoys parents, and staff do things. These were lovingly known in the trade as B-Days.

The ownership of the NHS was enshrined and spelt out in the Constitution, not formally drawn up until 2012 and re-visited in early 2021. The very first line of this quite simply states: 'The NHS belongs to the people.' This should be on the wall of every room in which the NHS treats its citizen/patients.

A few 'helpful' stats: about 1.5 million people work in the NHS (compared with 450,000 teachers), but that doesn't include 160,000 temporary/agency staff, 175,000 general practice staff including 42,000 GPs, 24,000 dentists and 12,000 opticians involved in NHS funded work. Spending on the health service is about 18 per cent of all government spending, education absorbs about 11 per cent, pensions and benefits about 34 per cent. Interestingly UK expenditure to the EU only accounts for 2 per cent of government spending and this doesn't include all of the financial support returned to us from Europe. Another myth to debunk is the level of spending inside the health service on faceless bureaucrats. Only 3 per cent of the workforce is involved in usually quite necessary accountancy, HR and other organisational functions.

The NHS, globally admired and envied, costs around £180bn a year to run, about £2,500 per person per annum. During the Blair/Brown years spending increased at around 6 per cent a year. It's been comparatively static since, according to the Office of National Statistics.

The CT+ for Blackburn with Darwen served more or less the same population, around 150,000 people, as did the borough council. But both organisations had their own organisational functions such as finance, HR, media and communications, estates, legal services and similarly had two separate chief executives: Graham Burgess, an excellent officer for the borough for the council, and Judith Griffin for the NHS. The duplication was wasteful and didn't make sense and I set about addressing these issues.

Another issue was that really the NHS wasn't effectively accessible or accountable to the public it served and didn't want to be. This lack of engagement again needed urgent and drastic attention.

Just as a starter, and this was a no-brainer, we imported what was the norm for Blackburn's style of democratic engagement – open access 'surgeries' for the public. This was subliminally resisted by the 'high-ups' in the local health service, until they realised I wasn't going to budge on it and we started on a monthly session where anybody could come and see me and I was accompanied by a probably initially reluctant NHS 'high-up'.

It was really quite easy, an advert in the local paper with a phone number to ring. The first run-through attracted five punters. What surprised me was that only three of them were local, another came from Bury and the fifth person from Rochdale, both in Greater Manchester and some twenty to twenty-five miles away! They told me they'd heard of nothing like this service before and travelled to gain our advice or support. We tried to put them onto the correct contact in their area. After this we restricted attendees to people living or with a GP in the Blackburn with Darwen area.

I also brought in from my earlier days as the lead on recreation, education, the college and crime and community safety, the practice of going out to see different sections or aspects of the workforce. This apparently caused great consternation amongst some GPs, dentists, pharmacists and others, who I wanted to see, to find out what they thought and what ideas they had. But it didn't take them long to realise that that was exactly why I wanted to see, speak and listen with them. I didn't want to restrict sourcing my organisational intelligence from the high-ups but to find out from those in the field too. This polarised the senior staff. Some said its brilliant the way your style gets folk to open up and talk openly, others tried to stop it in its tracks, actually saying we don't want you out there talking to others. I would win. Whilst leader of the council I'd had to remind council jobs-worths that there was a T on the front of town hall!

I started to poke my nose into things. For example, a patient's visit to a GP can be costed at around £30, 5 per cent of them are 'no shows'. That's a total of over fifteen million non-appointments, costing £200 million-plus. That's other people wasting clinicians time and our money. That money could fund over 58,000 hip replacements. Why should we tolerate others, without cause, wasting our taxes? I was going on the warpath. A Labour Party pal of mine, Bernard Mathews, no longer with us, worked in the NHS and was a stickler for not wasting any resources, however minuscule. I agree with Bernard!

After a certain length of time (ten to fifteen years), previously branded, i.e. pricey, drugs lose their patented status but not their efficacy. The price plummets for these 'generic' drugs, potentially saving the NHS millions, billions possibly. But people, including doctors and patients can be creatures of habit, or just plain lazy! Mrs Smith might like the pink pills, irrationally, and Dr Jones mightn't want to disappoint or challenge her to take the green, generic, cheaper, equally effective medicine. But our medicines management team developed and introduced systems and triggers to wean practitioners and patients off profligate prescribing. There was some daft resistance to this but when they saw we were resolute, common sense prevailed. We saved 70 per cent of our spending on statins when we restricted choice to the generic forms of the drug. We were making real differences, both at the margins, at the core and in the shop window too.

We also held our board meetings in public which would appear to be a novelty, so the public could see how the public's purse was spent. Meetings always had some requested key speakers to talk on key issues. Quite often the speakers sat patiently waiting their turn. They, NHS staff themselves, often admitted that they'd learned things, understood things better by being there! At the end of every meeting there was a public question and answer session putting everybody at the accountability of the people. I made it my business to relate as often as possible to the local media health journalists, appearing in the newspapers and on the local radio stations.

We began the process of merging people from what are known as 'back office' functions. HR (formerly known as personnel) and the media/comms inside the local NHS was weak and we began with a process of skill sharing and then a full merger. Funding regimes inside the NHS are complex and many specific to the needs of the organisation so we had to be more careful in our approach. Although not money focussed, I'd learned during my time as a service committee chair, the chairman of the finance committee, inside the college and at work that robust and reliable financial organisation was at the heart of any good public service.

Councils as well as the NHS all have a lot of property, a lot of land and sometimes they don't know exactly what they have got. The current term for that was estates. Within the council and the NHS we set up an analysis of things like: where were all our buildings, did we need them all, were they in the right place, were some more expensive to run than others, did all staff need to work in more expensive town centre buildings, could organisations share, lots of considerations that needed addressing.

Then came the biggest challenge, a full merger of two organisations, the first big step for which meant only having one chief executive. This could've been tricky, delicate and to some extent it was. In the end a due process was agreed, undertaken and the outcome was Graham Burgess becoming the new joint chief executive and Judith taking redundancy. The NHS leadership role went to Neil Matthewman, a good guy with a droll Yorkshire sense of humour, who knew the NHS well but also saw why, how and where I was trying to take it locally. We had a good productive relationship.

We were walking down the street in central Blackburn one teatime when this younger woman said, 'Hi Bill, have you got five minutes?' She took us inside a dilapidated building from which she ran her voluntary organisation. I quizzed her with Neil watching on. We were there half an hour. As we left I said 'I think Neil's got the picture now. Please can you investigate and report back in say a fortnight?' He undertook to do so.

As we walked to the car Neil enquired, 'Known her long?' I admitted to him that I didn't recollect meeting her ever before and was unsure of her role. But we afforded her time and left her feeling listened to, valued, satisfied and clear about the next steps. He said 'You handled that brilliantly, hit exactly the right note with her and that's not the first time I've seen you operate like that.'

* * *

The culture of the NHS was starkly very different to any other that I'd experienced.

Culture? You might ask. Yes. Every organisation established or informal, large or small, develops a culture all of its own. We all do it, our families develop a culture, groups of friends, businesses, large and small, nations, communities and neighbourhoods all develop cultures. There are rules of engagement, traditions, rituals, roles and even language and vocabulary and much, much more. We need to understand that. Take and observe a simple group of people stood around the bar in a pub: the time that they turn up or leave, what they wear, who does all the talking, who does all the listening, is it jokey or serious or a mixture of the two? Just watch a TV episode or stage performance of *Early Doors*, wonderfully observed and crafted by Craig Cash (he acted in this and also co-wrote and acted in *The Royle Family*) and Phil Mealey. Set phrases abound. For example, the lazy, old-school coppers Phil and Nige always resorting to radio phonetics to communicate to one another, 'Foxtrot Uniform Charley Kilo' being one of many examples. Inside the NHS I frequently heard phrases like 'deep dives' and 'heads up'. When I heard these it made me think that they were some form of sexual practice, which made me chuckle.

As journalist turned historian observed Max Hastings: 'Every culture cherishes its own narrative. That's not quite right since many people cling stubbornly to simple certainties until they die.'

These are all cultural norms, like it or like it not. Organisations also have a mindset, a way of thinking and operating – a micro culture. To me, from the outside, the NHS, full of very bright people, university trained and very intelligent, seemed very evidence-based in reaching their decisions and probably quite rightly so, given the life or death nature of every normal working day. But do they have soul? The answer must be Yes, initially.

I've spoken earlier about emotional intelligence, perhaps emotional literacy and how important it was in the genres of public service in which I had operated and with which I'd grown familiar. Youth work, being on the council, addressing communities, speaking as I have done in front of the microphone on radio or addressing 2,000 people, all have their own skills, techniques and approaches. Addressing large assemblies of people live, face to face must have an element of theatre within it if it's going to be successful. Talking on the radio in that manner would come over as totally pompous, so best you adopt a me talking to one person approach. Sender-Message-Receiver. No one has more than two ears and in effect, via the radio, you're only talking to one person all the time, multiplied by hundreds or thousands. The actual language, the pace at which you deliver, the tone of your voice, right down to the selection of individual words is crucial. I remember on BBC radio being asked what exactly a Comprehensive Performance Assessment was. If I had replied in local government speak, I would have lost my audience. So, from somewhere at the back of my mind, I grabbed an analogy that it was like a mega MOT of the council. Not only was I quite pleased with that instantly sprung to mind phrase but the council communications officer with me, Suzanne Halliwell, praised me for the fleet, applicable and easy to understand language I'd used.

In some ways coming into an organisation from a governance perspective is almost like being a guest, possibly seen as an uninvited intruder by some. You will need your cultural intelligence or cultural literacy wits about you. You may not 'get' the culture of the organisation to begin with, and that might be a deliberate obfuscating tactic by them, but you need to doggedly persevere and get an understanding of it, understand the language, processes and the individuals involved in it. You need not only to listen and understand what is being said, but by whom, how and why it is said. You need to pick out the obstinately obdurate, who will not budge, who will refuse to enable or sanction any shift of culture in their organisation which they run and they control because quite simply they think it's theirs! Because it's not theirs, it belongs to us, the people it's actually run for, who pay for it with their hard-earned taxes. Watch out also for more cunning cognitive dissonants. These are people who believe one thing but actually say and act at variance to that. This may be done unwittingly but the outcome of this activity is to try and outfox you, to try and get you to think they're actually on your side, when they aren't.

But you can go too far down the road of wearing the organisation's clothes. By that I mean, you can begin to adopt that culture, to be assimilated into it and imbued by it. My view is if you get to that point, you've gone too far, it might be a point of no return, time to leave. This is a very complex, delicate chemistry and you need to keep a balanced objective eye on it.

*   *   *

We embarked upon determined organisational integration, the council and the local NHS and clinicians streamlining. Not without difficulty we merged senior management under one chief exec, Graham Burgess, but also 'ball-bearing' functions such as finance, personnel, PR, legal. No need for two parallel teams of staff. We made savings, for example, by getting equally effective generic drugs prescribed by GPs not their expensive new on the market brand-name counterparts. We got our community pharmacies rightfully more integrated within our health family. Under Dominic Harrison, our director of public health, knowledgeable and eloquent, we got the local health service operating out more within communities.

Once again, as the CT+ developed and made great strides, we became a focus, a magnet for people to find out what we had done, why, and how had we done it. This included a very high-powered visit by the House of Commons Health Select Committee. Very senior politicians and civil servants came to see us, including two prominent current and future chairs of the committee, Stephen Dorrell and Dr Sarah Wollaston, both Tory MPs prominent in the world of health. In a private conversation they both told me they were well impressed with what they'd seen and wanted to see it replicated across the country. They left me feeling quite buoyed that what we had aspired to and achieved was recognised as a model of good practice to be disseminated nationally. Not the first time this has happened with little old Blackburn.

None of us reckoned with the advent of Andrew Lansley MP as the next Conservative health minister. He was appointed by David Cameron after the 2010 Conservative/Lib Dem General Election victory and only held the post for two years or so. That was long enough for him to have irrevocably introduced the Health and Social Care Act 2012. A piece of legislation that nobody asked for, nobody wanted, and seemed to make no sense or improvement whatsoever. It was described as, after the Great Wall of China, the only man-made thing visible from Outer Space!

It abolished NHS primary care trusts (PCTs) and Strategic Health Authorities (SHAs) and transferred between £60 billion and £80 billion of 'commissioning', or health care funds, from the abolished PCTs to several hundred (already defunct) GP led 'clinical commissioning groups'.

I'd previously offered locally to increase the representation of GPs on our board but that got their less than tepid response. I think a bit like good, child-centred teachers most community focussed GPs have no appetite or aspiration for strategic responsibility. Nationally GPs never asked for this and weren't really interested, tooled up for or used to taking overarching strategic decisions. However, *c'est la vie*. I likened it to the whole education system from the age of four through primary, secondary and tertiary adult, FE and HE being led, controlled by primary head school teachers. Just like one couldn't imagine universities allowing their junior counterparts to take control, it will be hard to see our health service flagships that is hospitals allowing neighbourhood-based general practitioners to call all the shots. It was opposed by the Royal College of Nursing, the BMA and many others.

Our CT+ and my leadership of it lasted four, perhaps five, years. It made great strides, many changes and much improvement, being acclaimed as the way forward for the future. It was the significant contributory factor in us once again winning, for an unprecedented second time, the national Council of the Year award in 2011. By 2013 all that we'd worked for, developed, delivered and improved disappeared, just as Andrew Lansley did, to be replaced by Jeremy Hunt. Lansley became Lord Lansley. His 'reforms' and the consequent restructuring and reorganisation were alleged to have cost £3 billion, mostly in substantial redundancy packages. Since 2013 it would appear that CCGs (Clinical Commissioning Groups), STPs (Sustainability and Transformation Plans) ICSs/ICPs (Integrated Care Systems/Partnerships) and PCNs (Primary Care Networks) have restructured, same old, same old, at least twice or three times. Same pattern: hit a brick wall you helped design and build, conjure up bright ideas to solve that as a problem, make the top tier redundant at considerable cost, reorganise and restructure, change name but still not doing as it says on the tin. I can't be alone in drawing the conclusion that this perpetual chopping and changing, on the hoof, demonstrated that it was ill conceived and designed from the outset?

Adult social care was much spoken about, much promised, on the steps of No 10 in late 2019, specifically by its new incumbent Boris Johnson. Guess what? Little or no action to resolve what is already an outrage and crisis. No meaningful public engagement, involvement or information. Almost complete 'radio silence' in the mainstream local and national media. Trade media ineffectually mainly only talking to themselves. Little understood and less said by local councils, council leaders or MPs.

* * *

2010 began totally unexpectedly.

Chapter 42

The Changes Brought About by the 2010 General Election

I'd like to help you in your struggle to be free.

After ten years as Chancellor of the Exchequer, Gordon Brown became the Prime Minister in June 1997.

Eventually, three years later, a general election was called for 6 May 2010.

Eventually? In 2007, as the Labour Party changed national 'Skipper', Brown had inherited Blair's fairly healthy parliamentary majority of sixty-six seats. Brown found himself enjoying something of a 'honeymoon period' with the electorate. He'd done a good job as Chancellor and perhaps should have gone to the people for his own mandate? He dithered and didn't.

As Rachel Sylvester, a *Times* columnist, said when writing for *Prospect* magazine in 2015:

> *It was the end of his reputation as a statesmanlike 'father of the nation' and a return to the idea that he was a tactical leader, indecisive, tortured and driven by self-interest. It was also the beginning of the Conservative recovery, following George Osborne's surprise party conference announcement of an inheritance tax cut, shifting the balance of power at Westminster. Labour was never ahead in the polls again after the election-that-never-was. Damian McBride, a former*

special adviser to Brown, in his book Power Trip *(Biteback 2014) describes this as 'the greatest misjudgement of Brown's long career, utterly changing the way he was perceived and defined'. But what if Brown had called an election in 2007, seeking his own mandate soon after taking over the leadership from Tony Blair?*

In June 2007 Jack Straw had successfully run Brown's leadership campaign. An article in 2010 by Toby Helm, the *Observer's* political editor, illustrated that:

The revelation that even Brown's most senior ally had given up on him by mid-2008 lays bare the extent to which confidence in the Prime Minister drained away within the Cabinet after a year marred by recriminations over his failure to call a snap autumn election in 2007, policy failures and by-election catastrophes.

This article goes on to explain that a variety of serving or former Cabinet Ministers felt Brown should exit as soon as possible. The names suggested included Stephen Byers, Charles Clarke, Frank Field, Patricia Hewitt, Geoff Hoon, David Miliband and James Purnell. Labour sustained successive and heavy by-election defeats in Crewe and Nantwich and Glasgow East in the spring and summer of 2008. Jack's name regularly cropped up either as advising Brown to go, as a potential replacement or both.

We went on holiday with me feeling like I was on 'Action Stations' to return to the UK to run any snap election in Blackburn, expecting Jack to be otherwise engaged.

In the end, all the newspaper conjecture, the Westminster whispers, snippets of insider information I'd gleaned, came to no avail. Gordon Brown neither jumped nor was pushed and no general election came to fruition.

In 2008 I began my eight-year tenure as chairman of the college board having been a 'back bencher', with one break, since 1981. A year later I was encouraged, sought and gained the chairmanship of the local NHS Care Trust Plus. These two fantastic roles were more than enough to keep me busy and engaged. I really enjoyed them both. They both also pitched me into wider regional and national roles within the associated educational and health service functions. But also my drift away from the local council, the Labour Group and party was now over five years old. Yes, I continued as both Jack's agent and constituency campaigns organiser but increasingly that drift of detachment widened.

Gordon Brown cut himself little flexible slack when it came to fixing the date in 2010. The latest date it could was in May and that's what the country relentlessly rumbled towards.

Anne was still working and so we took a school holiday pre-election break to our apartment in Spain. One morning my phone rang. I was sat on my bed, shutters down in the cool semi dark. It was Jack. 'How are you, Billy?'

'Fine thanks, we're taking a little pre-election break in Spain.'

'Excellent. I need to talk to you about you continuing as election agent.'

'But we've had the OK on that, confirmed in writing, from the Labour Party legal team, the NHS and the independent Appointments Commission.'

'My instinct though is that it's not viable, sustainable.'

I was having to process and assimilate these brief staccato sentences at speed. These are my recollections of the exchanges.

'You'd like me to finish? OK, I will.' No point stopping where you're not wanted, an inner voice told me.

I can, Jack, but is that the real reason, my inner voice was telling me again. 'Yes, I will. That's fine. Bye.'

I could feel a knot of emotional reaction welling up inside somewhere. I started to cry.

Anne walked in around this point. 'Who was that on the phone? What did they want? Why are you crying?'

'It was Jack sacking me after thirty-plus years as agent, spread over five decades' (from the 1970s to the 2010s, but where had that instant computation sprung from?).

'Bastards.' And then very little much more was said. I think I was taken out to one of our favourite roadside restaurants for a simple €9-10 Menu del Dia. Anne drove. I polished off a nice bottle of white, Albariño or Macabeo perhaps.

I guess I was actually in shock. This was a very stark way to end such a long and productive partnership. But there was probably no easy or good way to perform such a process. It did hurt, it hurt a lot. But it didn't take long for the intellectual processing to start overcoming the emotional.

I think Jack had come to this decision himself. I have yet to find a local party 'high-up' who admits they knew about this before it happened. But again, whether they did or didn't, doesn't really matter. The nettle was grasped. Thirty-plus years, all unpaid, one of few qualified agents in the country, dismissed in a two to three-minute phone call.

The decision? The right one. The process? No real alternative?

With immediate effect Phil Riley became the new constituency agent for the 2010 General Election. He still holds the post and, now retired from work, successfully operates as an exec member and deputy leader (now leader) too. A very clever and hard-working guy and, born on 29 February 1948, still not yet twenty years old! He always gets a birthday card from me!

I got my Sunday mornings back. They are still key to Labour's local success, I believe. The chairmanships at the college and within the NHS were plenty enough to engage my experiences, skills and talents and individually probably more than most have ever taken on. Suited me fine. Our 'kids' were off into their working and settled-down lives, Anne was about to retire after thirty-six years teaching. Things seemed just about a perfect balance!

Chapter 43

Into the Twenty-Teens

These events may have had some effect on the man with a girl by his side.

In the May 2010 General Election, David Cameron could not turn Labour's sixty-six-seat majority that Brown inherited from Tony Blair into outright victory with a clear parliamentary majority. There being 650 Westminster seats, 326 seats were needed to form a government and Cameron's Conservatives had 306 'in the bag' – not enough! Only the second 'hung' Parliament since the end of World War II (the other being in 1974). 149 sitting Labour MPs 'stood down', not seeking re-election. Labour lost ninety-one seats. Some 'horse trading' ensued. Brown resigned five days after polling day when it was clear that Cameron had brokered a coalition deal with Nick Clegg's Lib Dems, who, although losing a handful of seats, had fifty-seven seats to align with the Tories – 363 all together. Later, Clegg gained employment with Facebook; living in London and California, he's cited to be earning £2.8 million a year plus mega bonuses.

Locally in Lancashire of the sixteen parliamentary seats, Labour lost six of those they had held, notably Burnley, Pendle, Rossendale and Darwen and South Ribble.

In Blackburn, I didn't engage at all, to give Phil a clear run at his new role, and Jack did fine. There were eight candidates, the bottom five all losing their deposits (that means gaining less than 5 per cent of valid votes cast and therefore losing £500). That included Robin Evans, the BNP candidate, UKIP and three other 'Independents'. Jack had a majority of nearly 10,000, with local Tory councillor Michael Law-Riding coming second and the Skipton based Lib Dem candidate third.

But of course, this was my first general election campaign in more than thirty years in which I had no active role. No getting up as dawn broke, no getting to bed after midnight, no taking three weeks off work to coordinate the campaign, no taking photographs for use in election literature, no spending hours composing and setting out all election leaflets, spellchecking, sub-editing, etc., no hours spent at the printers, no loading of thousands and thousands of leaflets into my car, out of my car, into people's homes for distribution, no canvassing at teatime, in the morning or in the afternoon, no visiting people in their homes, their places of work, their places of worship, no Sunday morning meetings, no attending the count till goodness knows what time, none of those 1,001 tasks the job entailed.

And did I miss it? No, not at all. It was like having my life back. There were times when I wondered which people were doing what, but only fleetingly. I cast my vote (by post) and on the close of polls on election night sat and watched the TV for a while. It not making good viewing, I went off to bed. The picture was equally as bleak at breakfast time.

Labour, Brown and the people around him who did or didn't act, goofed, big style. Labour went into a self-led wilderness, with Ed Miliband and his acolytes and then Jeremy Corbyn and another set. Leftist parties can lurch as left as they like. But to change things they must convince the electorate to trust them with power. Cameron, Osborne, Clegg, then May and Johnson (later Truss and Sunak) were our national leaders. Where they led us? You decide!

So after thirteen years of Labour Government Dave and Nick went about creating their coalition which was the last for five years. Austerity was to be their buzzword. Worse, in my opinion, was to follow.

* * *

We had a lot of change ahead of us.

Anne retired after thirty-six years, teaching, we reckoned, 9,000 adolescent youngsters, who held her in high regard, along the way. I thought she'd miss it. I was wrong. She was due and ready for it.

Matt started work as a solicitor in Manchester, met Siân, bought a house and got married in 2011. They had Joshua in 2016 and Oliver in 2021.

Kit got her business degree from Manchester University, found a good job in the food industry, bought a house. She met and married engineer Gaz, they sold their own houses and bought one together. Alfie was born in 2016 and Harper in 2020.

Me? I'd got away from the youth and community service in 2006, did consultancy and inspection-type work. I was appointed pro bono chair of the college in 2008 and chair of the NHS Care Trust Plus in 2009. It was around then that my hip joints started to deteriorate causing excruciating pain requiring much pain management. I had both replaced in 2012 and 2013 at Wrightington Hospital. Not being in such extreme pain was a great relief.

Living in a large five-bedroomed house spread over four levels was not a good option for me, and later life may have other unexpected challenges, so we moved to what we hope is our last home, a little bungalow in the village of Pleasington on the western outskirts of Blackburn.

My mum died aged ninety in 2017. After fifty-five or so years in her home in Birmingham, I had brought her up to old folks' community living place Spring Bank Court a couple of miles away. She'd lived in *Dementia Land* which I didn't cope with so very well and moved into the Barrett family-run Magdalene House nursing home for around five years.

So, a lot of change yet to come and explore.

*　*　*

Tory Health Secretary Andrew Lansley introduced his NHS 'reforms', seen by many as sabotage.

The Health and Social Care Act was law in March 2012. By September the same year he was no longer Health Secretary. By October 2015 he was 'promoted' to the House of Lords.

I was encouraged to become involved in the post Lansley, yet another NHS reorganisation. I would have made £30–40k-plus pa as an honorarium in doing so, but it was so far a retrograde step and against my principles, that I declined. Many high-ranking and highly paid NHS officials walked off, shedding crocodile tears, with substantial redundancy deals, only to re-emerge somewhere else. Everyone else seemed simply to shift up a tier or two, sometimes an undeserved promotion without merit or movement.

I was invited to seek the voluntary position of chair of our local Healthwatch branch and was successful. At the time it felt like Healthwatch was designed not to succeed. Looking back now in fact destined to fail. They were poorly resourced at around a pound per head of the population that they served. In our case around about £160,000 a year, not far off the salary of one, perhaps two, local GPs or hospital consultants.

We had little or no support in reality but I was fortunate to have a vice-chairman imbued in the ways of the private sector, Paula Woodruff. Our other original (registered with Companies House 2014/15) volunteer directors included Ian Clarke from Twin Valleys, now Together Housing, Helen Humphreys former social services, Ashraf Kharbari from a mental health nursing and police background, Viv King from an FE/training agency background, Abdul Mulla (an ex-young person we'd worked with, then later youth worker, community worker and health development worker). We also had Anmol Mulla and Mahek Chisti, two pre-nursing FE students hoping to go off to university to study and obtain nursing degrees. They gave us their sixteen/seventeen-year-olds' perspectives on things but also, via me being chair of the college board, access to a range of students, different by age, ethnicity and background.

We were left almost entirely to our own devices. We acquired some existing IT equipment but had to secure our own servicing arrangements. But before that we had to form ourselves into a company and luckily with Paula Woodruff's expertise, we registered ourselves at Companies House. Then there were all the other things that companies must do such as HR support, business insurance, various policies such as employment procedures, health and safety and the many, many others. It took us months and whilst interesting it wasn't what Healthwatch was established to do.

Having put a great deal of expertise and energy into the early days of our Healthwatch and ensuring its solid organisational base, vice-chair Paula Woodruff had to return to fully committing her time to her business; she had to resign.

On doing so she sent me a lovely note:

I think in life you meet certain personalities whose presence/charisma are undeniable and who can move things forward. You, I do not doubt, are one of those people. I think the trust afforded to you from those around you is very much rooted in the years and foot leather you've put in.

There were thirty or forty Healthwatches across the north-west and I wondered if they were all struggling with the same building blocks – I'm running a very small company with a very big role.

To find that, I invited them all to attend a getting to know you meeting in Blackburn. Most groups attended. It must have worried the national Healthwatch because they sent our local regional support worker (based somewhere like Essex!) to find out what we were up to.

The meeting commenced and I was invited to chair it. The 'regional' person interjected, suggesting that we first listened to some highfaluting guest able to inform us from very high up Maslow's hierarchy of needs. I judged that this wasn't what we needed, yet another example in my life of 'high-ups' not having a clue what was needed 'on the ground'. I stepped in: 'Well, I thought what we might do was go round the table and give examples to each other of things that we've done quite well and things that we struggled with.' That was agreed and we set off in what was a very supportive, inquisitive, environment.

At its conclusion those in attendance asked please could we go round again because I've thought of things we've done quite well and thought of questions I'd like to ask. So that's what we did. The meeting was massively productive and probably lasted three hours. As it went on we 'drilled deeper' into the issues relevant to us. We took comprehensive notes which were issued for comment before becoming the minutes of the meeting and that became a regular feature of our bi-monthly meetings, chaired by me but held in different parts of the north-west.

Again the same old pattern seem to be forming: My childhood experiences, my personal education, becoming a youth worker and dealing with that hard-to-reach group, becoming a councillor, learning the ropes of that environment then that of schools, colleges, education, the voluntary sector, the police and NHS gave me a rich grounding of how to operate within and across these diverse environments. But I never forgot that I felt I was there, as far as I was concerned, as the champion of the client: the young person, a pupil or student, the individual, their family or their community. Once again it appeared to me that the NHS, although funded by and intended to serve the needs of the public, seemed to be designed and operating, in the main, for those employed within it. Bill, here is another brick wall, start banging your head against it!

Chapter 44

The Last Chapter

We talked about old times and drank ourselves some beers.

I began this process, putting 'pen to paper' in the spring of 2019, having no idea of its time commitment and emotional burden – it took four years. During that process I became aware that, as I approached thinking and writing about three events, my mum and dad's splitting up, my departure from the council and the spurious 'disciplinary' circumstances immediately prior to my seeking to leave my cherished career, I slowed down, grinding to a halt. I had to get back on those horses.

* * *

So, my writing process began in a time people recall as 'normality'! Theresa May was still Prime Minister, the prospect of Bullingdon Boris becoming PM barely imaginable. There was all that parliamentary palaver over Brexit followed by a divisive and deceitful campaign that got us a Johnson Government. Jo Cox MP was murdered. Labour, having wasted five years under the highly principled but totally unelectable Jeremy Corbyn, got a massive drubbing in the 2019 General Election. Johnson got a huge majority of eighty, taking many 'red wall' seats in the Midlands and North, previously always Labour constituencies. Corbyn resigned and Labour, with rediscovered common sense, elected lawyer, former director of public prosecutions and head of the Crown Prosecution Service, Sir Keir Starmer (now KC) as leader. The Johnson camp tried to convince us that Brexit was now (over and) done.

The Covid-19 pandemic resulted in three periods of lockdown that were generally observed across the nation but not in Downing Street. Patrick Vallance, Chris Whitty, Jonathan Van-Tam and Jenny Harries (all later deservedly honoured as knights and a dame) inter alia including Johnson and Health Minister Matt Hancock (until he went hands on elsewhere) appeared on TV every night to brief us about Covid. I became quite reclusive, physically and emotionally. We rarely left our home and I felt distanced and distant from neighbours, former pub pals, but most of all our family. I don't know about others, but despite whatever age they are or how far away they might live, I did feel frustrated not to be able to see them, feel how they were feeling, cuddle them. Perhaps my childhood and family upbringing influenced that?

The PM's special adviser Dominic Cummings drove himself to Barnard Castle to test his eyesight. He disappeared from view at the end of 2020 carrying a box down Downing Street. Donald Trump was forty-fifth US President, followed by Joe Biden. US citizens stormed the Capitol.

Prince Philip, Duke of Edinburgh, died in April 2021 and his widow Queen Elizabeth sat forlornly alone at his funeral in St George's Chapel, Windsor Castle. Sadly, some eighteen months later Her Majesty also left us after reigning for seventy years. The nation mourned and turned out in their hundreds of thousands to file past her lying in state, and to line the streets in Scotland, London and Windsor to pay last respects and say farewell to a woman held in high regard and deep affection. The Russians under Putin invaded Ukraine, causing great international consternation. Prices rocketed especially gas but also petrol, food, most things, causing a cost-of-living crisis. PM Johnson at his final time at the despatch box in July 2022, quoting actor Arnold Schwarzenegger in *Terminator 2*, bid the House of Commons '*Hasta la vista, Baby*'. The Tories then seemed to evaporate into thin air as they engaged in the process of determining their next leader and, for the rest of us, a Prime Minister. Were Sky's Beth Rigby and the BBC's Nick Eardley and Laura Kuenssberg the Cabinet for this period? Seemed like it! It took them eight weeks to whittle down eight original candidates to the two, Rishi Sunak and Liz Truss, to do the national hustings rounds of Tory Party members. This resulted in a victory for Mrs Truss by 81,000 votes to 60,000. It started badly, ended swiftly. And then the Tory party darling Liz, gave way to Sunak. We have yet to see how this ends.

What is 'normality'? Anyone remember?

*   *   *

In this our final chapter together, I want to take the opportunity to recap and review those that precede it. It is there you will have found more detail. I did advise at the outset that I didn't want to tell you exactly how to read the story. Here I want, not to repeat myself, but give some coherent connectivity to what you've read, hope you enjoyed, making you think about me, you, people and things around us, events that shape lives.

You hear people talk about 'their journey'. Aren't journeys supposed to have intended destinations with starting and staging points? Perhaps many people's stories aren't really 'journeys' at all? Finding starting and staging points and a definite destination isn't easy. I don't feel my 'journey' has reached its end. But there are clear footprints left where I made an impression.

I've done a lot, experienced a lot, learned loads and had numerous successes.

Molānā Jalāl ad-Dīn Muhammad Rūmī (known as Rūmī) was a thirteenth-century Islamic theologian, teacher, and poet, who travelled extensively in the Middle East observing, listening, thinking, learning and writing. He wrote:

'When setting out on a journey do not seek advice from someone who never left home.'

Let me start by dealing and disposing with the things that I think most people would perceive to be unexpected downsides.

* * *

My mum and dad parting company was trapped in being viewed and processed through the eyes, the moral compass and emotional sensitivities of a fourteen-year-old for many, probably too many, years. This clouded and moulded how I viewed that time and others in the future, some for the better, some possibly for the worse. Thinking, writing and talking about it more openly with others has helped, moved me on.

Please enable and empower youngsters around you to get things off their chest. With as little judgement as possible, please listen and hear what they are saying, aren't saying and how and why they are.

* * *

In mid-2003 I was sworn to a confidentiality protocol preventing me from divulging the imminent conferral of my knighthood to anyone. I had applied for an excellent, 'tailor-made', career-accelerating national role with the Innovation and Development Agency. I demurred at the final interview from disclosing my secret, very much a potential deal clincher for me. Wouldn't a knight in that staff team have enhanced their profile and reputation?

Should I have reneged on other responsibilities (shouldered of my own volition) of facing up to the successful electoral incursion of the far right National Party and opened up the opportunity of the job with the I&DeA? It was a career opportunity for which I felt massively suited, would enjoy and it was hugely well paid?

I didn't do. I didn't feel comfortable touting my impending honour (never have) and I had a greater sense of loyalty to the principles of equality and the diverse communities where I had plied my trade and served people. What would others, you, have done?

* * *

My departure from the council a year later, was it a defeat? Or a Pyrrhic victory for others?

Zamir Khan topped the polls in Audley Ward in 2004, standing as an Independent then Lib Dem and my two Labour colleagues were also elected. I was voted out, coming fourth. Khan was quoted in the local *Telegraph* stating 'mission accomplished'. I'm not sure I ever exactly understood what his mission was or what it accomplished? Then and ever since I've never felt malice towards the guy. Beyond the odd courteous handshake, I've never spoken with him. My thoughts are neutral towards him.

He'd 'chucked his cap into the ring' and that's kind of that. To suddenly no longer be on the council did shock me initially, I think most would think that would be a natural feeling. But in any contest, there are winners and losers. I had done my best, dispensed my various duties to the full, contributed to the electoral downfall of Evans of the far right, canvassed widely in the newly configured ward. I'd taken my diverse electorate at their word when, over a three to four-week campaigning period, to my face, they only ever told me that they were voting for all three Labour candidates.

Councillor Zamir Khan later switched from the Lib Dems to Independent then to Labour. At that time under the headline 'Man who ousted Sir Bill quits Lib Dems', he told reporter David Higgerson, on being asked if he was going to apply to become a Labour councillor, 'I will not rule anything out. For the time being I need to work out what is best for me.' It must've crossed a few minds that surely what was best for his constituents should have been more important. In the many ensuing years, water under many bridges now, I'm not sure if Councillor Khan has ever held councillor office with full executive responsibility, except to take his time-served turn as mayor. His electorate must be content with him twenty or so years and several elections later. He gained an MBE for his work for the Muslim Burial Society.

On the outside I think I appeared to take things with good grace. That evening I spoke well on the local BBC radio. Anne and I attended the reprehensible charade of the 'mayor making' two or three weeks later. It seemed very much that the rifts, ostensibly of high principle, allegedly caused by my electoral departure, had pragmatic sticking plasters placed over them.

I was dignified and measured in my dealings in the press during the ensuing unprincipled toing and froing of the 'Mahfia' months. I stood shoulder to shoulder with a potentially similarly vulnerable Jack Straw a year later as his agent at the 2005 General Election, my sixth and what proved to be my final performance of this key role.

Inside it was different. The moment of downfall was always likely to be a shock; although reconciled intellectually, it took a while to assimilate emotionally. I retreated into my emotional shell. It was the actions or inactions of others, my former comrades, that were the hardest to square. What I didn't understand was that they didn't understand. No apology, no gratitude, no goodbye, no courage or courtesy to even explain what had ensued and why. Whilst I had ensured 'closure' for Malcolm Doherty, Sue Reid and Gail Barton, no one appeared to possess the emotional intelligence to offer me similar.

That was the source of my greatest hurt, fuelled by frequently expressed compassionate comments from general party members of all backgrounds, town hall staff, others in Blackburn and beyond, anonymous shoppers in supermarkets who approached me and made their feelings very clear. Folk, from a variety of backgrounds expressed their anger and dismay. They felt I had been badly treated, the borough had suffered a great setback and community relations had been damaged. I stopped going out shopping for a year, nearly two.

My departure meant others moved up a political peg or two filling spaces left by me. I'm not sure of the impact on the party locally; my view of events was focussed from some considerable distance. There are many good, hard-working, principled, committed, selfless, talented folk there. But, like most organisations, there are also the workshy, who allow others to put in the 'hard miles', do all the graft until there's a press photo or social media opp. I'm not sure what social media-vaunted all-male trips to parties or banquets in Bradford, Leicester, Birmingham or 'delegations' abroad have to do with serving the pressing local needs of folk in Blackburn.

Alongside others, we had achieved fantastic things. There were still changes and improvements I wanted to address and accomplish on behalf of our local citizens. For example, I would have loved to have seen the

Metrolink tram extended to connect Blackburn and Darwen, via our Greater Manchester neighbour Bolton into Manchester, perhaps from Clitheroe. Trams every twelve minutes would have garnered a great environmental, social, commercial and economic positive impact. Not being able to do so was upsettingly frustrating. I had a massive omniscient grasp of things right across the council's reach, was well respected within the borough and far beyond, engaged with 'external' organisations including the private and voluntary sectors and handled the media skilfully. I was at 'the top of my game'. Democracy doesn't see or care about that, only crosses on paper count.

I had been centrally involved over twenty-five or so years in taking the local Labour Party from its post-war, white working-class, municipal administrative roots to a twenty-first-century vibrant, engaging, campaigning, ethnically diverse, fun, successful organisation. We were much better organised internally, recruited and welcomed fresh members with a more modern outlook, created a more inviting party office, developed policies and campaigned upon them; we went out to people, leafleted and not just at election time but street theatre, fun runs, soapbox sessions, community accountability meetings attended by hundreds on Friday evenings, many different 'surgeries' in many different parts of the constituency.

It was announced that a national enquiry by the Labour Party was to be conducted. Was it an external independent enquiry? I believe the answer to that is 'dubious'. Wouldn't most people expect, given the high community and media profile of events, for this to be handled with the utmost transparency? Clear and published terms of reference, the chief enquiry leader clearly identified, open access to all local folk to have their say, progress updates, a draft report circulated for comment, then published finally with a clear record of events, analysis and plan of action spelt out. Might my being called upon have been expected?

Please feel free to judge me for yourselves. I still feel the Labour Party nationally, regionally and locally, should have handled my departure and its aftermath with greater principle and dignity. That didn't transpire!

* * *

My departure from work was handled abominably too. No substantiation of ill-defined accusations. It was processed poorly, in an uncaring manner, procedures not followed, causing distress to me and my family, loyal friends and colleagues. I leave those who handled this to consider their actions and motives.

We had our tiny family, the four of us and my mum. Beyond that I felt I had three sets of *comrades*: the Lancashire Youth and Community Service, the Labour Party and Blackburn Golf Club. With them all, for different reasons and in different ways, I had felt a sharing of common values, an affinity, sense of belonging. The golf club didn't let me down!

In my last days in work, at my formal exit interview, I was told that what I said (and it was fully and carefully noted) was so controversial that it would have to be referred to senior personnel officers. I never heard another thing.

I experienced three big blows to me and the people close to me. Much less so these days, but at the time and for a long time, I wondered why. Perhaps you have while reading these accounts? My chosen life rendered me extremely busy; I had tried not to act arrogantly, complacently or without compassion. I always tried to put the needs of and engagement with all our citizens at the top of the party's local transformation. Did other people have legitimate grudges to avenge? Were there those (colleagues, friends, comrades even) who wanted me out of the way, to slow down (or derail) the Taylor creative and successful express, to do things their way, or simply just to be in charge. Did some view me with eyes green with envy?

Does it really matter? The outcome is exactly that. The outcome. If there were those whose sole intent was to hurt me, they must ponder that for themselves.

* * *

The seeds of this story were sown well before I was born.

What are the formative features of my life, the things that fashioned me? John Lennon once told us '*Life is what happens to you while you're busy making other plans*'. Think about yourself. Were there times when you didn't 'step up to the plate'? Why didn't you?

Shortly after the end of World War II I was born into a family that seemed permanently in tension. Did those who experienced world war, as combatants or civilians, really have a 'fighting' chance to adjust to the new post-war circumstances? I'm not sure if my mum and dad were ever entirely at one with one another, feasibly even themselves. But don't we all have to play the game of life with the cards that we get dealt?

What impact does someone being an only child or having many siblings, aunts and uncles, nieces, nephews and cousins have on the growing child, the emerging adult? I have none of these relatives, zilch.

I spent a great deal of time in my childhood on my own. Did that make me more independent, more resilient, more imaginative and creative? Or otherwise?

I was born into a post-war period generation known as baby boomers. The welfare state was very much still in its formative years. I believe most of that generation gained generally, but particularly for me, I derived great benefit from the NHS, good quality public housing and a 'free' state education from the age of five to twenty-one.

The generation that immediately preceded mine had experienced, first hand, the hell on earth of world war. Across our increasingly small world tens of millions had died (70 million-plus), or been wounded, permanently disabled, made homeless, widowed or orphaned, traumatised having witnessed the extremes of human atrocities and privations. Unimaginable. What a battering their 'normality' must have taken. My mum used to tell the story about her beloved brother and my Uncle George when he returned to fight in the war after a period of leave. Proudly in his uniform, he would kiss his wife, mum and sister goodbye, descend the dark tenement stairs. Emerging into the daylight, he would quick-march down Dalgety Avenue, never looking back to wave to his doting women, never. They would hang out of their front windows on the third floor cheering, waving and worrying about the most important man in their lives. George never looked back to wave to his adoring women, never. He did, only the once, turn, wave then continue on his way. They never saw him again.

These tragic experiences were compounded by further worldwide changes resultant from the transformation in post-colonial relationships and an emerging New World Order.

Looking back, and with the benefits that hindsight affords, three of the 'five great giants' provided me not with a featherbed or a safety net but more a launchpad into a very different future for me. I recognise that I am profoundly indebted for those great privileges, and I doubt a day goes by that I don't appreciate them and hope that I have done my best over the decades to open similar opportunities to others – young people, their families and their communities.

When does an event or episode become an experience, can an experience develop into a skill? Do we have to know that we've got it and are using it for it to be a skill? Can it be something intuitive that we've imbedded into our practice almost without knowing it? Think about the skills that professional sports people use. Do they know they've got them? Could they explain how they do it/how you could acquire the same skills? As the great Dutch and 1974 World Cup runner-up Johan Cruyff once said 'Playing football is very simple but playing simple football is the hardest thing there is'.

But are experiences and skills of little value unless you turn them into opportunities?

*   *   *

Our council flat in Leeds and then my mum's 'palace', a very modest two-bedroomed council house in Birmingham, provided warm, dry and affordable accommodation where a family could flourish. It brought tears to her eyes as she and I arrived from New Street Station by bus and a half mile walk. I don't remember us ever going hungry, except for that frugality-taken-too-far Christmas near miss! Although we did have the same tea Monday of every week, Tuesday and so on. We had a reasonable standard of living. Our garden was, if anything, too big and there were several parks within walking distance where we could play in *Parkie*-supervised safety.

Our neighbourhood was safe with the local police station less than a five-minute walk away and several police officers living as neighbours cheek by jowl amongst the rest of the community.

School, especially once we got inside toilets, was a good place, almost despite large (forty-five-plus) classes, militarily experienced and 'emergency' trained teachers and corporal punishment being de rigueur. The city council invested well in us with libraries and museums close at hand and totally accessible, free of charge. That thirst for information, knowledge and learning was instilled, deep rooted inside us school kids, from an early age. School trips opened our eyes and imaginations both to our history and the future.

Public transport, mainly in the shape of buses was plentiful, frequent, affordable, reliable and safe. On the No 11 Outer Circle route it was quite normal to reassuringly see half a mile in the distance, the next bus following the one you were catching. Buses carried 40 per cent-plus of all journeys made back then; it's less than 4 per cent now.

*   *   *

My first recollected scrape with authority was in 1957 in the confrontation with nursery head teacher Miss Jones during my very first minutes in state education in Birmingham; although this nascent rebel with accumulating causes had already ruffled feathers and tried to cheat the system by attempting to start his state education two years earlier in Leeds.

At the age of eight, I joined the Wolf Cubs, moving on to the Scouts until I was sixteen or more. My time, some eight or more years, in the Cubs and Scouts also stood me in great stead for the future. I acquired many new skills in this voluntary youth organisation, predominantly those of leadership, of having responsibility for others. I was helping with the younger-aged Cubs, when only aged fourteen or so myself. Trying lots of new things both indoors and out, learning new skills with the recognition of attainment, taking on responsibilities, visiting different places were all accomplished, adding to my skill base, especially self-confidence. Confidence and competence chase each other. The more competent you get, the more confident you are and so on!

Was rebelliousness my first instinct? Was it rebelliousness or a joint mission to challenge unjustifiable authority and defend the oppressed? Taking on any and all authority: teachers, head teachers, questioning blind adherence and complicity with Queen and Country, university academics, meddlesome council officials, 'dodging' becoming a schoolteacher, going into less institutionalised youth work instead, joining the Labour Party, sticking up for various 'under dogs'. Did that change? Did I somehow, somewhere, see or assimilate that some conformity, collaboration reaped more constructive benefits for more people?

Don't get me wrong here. I made mistakes, took the wrong decisions but the only way never to make any mistakes, I saw, was never to do anything. A mistake isn't totally a mistake if some learning comes from it.

I also benefitted from witnessing and examining the mistakes of others. Perhaps some of my teachers at junior school should have been less 'assertively' bullying in their dealings with me although I learned from that too, about how not to behave. Stand up to bullies. Seek out and sit with the imaginative and creative, the emotionally intelligent and literate.

I took and passed the eleven-plus exam that would enable me to go to a grammar school. I can only assume that was my dad's aspiration for me, to follow in his footsteps, as he had attended Roundhay Grammar School in Leeds.

But my secondary education was conducted at a massive, innovative and national education-leading comprehensive school known as Sheldon Heath Comprehensive. Fed by umpteen sprawling 1950s council estates built following slum clearance and/or Nazi bombing raids, there were 300 pupils in every year group of all abilities, that meant approaching 2,000 were on the school roll, with over a hundred teachers. I'm not sure I realised it at the time but there was a commitment, from the very top: national and local government, the head, management and staff, parents and the wider local community and a determination to make the school work for all of its students. Did I become intoxicated by the inspirational heady brew being fermented there? We saw Sheldon Heath Comprehensive had a mission, meant what it said and did it. I felt swept along by all of that energy and success. Did being at school, playing sport, spending time at the scout hut also mean escaping life at home?

I took a lot from those seven years at secondary school and hope I gave things back in return. I mixed with a lot of different people, played a lot of sport, not exceptionally well, but that brought social opportunities too. I took on leadership roles, normally as captain of school teams. But also, in clubs and societies for example, being involved in fledgling journalism, being secretary of the debating society, getting elected as the first chair of the sixth form.

I had several exchanges with our uber headmaster JE Smith CBE, all of them constructive even though most of them were difficult. He taking the trouble to come and seek me out and display humility by way of his apology over the issue of my 'long' hair meant a lot to me and taught me lessons about how to handle people. As did the student-instigated impromptu Monday afternoon alternative to his senior staff meeting session. We wanted to change our world. I wonder what Joe would think of me being Sir Bill? I bet a few have been surprised!

There were many excellent teachers at the school, role models for me then and for the future. Later in my life, reminiscing and relating the things they did for and with me brought public tears to my eyes. They wanted to change the world too. They went above and beyond the normal expectations of teachers and would have contravened many health and safety and child protection measures of today's world of risk assessment.

University was quite another experience, which perhaps in retrospect I wasn't ready for, not mature enough, but it brought a whole array of new issues and ideas. The freedoms and distractions of prolonged periods away from home, meeting dozens of new people from all sorts of different backgrounds, having girlfriends, drinking a lot of beer and totally different ways of studying (or not) and learning. As long-lost but refound university pal Steve Landles who hailed from the sleepy Cumbrian back water of Seascale said to me quite recently, 'Great days. We thought we were the first to discover most things. And we were earnest'.

I did learn through experience, how to speak to the press including being put in front of a media microphone. I also learned to address small, medium and large meetings with usually cogent, coherent arguments. I learned how to conduct meetings well as chair. My leadership and organisational skills were enhanced. Perhaps the causes were wrong, but I learned many things for future applicable use. I took courses in foreign policy analysis, strategic studies, force, violence and aggression, voting behaviour and other associated subjects. A waste of time? But I did learn the difference between strategy and tactics and when it was best to defend or attack depending on the prevailing situation.

Perhaps we were lulled or lured by music icons? As Thin Lizzy sang in the late seventies:

'There are people that will investigate you
They'll insinuate, intimidate and complicate you
Don't ever wait or hesitate to state the fate that awaits those who
Try to shake or take you
Don't let them break you
You can do anything you want to do.'

I don't know if getting involved with the world of student politics was a good or bad thing to happen. On balance, the former. It probably closed some doors to me but opened others? It seemed that the university professed an openness to knowledge and learning but practised something entirely different. Not only did a number of us learn from that, but it also stood us in good stead as to how we should handle ourselves in our future careers, especially in terms of our management values and practices as our diverse careers progressed.

Armed with what, in truth, was a pathetically mediocre honours degree, I set off into the world of work. What happened, peering backwards from the end of my thirty-three-year career, seemed very traditional, a few face-to-face jobs and then moving into management and training. But my inauspicious first day at work was exactly that, my first day at work! Thank goodness for Harold the Caretaker! I went on to thoroughly enjoy my time in youth and community work; it was wonderfully creative, imaginative and rewarding, except for periods with managers who neither valued or fostered creativity! They saw me not pulling my weight at work. What they didn't get or chose to ignore was my involvement in these various other things that enriched and enhanced my contributions to the youth work world too. A bit like when I once asked one of my stock chair of education questions, about how school had been that day, I recall one head teacher responding 'Great, there were no kids in!'

A small band of us moved what was really a profession in its infancy and transformed policy and practice certainly across Lancashire and probably beyond. Sadly and regrettably youth work as we grew it and knew it doesn't really exist any longer. Generations of adolescents may well be at risk from the pitfalls that can befall them without the guiding hand of a caring youth worker. Youth work doesn't cost a great deal of money, perhaps £100 a head per young person per year. Not investing in that way leads to millions upon millions being spent in the world of education, social services, the youth justice system, police and prisons, as well as all the personal and societal deficit cost, resulting in a downward spiral which can replicate itself down generations within chaotic families. I met up with a former young person I'd worked with in the seventies two or three years ago for a coffee. He is probably ten years my junior. We nattered for an hour or more as though we had kept in permanent touch. As we prepared to part company, after a hug, he said 'I've got to tell you something – You changed my life'. I walked away with tears welling.

Early on I joined our national professional association. By the quirks of opportunity that presented themselves, not for the first and most certainly not for the last time, at the age of twenty-two I found myself on the national executive and secretary of one of the key subcommittees, developing policies and liaising with other national bodies including local and central government.

I always said 'Yes' to opportunities that came my way and offered them on to others: developing curriculum and training youth workers, new councillors, public and voluntary sector staff, bringing agencies together to better serve their local clients and communities, training people from hard-to-reach groups to work within their communities to in turn support themselves and others, street theatre, mock job interviews and selection processes, taking young people out of an apparently inherited or self-constrained comfort zone to try new experiences, perhaps take on responsibilities, organise themselves and others, take a different career path, travel independently and abroad for example.

My work took me into most secondary schools locally. I got to know many teachers who, like me, were starting out in their careers. I met some local councillors and some of the officers in different departments in different councils. But not just meeting with them, talking with and listening to them, learning about what made them tick and the world of their working lives. We learn so much by carefully watching and listening to each other, especially our own and other people's youngsters.

Now please, if you think any of this was planned at its outset or during its development – STOP! I hadn't embarked on any of this with a plan, a map of where I was going and how I was going to get there. There were still plenty of forks in the road to choose, avenues to explore (some turned out to be cul-de-sacs), experiences to savour, new people to meet, friendships and relationships to forge, challenges to confront and turn into successes, mistakes to make and redress. What I didn't know was all that rich opportunity that was to come, how I would respond to it and what impact it would have. Surely it must be the same for us all? Pennies drop frequently – we don't always listen out for or hear them!

Why did I join the Labour Party? University pal Rick Dunning had joined years before me on a mission to save Suffolk's hedgerows. That had a strong influence on me joining Labour. I wanted to do something to help people. I wanted to pay back for the 'privileges' and experiences that had shaped my life and also to give mainly young people, similar openings and opportunities.

I chuckle to myself sometimes, knowing that an anagram of William Taylor is 'I am Tory law ill!'. Mildly risible, but what's happened to the Labour Party, really since Blair resigned, is no laughing matter. Culpably criminal might be a better description?

And here is another 'don't get me wrong'. I'm not urging anybody to join a political party or any particular political party. Neither am I advocating becoming local councillor. But don't just stand there, do something! Or as I once *Tweeted* – 'Don't just do something, stand there!' Like most things in my life, at the beginning of any experience, I entered into it naïvely. Most things I did or organisations I joined, I didn't understand at the outset. In some cases I didn't even twig I was joining an organisation and most certainly didn't 'get it'. Once again surely that must be the same for most of us?

So I chose to join a political party, the Labour Party. Councillor Ernest Gorton invited me to meet him in the smoke-smelly party rooms one Saturday morning in 1979. Emerging ten minutes later I was a local 'paper' (token) candidate in the Pleckgate area where we lived. I was further instructed to meet at 6 p.m. Monday on the corner of Briar Road and take a pencil. I did as I was told, turned up and met Jack Straw, the new parliamentary candidate. We did a couple of hours of canvassing, went for a quick beer and then returned home where Jack supped on Anne's hastily transformed career-anticipating home-made pie.

A few weeks later the General Election happened, Margaret Thatcher became the Prime Minister and Jack the local MP. I was invited to the election count and again really didn't understand what was going on. I didn't win the council seat I'd been hurriedly 'selected' to contest.

A few weeks after that I was appointed to the general management committee of the local party by Councillor Ernest Gorton.

Barely a further few weeks elapsed before Councillor Ernest Gorton fell poorly and I was approached by Jack Straw, who I'd known for barely two or three months, to stand in as secretary/agent. Temporarily, of course. Until 2010!

Within a year I'd taken and passed the National Agent's training and qualification, attended the 1979, post-Callaghan defeat, Labour Party Conference in Brighton as a delegate, both at my own cost and in my own time, and became a local councillor (aged twenty-eight).

Yet more dollops or oodles even of getting myself involved in things I didn't really understand. Is it hard to understand things when people only look from the outside?

Getting married really wasn't that different. Met this thoughtful, considerate, patient, pretty girl, we got on very well, decided to get married relatively quickly, bought a house. Three years after that we started to have kids. And forty-five-plus years later we find ourselves still married, having fun, travelling quite a lot and blessed with two no-longer kids, themselves married to great partners and now with families of their own.

In the council aspect of my life, I advanced comparatively quickly there too. Vice-chairman, quite soon chairman of a high-profile committee, then the youngest ever mayor (thirty-seven years old), later new and greater responsibilities on the council. All this seemed to be taken in my increasingly lengthy and swift stride.

Whilst off work and out of action due to illness, I was elected deputy leader of the council and then a few years later leader. This all enabled me to develop further, operating at sub-regional, regional, national and beyond multiple levels, deal with powerful local community pressure groups, Cabinet Ministers, high up civil service 'Mandarins', print, TV and radio journalists locally, the BBC, Sky, bring them all on. But with the same associated 'rookie' feelings of not really fully understanding things around me and with lots to learn. That never put me off, I thrived on new challenges. Built on them.

What did these challenges, achievements and successes on the council include?

+ Being a member, often in a leadership role, of some great teams of work colleagues, members and officers, many recognised with honours, from MBE and beyond.

+ Establishing a network of some thirty-plus neighbourhood centres and community bases across the borough – probably unrivalled elsewhere, where folks could meet, socialise, follow or try their favourite hobbies and other pursuits, organise themselves.

+ Enabling young people to have a voice. What we achieved in Blackburn was replicated across the country.

+ Beating off the transitory British National Party challenge but never being complacent about it.

+ Empowering young people and their communities, bringing art to people, putting roofs over young people's heads – Action Factory and Night Safe were established and developed and are still here thirty-plus years on.

+ Improving our schools, taking on and convincing initially reluctant heads and governors to see and play a wider, more corporate societal role. Identifying, celebrating and disseminating good practice and success, with many staff and their leadership recognised with honours.

+ Introducing community resourcing audit and analysis across the borough. This process identified all resources of the council, police, fire and rescue, the NHS, the Department of Work and Pensions, etc. Pooled all together this amounted to a figure four or five times that which the council alone spent, nearly a billion pounds. This was then apportioned down to electoral ward level and even smaller enumeration areas. Its findings were that the most resources went into white working-class communities. Again, this resource mapping was adopted as a national model of good practice for resource analysis.

- Again, we were ahead of the field in what became known as community cohesion. Our 'Belonging to Blackburn' where we promoted the concept of diversity with unity, again became a national model.

- Engaging with our communities whilst at the same time empowering them, via things like Friday night community accountability meetings, the 'exec on the road' initiative, council leader's Saturday morning surgeries. Many, Blair and Brown, John Prescott, the Deputy PM and various other Cabinet Ministers, the BBC's Jeremy Paxman, John Pienaar, Jim Hancock, Gordon Burns, Dave Guest, Annabel Tiffin and Elaine Dunkley, TV crews (including Panorama, Granada, Sky), print media political commentators and local government aficionados came to see.

- Again ground-breaking, our public private partnership with Capita brought extra flexibility to the way we provided services to our citizens. Other Capita jobs came into the borough too.

- Placing 9,000 council properties and tenants into the voluntary sector to secure for them a more stable and better future.

- Establishing local schools for members of all religious faiths.

- The recognition we gained for our achievements: twice being judged Council of the Year (and later, a third time), being awarded four beacon awards, an excellent Ofsted report for the LEA and being assessed as an 'Excellent' council following our comprehensive performance assessment inspections.

- And being knighted in 2003 not only for my contributions in public office but also in youth work.

I had had the broadest of experiences, I think polymath fits! Not just theoretical, not just policy, but successful practical application and the ability to teach this accessibly across various disciplines to young and old people, in communities and universities. I inspected, conducted peer reviews, witnessed and examined in many different fields.

People knew Bill Taylor, listened to what he had to say, liked, believed, and trusted him. Across different media and face-to-face, he exhibited confidence and coherence, convincing his various audiences.

I loved the challenge and 'job' satisfaction of being the constituency agent for thirty-plus years, stretching over five decades, to the Rt Hon Jack Straw MP. Many organisational and the motivating of other people skills were developed and with that came so much success and fun too.

The same really at work; new jobs, different jobs, the move from multi-cultural urban to more a rural environment, different and greater responsibility but still faced with imagination, creativity and success.

A great family life, humdrum but with a whole lot of love and a lot of fun. Taking the piss is the family *lingua franca*, with me the main target. But I think the best ribbing ever award goes to our hugely respectful offspring. Following Anne's attendance at several adult education classes run by local water colour artist, Harry Caunce, they irreverently dubbed her 'The Artist formerly known as Mum!'.

Much coveted and fondly remembered caravan holidays around Britain and France with loads of great experiences, meeting and forming enduring cherished friendships with other families; the Gordons, Taylors, Grahams, 'Finns' (long story), the Eldridges, Betty who isn't Betty (longer still) and many more and many more belly-aching laughs!

Hours and hours, over years and years home and away (including Cleethorpes and Burslem) with the Rovers (up to a 1,000 matches over thirty-plus years) and watching countless sports matches and practices (2,000-plus?), transporting ours and other people's children, committee attending, fundraising, kit washing.

And a trip to Buckingham Palace to be knighted by the heir to the throne. Surely that was the icing on the cake? Surely it was?

* * *

Quite by accident, or was it, I was instumental to four vital pieces of heritage of historical significance locally and beyond. The artefacts spread over many decades, as did securing and developing them.

How poor would the world be if the Edwardian Mitchell and Kenyon moving images had been chucked in a skip, the monster digital archive of our great Cotton Town hadn't been created and the seventy-year span of press, war, social and commercial Talbot images had been lost to the world? We've yet to see about my unique research resource archive, under the custodial stewardship of the college's management, staff and students there. That's about one person, his involvement in various communities, the Labour Party, the council, education, the college, our NHS, youth and community work, the private sector, voluntary sector.

* * *

I moved on to other things. In 2009 I was encouraged to apply and gained the chairmanship of the local but nationally ground-breaking NHS Care Trust Plus. With the college chair, two fantastic roles were more than enough to keep me busy and engaged. I really enjoyed them both and both flourished.

We set about shaping the NHS board, team building and priority setting. The board membership was a three-way split; local elected members, local NHS professionals and local 'lay' members drawn from the community, chaired by an independent me. We introduced many financial and clinically effective measures, streamlined management and 'back office' functions. We were recognised by national experts as the blueprint for the future. Until Andrew Lansley came along.

* * *

I had joined the college board in 1981, another culture I knew little of and had lots to learn. In 2008 I was asked to become chair. There was a great deal to do and under my stewardship we accomplished it all. I ruffled some feathers, some of the people I felt held distracting political or personal resentments against me.

In my eyes the college wasn't an educational establishment. It was probably the biggest engine of personal development and social mobility the borough had. We could offer people dreams and the capacity to fulfil them. What some in leadership/governance roles in any organisation need to understand is that their time there is transient. Others have been there before them and usually others follow. Leave it in better condition than you found it.

This vision/mission wasn't commonly held by all. Some governors only attended board meetings, not all of it and not all of them. Missing one could mean having no contact with the college for six months or more, not really fingers on the pulse stuff. I probably stayed a year too long as chair. In the digital version of the local paper I was described as having 'thrown the towel in'. This insightful comment was very close to the mark. I sensed a covert subliminal attritional erosion of my position. My continued presence wasn't helping the college and to be frank I'd simply had enough of it all!

After overseeing a £60 million-plus twenty-first-century transformation of the campus, I resigned in 2016 with some relief. In the local *Telegraph* Jack Straw said of me 'He has been chairman for some years and has fulfilled the role with great distinction. He has guided the college successfully through a period of great change and he is a great loss to the college'.

Hope Barnes, the student union president, wrote to me. The full text you have read earlier. But may I remind you of some of her strong but softly expressed sentiments:

> *… you were probably the person I was most nervous to meet. I had heard how lovely you were and all your other achievements. But I don't know why I was nervous because you made me feel at ease straightaway and you were so lovely to me…*
>
> *… I am very saddened by the news and knowing that you were in a students' union when you were younger. I will leave you with the promise to keep fighting for students' rights and work hard to make Blackburn College the place to be.*
>
> *You truly are an inspiration to me and many others*
> *Love with all my heart!*
> *Hope Barnes*
> *SU President*

I'll take Hope's version of events every time. Emotional intelligence.

*   *   *

I did my best. Made mistakes. I learned to trust more people more. As four-star Second World War US General George Patton observed 'Never tell people how to do things. Tell them what to do, and they will surprise you with their ingenuity.' I hope I didn't hurt anyone. I felt hurt often, but I assumed it came with the territory. I heard someone recently say, 'Don't regret what you've done, only what you haven't done.'

I've enjoyed most of what I did immensely! Immensely! Encouraged by others I chose to start writing this in 2019. It took me four years.

Thank you.

Thank you to so many people that I've met and worked with, mainly laughed but cried with sometimes too.

I wouldn't change very much. If I had got myself a heraldic shield the motto would have been '*Arte et Labore. In humilitate et humor*'.

'By skill and hard work. With humility and humour'.

And thank you for reading this.

I am only one in a million. Others have their stories yet to be heard.

Rūmī issued a challenge: 'And you? When will you begin that long journey into yourself?'

Go on, then! GOYA!